ZAGAT®

New York City Restaurants
2010

EDITORS
Curt Gathje and Carol Diuguid
COORDINATOR
Larry Cohn

Published and distributed by
Zagat Survey, LLC
4 Columbus Circle
New York, NY 10019
T: 212.977.6000
E: newyork@zagat.com
www.zagat.com

ACKNOWLEDGMENTS

We thank Jason Briker, Caren Weiner Campbell, Leigh Crandall, Mikola De Roo, Randi Gollin, Lynn Hazlewood, Bernard Onken, Steven Shukow, Kelly Stewart, Miranda Van Gelder and Kevin Zraly, as well as the following members of our staff: Josh Rogers (senior associate editor), Christina Livadiotis (assistant editor), Brian Albert, Sean Beachell, Maryanne Bertollo, Jane Chang, Sandy Cheng, Reni Chin, Bill Corsello, John Deiner, Caitlin Eichelberger, Alison Flick, Jeff Freier, Michelle Golden, Justin Hartung, Karen Hudes, Roy Jacob, Garth Johnston, Cynthia Kilian, Natalie Lebert, Mike Liao, Andre Pilette, Becky Ruthenburg, Stacey Slate, Jacqueline Wasilczyk, Yoji Yamaguchi, Sharon Yates, Anna Zappia and Kyle Zolner.

The reviews in this guide are based on public opinion surveys. The ratings reflect the average scores given by the survey participants who voted on each establishment. The text is based on quotes from, or paraphrasings of, the surveyors' comments. Phone numbers, addresses and other factual data were correct to the best of our knowledge when published in this guide.

Maps © 2009 GeoNova Publishing, Inc., except for p. 299 and front panel of foldout map copyright Zagat Survey, LLC

© 2009 Zagat Survey, LLC
ISBN-13: 978-1-60478-178-6
ISBN-10: 1-60478-178-5
Printed in the
United States of America

Contents

Ratings & Symbols

Zagat Top Spot	Name	Symbols	Cuisine	Zagat Ratings			
				FOOD	DECOR	SERVICE	COST

Area, Address & Contact

Z Tim & Nina's ◑ *Deli*   ▽ 23 | 9 | 13 | $15

W 50s | 4 Columbus Circle (8th Ave.) | 212-977-6000 | www.zagat.com

Review, surveyor comments in quotes

Nina's grandmother's "hobo stew" and Tim's mother's casserole at "brother-can-you-spare-a-dime" prices make for "endless lines" at this "dismal dive" down in the Columbus Circle IRT station; service is about "what you'd expect from the MTA", and the tableware is of the "Dixie Cup variety."

Ratings

Food, Decor and **Service** are rated on the Zagat 0 to 30 scale.

0	–	9	poor to fair
10	–	15	fair to good
16	–	19	good to very good
20	–	25	very good to excellent
26	–	30	extraordinary to perfection
	▽		low response | less reliable

Cost

Our surveyors' estimated price of a dinner with one drink and tip. Lunch is usually 25 to 30% less. For unrated **newcomers** or **write-ins,** the price range is shown as follows:

| I | $25 and below | E | $41 to $65 |
| M | $26 to $40 | VE | $66 or above |

Symbols

Z	highest ratings, popularity and importance
◑	serves after 11 PM
Ⓢ	closed on Sunday
Ⓜ	closed on Monday
⊄	no credit cards accepted

Maps

Index maps show restaurants with the highest Food ratings in those areas.

Menus, photos, voting and more – free at ZAGAT.com

About This Survey

Here are the results of our **2010 New York City Restaurants Survey,** covering 2,069 eateries throughout the five boroughs. Like all our guides, this one is based on input from avid local consumers – 38,868 all told. Our editors have synopsized their feedback and highlighted (in quotation marks within reviews) select comments. You can read full surveyor comments – and share your own opinions – on **ZAGAT.com,** where you'll also find the latest restaurant news plus menus, photos and more, all for free.

OUR PHILOSOPHY: Three simple premises underlie our ratings and reviews: First, we've long believed that the collective opinions of knowledgeable consumers are more accurate than the opinions of a single critic. (Consider, for example, that as a group our surveyors bring some 6.1 million annual meals' worth of experience to this Survey. They also visit restaurants year-round, anonymously – and on their own dime.) Second, as everyone knows, food quality is only part of the equation when choosing a restaurant, thus we ask surveyors to separately rate food, decor and service and report on cost. Finally, today more than ever, people need reliable information in a fast, easy-to-digest format, so we strive to be concise. Our Top Ratings lists (pages 9–23) and indexes (starting on page 278) are also designed to help you quickly choose the best place for any occasion.

JOIN IN: To improve this guide, **ZAGAT.com** or any aspect of our performance, we need your comments – after all, our business is based on customer feedback, so it's vital that we hear your opinions about how we can do a better job. Just contact us at **nina-tim@zagat.com.** We also invite you to join any of our surveys at **ZAGAT.com.** Do so and you'll receive a choice of rewards in exchange.

ABOUT ZAGAT: In 1979, we started asking friends to rate and review restaurants purely for fun. That hobby grew into Zagat Survey; 31 years later, we have over 350,000 surveyors and cover airlines, bars, dining, fast food, entertaining, golf, hotels, movies, music, resorts, shopping, spas, theater and tourist attractions in over 100 countries. Along the way, we evolved from being a publisher of print guides to a provider of digital content in a full range of formats: **ZAGAT.com,** the award-winning **ZAGAT.mobi** (for web-enabled mobile devices), **ZAGAT TO GO** (for smartphones) and **ZAGAT nru** (for Android phones). We also produce extensive content for corporate and custom clients. And of course, you can find us on Twitter (twitter.com/zagatbuzz), Facebook and other social media networks.

THANKS: We're grateful to editors Curt Gathje and Carol Diuguid, as well as Larry Cohn, who coordinates data collection, for their hard work over the years. We also sincerely thank the thousands of surveyors who participated – all of our content is really "theirs."

New York, NY
October 7, 2009

Nina and Tim Zagat

KEY NEWCOMERS

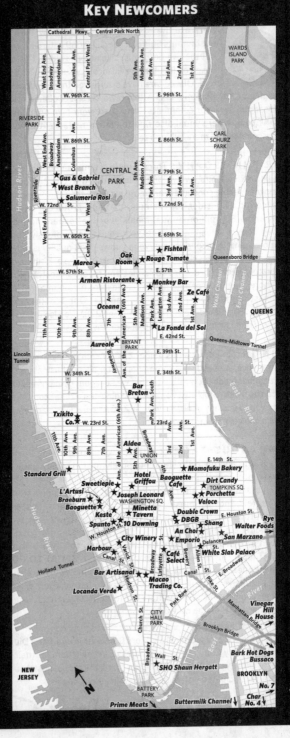

Menus, photos, voting and more - free at ZAGAT.com

Key Newcomers

Our editors' take on the year's top arrivals. See page 336 for a full list.

HAPPENING SCENES

Café Select
DBGB
Double Crown
Hotel Griffou
Marea
Minetta Tavern
Monkey Bar
Standard Grill
10 Downing
Ze Café

HOT CHEFS

Aureole | *Charlie Palmer*
Bar Artisanal | *Terrance Brennan*
Bar Breton | *Cyril Renaud*
DBGB | *Daniel Boulud*
Fishtail | *David Burke*
Gus & Gabriel | *Michael Psilakis*
Locanda Verde | *Andrew Carmellini*
Marea | *Michael White*
Salumeria Rosi | *Cesare Casella*
Shang | *Susur Lee*
SHO Shaun Hergatt | *Shaun Hergatt*
West Branch | *Tom Valenti*

STRIKING SPACES

Armani Ristorante
Harbour
La Fonda del Sol
Macao Trading Co.
Minetta Tavern
Monkey Bar
Oceana
Rouge Tomate
SHO Shaun Hergatt
Sweetiepie

LOCAL/SEASONAL

Aldea
Braeburn
Buttermilk Channel (Bklyn)
Dirt Candy
Rouge Tomate

PIZZA

Co.
Emporio
Keste
San Marzano
Spunto
Veloce

QUICK BITES

An Choi
Bark Hot Dogs (Bklyn)
Baoguette
Momofuku Bakery
Porchetta
Salumeria Rosi

SMALL WONDERS

Joseph Leonard
No. 7 (Bklyn)
Prime Meats (Bklyn)
Txikito
Vinegar Hill House (Bklyn)
White Slab Palace

WINE & SPIRITS FOCUS

Aureole
Bussaco (Bklyn)
Char No. 4 (Bklyn)
City Winery
L'Artusi
Rye (Bklyn)

BIG-NAME PROJECTS ON TAP:

Maialino – Italian from Danny Meyer in the Gramercy Park Hotel

Pulino's – Bowery pizzeria via Keith McNally

SD26 – Italian from Tony May opposite Madison Square Park

Ed's Chowder House – Seafooder opposite Lincoln Center from Jeffrey Chodorow

The Breslin – April Bloomfield's meat-and-charcuterie specialist in the Ace Hotel

Fatty 'Cue – Asian BBQ joint in Williamsburg via Zak Pelaccio

Bill's Bar & Burger – Meatpacking District American from Steve Hanson

Yet-to-be-named Midtown French-Vietnamese from David Chang

What's New

Since the economic meltdown began in 2008, there has been much gloom and doom expressed regarding the state of NYC's restaurant industry. But the real picture is much more nuanced.

Sure, many restaurants aren't enjoying the high times that characterized the recent boom years: 46% of surveyors say they are dining out less frequently, 41% are eating in less expensive places and 21% are cutting back on appetizers and/or desserts. The $200 bottle of wine is history. And lavish entertaining in private rooms has declined along with the stock of our banks.

But from the indicators we see, most restaurants are weathering the storm reasonably well. Eating out has become a norm for working people. They have no more time now to shop, cook and clean up afterwards than they did pre-crash. And some surveyors are finding upsides to the downturn: the many deals being offered by restaurants.

Other encouraging signs: there were 157 notable openings and 102 closings this year (vs. last year's 119 newcomers and 88 closures). And this year's newcomers were as varied as ever: there were luxury entries like **Harbour, Marea** and **SHO Shaun Hergatt**; instant scenes at **Hotel Griffou, Minetta Tavern, Monkey Bar** and the **Standard Grill**; neighborhood hits at **Flex Mussels, 10 Downing** and **West Branch**; and big-name chefs adding to their empires, in most cases at a lower price point than typical: Daniel Boulud (**DBGB**), Terry Brennan (**Bar Artisanal**), David Burke (**Fishtail**), David Chang (**Momofuku Bakery**) and Michael Psilakis (**Gus & Gabriel**). Indeed, price point was key last year, hence the plethora of new pizzerias (**Co., Keste, Veloce**) and small-plates options (**Bar Breton, La Fonda del Sol, Txikito**).

Of course, high-end dining didn't disappear, as this year's Survey winners confirm. Best Food honors went to **Le Bernardin**, for the sixth time in the past decade. The Most Popular restaurant was perennial favorite **Gramercy Tavern**, while **Asiate** took top Decor honors (for the third year running) and **Per Se** scored its fifth consecutive Best Service title.

But there are clearly changes afoot in the fine-dining realm. Those changes reached critical mass several years ago, when four Classic French paradigms – **La Caravelle, La Côte Basque, Lespinasse** and **Lutèce** – abruptly closed. It was the beginning of a sea change in the definition of fine dining, and its effects are ongoing (witness the recent shuttering of **Café des Artistes** and the **Rainbow Room**). Midtown, once home to the city's best dining, has lost much of its punch. Instead, a new generation of young diners is going Downtown (or to the outer boroughs) for dinner – and they're not dressing up and couldn't care less about tablecloths or tuxedoed waiters.

And the year ahead? There are several high-profile places in the pipeline from big names like David Chang, Steve Hanson, Tony May, Keith McNally and Danny Meyer. If anything, the restaurant revolution that so enriched our lives these past 30 years is as strong as ever.

New York, NY
October 7, 2009

Nina and Tim Zagat

Most Popular

A full list is plotted on the map at the back of this book.

1. Gramercy Tavern | *American*
2. Union Square Cafe | *American*
3. Peter Luger (Bklyn) | *Steak*
4. Le Bernardin | *French/Seafood*
5. Babbo | *Italian*
6. Daniel | *French*
7. Balthazar | *French*
8. Gotham B&G | *American*
9. Eleven Madison Park | *French*
10. Bouley | *French*
11. Jean Georges | *French*
12. Nobu | *Japanese*
13. Per Se | *American/French*
14. Blue Water Grill | *Seafood*
15. Café Boulud | *French*
16. Artisanal | *French*
17. Del Posto | *Italian*
18. Four Seasons | *American*
19. Buddakan | *Asian*
20. Becco | *Italian*
21. Rosa Mexicano | *Mexican*
22. Modern | *American/French*
23. Blue Hill | *American*
24. Atlantic Grill | *Seafood*
25. Aquagrill | *Seafood*
26. Palm | *Steak*
27. Il Mulino | *Italian*
28. Del Frisco's | *Steak*
29. 21 Club | *American*
30. Picholine | *French/Med.*
31. Carmine's | *Italian*
32. Chanterelle | *French*
33. Tabla | *Indian*
34. Aquavit | *Scandinavian*
35. Jean Georges' Nougatine | *Fr.*
36. Felidia | *Italian*
37. Shake Shack | *Burgers*
38. Bar Boulud | *French*
39. Blue Smoke | *BBQ*
40. La Grenouille | *French*
41. Sushi Yasuda* | *Japanese*

Top Food Ratings

28 | Le Bernardin | *French/Seafood*
Daniel | *French*
Jean Georges | *French*
Per Se | *American/French*
Chanterelle | *French*
L'Atelier/Joël Robuchon | *Fr.*
Bouley | *French*
Gramercy Tavern | *American*
Sasabune | *Japanese*
Sushi Yasuda | *Japanese*

Babbo | *Italian*
Gari/Sushi | *Japanese*
Picholine | *French/Med.*
Nobu | *Japanese*
Eleven Madison Park | *French*
Sripraphai (Qns) | *Thai*
Union Square Cafe | *American*
Mas | *American*
Milos | *Greek/Seafood*
Kuruma Zushi | *Japanese*

27 | Di Fara (Bklyn) | *Pizza*
Gotham Bar & Grill | *American*
Momofuku Ko | *American*
Corton | *French*
Sugiyama | *Japanese*
Kyo Ya | *Japanese*
Grocery (Bklyn) | *American*
Blue Hill | *American*
Annisa | *American*
Peter Luger (Bklyn) | *Steak*
Jean Georges' Nougatine | *Fr.*
La Grenouille | *French*
Tratt. L'incontro (Qns) | *Italian*
Il Mulino | *Italian*
Café Boulud | *French*

26 | Danny Brown (Qns) | *European*
Degustation | *French/Spanish*
15 East | *Japanese*
Masa | *Japanese*
Lucali (Bklyn) | *Pizza*
Roberto (Bronx) | *Italian*
Sushi Sen-nin | *Japanese*
Al Di La (Bklyn) | *Italian*
Il Giglio | *Italian*
Sushi Seki | *Japanese*
Bar Masa | *Japanese*
Marea | *Italian/Seafood*
Tomoe Sushi | *Japanese*
Sistina | *Italian*
Scalini Fedeli | *Italian*

Lists exclude places with low votes, unless indicated by a ∇; * indicates a tie with restaurant above

AMERICAN

28 Per Se
Gramercy Tavern
27 Gotham Bar & Grill
Momofuku Ko
Grocery (Bklyn)
Blue Hill

AMERICAN (REGIONAL)

26 Pearl Oyster Bar/NE
23 Mara's Homemade/Cajun
21 Carl's Steaks/Philly
Ed's Lobster Bar/NE
20 Michael's/Calif.
Great Jones Cafe/Cajun

BARBECUE

25 Fette Sau (Bklyn)
23 Daisy May's
22 Dinosaur BBQ
21 Blue Smoke
Hill Country
Smoke Joint (Bklyn)

BURGERS

24 burger joint
23 Shake Shack
22 DuMont (Bklyn)
Corner Bistro
21 Island Burgers
J.G. Melon

CARIBBEAN

23 Havana Alma/Cuban
Café Habana/Outpost/Cuban
22 Cuba/Cuban
21 Sofrito/Puerto Rican
Victor's Cafe/Cuban
Negril/Jamaican

CHINESE

24 Philippe
Tse Yang
23 Spicy & Tasty (Qns)
Oriental Garden
Shun Lee Palace
Phoenix Garden

DELIS

23 Barney Greengrass
Katz's Deli
Ess-a-Bagel
22 Mill Basin Deli (Bklyn)
2nd Ave Deli
Carnegie Deli

DESSERT

25 ChikaLicious
Chocolate Room* (Bklyn)
La Bergamote
23 L & B Spumoni (Bklyn)
22 Café Sabarsky
Lady Mendl's

DIM SUM

23 Oriental Garden
21 Ping's Seafood
Dim Sum Go Go
Chinatown Brasserie
Shun Lee Cafe
20 Mandarin Court

FRENCH

28 Le Bernardin
Daniel
Jean Georges
Per Se
Chanterelle
L'Atelier/Joël Robuchon
Bouley
27 Corton
Jean Georges' Nougatine
La Grenouille
Café Boulud
Eleven Madison Park

FRENCH (BISTRO)

25 JoJo
24 db Bistro Moderne
Raoul's
Tournesol (Qns)
23 Capsouto Frères
Bar Boulud

GREEK

27 Milos
26 Eliá (Bklyn)
25 Pylos
Taverna Kyclades (Qns)
Anthos
Avra

HOTEL DINING

28 Jean Georges (Trump Int'l)
L'Atelier/Joël (Four Seasons)
27 Café Boulud (Surrey)
26 Adour (St. Regis)
25 Norma's (Le Parker Meridien)
Gilt (NY Palace)

INDIAN

25 Tamarind
   Tabla
24 Amma
   Saravanaas
23 Dawat
   Yuva

ITALIAN

27 Trattoria L'incontro (Qns)
   Il Mulino
   Babbo
26 Roberto (Bronx)
   Al Di La (Bklyn)
   Il Giglio
   Marea
   Sistina
   Scalini Fedeli
   Convivio
   Pepolino
   Alto

JAPANESE/SUSHI

28 Sasabune
   Sushi Yasuda
27 Sugiyama
   Kyo Ya
   Gari/Sushi
   Nobu
   Kuruma Zushi
26 15 East
   Masa
   Sushi Sen-nin
   Sushi Seki
   Bar Masa

KOREAN

26 HanGawi
24 Moim (Bklyn)
23 Cho Dang Gol
22 Do Hwa
21 Kang Suh
   Bann

KOSHER

24 Azuri Cafe
22 Pongal
   Mill Basin Deli (Bklyn)
   Le Marais
   2nd Ave Deli
   Prime Grill

MEDITERRANEAN

27 Picholine
26 Little Owl
   Tanoreen (Bklyn)
25 Convivium Osteria (Bklyn)

24 Il Buco
   Alta

MEXICAN

24 Pampano
23 Maya
   Toloache
   El Paso Taqueria
   Itzocan
   Hell's Kitchen

MIDDLE EASTERN

26 Tanoreen (Bklyn)
24 Azuri Cafe
   ilili
23 Taboon
   Gazala Place
   Hummus Place

NEWCOMERS

26 Marea
24 Porchetta
23 Buttermilk Channel (Bklyn)
   Txikito
   Char No. 4 (Bklyn)
   Salumeria Rosi
   Fishtail
   DBGB
   Shang
22 Motorino
   Flex Mussels
   La Fonda del Sol

NOODLE SHOPS

25 Ippudo
24 Soba-ya
23 Momofuku Noodle Bar
22 Kampuchea
   Great NY Noodle
   Matsugen

PIZZA

27 Di Fara (Bklyn)
26 Lucali (Bklyn)
25 Zero Otto Nove (Bronx)
   Grimaldi's (Bklyn)
   Denino's (SI)
   Luzzo's
24 Lombardi's
   Franny's (Bklyn)
   ápizz
   Posto
   Joe & Pat's (SI)
   Adrienne's Pizza

RAW BARS

26 Aquagrill
   Pearl Oyster Bar

Marlow & Sons (Bklyn)
25 Esca
24 Blue Ribbon
Craftsteak

SEAFOOD

28 Le Bernardin
27 Milos
26 Marea
Aquagrill
Pearl Oyster Bar
25 Taverna Kyclades (Qns)

SMALL PLATES

28 L'Atelier/Joël Robuchon
26 Degustation
Marlow & Sons (Bklyn)
25 Maze
Casellula
Zenkichi (Bklyn)

SOUTH AMERICAN

24 Caracas
23 Churrascaria
22 Pio Pio
Buenos Aires
Chimichurri Grill
Empanada Mama

SOUTHERN/SOUL

23 Egg (Bklyn)
Char No. 4 (Bklyn)
22 Amy Ruth's
Pink Tea Cup
19 Sylvia's
Rack & Soul

SOUTHWESTERN

23 Mesa Grill
21 Canyon Road
18 Agave
17 Cilantro
16 Cowgirl

SPANISH/TAPAS

25 Tía Pol
Casa Mono

24 Socarrat Paella
Las Ramblas
23 Txikito
Boqueria

STEAKHOUSES

27 Peter Luger (Bklyn)
25 Sparks Steak
Wolfgang's
Strip House
Del Frisco's
BLT Steak

THAI

27 Sripraphai (Qns)
24 Kuma Inn
23 Joya (Bklyn)
Song (Bklyn)
Erawan (Qns)
22 Land

TURKISH

23 Turkish Kitchen
21 Beyoglu
Sahara (Bklyn)
Akdeniz
Ali Baba
Bereket

VEGETARIAN

26 HanGawi
24 Saravanaas
23 Candle 79
Blossom
Gobo
Hummus Place

VIETNAMESE

22 Nicky's Viet.
Omai
Baoguette
Nha Trang
21 Indochine
Nam

BY SPECIAL FEATURE†

BREAKFAST

27 Jean Georges' Nougatine
25 Norma's
23 Egg (Bklyn)
Balthazar
22 Locanda Verde
18 Regency∇

BRUNCH DOWNTOWN

26 Aquagrill
25 Clinton St. Baking Co.
24 Prune
Blue Ribbon Bakery
23 Balthazar
21 Bar Artisanal

† Editors' choices

BRUNCH MIDTOWN

25 Aquavit
23 Artisanal
22 Penelope
21 Water Club
20 Eatery
18 Cafeteria

BRUNCH UPTOWN

26 Telepan
25 David Burke Townhouse
23 Square Meal
20 Sarabeth's
   Nice Matin
19 West Branch

BUSINESS LUNCH/DTWN

28 Bouley
27 Gotham Bar & Grill
   Nobu
25 Wolfgang's
23 Delmonico's
21 City Hall

BUSINESS LUNCH/MIDTWN

28 Jean Georges
26 Marea
   Modern
   Four Seasons
22 21 Club
20 Michael's

CELEBRATIONS

28 Le Bernardin
   Daniel
   Bouley
26 Marea
   River Café
22 Terrace in the Sky

CELEBRITY SCENES

23 Rao's
20 Da Silvano
   Cipriani Downtown
   Minetta Tavern
19 Waverly Inn
18 Monkey Bar

CHILD-FRIENDLY

23 Shake Shack
   Otto
21 Blue Smoke
   Peanut Butter & Co.
18 Serendipity 3
16 Cowgirl

DINING AT THE BAR

27 Picholine
26 Del Posto
25 Hearth
   Perry Street
22 Oyster Bar
20 Centro Vinoteca

GROUP DINING

23 Buddakan
   Churrascaria Plataforma
   Stanton Social
22 Rosa Mexicano
21 Hill Country
18 Ruby Foo's

HIPSTER HANGOUTS

23 Spotted Pig
21 Freemans
   La Esquina
   Cafe Select∇
20 Double Crown
   Hotel Griffou∇

HISTORIC PLACES

27 Peter Luger
23 Barney Greengrass
   Katz's Deli
21 Barbetta
19 Waverly Inn
17 Walker's

HOTTEST SERVERS

25 Del Frisco's
23 Spice Market
21 Tao
   Pastis
18 Salute!
16 Brother Jimmy's

LATE DINING

24 Blue Ribbon
23 Spotted Pig
21 Bar Artisanal
   La Esquina
   Pastis
20 Minetta Tavern

MEET FOR DRINK/DTWN

25 Bond Street
22 Standard Grill
21 Bar Artisanal
18 Macao Trading
   City Winery
   Employees Only

MEET FOR DRINK/MIDTWN

27	Nobu 57
26	Modern
25	Maze
22	La Fonda del Sol
21	Barbounia
20	Michael Jordan's

MEET FOR DRINK/UPTWN

24	Ouest
23	Atlantic Grill
22	Geisha
20	Landmarc
	Cafe Luxembourg
16	Demarchelier

MILESTONES

25th	Sea Grill
	Union Square Cafe
20th	Bubby's
	Carmine's
	Savoy
	Tribeca Grill

POWER SCENES

26	Four Seasons (Grill Room)
25	Del Frisco's
24	Elio's
23	Smith & Wollensky
22	21 Club
20	Michael's

PRIVATE PARTIES

28	Le Bernardin
26	Four Seasons
24	Keens
	Le Cirque
	Harry's
23	Buddakan
	Megu
	Spice Market
22	21 Club
21	City Hall
	Patroon
18	City Winery

QUICK BITES

24	Caracas
	Porchetta
	Amy's Bread
22	Baoguette
21	Momofuku Bakery
20	Gray's Papaya

SENIOR APPEAL

26	Felidia
24	Le Cirque
22	Mr. K's
21	Barbetta
20	Chez Napoléon
19	Russian Tea Room

SINGLES SCENES

23	Stanton Social
21	Tao
	La Esquina
19	Kingswood
	Bagatelle
18	Macao Trading

SOCIETY WATCH

26	Four Seasons (Pool Room)
23	Lusardi's
	Le Bilboquet
	Harry Cipriani
22	Sant Ambroeus
18	Swifty's

TRANSPORTING

23	Balthazar
22	Matsuri
21	Tao
19	FireBird
18	Monkey Bar
17	Boathouse

24-HOUR

21	Kang Suh
	Bereket
19	Veselka (Second Ave.)
18	Cafeteria
17	French Roast
15	Empire Diner

VISITORS ON EXP. ACCT.

28	Daniel
	Jean Georges
	Per Se
26	Masa
	Marea
24	Gordon Ramsay

WINNING WINE LISTS

28	Daniel
26	Cru
	Veritas
	Alto
	Del Posto
22	21 Club

BY LOCATION

CHELSEA

26 Scarpetta
Del Posto
25 Morimoto
Tía Pol
La Bergamote
24 Da Umberto

CHINATOWN

23 Oriental Garden
Fuleen Seafood
Peking Duck
Nice Green Bo
22 Great NY Noodle
Big Wong

EAST 40s

28 Sushi Yasuda
27 Kuruma Zushi
26 Convivio
25 Grifone
Sparks Steak
Hatsuhana

EAST 50s

28 L'Atelier/Joël Robuchon
27 La Grenouille
26 Adour
Alto
Felidia
Four Seasons

EAST 60s

28 Daniel
26 Sushi Seki
Scalinatella
25 David Burke Townhouse
JoJo
24 Philippe

EAST 70s

28 Sasabune
27 Café Boulud
Gari/Sushi
23 Campagnola
Carlyle
Lusardi's

EAST 80s

26 Sistina
25 Erminia
Spigolo
Sandro's
Poke
24 Elio's

EAST 90s & 100s

25 Sfoglia
23 Square Meal
El Paso Taqueria
Nick's
Itzocan
22 Pio Pio

EAST VILLAGE

27 Momofuku Ko
Kyo Ya
26 Degustation
Kanoyama
25 Pylos
Jewel Bako

FINANCIAL DISTRICT

24 Harry's
MarkJoseph Steak
23 Adrienne's Pizza
Delmonico's
22 Bobby Van's
2 West

FLATIRON/UNION SQ.

28 Gramercy Tavern
27 Eleven Madison Park
Union Square Cafe
26 15 East
Tocqueville
Veritas

GARMENT DISTRICT

24 Keens
23 Uncle Jack's
Cho Dang Gol
22 Szechuan Gourmet
Frankie & Johnnie's
21 Kang Suh

GRAMERCY

25 Casa Mono
BLT Prime
24 Novitá
Yama
Posto
23 Ess-a-Bagel

GREENWICH VILLAGE

27 Gotham Bar & Grill
Blue Hill
Annisa
Il Mulino
Babbo
Mas

HARLEM

22 Dinosaur BBQ
Amy Ruth's
20 Papaya King
19 Sylvia's
Hudson River Café
Kitchenette

LITTLE ITALY

23 Il Cortile
Pellegrino's
Nyonya
Angelo's, Mulberry St.
21 Vincent's
La Esquina

LOWER EAST SIDE

25 Clinton St. Baking Co.
24 Frankies Spuntino
ápizz
wd-50
Kuma Inn
23 Falai

MEATPACKING

25 Valbella
24 Old Homestead
23 Spice Market
22 SEA
21 STK
Paradou

MURRAY HILL

26 Sushi Sen-nin
HanGawi
25 Wolfgang's
24 Mishima
Saravanaas
Primehouse NY

NOHO

25 Bond Street
24 Il Buco
Bianca
Aroma
22 Five Points
Sala

NOLITA

24 Lombardi's
Peasant
23 Kitchen Club
Café Habana
22 Public
21 Ed's Lobster Bar

SOHO

26 Aquagrill
Blue Ribbon Sushi
25 Aurora
24 Blue Ribbon
Snack
Savoy

TRIBECA

28 Chanterelle
Bouley
27 Corton
Nobu
26 Il Giglio
Scalini Fedeli

WEST 40s

27 Gari/Sushi
25 Sushi Zen
Del Frisco's
Esca
24 db Bistro Moderne
Triomphe

WEST 50s

28 Le Bernardin
27 Sugiyama
Nobu
Milos
26 Marea
Modern

WEST 60s

28 Jean Georges
Per Se
27 Jean Georges' Nougatine
Picholine
26 Masa
Bar Masa

WEST 70s

27 Gari/Sushi
26 Dovetail
23 Ocean Grill
Shake Shack
Salumeria Rosi
'Cesca

WEST 80s

25 eighty one
24 Ouest
23 Barney Greengrass
Celeste
Blossom
Momoya

WEST 90s & UP

24 Pisticci
   Gennaro
23 Hummus Place
22 Pio Pio
   Indus Valley
   Wondee Siam

WEST VILLAGE

26 Little Owl
25 dell'anima
   Wallsé
   Piccolo Angolo
   Perry Street
24 Mary's Fish Camp

OUTER BOROUGHS

BRONX

26 Roberto
25 Zero Otto Nove
23 Jake's
   Enzo's
   Dominick's
22 Pio Pio

BROOKLYN: BAY RIDGE

26 Tanoreen
   Eliá
24 Fushimi
   Tuscany Grill
23 Areo
   Agnanti

BROOKLYN: HTS/DUMBO

26 River Café
25 Grimaldi's
   Noodle Pudding
24 Henry's End
   Queen
   Jack the Horse

BKLYN: CARROLL GDNS./
BOERUM & COBBLE HILLS

27 Grocery
26 Lucali
   Saul
25 Chocolate Room
   Pó
24 Frankies Spuntino

BROOKLYN: FT. GREENE/
PROSPECT HEIGHTS

24 Franny's
23 Café Habana/Outpost
21 Smoke Joint
   Zaytoons
   Ici
   67 Burger

BROOKLYN: PARK SLOPE

26 Al Di La
   applewood
   Blue Ribbon Sushi
   Rose Water
25 Chocolate Room
   Stone Park Café

BKLYN: WILLIAMSBURG

27 Peter Luger
26 Marlow & Sons
25 Fette Sau
   Aurora
   Dressler
   Zenkichi

BROOKLYN: OTHER

27 Di Fara (Midwood)
24 Good Fork (Red Hook)
23 Tommaso (Dyker Heights)
   L & B Spumoni (Bensonhurst)
22 Farm on Adderley
   (Ditmas Park)

QUEENS: ASTORIA/L.I.C.

27 Trattoria L'incontro
25 Piccola Venezia
   Taverna Kyclades
24 Tournesol
23 Agnanti
   Elias Corner

QUEENS: OTHER

27 Sripraphai (Woodside)
26 Danny Brown (Forest Hills)
25 Grimaldi's (Douglaston)
24 Park Side (Corona)
   Sapori D'Ischia (Woodside)
   Don Peppe (Ozone Park)

STATEN ISLAND

26 Bocelli (Grasmere)
25 Denino's (Port Richmond)
24 Fushimi (Grant City)
   Joe & Pat's (Lower Todt Hill)
   Trattoria Romana
   (Dongan Hills)
23 Da Noi (Shore Acres/Travis)

Top Decor

29 Asiate	Tao
	Lady Mendl's
28 Daniel	Water's Edge (Qns)
Four Seasons	Tocqueville
Per Se	Megu
Gilt	Park Avenue . . .
La Grenouille	Rouge Tomate
River Café (Bklyn)	
	25 Boathouse
27 Buddakan	Gotham Bar & Grill
Zenkichi (Bklyn)	Marea
Le Bernardin	FireBird
Adour	Water Club
Eleven Madison Park	Cávo (Qns)
Jean Georges	Kings' Carriage
Chanterelle	Matsuri
	Public
26 One if by Land	South Gate
Del Posto	Porter House NY
Modern	Tabla
Bouley	L'Atelier/Joël Robuchon
Kittichai	Thalassa
Carlyle	Oak Room
Ajna Bar	Battery Gardens
Spice Market	EN Japanese
Le Cirque	Mas
Gramercy Tavern	
Morimoto	

PATIOS/GARDENS

25 Boathouse	Barolo
Battery Gardens	**21** Bryant Park Grill
23 New Leaf Cafe	Aurora (Bklyn)
Blue Hill	I Trulli
Barbetta	**20** Pure Food & Wine
Convivio	**19** Gascogne
22 Park	Inside Park
I Coppi	**18** Back Forty

ROMANCE

28 Daniel	Terrace in the Sky
La Grenouille	Erminia
River Café (Bklyn)	Petrossian
27 Chanterelle	Allen & Delancey
26 One if by Land	**23** Dressler (Bklyn)
Del Posto	Il Buco
Bouley	**22** Convivium Osteria (Bklyn)
Water's Edge (Qns)	Wallsé
Kings' Carriage	**20** Raoul's
Mas	Le Refuge
24 Scalini Fedeli	**19** Gascogne

VIEWS

29	Asiate			Battery Gardens
28	Per Se			View
	River Café (Bklyn)		24	Terrace in the Sky
26	Modern			Sea Grill
	Water's Edge (Qns)		22	A Voce (W 60s)
25	Boathouse		21	Metrazur
	Water Club			Alma (Bklyn)
	Porter House NY		20	Gigino Wagner Park

Top Service

<u>28</u> Per Se
Daniel
Jean Georges
Le Bernardin
Chanterelle

<u>27</u> La Grenouille
Gramercy Tavern
Bouley
Four Seasons
Adour
Eleven Madison Park
Mas
Sugiyama

<u>26</u> L'Atelier/Joël Robuchon
Picholine
Gilt
Corton
Blue Hill
Gotham Bar & Grill
Kyo Ya
Union Square Cafe
Cru
Café Boulud
Annisa
River Café (Bklyn)

Jean Georges' Nougatine
Carlyle

<u>25</u> Tocqueville
Del Posto
Asiate
Grifone
Degustation
Acappella
Erminia
Masa
San Pietro
Scalini Fedeli*
Il Giglio
Il Tinello
Trattoria L'incontro (Qns)
Zenkichi (Bklyn)
Grocery (Bklyn)
Le Perigord
Veritas
Modern
Babbo
Valbella

<u>24</u> Aquavit
One if by Land
Marea

Best Buys

Everyone loves a bargain, and NYC offers plenty of them. Bear in mind:
(1) lunch typically costs 25 to 30% less than dinner, (2) outer-
borough dining is less costly than in Manhattan, (3) most Indian restaurants offer affordable lunch buffets and (4) biannual Restaurant
Weeks (in January and July) are big bargains.

ALL YOU CAN EAT

23 Churrascaria
Chola
Turkish Kitchen
22 Becco
21 Yuka
Darbar
20 Sapphire Indian
Chennai Garden
La Baraka (Qns)
Utsav

BYO

26 Lucali
25 Poke
24 Kuma Inn
23 Phoenix Garden
Peking Duck (Chinatown)
Tartine
22 Cube 63▽ (LES)
21 Angelica Kit.
Tea & Sympathy
19 Nook▽

CHEAP DATES

24 Snack
Soba-Ya
22 Sala
21 Holy Basil
Klong
26 Seats
Sonia Rose▽
20 Nomad▽
19 Turkuaz
La Lanterna di Vittoria

EARLY-BIRD

25 Caviar Russe
23 La Sirène
Jean Claude
Uncle Jack's
Italianissimo
Artisanal
22 House
Kittichai
Sueños
Kefi

FAMILY-STYLE

26 Roberto (Bronx)
25 Piccolo Angolo
24 Patricia's (Bronx)
Don Peppe (Qns)
Pisticci
23 Oriental Garden
Nick's
Rao's
Dominick's (Bronx)
22 Asia de Cuba

PRE-THEATER

27 Sugiyama
Jean Georges/Nougatine
26 Telepan
25 Anthos
Avra
24 Ouest
23 Ocean Grill
Atlantic Grill
22 Molyvos
Bobby Van's

PRIX FIXE LUNCH

28 Sushi Yasuda ($23)
27 Gotham Bar & Grill ($25)
Jean Georges' Nougatine ($26)
Milos ($24)
26 15 East ($24)
Dovetail ($24)
Felidia ($30)
25 Tabla ($24)
Tía Pol ($16)
Maze ($28)

PRIX FIXE DINNER

28 Sushi Yasuda ($23)
26 Dovetail ($38)
HanGawi ($35)
Rose Water (Bklyn) ($28)
25 eighty one ($31)
JoJo ($35)
Bond Street ($40)
24 Allegretti ($39)
Petrossian ($35)
Aroma ($35)

BEST BUYS: FULL MENU

Alice's Tea Cup | *American*
Bereket | *Turkish*
Big Wong | *Chinese*
Brennan & Carr (Bklyn) | *Sandwiches*
Chickpea | *Mideastern*
Cubana Café | *Pizza*
Dim Sum Go Go | *Chinese*
Egg (Bklyn) | *Southern*
El Malecon | *Dominican*
Energy Kitchen | *Health Food*
Excellent Dumpling | *Chinese*
Fette Sau (Bklyn) | *BBQ*
Great NY Noodle | *Noodle Shop*
Hummus Place | *Israeli/Veg.*
Joe & Pat's | *Italian/Pizza*
Joya | *Thai*
Land | *Thai*
L & B Spumoni (Bklyn) | *Pizza*
La Taqueria | *Mexican*
La Taza de Oro | *Diner*
Mama's Food | *American*
Mandoo Bar | *Korean*
Maoz | *Vegetarian*
Mee | *Noodle Shop*
Menchanko-tei | *Noodle Shop*

Mill Basin Deli (Bklyn) | *Deli*
Nanoosh | *Mediterranean*
Nha Trang | *Vietnamese*
Nyonya | *Malaysian*
Penelope | *American*
Pepe | *Italian*
Pho Bang | *Vietnamese*
Pink Tea Cup | *Soul/Southern*
Pio Pio | *Peruvian*
Pump Energy | *Health Food*
Quantum Leap | *Health/Veg.*
Rai Rai Ken | *Noodle Shop*
Ramen Setagaya | *Noodle Shop*
Rice | *Eclectic*
Saigon Grill | *Vietnamese*
SEA | *Thai*
Smoke Joint (Bklyn) | *BBQ*
Song (Bklyn) | *Thai*
Spice | *Thai*
Sripraphai (Qns) | *Thai*
Thai Pavilion | *Thai*
Tom's (Bklyn) | *Diner*
Veselka | *Ukrainian*
Wondee Siam | *Thai*
Zaytoons | *Mideastern*

BEST BUYS: SPECIALTY SHOPS

Amy's Bread | *baked goods*
An Choi | *sandwiches*
Artichoke Basille's | *pizza*
Baoguette | *Viet./sandwiches*
Bôi | *sandwiches*
brgr | *burgers*
burger joint | *burgers*
Caracas | *arepas*
Carl's | *cheesesteaks*
Chipotle | *Mexican*
Corner Bistro | *burgers*
Defonte's | *sandwiches*
Denino's | *pizza*
Di Fara (Bklyn) | *pizza*
Dirty Bird to go | *chicken*
Dishes | *sandwiches*
Dumpling House | *dumplings*
Dumpling Man | *dumplings*
Empanada Mama | *empanadas*
Ess-a-Bagel | *deli*
Five Guys | *burgers*
goodburger | *burgers*
Gray's Papaya | *hot dogs*

Grimaldi's (Bklyn) | *pizza*
Hale & Hearty | *soup*
Hampton Chutney | *Indian*
Hanco's | *sandwiches*
Joe's Pizza | *pizza*
Kati Roll Co. | *Indian*
La Flor (Bronx) | *baked goods*
Lenny's | *sandwiches*
Momofuku Bakery | *dessert*
Nicky's Viet. | *sandwiches*
99 Miles to Philly | *cheesesteaks*
Papaya King | *hot dogs*
Peanut Butter | *sandwiches*
Pizza 33 | *pizza*
Porchetta | *sandwiches*
Press 195 | *sandwiches*
Rickshaw | *dumplings*
Roll-n-Roaster | *sandwiches*
Shake Shack | *burgers*
67 Burger | *burgers*
S'MAC | *mac 'n' cheese*
Two Boots | *pizza*
Waldy's | *pizza*

LUNCH: $35 OR LESS

A.J. Maxwell's	$30
Allegretti	24
Angelo & Maxie's	21
Anthos	28
AQ Kafé	15
Artisanal	24
Asiate	24
Atlantic Grill	24
Aureole	34
Avra	29
Bar Breton	24
Becco	18
Beppe	30
Bistro du Nord	19
Bobby Van's	30
Café de Bruxelles	15
Cafe Luxembourg	25
Cafe Un Deux/Le Petit	19
Centro Vinoteca	20
Chiam	21
Chinatown Brasserie	15
Chin Chin	27
Cibo	25
David Burke Townhouse	24
Del Frisco's	32
Demarchelier	16
Dovetail	24
Duane Park	24
Eleven Madison Park	28
etcetera etcetera	24
Felidia	30
15 East	24
FireBird	30
Five Points	25
Gallagher's Steak	28
Gascogne	21
Gavroche	20
Geisha	29
Giorgio's/Gramercy	20
Gotham Bar & Grill	25
HanGawi	20
Il Bastardo	15
Jean Georges' Nougatine	26
JoJo	24
Josephina	24
Kellari Taverna	24
Kings' Carriage	19
La Boîte en Bois	25
L'Absinthe	28
La Mangeoire	20
La Petite Auberge	20
Le Cirque	35
L'Ecole	28
Le Perigord	32
Le Relais/Venise	24
Lumi	28
Marea	34
Maze	28
Megu Midtown	24
Mercer Kitchen	24
Mia Dona	24
Milos	24
Molyvos	25
Mr. K's	28
Ocean Grill	24
Olives	24
Orsay	25
Osteria del Circo	28
Pampano	27
Parlor Steakhouse	25
Patroon	27
Periyali	26
Pongal	8
Quinto Quarto	20
Remi	24
Rouge Tomate	29
Russian Tea Room	35
Shun Lee Palace	24
Solera	29
Solo	24
Spice Market	24
Sushi Yasuda	23
Tabla	24
Tamarind	24
Tao	24
Tavern on the Green	39
T-Bar Steak	24
Telepan	22
Terrazz a Toscana	15
Thalia	17
Tía Pol	16
Tocqueville	24
Trata	25
Tratt. Dell'Arte	24
Tse Yang	28
Turkish Kitchen	17
21 Club	24
Uskudar	16
ViceVersa	24
Vong	24
West Bank Cafe	24
Zarela	17

DINNER: $40 OR LESS

PT = pre-theater only; where two prices are listed, the first is pre-theater and the second for normal dinner hours.

Abboccato/PT	$35	HanGawi	35
Akdeniz	22	ilili	35
Aki	30	Il Punto/PT	30
Algonquin/PT	39	Indochine/PT	32
Alias/PT	20	Japonais/PT	35
Allegretti	39	Jean Georges' Nougatine/PT	35
Alouette/PT	25	Jewel of India/PT	28
Apiary	35	JoJo	35
Aroma	35	Kefi/PT	17
Artisanal/PT	24/35	Kellari Taverna/PT	35
Avra/PT	39	Kittichai/PT	35
Bacchus (Bklyn)	25	La Boîte en Bois/PT	40
Bar Breton	35	La Bonne Soupe	24
Bay Leaf/PT	21	La Mangeoire	28
Becco	23	La Petite Auberge	29
Beppe	40	Le Rivage	37
Bistro Citron/PT	22	Le Singe Vert/PT	25
Bistro du Nord/PT	20	Maria Pia/PT	23
Bombay Palace	30	Marseille	35
Bond 45	35	McCormick & Schmick/PT	30
Bond Street	40	Métisse/PT	23
Brasserie Cognac/PT	30/40	Molyvos/PT	37
Brasserie Julien	22	Nios	35
Bryant Park/PT	35	Ocean Grill/PT	25
B. Smith's/PT	29	Osteria del Circo/PT	38
Bussaco (Bklyn)	23	Ouest/PT	34
Cafe Cluny/PT	30	Pascalou/PT	20
Café de Bruxelles/PT	25	Pasha/PT	24
Cafe Loup	28	Patroon	39
Cafe Un Deux Trois	28	Petrossian	35
Caffe Grazie	38	Pietrasanta	25
Capsouto Frères	40	Pomaire/PT	25
Cascina/PT	25	Quercy (Bklyn)	28
Caviar Russe/PT	30	Remi	35
Centro Vinoteca	35	Rose Water (Bklyn)	28
Chez Napoléon	30	Savann	16
Chinatown Brasserie	35	Shun Lee Palace	35
Chin Chin	35	Sueños/PT	30
Cibo	35	Sugiyama/PT	32
Cipriani Dolci	40	Sushi Yasuda	23
Cipriani Downtown	39	Table d'Hôte	29
Compass	35	Thalia/PT	35
dévi	35	Tommaso	25
Docks Oyster Bar/PT	28	Turkish Cuisine	27
Dovetail	38	21 Club	35
eighty one	31	Vatan	31
etcetera etcetera	35	ViceVersa	35
Gascogne/PT	27/29	Vincent's	28
Gavroche/PT	20	Vong	35
Gigino	30	Water Club	35
Haakon's Hall	14	West Bank Cafe	30

RESTAURANT
DIRECTORY

	FOOD	DECOR	SERVICE	COST

Abboccato Italian

21	20	20	$56

W 50s | Blakely Hotel | 136 W. 55th St. (bet. 6th & 7th Aves.) |
212-265-4000 | www.abboccato.com

A "consistent performer", this "cozy" Midtown "hideaway" plies its
"*favoloso*" Italian fare in a "convenient" location "across from City
Center" and near Carnegie Hall; yes, checks can get a "little pricey",
but the pre-theater prix fixe offers "good value."

Abigael's Eclectic

20	16	17	$49

Garment District | 1407 Broadway (bet. 38th & 39th Sts.) | 212-575-1407 |
www.abigaels.com

Chef Jeff Nathan continues to "prove that kosher food can be wonderful" at this steak-centric Garment Districter whose Eclectic menu is
augmented by sushi and Pan-Asian bites in an upstairs lounge; now if
only they'd do something about decor "in need of renovation" and often "just adequate" service.

Abigail American

▽ 20	20	17	$30

Prospect Heights | 807 Classon Ave. (St. Johns Pl.) | Brooklyn |
718-399-3200 | www.abigailbrooklyn.com

Convenient to the Brooklyn Museum, this "lovely", "affordable" Prospect
Heights yearling from chef Abigail Hitchcock (CamaJe) wins favor with
"tasty" New American cuisine, "jazz brunches" and an overall "posi-
tive vibe"; hopefully, it'll soon "work out the glitches" with service.

abistro Ⓜ African

▽ 25	13	21	$33

Fort Greene | 154 Carlton Ave. (bet. Myrtle Ave. & Willoughby St.) |
Brooklyn | 718-855-9455

The French-accented West African fare at this "tiny", "hidden" Fort
Greene "treasure" "couldn't be better", and the owners and crew
couldn't be more "welcoming"; factor in "affordable" checks, and the
"long waits are totally worth it."

Aburiya Kinnosuke Japanese

24	21	22	$53

E 40s | 213 E. 45th St. (bet. 2nd & 3rd Aves.) | 212-867-5454 |
aburiyakinnosuke.com

"Fantastic" robata-grill specialties and "homemade tofu" are the reasons to come to this sushi-free Japanese "den" in Midtown that's
"hard to find" (and "harder to pronounce") but "easy to love"; if some
declare it "a tad overpriced", it's way "cheaper than going to Tokyo"
with much the same effect.

Acappella Italian

25	22	25	$73

TriBeCa | 1 Hudson St. (Chambers St.) | 212-240-0163 |
www.acappella-restaurant.com

It's a "trip to Italy without the airfare" at this TriBeCan offering some of
the "best classic Italian in the city"; it's "old-fashioned", à la 1960,
and "pricey" too, but "excellent food and service" backed up by "free
grappa" at meal's end make it "one of the city's hidden treasures."

A Casa Fox ⊠Ⓜ Pan-Latin

▽ 20	19	20	$33

LES | 173 Orchard St. (Stanton St.) | 212-253-1900 | www.acasafox.com

Caterer Melissa Fox brings her Pan-Latin cooking to a wider audience
via this "warm, inviting" Lower Eastsider, where the "fairly priced" fare
ranges from *bocaditos* (small bites) to clay-pot dinners; the "charm-

ingly rustic", fireplace-enhanced space and "unrushed service" have all feeling "right at home."

Accademia di Vino *Italian*

19 | 19 | 18 | $50

E 60s | 1081 Third Ave. (bet. 63rd & 64th Sts.) | 212-888-6333 | www.accademiadivino.com

A "favorite" UES "gathering place", this "always-abuzz" bi-level enoteca/trattoria with a "wine cellar" feel offers "solid" (if "nothing special") Italian bites to go with its "impressive" vinos from The Boot; "spotty" service and tabs that can "rise quickly" don't dampen the "noisy", "fun scene"; N.B. a new UWS branch is planned for late 2009.

Acqua *Italian*

18 | 17 | 18 | $38

W 90s | 718 Amsterdam Ave. (95th St.) | 212-222-2752 | www.acquanyc.com

"Reliable" for an "evening in the neighborhood" is the word on this "casual" UWS "standby" plying wood-oven pizzas and other "basic" Italian fare at "decent prices"; maybe service is variable and the look "a little on the plain side", but most rate it "a safe bet."

Acqua at Peck Slip *Italian*

21 | 18 | 19 | $41

Seaport | 21 Peck Slip (Water St.) | 212-349-4433 | www.acquarestaurantnyc.com

On a "cute cobblestone" street a "little off the beaten" Seaport path, this "no-fuss" Italian's "pleasing" pastas and other "decent" dishes taste better when you "sit outside" and "watch the boats go by"; "reasonable" prices make occasionally "overwhelmed" service easy to take.

☑ Adour *French*

26 | 27 | 27 | $128

E 50s | St. Regis Hotel | 2 E. 55th St. (bet. 5th & Madison Aves.) | 212-710-2277 | www.adour-stregis.com

Although it's "probably the most authentic, most Parisian haute-cuisine restaurant in NY", Alain Ducasse's "refined", oenophile-oriented Midtown French isn't really adoured by the NY establishment; considering the overall "almost perfect" experience – David Rockwell's "elegant" glass "turn-of-the-century" decor, "dreamy food", "exceptional wines" and "courteous" pro service – it's no wonder the tabs can be "shockingly expensive."

Adrienne's Pizzabar ◑ *Pizza*

23 | 16 | 16 | $25

Financial District | 87 Pearl St. (bet. Coenties Slip & Hanover Sq.) | 212-248-3838 | www.adriennespizzabar.com

"Huge", "low-priced" pizzas keep this "fun" Financial District Italian "jam-packed" with Wall Street types, ergo the "harried service"; "get there early" at lunch to nab a seat out on "charming" "old Stone Street."

Afghan Kebab House *Afghan*

19 | 11 | 16 | $25

E 70s | 1345 Second Ave. (bet. 70th & 71st Sts.) | 212-517-2776
W 50s | 764 Ninth Ave. (bet. 51st & 52nd Sts.) | 212-307-1612
NEW Astoria | 25-89 Steinway St. (28th Ave.) | Queens | 718-777-7758
Jackson Heights | 74-16 37th Ave. (bet. 74th & 75th Sts.) | Queens | 718-565-0471

"Deliciously seasoned" "quality" kebabs are the "highlight" at these "reliable" Middle Eastern storefronts; sure, they're "divey" with "so-so" service, but "unbeatable prices" ensure that most people "keep going back" to these "tiny" contenders.

	FOOD	DECOR	SERVICE	COST

Agave *Southwestern*

18 | **18** | **17** | **$39**

W Village | 140 Seventh Ave. S. (bet. Charles & W. 10th Sts.) |
212-989-2100 | www.agaveny.com

A prime location, lots of "singles" and "fantastic tequilas" add up to a
"vibrant" (sometimes "deafening") scene at this Village Southwesterner;
given the mostly "just ok" eats, "mediocre" service and decor "need-
ing a face-lift", though, "you'd better be here to party."

Agnanti *Greek*

23 | **15** | **19** | **$35**

Bay Ridge | 7802 Fifth Ave. (78th St.) | Brooklyn | 718-833-7033
Astoria | 19-06 Ditmars Blvd. (19th St.) | Queens | 718-545-4554
www.agnantimeze.com

For the "cheapest trip to Greece you'll ever have" try these "traditional"
Astoria–Bay Ridge tavernas, where "whole grilled fish are a highlight"
but there are also "some unusual dishes from Asia Minor" on offer; in
summer, ask for a table "out next to the park" at the Queens original.

NEW Agua Dulce ● *Pan-Latin*

- | **-** | **-** | **M**

W 50s | 802 Ninth Ave. (bet. 53rd & 54th Sts.) | 212-262-1299 |
www.aguadulceny.com

Awash in bright pastels and glistening tile, this West 50s newcomer
takes its name ('fresh water') literally, pouring its own filtered, flavor-
infused agua to accompany midpriced Pan-Latin fare like citrus-salmon
ceviche; the crisp interior is making its own splash, with a bustling bar
beneath a two-story atrium and moody, multilevel dining room.

Aja ● *Pan-Asian*

20 | **21** | **18** | **$40**

E 50s | 1068 First Ave. (58th St.) | 212-888-8008 | www.ajaasiancuisine.com

"Koi fish" swimming under "see-through floors" and a "giant Buddha"
statue add "very cool" atmosphere to this relatively "reasonable" Sutton
Place eatery plying "innovative sushi" and Pan-Asian bites; just know
that "loud" noise levels can "undo" the "Zen-like" mood.

Aji Sushi *Japanese*

21 | **14** | **20** | **$30**

Murray Hill | 519 Third Ave. (bet. 34th & 35th Sts.) | 212-686-2055 |
www.ajisushinyc.com

In a neighborhood swimming with sushi choices, this "tiny" Murray
Hill Japanese "stands out" for its "affordable" rolls comprising catch so
fresh it's "still snapping"; those unimpressed with the "nothing-to-look-
at" digs should know the "efficient service" extends to "quick delivery."

A.J. Maxwell's Steakhouse *Steak*

22 | **19** | **21** | **$63**

W 40s | 57 W. 48th St. (bet. 5th & 6th Aves.) | 212-262-6200 |
www.ajmaxwells.com

"Bring your appetite" because the "delicious", "pricey" slabs are "huge"
at this "classy yet casual" Rock Center meatery decorated with a mural
from the space's days as the Forum of the Twelve Caesars; a few shrug
"nothing special", but the "friendly" service pleases most.

Ajna Bar ● *Asian Fusion*

19 | **26** | **18** | **$63**

(fka Buddha Bar)

Meatpacking | 25 Little W. 12th St. (bet. 9th Ave. & Washington St.) |
212-647-7314

The "giant Buddha" is gone and the name has changed, but the jellyfish
tanks and other "dramatic" decor elements remain at this "happen-

| | FOOD | DECOR | SERVICE | COST |

ing" Meatpacking resto-bar that's a "sight to behold" – as are the "gorgeous" patrons "hobnobbing" with "models and bottles"; the "decent" Asian fusion fare and "snooty" service don't "quite live up" to the "noisy" "scene", but "what could?"

Akdeniz ☒ Turkish
21 | **12** | **19** | **$31**

W 40s | 19 W. 46th St. (bet. 5th & 6th Aves.) | 212-575-2307 | www.akdenizturkishusa.com

"Tasty" and "plentiful" Turkish fare at "bang-for-your-buck" prices makes this "accommodating" eatery a Theater District "find"; it's "ideal for a quick lunch" or "satisfying" prix fixe dinner ($22), and if the decor were better it "wouldn't be so cheap."

Aki Japanese
24 | **14** | **22** | **$45**

G Village | 181 W. Fourth St. (bet. Barrow & Jones Sts.) | 212-989-5440

Treasured as a "wonderful" Greenwich Village "hidden gem", this "quirky" nook offers "inventive" Japanese sushi with a Caribbean accent, plus service "with a smile"; "sparse", "elevator-size" digs don't deter many when the prices are this "economical" for the quality.

A La Turka Turkish
19 | **13** | **16** | **$36**

E 70s | 1417 Second Ave. (74th St.) | 212-744-2424 | www.alaturkarestaurant.com

"A la delightful" declare partisans of this "casual" UES Turk where "plentiful portions" of "delish" "homey" classics at "recession-bustser" prices mean business is "bustling"; those who object to its "so-so" surroundings and "hit-or-miss" service get it "to go."

Alberto Italian
▽ **23** | **20** | **23** | **$50**

Forest Hills | 98-31 Metropolitan Ave. (bet. 69th & 70th Aves.) | Queens | 718-268-7860

This Forest Hills "longtime neighborhood staple" has built its "loyal following" with "*delizioso*" "old-school" Northern Italian dishes and staffers "caring" enough to make you feel "like a guest in their home"; a "romantic", stained-glass-window-enhanced interior and fair prices make "reservations a must."

Alchemy American
19 | **18** | **18** | **$29**

Park Slope | 56 Fifth Ave. (bet. Bergen St. & St. Marks Pl.) | Brooklyn | 718-636-4385 | www.alchemybrooklyn.com

Relied on as a "quaint neighborhood" "hangout", this "friendly" New American gastropub in Park Slope has a solid beer selection and a "cozy", "dark" setup complete with "back garden" as its chief virtues; skeptics cite "just ok" food and "sweet-but-strained" service, but given the modest prices, "good vibes" prevail.

NEW Aldea ☒ Portuguese
▽ **26** | **20** | **23** | **$61**

Flatiron | 31 W. 17th St. (bet. 5th & 6th Aves.) | 212-675-7223 | www.aldearestaurant.com

Exhibiting more elegance than its name ('village') may suggest, this Flatiron arrival's "spare" clean-lined space culminates in a wide-open back kitchen; the "superb" "nouveau" Portuguese cuisine showcasing seasonal and greenmarket ingredients is surprisingly well-priced given its high quality and sophistication; P.S. sit at the back bar to watch the chefs "work their magic."

	FOOD	DECOR	SERVICE	COST

☑ Al Di La *Italian*
26 | 18 | 22 | $47

Park Slope | 248 Fifth Ave. (Carroll St.) | Brooklyn | 718-783-4565 |
www.aldilatrattoria.com

Apart from the "inevitable long wait" ("if only they took reservations!"), pretty much "nothing beats" this "laid-back" Park Sloper's "top-notch" Venetian cuisine, "reasonable" prices and "accommodating" service; the "whole wonderful experience" is enough to make you want to go "al di time" – including during "recently begun lunch service", when tables are easier to come by.

Aleo *Italian/Mediterranean*
▽ 19 | 16 | 19 | $42

Flatiron | 7 W. 20th St. (bet. 5th & 6th Aves.) | 212-691-8136 |
www.aleorestaurant.com

The combination of "well-prepared" Italian-Med cuisine, "personal service" and "moderate prices" "works well" at this "reliable" (if "predictable") Flatironer; the interior is "pleasant" enough, but nab a seat out in the garden and you may "feel like you've escaped NYC."

Alfredo of Rome *Italian*
18 | 18 | 17 | $49

W 40s | 4 W. 49th St. (bet. 5th & 6th Aves.) | 212-397-0100 |
www.alfredos.com

This "spacious" Rock Center Italian may cater largely to the "tourist" trade (don't forget your "'I Love NY' tee"), but there's "decent" fare to be had once you get past the "noise" and "spotty" service; as for the namesake fettuccine, one diner's "must" is another's "long way from Rome."

Algonquin Hotel Round Table *American*
17 | 24 | 20 | $57

W 40s | Algonquin Hotel | 59 W. 44th St. (bet. 5th & 6th Aves.) |
212-840-6800 | www.algonquinhotel.com

You go to this Theater District "institution" move for its "rich history" than for the "average", "expensive" American eats (maybe "Dorothy Parker didn't much care about food"); most just "soak in" the "civilized", "old-NY" vibe and "fine drinks" until the "literary ghosts" inspire them to head home and "read."

Alias *American*
▽ 21 | 15 | 20 | $37

LES | 76 Clinton St. (Rivington St.) | 212-505-5011 |
www.aliasrestaurant.com

American comfort food "prepared with care" and boasting "original flavors" ensures this "tiny" LES storefront remains a "standby" – and the "friendly" service and "accessible prices" don't hurt either; don't miss the "phenomenal brunch" and "can't-go-wrong" $30 Sunday night prix fixe.

Ali Baba *Turkish*
21 | 15 | 18 | $32

E 40s | 862 Second Ave. (46th St.) | 212-888-8622 |
www.alibabasterrace.com ●

Murray Hill | 212 E. 34th St. (bet. 2nd & 3rd Aves.) | 212-683-9206 |
www.alibabaturkishcuisine.com

"Delectable" edibles "like in Istanbul" at "value" prices (no "40 thieves" here) ensure these "without-frills" East Side Turks are perpetually "packed"; "pleasant"-but-"rushed" service is part of the deal, as are "tight" conditions – though in summer the U.N.-area offshoot's rooftop terrace is a good option.

Menus, photos, voting and more – free at ZAGAT.com

	FOOD	DECOR	SERVICE	COST

Aliseo Osteria del Borgo Ⓜ *Italian* ▽ 23 | 20 | 20 | $48

Prospect Heights | 665 Vanderbilt Ave. (bet. Park & Prospect Pls.) | Brooklyn | 718-783-3400

"Charming, but not pretentious", this "tiny" Prospect Heights Italian proffers seasonal fare inspired by Italy's Marche region; the "freshest" possible ingredients, "attentive" service and the presence of a "lovely" (some say "zany") owner complete the "homey" picture.

Allegretti Ⓩ *French* 24 | 22 | 23 | $71

Flatiron | 46 W. 22nd St. (bet. 5th & 6th Aves.) | 212-206-0555 | www.allegrettinyc.com

"Exciting", "sophisticated" Niçoise cuisine by "hot chef" Alain Allegretti (ex Le Cirque, Atelier) shines at this "high-end" Gallic parked on a "nondescript" Flatiron block; the "omnipresent" servers are "gracious" and the setting "elegant" if "stark" – "but oh, those prices."

Allen & Delancey *American* 23 | 24 | 21 | $67

LES | 115 Allen St. (Delancey St.) | 212-253-5400 | www.allenanddelancey.net

"Velvet curtains", "dim lighting", "candles all over" – this LES New American is "one of the sexiest restaurants in the city", and perhaps the "ultimate date spot" for "hip" couples; however, know that the "nights to remember" here are "expensive"; N.B. the post-Survey arrival of chef Ryan Skeen (ex Irving Mill) puts the Food rating in play.

Alloro *Italian* 22 | 18 | 22 | $51

E 70s | 307 E. 77th St. (bet. 1st & 2nd Aves.) | 212-535-2866 | www.alloronyc.com

"Delightful" declare early visitors to this "alluring" Upper East Side yearling from the Cacio e Pepe folks, citing "imaginative" takes on "traditional Italian cuisine" coupled with "gracious", "treat-you-like-family" service; however, the "vibrant", verdant modern decor has many musing "what's with all the green?"

Alma *Mexican* 20 | 21 | 19 | $36

Carroll Gardens | 187 Columbia St., 2nd fl. (Degraw St.) | Brooklyn | 718-643-5400 | www.almarestaurant.com

"Holy guacamole", check out the "magical rooftop views" of Manhattan from this "transporting" Mexican eatery that's a longtime West Carroll Gardens "fave"; despite "long waits", most say *muy bueno* about the "semi-upscale" fare and semi-downscale tabs – "deliciously strong margaritas" certainly help.

NEW Almond *French* 20 | 19 | 20 | $48

Flatiron | 12 E. 22nd St. (bet. B'way & Park Ave. S.) | 212-228-7557 | www.almondnyc.com

A "spin-off" of the "popular" Bridgehampton eatery, this latest arrival to a revolving-door Flatiron space retains the "whitewashed" summer cottage vibe of its predecessor, Borough Food & Drink; "solid" French bistro fare at relatively "modest" rates is garnering it a "noisy, young" following.

Alouette ◗ *French* 20 | 17 | 20 | $44

W 90s | 2588 Broadway (bet. 97th & 98th Sts.) | 212-222-6808 | www.alouettenyc.com

"Still a neighborhood secret" "after all these years", this "sweet" UWS French bistro "pleases palates and pocketbooks" with "delicious", "af-

"fordable" classics; the "duplex" space can feel "cramped", but the "thoughtful" service ensures an overall "easygoing" vibe.

Alta *Mediterranean*
24 | 23 | 21 | $50

G Village | 64 W. 10th St. (bet. 5th & 6th Aves.) | 212-505-7777 | www.altarestaurant.com

"Fun for groups" and "dates", this "rustic", fireplace-equipped Village "retreat" turns out Med tapas that "dazzle with creativity and flavor" (even the Brussels sprouts are "ah-maaazing"); just know that it gets "loud" and the bill can "mount" when "everyone's having a good time."

☑ Alto ⌨ *Italian*
26 | 23 | 24 | $98

E 50s | 11 E. 53rd St. (bet. 5th & Madison Aves.) | 212-308-1099 | www.altorestaurant.com

"Excellent in all respects" – from chef Michael White's "divine" prix fixe-only Italian cuisine backed by an "incredible wine selection" to the "elegant, modern" space and "attentive yet unobtrusive" service – this "top-notch" Midtowner is deemed "better than ever"; however, it's perhaps best suited to "special occasions" and "power lunches", because the "over-the-top" prices "challenge the limits" of most credit cards.

Amaranth ◐ *Mediterranean*
18 | 17 | 17 | $60

E 60s | 21 E. 62nd St. (bet. 5th & Madison Aves.) | 212-980-6700 | www.amaranthrestaurant.com

"Frilly" "young lovelies" "out of the society pages" and other "Park Avenue types" make for a "see-and-be-seen" scene at this "pricey" East Side Med; if you can focus on it, the "simple" food is "good" enough, but, no surprise, service is "better if you're a frequent customer."

Amazing 66 *Chinese*
22 | 11 | 15 | $25

Chinatown | 66 Mott St. (bet. Bayard & Canal Sts.) | 212-334-0099

This "popular" Chinatown eatery distinguishes itself with "original" Cantonese offerings, including "selections for the daring", at prices that are a "pittance"; "brusque" servers are always in a "rush" and there's no decor to speak of, but "who cares when the food's this good?"

Amber ◐ *Pan-Asian*
20 | 20 | 19 | $37

E 80s | 1406 Third Ave. (80th St.) | 212-249-5020 | www.orderamberuppereast.com

NEW **G Village** | 432 Sixth Ave. (bet. 9th & 10th Sts.) | 212-477-5880

Murray Hill | 381 Third Ave. (bet. 27th & 28th Sts.) | 212-686-6388 | www.ambernyc.net

W 70s | 221 Columbus Ave. (70th St.) | 212-799-8100 | www.ambercolumbus.com

"Snazzy" setups ("love the giant Buddha"), "enticing" Pan-Asian "fusion" dishes and "fresh" sushi at "inexpensive" rates are the draw at these "trendy" "favorites"; service is variable and the music "deafening", but the "young clientele" doesn't seem to mind.

Amma *Indian*
24 | 18 | 23 | $47

E 50s | 246 E. 51st St. (bet. 2nd & 3rd Aves.) | 212-644-8330 | www.ammanyc.com

"Upscale" Northern Indian cuisine elevated to "new levels" is the deal at this "warm, welcoming" East Midtowner "hidden among brownstones" – especially if you go for the tasting menu; however, though its name means "mother", unlike at ma's table, you'll need to "be prepared to pay."

Ammos 🅱 *Greek*

FOOD	DECOR	SERVICE	COST
21	21	19	$55

E 40s | 52 Vanderbilt Ave. (bet. 44th & 45th Sts.) | 212-922-9999 | www.ammosnewyork.com

"Light, bright", "modern" Greek cuisine, including "fresh, well-presented" seafood, is the draw at this "handsome" Grand Central-area standby; service is "good", if occasionally "condescending", but watch for per-pound prices that can "blow the budget."

Amor Cubano ❶ *Cuban*

	FOOD	DECOR	SERVICE	COST
▽	22	20	23	$35

Harlem | 2018 Third Ave. (111th St.) | 212-996-1220 | www.amorcubanorestaurant.com

"Step right into" old Havana for a night at this "upbeat", "friendly" East Harlem Cuban; its "homestyle" "favorites" and "strong drinks" are delivered by "colorful costume"–clad servers who dance to Latin music of yesteryear – "what more could you ask for?"

Amorina *Pizza*

	FOOD	DECOR	SERVICE	COST
▽	25	15	22	$24

Prospect Heights | 624 Vanderbilt Ave. (Prospect Pl.) | Brooklyn | 718-230-3030 | www.amorinapizza.com

"Outstanding" thin-crust pizzas with "fresh", "unconventional" toppings at "recession-friendly" rates cement this Prospect Heights pie place's status as a local "go-to"; "friendly" staffers, checkered tablecloths and "Italian ephemera hanging on the walls" complete the "homey" vibe.

Amy Ruth's *Soul Food*

FOOD	DECOR	SERVICE	COST
22	13	18	$26

Harlem | 113 W. 116th St. (bet. Lenox & 7th Aves.) | 212-280-8779 | www.amyruthsharlem.com

When you need some "soul food in the city", this "honest-to-goodness" "down-home" Harlem "standby" will provide your "fatty fix" of ribs, waffles and chicken and such at a "reasonable" price; maybe the digs are "nothing special", but that doesn't slow the "lines" for the "sumptuous Sunday brunch."

Amy's Bread *Bakery/Sandwiches*

FOOD	DECOR	SERVICE	COST
24	12	18	$13

Chelsea | Chelsea Mkt. | 75 Ninth Ave. (bet. 15th & 16th Sts.) | 212-462-4338
G Village | 250 Bleecker St. (Leroy St.) | 212-675-7802
W 40s | 672 Ninth Ave. (bet. 46th & 47th Sts.) | 212-977-2670
www.amysbread.com

Some of the "most awesome bread ever", "fresh sandwiches" and "tasty sweets" at "fair" prices make these "casual" bakeries/cafes a "carb-lover's dream" and a "NY staple" – ergo the "lines out the door"; "seductive aromas" lure 'em in, but "drab" setups with "few seats" keep visits "quick."

NEW An Choi Ⓜ *Vietnamese*

	FOOD	DECOR	SERVICE	COST
▽	21	18	20	$25

LES | 85 Orchard St. (bet. Broome & Grand Sts.) | 212-226-3700 | www.anchoinyc.com

With a purposely minimalist look – exposed brick, bare bulbs, a glass-walled kitchen – this LES Vietnamese is drawing hipsters and bankers alike; though by the standards of nearby Chinatown its *banh mi* and pho might be a tad pricey, most deem it a "bargain" all the same.

	FOOD	DECOR	SERVICE	COST

NEW André *French*
— — — M

E 50s | Renaissance Hotel 57 | 130 E. 57th St., 2nd fl. (bet. Lexington & Park Aves.) | 212-688-3939 | www.opiarestaurant.com

On the Renaissance Hotel's second floor, behind the lounge Opia, this new Franco-American plies midpriced, seasonal fare in airy digs; with a former La Goulue chef in the kitchen and live jazz on Monday nights, it's already filling up with hotel guests and East Side suits.

NEW Anella ▣⇱ *Italian*
— — — M

Greenpoint | 222 Franklin St. (bet. Green & Huron Sts.) | Brooklyn | 718-389-8100 | www.anellabrooklyn.com

A Chanterelle alum revives Greenpoint's erstwhile Queen's Hideaway space with this new Italian vending pizzas, pastas and hearty dishes from a brick oven; its already-bustling interior is fashionably dishabille, with a reclaimed wood bar and patio seating.

Angelica Kitchen ⇱ *Vegan/Vegetarian*
21 | 15 | 18 | $25

E Village | 300 E. 12th St. (bet. 1st & 2nd Aves.) | 212-228-2909 | www.angelicakitchen.com

You "can't help feeling virtuous" at this "1970s"-era East Village vegan, whose "healthy food at its finest" is a "favorite" of "hippies" and "detoxing" "skinny models" alike; sometimes-"bland" flavors, iffy decor and "erratic" service are balanced by the "value" prices and BYO policy.

Angelina's ▣ *Italian*
21 | 20 | 18 | $53

Staten Island | 399 Ellis St. (off Arthur Kill Rd.) | 718-227-2900 | www.angelinasristorante.com

Ensconced in "pleasant" Tottenville digs boasting "amazing" waterfront views, this plush, tri-level Staten Islander pleases patrons with "delicious" Italian fare and "live music on most nights"; "personal" service helps take the edge off "Manhattan-high" prices.

Angelo & Maxie's *Steak*
22 | 19 | 20 | $57

Flatiron | 233 Park Ave. S. (19th St.) | 212-220-9200

Maxie's Bar & Grill ☻ *American*
Flatiron | 233 Park Ave. S. (19th St.) | 212-979-7800
www.angelo-maxies.com

"Enormous" drinks and "mega"-size steaks fuel a "high-energy" scene at this "rollicking" Flatiron meatery packed with "miles of men and martinis"; the "waiters aim to please", but it's the "less-than-the-big-boys'" tabs that ensure it remains a "solid" hit; P.S. the "low-key" next-door bar-and-grill focuses on burgers.

Angelo's of Mulberry Street ▣ *Italian*
23 | 16 | 20 | $46

Little Italy | 146 Mulberry St. (bet. Grand & Hester Sts.) | 212-966-1277 | www.angelomulberry.com

An "oasis" of "authenticity" among Little Italy's "tourist traps", this red-saucer dating back to 1902 "remains the same" "jammed" joint "despite recession or depression", with "friendly" waiters ferrying "primo" Neapolitan basics; the "slightly tacky" setting notwithstanding, to most it's "worth the wait every time."

Angelo's Pizzeria *Pizza*
21 | 12 | 16 | $25

E 50s | 1043 Second Ave. (55th St.) | 212-521-3600
W 50s | 117 W. 57th St. (bet. 6th & 7th Aves.) | 212-333-4333

(continued)

Angelo's Pizzeria

W 50s | 1697 Broadway (bet. 53rd & 54th Sts.) | 212-245-8811
www.angelospizzany.com

These "nothing-fancy" Midtown pizzerias have "office" types "hooked" on their "fresh, thin-crust" pies piled with "delicious toppings" at "just-right" prices; "wave down" the "slow" servers and look past the "minimal" decor, because in these parts such "bargains" are hard to come by.

Angus McIndoe ● *American*

17 | 16 | 19 | $41

W 40s | 258 W. 44th St. (bet. B'way & 8th Ave.) | 212-221-9222 | www.angusmcindoe.com

Broadway "celebs abound" at this "friendly", tri-level "pre- and post-theater" Times Square "favorite"; sure, the American eats are "ordinary", but "fabulous" "stargazing" and a "convenient-for-curtain-time" locale "make up for any disappointments."

Annisa *American*

27 | 22 | 26 | $78

G Village | 13 Barrow St. (bet. 7th Ave. S. & W. 4th St.) | 212-741-6699 | www.annisarestaurant.com

A "top" spot among "foodies", chef Anita Lo's "high-end" Village New American earns praise for "sublime", "imaginative" East-meets-West cuisine and "first-class" service, not to mention its signature wine list starring "female vintners"; such "magical" experiences are bound to come with an "expensive price tag"; N.B. a renovation is underway following a recent fire.

NEW Anselmo's Pizza ⌘ *Pizza*

∇ 16 | 12 | 17 | $21

Red Hook | 354 Van Brunt St. (Sullivan St.) | Brooklyn | 347-804-0102 | www.anselmospizza.com

This no-frills, affordable Red Hook "new kid on the block" specializes in "crispy" thin-crust pies ("no slices") topped with mozz imported from Italy; Anselmo himself presides over the huge oven in the corner, an antique unearthed during recent building renovations.

Anthos ☒ *Greek*

25 | 21 | 23 | $64

W 50s | 36 W. 52nd St. (bet. 5th & 6th Aves.) | 212-582-6900 | www.anthosnyc.com

"Food from the gods" is the verdict on "amazing chef" Michael Psilakis' "nouvelle Greek" cuisine at this "modern, luxurious" Midtowner co-owned by restaurateur Donatella Arpaia; the pro staff is "smooth and unpretentious", leaving "pricey" tabs as the only rub – fortunately, the more casual upstairs' mezes offer serious "value."

Antica Venezia *Italian*

23 | 21 | 24 | $55

W Village | 396 West St. (W. 10th St.) | 212-229-0606 | www.avnyc.com

"Make the trek" to this "romantic", "old-world" Italian that's "so far west" in the West Village, you're "almost in the Hudson"; it "surprises and delights" with "caring", "genteel" service, "delicious" pastas and seafood, free "nibbles" and grappa to "cap the joyful experience."

Antonucci *Italian*

21 | 17 | 20 | $53

E 80s | 170 E. 81st St. (bet. Lexington & 3rd Aves.) | 212-570-5100

This UES "neighborhood favorite" is appreciated for "fresh, modern" Italian fare and "friendly" staffers; sure, "tables are on top of one an-

| | FOOD | DECOR | SERVICE | COST |

other" and the "din is overwhelming" "when the place is full" (i.e. "always"), but the favorable-for-the-area "price point" will distract you.

A.O.C. ◐ *French*   20 | 18 | 18 | $41
W Village | 314 Bleecker St. (Grove St.) | 212-675-9463 |
www.aocnyc.com

A.O.C. Bistro ◐ *French*
Park Slope | 259 Fifth Ave. (Garfield Pl.) | Brooklyn | 718-788-1515 |
www.aocbistro.com

"You're in Paris" at these "real-deal" West Village–Park Slope bistros given their "vast" menus of "decent" "classic" dishes, "noisy" crowds and "French-speaking" staffers; "fair" prices make up for "take-it-or-leave-it" service – as does the "lovely" back garden at the Bleecker Street original.

NEW Aperitivo *Pizza*   ∇ 20 | 19 | 19 | $33
E 40s | 780 Third Ave. (48th St.) | 212-758-9402 |
www.aperitivonyc.com

Midtown office types are thankful for the arrival of this "class-act" Italian on the East 40s lunch and after-work scenes; "delicious" pizzas, "upscale ambiance", a "beautiful bar" and "reasonable prices" are the reason – given a little time, it just might be "a home run."

Apiary *American*   22 | 21 | 21 | $53
E Village | 60 Third Ave. (bet. 10th & 11th Sts.) | 212-254-0888 |
www.apiarynyc.com

With chef Scott Bryan (ex Veritas) in the kitchen, this "hip" East Village New American has "taken off" with "delicious", "inventive" cuisine, "courteous" staffers and a "cutting-edge" space by partner Ligne Roset, the Italian furniture retailer; just know that it "hums like a hive" when crowded and its prices can sting.

ápizz *Italian*   24 | 21 | 20 | $48
LES | 217 Eldridge St. (bet. Rivington & Stanton Sts.) | 212-253-9199 |
www.apizz.com

For "ápizz of heaven", head "down a little side street" and unearth this "terrific" Lower East Side Italian hiding behind an "unassuming facade"; the "thin-crust pies" and other "wood-fired" dishes are deemed "worth the search", and the staff is as "welcoming" as the "warm", "intimate" digs. .

Z applewood M *American*   26 | 21 | 23 | $47
Park Slope | 501 11th St. (bet. 7th & 8th Aves.) | Brooklyn | 718-788-1810 |
www.applewoodny.com

A "favorite" of the "locally grown–obsessed", this "homey", "pricey" Park Slope New American standout delivers "creative" cuisine highlighting "just-off-the-farm-fresh" ingredients (including an "outstanding" brunch); the "nothing-fancy" digs get "a tad too loud" and "tight" when the "local hipster" crowd converges – but "caring" service eases the pain.

NEW AQ Kafé *Scandinavian*   19 | 17 | 18 | $22
W 50s | 1800 Broadway (bet. CPS & 58th St.) | 212-541-6801 |
www.aqkafe.com

"Sweden comes to Columbus Circle" via this "A-ok" cafe that's something of a "Scandinavian Le Pain Quotidien", down to the "fantastic"

| | FOOD | DECOR | SERVICE | COST |

breads and pastries sold at a front counter; it's "fast" and "affordable" for "smorgasbord platters" and such, but note that its "simple", "Ikea"-esque digs close up "early" (8 PM).

⚡ Aquagrill *Seafood* | 26 | 19 | 23 | $60 |
SoHo | 210 Spring St. (6th Ave.) | 212-274-0505 |
www.aquagrill.com

For "some of the best seafood" in NYC, plus an "amazing raw bar", head to this "casual", "friendly" SoHo "neighborhood" grill; despite "cramped, noisy" quarters, finatics attest "it doesn't get any better" – certainly not for less – so no surprise it's often "jam-packed."

Aquamarine ◐ *Pan-Asian* | 21 | 20 | 19 | $36 |
Murray Hill | 713 Second Ave. (bet. 38th & 39th Sts.) | 212-297-1880 |
www.orderaquamarine.com

"Cool for the 'hood", this "trendy" Murray Hill Pan-Asian is home to "surprisingly good" sushi and "fusion" dishes, a happening "bar scene" and "Zen-like" decor that's all "bamboo and waterfalls"; add "affordable" checks, and no wonder it's "busy and popular."

⚡ Aquavit *Scandinavian* | 25 | 24 | 24 | $76 |
E 50s | 65 E. 55th St. (bet. Madison & Park Aves.) | 212-307-7311 |
www.aquavit.org

"Stylish in a subdued way", this "sleek" Midtown Scandinavian generates raves for celebrated chef Marcus Samuelsson's cuisine (he may have been born in Ethiopia, but he "learned to cook in Swedish heaven"); for "the full treatment" you'll have to "splurge" on prix fixe-only dinner, though the "more casual" à la carte front cafe is a "reasonable" alternative.

NEW Arcane ◐ *Caribbean/French* | – | – | – | M |
E Village | 111 Ave. C (bet. 7th & 8th Sts.) | 212-777-0477

To the East Village's Avenue C nightlife row comes this casual, mid-priced newcomer serving French-Caribbean dishes like meat and fish cooked à la plancha; the interior is snug, with pitch-black walls and a handsome wooden bar set amid a smattering of tropical plants.

Areo ◐Ⓜ *Italian* | 23 | 19 | 21 | $53 |
Bay Ridge | 8424 Third Ave. (bet. 84th & 85th Sts.) | Brooklyn |
718-238-0079

Turning out "robust pastas" and such in "generous portions", this "Bay Ridge favorite" is overseen by a "like-family" staff that ensures you "leave fat and happy"; maybe the decor is on the "drab side", but given the "noisy" acoustics and "bling"-and-"high-hair" clientele, there's "energy" to spare.

Arirang Hibachi Steakhouse *Japanese* | 20 | 18 | 21 | $37 |
Bay Ridge | 8814 Fourth Ave. (bet. 88th & 89th Sts.) | Brooklyn |
718-238-9880
Staten Island | 23A Nelson Ave. (Locust Pl.) | 718-966-9600
www.partyonthegrill.com

"Every table is celebrating a birthday" at these "Benihana knockoffs", where "hilarious" hibachi chefs toss off "tasty" Japanese steak-house classics with theatrical "chopping and flipping" sure to "entertain" "kids of all ages"; certainly you "get your money's worth", but "watch those flames."

	FOOD	DECOR	SERVICE	COST

NEW Armani Ristorante *Italian*   ▽ 23 | 26 | 21 | $61

E 50s | Armani/5th Ave. | 717 Fifth Ave., 3rd fl. (56th St.) | 212-207-1902 | www.armani5thavenue.com

Frock star Giorgio Armani unveils this "super-stylish" Italian eatery hidden on the third floor of his new Midtown flagship store; while the "pricey", seafood-heavy fare is "delicious", it's outshined by the room's "*molta bella*" "Euro" mod design – not to mention the clientele ("be sure to dress the part!").

Arno ☒ *Italian*   20 | 16 | 21 | $50

Garment District | 141 W. 38th St. (bet. B'way & 7th Ave.) | 212-944-7420 | www.arnoristorante.com

"Straightforward" Italian fare and servers who "aim to please" translate into perpetual "good buzz" at this Garment District "staple"; once decor-challenged, it's now "remodeled and looking good" – but upstarts claim the kinda "pricey" menu "could use some fresh notes."

Aroma ● *Italian*   24 | 18 | 21 | $40

NoHo | 36 E. Fourth St. (bet. Bowery & Lafayette St.) | 212-375-0100 | www.aromanyc.com

It's "worth holding your breath" to "squeeze into" this "cute" but "Lilliputian" NoHo Italian where the "sophisticated" "artisanal" fare and "huge wine selection" packed with "regional stars" are the draw; "friendly" service, "reasonable prices" and an "infectiously hip" vibe have most "headed back."

Arqua *Italian*   22 | 21 | 22 | $57

TriBeCa | 281 Church St. (White St.) | 212-334-1888 | www.arquaristorante.com

Those seeking "a taste of Italy without the airfare" tout this "relaxing" TriBeCa Northern Italian that still delivers "terrific" "fresh" preparations and "warm" service "after all these years"; despite the tabs, most find themselves "sighing with satisfaction" at the simpatico experience.

Arté *Italian*   18 | 18 | 19 | $43

G Village | 21 E. Ninth St. (bet. 5th Ave. & University Pl.) | 212-473-0077

This "longtime" Village Italian "neighborhood joint" gets points for its "inexpensive" lineup of "well-prepared" (if "predictable") pastas and such that makes it a staple among "locals"; try for the "lovely" garden, "weather permitting", because the interior could perhaps use "a renovation."

Arté Café *Italian*   18 | 18 | 18 | $36

W 70s | 106 W. 73rd St. (bet. Amsterdam & Columbus Aves.) | 212-501-7014 | www.artecafenyc.com

"The price is right" at this "exposed-brick" UWS Italian "old standby" that "abounds with regulars" thanks to its "reliable", if "unspectacular", eats; maybe "service could be better" too, but given its location "within walking distance" of Lincoln Center, most "go back again and again."

Artichoke Basille's Pizza ●⊯ *Pizza*   23 | 6 | 12 | $10

E Village | 328 E. 14th St. (bet. 1st & 2nd Aves.) | 212-228-2004 | www.artichokepizza.com

Its "namesake" "artichoke-dip" pizza is one of the "standouts" at this "no-frills" East Village slice joint, where "painfully inefficient" service and a lack of tables don't keep "insane lines" of "inebriated folk" and others from their "slice of heaven"; call ahead for pickup, or plan to "wait forever."

Artie's Deli *Deli*

FOOD	DECOR	SERVICE	COST
18	10	15	$24

W 80s | 2290 Broadway (bet. 82nd & 83rd Sts.) | 212-579-5959 | www.arties.com

"If it's Jewish deli you crave", this "hectic" Upper Westsider is "reliable" for "overstuffed sandwiches" and other "classic" noshes provided by an authentically "surly" staff in a "faux-retro" space; connoisseurs conclude "not bad, but not best."

☑ Artisanal *French*

FOOD	DECOR	SERVICE	COST
23	20	20	$54

Murray Hill | 2 Park Ave. (enter on 32nd St., bet. Madison & Park Aves.) | 212-725-8585 | www.artisanalbistro.com

Yes, it's a "cheese-lover's paradise", but don't count out the other "excellent" menu selections at this Murray Hill French brasserie considered "well priced for the quality"; the "like-in-Paris" digs get "a bit noisy", but it earned its "good vibes" honestly; P.S. don't miss the "fab fondue", and "thank God for Lipitor."

Arturo's Pizzeria ◑ *Pizza*

FOOD	DECOR	SERVICE	COST
22	13	16	$26

G Village | 106 W. Houston St. (Thompson St.) | 212-677-3820

Visits to this "divey" pizzeria are "like going back in time" to "'60s Greenwich Village", complete with "kitschy" artwork and "live jazz"; its "crisp" coal-oven pies are a perpetual hit with "NYU" students and other lovers of "cheap" food and wine and "late-night" hours.

☑ Asia de Cuba *Asian/Cuban*

FOOD	DECOR	SERVICE	COST
22	24	20	$61

Murray Hill | Morgans Hotel | 237 Madison Ave. (bet. 37th & 38th Sts.) | 212-726-7755 | www.chinagrillmgt.com

It's still one of the "hottest spots north of Havana" – even if it's also a Murray Hill "fixture" – so "dress swanky", "sit at the communal table" and enjoy the "clever" Asian-Cuban fusion fare, "gorgeous" all-white digs and "hot" "young" patrons; a few sniff it's "becoming more of a chain", but all agree it's still singularly "splurge"-worthy.

☑ Asiate *American/Asian*

FOOD	DECOR	SERVICE	COST
24	29	25	$111

W 60s | Mandarin Oriental Hotel | 80 Columbus Circle, 35th fl. (60th St. at B'way) | 212-805-8881 | www.mandarinoriental.com

A space with views over Central Park so "gorgeous" it's rated NYC's No. 1 for Decor, "neo-fusion food at its best" and "gracious" service combine to make this Asian–New American aerie high in Columbus Circle's Mandarin Oriental Hotel a "wonderful place to impress out-of-town guests" or "to work on a romance"; although it's "a splurge" for the prix fixe–only dinner, the $24 weekday lunch deal is a must-try.

☑ Atlantic Grill *Seafood*

FOOD	DECOR	SERVICE	COST
23	19	21	$54

E 70s | 1341 Third Ave. (bet. 76th & 77th Sts.) | 212-988-9200 | www.brguestrestaurants.com

"Hands-down one of the best seafood restaurants on the Upper East Side", this "standby" is praised for its "neighborhood feel" and "terrific" brunch; boasting a "big bar scene", it's "a good place to meet, greet and people-watch" – though "noisy, crowded" conditions are as much part of the catch as waves in the ocean.

	FOOD	DECOR	SERVICE	COST

NEW At Vermilion | Indian/Nuevo Latino

▽ 18 | 19 | 17 | $55

E 40s | 480 Lexington Ave. (46th St.) | 212-871-6600 |
www.thevermilionrestaurant.com

East Midtown's former Django space now houses this stylish Chicago import serving "bold", "spicy" (and "pricey") Indo-Latin fusion cuisine; both levels – the ground-floor lounge and the "huge" upstairs dining room – sport a "minimalist" look with lots of white, metal and black-and-white photography.

August | European

22 | 21 | 20 | $48

W Village | 359 Bleecker St. (bet. Charles & W. 10th Sts.) | 212-929-8727 |
www.augustny.com

As "darling" as "the cafes you stumble across" abroad, this "rustic" West Villager has a far-ranging menu that provides a "delicious" "gastronomic tour of Europe", plus wood-fired specialties, at "reasonable" prices; insiders attest the "garden room in back" is "the place to sit."

NEW Aureole | American

▽ 29 | 24 | 28 | $109

W 40s | Bank of America Tower | 135 W. 42nd St. (bet. B'way & 6th Ave.) | 212-319-1660 | www.charliepalmer.com

Charlie Palmer's flagship American "foodie mecca" recently departed its UES home of 20-plus years and debuted within Adam Tihany–designed space in Midtown's Bank of America Tower; in addition to its "modern", glassy makeover, it has a new chef, Christopher Lee (ex Gilt), whose output early-goers rate "extraordinary"; N.B. the main dining room is prix fixe–only, but the barroom offers an à la carte menu.

Aurora | Italian

25 | 21 | 22 | $52

SoHo | 510 Broome St. (bet. Thompson St. & W. B'way) | 212-334-9020
Williamsburg | 70 Grand St. (Wythe Ave.) | Brooklyn | 718-388-5100 ⊅
www.aurorAristorante.com

Fans of these SoHo and Brooklyn "winners" would like to keep them a "secret", but realize that the "refined, creative" Italian cuisine, pleasingly "rustic" setups, "gracious" service and "doable" tabs are too good not to share; the Williamsburg location has a beautiful "outdoor arbor" but comes with "cash-only" hassle.

Austin's Steakhouse 🗷 | Steak

19 | 16 | 18 | $51

Bay Ridge | 8915 Fifth Ave. (90th St.) | Brooklyn | 718-439-5000 |
www.austinssteakhouseny.com

Maybe it's a bit "pricey" for Bay Ridge, but this "local steakhouse" offers solid "value for money spent" given its "big" slabs served amid "comfy" environs; now if it would only hire more staffers – and maybe the decor could be "raised a notch" too.

A Voce | Italian

24 | 22 | 22 | $65

Flatiron | 41 Madison Ave. (26th St.) | 212-545-8555 🗷
NEW W 60s | Time Warner Ctr. | 10 Columbus Cir., 3rd fl.
(60th St. at B'way) | 212-823-2523
www.avocerestaurant.com

New chef Missy Robbins "picks up where" former chef Andrew Carmellini "left off" at this "sophisticate" off Madison Square Park, where "gorgeous" seasonal Italian fare comes in "elegantly minimalist" environs; the service is "pro", but just watch out for "high" tabs and noise levels; N.B. the Time Warner Center branch opened post-Survey.

Avra ● *Greek*   25 | 21 | 21 | $59

E 40s | 141 E. 48th St. (bet. Lexington & 3rd Aves.) | 212-759-8550 | www.avrany.com

The "freshest fish" – like "you'd find in Santorini" – is the highlight of this "upscale" Midtown Greek whose eye-catching display of seafood is "almost better than snorkeling"; other bonuses are "airy" digs, "professional" staffers and patio seating – but "you do pay for the privilege."

Awash *Ethiopian*   22 | 12 | 16 | $25

E Village | 338 E. Sixth St. (bet. 1st & 2nd Aves.) | 212-982-9589 ●
W 100s | 947 Amsterdam Ave. (bet. 106th & 107th Sts.) | 212-961-1416 www.awashnyc.com

"Awash your hands" before you "eat with them" at these Ethiopian twins known for "nicely spiced" stews "served on spongy injera bread" in a "shabby" space; what the staff lacks in "efficiency" it makes up for in "friendliness" – and you "can't beat the deal" pricewise.

Azul Bistro ● *Argentinean/Steak*   ▽ 22 | 18 | 19 | $42

LES | 152 Stanton St. (Suffolk St.) | 646-602-2004 | www.azulnyc.com

Meat is the strong suit of this "cute and dark" LES Argentine "filled with hip carnivores" who come for "deliciously prepared steaks" and "great red wines" at fair prices; those who've discovered it have fingers crossed that it "stays off the radar."

☒ Azuri Cafe ⊅ *Israeli*   24 | 5 | 11 | $14

W 50s | 465 W. 51st St. (bet. 9th & 10th Aves.) | 212-262-2920

Falafel fanatics trek to west Hell's Kitchen for "superb overstuffed sandwiches" prepared according to "high standards" at this Israeli-kosher "hole-in-the-wall"; just focus on the "fresh" flavors and "made-for-the-recession" prices and not the "terrible decor" or "grouchy" service.

☒ Babbo ● *Italian*   27 | 23 | 25 | $79

G Village | 110 Waverly Pl. (bet. MacDougal St. & 6th Ave.) | 212-777-0303 | www.babbonyc.com

Brought to you by the Batali-Bastianich team, this Greenwich Village "classic" set in a "lovely" "carriage house" is just about "as good as it gets" for "upscale" Italian food and wine – "you could eat here every night without getting bored"; it's "almost impossible to get in", and when you do it's often "crowded, hectic" and "noisy", but for most it's still "on top of the wish list."

Bacchus *French*   ▽ 23 | 19 | 20 | $37

Boerum Hill | 409 Atlantic Ave. (bet. Bond & Nevins Sts.) | Brooklyn | 718-852-1572 | www.bacchusbistro.com

Boerum Hillers feel "lucky to have a local spot" like this "tiny" French bistro "charmer", where the "delicious" "classic" dishes pair well with "reasonable" wines; there's a "deal" of a dinner prix fixe ($25), live music and a "delightful" garden – "what more could you ask for?"

Baci & Abbracci ● *Italian*   ▽ 21 | 18 | 21 | $33

Williamsburg | 204 Grand St. (bet. Bedford & Driggs Aves.) | Brooklyn | 718-599-6599 | www.baciny.com

At this "fun" "little" Williamsburg Neapolitan, the "like-you'd-get-in-Italy" wood-oven pizzas are the menu standouts and the "wonderful back garden" is the place to sit in summer; with a "considerate staff" and "fair prices" to boot, it has patrons wanting to "kiss and hug it back."

Back Forty *American*
21 | 18 | 19 | $38

E Village | 190 Ave. B (bet. 11th & 12th Sts.) | 212-388-1990 | www.backfortynyc.com

For an "affordable" "locavore love fest", try Peter Hoffman's "buzzing" East Village New American, where "hipsters" dig into "simple", "del-ish", "ingredient"-driven fare (including "awesome burgers"); its "farmhouse"-inspired interior is "pleasant" enough, but the back garden is a real "retreat from the asphalt jungle."

Bagatelle *French*
19 | 22 | 16 | $73

Meatpacking | 409 W. 13th St. (bet. 9th Ave. & Washington St.) | 212-675-2400 | www.bistrotbagatelle.com

At this Meatpacking "scene", the "beautiful Europeans" don't mind that the DJ's "booming" tunes "overshadow" the "decent" New French nibbles – especially at Saturday brunch when the "champagne flows" and everyone "dances on tables"; prices here "rival St. Tropez", so bring your "non-hard-earned euros."

☒ Balthazar ● *French*
23 | 23 | 20 | $56

SoHo | 80 Spring St. (bet. B'way & Crosby St.) | 212-965-1414 | www.balthazarny.com

"A rare find this side of the Atlantic", Keith McNally's "Paris-in-NY" SoHo brasserie is "a feast for all the senses" with "wonderful" French classics and a "happening scene" brimming with "celeb sightings"; in sum, it's a "perennial winner" that does everything right – "what Paris' La Coupole used to be" – plus it's a "power breakfast" favorite.

Baluchi's *Indian*
17 | 13 | 15 | $28

E 50s | 224 E. 53rd St. (bet. 2nd & 3rd Aves.) | 212-750-5515
E 80s | 1724 Second Ave. (bet. 89th & 90th Sts.) | 212-996-2600
G Village | 361 Sixth Ave. (bet. Washingon Pl. & W. 4th St.) | 212-929-2441
G Village | 90 W. Third St. (bet. Sullivan & Thompson Sts.) | 212-529-5353
Murray Hill | 329 Third Ave. (bet. 24th & 25th Sts.) | 212-679-3434
SoHo | 193 Spring St. (bet. Sullivan & Thompson Sts.) | 212-226-2828
TriBeCa | 275 Greenwich St. (Warren St.) | 212-571-5343
W 50s | 240 W. 56th St. (bet. B'way & 8th Ave.) | 212-397-0707
NEW Park Slope | 310 Fifth Ave. (bet. 2nd & 3rd Sts.) | Brooklyn | 718-832-5555
Forest Hills | 113-30 Queens Blvd. (bet. 76th Ave. & 76th Rd.) | Queens | 718-520-8600
www.baluchis.com
Additional locations throughout the NY area

Seemingly "all over town", this "reliable" Indian "mini-chain" is a "safe choice" for "standard" fare that doesn't "break the budget"; the "50% off" dine-in lunch deal will have you happily overlooking the "dreary atmosphere" and "friendly" but often "glacial" service.

Bamonte's *Italian*
23 | 17 | 22 | $44

Williamsburg | 32 Withers St. (bet. Lorimer St. & Union Ave.) | Brooklyn | 718-384-8831

For "red sauce and a sense of history", step into this circa-1900, "still-Bamonte-run" Williamsburg "institution" whose "old-school Italian cooking" is like "nonna" made; tuxedoed "career" waiters and "tired" "*Godfather*" "movie set" decor only "add character" – ya gotta "try it at least once."

Banjara ● *Indian* | 23 | 15 | 18 | $34 |

E Village | 97 First Ave. (6th St.) | 212-477-5956 |
www.banjaranyc.com

It's a "subcontinent apart" from its "Sixth Street neighbors" say supporters of this "crowded" Northern Indian and its "superb range" of "fabulous", "nuanced" dishes; service is inconsistent and the "desert"-toned digs are "nothing to write home about", but it's all about those "flavors."

Bann *Korean* | 21 | 22 | 20 | $50 |

W 50s | Worldwide Plaza | 350 W. 50th St. (bet. 8th & 9th Aves.) |
212-582-4446 | www.bannrestaurant.com

"Fresh ingredients" you "cook yourself" at hibachi tables is the deal at this "modern", "serene" Korean in Worldwide Plaza, a Midtown sister to SoHo's Woo Lae Oak; no, these "tasty" eats "ain't cheap" – but you're "paying for the upscale ambiance" you "don't get in K-town."

Bann Thai *Thai* | 20 | 18 | 20 | $30 |

Forest Hills | 69-12 Austin St. (67th Dr.) | Queens | 718-544-9999 |
www.bannthairestaurant.com

"Consistently good" Thai fare in "colorful" "tropical" environs is the deal at this standby situated "slightly off" Forest Hills' "main stretch"; it wins favor with "polite" service and "bargain prices", and better still you usually "can get a seat without having to wait long."

NEW Baoguette ⌷ *Vietnamese* | 22 | 8 | 15 | $11 |

Murray Hill | 61 Lexington Ave. (bet. 25th & 26th Sts.) | 212-532-1133 ⌷
W Village | 120 Christopher St. (Bedford St.) | 212-929-0877

NEW Baoguette Cafe ●⌷ *Vietnamese*

E Village | 37 St. Marks Pl. (bet. 2nd & 3rd Aves.) | 212-380-1487
www.baoguette.com

Furthering NYC's "Vietnamese sandwich craze", Michael 'Bao' Huynh rolls out this new minichain supplying *banh mi* "perfection", in versions both traditional and creative, to already-"addicted" customers at "bargain" rates; service is "quick", but the "no-frills" decor has many opting out – as in "takeout."

Bao Noodles *Vietnamese* | 19 | 12 | 16 | $27 |

Gramercy | 391 Second Ave. (bet. 22nd & 23rd Sts.) | 212-725-7770 |
www.baonoodles.com

A "treat" for the taste buds is what noodle-loving loyalists say about the "phantastic pho" and other Viet vittles at this "fun" Gramercy vet; it's totally "plain-looking" and the service leaves something "to be desired" – but what do you expect at such "bargain-basement" prices?

⊠ Bar Americain *American* | 23 | 23 | 22 | $62 |

W 50s | 152 W. 52nd St. (bet. 6th & 7th Aves.) | 212-265-9700 |
www.baramericain.com

"Flay-tastic" "twists" on American classics are the signature of Bobby Flay's "big", "boisterous" Midtowner whose "swanky" space is "loaded" with everyone from "media execs" to "tourists"; "polished service" is assured, but just be prepared to "Throwdown some cash."

		FOOD	DECOR	SERVICE	COST

Baraonda ● *Italian*
18 | 17 | 16 | $48

E 70s | 1439 Second Ave. (75th St.) | 212-288-8555 | www.baraondany.com
The late-night "bacchanalia" complete with "dancing on tabletops" is what keeps the Euros and "bachelorettes" coming to this otherwise "ho-hum" UES Italian; maybe the price and the service are a bit "pushy", but it's "always packed", and if you "want to be seen, not heard", this is your place.

NEW Bar Artisanal ● *French*
21 | 22 | 17 | $50

TriBeCa | 268 W. Broadway (6th Ave.) | 212-925-1600 | www.barartisanal.com
Lactic legend Terrance Brennan (Picholine, Artisanal) strikes again with this "cavernous", "airy" new TriBeCan that focuses on "delightful" French sharable plates and artisanal cheeses; a menu with no item over $20 and a bar serving late-night snacks keep it "jumping" at all hours.

NEW BarBao *Vietnamese*
21 | 21 | 21 | $48

W 80s | 100 W. 82nd St. (bet. Amsterdam & Columbus Aves.) | 212-501-0776 | www.barbaonyc.com
Michael 'Bao' Huynh (Bún) and his "innovative", "sophisticated" French-Vietnamese fare venture to the UWS with this arrival in the re-vamped former Rain space; factor in "pleasant" service and a "spacious bar" mixing "fab" drinks, and the "upscale" rates don't seem so bad.

NEW Barberry ⓂⒹ *American/Mediterranean*
- | - | - | M

Williamsburg | 152 Metropolitan Ave. (Berry St.) | Brooklyn | 718-599-3027 | www.barberryny.com
Williamsburg's former tapas spot Zipi Zape has been lightly made over into this midpriced Med–New American, whose tin-plated walls are lined with a mishmash of antique photos; the same chef mans the kitchen, but he's expanded the menu with eclectic options that go beyond the borders of Spain.

Barbès ● *French/Moroccan*
20 | 19 | 20 | $43

Murray Hill | 21 E. 36th St. (bet. 5th & Madison Aves.) | 212-684-0215 | www.barbesrestaurantnyc.com
Quite a "find" on an "unlikely" block near the Morgan Library, this Murray Hiller excels at "interesting tagines" and other French-Moroccan specialties; with a "dark", "sexy" vibe and "pleasant" service, it's a "sleeper" that can get "noisy" when its "cozy" digs fill up.

Barbetta ●ⒷⓂ *Italian*
21 | 23 | 22 | $63

W 40s | 321 W. 46th St. (bet. 8th & 9th Aves.) | 212-246-9171 | www.barbettarestaurant.com
"There's nothing better than dining in the garden" of this "reliable" Italian that's been a Theater District standby since 1925; its "old-world European charm", "well-executed" Italian food and "civilized, professional" service make it a good bet anytime, especially for its "outstanding" $55 pre-theater dinner.

Bar Blanc Bistro *American*
22 | 22 | 21 | $60

G Village | 142 W. 10th St. (bet. Greenwich Ave. & Waverly Pl.) | 212-255-2330 | www.barblanc.com
Recently recast as a more "casual" New American bistro, this "posh" Villager wins favor with "sophisticated" "seasonal" cooking from chef

| | FOOD | DECOR | SERVICE | COST |

Sebastiaan Zijp (a "Bouley refugee") and "friendly" service; however, though it's less expensive than before, it's still far from cheap.

Barbone ⏺ *Italian* ▽ 24 | 18 | 23 | $43

E Village | 186 Ave. B (bet. 11th & 12th Sts.) | 212-254-6047 | www.barbonenyc.com

"In a neighborhood of trattorias", this midpriced East Village Italian "stands out" with "impeccable" pastas and a "treasure trove" of "reasonable" wines, not to mention "wonderful" "personal" service and a "delightful" garden; however, its greatest asset may be the owner, a "prince among hosts."

🅩 Bar Boulud *French* 23 | 20 | 21 | $60

W 60s | 1900 Broadway (bet. 63rd & 64th Sts.) | 212-595-0303 | www.danielnyc.com

The "best thing on the Lincoln Center scene since they put translations on the seat backs" at the Met, this "clean"-lined wine bar from star chef Daniel Boulud serves "casual" French bistro fare with "life-altering charcuterie" and "fantastic wines" as the focus – it's "a bit pricey, but so worth it"; a few find the "narrow" setting "overly noisy", but the fact that it's "crowded almost all the time" speaks for itself.

Barbounia *Mediterranean* 21 | 23 | 19 | $49

Flatiron | 250 Park Ave. S. (20th St.) | 212-995-0242 | www.barbounia.com

Yes, the Med eats at this "big", "sexy" Flatironer are "reliably delicious", but it's the "innovative cocktails", "hot crowd" and "gorgeous" decor – from the "vaulted ceilings" to the "glittery" bar – that draw raves; yes, it's a "bit high-priced" and "noisy", but for "frolicking" and "people-watching", it "doesn't disappoint."

🆕 Bar Breton *French* 18 | 14 | 17 | $43

Chelsea | 254 Fifth Ave. (bet. 28th & 29th Sts.) | 212-213-4999 | www.barbreton.com

Having folded Fleur de Sel, French chef Cyril Renaud takes his Breton cookery to this more "casual", "affordable" North Chelsea "successor", which splits surveyors: some "love" the "delicious" crêpes and galettes, but a "disappointed" contingent cites "uncomfortable" digs and "spotty" service; your call.

Barbuto *Italian* 22 | 18 | 19 | $51

W Village | 775 Washington St. (bet. Jane & W. 12th Sts.) | 212-924-9700 | www.barbutonyc.com

"Culinary legend" Jonathan Waxman delivers "delicious", "unfussy", "seasonal" fare at this "friendly", "rollicking" West Village Italian; the "industrial" setting can get "noisy", but most agree "eating in a [former] garage was never so good" – especially in "mild weather" when they "roll up the doors."

Bar Carrera ⏺ *Spanish* ▽ 22 | 21 | 23 | $37

E Village | 175 Second Ave. (bet. 11th & 12th Sts.) | 212-375-1555
G Village | 146 W. Houston St. (MacDougal St.) | 212-253-9500
www.barcarrera.com

"Addictive", affordable "Spanish nibbles" and a sizable selection of "hard-to-find" wines are the draw at these "rockin'" cross-Village Basque tapas twins; on prime nights a "fun" scene heats up, but the "friendly, informative" staff keeps things "relaxed."

	FOOD	DECOR	SERVICE	COST

NEW Bark Hot Dogs ◐ *Hot Dogs*
| - | - | - | I |

Park Slope | 474 Bergen St. (bet. 5th & 6th Aves.) | Brooklyn | 718-789-1939 |
www.barkhotdogs.com

The humble hot dog goes local, artisanal and sustainable at this
new Park Sloper, where the franks come from an old-world Upstate
butcher, the accompaniments are housemade or locally sourced and
there are Brooklyn craft beers on tap; it's pricier than your average
dog shop, but the recycled-wood tables in its spare-but-stylish space
are already packed.

Barking Dog *American*
| 15 | 13 | 15 | $25 |

E 70s | 1453 York Ave. (77th St.) | 212-861-3600
E 90s | 1678 Third Ave. (94th St.) | 212-831-1800 ⊅
Murray Hill | Affinia Dumont | 150 E. 34th St. (bet. Lexington & 3rd Aves.) |
212-871-3900 ◐

A "must" for "dog-lovers" – and "stroller"-pushers – this "canine-
themed" trio dispenses "mounds" of "cheap" American "comfort"
classics rated a "step up" from a standard diner's; they're "crowded"
(especially at brunch), and adventurous eaters should "bark up another tree", but "they serve their purpose."

barmarché ◐ *American*
| 18 | 19 | 17 | $41 |

NoLita | 14 Spring St. (Elizabeth St.) | 212-219-2399 |
www.barmarche.com

"Delicious libations", *bon marché* tabs and a "chill vibe" draw "young,
funky" types to this "shabby-chic" NoLita New American; the "romantic" atmosphere presents "date spot" potential, but "just-ok" edibles
and "slow" service are also part of the picture.

☑ Bar Masa ⊠ *Japanese*
| 26 | 22 | 23 | $99 |

W 60s | Time Warner Ctr. | 10 Columbus Circle, 4th fl. (60th St. at B'way) |
212-823-9800 | www.masanyc.com

The next-door, somewhat "cheaper" adjunct to Masa, this "casual"
Time Warner Center Japanese sushi star presents "exquisite" à la
carte offerings that include some items from the mother ship's menu;
its "spartan"-yet-"elegant" setting and "exceptional" service make for
an overall "serene" vibe – at least until the check comes.

☑ Barney Greengrass Ⓜ⊅ *Deli*
| 23 | 8 | 15 | $28 |

W 80s | 541 Amsterdam Ave. (bet. 86th & 87th Sts.) | 212-724-4707 |
www.barneygreengrass.com

Setting "the gold standard for pickled herring, smoked fish and Sunday
brunch", this UWS "Jewish comfort food" institution, dating back to
1908 and "still in the Greengrass family", is "everything a deli should
be": "crowded, loud, delicious and fun"; despite "old, drab" decor and
"Woody Allen waiters", customers brave "crazy lines on weekends" –
"some things never change, thank God!"

Barolo *Italian*
| 18 | 22 | 18 | $56 |

SoHo | 398 W. Broadway (bet. Broome & Spring Sts.) | 212-226-1102 |
www.nybarolo.com

Dining "under the spring cherry blossoms" in the "magical", "reason-to-
go" back garden of this Italian vet is as close to "heaven" as it gets in
SoHo; "decent" fare and "fine wines" satisfy its mix of "air-kissing"
Euros, tourists and shoppers, who don't bat an eye at "hefty price tags."

	FOOD	DECOR	SERVICE	COST

Barosa *Italian* ▽ 23 | 18 | 21 | $37

Williamsburg | 312 Graham Ave. (bet. Ainslie & Devoe Sts.) | Brooklyn | 718-218-7236 Ⓜ

Rego Park | 62-29 Woodhaven Blvd. (62nd Rd.) | Queens | 718-424-1455 | www.barosas.com

These outer-borough Italians "consistently please" with their "home"-style classics, "cheerful, unrushed" service and "Sinatra"-worthy vibes; on weekends it can be "tough to get a table" at the Rego Park original, and the newer Williamsburg offshoot is gaining a following too.

Bar Pitti ●⇔ *Italian* 23 | 15 | 17 | $40

G Village | 268 Sixth Ave. (bet. Bleecker & Houston Sts.) | 212-982-3300

"Go for the scene", stay for the "crazy-amazing pastas" at this street-side Village Italian known for its prime "celeb"/"model"-watching; its "minimal" digs are "overcrowded" and the "cute" waiters may "shoo you through your meal", but legions "keep coming back" nonetheless.

Barrio *Mexican* ▽ 17 | 16 | 17 | $34

Park Slope | 210 Seventh Ave. (3rd St.) | Brooklyn | 718-965-4000 | www.barriofoods.com

Park Slopers have "welcomed" this Mexican that pleases its "young crowd" with "novel drinks" that can overshadow the "creative" edibles (which include a "two-thumbs-up" kids' menu); some say "it's still finding its way", but the fact that its patio is usually packed speaks for itself.

Bar Stuzzichini *Italian* 19 | 17 | 18 | $43

Flatiron | 928 Broadway (bet. 21st & 22nd Sts.) | 212-780-5100 | www.barstuzzichini.com

"Try a little bit of everything" at this "buzzy" Flatiron Italian whose *delizioso* small plates are designed to accompany a "good glass of vino" or two; if the vaguely "chain"-like decor and variable service are a "letdown" for some, "fairly reasonable prices" may mollify.

Bar Toto ● *Italian* 18 | 18 | 18 | $27

Park Slope | 411 11th St. (6th Ave.) | Brooklyn | 718-768-4698 | www.bartoto.com

"Good vibes" abound at this "welcoming" Park Slope "local joint" whose "tin-ceilinged" interior and sidewalk tables are "pleasant" for "solid" "casual" Italian eats at toto-ally tempting rates; just know it's big with "families", meaning the "early evening hours" tend to be "kid-dominated."

Bar Vetro ⊠ *Italian* ▽ 20 | 17 | 22 | $40

E 50s | 222 E. 58th St. (bet. 2nd & 3rd Aves.) | 212-308-0112 | www.barvetro.com

"Surprised it's not more popular" say those in-the-know about this "approachable" Italian Eastsider, "convenient" for a "casual", well-priced bite "near Bloomie's"; a "cordial" staff mans its "space-age-Milano" room, and there's usually a "lively" scene at the green-glass bar.

Basilica ● *Italian* 20 | 14 | 20 | $33

W 40s | 676 Ninth Ave. (bet. 46th & 47th Sts.) | 212-489-0051 | www.basilicarestaurant.com

It's such a "squeeze", you may end up "in a stranger's lap" at this "homey", "impossibly narrow" Hell's Kitchen Italian, but "savory" fare

| | FOOD | DECOR | SERVICE | COST |

and "fast, friendly" service overcome all; the prices are "hard to beat" too – and the $28 pre-theater deal that "includes a bottle of wine" is a "no-brainer."

Basso56 ● *Italian* — 22 | 17 | 23 | $50
W 50s | 234 W. 56th St. (bet. B'way & 8th Ave.) | 212-265-2610 | www.basso56.com

"Convenient to Carnegie Hall", this Italian dishes up a "diverse" balance of "inventive" and "traditional" dishes at relatively "reasonable" rates; thinking positively, the "somewhat spartan" decor can be a "welcome retreat from the Midtown visual assault" – and the "pro" staff's "warm" attention further soothes.

Basta Pasta *Italian* — 23 | 17 | 20 | $43
Flatiron | 37 W. 17th St. (bet. 5th & 6th Aves.) | 212-366-0888 | www.bastapastanyc.com

This "sleek" Flatironer's "sophisticated", "knock-your-socks-off" Japanese-Italian fusion dishes ("definitely not your mom's red sauce") are hailed as an "idiosyncratic marvel"; the open-kitchen look is "spare", but the mood is "friendly" and the prices "don't break the bank."

NEW Bati *Ethiopian* — - | - | - | I
Fort Greene | 747 Fulton St. (bet. S. Elliott Pl. & S. Portland Ave.) | Brooklyn | 718-797-9696 | www.batikitchen.com

Traditional Ethiopian dishes – many of them vegetarian – abound at this tiny, warmly lit Fort Greene arrival; it's already drawing droves of neighborhood types willing to sit on top of each other to nibble affordable, health-focused fare in laid-back environs.

Battery Gardens *American/Continental* — 18 | 25 | 19 | $50
Financial District | SW corner of Battery Park (State St.) | 212-809-5508 | www.batterygardens.com

The American-Continental eats at this Battery Park dweller get "respectable" marks, but it's the "perfect view of Lady Liberty" and the harbor that'll "charge your romantic battery"; "warm" service and "fair prices" also don't hurt, but on a "gorgeous day", the vista is "what you'll remember."

Bay Leaf *Indian* — 21 | 17 | 19 | $39
W 50s | 49 W. 56th St. (bet. 5th & 6th Aves.) | 212-957-1818 | www.bayleafnyc.com

"Plentiful portions" of "attentively prepared" regional "staples" place this "low-key" Midtown Indian "a cut above"; even though "nothing about the decor says 'wow'", the "helpful" service and "gentle pricing" – especially the "bargain" $16 lunch buffet – garner an enthusiastic "thumbs-up."

Bayou *Cajun* — ∇ 22 | 18 | 20 | $39
Staten Island | 1072 Bay St. (bet. Chestnut & St. Mary's Aves.) | 718-273-4383 | www.bayoustatenisland.com

"N'Awlins comes to Staten Island" via this "fun 'n' funky" Rosebank "gem", where the "fantastic" "down-home" Cajun-Creole specialties come at pleasing "bargain" rates; the quarters may be "small", but a "festive" mood prevails, especially when one of the "live bands" takes the stage.

	FOOD	DECOR	SERVICE	COST

NEW b-bap *Korean*

	-	-	-	I

W 50s | 830 Ninth Ave. (bet. 54th & 55th Sts.) | 212-315-0033 | www.b-bap.com

"Twists on bibimbop" are the specialty of this Hell's Kitchen counter-service arrival that lets diners customize bowls of the popular Korean dish with a choice of rices and "fresh", "innovative" ingredients; if the "sci-fi" setup with a smattering of tables is too "weird" for you, there's always "amazingly fast" delivery.

B. Café *Belgian*

	21	18	20	$40

E 70s | 240 E. 75th St. (bet. 2nd & 3rd Aves.) | 212-249-3300
NEW **W 80s** | 566 Amsterdam Ave. (bet. 87th & 88th Sts.) | 212-873-1800
You have to hustle to get your "mussels from Brussels" at these "friendly", "crowded" crosstown Belgian bistros boasting "terrific frites" and beatific beers to go with the bivalves; the "narrow" environs are "not for the claustrophobic", but "attentive" servers deserve a B-plus.

Beacon *American*

	23	21	21	$60

W 50s | 25 W. 56th St. (bet. 5th & 6th Aves.) | 212-332-0500 | www.beaconnyc.com

Waldy Malouf's Midtown New American "continues to shine" with trademark "excellent" wood-grilled dishes, "impressive", multilevel digs and "gracious" service; big with the "business" crowd at lunch and "theatergoers" in the evening, it comes with "expense account"-level tabs, unless you go prix fixe.

Beast *Mediterranean*

	∇ 21	14	20	$32

Prospect Heights | 638 Bergen St. (Vanderbilt Ave.) | Brooklyn | 718-399-6855 | www.brooklynbeast.com

A Prospect Heights "local gathering place", this "dark", "quirky" tapas joint packs 'em in with "awesome drinks" and "delicious" Mediterranean tidbits, plus a popular brunch; its "comfortable" atmosphere makes "slow service" easy to endure.

☒ Becco ◐ *Italian*

	22	18	21	$45

W 40s | 355 W. 46th St. (bet. 8th & 9th Aves.) | 212-397-7597 | www.becco-nyc.com

At Joe and Lidia Bastianich's "terrific" Restaurant Row Italian, "everyone raves about" the "amazing" $23 "all-you-can-eat" pasta "sampler", not to mention the "everything's $25" wine list; no wonder it's "crowded and noisy", but still the "efficient" staffers get theatergoers "in and out" on time.

Beccofino *Italian*

	∇ 22	16	20	$35

Bronx | 5704 Mosholu Ave. (bet. Fieldston Rd. & Spencer Ave.) | 718-432-2604

One of Riverdale's "best", this "cute" Bronx Italian has a "big following" for its "expertly prepared" "homestyle" cooking offered up in "big portions" at low prices; however, "small" dimensions, "friendly" but "slow" service and a no-reservations policy mean there's often a "wait."

Belcourt *European*

	20	18	18	$40

E Village | 84 E. Fourth St. (2nd Ave.) | 212-979-2034 | www.belcourtnyc.com

"Cozy" "French antique decor" is paired with up-to-date "seasonal" Pan-European dishes at this "pleasant", "casual" East Villager; the "reasonable prices" and "carefully mixed cocktails" may help patrons abide the "noisy" acoustics and "friendly"-but-"slow" service.

Bella Blu ◐ *Italian* | 20 | 17 | 18 | $51 |

E 70s | 967 Lexington Ave. (bet. 70th & 71st Sts.) | 212-988-4624 | www.baraondany.com

The "wonderful" brick-oven pizzas are "not to be missed" at this UES Northern Italian, a local "favorite" bedecked with "interesting" murals and populated by a "lively", "attractive" crowd; however, some say it's "more expensive than expected" and suggest "bring earplugs."

Bella Via *Italian* | 22 | 16 | 18 | $31 |

LIC | 47-46 Vernon Blvd. (48th Ave.) | Queens | 718-361-7510 | www.bellaviarestaurant.com

"Consistently satisfying" pastas and "done-to-perfection" coal-oven pizzas are the hallmark of this "friendly", "casual" LIC Italian; "small-ish" though it may be, locals are "happy" to crowd in to this standby that's "much needed" given the area's lack of "decent options."

Bellavitae *Italian* | 23 | 18 | 21 | $52 |

G Village | 24 Minetta Ln. (bet. MacDougal St. & 6th Ave.) | 212-473-5121 | www.bellavitae.com

One of the Village's "best-kept secrets" is this "intimate", "hidden" Italian proffering "beautifully prepared" small plates and "interesting wines" that leave diners "feeling well fed and contented"; its "knowledgeable" staff also "deserves accolades", but "be warned": "little plates do not mean a little bill."

Belleville *French* | 19 | 21 | 17 | $36 |

Park Slope | 330-332 Fifth St. (5th Ave.) | Brooklyn | 718-832-9777 | www.bellevillebistro.com

The "triplets would love" this "reliable", well-priced bistro, whose "cute" "Balthazar look" brings a "little corner of France to Park Slope"; while the staff is improving, the experience still may come "complete with Parisian attitude"; N.B. check out its new around-the-corner lounge.

Bellini *Italian* | 18 | 14 | 18 | $36 |

W 80s | 483 Columbus Ave. (bet. 83rd & 84th Sts.) | 212-724-4615 | www.bellininyc.com

"Simple but tasty" Italian classics delivered by an "attentive" crew is the deal at this BYO Upper Westsider, where brick-oven pizzas with "pizzazz" are the highlight; it's "narrow as a shoebox", but no one minds much given the pricing "perfect for recession-era budgets."

Bello *Italian* | 21 | 16 | 21 | $47 |

W 50s | 863 Ninth Ave. (56th St.) | 212-246-6773 | www.bellorestaurant.com

"Forget the calories" and tuck into "fresh, delicious" pastas and other "plentiful" classics at this "friendly", "old-fashioned" Hell's Kitchen Italian; sure, it's a bit "staid", but the perk of "free parking" after 5 PM is practically "worth the cost of the meal alone."

Bello Sguardo ◑ *Mediterranean* | 20 | 16 | 17 | $37 |

W 70s | 410 Amsterdam Ave. (bet. 79th & 80th Sts.) | 212-873-6252 | www.bellosguardony.com

"Small plates equal big taste" at this "terrific" UWS Mediterranean, where the "ample choices" come via a "cordial" crew, and where "rea-

	FOOD	DECOR	SERVICE	COST

"sonable prices" are made "even more so" by the $20 dinner prix fixe; critics citing "so-so" decor should know a "freshen-up" is in the works.

Ben & Jack's Steak House *Steak*
23 | 18 | 21 | $71

E 40s | 219 E. 44th St. (bet. 2nd & 3rd Aves.) | 212-682-5678
NEW Murray Hill | 255 Fifth Ave. (bet. 28th & 29th Sts.) | 212-532-7600
www.benandjackssteakhouse.com

These "congenial" East Side Luger wannabes deliver "melt-in-your-mouth" steaks and "even better" sides at an "efficient pace"; prices are predictably "high-end", but if "tenderloin and testosterone" tempt you, just pack the "company card."

Ben Benson's *Steak*
23 | 18 | 22 | $70

W 50s | 123 W. 52nd St. (bet. 6th & 7th Aves.) | 212-581-8888 |
www.benbensons.com

"Oozing testosterone", this Midtown West "meat fest" is a "fantastic", "no-b.s." place for "strong drinks", steaks with "perfectly prepared accompaniments" and "surprisingly good fish dishes"; despite a few beefs about "noisy" acoustics and "crusty waiters", most advise "bring your wallet and your appetite – you won't be sorry."

Benjamin Steak House *Steak*
24 | 21 | 23 | $72

E 40s | Dylan Hotel | 52 E. 41st St. (bet. Madison & Park Aves.) |
212-297-9177 | www.benjaminsteakhouse.com

Housed in Midtown's Dylan Hotel, this "refined" chop shop delivers "high-quality", "pricey" beef and "surpassing" service in capacious, rather "elegant" digs; that it "hits the right notes" in the challenged area around Grand Central is a "pleasant surprise."

Benoit Ⓢ *French*
19 | 20 | 19 | $62

W 50s | 60 W. 55th St. (bet. 5th & 6th Aves.) | 646-943-7373 |
www.benoitny.com

Having "received mixed reviews" when it opened, Alain Ducasse's Midtown replica of the renowned Paris bistro has "gotten better since chef Pierre Schaedelin's arrival"; however, despite having "good food, decor and service", plus a "true steal" $19 prix fixe lunch, many still find the venture "uneven" and "disappointing" for the price.

Ben's Kosher Deli *Deli*
18 | 11 | 14 | $25

Garment District | 209 W. 38th St. (bet. 7th & 8th Aves.) | 212-398-2367
Bayside | Bay Terrace | 211-37 26th Ave. (211th St.) | Queens |
718-229-2367
www.bensdeli.net

"You don't have to be Jewish" to fress at these "quintessential" Garment District–Bayside kosher delis, where "early-bird specials" cater to "old-timers"; with "monster sandwiches", "abrupt" service and "shabby" digs, there are "no surprises" here, but when you're "kvelling over your kreplach", "do you really want any?"

Beppe Ⓢ *Italian*
23 | 20 | 22 | $58

Flatiron | 45 E. 22nd St. (bet. B'way & Park Ave. S.) | 212-982-8422 |
www.beppenyc.com

One of the Flatiron's "tastier, friendlier" options is this "like-in-Italy" Tuscan, where the "fantastic" "rustic" fare is backed by an impressive wine list; "warm", "open-hearthed" "farmhouse" digs are the crowning touch, which, despite "high prices", folks "keep coming back" to.

	FOOD	DECOR	SERVICE	COST

Bereket ● ⇜ *Turkish* — 21 | 4 | 13 | $13

LES | 187 E. Houston St. (Orchard St.) | 212-475-7700

Cabbies and club-hoppers satisfy their "late-night" "cravings" at this "cheap"-yet-"delicious" 24/7 Lower East Side Turk; it's "perfect" for a "quick fix" or "to sober up after partying", and at 3 AM, no one notices the "no-frills" decor.

Bettola ● *Italian* — 21 | 16 | 18 | $36

W 70s | 412 Amsterdam Ave. (bet. 79th & 80th Sts.) | 212-787-1660 | www.bettolanyc.com

All the "right ingredients" make for "terrific" thin-crust pizzas at this UWS "old reliable", which also purveys pasta "standards"; decorwise it's "not much", but it's "welcoming" and "surprisingly affordable", and "when the weather's good" its sidewalk seats can't be beat.

Beyoglu *Turkish* — 21 | 17 | 18 | $36

E 80s | 1431 Third Ave. (81st St.) | 212-650-0850

"What's not to like?" muse mavens of the "amazing" meze at this UES Turkish "delight", where even a "poor man" can gorge on a "complexity of flavors" delivered "fast"; it's "always packed" and often "hectic", so if "noise isn't your thing", try the "quieter upstairs."

Bianca ⇜ *Italian* — 24 | 17 | 19 | $33

NoHo | 5 Bleecker St. (bet. Bowery & Elizabeth St.) | 212-260-4666

"Pasta is the way to go" at this "tiny", "charming" cash-only NoHo Italian, where a "courteous" crew delivers "incredible" Emilia-Romagnan dishes priced "cheap"; however, the "secret is out", so expect "packed" quarters and a "wait" – to most it's well "worth the inconvenience."

Bice ● *Italian* — 21 | 20 | 20 | $64

E 50s | 7 E. 54th St. (bet. 5th & Madison Aves.) | 212-688-1999 | www.bicenewyork.com

"Still packing 'em in" after "all these years", this East Side Northern Italian is a "suit"-filled "power-lunch" place by day that morphs into a "Euro"-centric "scene" in the evening; those who can focus on the "costly" food say it's "quite good", though it comes with "a side of hedge funds" and "snooty" service.

Big Nick's Burger Joint ● *Burgers* — 17 | 5 | 13 | $18

W 70s | 2175 Broadway (77th St.) | 212-362-9238 | www.bignicksnyc.com
W 70s | 70 W. 71st St. (Columbus Ave.) | 212-799-4444 | www.bignicksny.com

After nearly 50 years, these separately owned UWS "greasy spoons" continue to produce "terrific" "sumo burgers" and pizzas off a menu as "long as the Epic of Gilgamesh" ("it'll take you a couple of months to read"); open 24/7 and "always crowded at 4 AM", they're the kind of "real-NY" "holes-in-the-wall" that are ideal when "everyone wants to eat something different" and price matters.

Big Wong ⇜ *Chinese* — 22 | 5 | 11 | $15

Chinatown | 67 Mott St. (bet. Bayard & Canal Sts.) | 212-964-0540

Hailed as one of the "best dives" around, this "chaotic", unfortunately named Chinese "joint" offers the "quintessential Chinatown experience" and serves as an unofficial "jury duty" canteen too; its "quick" "feasts" of "dirt-cheap" "deliciousness" are "well worth" the "nonexistent decor" and "graceless" service.

Bistro Cassis *French*

| 20 | 17 | 17 | $44 |

W 70s | 225 Columbus Ave. (bet. 70th & 71st Sts.) | 212-579-3966
"Practice your French on the waiters" at this "solid", "lively" UWS Gallic, which proffers "well-prepared" bistro "classics"; service veers from "adequate" to attitudinal, and some "wish they took reservations" – but the prices get no complaints.

Bistro Chat Noir *French*

| 18 | 19 | 19 | $56 |

E 60s | 22 E. 66th St. (bet. 5th & Madison Aves.) | 212-794-2428 | www.bistrochatnoir.com
This "inviting" little Upper Eastsider from the La Goulue folks wins favor with "simple" but "decent" French fare and a "charming host"; maybe it's "expensive for what it is", but hey, it's a "pricey neighborhood" – most locals happily let this cat "cross their path."

Bistro Citron *French*

| 20 | 18 | 19 | $43 |

W 80s | 473 Columbus Ave. (bet. 82nd & 83rd Sts.) | 212-400-9401 | www.bistrocitronnyc.com
You "can't go wrong with the moules" and other "French basics" at this "comfortable" UWS bistro, the "friendly" "sister" to Bistro Cassis; though the service quality "depends on your waiter", overall it's deemed a local "delight", with moderate prices as the crowning touch.

Bistro du Nord *French*

| 18 | 15 | 17 | $47 |

E 90s | 1312 Madison Ave. (93rd St.) | 212-289-0997
Perfect "before visiting Museum Mile", this "cozy" Carnegie Hill duplex is "classic Parisian" from the "dependable, no-surprises" French bistro fare to the "noisy" quarters; prix fixe menus that are a "steal" take the edge off of "so-so" service and "postage stamp"–size digs.

Bistro Les Amis ◐ *French*

| 21 | 18 | 22 | $44 |

SoHo | 180 Spring St. (Thompson St.) | 212-226-8645 | www.bistrolesamis.com
"Everything a neighborhood bistro should be", this "comforting" SoHo boîte is true to its name with "friendly" service and "tasty" eating "without crazy waits"; it can get "crowded" during prime times, but in clement weather there's always the "pleasant" outside tables.

Bistro 61 *French*

| 20 | 16 | 20 | $42 |

E 60s | 1113 First Ave. (61st St.) | 212-223-6220 | www.bistro61.com
"Relaxed" and "under the radar", this East Side "slice of Paris" near the Queensboro Bridge specializes in "pleasant" French bistro fare with a "Moroccan accent"; "tight quarters" notwithstanding, the "prices are right" and the vibe is "warm."

Bistro Ten 18 *American*

| 19 | 18 | 19 | $40 |

W 100s | 1018 Amsterdam Ave. (110th St.) | 212-662-7600 | www.bistroten18.com
Just "steps from St. John the Divine", this "friendly" Morningside Heights "standout" draws "Columbia U." types with its "pleasant" New American fare and "cozy" setting stoked by a "lovely fireplace"; "not-too-expensive" tabs and "friendly" servers are added allures.

	FOOD	DECOR	SERVICE	COST

Bistro 33 *French/Japanese* ▽ 23 | 18 | 23 | $36

Astoria | 19-33 Ditmars Blvd. (21st St.) | Queens | 718-721-1933 |
www.bistro33nyc.com

"Still shining on its Astoria corner", this "off-the-beaten-path" Japanese-French bistro proffers "fusion" dishes that generally "hit the bull's-eye"; in "warm weather" the patio augments its "tiny" digs, while modest tabs and "friendly" service make it a year-round local "standout."

NEW Bistrouge Ⓜ *Eclectic* ▽ 24 | 21 | 24 | $30

E Village | 432 E. 13th St. (bet. Ave. A & 1st Ave.) | 212-677-2200 |
www.bistrouge.com

Early visitors to this "cozy" new East Villager tout its "amazing cocktails" and "excellent", "inexpensive" rustic European-Eclectic dishes that borrow flavors from around the Mediterranean; "accommodating" service and an overall "warm" vibe are other selling points.

NEW Bizaare Avenue Café ● *Eclectic* - | - | - | M

Astoria | 35-01 36th St. (35th Ave.) | Queens | 718-937-1234 |
www.bizaareny.com

Everything that isn't bolted down is for sale (hence the dangling price tags) at this sprawling arrival across from Astoria's Museum of the Moving Image; it replaces the erstwhile Cup's diner kitsch with a loungey souk look, and its globe-trotting menu – including items from a sushi bar – is just as Eclectic.

Black Duck *American/Seafood* 20 | 19 | 20 | $46

Murray Hill | Park South Hotel | 122 E. 28th St. (bet. Lexington Ave. & Park Ave. S.) | 212-448-0888 | www.blackduckny.com

All's "ducky" at this "quaint" New American in a Murray Hill "boutique" hotel, where the "delicious" seafood-heavy offerings come via a "caring" crew; "live jazz" on weekends invigorates the "pub" ambiance that takes you back to "foggy London" – but "with better food."

Black Iron Burger Shop ●⇄ *Burgers* ▽ 21 | 16 | 18 | $19

E Village | 540 E. Fifth St. (bet. Aves. A & B) | 212-677-6067 |
www.blackironburger.com

"Damn fine" "all-American burgers" and "fries and onion rings with just the right amount of grease" are winning points for this "friendly" East Village yearling; a "thoughtful beer selection" compensates for "dive-bar" atmosphere and sides that "jack up the price fast."

Blaue Gans ● *Austrian/German* 21 | 18 | 20 | $47

TriBeCa | 139 Duane St. (bet. Church St. & W. B'way) | 212-571-8880 |
www.kg-ny.com

One taste of the "sophisticated" spins on Austro-German classics at chef Kurt Gutenbrunner's "energetic" TriBeCa "blue goose" "explains why" its "informal", "arty" digs are "always packed"; "top-notch treatment" at relatively "wallet-friendly" prices makes it the "perfect" place "to get your schnitzel fix."

Blockheads Burritos *Mexican* 16 | 10 | 14 | $19

E 50s | 954 Second Ave. (bet. 50th & 51st Sts.) | 212-750-2020
E 80s | 1563 Second Ave. (bet. 81st & 82nd Sts.) | 212-879-1999
Financial District | Courtyard at 4 World Financial Ctr. (North & Vesey Sts.) | 212-619-8226
Murray Hill | 499 Third Ave. (bet. 33rd & 34th Sts.) | 212-213-3332

(continued)

Blockheads Burritos

W 50s | Worldwide Plaza | 322 W. 50th St. (bet. 8th & 9th Aves.) | 212-307-7029
W 100s | 951 Amsterdam Ave. (bet. 106th & 107th Sts.) | 212-662-8226
www.blockheads.com

"Casual cantinas" plying "gringo-ized" Mexicana, "cinderblock"-size burritos and "zingy" margaritas for "next-to-nothing" tabs; their "loud", "young" crowd reports that the "low-rent" digs and "slow" service make "prompt delivery" all the more appealing.

Blossom *Vegan/Vegetarian*

23	18	21	$35

Chelsea | 187 Ninth Ave. (bet. 21st & 22nd Sts.) | 212-627-1144 | www.blossomnyc.com
W 80s | 466 Columbus Ave. (bet. 82nd & 83rd Sts.) | 212-875-2600 | www.blossomcafe.com

Converts who "never knew vegetables could taste this fantastic" say the "scrumptious" vegan vittles from these Chelsea-UWS siblings prove that "healthy food" with "first-rate" flavors is not an oxymoron; "calm" "New Agey" decor and "friendly" service boost the overall "pleasant" experience.

BLT Burger *Burgers*

20	15	17	$27

G Village | 470 Sixth Ave. (bet. 11th & 12th Sts.) | 212-243-8226 | www.bltburger.com

Laurent Tourondel's "no-frills" outpost in the Village is a perpetual "zoo" thanks to its "tasty" takes on "quality" burgers and "absolutely genius" "boozy shakes"; "inconsistent" service aside, it's a "fun scene" and way more "affordable" than its Uptown siblings.

BLT Fish 🄴 *Seafood*

23	20	22	$64

Flatiron | 21 W. 17th St. (bet. 5th & 6th Aves.) | 212-691-8888 | www.bltfish.com

Finatics "can't stay away" from Laurent Tourondel's "festive" Flatiron seafooder, where the "sublime", "super-fresh" catch swims to the table via a "smooth", "relaxed" crew; should the price tags "frighten", there's always the "casual" "New England fish shack" downstairs.

BLT Market *American*

23	21	22	$69

W 50s | Ritz-Carlton | 1430 Sixth Ave. (CPS) | 212-521-6125 | www.bltmarket.com

"Another triumph for chef Tourondel", this "delightful" New American in Midtown's Ritz-Carlton delivers "wonderful" "market-driven" cuisine amid "upscale-homey" "farmhouse" surroundings; the "attentive" service and "view of Central Park" help admirers overlook the "haute prices."

BLT Prime *Steak*

25	22	23	$74

Gramercy | 111 E. 22nd St. (bet. Lexington Ave. & Park Ave. S.) | 212-995-8500 | www.bltprime.com

Carnivores "rejoice" over the "outstanding" cuts at Laurent Tourondel's "sharp-looking" Gramercy steakhouse, where the "popovers alone" are "worth a trip"; "spot-on" service and "wonderful" wines seal the deal at this "primal" "winner" – so long as you "don't have a cow" when the bill comes.

	FOOD	DECOR	SERVICE	COST

🅉 BLT Steak 🅉 *Steak* — 25 | 22 | 22 | $75

E 50s | 106 E. 57th St. (bet. Lexington & Park Aves.) | 212-752-7470 | www.bltsteak.com

Nothing "outstrips the strip sirloin" and other "amazing", "aged" steaks at Laurent Tourondel's original chophouse in Midtown, though the "stylish" decor and "attentive" service also "fire on the right cylinders"; just "bring your Lipitor" and the "corporate card" – if you still have one.

bluechili & Siam Inn ● *Pan-Asian* — 20 | 16 | 18 | $39

W 50s | 251 W. 51st St. (bet. B'way & 8th Ave.) | 212-246-3330 | www.bluechilinewyork.com

"Solid", "affordable" Pan-Asian eats and a "convenient" Theater District location ensure this "trendy" "hideaway" remains a pre-show "staple"; however, surveyors split over the "techno" decor featuring "constantly changing" colored lighting ("very cool" vs. "makes you think you've had one too many").

Blue Fin ● *Seafood* — 22 | 22 | 20 | $56

W 40s | W Times Sq. | 1567 Broadway (47th St.) | 212-918-1400 | www.brguestrestaurants.com

There's "nothing blue" about Steve Hanson's "upbeat" Times Square seafooder, which presents "quality" fish in a "beautiful setting" – with prices to match; service can be "spotty" and the ground level can get "hectic", but the upstairs area is a "surprising retreat" from Broadway "chaos."

Blue Ginger *Japanese/Pan-Asian* — 21 | 16 | 19 | $39

Chelsea | 106 Eighth Ave. (bet. 15th & 16th Sts.) | 212-352-0911

This "bustling" Chelsea Pan-Asian spotlights "creative" sushi that's "not too tough on the wallet"; its "dark", "low-key" quarters are "nothing special", but "efficient" service and a Joyce Theater–convenient location make it "worth a visit" if you're in the area.

🅉 Blue Hill *American* — 27 | 23 | 26 | $77

G Village | 75 Washington Pl. (bet. MacDougal St. & 6th Ave.) | 212-539-1776 | www.bluehillfarm.com

Chef Daniel Barber "wows" his well-heeled clients (including the Obamas) with "inspired" New American cooking based on "exquisitely fresh" seasonal ingredients; though its "intimate", "tasteful" quarters are in the middle of Greenwich Village, you feel you're "so close to the farm, you might have to harvest the food yourself" – that is if the "helpful" staff weren't there to provide "everything you need, with a smile."

Blue Ribbon ● *American* — 24 | 18 | 22 | $53

SoHo | 97 Sullivan St. (bet. Prince & Spring Sts.) | 212-274-0404
Park Slope | 280 Fifth Ave. (bet. 1st St. & Garfield Pl.) | Brooklyn | 718-840-0404
www.blueribbonrestaurants.com

"Still fresh after all these years", these ever-"popular" SoHo–Park Slope New Americans from the Brombergs are best known for their "excellent", "very diverse" menus and some of the "best late-night dining in NYC"; "warm" service helps make the "long waits" and "pricey" tabs easier to swallow.

	FOOD	DECOR	SERVICE	COST

Blue Ribbon Bakery ● *American* | 24 | 19 | 20 | $42 |

G Village | 35 Downing St. (Bedford St.) | 212-337-0404 |
www.blueribbonrestaurants.com

"There are no misses" at this "casual-yet-classy" Bromberg New American Villager, where the "cozy" vibe is abetted by the "smell of fresh bread" baking; "crowds and noise" are part of the "convivial" picture, especially during its "amazing brunch."

Z Blue Ribbon Sushi ● *Japanese* | 26 | 19 | 21 | $58 |

SoHo | 119 Sullivan St. (bet. Prince & Spring Sts.) | 212-343-0404
Park Slope | 278 Fifth Ave. (bet. 1st St. & Garfield Pl.) | Brooklyn |
718-840-0408
www.blueribbonrestaurants.com

This "serene" SoHo–Park Slope Japanese twosome from the versatile Bromberg siblings owes its stellar reputation to "exquisite", "like-it-was-caught-that-morning" fresh fish and appealingly "no-fuss" service; for such "top-notch" meals, sushiphiles willingly brave "long waits" and serious tabs.

Blue Ribbon Sushi Bar & Grill ● *Japanese* | 24 | 20 | 21 | $61 |

W 50s | 6 Columbus Hotel | 308 W. 58th St. (bet. 8th & 9th Aves.) |
212-397-0404 | www.blueribbonrestaurants.com

"Delectable" sushi is the thing at this "terrific", "pricey" Columbus Circle outpost of the Bromberg empire, though the "outstanding" grill items are "a bonus" for the "sushiphobic"; a "rockin' bar scene" and "knowledgeable servers" up the ante.

Z Blue Smoke *BBQ* | 21 | 17 | 19 | $42 |

Murray Hill | 116 E. 27th St. (bet. Lexington Ave. & Park Ave. S.) |
212-447-7733
NEW Flushing | Citi Field | 126th St. & Roosevelt Ave.
(behind the scoreboard) | Queens
www.bluesmoke.com

"Gets better every year" gush groupies of Danny Meyer's "popular" (i.e. "crowded and noisy") BBQ joint, where the "mmm" ribs and such are smoked "in all different styles" and served in an "attractive" space with live music downstairs at the Jazz Standard; still, a few wonder "is upscale BBQ an oxymoron" or just a "way to clog a vein"?; N.B. the new Citi Field branch is a hit with game-goers.

Z Blue Water Grill *Seafood* | 23 | 22 | 21 | $56 |

Union Sq | 31 Union Sq. W. (16th St.) | 212-675-9500 |
www.brguestrestaurants.com

Set in a "spectacular" marble-clad former bank space, this "bustling, happy" Union Square seafood standout scores with "consistently delicious" cooking, especially at brunch; if "not quite Le Bernardin, it's easier to score a reservation" and lighter on your budget; for prime "people-watching", "sit outside" on the veranda – and don't miss the "sexy" downstairs jazz room.

Boathouse *American* | 17 | 25 | 18 | $56 |

E 70s | Central Park | Central Park Lake, enter on E. 72nd St. (Park Dr. N.) |
212-517-2233 | www.thecentralparkboathouse.com

Overlooking Central Park Lake, this American "classic" is "like no other place in the city" and "spectacular in any season"; it's ideal for a "special date", "brunch with friends" or "just for a drink on the deck", and "it almost doesn't matter" that the "overpriced" fare "isn't fantastic" given this view.

Bobby Van's Steakhouse *Steak* | 22 | 19 | 21 | $68 |

E 40s | 230 Park Ave. (46th St.) | 212-867-5490 🖂
E 50s | 131 E. 54th St. (bet. Lexington & Park Aves.) | 212-207-8050
Financial District | 25 Broad St. (Exchange Pl.) | 212-344-8463 🖂
NEW Jamaica | JFK Airport | American Airlines Terminal 8 | Queens | 718-553-2100

Bobby Van's Grill *Steak*

W 50s | 135 W. 50th St. (bet. 6th & 7th Aves.) | 212-957-5050 | www.bobbyvans.com

"Superb" steaks and "divine" wines are delivered by an "energetic" staff at these "boisterous", "masculine-but-attractive" chophouses; given that the "meat lover's fiesta" comes at a "high" price, it seems suitable that you "dine in an old bank vault" at the Financial District branch.

Bobo *American* | 22 | 25 | 22 | $60 |

W Village | 181 W. 10th St. (7th Ave. S.) | 212-488-2626 | www.bobonyc.com

A magnet for "fashionistas", "editors" and "Euros", this "sexy" Villager's brownstone setting features a happening downstairs bar and an "intimate" antiques-filled dining room above; good news: the "pricey" food "has been getting better" since shifting from European to New American.

Boca Chica *Pan-Latin* | 19 | 14 | 16 | $30 |

E Village | 13 First Ave. (1st St.) | 212-473-0108

Perpetually "hopping", this East Village vet is beloved for its "cheap", "delicious" Pan-Latin *comida* in "plentiful" portions; "wickedly strong" cocktails help its "undergrad"-heavy clientele "tolerate" the "frequent long waits" and "loud", "elbow-crunching" conditions.

Bocca *Italian* | 21 | 18 | 22 | $41 |

Flatiron | 39 E. 19th St. (bet. B'way & Park Ave. S.) | 212-387-1200 | www.boccanyc.com

From the owner of Cacio e Pepe comes this "personable" Flatiron arrival offering "well-priced" Roman fare that shows a little "imagination" and is delivered by a "charming" staff; early-goers say "you'd expect to pay more", especially given the sleek space's "cool vibe."

Bocca di Bacco ◗ *Italian* | 21 | 20 | 18 | $43 |

W 50s | 828 Ninth Ave. (bet. 54th & 55th Sts.) | 212-265-8828 | www.boccadibacconyc.com

"Wonderful" Italian fare from chef Roberto Passon and a lengthy vino list set this "understated lair" in Hell's Kitchen "apart from the riff-raff"; the "refreshingly mellow" staffers "know their wines", and best of all, you'll pay "less than you'd think."

Bocca Lupo ◗ *Italian* | 24 | 20 | 20 | $33 |

Cobble Hill | 391 Henry St. (Warren St.) | Brooklyn | 718-243-2522
Cobble Hill locals "feel lucky" to have this "well-hidden" supplier of "delicious, reasonable" Italian small plates and "nice wines" in their midst; "cute" and "urbane", it's a brunch "favorite" that's also "open late" – and is equally "terrific for families or drinks with friends."

	FOOD	DECOR	SERVICE	COST

Bocelli *Italian* — 26 | 23 | 23 | $51

Staten Island | 1250 Hylan Blvd. (bet. Old Town Rd. & Parkinson Ave.) | 718-420-6150 | www.bocellirest.com

This "fine" Italian in SI's Grasmere "never disappoints" with its "generous portions" of "out-of-this-world" seafood; from the "impeccable" service and "upscale" feel to the valet parking, it offers "quality" "all the way around" – and "pricey" tabs come with the territory.

Bodrum *Mediterranean/Turkish* — 19 | 15 | 19 | $37

W 80s | 584 Amsterdam Ave. (bet. 88th & 89th Sts.) | 212-799-2806 | www.bodrumnyc.com

Known for its "exceptional" bread and Turkish-style "brick-oven pizzas", this "fair-priced" UWS Mediterranean sure "won't leave you hungry"; those put off by the "cramped" interior can always turn to the "quick, courteous" staff to help them "wrangle an outside table."

Bogota Latin Bistro *Pan-Latin* — 20 | 17 | 17 | $30

Park Slope | 141 Fifth Ave. (bet. Lincoln & St. Johns Pls.) | Brooklyn | 718-230-3805 | www.bogotabistro.com

With an "eclectic" menu offering something *delicioso* for every palate, this "reasonable" Park Slope Pan-Latin also "has everyone feeling good" with its "all-night happy hours"; no surprise it's "often loud", but the year-round back patio is a retreat from the *caliente* bar scene.

Bôi *Vietnamese* — 20 | 16 | 19 | $37

E 40s | 246 E. 44th St. (bet. 2nd & 3rd Aves.) | 212-681-6541

Bôi Sandwich ⊅ *Vietnamese*

NEW **E 40s** | 708 Third Ave. (bet. 44th & 45th Sts.) | 212-682-1117

Bôi to Go 🅂 *Vietnamese*

E 40s | 800 Second Ave. (bet. 42nd & 43rd Sts.) | 212-681-1122
www.boi-restaurant.com

Always "packed at lunch", this "small", "straight-from-Saigon" standout near Grand Central delivers with "lovely", "reasonable" Vietnamese cuisine and "warm" service; however, if "cramped togetherness" isn't your style, hit its nearby "to-go storefront" counterparts instead.

NEW Boka ● *Korean* — ▽ 23 | 18 | 15 | $25

E Village | 9 St. Marks Pl. (bet. 2nd & 3rd Aves.) | 212-228-2887

The transformation of the East Village's St. Marks Place into a Japanese-Korean enclave continues with the arrival of this "mod" new Korean; its sleek, spare setup puts the focus on the food, notably "outstanding" "hand-lacquered" fried chicken from the BonChon franchise.

Bombay Palace *Indian* — 20 | 18 | 19 | $40

W 50s | 30 W. 52nd St. (bet. 5th & 6th Aves.) | 212-541-7777 | www.bombay-palace.com

"Standard curry fixes" are found at this "quiet" Midtown Indian staffed by a "smiling" crew; ok, the "retro Bombay" decor is on the "cheesy" side, but the $15 lunch buffet is undeniably a "good deal."

Bombay Talkie *Indian* — 20 | 18 | 17 | $37

Chelsea | 189 Ninth Ave. (bet. 21st & 22nd Sts.) | 212-242-1900 | www.bombaytalkie.com

"Casual but sleek", this Chelsea Indian slings "authentic Bombay street" fare plus "creative cocktails" in a "trendy", "Bollywood-themed" setting; portions are "small" and the service can be "lacking", but the "delicious" flavors and "festive" vibe compensate.

Bond 45 ◑ *Italian* | 20 | 18 | 19 | $51

W 40s | 154 W. 45th St. (bet. 6th & 7th Aves.) | 212-869-4545 | www.bond45.com

A "throwback to old NY", this "cavernous" Italian housed in Times Square's former Bond's clothing store "hustles and bustles" with "tourists" and theatergoers; the din is "deafening" and it's "pricey for what it is", but "good" food and "expedient" service make it a "solid" bet.

Bondi Road ◑ *Australian* | ▽ 18 | 14 | 18 | $31

LES | 153 Rivington St. (bet. Clinton & Suffolk Sts.) | 212-253-5311 | www.bondiroad.com

"Solid" fish 'n' chips and other pub basics "soak up" the "dangerous" drinks at this "popular", "inexpensive" LES Aussie; the young things who "pack" in look past the "surfer-dude decor" and focus on the "flirtatious staff" and all-around "fun" time.

Bond Street ◑ *Japanese* | 25 | 22 | 20 | $67

NoHo | 6 Bond St. (bet. B'way & Lafayette St.) | 212-777-2500

"Beautiful fish" ferried by "even more beautiful" staffers is the deal at this "stylish" NoHo Japanese sushi star that's "still cool after all these years"; in the "chic" upstairs dining rooms and lounge below, its "celeb"/ "jet-setter" crowd provides an eyeful at predictably "high prices."

Boqueria ◑ *Spanish* | 22 | 18 | 19 | $46

Flatiron | 53 W. 19th St. (bet. 5th & 6th Aves.) | 212-255-4160
NEW SoHo | 171 Spring St. (bet. Thompson St. & W. B'way) | 212-343-4255
www.boquerianyc.com

The "cool" crowd wants *"mas"* of the "delish" "inventive" tapas turned out by this "modern" Flatiron Spaniard and its new SoHo clone; critics cite "cramped" settings, "long waits" and tabs that "add up", but "friendly" service and a "sparkly" "Barcelona" vibe prevail.

Borgo Antico ◑ *Italian* | 18 | 16 | 19 | $44

G Village | 22 E. 13th St. (bet. 5th Ave. & University Pl.) | 212-807-1313 | www.borgoanticony.com

A "big favorite" among locals, this "reasonable" bi-level Village Italian's "good", "no-surprises" dishes come via an "accommodating" staff in "comfortable" environs; ok, the decor is a bit "run-down" and maybe you "won't be wowed" – but you will be "satisfied."

NEW Bossa Nova Brazil ◑ *Brazilian* | ▽ 21 | 18 | 19 | $39

W 50s | 772 Ninth Ave. (bet. 51st & 52nd Sts.) | 212-586-5006 | www.bossanovabrazilny.com

Brazilian music and the smell of garlic fill the air at this Hell's Kitchen arrival offering churrasco-grilled meats and other well-priced classics; its narrow digs include a lively bar, with a singer on Thursday–Saturday nights and caipirinhas that flow steadily as the Amazon.

Bottega del Vino *Italian* | 22 | 20 | 22 | $63

E 50s | 7 E. 59th St. (bet. 5th & Madison Aves.) | 212-223-2724 | www.bottegadelvinonyc.com

Taking its cues from the "Verona original", this "swanky" (as in "pricey") Midtowner pours "superb" wines that "pair beautifully" with

	FOOD	DECOR	SERVICE	COST

the "authentic" Italian fare; its "medieval" "Alpine" decor and chic "Euro" crowd "transport you to Italy" – but "without airport hassles."

Bottino *Italian*

| | 18 | 16 | 16 | $45 |

Chelsea | 246 10th Ave. (bet. 24th & 25th Sts.) | 212-206-6766 | www.bottinonyc.com

"Popular" post-"gallery crawl", this Chelsea "standby" sates the "art crowd" with "tasty" Tuscan standards; the setting has "seen better days" and the servers are "as concerned about picking up dates as they are about picking up plates", but the "charming garden" is a perennial "highlight."

Bouchon Bakery *American/French*

| | 23 | 15 | 18 | $29 |

W 60s | Time Warner Ctr. | 10 Columbus Circle, 3rd fl. (60th St. at B'way) | 212-823-9366 | www.bouchonbakery.com

Thomas Keller's cafe/patisserie in the Time Warner Center dishes up "dreamy" shopping breaks with its New American sandwiches, salads and "decadent" desserts; the "middle-of-the-mall" setting and just-"serviceable" staff don't make it any less of a "gourmet" experience.

⧢ Bouley ◑ *French*

| | 28 | 26 | 27 | $100 |

TriBeCa | 163 Duane St. (Hudson St.) | 212-964-2525 | www.davidbouley.com

Evoking endless enthusiasm ("truly divine", a "fairy tale", "mecca") in "gorgeous" new digs around the corner from its former space, David Bouley's "transcending" TriBeCa restaurant comes as close to du-plicating the three-star French country dining experience as you'll find this side of the Atlantic; naturally, its "exceptional" "haute" cui-sine and "nearly psychic" pro service come at "splurge"-worthy prices, but the six-course, $48 prix fixe lunch may be New York City's "single best bargain."

⧢ Bouley Upstairs *Eclectic*

| | 26 | 17 | 20 | $48 |

TriBeCa | 130 W. Broadway (Duane St.) | 212-608-5829 | www.davidbouley.com

"Now downstairs too" due to a recent expansion, David Bouley's "in-formal" eatery with two separate kitchens – one for Japanese dishes, one for contemporary French-American – presents "amazing value" yet is one of "the best-kept secrets in NYC"; it's absolutely "not to be missed" since when "Bouley gets it right", he really gets it right.

Bourbon Street Café *Cajun/Southern*

| | 18 | 16 | 18 | $33 |

Bayside | 40-12 Bell Blvd. (bet. 40th & 41st Aves.) | Queens | 718-224-2200 | www.bourbonstreetny.com

"Every day is Mardi Gras" at this "festive" Bayside "hangout", where the kitchen is "generous with spices" in its "surprisingly tasty" Cajun classics; maybe the decor is "nothing special", but "moderate" prices and "helpful" service create an overall "happy" vibe.

Braai ◑Ⓜ *South African*

| | ▽ 19 | 21 | 19 | $43 |

W 50s | 329 W. 51st St. (bet. 8th & 9th Aves.) | 212-315-3315 | www.braainyc.com

From the owners of Xai Xai Wine Bar comes this "well-priced" Hell's Kitchen yearling, a South African braai (or BBQ) joint plying "de-licious" game meats; housed in an "exotic bamboo hut"-like space, it's a "welcome addition to the pre-theater" scene.

	FOOD	DECOR	SERVICE	COST

NEW Braeburn American
21 | 20 | 20 | $56

W Village | 117 Perry St. (Greenwich St.) | 212-255-0696 |
www.braeburnrestaurant.com

West Villagers have "another gem" in this "sweet", "quiet" New
American arrival from Brian Bistrong (ex The Harrison), whose
"comfort"-oriented fare pleases "locavores" and "plain good food"-
lovers alike, including during "super brunch"; "pleasant" service and a
"stylish" "Adirondacks"-esque setup are other pluses.

Brasserie French
20 | 21 | 20 | $53

E 50s | Seagram Bldg. | 100 E. 53rd St. (bet. Lexington & Park Aves.) |
212-751-4840 | www.patinagroup.com

This "retro-future" Midtown "spaceship" of brasserie cuisine remains
an "iconic" destination for "tourists" and "dealmakers" seeking "dependable" French favorites; "pleasant" service boosts the "jovial"
vibe – though "loud" decibels and "high prices" detract.

Brasserie Cognac ● French
18 | 20 | 17 | $52

W 50s | 1740 Broadway (55th St.) | 212-757-3600 |
www.cognacrestaurant.com

Convincing "faux" brasserie trappings make for a "charming" feel, but
proximity "to Carnegie Hall and City Center" may be the greatest asset
of this "pleasant" yearling from the Serafina folks; given its "solid" Gallic
classics served three squares a day, most overlook the "spotty" service.

Brasserie 8½ French
21 | 23 | 22 | $58

W 50s | 9 W. 57th St. (bet. 5th & 6th Aves.) | 212-829-0812 |
www.patinagroup.com

"Bergdorf blonds" and businesspeople bond over "fine" modern French
cuisine at this Midtown cellar dweller, where descending the "glam"
Jetsons-esque curved staircase makes even "working stiffs" feel like
"Hollywood royalty"; overseen by a "pro staff", it has an "energetic" vibe
(abetted by the "busy bar") but is still "quiet enough for conversation."

Brasserie 44 American
20 | 20 | 20 | $60

W 40s | Royalton Hotel | 44 W. 44th St. (bet. 5th & 6th Aves.) |
212-944-8844 | www.brasseriefortyfour.com

"Hot" at lunch but a "sleeper" come dinnertime, this eatery in the
Royalton lobby (aka "the old 44") serves its "very good" New American
fare in "hip", "modern" digs; those who find it "overpriced" just go for
"fab drinks" and "people-watching" at the adjacent bar.

Brasserie Julien French
18 | 18 | 18 | $44

E 80s | 1422 Third Ave. (bet. 80th & 81st Sts.) | 212-744-6327 |
www.brasseriejulien.com

An appealing '20s "Paris feel" and "tasty", "reasonable" (for the zip
code) Gallic fare delivered by a "reliable" crew ensure that this "relaxing" "UES standard" remains a favored "neighborhood haunt"; expect
a "big turnout" on weekend nights when there's live jazz.

Brasserie Ruhlmann French
18 | 21 | 17 | $56

W 50s | 45 Rockefeller Plaza (enter on 50th St., bet. 5th & 6th Aves.) |
212-974-2020 | www.brasserieruhlmann.com

It's "all about the location" at this Rockefeller Center brasserie whose
"art deco wonder" of a room is augmented with an "unbeatable" patio;

it's a "safe bet", given chef Laurent Tourondel's "consistent" fare, though there are grumbles about "spotty" service and tabs that raise the question, "where's my TARP?"

NEW Brasserie 1605 *American*

FOOD	DECOR	SERVICE	COST
-	-	-	M

W 40s | Crowne Plaza Times Sq. Hotel | 1605 Broadway, 2nd fl. (bet. 48th & 49th Sts.) | 212-315-6000 | www.cpmanhattantimessquare.com

Though it looks out on the frantic, colossal M&M's World sign across Broadway, this New American arrival serves as a quiet haven from the hustle-bustle below; the midpriced comfort dishes like Kobe burgers are crowd-pleasers, but it's the eye-popping views of Times Square that take center stage here.

Bravo Gianni *Italian*

FOOD	DECOR	SERVICE	COST
22	16	23	$66

E 60s | 230 E. 63rd St. (bet. 2nd & 3rd Aves.) | 212-752-7272 | www.bravogiannirestaurant.com

This "old-school", "real-deal-NY" Upper Eastsider "continues to please" with its Northern Italian classics "served with aplomb"; the eponymous chef-owner "meets and greets" a longtime clientele "right out of central casting" – but outsiders opine "if you don't know Gianni, it's not so bravo", especially given the price.

Bread Tribeca *Italian*

FOOD	DECOR	SERVICE	COST
19	17	18	$37

TriBeCa | 301 Church St. (Walker St.) | 212-334-8282 | www.breadtribeca.com

Bread ● *Sandwiches*

NoLita | 20 Spring St. (bet. Elizabeth & Mott Sts.) | 212-334-1015

TriBeCans toast the "tremendous" bread at this "funky, chic" Italian proffering "inventive" panini and other "basic", "reasonably priced" dishes; "polite" staffers preside over the "bright", "upscale" room – and there's also a bite-size NoLita affiliate.

Breeze *French/Thai*

FOOD	DECOR	SERVICE	COST
21	15	19	$30

W 40s | 661 Ninth Ave. (bet. 45th & 46th Sts.) | 212-262-7777 | www.breezenyc.com

"Creative" French-Thai fusion fare via a "responsive" crew makes this Hell's Kitchen storefront a "standout", especially for theatergoers seeking "value" and "quick turnaround"; design touches like "kooky" menus in CD cases and on old "recycled" records add a "fun spin."

Brennan & Carr ●⊟ *Sandwiches*

FOOD	DECOR	SERVICE	COST
21	9	16	$18

Sheepshead Bay | 3432 Nostrand Ave. (Ave. U) | Brooklyn | 718-646-9559

Specializing in "soppy", "savory" roast beef sandwiches since 1938, this "no-frills" Sheepshead Bay "gravy pit" remains an "old-school Brooklyn" "institution"; "hardening of the arteries" and "dive" decor that seemingly "hasn't changed since they opened" are part of the experience.

brgr *Burgers*

FOOD	DECOR	SERVICE	COST
19	12	14	$16

Chelsea | 287 Seventh Ave. (bet. 26th & 27th Sts.) | 212-488-7500 | www.brgr.us

Aside from the "vowels in its name", "nothing is missing from the burger experience" at this "courteous" Chelsea counter-service joint offering "almost any topping" on "cooked-to-order" turkey, beef and veggie patties, plus "hvnly" shakes; still, some who compare it to a "noisy", "upscale McDonald's" wonder "what all the buzz is about."

	FOOD	DECOR	SERVICE	COST

Bricco *Italian* | 20 | 17 | 20 | $46 |

W 50s | 304 W. 56th St. (bet. 8th & 9th Aves.) | 212-245-7160 |
www.bricconyc.com

Long a Hell's Kitchen "standby", this "solid" trattoria specializes in
"excellent wood-fired pizzas" ferried by "friendly" staffers strategi-
cally synchronized to make your curtain; whether you consider it "romantic" or not, the owner often invites "pretty women" to plant lipstick
"kisses on the ceiling."

Brick Cafe *French/Italian* | 21 | 20 | 19 | $32 |

Astoria | 30-95 33rd St. (31st Ave.) | Queens | 718-267-2735 |
www.brickcafe.com

A "popular" Astoria "neighborhood joint" – "especially in summer"
when there's sidewalk seating – this "affordable" "SoHo-esque"
French-Italian is "perfect for brunch"; an underwhelmed few may
shrug "nothing to rave about", but it's "always crowded for a reason."

Brick Lane Curry House *Indian* | 21 | 15 | 16 | $30 |

E 50s | 235 E. 53rd St. (bet. 2nd & 3rd Aves.) | 212-339-8353 |
www.bricklanetoo.com

E Village | 306-308 E. Sixth St. (bet. 1st & 2nd Aves.) | 212-979-2900 |
www.bricklanecurryhouse.com

Those who "like it hot" head for this "superior" Sixth Street Indian
known for its "incendiary" U.K.-style curries – specifically the "mind-
blastingly hot *phaal*" – though there are "less spicy dishes" too; now
Midtowners have their own "minimalist" BYO branch.

Bridge Cafe *American* | 21 | 20 | 21 | $49 |

Financial District | 279 Water St. (Dover St.) | 212-227-3344 |
www.bridgecafenyc.com

"Delicious", "hearty" New Americana, "friendly" service and "cozy"
circa-1794 tavern digs ensure that this "landmark under the Brooklyn
Bridge" remains a "standby"; given its proximity to the Seaport, some
are surprised there "aren't many tourists."

Brio *Italian* | 18 | 14 | 17 | $40 |

E 60s | 137 E. 61st St. (Lexington Ave.) | 212-980-2300 | www.brionyc.com

"Especially good pizzas" and other "fair-priced" Italian standards have
"Bloomingdale's shoppers" and others popping into this "hopping" Upper Eastsider, especially at lunchtime; however, despite the "convivial"
mood, some suggest that the decor and service "need improvement."

Brioso *Italian* | ▽ 24 | 18 | 19 | $49 |

Staten Island | 174 New Dorp Ln. (9th St.) | 718-667-1700 |
www.briosoristorante.com

"Superb" specials augment the "terrific" Italian standards at this "welcoming" New Dorp trattoria deemed "one of Staten Island's best";
other pluses are comparatively "upscale" digs and "pro" service – but
now that "the secret's out", "noise" and weekend "crowds" also figure in.

Broadway East *American* | ▽ 22 | 22 | 20 | $44 |

LES | 171 E. Broadway (bet. Jefferson & Rutgers Sts.) | 212-228-3100 |
www.broadwayeast.com

A "living wall of greenery" is the "beautiful" dining room's focal point
at this "vegetarian-oriented" LES New American; though we hear a

new chef may shake things up a bit, the "hipster"-magnet downstairs lounge (open till 4 AM) shouldn't be affected.

Brooklyn Diner USA ◑ *Diner* | 17 | 15 | 17 | $33 |

W 40s | 155 W. 43rd St. (bet. B'way & 6th Ave.) | 212-265-5400
W 50s | 212 W. 57th St. (bet. B'way & 7th Ave.) | 212-977-2280
www.brooklyndiner.com

This "friendly", "theatrical" Midtown diner duo from Shelly Fireman "satisfies" with "Jewish comfort" fare and "stick-to-your-ribs" Americana served from breakfast till late in the evening; given its "humongous", "mouthwatering" choices, "if you share, it's a great buy", if you don't, it's "doggy bag" time; P.S. bring "your cardiologist's number."

Brooklyn Fish Camp Ⓜ *Seafood* | 22 | 15 | 18 | $42 |

Park Slope | 162 Fifth Ave. (bet. Degraw & Douglass Sts.) | Brooklyn | 718-783-3264 | www.brooklynfishcamp.com

"Simple" yet "sophisticated" seafood (including signature lobster rolls) reels in regulars at this Park Slope sibling of Mary's Fish Camp, overseen by a sometimes-"zany" crew; the "stripped-down" interior is augmented by a front bar and "wonderful back garden."

🆕 Brooklyn Star *Southern* | – | – | – | M |

Williamsburg | 33 Havemeyer St. (bet. N. 7th & 8th Sts.) | Brooklyn | 718-599-9899 | www.thebrooklynstar.com

Southern food from a Momofuku alum takes center stage at this mid-priced arrival in the former Brick Oven Gallery space, where the pizza oven is now used to crank out the likes of cornbread and mac 'n' cheese served in hot skillets; its tiny digs are Billyburg-minimal.

Brother Jimmy's BBQ *BBQ* | 16 | 12 | 14 | $26 |

E 40s | Grand Central | lower level (42nd St. & Vanderbilt Ave.) | 212-661-4022
E 70s | 1485 Second Ave. (bet. 77th & 78th Sts.) | 212-288-0099 ◑
E 90s | 1644 Third Ave. (92nd St.) | 212-426-2020 ◑
Garment District | 416 Eighth Ave. (31st St.) | 212-967-7603 ◑
Murray Hill | 181 Lexington Ave. (31st St.) | 212-779-7427 ◑
W 80s | 428 Amsterdam Ave. (bet. 80th & 81st Sts.) | 212-501-7515 ◑
www.brotherjimmys.com

"Down-home BBQ" and "cheap beer" fuel the "frat-house" scene at this smokin' sextet that's "hog heaven" for the "under-30" set; however, the "super-cute waitresses" are so "slow", even drooling dudes admit "it might be faster to drive to Carolina."

Brown Café *American* | ∇ 23 | 14 | 18 | $37 |

LES | 61 Hester St. (bet. Essex & Ludlow Sts.) | 212-477-2427 | www.greenbrownorange.com

At this LES "culinary gold mine", a talented kitchen turns the "freshest" organic ingredients into "innovative" New American eats, served by "personable" staffers "carefully selected for their hipness"; "unassuming", rough-hewn digs are "intimate" to some, "cramped" to others – but all agree about the "excellent value."

Bruckner Bar & Grill ◑ *American* | – | – | – | I |

Bronx | 1 Bruckner Blvd. (3rd Ave.) | 718-665-2001 | www.brucknerbar.com

A "worthwhile stop" in a "gentrifying" Bronx "artist community", this "great hideaway" below the Third Avenue Bridge offers casual New

American eats in a basic storefront setting; its "crowd and ambiance" may have you thinking "you're in the East Village."

Bryant Park Grill/Cafe *American* 17 | 21 | 17 | $48

W 40s | behind NY Public Library | 25 W. 40th St. (bet. 5th & 6th Aves.) | 212-840-6500 | www.arkrestaurants.com

"The city is the decor" at Bryant Park's "lovely" American duo, which includes the "airy", more upscale Grill, suitable for a "business lunch", and the outdoor Cafe offering a "limited" menu plus plenty of "people-watching"; in both cases, most "wish the food and service matched" the setting.

B. Smith's Restaurant Row *Southern* 19 | 19 | 19 | $50

W 40s | 320 W. 46th St. (bet. 8th & 9th Aves.) | 212-315-1100 | www.bsmith.com

"Dependable" "nouveau" Southern fare served in "casual" digs ensures that Barbara Smith's midpriced Restaurant Row vet is still the "belle of the ball"; the staff will "get you to your curtain", so the only danger is "sleeping during the show" after all that hearty "comfort food."

Bubba Gump Shrimp Co. ● *American/Seafood* 14 | 15 | 16 | $31

W 40s | 1501 Broadway (bet. 43rd & 44th Sts.) | 212-391-7100 | www.bubbagump.com

It certainly "*looks* like a place built by a lovable dimwit" and the "awesome" Times Square view resembles a "big video game", so "kids tend to like" this "touristy" theme seafooder where "enthusiastic" staffers sling "mass-produced" catch in cacophonous quarters; however, crabby critics call it "Bubba Dump."

Bubby's *American* 18 | 15 | 15 | $30

TriBeCa | 120 Hudson St. (N. Moore St.) | 212-219-0666
Dumbo | 1 Main St. (bet. Plymouth & Water Sts.) | Brooklyn | 718-222-0666 ⓜ🚇
www.bubbys.com

TriBeCa "families" and Dumbo dwellers dig this duo's "heartwarming" American "comfort" fare that's "affordable" and especially "popular" at Sunday brunch (with lines so long you may have to "wait until Monday"); doubters "dodge strollers" and dismiss this "hip IHOP" as a "diner with pretensions."

🄩 Buddakan ● *Asian* 23 | 27 | 21 | $64

Chelsea | 75 Ninth Ave. (16th St.) | 212-989-6699 | www.buddakannyc.com
It's a "total scene", but "you probably need to be younger than 30" and "good-looking" to get the most out of Stephen Starr's "stunning", "cavernous" Chelsea "movie set"; "always fun" and usually "crowded", it offers "creative, delicious", "pricey" modern Asian cooking that continues to be "surprising" – even if its "happening" bar action isn't.

Buenos Aires ● *Argentinean/Steak* 22 | 14 | 21 | $41

E Village | 513 E. Sixth St. (bet. Aves. A & B) | 212-228-2775 | www.buenosairesnyc.com

"You can taste the pampas" in the "succulent" "grass-fed" steaks and "robust" regional Malbecs at this East Village Argentine, where a "convivial" vibe, "unpretentious" service and "great value" make up for "lacking" decor; small wonder this "neighborhood gem" is always "crowded" (expect "marathon waits").

	FOOD	DECOR	SERVICE	COST

Bukhara Grill *Indian* 22 | 15 | 18 | $38

E 40s | 217 E. 49th St. (bet. 2nd & 3rd Aves.) | 212-888-2839 | www.bukharany.com

At this U.N.-area Indian, the "well-spiced" dishes are full of "evocative flavors", and the "excellent" $17 lunch buffet "can't be beat"; maybe it looks a little "dowdy", but given that the "attentive" waiters are "ready to please", most don't mind much.

Bull & Bear ❶ *Steak* 20 | 22 | 21 | $68

E 40s | Waldorf-Astoria | 570 Lexington Ave. (49th St.) | 212-872-1275 | www.bullandbearsteakhouse.com

A favored financier "hangout", this "clubby" Waldorf-Astoria "institution" proffers "solid" steaks and chops, "outstanding" cocktails, "courteous" service and an "old-school" "robber-baron" appeal; still, those not "on expense accounts" wish the "spendy" tabs were more "bear-a-bull."

Bún ❶ *Vietnamese* ▽ 20 | 16 | 18 | $30

SoHo | 143 Grand St. (bet. Crosby & Lafayette Sts.) | 212-431-7999 | www.eatbun.com

At Michael Huynh's "friendly", low-budget eatery on the SoHo-Chinatown border, the "twists" on Vietnamese classics, including the namesake noodle dish, are "imaginative" yet "traditional enough to satiate a craving"; however, the mod, bamboo-trimmed interior (think *The Jetsons* goes to Vietnam") gets mixed reviews.

Burger Heaven *Burgers* 16 | 9 | 14 | $19

E 40s | 20 E. 49th St. (bet. 5th & Madison Aves.) | 212-755-2166
E 40s | 291 Madison Ave. (bet. 40th & 41st Sts.) | 212-685-6250
E 50s | 536 Madison Ave. (bet. 54th & 55th Sts.) | 212-753-4214
E 50s | 9 E. 53rd St. (bet. 5th & Madison Aves.) | 212-752-0340
E 60s | 804 Lexington Ave. (62nd St.) | 212-838-3580
E 80s | 1534 Third Ave. (bet. 86th & 87th Sts.) | 212-722-8292
www.burgerheaven.com

If not exactly "heaven on earth" – more like "burgertory" – this "glorified coffee shop" chainlet remains a "staple" for its "reliable", "fresh" patties, salads and such at "fair prices"; "prompt" servers "move you out quick", a blessing for "office" types on the go.

🆉 burger joint at Le Parker Meridien ❶🍴 *Burgers* 24 | 10 | 13 | $16

W 50s | Le Parker Meridien | 119 W. 56th St. (bet. 6th & 7th Aves.) | 212-708-7414 | www.parkermeridien.com

Burger-meisters savor the "delicious juxtaposition" of this counter-service "dive" concealed in a "plush" Midtown hotel lobby while downing "mouthwatering" patties and "great shakes"; it's "not so secret" these days, though, so "Disneyland"-esque lines, "harried" staffers and "packed" seating are part of the "bargain."

NEW Bussaco Ⓜ *American* ▽ 22 | 21 | 20 | $46

Park Slope | 833 Union St. (bet. 6th & 7th Aves.) | Brooklyn | 718-857-8828 | www.bussacobklyn.com

"Innovative but not outrageous" New American creations paired with "excellent" wines make this new Park Sloper "worth checking out"; to most, the "attentive" service and "simple, calm" space are equally

FOOD DECOR SERVICE COST

"satisfying", but skeptics say a "limited menu" and "inconsistent" cooking bespeak "unrealized potential."

NEW Butcher Bay Ⓜ *Seafood* ▽ 14 | 12 | 14 | $35
E Village | 511 E. Fifth St. (bet. Aves. A & B) | 212-260-1333 | www.butcherbaynyc.com
At this new wood-planked East Village seafood shack, the sidewalk sounds of boisterous passersby stand in for the roar of the ocean; most of the affordable fin fare is fried, but there are a few exceptions like the market fish of the day for those aiming to fit into skinny jeans.

Butter Ⓩ *American* 20 | 23 | 18 | $61
E Village | 415 Lafayette St. (bet. Astor Pl. & 4th St.) | 212-253-2828 | www.butterrestaurant.com
"Gorgeous" "you're-in-the-woods" decor and "enticing" New American eats mean this Astor Place hot spot offers more than a "happening" bar scene; its "young crowd" pays "high tabs" to see "Hollywood" types "slumming it", and doesn't bat an eye at "blaring music" and serious staff "attitude."

NEW Buttermilk Channel Ⓜ *American* 23 | 22 | 23 | $41
Carroll Gardens | 524 Court St. (Huntington St.) | Brooklyn | 718-852-8490 | www.buttermilkchannelnyc.com
Employing "excellent" local ingredients, this Carroll Gardens arrival nails the New American upscale "comfort" genre, and at "reasonable" rates to boot; its "lovely" "buttermilk-colored" room wears a "warm glow", ditto the "gracious" owner and staff, but it gets "packed" and "loud", with waits "bordering on the ridiculous."

BXL Café ❶ *Belgian* ▽ 20 | 20 | 18 | $32
W 40s | 125 W. 43rd St. (bet. B'way & 6th Ave.) | 212-768-0200
BXL East ❶ *Belgian*
NEW E 50s | 210 E. 51st St. (bet. 2nd & 3rd Aves.) | 212-888-7782 | www.bxlcafe.com
Amis advise "don't bother ordering anything" but the "amazing" mussels at these "convenient", "friendly" Midtown Belgians, also appreciated for their "awesome" regional ales; after the $20 all-you-can-eat *moules* on Sundays and Mondays, one emerges "full, happy and with money left over."

Cabana ❶ *Nuevo Latino* 21 | 18 | 18 | $38
E 60s | 1022 Third Ave. (bet. 60th & 61st Sts.) | 212-980-5678
Seaport | Pier 17 | 89 South St. (Fulton St.) | 212-406-1155
Forest Hills | 107-10 70th Rd. (bet. Austin St. & Queens Blvd.) | Queens | 718-263-3600
www.cabanarestaurant.com
The "generous" portions of Nuevo Latino *comida* are "zesty" and "filling" at this "colorful" trio that's "always" "hopping"; waits are made "more bearable" by mojitos "straight out of Havana" and, at the Seaport branch, "incredible" harbor views from the "spacious" deck.

Cabrito ❶ *Mexican* 18 | 13 | 16 | $35
G Village | 50 Carmine St. (bet. Bedford & Bleecker Sts.) | 212-929-5050 | www.cabritonyc.com
Amigos appreciate the "imaginative" Mexican eats – including the "delicious" namesake roast goat – at this "funky", "friendly" Villager

with a "loud" bar scene; however, the "too-crowded" setting and "lackadaisical" service get some surveyors' goat.

Cacio e Pepe *Italian*

FOOD	DECOR	SERVICE	COST
20	14	18	$41

E Village | 182 Second Ave. (bet. 11th & 12th Sts.) | 212-505-5931
When at this "warm", "unpretentious" East Village trattoria, do as the Romans do: *mangia* the "authentic" namesake pasta served "in a large cheese wheel" and pair it with an "affordable" Italian vino; in summer, cognoscenti dine alfresco in the "terrific back garden."

Cacio e Vino ● *Italian*

FOOD	DECOR	SERVICE	COST
21	15	19	$39

E Village | 80 Second Ave. (bet. 4th & 5th Sts.) | 212-228-3269 | www.cacioevino.com
Pie partisans "pop in" to this "casual", "cozy" East Village Sicilian for "terrific" wood-fired pizzas and calzones, all "very fresh"; exposed-brick walls make for "bad acoustics" when it's "packed", but "decent prices" and sincere service silence those objections.

Cafe Asean ⊭ *SE Asian*

FOOD	DECOR	SERVICE	COST
20	14	18	$28

G Village | 117 W. 10th St. (bet. Greenwich & 6th Aves.) | 212-633-0348
For "delish" "home"-style meals "away from home", Villagers vaunt this "informal" SE Asian "standby" in the shadow of Jefferson Market Library; an "adorable" back garden redeems the "quirky" interior, and though service is as "laid-back" as the vibe, the "price is right."

Cafe Bar ● *Greek/Mediterranean*

FOOD	DECOR	SERVICE	COST
∇ 18	17	16	$24

Astoria | 32-90 36th St. (34th Ave.) | Queens | 718-204-5273 | www.cafebarastoria.com
"Locals, Manhattan refugees" and "night owls" gravitate to this "arty" Astoria Greek-Med for sandwiches and salads served on "mis-matched" china, plus "fancy coffee", wine and cocktails; the updated "eclectic" digs now have booths and a communal table, but service is still "lackluster."

☑ Café Boulud *French*

FOOD	DECOR	SERVICE	COST
27	23	26	$80

E 70s | Surrey Hotel | 20 E. 76th St. (bet. 5th & Madison Aves.) | 212-772-2600 | www.danielnyc.com
"Melding the modern and relaxed with the traditional and classy", Daniel Boulud's "less-formal" Upper Eastsider features Gavin Kaysen's "outstanding" "haute Nouveau French" cuisine delivered by a "superb" staff; it costs "much less" than the flagship, but is still mostly for those who "haven't figured out there's a recession on"; N.B. renovations underway are expected to add a new bar and two private rooms.

Cafe Centro ☒ *Mediterranean*

FOOD	DECOR	SERVICE	COST
20	19	20	$50

E 40s | MetLife Bldg. | 200 Park Ave. (45th St.) | 212-818-1222 | www.patinagroup.com
Thanks to its "well-executed" Med menu and "attentive" service, this "big, bright", "bustling" brasserie next to Grand Central remains a "tried-and-true" destination for a "business lunch" or "quiet" dinner "with commuting pals"; ample outdoor seating provides "added pleasure."

Cafecito ⊭ *Cuban*

FOOD	DECOR	SERVICE	COST
∇ 23	15	18	$29

E Village | 185 Ave. C (bet. 11th & 12th Sts.) | 212-253-9966
"Delicious" Cuban cooking and "effective cocktails" reward the "hike" out to this "small" but "wonderful" Alphabet City Latin lair; the "value"

pricing figures heavily in its "popularity", which is poised to grow with the addition of a take-out satellite that's in the works.

Cafe Cluny ❶ *American/French*   21 | 20 | 20 | $49

W Village | 284 W. 12th St. (W. 4th St.) | 212-255-6900 |
www.cafecluny.com

This "trendy but friendly" West Villager's "satisfying" French-American bistro fare and "bleached-wood" digs – plus a smattering of "celebs" – draw droves, especially for the "perfect" brunch; its snug space strikes some surveyors as "intimate" and "lively" but others as "tight" and "loud" – all are equally "annoyed" by "long waits."

Cafe Colonial *Brazilian*   19 | 17 | 16 | $37

NoLita | 276 Elizabeth St. (Houston St.) | 212-274-0044 |
www.cafecolonialny.com

"Rich and flavorful" stews and "the best cheese bread around" keep it Rio at this "unpretentious" NoLita Brazilian that's a good choice for a "casual" date or brunch; service may be "slow", but hey, the "quaint" digs are so "tiny" you won't have trouble "finding the waitress."

Cafe Con Leche *Cuban/Dominican*   18 | 11 | 16 | $25

W 80s | 424 Amsterdam Ave. (bet. 80th & 81st Sts.) | 212-595-7000
W 90s | 726 Amsterdam Ave. (bet. 95th & 96th Sts.) | 212-678-7000

"Wear stretchy pants" to this "friendly", "reliable" UWS duo known for its "hefty" helpings of "simple, tasty", "cheap" Cuban-Dominican grub, plus "terrific" namesake coffee; "yummy cocktails" take the edge off "noisy", kinda "shabby" digs – and "fast delivery" is also an option.

Café d'Alsace ❶ *French*   21 | 18 | 19 | $47

E 80s | 1695 Second Ave. (88th St.) | 212-722-5133 |
www.cafedalsace.com

"If ya gotta have choucroute", head for this Yorkville French brasserie plying "dependable" Alsace classics plus "outstanding" suds overseen by a "beer sommelier"; given its "pretty sidewalk dining area" and the "dearth of good eating" options nearby, it's "always busy."

Café de Bruxelles ❶ *Belgian*   21 | 16 | 19 | $44

W Village | 118 Greenwich Ave. (13th St.) | 212-206-1830 |
www.cafebruxellesonline.com

When you're craving "mussels, frites and a good beer", this "comfortable" Village vet – "the best west of Antwerp" – "never fails to satisfy"; "decade after decade", its "authentic" "homestyle" Belgian cooking, "charming" setting, "unhurried" service and "affordable" prices have kept it a beloved "local hangout."

Café du Soleil *French/Mediterranean*   18 | 16 | 15 | $39

W 100s | 2723 Broadway (104th St.) | 212-316-5000 |
www.cafedusoleilnyc.com

With a "sunny" setup "to match its name", this "pleasant" UWS bistro draws "locals" for its "serviceable", "well-priced" French-Med rotation, including a "safe-bet" brunch; sidewalk seats provide relief from the "noise" inside, though there's no escaping the "spotty" service.

Cafe Español ❶ *Spanish*   20 | 15 | 20 | $37

G Village | 172 Bleecker St. (bet. MacDougal & Sullivan Sts.) |
212-505-0657

(continued)

Cafe Español

G Village | 78 Carmine St. (bet. Bedford St. & 7th Ave. S.) | 212-675-3312 | www.cafeespanol.com

"Reliable year after year", these "unpretentious", separately owned Village Spaniards supervised by "accommodating" hosts endure by delivering "more than your money's worth" of "tasty" Iberian eats; the "great sangria" is also credited with helping patrons "leave happy."

Café Evergreen *Chinese*   18 | 12 | 19 | $32

E 60s | 1288 First Ave. (bet. 69th & 70th Sts.) | 212-744-3266

Saving themselves a "schlep" to C-town, Eastsiders head to this "authentic" neighborhood Cantonese for "delightful" dim sum and "surprisingly good" wine choices at "reasonable" rates; fortunately, the chow is "delivered quickly" because there's "not much atmosphere" to take in.

Cafe Fiorello ● *Italian*   20 | 17 | 19 | $51

W 60s | 1900 Broadway (bet. 63rd & 64th Sts.) | 212-595-5330 | www.cafefiorello.com

At this Italian "institution", an antipasto bar and "divine" thin-crust pizzas plus sidewalk seating supply a "satisfying" prelude to Lincoln Center performances; "quick" turnaround keeps the pre-theater "mob" moving, but doesn't quiet gripes about "rising prices."

Café Frida *Mexican*   19 | 15 | 17 | $39

W 70s | 368 Columbus Ave. (bet. 77th & 78th Sts.) | 212-712-2929 | www.cafefrida.com

Westsiders weary of "standard taco places" turn up at this "festive" Mexican specializing in "slightly upscale" south-of-the-border dishes with prices to match; "potent" margaritas also fuel the "fun", though "slow" service and "way-dark" lighting dim the mood for some.

Café Gitane ●⇄ *French/Moroccan*   20 | 17 | 15 | $28

NoLita | 242 Mott St. (Prince St.) | 212-334-9552

Don your "sunglasses and stilettos" for a trip to this "über-hip", cash-only NoLita boîte whose perpetual "preen" "scene" practically upstages the "tasty, inexpensive" French-Moroccan eats; count on "oblivious" service, and unless you're "Lenny Kravitz", "long waits" for a table too; N.B. a branch in the West Village's new Jane Hotel is in the works.

Café Habana ● *Cuban/Mexican*   23 | 12 | 15 | $25

NoLita | 17 Prince St. (Elizabeth St.) | 212-625-2001

Habana Outpost ●⇄ *Cuban/Mexican*

Fort Greene | 755-757 Fulton St. (S. Portland Ave.) | Brooklyn | 718-858-9500 | www.ecoeatery.com

"The grilled corn is an experience" and ditto the "wait" to try it at this "tiny", "mobbed" NoLita Mexican-Cuban; for the same "cheap" reward "without the hassle", hit up the "more relaxing" Fort Greene outpost.

Café Henri ● *French*   ∇ 21 | 16 | 18 | $24

G Village | 27 Bedford St. (Downing St.) | 212-243-2846
LIC | 10-10 50th Ave. (bet. Jackson Ave. & Vernon Blvd.) | Queens | 718-383-9315

The "amazing crepês" alone are "worth the trip" to these "cozy" Village-LIC French cafes specializing in "light" munchies and brighten-your-

	FOOD	DECOR	SERVICE	COST

day coffee; though seating's limited, the "Parisian"-style "no-hurry" hospitality ensures "a table's yours until you feel like giving it up."

Cafe Joul *French*
18 | 13 | 18 | $44

E 50s | 1070 First Ave. (bet. 58th & 59th Sts.) | 212-759-3131

Though it's not much to look at, this "decent", "low-key" Sutton Place bistro keeps it real with "reliable", moderately priced French "classics" enjoyed amid a "friendly" atmosphere; the "crowded brunch" scene suggests its "mainstay" status is secure.

Café Katja *Austrian*
▽ 23 | 17 | 24 | $33

LES | 79 Orchard St. (bet. Broome & Grand Sts.) | 212-219-9545 | www.cafe-katja.com

Some of the "best wurst for your buck" awaits at this "real-deal" LES Austrian, a "laid-back" "gem" run by "knowledgeable" staffers who "really care"; factor in "excellent" beers, and "flashbacks to your backpacking trip through Europe" are only a gulp away.

Cafe Loup ❶ *French*
19 | 18 | 20 | $44

G Village | 105 W. 13th St. (bet. 6th Ave. & 7th Ave. S.) | 212-255-4746

"Everyone seems to know each other" at this "been-around-forever" Village "neighborhood haunt" that pleases the pack with "dependable" French bistro fare and "attitude-free" "pro" service; sound hounds especially dig Sunday's live jazz during both "delightful brunch" and dinner.

Cafe Luluc ❶⊄ *French*
19 | 15 | 18 | $28

Cobble Hill | 214 Smith St. (Baltic St.) | Brooklyn | 718-625-3815

A "pleasant stop on the Smith Street restaurant parade", this "quaint" Cobble Hill Gallic hits the mark "any time of day" dishing up "no-frills" standards ("the pancakes are magical") in "unrushed" environs; its "packed brunch" scene suggests the cash-only policy is easy to overluc.

Cafe Luxembourg ❶ *French*
20 | 18 | 19 | $52

W 70s | 200 W. 70th St. (bet. Amsterdam & West End Aves.) | 212-873-7411 | www.cafeluxembourg.com

"Never conceding to fads", this Lincoln Center–area "institution" maintains its "long-running success" streak, drawing legions of loyalists "happy to drop coin" for "unfussy" French bistro fare in "casual, lively" surroundings; the service "isn't always the greatest", and the "packed" digs get "noisy" – except when a "celeb sighting" renders the crowd "speechless."

Cafe Mogador ❶ *Moroccan*
21 | 15 | 17 | $29

E Village | 101 St. Marks Pl. (bet. Ave. A & 1st Ave.) | 212-677-2226 | www.cafemogador.com

"Still going strong" after more than a quarter-century in business is this "constantly packed" East Village Moroccan, where "delicious", "down-to-earth" cooking that's "priced right" plays in a "cozy" setting; luckily for the "hordes" lined up to get in, it's open late.

Cafe Moutarde *French*
19 | 20 | 19 | $42

Park Slope | 239 Fifth Ave. (Carroll St.) | Brooklyn | 718-623-3600

Park Slopers play Parisians at this "pleasant" bistro where a "well-priced" rotation of "dependable" Gallic fare plus an "authentic" setting simulate a "trip to France" *sans* the flight; come weekend brunch, "crowds" put the "friendly" staff to the test.

	FOOD	DECOR	SERVICE	COST

Cafe Ronda *Mediterranean/S American* | 19 | 15 | 17 | $37 |

W 70s | 249-251 Columbus Ave. (bet. 71st & 72nd Sts.) | 212-579-9929 |
www.caferonda.com

"Locals" feed their fancy for a "change of pace" at this "lively" "little"
UWS cafe serving a "varied" Med–South American menu comprising
"tapas and more"; though service can appear "rudderless" at times,
the sidewalk seating and "great brunch" seal the deal.

Café Sabarsky/Café Fledermaus *Austrian* | 22 | 24 | 19 | $43 |

E 80s | Neue Galerie | 1048 Fifth Ave. (86th St.) | 212-288-0665 |
www.wallse.com

"A veritable *schlag*-fest" is yours if you "save room for the outstanding pastries" at chef Kurt Gutenbrunner's "old-world", "worth-
the-wait" Neue Galerie Viennese cafe "overlooking Central Park";
Fledermaus downstairs offers the same menu in "less-plush" digs.

NEW **Café Select** ● *Swiss* | ▽ 21 | 20 | 19 | $32 |

SoHo | 212 Lafayette St. (bet. Broome & Spring Sts.) | 212-925-9322 |
www.cafeselectnyc.com

The latest from "the La Esquina gang", this "small" but "stylish" SoHo
newcomer woos "Swiss expats" and assorted "cool" cats with a roster
of "reasonably priced" Alpine fare ferried by "skinny servers"; among
trendoids, the "hidden back room" is most select.

Cafe Spice *Indian* | 18 | 15 | 16 | $28 |

E 40s | Grand Central | lower level (42nd St. & Vanderbilt Ave.) |
646-227-1300
G Village | 72 University Pl. (bet. 10th & 11th Sts.) | 212-253-6999
www.cafespice.com

Its cuisine may be "toned down for Westerners", but "if you're near
NYU and looking for Indian", this "reliable" Villager furnishes an "inexpensive" fix; over at the Grand Central outpost, commuters count
on the take-out branch to "hit the spot" on the way home.

Cafe Steinhof *Austrian* | 18 | 15 | 18 | $29 |

Park Slope | 422 Seventh Ave. (14th St.) | Brooklyn | 718-369-7776 |
www.cafesteinhof.com

With its "bargain"-priced parade of "Austrian comfort food" plus
"solid" suds, this "lively" Park Sloper is always "satisfying"; frequent live
music and movie screenings are other reasons it's usually "crowded."

Cafeteria ● *American* | 18 | 15 | 14 | $32 |

Chelsea | 119 Seventh Ave. (17th St.) | 212-414-1717 |
www.cafeteriagroup.com

"Eye candy" abounds at this "round-the-clock" Chelsea American
where the "comfort classics" come with a side of "pretentiousness"; it
may have "lost some swagger" of late, but not its "great mac 'n' cheese."

Cafe Un Deux Trois ● *French* | 16 | 16 | 17 | $43 |

W 40s | 123 W. 44th St. (bet. B'way & 6th Ave.) | 212-354-4148 |
www.cafeundeuxtrois.biz
Le Petit Un Deux Trois ● *French*
NEW **W 40s** | 403 W. 43rd St. (bet. 9th & 10th Aves.) | 212-489-4900 |
www.lepetitundeuxtrois.com

"Stodgy" but "dependable", this Times Square "mainstay" hooks up a
"quick" pre-theater "in-and-out" with French bistro classics packaged

	FOOD	DECOR	SERVICE	COST

into "economical" prix fixes, plus "crayons for doodling" between courses; the new Petite spin-off comes with a "darling" enclosed garden.

Caffe Cielo ◐ *Italian* — 20 | 17 | 21 | $45

W 50s | 881 Eighth Ave. (bet. 52nd & 53rd Sts.) | 212-246-9555 | www.caffecielonyc.com

Being "close to" but not in the Theater District gives this "welcoming" Hell's Kitchen Italian a "neighborhood" feel while also making it a "reliable" option for ticket-holders "in a hurry"; the food's "solid" and "affordable" too, explaining why it's "been around a while."

Caffe Grazie *Italian* — 19 | 17 | 22 | $48

E 80s | 26 E. 84th St. (bet. 5th & Madison Aves.) | 212-717-4407 | www.caffegrazie.com

"Museum-hoppers" and "well-dressed" locals seek "quiet" meals served by "attentive" staffers at this "reliable", "sleepy" Italian quartered in a "lovely" townhouse "within striking distance of the Met"; prices are "a little steep", but the $15 lunch special presents "good value."

NEW Calexico Ⓜ✍ *Mexican* — - | - | - | I

Carroll Gardens | 122 Union St. (bet. Columbia & Hicks Sts.) | Brooklyn | 718-488-8226 | www.calexicocart.com

A stationary sibling to the taco trucks in SoHo and NoLita, this funky, cash-only newcomer brings much the same Cal-Mex menu to West Carroll Gardens; it boasts a self-serve salsa bar, but otherwise is as no-frills as its mobile counterparts and just as cheap – no surprise its few seats fill up fast.

Calle Ocho *Nuevo Latino* — 21 | 21 | 19 | $47

W 80s | 446 Columbus Ave. (bet. 81st & 82nd Sts.) | 212-873-5025 | www.calleochonyc.com

"Always jumpin'", this UWS joint joins "killer" Nuevo Latino cuisine and "fun cocktails" in a "cavernous", "tropical" space; tabs tilt upwards, but there's always the "all-you-can-drink sangria" during brunchtime to obliterate any cash concerns.

CamaJe ◐ *American/French* — ∇ 20 | 15 | 20 | $39

G Village | 85 MacDougal St. (bet. Bleecker & Houston Sts.) | 212-673-8184 | www.camaje.com

"Well-prepared" French-American fare that "won't break the bank" arrives at a "leisurely" pace amid "worn-out couches" and other "quirky" set pieces at this "cutesy" Village bistro; there's a "tasty jazz brunch" come Sundays and a full roster of "fun cooking classes" for DIYers.

Campagnola ◐ *Italian* — 23 | 18 | 21 | $68

E 70s | 1382 First Ave. (bet. 73rd & 74th Sts.) | 212-861-1102

"Old-school" Italiana just "like mama made" stars at this "classy" Eastsider that's *molto* popular among "Soprano wannabes", "May-December couples" and "voyeur" types; "amiable" staffers are more so "if you're a regular", but no matter what, "deep pockets" are a must.

Campo *Italian* — 18 | 17 | 18 | $30

W 100s | 2888 Broadway (bet. 112th & 113th Sts.) | 212-864-1143 | www.camponyc.com

"Columbia students" looking for a "convenient" carb-up hit this "friendly" Upper West Side trattoria where "yummy" thin-crust pizzas and other "decent" Italian standards get the job done at "reasonable prices"; all-you-can-eat specials and twice-daily happy hours keep it "lively" until "late."

	FOOD	DECOR	SERVICE	COST

Canaille ☑ *French* ▽ 22 | 17 | 18 | $40

Park Slope | 78 Fifth Ave. (bet. Prospect & St. Marks Pls.) | Brooklyn | 718-789-8899 | www.canaillebistro.com

"Lovely" classic fare in an "intimate" setting sums up the "absolutely Parisian" essence of this French bistro on Park Slope's Restaurant Row; most agree it shows real "promise", but opinions diverge over the owner-host, who is either "charming" or "obtrusive" depending on whom you ask.

Canaletto *Italian* 21 | 16 | 21 | $54

E 60s | 208 E. 60th St. (bet. 2nd & 3rd Aves.) | 212-317-9192

Eastsiders "on break from power-shopping at Bloomie's" duck into this "respectable" "neighborhood" Italian for "on-the-mark" meals handled by staffers who "go out of their way to please"; if the experience seems "unexciting" to some, to regulars "that's the best thing about it."

Candle Cafe *Vegan/Vegetarian* 22 | 14 | 20 | $32

E 70s | 1307 Third Ave. (bet. 74th & 75th Sts.) | 212-472-0970 | www.candlecafe.com

"Well-prepared" vegan and vegetarian eats crop up in a "variety" of iterations "tasty" enough to make carnivores "come to their senses" at this "dressed-down" UES sister of nearby Candle 79; it's "cramped", but "helpful" staffers ensure everyone gets a crack at "body and soul purity."

Candle 79 *Vegan/Vegetarian* 23 | 20 | 22 | $45

E 70s | 154 E. 79th St. (bet. Lexington & 3rd Aves.) | 212-537-7179 | www.candlecafe.com

Ethical epicures indulge in "creatively spun" "meatless delights" presented by a "fine" staff at this "elegant" UES "temple" of "grown-up" vegetarian and vegan cuisine; tabs may seem "steep" for the genre, but as it's "one of the best" going, most willingly spring for "carrots priced like karats."

Canyon Road *Southwestern* 21 | 17 | 18 | $37

E 70s | 1470 First Ave. (bet. 76th & 77th Sts.) | 212-734-1600 | www.arkrestaurants.com

"Tasty" Southwestern grub and "killer" margs rule the road at this "friendly" Upper Eastsider that's generally "packed" with "locals" and "post-collegians" on "blind dates" (prepare to "eavesdrop"); for "great food and drink specials", hit the "fun bar" at happy hour.

Capital Grille *Steak* 23 | 22 | 23 | $69

E 40s | 155 E. 42nd St. (bet. Lexington & 3rd Aves.) | 212-953-2000
NEW **W 50s** | 120 W. 51st St. (bet. 6th & 7th Aves.) | 212-246-0154
www.thecapitalgrille.com

Inside the "iceberg"-like Trylon Towers adjacent to the Chrysler Building resides this "high-end" steakhouse, a meaty magnet for "corporate" types boasting "solid" beef, "fab wines" and "attentive service"; most agree it displays "remarkable consistency for a chain" link – and now it's been joined (post-Survey) by a West Midtown branch.

	FOOD	DECOR	SERVICE	COST

Capsouto Frères *French* | 23 | 23 | 24 | $58 |

TriBeCa | 451 Washington St. (Watts St.) | 212-966-4900 |
www.capsoutofreres.com

"Soulful" French cooking and "amazing" wines – not to mention the
"best soufflé anywhere" – are yours provided "you can find" this "favorite" bistro located totally "out of the way" in TriBeCa ("even seasoned cabbies" may need a GPS); rewards include "superb" service,
"spacious" environs and "easy parking."

Z Caracas Arepa Bar *Venezuelan* | 24 | 14 | 17 | $20 |

E Village | 93½ E. Seventh St. (bet. Ave. A & 1st Ave.) |
212-529-2314

Z Caracas Brooklyn *Venezuelan*

NEW Williamsburg | 291 Grand St. (bet. Havemeyer & Roebling Sts.) |
Brooklyn | 718-218-6050

Z Caracas to Go *Venezuelan*

E Village | 91 E. Seventh St. (1st Ave.) | 212-228-5062
www.caracasarepabar.com

For a "thoroughly satisfying", low-cost "alternative to the sandwich
grind", try the "delicious" arepas at these "popular" Venezuelans; to
avoid "cramped" digs at the East Village original, either "get it to go"
next door or hit the "roomier" new Williamsburg outpost.

Cara Mia *Italian* | 20 | 15 | 19 | $38 |

W 40s | 654 Ninth Ave. (bet. 45th & 46th Sts.) | 212-262-6767 |
www.caramiany.com

"Reasonable" Italian eats and turnaround that has you "out in time for
your show" are "well worth" the "tight fit" at this "small"-but-
"welcoming" Hell's Kitchen "pre-theater staple"; those who prefer an
"unrushed" repast go after curtain time, when it "empties out."

NEW Caravaggio *Italian* | - | - | - | E |

E 70s | 23 E. 74th St. (bet. 5th & Madison Aves.) | 212-288-1004

Sistina's owners have opened this new standout in the very UES former
Coco Pazzo space, sprucing it up with murals by Donald Baechler but
retaining its old-NY glam – which extends to its well-heeled clientele;
as the name implies, its menu is comprised of pricey Italian dishes that
pay homage to the classics.

Caravan of Dreams *Vegan/Vegetarian* | 20 | 12 | 18 | $29 |

E Village | 405 E. Sixth St. (1st Ave.) | 212-254-1613 |
www.caravanofdreams.net

Vegans track down "healthy, flavorful" fare that's "reasonably priced"
and kosher too at this "ethically sound", if decor-challenged, East
Villager; hospitality is appropriately "easygoing", with additional "hip-
pie" vibes transmitted via live music performances and yoga classes.

Carl's Steaks *Cheesesteaks* | 21 | 6 | 12 | $13 |

Murray Hill | 507 Third Ave. (34th St.) | 212-696-5336 ◑
TriBeCa | 79 Chambers St. (bet. B'way & Church St.) | 212-566-2828
www.carlssteaks.com

The "greasy", "gut-busting" cheesesteaks at this TriBeCa–Murray Hill
duo are "as good as they get" short of "a drive to Philly", and hit the
spot "after a night at the bars" (bring "Pepto"); decor and elbow room
are next to "nonexistent", so "eat quick" or go "takeout."

	FOOD	DECOR	SERVICE	COST

☑ Carlyle Restaurant *French*   23 | 26 | 26 | $85

E 70s | Carlyle Hotel | 35 E. 76th St. (Madison Ave.) | 212-570-7192 |
www.thecarlyle.com

"One of the true class acts in NYC", this UES hotel dining room is a
"paean to another era" supplying "surprisingly good" French classics
delivered by a "more-than-courteous" crew in "elegant", "spacious",
"haven-of-calm" environs; the "lovely experience" may prove "costly",
but not if you recognize it as a trip to the Golden Age.

Carmine's *Italian*   20 | 16 | 18 | $40

W 40s | 200 W. 44th St. (bet. B'way & 8th Ave.) | 212-221-3800 ◑
W 90s | 2450 Broadway (bet. 90th & 91st Sts.) | 212-362-2200
www.carminesnyc.com

"Heaping platters" of "garlic-laden", "homestyle" Italian classics keep
it "crowded" and "noisy" at these "festive" Westsiders, built in the
style of Little Italy in 1900; "go with a group" and remember that "old-
fashioned", "good-value" food is "meant to be shared."

☑ Carnegie Deli ◑♥ *Deli*   22 | 10 | 14 | $29

W 50s | 854 Seventh Ave. (55th St.) | 212-757-2245 | www.carnegiedeli.com
A circa-1937 "NY icon" featuring "mile-high" sandwiches, "serious"
pickles, "gold-standard" cheesecake, "communal tables" and "colorful" waiters, this "crowded, noisy" Midtown Jewish deli is a "can't-
miss for locals and tourists"; yes, it's "expensive", but "huge portions"
and the chance to see Woody Allen make it a good buy.

Carol's Cafe ⊠Ⓜ *Eclectic*   ▽ 25 | 17 | 21 | $59

Staten Island | 1571 Richmond Rd. (bet. Four Corners Rd. & Seaview Ave.) |
718-979-5600 | www.carolscafe.com
It's "like you've got your own personal cook" at this "top-notch" Dongan
Hills Stand Islander where chef-owner Carol Frazzetta "thrills" with
her "creative" Eclectic entrees and "divine desserts"; prices say "special
occasion", but the semi-weekly $22 prix fixe is an "excellent value."

NEW Casa La Femme ◑ *Egyptian*   ▽ 20 | 25 | 19 | $53

W Village | 140 Charles St. (bet. Greenwich & Washington Sts.) |
212-505-0005 | www.casalafemmeny.com
"Romance" can once again blossom in Bedouin-style "private tents"
amid belly dancers, hookahs and "pretty good" Egyptian eats at this
"sexy", newly relocated Village hot spot; you'll spend like a sultan for
such "decadence", but there are few surer ways to "impress a date."

Casa Mono ◑ *Spanish*   25 | 18 | 20 | $54

Gramercy | 52 Irving Pl. (17th St.) | 212-253-2773 | www.casamononyc.com
Always a "crazy scene", Mario Batali's "tiny" Gramercy Spaniard has
"adventurous eaters" piling in – the lucky sit "by the open kitchen" – to
sample "sublime" tapas and wines with guidance from a "knowledgeable" staff; *sí sí*, "you'll pay" for the "pleasure", and the "wait can be a
pain" – unless you spend it "around the corner" at its sib, Bar Jamon.

Cascina ◑ *Italian*   19 | 17 | 19 | $40

W 40s | 647 Ninth Ave. (bet. 45th & 46th Sts.) | 212-245-4422 |
www.cascina.com
For a "reliable" "pre-theater" pit stop, this Hell's Kitchen standby's
"homestyle" Italian cooking in "cozy" quarters gets the job done "in

time for your show"; "fine wines" from its own vineyard and an ample grappa selection set it apart from its peers.

Casellula ● *American*

	FOOD	DECOR	SERVICE	COST
	25	19	20	$40

W 50s | 401 W. 52nd St. (bet. 9th & 10th Aves.) | 212-247-8137 | www.casellula.com

There's "sophisticated" snacking to be had at this "hip" Hell's Kitchen wine bar where "knowledgeable" staffers help you assemble "wonderful" wine-and-cheese pairings and navigate an assortment of fromage-focused New American small plates; it's a "tiny gem" where reservations aren't accepted, so anticipate a "line."

Casimir ● *French*

	FOOD	DECOR	SERVICE	COST
	▽ 19	19	16	$39

E Village | 103-105 Ave. B (bet. 6th & 7th Sts.) | 212-358-9683 | www.casimirrestaurant.com

"Cool" cats collect at this "tucked-away" East Villager offering "decent" French bistro fare in a "cozy" space, the highlight of which is a "romantic" back garden; "good prices" and groovy house music help compensate for service that's "not the greatest."

Caviar Russe *American*

	FOOD	DECOR	SERVICE	COST
	25	23	23	$84

E 50s | 538 Madison Ave., 2nd fl. (bet. 54th & 55th Sts.) | 212-980-5908 | www.caviarrusse.com

Up the stairs and into a "magical" room out of a "Russian fairy tale" is the route to "decadence defined" at this Midtown New American dispensing "excellent" caviar and sushi; be careful lest the excursion "melt your credit card" – though the $20 prix fixe lunch is really cool.

Cávo ● *Greek*

	FOOD	DECOR	SERVICE	COST
	21	25	20	$46

Astoria | 42-18 31st Ave. (bet. 42nd & 43rd Sts.) | Queens | 718-721-1001 | www.cavoastoria.com

Between its "breathtaking" decor and "delicious" Greek food, this "super-large" Astoria eatery-cum-nightclub is both a dining hub and a "place to party"; if tabs seem sizable, it "can get away with it" given the "fab" setting including a "transporting" outdoor waterfall garden.

Celeste ⊘ *Italian*

	FOOD	DECOR	SERVICE	COST
	23	11	15	$34

W 80s | 502 Amsterdam Ave. (bet. 84th & 85th Sts.) | 212-874-4559

Find out "what you'll put up with" for "delectable" Neapolitan fare priced "cheap" at this "mobbed" Westsider that spurns credit cards and reservations yet sports a "neverending line"; no, it "doesn't hang out the welcome mat", but the "entertaining" owner provides "his own show."

Cellini *Italian*

	FOOD	DECOR	SERVICE	COST
	22	18	22	$59

E 50s | 65 E. 54th St. (bet. Madison & Park Aves.) | 212-751-1555 | www.cellinirestaurant.com

Whether it's time for a "power lunch" or simply a "quiet dinner", "you can't go wrong" with this "versatile" East Midtown Italian; "solid" fare, "attentive" service and "no flights of fancy" add up to "quality" ("if unexciting") dining that's "worth the price."

Centolire *Italian*

	FOOD	DECOR	SERVICE	COST
	21	20	21	$61

E 80s | 1167 Madison Ave. (bet. 85th & 86th Sts.) | 212-734-7711 | www.pinoluongo.com

Ok, maybe it's "not a happening place", but Eastsiders "love" the "elegant" upstairs room at Pino Luongo's Carnegie Hill Italian, where "attentive" servers present "sophisticated" Tuscan specialties at "up-scale" rates; the ground-floor component has become a "less-formal" panini purveyor, but either floor is a good neighbor.

Centrico *Mexican*

20 | 18 | 19 | $47

TriBeCa | 211 W. Broadway (Franklin St.) | 212-431-0700 | www.myriadrestaurantgroup.com

There's a "lively", youth-centric "scene" at this "high-end" TriBeCa Mexican where the "innovative" takes on "traditional" dishes match up with "knockout margaritas"; the "high-ceilinged" space "can get noisy", though, making the calmer outdoor dining option "especially nice" when available.

Centro Vinoteca ◑ *Italian*

20 | 18 | 18 | $52

W Village | 74 Seventh Ave. S. (Barrow St.) | 212-367-7470 | www.centrovinoteca.com

It's "small-plate heaven" at this "hip", "good-for-groups" Village Italian furnishing "innovative", midpriced bites and "excellent" wines in a "buzzing", "crowded bar"–centered room (plus a "more sedate" one upstairs); chef Anne Burrell "is missed", but former *Top Chef* contender Leah Cohen "rocks on" in her stead.

Cercle Rouge ◑ *French*

19 | 18 | 17 | $45

TriBeCa | 241 W. Broadway (N. Moore St.) | 212-226-6252 | www.cerclerougeresto.com

"*Ordinaire*" or positively "Pastis-like" is the split verdict on this midpriced TriBeCa brasserie that, either way, is deemed a "keeper" thanks to "decent" food and comfortable quarters; for a "funky" twist, "they have a magic show" during weekend brunch, so bring the "baby buggies" by.

'Cesca *Italian*

23 | 22 | 22 | $61

W 70s | 164 W. 75th St. (Amsterdam Ave.) | 212-787-6300 | www.cescanyc.com

"Aging well", this "classy" UWS Southern Italian offers "rich", "expertly prepared" cuisine via a "friendly" staff; all told, the "crowded" bar, "open kitchen" and banquettes provide a "warm" ambiance attracting a "sophisticated", "lively" crowd, including neighbors like Katie Couric and Renée Fleming.

Chadwick's *American*

22 | 20 | 22 | $46

Bay Ridge | 8822 Third Ave. (89th St.) | Brooklyn | 718-833-9855 | www.chadwicksny.com

At this "long-standing" Bay Ridge "institution", dining is done the "old-school" way, with "fine" Traditional American food (including "terrific steaks") and "accommodating" service in a "clubby", "white-tablecloth" setting; regulars tout the lunch ($17) and early-bird ($23) prix fixe deals, not to mention the "valet parking."

Chance *Pan-Asian*

▽ 22 | 19 | 19 | $35

Boerum Hill | 223 Smith St. (Butler St.) | Brooklyn | 718-242-1515 | www.chancecuisine.com

"Thoughtfully done" Pan-Asian dishes meet "fun cocktails", "stylish" decor and "blaring music" at this Boerum Hill joint that's big with the "younger set"; "value" lunches and a dim sum scene that's "less chaotic than in Chinatown" are your safest chances here.

	FOOD	DECOR	SERVICE	COST

🄩 Chanterelle *French* — **28 | 27 | 28 | $106**

TriBeCa | 2 Harrison St. (Hudson St.) | 212-966-6960 |
www.chanterellenyc.com
Now in its 31st year, David and Karen Waltuck's TriBeCa French star
continues to provide just about "as fine a dining experience as you can
get in NY"; its "exceptional food", near-"unparalleled" service and "elegant", "understated" setting "define the difference between dining
and eating" and "attest to the fact that you get what you pay for" in
life; N.B. a revamp scheduled to be completed by winter 2009 will
usher in a new front bar/cafe and an expanded menu.

NEW Charles 🄩 *American/Mediterranean* — **∇ 18 | 23 | 17 | $63**

W Village | 234 W. Fourth St. (10th St.) | www.restaurantcharles.com
It shed a bit of its "mystique" when it removed the papers from its windows, but this Village "Waverly Inn" wannabe still woos "fashionable"
types with its "sexy", "speakeasy"-like setting and aloof rez policy (by
e-mail or in person only); oh, and there is Med-inflected New American
food, at prices sure to make the "plebes feel out of place."

NEW Char No. 4 ● *Southern* — **23 | 20 | 21 | $41**

Cobble Hill | 196 Smith St. (bet. Baltic & Warren Sts.) | Brooklyn |
718-643-2106 | www.charno4.com
"Pork and whiskey" reign at this Cobble Hill arrival, where a "breathtaking" array of bourbons shines at the front bar, while the dining area
serves "fantastic" "dressed-up" Southern food with a focus on the
"swine"; the decor is "minimalist", but, considering the "small portions", the prices ain't.

Chef Ho's Peking Duck Grill *Chinese* — **23 | 15 | 20 | $32**

E 80s | 1720 Second Ave. (bet. 89th & 90th Sts.) | 212-348-9444
Long a Yorkville "favorite", this "old-school" Chinese stands "a cut
above" the "ho-hum" area options with "tasty" cuisine (the namesake
dish especially) at "can't-be-beat" prices; "rapid" service leaves little
time to dwell on the "modest" digs.

Chennai Garden *Indian/Vegetarian* — **21 | 12 | 15 | $23**

Murray Hill | 129 E. 27th St. (Park Ave. S.) | 212-689-1999
Kosher vegetarian Indian food "may sound bland", but the "spicy",
"satisfying" dishes at this Curry Hiller are so "tasty", even carnivores say
they "could live happily without meat"; "stark" digs and variable service
put the focus on the flavors – particularly the "lavish" $7 lunch buffet.

Chestnut 🄜 *American* — **24 | 19 | 22 | $47**

Carroll Gardens | 271 Smith St. (bet. Degraw & Sackett Sts.) | Brooklyn |
718-243-0049 | www.chestnutonsmith.com
Something of an "unsung hero" on the "neverending" Smith Street strip,
this midpriced Carroll Gardens New American shines with "creative",
"seasonal" upscale fare and "lovely" service; a recent expansion added a
"cozy bar" area, which ups the "warmth" of its somewhat "plain" space.

Chez Jacqueline *French* — **21 | 19 | 20 | $51**

G Village | 72 MacDougal St. (bet. Bleecker & Houston Sts.) | 212-505-0727 |
www.chezjacquelinerestaurant.com
"Cozy" and "welcoming" as a "bistro in Provence", this Village "favorite" "still turns out French classics with flair" three decades on;

some claim it's getting "tired" and a bit *cher*, but most are "glad it's around", since sanctuaries for "real conversation" seem like an "endangered species."

Chez Josephine ●Ⓜ *French*

20 | 22 | 21 | $53

W 40s | 414 W. 42nd St. (bet. 9th & 10th Aves.) | 212-594-1925 |
www.chezjosephine.com

A "Theater District favorite" for "unique bistro decor, piano music and fine food", Jean-Claude Baker's tribute to his adoptive mother, the renowned Josephine Baker, is a "true NY experience" suffused with "French flavor"; from the moment you meet the "charming", "campy" host, you'll feel "transported" to another "cosmopolitan" "romantic" era.

Chez Napoléon Ⓩ *French*

20 | 15 | 21 | $46

W 50s | 365 W. 50th St. (bet. 8th & 9th Aves.) | 212-265-6980 |
www.cheznapoleon.com

If you "don't believe in time warps", stepping into this circa-1960 Theater District French bistro will change your mind with its "genuine-article" fare, "welcoming" staff and retro prices; yes, the decor is dated, but loyalists who "love that" "hope it stays unchanged forever."

Chez Oskar ● *French*

17 | 17 | 17 | $34

Fort Greene | 211 DeKalb Ave. (Adelphi St.) | Brooklyn | 718-852-6250 |
www.chezoskar.com

The "funky", "laid-back" vibe that's in tune with Fort Greene's "eclectic" character makes this "cozy" French bistro a "neighborhood fave" as well as a "pleasant" pick for "pre-BAM" dining; the "decent" fare can seem "uninspired", so some look to the "live music" to add spice.

Chiam Chinese Cuisine *Chinese*

21 | 19 | 21 | $47

E 40s | 160 E. 48th St. (bet. Lexington & 3rd Aves.) | 212-371-2323 |
www.chiamnyc.com

"It costs more than your average Chinese", but this "upscale" Midtowner is "worth it" given its "well-prepared" staples served by a "considerate" crew; it's especially "convenient for business-lunchers" and anyone else game for the $21 midday prix fixe.

Chianti Ⓩ *Italian*

22 | 18 | 21 | $40

Bay Ridge | 8530 Third Ave. (bet. 85th & 86th Sts.) | Brooklyn |
718-921-6300 | www.chianti86.com

At this "friendly" Bay Ridge "staple" catering to "groups", "plentiful" portions of "very good", "modestly priced" Italian eats (in either family-style or individual portions) mean you need only "come hungry", not loaded; just know that its "pleasant" atmosphere features "lots of noise and people."

Chickpea *Mideastern*

18 | 10 | 15 | $12

E Village | 210 E. 14th St. (bet. 2nd & 3rd Aves.) | 212-228-3445
NEW **Flatiron** | 688 Sixth Ave. (bet. 21st & 22nd Sts.) | 212-243-6275 ●
LES | 147 E. Houston St. (bet. Eldridge & Forsyth Sts.) |
212-260-8010
www.getchickpea.com

"Fresh, fast and cheap" says it all about these "no-frills" Mideasterners whose "baked-not-fried" falafel caters to "healthy" hummus fanciers; others favor the shawarma, but all acknowledge that the "delicious" goods come in "nothing-fancy" digs well suited for takeout.

	FOOD	DECOR	SERVICE	COST

ChikaLicious *Dessert*
25 | 17 | 21 | $24

E Village | 203 E. 10th St. (bet. 1st & 2nd Aves.) | 212-995-9511 | www.chikalicious.com
E Village | 204 E. 10th St. (bet. 1st & 2nd Aves.) | 212-475-0929 | www.dessertclubchikalicious.com ◖

Go way beyond "Betty Crocker" at this "teeny-tiny" dessert bar offering an "exquisite", "costly" three-course prix fixe "sugar rush" that's prepared "before your eyes" and offered with "wine pairings"; to avoid the "long wait", "go early" or hit the take-out satellite across the street.

Chimichurri Grill ◖ *Argentinean/Steak*
22 | 15 | 19 | $50

W 40s | 609 Ninth Ave. (bet. 43rd & 44th Sts.) | 212-586-8655 | www.chimichurrigrill.com

It's "beef galore" – but space, not so much – at this recently relocated, "affordable" Hell's Kitchen Argentine boasting "quality" steaks doused in that "wonderful" signature sauce; the "efficient" staff ensures theatergoers in a hurri get there in time.

NEW Chimney Barbecue *Eclectic*
- | - | - | M

E 100s | 2056 Second Ave. (bet. 105th & 106th Sts.) | 212-360-1988 | www.chimneybbq.com

Spanish Harlem is home to this Eclectic arrival whose all-over-the-place menu offers everything from sushi to entrees like strawberry barbecue–glazed hanger steak; its unassuming, brick-lined space includes a bar area as well as an upstairs lounge.

Chimu *Peruvian*
∇ 22 | 14 | 19 | $34

Williamsburg | 482 Union Ave. (bet. Meeker & Metropolitan Aves.) | Brooklyn | 718-349-1208

In an out-of-the-way corner of Williamsburg near the BQE, this Peruvian "rocks" with "sumptuous" ceviche and "meat feasts" at good rates; the setup is unremarkable apart from the "fountain"-enhanced patio, perhaps explaining why it's "not a total hipster hangout."

China Fun *Chinese*
15 | 10 | 13 | $25

E 60s | 1221 Second Ave. (64th St.) | 212-752-0810
W 70s | 246 Columbus Ave. (bet. 71st & 72nd Sts.) | 212-580-1516
www.chinafun-ny.com

At this "bustling" crosstown pair, "unusual dim sum" plus "predictable" "Chinese standards" and a sprinkling of sushi make up the "vast", crowd-pleasingly priced menu; those who find "gruff" service and "crazed" ambiance "not that much fun" tend to "take out."

China Grill *Asian*
22 | 21 | 19 | $58

W 50s | 60 W. 53rd St. (bet. 5th & 6th Aves.) | 212-333-7788 | www.chinagrillmgt.com

As "hectic as ever", this Midtown "pioneer" delivers "terrific", "high-fashion Asian fare" to "corporate" folk, "Gen-Xers", trendies and "tourists" happy to "pony up" for the experience; the "soaring", "sexy" space is reliably "lively", but the decibels can be "deafening."

China 1 Ⓜ *Chinese*
∇ 17 | 16 | 13 | $34

E Village | 50 Ave. B (bet. 3rd & 4th Sts.) | 212-375-0665 | www.china1nyc.com

Best known for the "late-night scene" in its underground lounge, this "trendy" East Villager does operate as a "real restaurant", plying "good" (if "not memorable") Chinese fare at affordable prices; servers who take their time "acknowledging" your presence are the number one drawback.

Chinatown Brasserie *Chinese*

| | 21 | 23 | 18 | $48 |

NoHo | 380 Lafayette St. (Great Jones St.) | 212-533-7000 | www.chinatownbrasserie.com

The "moody" vibe is "old Shanghai" at this NoHo Chinese, where the "fancified" fare from "designer dim sum" to "wonderful Peking duck" is presented with "pizzazz"; tabs are "astronomical compared to C-town", but the food "quality" and "snazzy" setting – including an "enjoyable" sidewalk section – add value.

Chin Chin ● *Chinese*

| | 23 | 18 | 22 | $51 |

E 40s | 216 E. 49th St. (bet. 2nd & 3rd Aves.) | 212-888-4555 | www.chinchinny.com

Favored by "corporate T&E" types, this "longtime" "upscale" Midtown Chinese standby still "hits the spot" with its "fine" cuisine (ask for the "outstanding Grand Marnier shrimp") via an "attentive" crew; in all, the package is win-win because "you get what you pay for."

Chinese Mirch *Asian Fusion*

| | 19 | 11 | 15 | $29 |

NEW E 90s | 1830 Second Ave. (bet. 94th & 95th Sts.) | 212-828-6400 Ⓜ
Murray Hill | 120 Lexington Ave. (28th St.) | 212-532-3663
www.chinesemirch.com

Seekers of novel "gastronomic experiences" hit this Murray Hill Asian fusion joint blending Chinese and Indian flavors into "bold", "fiery" fare; "cheap" prices have most overlooking "hit-or-miss" service and no-frills digs; N.B. the new UES branch is mostly takeout.

Chipotle *Mexican*

| | 18 | 10 | 13 | $13 |

E 40s | 150 E. 44th St. (bet. Lexington & 3rd Aves.) | 212-682-9860
E 50s | 150 E. 52nd St. (bet. Lexington & 3rd Aves.) | 212-755-9754
E Village | 19 St. Marks Pl. (bet. 2nd & 3rd Aves.) | 212-529-4502
Financial District | 2 Broadway (Stone St.) | 212-344-0941
Flatiron | 680 Sixth Ave. (bet. 21st & 22nd Sts.) | 212-206-3781
Garment District | 304 W. 34th St. (8th Ave.) | 212-268-4197
Garment District | Empire State Bldg. | 350 Fifth Ave. (34th St.) | 212-695-0412
SoHo | 200 Varick St. (bet. Houston & King Sts.) | 646-336-6264
W 40s | 9 W. 42nd St. (bet. 5th & 6th Aves.) | 212-354-6760
Brooklyn Heights | 185 Montague St. (Clinton St.) | Brooklyn | 718-243-9109
www.chipotle.com
Additional locations throughout the NY area

The "motherlode" of "healthy-ish", "football-size" burritos, this Mexican chain vends "mean roll-ups" that are "custom-made" with "wham-bam" "assembly-line precision" – and at "recession-buster" rates; naturally lunchtime's a "zoo", but an e-mailed order can "expedite" things.

ChipShop *British*

| | 19 | 15 | 18 | $22 |

Brooklyn Heights | 129 Atlantic Ave. (Henry St.) | Brooklyn | 718-855-7775
Park Slope | 383 Fifth Ave. (bet. 6th & 7th Sts.) | Brooklyn | 718-832-7701 ⊕
www.chipshopnyc.com

"Traditional" fish 'n' chips and other "loverly", "artery-clogging" Brit chow lures expats and Anglophiles to this "smashing" Park Slope-Brooklyn Heights duo; add "outrageous" "deep-fried candy bars", "kitschy" "pub" setups and easygoing tabs, and you've got yourself a "jolly ol' time."

Chiyono ●Ⓜ *Japanese*   ▽ 25 | 18 | 22 | $34

E Village | 328 E. Sixth St. (bet. 1st & 2nd Aves.) | 212-673-3984 | www.chiyono.com

At this minimalist East Village "gem", "simple, elegant" Japanese cooking comes at a "large communal table" via a "patient" staff; don't expect sushi, just the "subtle flavors" and "super-fresh ingredients" of fine "homestyle" dishes, all at "affordable", near-homestyle rates.

ⓩ Chocolate Room *Dessert*   25 | 19 | 20 | $18

Cobble Hill | 269 Court St. (bet. Butler & Douglass Sts.) | Brooklyn | 718-246-2600

Park Slope | 86 Fifth Ave. (bet. Prospect Pl. & St. Marks Ave.) | Brooklyn | 718-783-2900

www.thechocolateroombrooklyn.com

Suppliers of "sheer bliss", these Park Slope–Cobble Hill dessert destinations are a "chocolate-lover's paradise" "updated for grown-up tastes" and paired with "wonderful" dessert wines; with "classy" service and "candlelight", they're a perfect "place to end the evening."

Cho Dang Gol *Korean*   23 | 16 | 18 | $30

Garment District | 55 W. 35th St. (bet. 5th & 6th Aves.) | 212-695-8222 | www.chodanggolny.com

"Tofu never tasted so good" as at this "reliable", priced-right Garment District Korean where the "homemade" "silk for the mouth" stars in a wide variety of "healthy, hot, delicious" dishes; a "warm" vibe and "well-meaning" staff help make it "the real thing."

Chola *Indian*   23 | 16 | 19 | $39

E 50s | 232 E. 58th St. (bet. 2nd & 3rd Aves.) | 212-688-4619 | www.fineindiandining.com

"Imaginative" twists and "unusual spicing" elevate this "upscale" East Side Indian's output "worlds above the usual curry and samosa"; service is "solicitous", and if the decor is "undistinguished", the "copious" $14 lunch buffet is well "out of the ordinary."

Chow Bar *Asian Fusion*   20 | 17 | 18 | $42

W Village | 230 W. Fourth St. (W. 10th St.) | 212-633-2212

"Young" things wash down "trendy", "tasty" Asian fusion eats with "killer" cocktails at this "upbeat" West Village "mainstay"; the space may "need an update", but it's "comfy" and manned by a "solid" crew – and the bar scene keeps things "lively" (i.e. "loud").

Christos Steak House ● *Steak*   23 | 17 | 22 | $61

Astoria | 41-08 23rd Ave. (41st St.) | Queens | 718-777-8400 | www.christossteakhouse.com

"Mykonos meets Dallas" at this "memorable" Astoria steakhouse where "great Greek appetizers" pave the way for "juicy", Texas-size cuts of beef; a few bemoan "Manhattan prices", but "responsive" service, "outdoor seating in warm weather" and "valet parking" compensate.

Churrascaria Plataforma ● *Brazilian/Steak*   23 | 20 | 22 | $73

W 40s | 316 W. 49th St. (bet. 8th & 9th Aves.) | 212-245-0505 | www.churrascariaplataforma.com

(continued)

Churrascaria TriBeCa ● *Brazilian/Steak*

TriBeCa | 221 W. Broadway (bet. Franklin & White Sts.) | 212-925-6969 |
www.churrascariatribeca.com

"Swashbuckling" servers keep the "delectable" all-you-can-eat grilled
meats coming ("until your buttons pop") at these "expansive, expensive" Brazilian rodizios in Midtown and TriBeCa, where even the
"tempting" salad bar is "a meal in itself"; it's like a "party at every table",
so "go hungry and leave happy."

Ciaobella ● *Italian* | 21 | 16 | 17 | $37 |

E 80s | 1640 Second Ave. (85th St.) | 212-794-9494 | www.ciaobellanyc.com
Already "humming", this "trendy" UES yearling from the owners of
Baraonda and Per Lei is drawing "attractive" types for "well-prepared",
"reasonable" Italian fare in digs bedecked with chandeliers and mosa-
ics; despite some service glitches, it's deemed a "welcome addition."

Cibo *American/Italian* | 20 | 18 | 21 | $47 |

E 40s | 767 Second Ave. (41st St.) | 212-681-1616
A "good bet" for "grown-up dining", this "soothing" Tuscan–New
American "standby" near Grand Central delivers "tasty" food and
"plenty of it" via a "skillful" staff; it's "fairly priced" anyway, but the
prix fixe menus are a "steal."

Cilantro ● *Southwestern* | 17 | 15 | 18 | $31 |

E 70s | 1321 First Ave. (71st St.) | 212-537-4040
E 80s | 1712 Second Ave. (bet. 88th & 89th Sts.) | 212-722-4242
W 80s | 485 Columbus Ave. (bet. 83rd & 84th Sts.) | 212-712-9090
www.cilantronyc.com

"Cheap","cheerful" and "noisy" sums up this "casual" Southwestern
trio dispensing "dependable" dishes in "generous" servings; the
"friendly" staff is good with "little ones", while "jumbo margaritas"
keep big ones "boisterous", so nobody cares much about "cheesy",
"sombrero"-driven decor.

Cipriani Dolci ● *Italian* | 20 | 20 | 18 | $57 |

E 40s | Grand Central | West Balcony (42nd St. & Vanderbilt Ave.) |
212-973-0999 | www.cipriani.com

"Sure, it's touristy", but this "upbeat", upmarket mezzanine Italian
"under Grand Central's dome" offers "people-watching galore" along
with "tasty" eats; even with sometimes-"snooty" service, it's enjoy-
ably "energizing", especially for its signature Bellinis.

Cipriani Downtown ● *Italian* | 20 | 19 | 18 | $70 |

SoHo | 376 W. Broadway (bet. Broome & Spring Sts.) | 212-343-0999 |
www.cipriani.com

"Air kisses fly" at this "glam" SoHo Italian as "supermodels", "jet-
setters", "celeb wannabes" and other "beautiful" types "swarm" in;
it's "crazy-overpriced" and staffed by an "egoistic" crew, yet "the
kitchen knows what it's doing" and the Bellinis are "superb."

Circus *Brazilian/Steak* | 20 | 18 | 20 | $53 |

E 60s | 132 E. 61st St. (bet. Lexington & Park Aves.) | 212-223-2965 |
www.circusrestaurante.com

"Marvelous caipirinhas" boost the "lively" vibe at this "inviting" East
Side Brazilian, where the "delicious" food is more "serious" than the

"kitschy" "clown"-themed decor suggests; it's "expensive" for a "neighborhood place", but a "super-friendly" staff ensures it's "always fun."

Citrus Bar & Grill *Asian/Nuevo Latino*
20 | 18 | 18 | $40

W 70s | 320 Amsterdam Ave. (75th St.) | 212-595-0500 | www.citrusnyc.com
There's "something for everyone" at this "peppy" UWS Latin-Asian whose "novel" mix spans "chops to sushi", with "amazing drinks"; at prime times, the "sleek" setting is a bit of a squeeze with "young", "high-volume" habitués who tout the "value" as much as the "mingling."

City Bakery *Bakery*
22 | 12 | 14 | $20

Flatiron | 3 W. 18th St. (bet. 5th & 6th Aves.) | 212-366-1414 | www.thecitybakery.com
"Ambrosial" hot chocolate, "irresistible" baked goods and an "unparalleled" salad bar/buffet make this "cafeteria-style" Flatironer "perfect" for a "quick" nosh; devotees take in stride occasional "sticker shock", "grumpy" service and "madhouse" conditions – though "grab and go" is always an option.

City Crab & Seafood Co. *Seafood*
18 | 16 | 17 | $48

Flatiron | 235 Park Ave. S. (19th St.) | 212-529-3800 | www.citycrabnyc.com
An "easy fix for crustacean addicts" and fish "fanatics", this "solid" Flatiron seafooder also offers "fair prices" and "gigantic drinks" that keep the "wharflike" space "jumping" (and "noisy"); apart from "ditzy" service, there's really "nothing to crab about."

City Hall ⊠ *Seafood/Steak*
21 | 21 | 21 | $58

TriBeCa | 131 Duane St. (bet. Church St. & W. B'way) | 212-227-7777 | www.cityhallnyc.com
"Outstanding" "steakhouse victuals" served in a "clubby" setting suit "local politicos", financial wizards and other "power-lunchers" at Henry Meer's "handsome" TriBeCa surf 'n' turfer; a "courteous" crew works the "airy" room done up to "evoke old NY", while "high prices" further hint this is a "class act."

City Island Lobster House ● *Seafood*
19 | 16 | 17 | $46

Bronx | 691 Bridge St. (City Island Ave.) | 718-885-1459 | www.cilobsterhouse.com
If you squint, it's "Cape Cod in NY" at this City Island seafooder, where the fish is "really fresh" and portions ensure "you get your money's worth"; maybe the "gaudy" decor and service "could be better", but "terrific views" from the deck make it "worth the trip."

City Lobster & Steak *Seafood*
19 | 17 | 18 | $51

W 40s | 121 W. 49th St. (6th Ave.) | 212-354-1717
A "find" near Radio City, this "roomy" midpriced Midtowner delivers "reliably good" versions of what its name promises for an audience of "out-of-towners" and "business-lunchers"; although the service isn't quite "down pat" and the decor's "nothing much", it's really handy "if you're catching a show."

⦿ City Winery ● *Mediterranean*
18 | 22 | 16 | $37

SoHo | 155 Varick St. (Vandam St.) | 212-608-0555 | www.citywinery.com
Totally "unique" in New York City, this "cavernous" new West SoHo winery/eatery/performance space not only stocks a "huge" wine se-

lection, it also makes its own on-site; the 21,000-sq.-ft. "warehouse-chic" space includes multiple rooms, bars, a stage and a vast wine cellar – oh, and there are also Mediterranean eats and on Sundays a "great klezmer brunch."

NEW Civetta ● *Italian/Mediterranean* ▽ 19 | 22 | 18 | $57

NoLita | 98 Kenmare St. (bet. Lafayette & Mulberry Sts.) | 212-274-9898 | www.civettarestaurant.com

From the owners of Bottega del Vino and Via Quadronno, this pricey new NoLita Med-Italian offers copious antipasti plus some pastas and entrees; the bi-level space includes an "old-school" rustic Tuscan dining room and downstairs a cavernous, "Casanova"-worthy lounge.

NEW Clerkenwell ●Ⓜ *British* - | - | - | M

LES | 49 Clinton St. (bet. Rivington & Stanton Sts.) | 212-614-3234 | www.clerkenwellny.com

Economical English gastropub fare that suits comfort-seekers is the thing at this congenial LES newcomer plying dinner till midnight, small plates afterwards and brunch on weekends; window seats flanking the entrance are a boon left over from the space's past life as a shoe store – more recently it housed aKa Cafe and Summers Bar.

Ⓩ Clinton St. Baking Co. *American* 25 | 13 | 16 | $26

LES | 4 Clinton St. (bet. Houston & Stanton Sts.) | 646-602-6263 | www.greatbiscuits.com

Relied upon as a "brunch mecca", this "tiny" LES American bakery/cafe is "bursting at the seams" on weekends as "crowds" tuck into "sublime" pancakes and other "scrumptious" "reimagined favorites"; though waits can be "painful" at prime times, it's usually a "breeze" to get in on weekdays or at dinner.

Club A Steak House ●Ⓢ *Steak* ▽ 25 | 23 | 26 | $71

E 50s | 240 E. 58th St. (bet. 2nd & 3rd Aves.) | 212-688-4190 | www.clubasteak.com

The former Bruno Ristorante has morphed into this East Side steakhouse, drawing "devout carnivores" with chop-shop classics "cooked to perfection" and smoothly served in "beautiful red" environs enlivened by a piano player; no membership is required, but you may "need a corporate card" to get the full effect.

NEW Co. *Pizza* 22 | 16 | 18 | $32

Chelsea | 230 Ninth Ave. (24th St.) | 212-243-1105 | www.co-pane.com

A new "pizza temple" is born in this Chelsea arrival from Sullivan Street Bakery's Jim Lahey, whose "creative" pies have 'em lining up and "squeezing in"; look for a "simple" space, "sociable" communal tables, lots of "noise" and a few service "kinks" as the "aspiring actor" staff learns the part.

Coals ⓈⓂ *Pizza* ▽ 25 | 16 | 18 | $21

Bronx | 1888 Eastchester Rd. (Morris Park Ave.) | 718-823-7002 | www.coalspizza.com

What's "different" at this "cheery", "no-attitude" Bronx "hangout" is that the "terrific thin-crust" pizzas are "grilled"; add an "affordable" assortment of panini and salads, "unusual beers" on tap and occasional karaoke and you've got a "winning combination."

| | FOOD | DECOR | SERVICE | COST |

Coco Roco Peruvian
20 15 15 $28

Cobble Hill | 139 Smith St. (bet. Bergen & Dean Sts.) | Brooklyn | 718-254-9933
Park Slope | 392 Fifth Ave. (bet. 6th & 7th Sts.) | Brooklyn | 718-965-3376
"Fabulous, juicy" rotisserie chicken is the "main event" at these Cobble Hill–Park Slope "neighborhood faves" offering "tasty" "true Peruvian" eats for "cheap"; sure, the decor is "minimal" and service "glacial", but after one of the "super-strong" cocktails, you "won't care" a bit.

Coffee Shop ● American/Brazilian
15 13 12 $31

Union Sq | 29 Union Sq. W. (16th St.) | 212-243-7969
It's mostly about "visual entertainment" at this "laid-back" Union Square American-Brazilian, where "eye-candy" servers reluctantly ferry "basic", low-cost food in "dark", "deafening", dingy digs; the "gawker-to-supermodel ratio has skewed" of late, but "it's still a scene."

Cole's Dock Side Continental/Seafood
∇ 20 15 21 $39

Staten Island | 369 Cleveland Ave. (Hylan Blvd.) | 718-948-5588 | www.colesdockside.com
A "harborside" location, "excellent" "fresh" catch at "reasonable" prices and "helpful" service are the "formula for a good time" at this "quaint" Continental seafooder in Staten Island's Great Kills; the prospect of "a table on the porch" in warm weather also reels 'em in.

Commerce American
22 21 20 $58

W Village | 50 Commerce St. (Barrow St.) | 212-524-2301 | www.commercerestaurant.com
The "high-end" New American "comfort" fare at this West Village "hot spot" lures "savvy" sorts who don't mind sitting "cheek-to-jowl" to sample it; a "smart" crew works the "gorgeous", snug room, so the only problem is "nightclub"-level decibels; N.B. it no longer takes cash.

Community Food & Juice American
21 17 18 $33

W 100s | 2893 Broadway (bet. 112th & 113th Sts.) | 212-665-2800 | www.communityrestaurant.com
Newly reopened following a kitchen fire, this "godsend" to Morningside Heights presents its "locavore"-oriented, "reasonably priced" New American fare in "open", "airy" digs – now minus the juice bar; the "friendly" service can be "slow" and the acoustics "loud", but it's "always crowded" nonetheless (expect to "wait at peak times").

Compass American
22 23 22 $59

W 70s | 208 W. 70th St. (bet. Amsterdam & West End Aves.) | 212-875-8600 | www.compassrestaurant.com
Among "the best near Lincoln Center", this "comfortable"-yet-"sophisticated" New American offers "top-notch" cooking and "seamless service" in "peace and quiet"; its "excellent three-pound lobster" and "bargain" prix fixe menus are "worth every penny", ditto its wines.

☑ Convivio Italian
26 23 24 $73

E 40s | 45 Tudor City Pl. (42nd St., bet. 1st & 2nd Aves.) | 212-599-5045 | www.convivionyc.com
"Compliments to the chef" abound at this "extraordinary" Tudor City Southern Italian, where Michael White has created a "worthy successor to L'Impero" with "fabulous" fare you can explore in a "knockout"

four-course, $59 prix fixe menu; "attention to detail" is evident in the "superior" service and "bright", "welcoming" setting, meaning this "winner" is "aptly named."

Convivium Osteria *Mediterranean*   25 | 22 | 22 | $50

Park Slope | 68 Fifth Ave. (bet. Bergen St. & St. Marks Ave.) | Brooklyn | 718-857-1833 | www.convivium-osteria.com

"Delectable" Mediterranean "country fare" served in "quaint, rustic" environs gives this "under-the-radar" Park Sloper its "farmhouse-in-Sardinia" feel; the "lovely" garden, wine cellar "hideaway" and "warm", "well-trained" staff make this "labor of love" "one of the most romantic places" around.

Cookshop ● *American*   22 | 19 | 21 | $51

Chelsea | 156 10th Ave. (20th St.) | 212-924-4440 | www.cookshopny.com

Diners with a "passion" for "regional, farm-fresh" fare are "thrilled" with this "unpretentious" West Chelsea American providing "virtuous eating at its best"; there's "enthusiastic" service and "good energy" in the "airy" digs, but it gets "louder than a bomb" when "mobbed" at the "amazing brunch."

Coppola's *Italian*   20 | 15 | 19 | $38

Murray Hill | 378 Third Ave. (bet. 27th & 28th Sts.) | 212-679-0070 ●
W 70s | 206 W. 79th St. (bet. Amsterdam Ave. & B'way) | 212-877-3840
www.coppolas-nyc.com

"Stick to the basics", and you'll "feast" on "tasty" "red-sauce" Italian standards delivered by an "efficient" team at these "comfortable" UWS–Murray Hill eateries; maybe there are "no bells and whistles", but "what's not to like about reasonable and reliable?"

Cornelia Street Cafe ● *American/French*   19 | 16 | 18 | $37

G Village | 29 Cornelia St. (bet. Bleecker & W. 4th Sts.) | 212-989-9319 | www.corneliastreetcafe.com

Really the "quintessential Village bistro", this "quirky", "down-to-earth" French-American has "been there forever" (actually since 1977) dispensing "affordable", "homey" staples, especially at its "lovely brunch"; an "affable" staff and "nightly music or poetry" keep the "convivial" "regulars" coming.

NEW Cornelius ● *American*   ▽ 18 | 14 | 20 | $38

Prospect Heights | 565 Vanderbilt Ave. (Pacific St.) | Brooklyn | 718-398-6662 | www.corneliusbrooklyn.com

The folks behind Soda Bar and Le Gamin have collaborated on this polished new gastropub along Prospect Heights' Vanderbilt strip; early-goers call it a "wonderful addition" to the scene thanks to its "decent", reasonable American comfort fare, "whiskey-connoisseur's-heaven" cocktails and "hip" speakeasy vibe.

Corner Bistro ●⇗ *Burgers*   22 | 10 | 12 | $18

W Village | 331 W. Fourth St. (Jane St.) | 212-242-9502

"Legendary", "giant", multi-napkin burgers rated some of the "best in the city", plus "frosty mugs of beer" and "chili fries", are the highlights of this "old-time" West Village "institution"; "mind-boggling waits", "paper plates, plastic silverware", "dive" decor and "grumpy" service notwithstanding, it's a NYC "tradition."

	FOOD	DECOR	SERVICE	COST

Cortina *Italian*   ▽ 16 | 15 | 18 | $35

E 70s | 1448 Second Ave. (bet. 75th & 76th Sts.) | 212-517-2066 |
www.ristorantecortina.com

"Standard Northern Italian" dishes plus housemade desserts and ice
cream "keep folks returning" to this "quiet", "non-fancy" UES eatery;
it's a "pleasant neighborhood place", where the owner adds "a personal touch" and the "prices are right."

☑ Corton ⓩ *French*   27 | 25 | 26 | $114

TriBeCa | 239 W. Broadway (bet. Walker & White Sts.) | 212-219-2777 |
www.cortonnyc.com

"Everything about" Drew Nieporent's TriBeCa yearling "feels right", from
"mad genius" chef Paul Liebrandt's "exceptional", "new-generation"
French cuisine to David Rockwell's "understated" decor and the "flawless" pro staff; naturally it's "pricey" (prix fixe-only options start at
$79), but "wowed" surveyors say it's "worth every penny."

Cosette *French*   20 | 15 | 21 | $41

Murray Hill | 163 E. 33rd St. (bet. Lexington & 3rd Aves.) | 212-889-5489

"Eager-to-please" staffers "cosset" customers at this "petite" Murray
Hill French "charmer" offering such "authentic" bistro "basics" that you
may "imagine you're in Paris"; a "welcoming" vibe and "exceptional
value" have loyal locals declaring *mais oui* for this "favorite."

Così *Sandwiches*   16 | 10 | 12 | $15

E 40s | 38 E. 45th St. (bet. Madison & Vanderbilt Aves.) | 212-370-0705
E 50s | 60 E. 56th St. (bet. Madison & Park Aves.) | 212-588-1225
Financial District | World Financial Ctr. | 200 Vesey St. (West St.) |
212-571-2001
Flatiron | 700 Sixth Ave. (bet. 22nd & 23rd Sts.) | 212-645-0223
G Village | 53 E. Eighth St. (bet. B'way & Mercer St.) | 212-260-1507
G Village | 841 Broadway (13th St.) | 212-614-8544 ◑
Murray Hill | 461 Park Ave. S. (31st St.) | 212-634-3467
W 40s | 11 W. 42nd St. (bet. 5th & 6th Aves.) | 212-398-6662
W 50s | Paramount Plaza | 1633 Broadway (50th St.) | 212-397-9838
W 70s | 2186 Broadway (bet. 76th & 77th Sts.) | 212-595-5616
www.getcosi.com
Additional locations throughout the NY area

"Lunch on the run" comes with "free WiFi" at these "default" sandwich
shops known for "terrific" made-on-premises flatbread stuffed with
"unusual fillings"; "poor traffic flow", "undertrained" staffers and "generic", "Starbucks-like" decor are the downsides.

Counter ◑ *Vegan/Vegetarian*   20 | 17 | 20 | $39

E Village | 105 First Ave. (bet. 6th & 7th Sts.) | 212-982-5870 |
www.counternyc.com

"One of the fancier vegetarians" – and "less crunchy than your average" vegan joint – this "appealing" East Villager offers "delicious",
"satisfying" fare at a fair price; its "solicitous" staff and monthly organic wine dinners are other reasons that "even omnivores" tout it.

Country *American*   21 | 21 | 19 | $64

Murray Hill | Carlton Hotel | 90 Madison Ave. (29th St.) | 212-889-7100 |
www.countryinnewyork.com

"Well-executed" New American cooking makes this "posh" subterranean cafe in Murray Hill's Carlton Hotel a "business-lunch" staple;

"polite" but sometimes "lacking" service and "high prices" leave some "underwhelmed", but others claim it's the "perfect place" to unwind, especially given the "true artists" behind the bar.

Covo ● *Italian* ▽ 23 | 22 | 20 | $33

Harlem | 701 W. 135th St. (12th Ave.) | 212-234-9573 | www.covony.com

"Dreamy" wood-fired pizzas are the "hits" at this "worth-the-trek" West Harlem "hideaway", though the "rustic" Italian dishes are "good all around"; a "friendly" ambiance and "value" pricing keep the "super-cool" converted train station setup with its "clubby" upstairs lounge oh-so-"happening."

Cowgirl *Southwestern* 16 | 17 | 17 | $29

W Village | 519 Hudson St. (W. 10th St.) | 212-633-1133 | www.cowgirlnyc.com

Cowgirl Sea-Horse *Southwestern*

NEW Seaport | 259 Front St. (Dover St.) | 212-608-7873

"Sassy" sums up this "jumping", "affordable" West Villager dispensing "huge portions" of Southwestern "comfort food" in "faux"-Texan digs; early on, kids have "a roaring good time", then later it's "giddy-up" for the grown-ups when the "huge margaritas" start to flow; N.B. the seafood-oriented Seaport outpost opened post-Survey.

⚡ Craft *American* 25 | 24 | 24 | $80

Flatiron | 43 E. 19th St. (bet. B'way & Park Ave. S.) | 212-780-0880 | www.craftrestaurant.com

Tom (*Top Chef*) Colicchio's home base is this "cool" Flatiron New American "flagship", where you "mix and match" from a menu of "simple" but "divine dishes" whose "high-quality" ingredients "are allowed to shine" through; the "sleek, modern setting" and "perfectly paced" service contribute to the "magical" experience that our expert panel says justifies those "eye-popping prices."

Craftbar *American* 22 | 19 | 21 | $51

Flatiron | 900 Broadway (bet. 19th & 20th Sts.) | 212-461-4300 | www.craftrestaurant.com

A "lively" crowd gets its "*Top Chef*" fix at Tom Colicchio's "less-fussy" Flatiron New American, an around-the-corner "alternative" to Craft; the "barnlike space" is "noisy" and service "relaxed", yet the "gourmet-*sans*-frills" experience comes with a "nice buzz" and minimal "sticker shock."

Craftsteak *Steak* 24 | 24 | 23 | $82

Chelsea | 85 10th Ave. (bet. 15th & 16th Sts.) | 212-400-6699 | www.craftrestaurant.com

The "soaring space" divided by wine bottle–filled glass walls gives Tom Colicchio's "plush" West Chelsea steakhouse lots of "eye appeal", and its "overwhelming" selection of beef (made accessible by a "stellar" staff) gives it mouth appeal; yes, "prices are high", but "the new half-steak menu" in the bar suits "daintier" diners and the less deep of pocket.

Crema *Mexican* 21 | 18 | 19 | $47

Chelsea | 111 W. 17th St. (bet. 6th & 7th Aves.) | 212-691-4477 | www.cremarestaurante.com

"Haute" Nuevo Mexican cuisine reaches "new heights" at this "inviting" Chelsea eatery, where chef Julieta Ballesteros "aces the flavors" by adding French "spin" to dishes almost "too pretty to touch"; factor in "delightful" service and "delicious" drinks, and it's "worth the pesos."

Crispo ● *Italian*

W Village | 240 W. 14th St. (bet. 7th & 8th Aves.) | 212-229-1818 | www.crisporestaurant.com

They "never let you down" at this "thoroughly enjoyable" West Villager serving "hearty-yet-refined" Northern Italian fare in a "homey" setting; a "courteous staff" and good "value" incline partisans to overlook the "din", while the "adorable" garden room "is the icing on the cake."

☑ Cru 🅂🅼 *European*

G Village | 24 Fifth Ave. (bet. 9th & 10th Sts.) | 212-529-1700 | www.cru-nyc.com

"Superb" Modern European cuisine "pairs well" with an "amazing", "phone book–size" wine list at this Village "luxury experience"; patrons are "treated royally" in a "beautiful", "formal" room, so no surprise the prices are "way up there" – especially if you go for the tasting menu – but to most it's "worth the splurge"; N.B. a new chef arrived post-Survey, putting the above Food score in question.

NEW Crudo *Caribbean/European*

Garment District | Wingate Hotel | 235 W. 35th St. (bet. 7th & 8th Aves.) | 212-695-9001 | www.crudonyc.com

Colorful Euro-Caribbean cuisine is the thing at this arrival in the Garment District's Wingate Hotel, where somewhat high prices fetch huge portions; a small streetside patio precedes a narrow barroom, a formal dining room with a crudo-and-ceviche bar and a rear garden with live entertainment on some nights.

Cuba *Cuban*

G Village | 222 Thompson St. (bet. Bleecker & W. 3rd Sts.) | 212-420-7878 | www.cubanyc.com

"Rich" Cuban food, "addictive" mojitos and "live Latin music" add up to a "heady experience" at this "cute" Village "Little Havana"; it's "festive" (read: "noisy") with "affordable" prices, "warm" service and a free, "fresh-rolled cigar", so everyone "leaves happy."

Cuba Cafe *Cuban*

Chelsea | 200 Eighth Ave. (bet. 20th & 21st Sts.) | 212-633-1570 | www.chelseadining.com

Those fancying "flavorful Cuban" fare for "cheap" are enticed to this "energetic" Chelsea joint whose renditions are reminiscent of "mama's cooking"; a "down-to-earth" staff works the "funky" space, while "great mojitos" fuel the "spirited" vibe.

Cubana Café ⊅ *Cuban*

G Village | 110 Thompson St. (bet. Prince & Spring Sts.) | 212-966-5366
Carroll Gardens | 272 Smith St. (bet. Degraw & Sackett Sts.) | Brooklyn | 718-858-3980 ●

Evoking "1950s Havana", this "colorful" Village–Carroll Gardens duo dispenses "abundant, tasty" Cuban eats at "crazy-reasonable" (cash-only) rates; "crowds" ignore the "cramped" conditions and "lackadaisical" service as they sip "strong" "Caribbean cocktails" and practice "lip reading" when the mood gets "lively."

	FOOD	DECOR	SERVICE	COST

Cube 63 *Japanese*
▽ 22 | 14 | 15 | $36

LES | 63 Clinton St. (bet. Rivington & Stanton Sts.) | 212-228-6751 ◑🅷
Cobble Hill | 234 Court St. (bet. Baltic & Warren Sts.) | Brooklyn |
718-243-2208

Digs the "size of a cardboard box" don't deter fans of these "loud" LES-Cobble Hill Japanese joints offering "high-quality sushi served straight up"; there's beer, wine and sake at the Brooklyn branch, while BYO keeps the bill extra-"affordable" in Manhattan.

Curry Leaf *Indian*
20 | 11 | 16 | $28

Murray Hill | 99 Lexington Ave. (27th St.) | 212-725-5558 |
www.curryleafnyc.com

"Well-spiced", "fresh, varied" Indian eats "two cuts above" the norm make this "always-packed" Murray Hill standout from the Kalustyan's folks a "solid choice"; it's "short on charm" with service that says "don't linger", but "wow, what a bargain."

Da Andrea *Italian*
23 | 16 | 21 | $38

G Village | 35 W. 13th St. (bet. 5th & 6th Aves.) | 212-367-1979 |
www.biassanot.com

Now in "more commodious", "country-style" Village quarters, this "convivial" Italian provides the same "superior" "homestyle" Emilian fare for which it's long been "beloved"; the "animated" scene gets "loud" at times, but "welcoming" staffers and "unbelievably reasonable" checks compensate.

Da Ciro *Italian/Pizza*
21 | 14 | 20 | $45

Murray Hill | 229 Lexington Ave. (bet. 33rd & 34th Sts.) | 212-532-1636
A longtime Murray Hill Italian "favorite" in "old-world" duplex digs, this "reliable standby" presents a "balanced menu" ranging from "surefire-winner" pizzas and focaccia Robiola to "solid" classics; a "friendly" staff and "abundant servings" offset slightly "pricey" tabs.

Da Filippo *Italian*
21 | 18 | 22 | $54

E 60s | 1315 Second Ave. (bet. 69th & 70th Sts.) | 212-472-6688 |
www.dafilipporestaurant.com

"Even first-timers feel like regulars" at this "upscale" UES Northern Italian "stalwart", thanks to owner Carlo Meconi and his "amiable staff"; it's a "little expensive", but "terrific" cooking, "lots of specials" and a "cozy" setting secure its "local" "treasure" status.

Daisy May's BBQ USA *BBQ*
23 | 7 | 13 | $25

W 40s | 623 11th Ave. (46th St.) | 212-977-1500 | www.daisymaysbbq.com
"One of NYC's best BBQ" joints, this way West Hell's Kitchen "rib shack" has surveyors swooning over its "scrumptious" smoked meats and "terrific" sides; "cafeteria-style" service and almost "nonexistent decor" come with the "budget prices" and a "real Southern feel."

Dallas BBQ ◐ *BBQ*
15 | 9 | 14 | $23

Chelsea | 261 Eighth Ave. (23rd St.) | 212-462-0001
E 70s | 1265 Third Ave. (bet. 72nd & 73rd Sts.) | 212-772-9393
E Village | 132 Second Ave. (St. Marks Pl.) | 212-777-5574
Washington Heights | 3956 Broadway (bet. 165th & 166th Sts.) |
212-568-3700
W 40s | 241 W. 42nd St. (bet. 7th & 8th Aves.) | 212-221-9000
(continued)

(continued)

Dallas BBQ

W 70s | 27 W. 72nd St. (bet. Columbus Ave. & CPW) | 212-873-2004
NEW Bronx | 281 W. Fordham Rd. (Major Deegan Expwy.) | 718-220-2822
Downtown Bklyn | 180 Livingston St. (bet. Hoyt & Smith Sts.) | Brooklyn |
718-643-5700
www.dallasbbq.com

This "cheap and cheerful" BBQ chain churns out "sweet, mildly spiced"
'cue that "slides down easy" and "fishbowl"-size margaritas at
"practically-giving-it-away" prices; they're "noisy" and "no-frills", to put
it mildly, but they "hit the spot" when you want a "quick eat and run."

Danal *Mediterranean*

20 | 20 | 20 | $42

G Village | 59 Fifth Ave. (bet. 12th & 13th Sts.) | 212-982-6930 |
www.danalnyc.com

A "charming host" presides over this "shabby-chic" Village "standby",
whose "solid bourgeois" French-Med fare is served up in "ample" new-
ish digs that still feel "serene" and "homey"; no wonder "locals return
frequently", especially for the "delicious" daily brunch.

Da Nico *Italian*

21 | 18 | 20 | $40

Little Italy | 164 Mulberry St. (bet. Broome & Grand Sts.) | 212-343-1212 |
www.danicoristorante.com

You can "roll up your sleeves" and tuck into "classic" Italiano "like your
mama cooked" at this longtime "Little Italy go-to"; service is "accommodating" and the "comfortable" digs include a "lovely back garden"
that makes a fine "refuge" from the Mulberry Street "craziness."

ⓩ Daniel Ⓢ *French*

28 | 28 | 28 | $137

E 60s | 60 E. 65th St. (bet. Madison & Park Aves.) | 212-288-0033 |
www.danielnyc.com

"Well deserving of its top ratings year after year", Daniel Boulud's UES
New French "phenomenon" has many who consider it "the best in
NYC" for "elegant", "jackets-required" dining; everything here is
"memorable", from the "amazingly creative and varied" cuisine and
"extraordinary" wine list to the "polished, cordial" service and "new
and improved" "luxe" decor – and even the bill; N.B. it's prix fixe-only,
though you can order à la carte in the "less-formal" lounge.

ⓩ Danny Brown
Wine Bar & Kitchen Ⓜ *European*

26 | 21 | 24 | $47

Forest Hills | 104-02 Metropolitan Ave. (71st Dr.) | Queens | 718-261-2144 |
www.dannybrownwinekitchen.com

"Groundbreaking" for Forest Hills, this "upscale" "favorite" wins
hearts with the eponymous chef-owner's "exceptional" Modern
European cuisine, "superb" wines and service that's always "in the
groove"; a "soothing setting" completes the "sophisticated", "romantic" experience that requires no "schlep to Manhattan."

Da Noi *Italian*

23 | 19 | 22 | $46

Staten Island | 138 Fingerboard Rd. (Tompkins Ave.) | 718-720-1650
Staten Island | 4358 Victory Blvd. (Service Rd.) | 718-982-5040
www.danoirestaurant.com

Expect a "friendly welcome" at this "standout" Staten Island twosome
whose "wonderful", "flavorful" Northern Italian classics have won a

"large following" – i.e. prepare for "a wait" on weekends; "attentive" service and "comfortable" setups give it "pleasant" "family" appeal.

Darbar *Indian*　　　　　　　　21 | 16 | 19 | $32

E 40s | 152 E. 46th St. (bet. Lexington & 3rd Aves.) | 212-681-4500 | www.darbarny.com

Darbar Grill *Indian*

NEW E 50s | 157 E. 55th St. (bet. Lexington & 3rd Aves.) | 212-751-4600 | www.darbargrill.com

This Grand Central–area Indian and its new East 50s offshoot "distinguish themselves" with "well-balanced" cooking and "pleasant" service; the "outstanding" $12 lunch buffet is "one of the best deals" going.

NEW Dardanel *Mediterranean*　　　▽ 18 | 13 | 18 | $37

E 50s | 1071 First Ave. (bet. 58th & 59th Sts.) | 212-888-0809 | www.dardanelnyc.com

"Fresh", "innovative" seafood dishes top the menu of "unusual" Mediterranean offerings at this "quiet" newcomer in the shadow of the Queensboro Bridge; service is "sweet, if slow", and "takeout is an option" for style mavens who are iffy on the nautical decor.

Da Silvana Ⓜ *Italian*　　　　　▽ 20 | 16 | 21 | $42

Forest Hills | 71-51 Yellowstone Blvd. (bet. Clyde & Dartmouth Sts.) | Queens | 718-268-7871 | www.dasilvana.com

Forest Hills locals "nostalgic" for "classic, old-school red-sauce" Italian are "regulars" at this "small", "quiet" "neighborhood" joint offering "solid" eats in "generous" servings; a contingent claims it's "seen better days", but all agree the staff "can't be beat for friendliness."

Da Silvano ● *Italian*　　　　　　20 | 16 | 18 | $64

G Village | 260 Sixth Ave. (Bleecker St.) | 212-982-2343 | www.dasilvano.com

Yes, it offers "solid" Tuscan fare, but this Village "people-watching paradise" is "definitely about the scene" complete with "celebs" and "paparazzi lining the front sidewalk", best viewed from the outdoor seats; if you're not part of the shtick, you may be turned off by the "palpable snobbery" and prices as "fancy" as the clientele.

Da Tommaso ● *Italian*　　　　　20 | 14 | 20 | $47

W 50s | 903 Eighth Ave. (bet. 53rd & 54th Sts.) | 212-265-1890

"Delicious" Northern Italian "basics" meet "old-world charm" at this Theater District vet; maybe it looks "a little long in the tooth", but never mind – the "cordial" staff will have you "seated and served in plenty of time to make your show."

Da Umberto Ⓢ *Italian*　　　　　24 | 18 | 23 | $67

Chelsea | 107 W. 17th St. (bet. 6th & 7th Aves.) | 212-989-0303

This "old-style" Chelsea Northern Italian has been delivering "magnificent" classics via an "attentive" pro staff "for a very long time"; it's "expensive" and may "need a face-lift", but to most it remains "rock-solid" – "they don't make 'em like this anymore."

David Burke Townhouse *American*　　25 | 24 | 24 | $73

E 60s | 133 E. 61st St. (bet. Lexington & Park Aves.) | 212-813-2121 | www.davidburketownhouse.com

"Fashionable", "very UES" types gather at David Burke's New American eatery, which is "still fabulous, even sans partner Donatella", from the "remarkable" fare and "posh", recently revamped (post-Survey) townhouse setting to the "polished" service; it's "expensive", but the "incredible" "$24 prix fixe lunch" will leave you "smiling from ear to ear."

Dawat Indian

	FOOD	DECOR	SERVICE	COST
	23	19	21	$48

E 50s | 210 E. 58th St. (bet. 2nd & 3rd Aves.) | 212-355-7555 | www.dawatrestaurant.com

"Sophisticated" Indian cuisine full of "mouthwatering" "subtle touches" is on offer at cookbook author Madhur Jaffrey's "venerable" East Midtowner; a "gracious" staff gives guidance to novices, while "crisp linens" in the "pretty", "minimalist" space confirm it's a "class" act.

☑ db Bistro Moderne French

	FOOD	DECOR	SERVICE	COST
	24	21	22	$65

W 40s | City Club Hotel | 55 W. 44th St. (bet. 5th & 6th Aves.) | 212-391-2400 | www.danielnyc.com

"Foodies", "fashionistas and publishing types" create a "fizzy" vibe at Daniel Boulud's Theater District French "superbistro", where the "outstanding" fare comes via a "caring" staff; prices can "stun" (e.g. that "famous" $32 "enhanced burger"), but the $45 pre-theater prix fixe is a "deal" – either way, "treat yourself" because this is "one of d-best."

☑ NEW DBGB ◐ French

	FOOD	DECOR	SERVICE	COST
	23	22	22	$46

E Village | 299 Bowery (bet. 1st & Houston Sts.) | 212-933-5300 | www.danielnyc.com

Daniel Boulud hits the Bowery with his most "casual" venture yet, bearing a moniker that references the street's legendary punk music hall and dishing up "fantastic" rustic French fare that's a mix of housemade charcuterie, craft beers and "comfort" items like burgers; centered around a huge "open kitchen", its "loud, bustling", "industrial" space features kitchenware for decor, another nod to the neighborhood.

Dean's Pizza

	FOOD	DECOR	SERVICE	COST
	17	15	15	$27

E 40s | 801 Second Ave. (bet. 42nd & 43rd Sts.) | 212-878-9600
TriBeCa | 349 Greenwich St. (bet. Harrison & Jay Sts.) | 212-966-3200
W 80s | 215 W. 85th St. (bet. Amsterdam Ave. & B'way) | 212-875-1100
www.deansnyc.com

"It's all about the pizza" at this trio of "reasonable" joints, which are large enough "for a crowd" and "havens" for those with kids; regulars advise "try the square pie", come "after 7 PM" when "it quiets down" and be patient with the "overworked staff."

Dee's Brick Oven Pizza Ⓜ Mediterranean/Pizza

	FOOD	DECOR	SERVICE	COST
	21	17	18	$28

Forest Hills | 107-23 Metropolitan Ave. (74th Ave.) | Queens | 718-793-7553 | www.deesnyc.com

"Incredible salads" and "wonderful appetizers" are on the menu at this "laid-back", "family-friendly" Forest Hills Mediterranean, but "topnotch brick-oven pizzas" are the main draw; "aim-to-please" service and "affordable" prices are other reasons it's "always crowded."

Defonte's Sandwich Shop Ⓢ Italian

	FOOD	DECOR	SERVICE	COST
	24	9	19	$13

NEW Gramercy | 261 Third Ave. (21st St.) | 212-614-1500
Red Hook | 379 Columbia St. (Luquer St.) | Brooklyn | 718-625-8052 ⊄
www.defontesofbrooklyn.com

There's "no skimping" on the "ultrafresh ingredients" in the "crazygood" "mega"-heros dispensed at these "old-fashioned" Italian sandwich emporiums, one a Red Hook "oasis" since 1922, the other a "new Gramercy outpost that's just as good"; scant seating suggests "take-out", while service amounts to "organized chaos with a smile."

DeGrezia ⊠ Italian
23 | 21 | 24 | $63

E 50s | 231 E. 50th St. (bet. 2nd & 3rd Aves.) | 212-750-5353 | www.degreziaristorante.com

An "elegant" "stalwart", this "small" East Midtown downstairs "hide-away" offers "outstanding" Italian "classics" that have "not been Americanized", delivered by a "white-glove" staff; though it's "pricey", a "relaxing" atmosphere that "permits intimate conversation" makes it a "romantic" "treasure" for many.

☒ Degustation ⊠ French/Spanish
26 | 22 | 25 | $71

E Village | 239 E. Fifth St. (bet. 2nd & 3rd Aves.) | 212-979-1012

"It's like dinner theater" for gourmands at Grace and Jack Lamb's "teeny" East Village tapas "gem", where "brilliant bites" of "adven-turous" Franco-Spanish fare are prepared in front of the 16 diners seated at the "tasting bar around the open kitchen"; though the cost of these "small masterpieces" quickly adds up, "this is what being a foodie is all about."

☒ Del Frisco's ● Steak
25 | 23 | 23 | $75

W 40s | 1221 Sixth Ave. (bet. 48th & 49th Sts.) | 212-575-5129 | www.delfriscos.com

An "electric" Midtown "power scene", this "steakhouse on steroids" serves "he-man portions" of "A+", "succulent" beef in a "mammoth" multilevel mahogany setting with a "stellar" staff; "everything's big" – from the "roar" in the room to "the bucks" you'll spend – although the $50 "pre-theater package" is a "real money-saver."

Delhi Palace Indian
▽ 22 | 12 | 16 | $24

Jackson Heights | 37-33 74th St. (bet. 37th Ave. & 37th Rd.) | Queens | 718-507-0666

"Those in-the-know" in Jackson Heights swear by this "old standby" dispensing "excellent", "well-prepared" Indian classics; maybe the de-cor "needs a rehab", but the "welcome" is "warm" and the rates "dirt-cheap", especially for grazers at the "don't-miss" $10 lunch buffet.

Delicatessen ● American
18 | 20 | 17 | $38

NoLita | 54 Prince St. (Lafayette St.) | 212-226-0211 | www.delicatessennyc.com

"Stylish" "younger" types convene at Cafeteria's "trendy" NoLita off-shoot to nosh on New American "comfort food with character" in a "cool" setting that has a "surprise" "cocktail lounge downstairs" and walls that open in summer; it's a "total scene", especially late, when the service gets a little "pokey."

dell'anima ● Italian
25 | 19 | 21 | $53

W Village | 38 Eighth Ave. (Jane St.) | 212-366-6633 | www.dellanima.com

"Phenomenal" Italian fare, "dynamite wines" and a "good-time" vibe keep this "teeny", "energetic" West Villager "packed to the gills with twentysomethings" most nights; "elbow-bumping" and "noise" are givens, but service is "sharp", and a seat at the "chef's counter" is "a must" to see how it's done.

	FOOD	DECOR	SERVICE	COST

Delmonico's ☒ *Steak*
`23` `22` `23` `$64`

Financial District | 56 Beaver St. (S. William St.) | 212-509-1144 | www.delmonicosny.com

"Old NY lives" on at this "landmark" Financial District steakhouse that's been "feeding business folk for generations"; "supreme" beef, "decadent sides", "accommodating" service and all the "history" in the "well-appointed" "gentleman's club" setting make it "one of the city's greats" – "Diamond Jim would be proud."

☑ Del Posto *Italian*
`26` `26` `25` `$93`

Chelsea | 85 10th Ave. (16th St.) | 212-497-8090 | www.delposto.com

You "walk in and immediately feel like you're in Roma" at this way West Chelsea "Batali-Bastianich masterpiece" that's an "experience not to be missed"; its marble-and-mahogany "transplanted palazzo" decor, "heavenly" food and wines and "top-notch" service supply "the OMG factor" big time – and though tabs are "stiff", the enoteca section is a "relative bargain."

Delta Grill ❶ *Cajun/Creole*
`20` `14` `18` `$33`

W 40s | 700 Ninth Ave. (48th St.) | 212-956-0934 | www.thedeltagrill.com

The "good times roll" at this "noisy" Hell's Kitchen "hangout", where "hearty", "spicy-hot" Cajun-Creole "comfort food" is washed down with cold "Abita on tap"; it's easy to forget the "dumpy" digs and "so-so" service when the "hard-stomping" bands start up on weekends.

Demarchelier *French*
`16` `15` `16` `$48`

E 80s | 50 E. 86th St. (bet. Madison & Park Aves.) | 212-249-6300 | www.demarchelierrestaurant.com

"Steak frites cravings" are "reliably" sated at this "lively" UES French bistro where the "simple" meals come with a side of "people-watching"; "tired" digs and a "snarly" staff don't deter "loyal" regulars, who cite the "civilized" $26 prix fixe "deal" and "Paris feel" as reasons to go.

Denino's Pizzeria ⊘ *Pizza*
`25` `10` `18` `$20`

Staten Island | 524 Port Richmond Ave. (bet. Hooker Pl. & Walker St.) | 718-442-9401

"Top-notch" thin-crust pies with "honest toppings" have made this "family-run" "pizza joint" in Port Richmond a "tradition" for Staten Islanders; "no-nonsense" service and a "no-frills" setup do nothing to thin the pie-eyed "crowds", so be prepared to "wait at the door."

Dervish ❶ *Mediterranean*
`18` `15` `19` `$37`

W 40s | 146 W. 47th St. (bet. 6th & 7th Aves.) | 212-997-0070 | www.dervishrestaurant.com

It introduced a new Mediterranean menu recently, but you'll still find some "Turkish delights" at this "pleasant" Theater District standby; "pretty it's not", but "fast", "friendly" service and a $28 pre-theater prix fixe make it worth your giving it a whirl.

NEW de Santos ☒ *Italian*
`▽` `21` `17` `18` `$54`

G Village | 139 W. 10th St. (bet. Greenwich Ave. & Waverly Pl.) | 212-206-9229 | www.desantosnyc.com

With successful restaurants in Mexico under his belt, rock star Alex González (of Maná fame) brings this "delicious" new midpriced modern Italian to the Village; a "young" clientele and "loud", "sexy" soundtrack lend a "clubby" vibe to its brownstone space complete with "garden seating."

DeStefano's Steakhouse Ⓜ Steak
▽ 23 | 19 | 22 | $57

Williamsburg | 89 Conselyea St. (Leonard St.) | Brooklyn | 718-384-2836 | www.deesteakhouse.com

"Nothing too fancy", just "excellent beef" and "generous" chops "done well" are on offer at this "old-fashioned" Williamsburg steakhouse; the "warm", "no-attitude" staff "makes you feel like you belong" while its prix fixe deals are downright "neighborly."

Destino Ⓢ Italian
19 | 19 | 18 | $58

E 50s | 891 First Ave. (50th St.) | 212-751-0700 | www.destinony.com

A "neighborhood" go-to for Sutton Place "swells", this "upscale", "home style" Italian is a "must for the meatballs" made by a Rao's alum; the bar's "inviting", the live music's "jazzy" and Justin Timberlake is an owner, yet somehow it "misses the cool factor."

Deux Amis French
20 | 17 | 21 | $48

E 50s | 356 E. 51st St. (bet. 1st & 2nd Aves.) | 212-230-1117

This "cozy" East Midtown "clone of a Parisian bistro", delivers "tasty" "country French" fare with "delicious" "couscous dishes as an extra treat"; a "charming owner" boosts the "lovely atmosphere", while outdoor seating in summer is even more "pleasant."

dévi Indian
23 | 20 | 21 | $59

Flatiron | 8 E. 18th St. (bet. B'way & 5th Ave.) | 212-691-1300 | www.devinyc.com

"Culinary wizards" Suvir Saran and Hemant Mathur cook up "seriously haute", "innovative takes" on the "tastes of India" at their Flatiron "mecca" overseen by a "delightful" crew; it's not "cheap", but an "elegant" setting and a $35 prix fixe dinner make for serious "value."

NEW Dhaba Indian
▽ 22 | 16 | 16 | $29

Murray Hill | 108 Lexington Ave. (bet. 27th & 28th Sts.) | 212-679-1284 | www.highwaydhaba.com

A "lively", "lower-cost" sibling to Chola, this "standout" Murray Hill newcomer is "quickly building a name for itself" with "unusual", "wonderfully spiced" Indian fare; service can be "slow" in the "Bollywood-bright" space, although "excellent value" overall and an "amazing" $10 lunch buffet compensate.

Dieci Italian
▽ 22 | 16 | 20 | $42

E Village | 228 E. 10th St. (bet. 1st & 2nd Aves.) | 212-387-9545 | www.dieciny.com

Scoring "points for creativity", this "tiny" East Village Italian turns out a "limited menu" of small plates with "large tastes", including a few twists that reflect the Japanese owners' heritage; go early and "snag a table" or join the young crowd at the counter.

Ⓩ Di Fara Ⓜ🍴 Pizza
27 | 4 | 8 | $16

Midwood | 1424 Ave. J (15th St.) | Brooklyn | 718-258-1367 | www.difara.com

Word is that "even God waits for service" at this circa-1964 Midwood "institution" whose "heavenly" pizzas are voted NYC's No. 1;

the "hole-in-the-wall" setup is beyond "dingy", and "it seems like for-ever before your pie is ready", but watching Dom DeMarco "work his magic" before "crowds of waiting admirers" is an "experience" in itself.

Dim Sum Go Go *Chinese*
21 | 11 | 14 | $24

Chinatown | 5 E. Broadway (Chatham Sq.) | 212-732-0797
"Marvelous" dim sum "cooked to order" comes à la carte "instead of off a cart" at this "change-of-pace" C-towner; true, the decor needs "sprucing up" and service can be "gruff", but even those who "miss the trolleys" suggest "go go" anyway.

Diner ● *American*
24 | 18 | 19 | $37

Williamsburg | 85 Broadway (Berry St.) | Brooklyn | 718-486-3077 | www.dinernyc.com
"People flock from all over" for the "adventurous", "delicious" sea-sonal New American eats at this "classic", circa-1927 "boxcar diner" under the Williamsburg bridge; expect a "low-key" vibe, "fair" prices, "ginormous Bloody Marys" at its "perfect brunch" and servers who match the "gorgeous hipster clientele."

Dinosaur Bar-B-Que *BBQ*
22 | 15 | 17 | $31

Harlem | 646 W. 131st St. (12th Ave.) | 212-694-1777 | www.dinosaurbarbque.com
"Yeehaw!" – be ready to "abandon decorum" at this "hopping", "Texas roadhouse"–like West Harlem import from Upstate dispensing "T. rex-size", "bone-shaking BBQ", "soulful sides" and "terrific draft beers" at "dyno-mite" prices; expect "looong waits" and prepare to get "down and dirty", and as for service, sometimes it's "not so great."

NEW Dirt Candy 🅂Ⓜ *Vegetarian*
▽ 23 | 17 | 23 | $45

E Village | 430 E. Ninth St. (bet. Ave. A & 1st Ave.) | 212-228-7732 | www.dirtcandynyc.com
"Exceptionally good" victuals "that happen to be vegetarian" are the deal at this "clever" new East Villager turning out "whimsical, original" vegetable dishes – "as opposed to mock meats" and such; draw-backs are slightly "pricey" tabs and "beyond-small" digs that are often "hard to get into."

Dirty Bird to-go *Chicken*
18 | 5 | 13 | $18

W Village | 204 W. 14th St. (7th Ave. S.) | 212-620-4836 | www.dirtybirdtogo.com
The "savory" fried or rotisserie organic chicken and seductive sides at this West Village "hole-in-the-wall" give take-out "fast food a good rap"; some complain it takes "too much scratch" given the "small por-tions", but most surveyors couldn't give a flap about that.

Dishes *Sandwiches*
22 | 14 | 13 | $17

E 40s | 6 E. 45th St. (bet. 5th & Madison Aves.) | 212-687-5511 🅂
E 40s | Grand Central | lower level (42nd St. & Vanderbilt Ave.) | 212-808-5511
E 50s | Citigroup Ctr. | 399 Park Ave. (53rd St.) | 212-421-5511 🅂
www.dishestogo.com
"Creative soups, fresh salads and sublime sandwiches" draw the "still-employed" to this "upscale" Midtown trio, where "brusque" service doesn't deter the "maddening" lunchtime crowds; it's "expensive for what it is" too, though regulars say you "get what you pay for."

	FOOD	DECOR	SERVICE	COST

Ditch Plains ● *Seafood*
| | 18 | 16 | 16 | $36 |

G Village | 29 Bedford St. (Downing St.) | 212-633-0202 |
www.ditch-plains.com

Marc Murphy's Village seafooder "named after a Montauk surf spot"
serves up "shore and landlocked" "comfort" American in "dark", "minimalist" digs; a "busy bar scene" makes it a "wave to catch" for "twentysomethings" who don't sweat the "indifferent" service.

Docks Oyster Bar *Seafood*
| | 19 | 18 | 18 | $51 |

E 40s | 633 Third Ave. (40th St.) | 212-986-8080 |
www.docksoysterbar.com

Raw or cooked, "wonderfully fresh" seafood "any way you enjoy it" can
be found at this "cavernous" Midtown "mainstay" (fans "still mourn the
loss of the UWS location"); the "jumping" "bar scene" gets "noisy",
but "affable" service and "decent" prices make it "easy to take."

Do Hwa *Korean*
| | 22 | 19 | 20 | $42 |

G Village | 55 Carmine St. (Bedford St.) | 212-414-1224 |
www.dohwanyc.com

"Scrumptious bibimbop", Korean BBQ and "traditional" dishes, plus
the chance to "grill on your own table", are the lure at this "upscale"
Villager; yes, such fare comes "cheaper in Koreatown", but here you
get "hipster servers", "comfortable" digs and "inventive cocktails."

Dok Suni's ●⊘ *Korean*
| ∇ 22 | 17 | 18 | $32 |

E Village | 119 First Ave. (bet. St. Marks Pl. & 7th St.) | 212-477-9506
The mood's "mellow" at this "funky" "little" East Village Korean, but
some of the "fantastic", "flavorful", "homestyle" dishes on offer will
"light your mouth on fire"; "good drinks" and "cheap-ish" checks ensure it's "still a go-to place."

Dominick's ⊘ *Italian*
| | 23 | 11 | 17 | $37 |

Bronx | 2335 Arthur Ave. (bet. Crescent Ave. & E. 187th St.) | 718-733-2807
"Don't expect fancy" at this "over-the-top" Italian example of Bronx
"brashness" – just "bountiful", "deeply comforting" eats; "the waiters
are a scream", and since the "shtick" is "no menus, no prices", you
"eat what they tell you to", "squeezed in" at a communal table, then
pay up in "cash."

Donguri Ⓜ *Japanese*
| ∇ 26 | 15 | 25 | $66 |

E 80s | 309 E. 83rd St. (bet. 1st & 2nd Aves.) | 212-737-5656 |
www.dongurinyc.com

"Divine" dishes of "delicious simplicity" – but no sushi – are the thing
at this Upper East Side "little slice of Japan" specializing in "wonderful, high-priced" Kansai fare (including "soba and udon done to perfection"); its "super-tiny" room's "cozy" feel is made even more so by
the "gracious" staff.

Don Pedro's *Caribbean/European*
| | 21 | 16 | 20 | $41 |

E 90s | 1865 Second Ave. (96th St.) | 212-996-3274 |
www.donpedros.net

"Inventive", "reliably delectable" Euro-Caribbean fare in "enormous
portions" makes this "cute" Upper Eastsider a "real treat"; factor in
"terrific sangria", "generous cocktails" and "hospitable service", and
the "super-satisfied" call it an "out-of-the-way" "oasis."

	FOOD	DECOR	SERVICE	COST

Don Peppe ⓂⒹ Italian
24 | 11 | 18 | $45

Ozone Park | 135-58 Lefferts Blvd. (bet. 135th & 149th Aves.) |
Queens | 718-845-7587

It's a "family-style garlic fest" at Ozone Park's Italian "favorite", famed
for its "gargantuan" platters of "outrageous" "red-sauce" fare; it
"doesn't look like much", but "amiable" waiters keep the "rowdy"
"cast of characters" plied with "very drinkable" housemade wine,
ensuring its "popularity."

Dos Caminos Mexican
20 | 19 | 18 | $44

E 50s | 825 Third Ave. (bet. 50th & 51st Sts.) | 212-336-5400
Murray Hill | 373 Park Ave. S. (bet. 26th & 27th Sts.) | 212-294-1000
SoHo | 475 W. Broadway (bet. Houston & Prince Sts.) | 212-277-4300
www.brguestrestaurants.com

"Hot and spicy" describes both "scene" and eats at Steve Hanson's
"appealing" trio of "party-style" Mexicanos, where "made-at-your-
table" guacamole is "the star"; the "slick setting" gets its "buzz" from
a "young", "good-looking" crowd downing "potent potables" but overlooking sometimes "so-so" service.

NEW Double Crown Eclectic
20 | 23 | 19 | $52

NoHo | 316 Bowery (Bleecker St.) | 212-254-0350 |
www.doublecrown-nyc.com

Bangers and mash meet tandoori foie gras at NoHo's "hot" new sibling
of Public, where an "exciting" Eclectic Indo-Asian menu reflects
British "colonial imperialism" on the plate; "fabulous" types quaffing
"delicious cocktails" in the "breathtaking" industrial-vintage space
add to the "exotic" experience.

Ⓩ Dovetail American
26 | 21 | 24 | $72

W 70s | 103 W. 77th St. (Columbus Ave.) | 212-362-3800 |
www.dovetailnyc.com

Proving that a dining "destination on the UWS" is not an oxymoron,
this New American yearling offers "a perfect purée of informality, sophistication and deliciousness" compliments of "innovative" chef John
Fraser; it's "pricey", but finding "playful, thoroughly enjoyable meals"
this near the Museum of Natural History has most "amazed"; P.S. the
Sunday 'suppa' may be "the best value ever."

Dressler American
25 | 23 | 23 | $55

Williamsburg | 149 Broadway (bet. Bedford & Driggs Aves.) | Brooklyn |
718-384-6343 | www.dresslernyc.com

"Smart, hip and very Williamsburg", this "upscale" New American
blends "deftly" prepared, "delicious" cuisine, "delightful" service and a
"gorgeous" setting dressed up with "artistic ironwork"; "it would be a hit
anywhere", but being in Brooklyn means the prices pack "extra" "value."

Duane Park American
23 | 21 | 22 | $58

TriBeCa | 157 Duane St. (bet. Hudson St. & W. B'way) | 212-732-5555 |
www.duaneparknyc.com

Too "often overlooked", this "pleasant" TriBeCan offers "extraordinary" "Southern-accented" New American cuisine in a "pretty" room
done up in "neo-classical" style; prices are "reasonable", and "cheerful" servers "aim to please", while "cool jazz" and "fun burlesque
nights" supply a little "thrill."

	FOOD	DECOR	SERVICE	COST

NEW Ducale *Italian* ▽ 16 | 18 | 17 | $50

W 70s | 392 Columbus Ave. (79th St.) | 212-787-7150
Off to a "shaky start but showing potential", this "quiet", midpriced
UWS Italian turns out "good, simple" fare in "tasteful", bi-level digs
adorned with "beautiful" photos of Venice; "slow" but "well-meaning"
service makes it a good bet "for an unrushed meal."

Due ● *Italian* 21 | 17 | 21 | $47

E 70s | 1396 Third Ave. (bet. 79th & 80th Sts.) | 212-772-3331
Getting "more comfortable with each passing year", this "laid-back"
UES Northern Italian offers "tasty" cuisine at a "fair price", served by
"congenial" staffers in "quiet", "pleasant" environs; no wonder locals
consider it a "neighborhood" "treasure."

DuMont *American* 22 | 16 | 18 | $29

Williamsburg | 432 Union Ave. (bet. Devoe St. & Metropolitan Ave.) |
Brooklyn | 718-486-7717

DuMont Burger ● *American*

Williamsburg | 314 Bedford Ave. (bet. S. 1st & 2nd Sts.) | Brooklyn |
718-384-6127
www.dumontnyc.com
Despite "off-the-meter hipness", there's "no dreaded attitude" at this
"adorable" Williamsburg "hangout" dispensing "flavorful, filling",
"low-cost" New American "comfort" eats; aficionados "elbow" in,
spread out in the garden or hit the Bedford Avenue spin-off for one of
its "trademark" burgers or sandwiches.

Dumpling House *Chinese* 22 | 6 | 11 | $11

LES | 118A Eldridge St. (bet. Broome & Grand Sts.) | 212-625-8008
"Order fast" to keep the "big line" moving at this "chaotic" LES Chinese
purveyor known for its "hot-from-the-wok" dumplings; the dumpy decor
is almost "laughable", but then so are the "next-to-nothing" prices.

Dumpling Man ● *Chinese* 19 | 7 | 13 | $12

E Village | 100 St. Marks Pl. (bet. Ave. A & 1st Ave.) | 212-505-2121 |
www.dumplingman.com
"Yummy things come in small packages" at this East Village Chinese
"dive" where you can "watch the dumplings being made" in all their
"mouthwatering" "variety"; rather than "fight for space", most craving
a "cheap bite" get it "to go."

Dylan Prime *Steak* 24 | 23 | 22 | $70

TriBeCa | 62 Laight St. (Greenwich St.) | 212-334-4783 |
www.dylanprime.com
Despite "top-notch" "prime cuts" and "inspired cocktails" ferried by a
"charismatic" crew, a "touch of cool" at this "sexy", "modern" TriBeCan
signals that it's "not your father's steakhouse"; its "young" patrons report that it costs a "pretty penny", but say "it's worth it."

Earthen Oven *Indian* 21 | 13 | 18 | $35

W 70s | 53 W. 72nd St. (bet. Columbus Ave. & CPW) | 212-579-8888
"Distinctive", "high-quality" Indian fare and an array of "unusual" regional dishes keep this "low-key" UWS spot "busy"; "courteous" service warms up the "coffee-shop ambiance", while the "bargain" lunch
buffet and "prix fixe deals" are extra draws.

	FOOD	DECOR	SERVICE	COST

East Manor *Chinese*
19 | 13 | 13 | $26

Flushing | 46-45 Kissena Blvd. (bet. Kalmia & Laburnum Aves.) | Queens | 718-888-8998

Carts bearing "traditional" dim sum "speed by your table" at this "cavernous" Flushing Chinese, however, there's also a "dazzling variety" of choices at the buffet; despite "dingy" digs and service that's "lacking", the place is "packed to the brim" on weekends.

E.A.T. *American*
19 | 11 | 14 | $40

E 80s | 1064 Madison Ave. (bet. 80th & 81st Sts.) | 212-772-0022 | www.elizabar.com

Providing a "true NY experience", Eli Zabar's "UES classic" serves as a "high-class" pit stop offering a "large variety" of "delicious" "fresh" sandwiches and other deli fare; "surly service" and "scandalous prices" don't keep it from being "crammed" (especially at brunch) with museumgoers and "affluent" neighbors – not to mention the occasional hungry "celebrity."

Eatery ● *American*
20 | 15 | 17 | $32

W 50s | 798 Ninth Ave. (53rd St.) | 212-765-7080 | www.eaterynyc.com

"Grown-up" "comfort food", e.g. "gourmet mac 'n' cheese", lures "crowds of twentysomethings" to this "happening" Hell's Kitchen New American; service from the equally "young crew" can be "lax" and "decibels" "earsplitting" in its "funky-modern" digs, yet "fair prices" help keep the mood "happy."

Ecco 🗷 *Italian*
23 | 20 | 22 | $55

TriBeCa | 124 Chambers St. (bet. Church St. & W. B'way) | 212-227-7074

"Pols" and "businesspeople in-the-know" hit this "vintage" TriBeCa Italian for "classic" "good eats" delivered by "waiters always at the ready"; tin ceilings, a "beautiful wood bar" and a piano player on weekends evoke "old NY", though the prices are perfectly up to date.

Edison Cafe ⇇ *Coffee Shop*
16 | 8 | 13 | $22

W 40s | Edison Hotel | 228 W. 47th St. (bet. B'way & 8th Ave.) | 212-840-5000

You'll likely spot "an actor" or two at this "throwback" Theater District coffee shop "fondly called the Polish Tearoom" – but it's the "matzo ball soup" that stars here, with a supporting cast of "reliable", "Jewish deli" faves; it's "crazy busy" and "not so beautiful", but a boon to the "budget-conscious."

Ed's Lobster Bar *Seafood*
21 | 16 | 18 | $43

NoLita | 222 Lafayette St. (bet. Kenmare & Spring Sts.) | 212-343-3236 | www.lobsterbarnyc.com

"Fantastic" "overstuffed" lobster rolls, "fabulous fish" and a "Cape Cod look" make this "cheery" NoLita seafooder "feel like the beach"; it can get "cramped" in its "tiny" space, so afishionados know to "go early to avoid the crowds."

Egg ⇇ *Southern*
23 | 12 | 18 | $20

Williamsburg | 135A N. Fifth St. (bet. Bedford Ave. & Berry St.) | Brooklyn | 718-302-5151 | www.pigandegg.com

"Satisfy your cravings" for "unadorned", "egg-centric" Southern cooking at this "bare-bones", "wallet-friendly" Williamsburg joint favored for "ham-and-grits" breakfasts and "down-home" dinners (Wednesday-

Sunday); it's most beloved for its "delicious" weekend brunch, but between "sluggish service" and all the "hype" waits can be "horrendous."

Eight Mile Creek ◑ Australian

▽ | 20 | 16 | 20 | $41

NoLita | 240 Mulberry St. (bet. Prince & Spring Sts.) | 212-431-4635 | www.eightmilecreek.com

"Authentically Australian" fare is the "enjoyable" specialty of this NoLita "hangout"; what with "friendly service", "good beers", "BBQ Sundays in the backyard" in summer and the "lively" pub downstairs, you can bet it's "fun", mate – but don't ask for the kangaroo.

eighty one American

25 | 23 | 24 | $75

W 80s | Excelsior Hotel | 45 W. 81st St. (bet. Columbus Ave. & CPW) | 212-873-8181 | www.81nyc.com

Opposite the Museum of Natural History, Ed Brown's "class-act" New American yearling has "given the UWS something to brag about"; perfect for "a cozy dinner", it's "refined without being stuffy", from the "elegant" setting to the "attentive" service – and while it's "not inexpensive", the $31 dinner prix fixe is an "unbelievable deal."

EJ's Luncheonette ⇌ Diner

16 | 10 | 14 | $23

E 70s | 1271 Third Ave. (73rd St.) | 212-472-0600
W 80s | 447 Amsterdam Ave. (bet. 81st & 82nd Sts.) | 212-873-3444

"Whatever your pleasure, it's on the menu" at these crosstown "retro" diners, where portions are "heaping", service "quick" and specials "recession-busters"; just plan to tangle with "Hummer-size strollers", not mention a "cash-only" policy and "long" weekend lines.

Elaine's ◑ American/Italian

13 | 14 | 15 | $57

E 80s | 1703 Second Ave. (bet. 88th & 89th Sts.) | 212-534-8103

Elaine Kaufman's UES Italian-American cafe over the years has become "a NYC institution" because "it's like walking into an Irwin Shaw novel" – "cranky" and "masculine" and "celebrity"-centric; some people, presumably writer-regulars, even praise the "pricey" food, but as ratings show, it can be "a letdown" for the rest of us.

NEW El Almacén ◑⇌ Argentinean

- | - | - | M

Williamsburg | 557 Driggs Ave. (bet. N. 6th & 7th Sts.) | Brooklyn | 718-218-7284

The words 'fiambreria' and 'queseria' on the windows suggest a Latin meat-and-cheese shop, as do the pantry shelves and hanging sausages, but in fact this well-priced Williamsburg arrival is an Argentine eatery serving a beefy menu; its railroad-style room is already filing up.

El Boqueron Spanish

▽ | 23 | 14 | 23 | $45

Astoria | 31-01 34th Ave. (31st St.) | Queens | 718-956-0107 | www.elboquerontapas.com

"Everyone feels like a regular" at this "unpretentious" Astoria Spaniard as they enjoy the "varied" tapas or other items from the "stylish menu" and get coddled by the "friendly staff"; never mind if the space "could use a face-lift" – it's a "local favorite."

El Charro Español Spanish

▽ | 22 | 14 | 21 | $45

G Village | 4 Charles St. (bet. Greenwich Ave. & Waverly Pl.) | 212-242-9547

"Still going strong", this "under-the-radar" Villager has been turning out "plentiful portions" of "wonderful", "true Spanish food" at "good prices" since 1925; a "happy" staff brightens the "old-fashioned" subterranean setting, leaving longtime fans "hoping it never changes."

Elephant, The ●Ⓜ French/Thai
▽ 20 | 16 | 16 | $36

E Village | 58 E. First St. (bet. 1st & 2nd Aves.) | 212-505-7739 | www.elephantrestaurant.com

It's so "tiny", you may "feel like an elephant" yourself at this "funky", "vibrant" East Village Thai-French; it's "always loud and crowded", and service is "iffy" too, but the "delicate" fare and "jovial" vibe "more than make up for" any deficiencies.

Elephant & Castle ● Pub Food
17 | 14 | 16 | $29

G Village | 68 Greenwich Ave. (bet. Perry St. & 7th Ave. S.) | 212-243-1400 | www.elephantandcastle.com

Showing serious "staying power", this "mellow", "tried-and-true" Villager has offered "reliable" pub grub and a "dandy weekend brunch" for 35 years; it's "so tiny you have to go in sideways", but it's as "comfortable" as an "old sweater", and it "won't empty your wallet" either.

❷ Eleven Madison Park Ⓧ French
27 | 27 | 27 | $114

Flatiron | 11 Madison Ave. (24th St.) | 212-889-0905 | www.elevenmadisonpark.com

At Danny Meyer's "elegant, refined" Madison Square Park New French, a "spectacular" "cathedral-like" former bank space with miles of "marble and granite" is made to feel "warm and welcoming" thanks to the attentions of an "impeccable" staff; "perfectly suited" to the room is Daniel Humm's "sublime", "creative" prix fixe-only cooking backed by a "superb" wine list, all adding up to a serious but "wonderful" splurge – though the $28 lunch prix fixe may be "the best deal in NY."

El Faro ●Ⓜ Spanish
22 | 11 | 19 | $41

W Village | 823 Greenwich St. (bet. Horatio & Jane Sts.) | 212-929-8210 | www.elfaronyc.com

"Around forever", or at least since 1927, this "reasonable" West Village Spaniard "has won New Yorkers' hearts" with "delicious", "garlicky" tapas and other classics served by a "friendly" crew – and "for being a staple in the ever-changing restaurant scene"; maybe the decor "leaves something to be desired", but "with a little imagination, you're on a Madrid sidestreet."

Eliá Ⓜ Greek
26 | 21 | 23 | $47

Bay Ridge | 8611 Third Ave. (bet. 86th & 87th Sts.) | Brooklyn | 718-748-9891 | www.eliarestaurant.com

"Wonderful", "well-prepared" Hellenic cuisine and the "freshest fish" are hallmarks at this "lovely little" Bay Ridge "oasis", where "solicitous", "hands-on owners" set a "welcoming" tone; it's so "relaxing", especially amid the flowers on the deck, that you may feel "you're on a Greek island."

Elias Corner ●⊟ Greek/Seafood
23 | 9 | 15 | $38

Astoria | 24-02 31st St. (24th Ave.) | Queens | 718-932-1510

"Simple, unadorned" and "beautifully grilled" fish "as fresh as it gets" is this Astoria Greek taverna's claim to fame; the digs are "a little seedy", there's "no menu" ("waiters rattle off" the options) and it's "cash only", but in summer the "patio is like a party."

	FOOD	DECOR	SERVICE	COST

⚡ Elio's ◑ _Italian_
24 | 17 | 20 | $64

E 80s | 1621 Second Ave. (bet. 84th & 85th Sts.) | 212-772-2242

"Terrific" Italian classics, "great people-watching" and a "clubby" UES feel have convinced tony neighbors that "this is the real deal"; it's "expensive" and "noisy", but "loyal patrons" crowd in all the same, reporting they've "never had a bad meal there" – and you "never know who you might dine next to" ("Gwyneth, Madonna, Matt").

Elizabeth ◑ _Eclectic_
▽ 19 | 22 | 18 | $48

NoLita | 265 Elizabeth St. (bet. Houston & Prince Sts.) | 212-334-2426 | www.elizabethny.com

Sporting a "hip" bar and a "peaceful" back garden, this NoLita Eclectic arrival lets you choose between "trendy" or "romantic" backdrops for its "high-end comfort" fare; some report glitches as the place "evolves", but "sinful" cocktails and a staff that "tries hard" compensate.

El Malecon ◑ _Dominican_
21 | 8 | 14 | $20

Washington Heights | 4141 Broadway (175th St.) | 212-927-3812
W 90s | 764 Amsterdam Ave. (bet. 97th & 98th Sts.) | 212-864-5648
Bronx | 5592 Broadway (231st St.) | 718-432-5155

Rotisserie chicken "worth crossing the road for" is the "crowd-pleasing" specialty at this Uptown-Bronx threesome that also dispenses other "authentic Dominican" grub – and "lots of it" – "for cheap"; those who don't dig "diner decor" get takeout or "lightning-speed" delivery.

elmo ◑ _American_
16 | 16 | 16 | $36

Chelsea | 156 Seventh Ave. (bet. 19th & 20th Sts.) | 212-337-8000 | www.elmorestaurant.com

The "tarted-up comfort food" is "almost a distraction" at this "airy" Chelsea New American "scene", where "drinks flow" and the waiters are part of the "eye candy"; just beware – "boys will be boys", so this "party" can be "deafening."

El Parador Cafe _Mexican_
21 | 17 | 21 | $44

Murray Hill | 325 E. 34th St. (bet. 1st & 2nd Aves.) | 212-679-6812 | www.elparadorcafe.com

"One of the best-kept secrets" in Murray Hill, this "unassuming" Mexican has been dispensing "enticing" fare for half a century; it "doesn't look like much", but the "relaxed tempo", "cheerful" service, "killer margaritas" and "unbeatable prices" mean it "still satisfies."

El Paso Taqueria _Mexican_
23 | 11 | 16 | $25

NEW **E 100s** | 1643 Lexington Ave. (104th St.) | 212-831-9831 ◑
E 90s | 64 E. 97th St. (Park Ave.) | 212-996-1739
Harlem | 237 E. 116th St. (3rd Ave.) | 212-860-4875 ◑
www.elpasotaqueria.com

The "hearty, tasty", "real Mexican food" at this Harlem-UES trio earns the "seal of approval" from expats who know "_autentico_" when they eat it; considering the "outstanding" deals, amigos "look past" "claustrophobic" digs with "tiny tables" or get it to go.

El Quijote ◑ _Spanish_
20 | 14 | 18 | $44

Chelsea | 226 W. 23rd St. (bet. 7th & 8th Aves.) | 212-929-1855

"Mountains of paella", "delicious lobsters" and "zesty" Spanish preparations at "the right price" mean this "quirky" circa-1930 "Chelsea institution" is a "zoo" much of the time; it's a "hoot" too, thus few care about "sketchy" service and decor "so outdated it's almost fashionable again."

El Quinto Pino ● Spanish

FOOD	DECOR	SERVICE	COST
21	16	18	$37

Chelsea | 401 W. 24th St. (bet. 9th & 10th Aves.) | 212-206-6900 | www.elquintopinonyc.com

"Top-of-the-line tapas" and a "great selection" of Spanish wines have 'em "squeezing in" at this "adorable" Chelsea offshoot of Tía Pol; be forewarned, those little plates "can add up", and even with "prompt service" it's "hard to get a stool" in the table-free, "postage-stamp" space.

El Rio Grande Tex-Mex

FOOD	DECOR	SERVICE	COST
18	15	16	$35

Murray Hill | 160 E. 38th St. (bet. Lexington & 3rd Aves.) | 212-867-0922 | www.arkrestaurants.com

Representing Texas in one half and Mexico in the other, this "lively" Murray Hill eatery fittingly dishes up "dependable" Tex-Mex, although "margaritas that knock you for a loop" are probably what keeps it a "hot spot"; it's usually "elbow-to-elbow" and a "ton of fun."

Embers Steak

FOOD	DECOR	SERVICE	COST
21	14	19	$50

Bay Ridge | 9519 Third Ave. (bet. 95th & 96th Sts.) | Brooklyn | 718-745-3700

A "long-established" "favorite", this Bay Ridge steakhouse "holds its own" with "sizzling, drenched-in-butter" hunks of beef in portions that scream "doggy bag"; the "cramped" space "could use sprucing up", but "terrific" prices warm the heart.

Empanada Mama ● South American

FOOD	DECOR	SERVICE	COST
22	11	14	$18

W 50s | 763 Ninth Ave. (bet. 51st & 52nd Sts.) | 212-698-9008 | www.empmamanyc.com

"Little pockets of heaven" (aka empanadas) in a "multitude" of varieties including dessert are dispensed "super cheap" at this "hole-in-the-wall" Hell's Kitchen South American; service as "flaky as the crusts" and "out-the-door crowds" make "takeout" preferable for many.

Empire Diner ● Diner

FOOD	DECOR	SERVICE	COST
15	15	15	$27

Chelsea | 210 10th Ave. (22nd St.) | 212-243-2736 | www.empire-diner.com
The "authentic" circa-1929 "art deco" digs and "sidewalk seating" are "reason enough" to hit this Chelsea diner dispensing classic "favorites" 24/7; it's a "pre-dawn revelers' delight" and "there when you need it", so never mind if the food is "just ok" and service may be "petulant" at times.

Empire Szechuan ● Chinese

FOOD	DECOR	SERVICE	COST
15	8	13	$24

G Village | 15 Greenwich Ave. (bet. Christopher & W. 10th Sts.) | 212-691-1535
G Village | 173 Seventh Ave. S. (bet. Perry & W. 11th Sts.) | 212-243-6046
Washington Heights | 4041 Broadway (bet. 170th & 171st Sts.) | 212-568-1600
W 60s | 193 Columbus Ave. (bet. 68th & 69th Sts.) | 212-496-8778
W 100s | 2642 Broadway (100th St.) | 212-662-9404
www.empiretogo.com
An "expansive" menu for an "inexpensive" sum is the formula at this all-over-town mini-chain where the "basic" Chinese chow is "adequate but not exceptional"; "'70s moderne" decor and "toss-it-on-the-table service" render it "better for takeout."

	FOOD	DECOR	SERVICE	COST

Employees Only ● *European* | 18 | 21 | 19 | $45

W Village | 510 Hudson St. (bet. Christopher & W. 10th Sts.) | 212-242-3021 | www.employeesonlynyc.com

"Serious mixologists" create such "fancy-schmancy" tipples at this Villager that they almost "eclipse" the "surprisingly good" European eats served until "late"; "young professionals" "crank up the noise" in its "speakeasy-esque" setting, but it's quieter (and "lovely for brunch") in the back garden.

NEW Emporio ● *Italian* | ▽ 22 | 21 | 20 | $39

NoLita | 231 Mott St. (bet. Prince & Spring Sts.) | 212-966-1234 | www.auroraristorante.com

A "welcome addition" to NoLita, this offshoot of Williamsburg's Aurora serves the same "simple, fresh" Italian fare and the "thinnest-crusted pizza on the planet" till the wee hours; a "sweet", "low-key" crew presides over the "rustic" space, boosting the overall "homey feel."

Energy Kitchen *Health Food* | 17 | 8 | 15 | $15

Chelsea | 307 W. 17th St. (bet. 8th & 9th Aves.) | 212-645-5200
E 40s | 300 E. 41st St. (2nd Ave.) | 212-687-1200
E 50s | 1089 Second Ave. (bet. 57th & 58th Sts.) | 212-888-9300
NEW E 80s | 1628 Second Ave. (bet. 84th & 85th Sts.) | 212-288-8484
Financial District | 71 Nassau St. (bet. Fulton & John Sts.) | 212-577-8989 🛇
NEW Flatiron | 18 W. 23rd St. (bet. 5th & 6th Aves.) | 212-989-2323
W 40s | 417 W. 47th St. (bet. 9th & 10th Aves.) | 212-333-3500
W Village | 82 Christopher St. (bet. Bleecker St. & 7th Ave. S.) | 212-414-8880
www.energykitchen.com

"Healthy and tasty" are "not mutually exclusive" at this "nutritious" mini-chain that's a magnet for "gym rats and vegetarians"; while the "customizable" wraps and burgers offered are "not exactly fine dining", they're "not bad" if you're "trying to count calories" – and can ignore the "locker room" settings.

EN Japanese Brasserie *Japanese* | 23 | 25 | 22 | $60

W Village | 435 Hudson St. (Leroy St.) | 212-647-9196 | www.enjb.com

The en-lightened "skip the sushi" and go for the Japanese small plate "delicacies" at this "amazing" West Villager famed for its "wonderful housemade tofu" and "premium sakes"; a "spectacular", "minimalist" space and "helpful" staffers add to an "indulgence" that's "totally worth the Benjamins."

Ennio & Michael *Italian* | 21 | 16 | 23 | $49

G Village | 539 La Guardia Pl. (bet. Bleecker & W. 3rd Sts.) | 212-677-8577 | www.ennioandmichael.com

"Good, honest" Italian cooking keeps regulars coming to this "venerable" Village "favorite", where an "amiable" staff makes everyone "comfortable"; the decor may be "bland", but "fair prices" and primo "people-watching" on the patio are anything but.

Enoteca Maria Ⓜ *Italian* | ▽ 23 | 18 | 21 | $42

Staten Island | 27 Hyatt St. (Central Ave.) | 718-447-2777 | www.enotecamaria.com

"The menu changes daily" at this "quaint little" Italian wine bar–cum-small plates specialist in Staten Island's St. George; a "rotating

| | FOOD | DECOR | SERVICE | COST |

cast" of "authentic nonnas" does the cooking, providing a "tour" of "regional" specialties, and a staff that "couldn't be nicer" adds to the "pleasant" ambiance.

Enzo's *Italian*
23 | 16 | 22 | $40

Bronx | 1998 Williamsbridge Rd. (Neill Ave.) | 718-409-3828 🅜
Bronx | 2339 Arthur Ave. (bet. Crescent Ave. & E. 186th St.) | 718-733-4455
www.enzosofthebronx.com

"Bountiful" portions of "old-fashioned" Italian "classics" give these Bronx trattorias a "comfortable" "dining-with-family" feel; though the no-rez policy produces weekend waits and the digs "aren't much to look at", "friendly" service is a "bright spot."

Epices du Traiteur *Mediterranean/Tunisian*
20 | 16 | 20 | $44

W 70s | 103 W. 70th St. (Columbus Ave.) | 212-579-5904

"Handy to Lincoln Center", this "convivial" UWS eatery offers "a change of pace" with Med-Tunisian dishes at "decent" prices; a "gracious" staff works the "cozy", "crowded", "narrow" room, while a "pretty garden" in back provides a refuge, weather permitting.

Erawan *Thai*
23 | 21 | 21 | $38

Bayside | 213-41 39th Ave. (Bell Blvd.) | Queens | 718-229-1620 🅜
Bayside | 42-31 Bell Blvd. (bet. 42nd & 43rd Aves.) | Queens | 718-428-2112

"You can't go wrong" ordering any of the "top-flight" Thai dishes "creatively presented" at this Bayside duo, whether it's "traditional" or Siam-style steakhouse fare at the larger 39th Avenue branch; "courteous" service, "beautiful" digs and a "relaxing" vibe give them "date spot" potential.

Erminia 🅈 *Italian*
25 | 24 | 25 | $67

E 80s | 250 E. 83rd St. (bet. 2nd & 3rd Aves.) | 212-879-4284 | www.erminiaristorante.com

"Mastering the art of mood", this "transporting" UES Italian melds "superb" Roman cuisine, "charming" service and a "tiny" "candlelit" room into a "magical" experience "oozing with romance"; just remember to "reserve ahead" if you want to taste "la dolce vita."

🆉 Esca ◐ *Italian/Seafood*
25 | 21 | 23 | $71

W 40s | 402 W. 43rd St. (9th Ave.) | 212-564-7272 | www.esca-nyc.com

From the Bastianich-Batali-Pasternack team, this Theater District Italian "favorite" has developed a reputation as "one of the city's best seafooders", excelling with an "amazing" selection of "super-fresh crudo" and "wonderful pastas" too; high marks across the board explain the "crowds", and help justify the price tag.

Ess-a-Bagel *Deli*
23 | 7 | 12 | $11

E 50s | 831 Third Ave. (bet. 50th & 51st Sts.) | 212-980-1010
Gramercy | 359 First Ave. (21st St.) | 212-260-2252
www.ess-a-bagel.com

"It's carb heaven" at these East Side delis where "fresh", "scrumptious" bagels "the size of tires" come topped with a "dizzying array of schmears"; they've gained a "cult following" among those who consider "bare-bones" setups, "grumpy" service and "standing in line" just "part of the experience."

	FOOD	DECOR	SERVICE	COST

Essex ◑ *American* — 18 | 15 | 16 | $33

LES | 120 Essex St. (Rivington St.) | 212-533-9616 | www.essexnyc.com
Famous for its three-drink "boozy brunch" specials, this "energetic" LES New American also turns out "well-priced" dinner fare with Jewish-Latin touches; it's a "hot spot" for "youthful", "sceney" types, but even they complain of the "interminable waits" and "cacophony" in its "loftlike" quarters.

Etats-Unis *American* — 23 | 16 | 21 | $64

E 80s | 242 E. 81st St. (bet. 2nd & 3rd Aves.) | 212-517-8826 | www.etatsunisrestaurant.com
"First-rate" New American fare and a "quietly competent" staff make this "tiny", "unassuming" vet a "top choice" among the "older UES crowd"; those "a bit more hip" hit the "teeny" "wine bar across the street", where prices for "equally delicious food" are less daunting.

etcetera etcetera Ⓜ *Italian* — 20 | 18 | 20 | $47

W 40s | 352 W. 44th St. (bet. 8th & 9th Aves.) | 212-399-4141 | www.etcrestaurant.com
A "sister of ViceVersa and just as gooda gooda" (if "less chic"), this "dynamic" Theater District Italian delivers "creative pickings" at "fair prices" via a "cheerful" staff; if decibels in the "modern" digs become an "ouch for the ears", ask for the "lovely, quiet upstairs room."

Ethos *Greek* — 22 | 16 | 18 | $42

NEW **E 50s** | 905 First Ave. (51st St.) | 212-888-4060
Murray Hill | 495 Third Ave. (bet. 33rd & 34th Sts.) | 212-252-1972 ◑
www.ethosrestaurants.com
"Deservedly popular", this "unassuming" Murray Hill Greek and its roomier, "more attractive" new East 50s spin-off both feature the same "incredibly fresh" fish "grilled the Med way" plus other "taverna classics"; "welcoming" vibes and solid "value" are other endearments.

Euzkadi *Spanish* — ▽ 21 | 18 | 18 | $39

E Village | 108 E. Fourth St. (bet. 1st & 2nd Aves.) | 212-982-9788 | www.euzkadirestaurant.com
"Wonderful tapas" and other "traditional" Basque specialties keep diners "basking in the warm" glow of this "charming" East Village "hole-in-the-wall"; there's live flamenco on Tuesdays and "bachelorette parties abound", but the mood's generally "friendly" and "relaxing."

Excellent Dumpling House ⊄ *Chinese* — 20 | 5 | 12 | $16

Chinatown | 111 Lafayette St. (bet. Canal & Walker Sts.) | 212-219-0212
"Jurors rejoice" and "tourists" converge at this "crowded" Chinatown "favorite" doling out "savory, juicy" dumplings and Shanghainese eats at "giveaway prices"; they "rush you in, rush you out", but that's ok considering the "cramped" communal tables and "close-your-eyes" decor.

Extra Virgin *Mediterranean* — 22 | 18 | 17 | $42

W Village | 259 W. Fourth St. (bet. Charles & Perry Sts.) | 212-691-9359 | www.extravirginrestaurant.com
"Buzzing" with the "din" of "stylish locals come to play", this "cute" West Villager serves up "simply delicious" "moderately priced" Med dishes and a "divine" brunch; waits can be "painful" and "service isn't the best", but the "people-watching" is "perfect", as are "those outdoor tables."

	FOOD	DECOR	SERVICE	COST

Fabio Piccolo Fiore *Italian*
▽ 21 | 19 | 21 | $49

E 40s | 230 E. 44th St. (bet. 2nd & 3rd Aves.) | 212-922-0581 | www.fabiopiccolofiore.com

"Gracious hospitality" is the trademark of this "cheerful" Grand Central-area Italian whose "excellent" eats come via a "sweet" chef who "gladly prepares" "anything you can describe"; it's a "spot to chat" or listen to "unobtrusive live piano", so it may not be "undiscovered" for long.

Fairway Cafe *American*
18 | 9 | 12 | $28

W 70s | 2127 Broadway, 2nd fl. (74th St.) | 212-595-1888
Red Hook | 480-500 Van Brunt St. (Reed St.) | Brooklyn | 718-694-6868
www.fairwaymarket.com

Offering the perfect "shopping pit stop", these cafes "fortify" with "quality" American fare (and "good steak" at the UWS branch) at "more than reasonable" rates; expect "slow" service and seriously "plain" decor, though in Red Hook factor in a "million-dollar" view of the harbor and "Lady Liberty."

Falai *Italian*
23 | 18 | 19 | $47

LES | 68 Clinton St. (bet. Rivington & Stanton Sts.) | 212-253-1960

Falai Panetteria *Italian*

LES | 79 Clinton St. (Rivington St.) | 212-777-8956

Caffe Falai *Italian*

SoHo | 265 Lafayette St. (Prince St.) | 212-274-8615
www.falainyc.com

"Simple" Italian cooking that "dazzles" is chef Iacopo Falai's signature, whether it's a "memorable" dinner in his "fashionable" LES original, at the casual Panetteria "spin-off" nearby or the Caffe "respite" in SoHo (both of which also serve breakfast and lunch); "warm service" offsets "tight, white" "minimalist" setups.

F & J Pine Restaurant *Italian*
22 | 20 | 20 | $36

Bronx | 1913 Bronxdale Ave. (bet. Matthews & Muliner Aves.) | 718-792-5956 | www.fjpine.com

There's "plenty to cheer about" at this "down-to-earth" Bronx Italian "landmark", from the "tremendous, tasty portions" laden with "red sauce and cheese" to the "sports memorabilia" and "Yankee" sightings; "friendly" staffers, "good value" and cartloads of "leftovers" ensure it's worth the "crazy wait."

Farm on Adderley *American*
22 | 19 | 21 | $37

Ditmas Park | 1108 Cortelyou Rd. (bet. Stratford & Westminster Rds.) | Brooklyn | 718-287-3101 | www.thefarmonadderley.com

"Fabulous", "farm-fresh" New American fare at "modest prices" makes this Ditmas Park bistro a "novelty" in a "sleepy, old-time neighborhood"; "obliging" service, a "comfortable", "informal" setting with a "jovial" vibe plus a "lovely garden" help explain why it's "usually crowded."

NEW Fat Hippo ● *Diner*
▽ 20 | 16 | 18 | $33

LES | 71 Clinton St. (bet. Rivington & Stanton Sts.) | 212-228-0994 | www.fathipponyc.com

The long-vacant 71 Clinton space on the LES is now home to this modern diner slinging fancied-up comfort "basics" like free-range turkey meatloaf; given its late-night hours and comfortable "price point", it's a perfect pit stop for area bar-hoppers.

	FOOD	DECOR	SERVICE	COST

Fatty Crab ◐ *Malaysian*   22 | 13 | 18 | $42
NEW **W 70s** | 2170 Broadway (77th St.) | 212-496-2722
W Village | 643 Hudson St. (bet. Gansevoort & Horatio Sts.) | 212-352-3590
www.fattycrab.com
There's now a roomier UWS location to join the "hip", "funky" West
Village original, and both offer "terrific" "interpretations" of Malaysian
"street food" packing "flavors that'll blow you away"; the vibe is "fun"
and "informal" – and often "jammed" and "noisy" too.

Fatty's Cafe *American/Eclectic*   ▽ 22 | 17 | 20 | $24
Astoria | 25-01 Ditmars Blvd. (Crescent St.) | Queens | 718-267-7071 |
www.fattyscafenyc.com
"Every nabe should have a Fatty's" declare fans of Astoria's "popular
watering hole" famed for "excellent" American eats with "Latin twists"
at "great prices"; a "super staff" serves in "relaxed" digs dressed up
with "rotating local art", or out in the "backyard" "escape."

NEW **Favela Cubana** ◐⊅ *Brazilian/Cuban*   - | - | - | M
G Village | 543 La Guardia Pl. (bet. Bleecker & W. 3rd Sts.) | 212-777-6500 |
www.favelacubana.com
At this lively, colorful new Village Brazilian-Cuban, look for "enjoyable", moderately priced food and cocktails made for collegiate types
(there's an NYU dorm across the street); live music on weekends and
patio seating in warmer months are further enticements.

Felice ◐ *Italian*   20 | 21 | 20 | $44
E 60s | 1166 First Ave. (64th St.) | 212-593-2223 | www.felicewinebar.com
"Downtown" style comes to the UES via this "cool", "rustic" Italian
whose "attractive exposed-brick" setup "screams 'wine bar'"; "spot-
on" service, "tasty" nibbles and "luscious", "affordable" vinos make it
an "easy", "inviting spot to meet friends."

Z **Felidia** *Italian*   26 | 22 | 24 | $78
E 50s | 243 E. 58th St. (bet. 2nd & 3rd Aves.) | 212-758-1479 |
www.lidiasitaly.com
"Lidia, I love you" declare devotees of "TV chef" Lidia Bastianich and
her East Side Italian that's "still excellent after all these years"; its
"wonderful" townhouse setting can feel "a bit cramped", but that's
easily overlooked given such "exquisite" "high cuisine", "exceptional"
wines and "classy" pro service; naturally it's "costly", but the $30 prix
fixe lunch is a "bargain" for a virtual trip to Italy.

Félix ◐ *French*   16 | 17 | 15 | $43
SoHo | 340 W. Broadway (Grand St.) | 212-431-0021 | www.felixnyc.com
"Hip SoHo" types mingle with "Euros" and kick up a "raucous scene"
at this perennially "fun" French bistro; the food's "nothing special" and
service can be "spotty", but brunching and "watching the world go by"
when "the doors are open on a sunny day" is "unbeatable."

Z **Fette Sau** *BBQ*   25 | 16 | 15 | $25
Williamsburg | 354 Metropolitan Ave. (bet. Havemeyer & Roebling Sts.) |
Brooklyn | 718-963-3404
A "primal carnivorous" vibe prevails at this "funky" Williamsburg BBQ
"joint" – NYC's No. 1 – where "hipsters" pile in for "fantastic", "slow-
cooked meats" "by the pound", "classy" beers by the gallon and "a whole

slew of whiskeys"; if "zero-patience", "cafeteria-style" service and "free-for-all picnic tables" sound "stressful", there's always "takeout."

▣ 15 East ⓩ *Japanese*   26 | 22 | 23 | $84

Union Sq | 15 E. 15th St. (bet. 5th Ave. & Union Sq. W.) | 212-647-0015 | www.15eastrestaurant.com

"Sit at the sushi bar" and "go for the omakase" at this "exceptional" Union Square Japanese from the Tocqueville folks, where chef Masato Shimizu "wows" with his "brilliant tidbits" and "witty repartee"; "Zen"-like decor and a "friendly" staff notwithstanding, it helps if "somebody else is picking up the tab."

Fig & Olive *Mediterranean*   20 | 20 | 18 | $46

E 50s | 10 E. 52nd St. (bet. 5th & Madison Aves.) | 212-319-2002
E 60s | 808 Lexington Ave. (bet. 62nd & 63rd Sts.) | 212-207-4555
Meatpacking | 420 W. 13th St. (bet. 9th Ave. & Washington St.) | 212-924-1200
www.figandolive.com

"Wonderful nibbling" in "snazzy" digs is the deal at these "cheery" Mediterraneans where the "tasty small plates" are dominated by "olive oils galore"; never mind if tabs "add up quickly" and service can be "haphazard" – the "capacious" Meatpacking outpost is a "party", and the Eastsiders are "civilized" spots to meet "chums."

Filippo's Ⓜ *Italian*   ▽ 24 | 18 | 21 | $57

Staten Island | 1727 Richmond Rd. (bet. Buel & Seaver Aves.) | 718-668-9091 | www.filipposrestaurant.com

One of Staten Island's "more creative" Italians, this Dongan Hills "strip-mall trattoria" transforms "top-notch ingredients" into "delicious" dishes ferried by an "attentive" staff; the "cozy, romantic" feel belies the locale, as do somewhat "startling" tabs – though most attest "you get what you pay for."

F.illi Ponte ⓩⓂ *Italian*   23 | 21 | 22 | $71

TriBeCa | 39 Desbrosses St. (bet. Washington & West Sts.) | 212-226-4621 | www.filliponte.com

"Breathtaking views of the Hudson" and an "elegant" space make a "romantic" backdrop for "sumptuous" Italian cuisine at this "out-of-the-way" West TriBeCan; some detect echoes of "gangster chic", but "lovely" service and a "leisurely" pace leave deep-pocketed diners fully "satisfied."

Fiorentino's *Italian*   19 | 15 | 18 | $34

Gravesend | 311 Ave. U (bet. McDonald Ave. & West St.) | Brooklyn | 718-372-1445

"Not for tourists or trendies", this Gravesend "neighborhood joint" doles out "ample" portions of "affordable", "old-school" Neapolitan cooking that's just right for "family meals"; "tuxedoed" waiters oversee the "noisy", "overcrowded", "'50s-time-warp" digs, but even these "pros" can't prevent occasional "waits."

Fiorini ⓩ *Italian*   20 | 18 | 21 | $61

E 50s | 209 E. 56th St. (bet. 2nd & 3rd Aves.) | 212-308-0830 | www.fiorinirestaurant.com

Lello Arpaia's somewhat "unsung" East Midtowner is "tasteful in all respects", from the "right-on" Neapolitan repasts to the "smooth, experienced" service; maybe the decor "leaves a bit to be desired", but it's conducive to "lingering" and "conversation" during a "pleasant", if "pricey", evening out.

FireBird ⓜ Russian
19 | 25 | 21 | $64

W 40s | 365 W. 46th St. (bet. 8th & 9th Aves.) | 212-586-0244 | www.firebirdrestaurant.com

"Fit for a czar" (or at least a czar wannabe), this "elegant" Restaurant Row Russian offers its "very good", "expensive" fare in a "dazzling" duplex "decorated like the imperial court" and overseen by "attentive" "costumed" waiters; copious "caviar, blintzes and vodka" ensure everyone's having "fun" – in short, it's a natural for a blowout "celebration."

Firenze ◑ Italian
20 | 19 | 23 | $52

E 80s | 1594 Second Ave. (bet. 82nd & 83rd Sts.) | 212-861-9368

This "sweet" UES Tuscan sends its "well-made classics" out into "quaint" quarters overseen by a "solicitous", "never-rushed" staff; true, the "intimate" room is a little "tight", but its "subdued", "candlelit" vibe inspires "romance" – as does occasional "grappa on the house" at tab time.

Fish Seafood
22 | 14 | 19 | $39

G Village | 280 Bleecker St. (Jones St.) | 212-727-2879

"They've done the fishing for you" at this "Cape Cod"-style Villager, an "unpretentious" source of "palatable" "basic seafood" and raw-bar fare served amid "divey" "nautical" decor; if "you're watching your pennies", the "oyster special is amazing."

NEW Fishtail ◑ Seafood
23 | 22 | 22 | $66

E 60s | 135 E. 62nd St. (bet. Lexington & Park Aves.) | 212-754-1300 | www.fishtaildb.com

"David Burke has done it again" at this new East Side townhouse seafooder, a "bright" "sophisticate" where the "creative" (if "costly") fin fare and "courteous" service are likely to "capture you hook, line and sinker"; it's still "getting its sea legs" following a recent chef change, but early tidings suggest a "winner."

Five Front ⓜ American
19 | 17 | 19 | $42

Dumbo | 5 Front St. (Old Fulton St.) | Brooklyn | 718-625-5559 | www.fivefrontrestaurant.com

For "fine" "comfort-style" food served with "aplomb", Dumbo's "laid-back" "neighborhood" types have this "affordable" New American bistro on the front burner; the "delightful" bamboo garden tucked beneath the Brooklyn Bridge is an especially "sweet retreat."

Five Guys Burgers
20 | 8 | 14 | $13

G Village | 496 La Guardia Pl. (bet. Bleecker & Houston Sts.) | 212-228-6008
W 50s | 43 W. 55th St. (bet. 5th & 6th Aves.) | 212-459-9600
W Village | 296 Bleecker St. (7th Ave. S.) | 212-367-9200 ◑
NEW Bay Ridge | 8510 Fifth Ave. (bet. 85th & 86th Sts.) | Brooklyn | 718-921-9380
Brooklyn Heights | 138 Montague St. (bet. Clinton & Henry Sts.) | Brooklyn | 718-797-9380
Park Slope | 284 Seventh Ave. (bet. 6th & 7th Sts.) | Brooklyn | 718-499-9380

(continued)

(continued)

Five Guys

College Point | 132-01 14th Ave. (132nd St.) | Queens | 718-767-6500

NEW **Glendale** | 73-25 Woodhaven Blvd. (bet. 74th & Rutledge Aves.) | Queens | 718-943-3483

www.fiveguys.com

"Runs circles around" its fast-food rivals say supporters of this DC-based franchise furnishing "killer" burgers dressed with "toppings galore" plus "addictive" fries and "free peanuts" for the wait; setups are "stark", but when you seek a "bazillion calories" on the "cheap", these guys "rock."

NEW **Five Leaves** ◑ *American*   ▽ 23 | 21 | 20 | $33

Williamsburg | 18 Bedford Ave. (bet. Lorimer St. & Manhattan Ave.) | Brooklyn | 718-383-5345 | www.fiveleavesny.com

Conceived by the late Heath Ledger, this new Williamsburg "hipster spot" serves "outta-sight" New American fare with "interesting" Aussie accents in a "neat" "nautical" setting; the "skinny jeans" contingent keeps it "lively", though given the "close quarters", "not always comfy."

5 Napkin Burger ◑ *Burgers*   21 | 18 | 18 | $29

W 40s | 630 Ninth Ave. (45th St.) | 212-757-2277 | www.5napkinburger.com

Forget napkins – "you'll need a big towel" to eat one of the "exceptional" burgers at this "crowded", "affordable", "theater-convenient" Hell's Kitchen "diner plus"; add "pleasant" "butcher shop" decor, "speedy" service and "amazing shakes", and it's no wonder this yearling is such a "smash success."

5 Ninth *American*   19 | 22 | 18 | $52

Meatpacking | 5 Ninth Ave. (bet. Gansevoort & Little W. 12th Sts.) | 212-929-9460 | www.5ninth.com

When "fashionistas" "need a break" from Meatpacking District "shopping sprees", this "charming" three-level townhouse and its "satisfying" "seasonal" New American fare fill the bill; if "unfocused" service and "pricey" tabs detract, just "go for a cocktail" in the "not-to-be-missed" back garden.

NEW **508** ◑ *Italian/Mediterranean*   ▽ 19 | 20 | 18 | $37

SoHo | 508 Greenwich St. (bet. Canal & Spring Sts.) | 212-219-2444 | www.508nyc.com

With new owners, this West SoHo Italian-Med has simplified its predecessor Giorgione 508's name, but not its menu of "well-priced" small bites and pastas; the "charming" candlelit interior suits for occasions from after-work drinks at the bar to family dinners and dates.

Five Points ◑ *American/Mediterranean*   22 | 21 | 21 | $49

NoHo | 31 Great Jones St. (bet. Bowery & Lafayette St.) | 212-253-5700 | www.fivepointsrestaurant.com

They "have it down pat" at this "vibrant" NoHo "favorite", where "capable" staffers serve "first-rate", "fairly priced" Med–New American fare in a "lovely setting" featuring a "babbling creek"; it "can get crowded", most pointedly during the "knock-your-socks-off" brunch.

	FOOD	DECOR	SERVICE	COST

Flatbush Farm *American*   20 | 19 | 19 | $36

Park Slope | 76 St. Marks Ave. (Flatbush Ave.) | Brooklyn | 718-622-3276 | www.flatbushfarm.com

Park Slope veers a little bit "country" at this "homey" New American, where the "tasty" "seasonal menu" incorporates "fresh" local and organic ingredients; service can get a bit "too laid-back", but the "wonderful" back garden "keeps all the cows coming home."

Flea Market Cafe ● *French*   ▽ 21 | 19 | 19 | $31

E Village | 131 Ave. A (bet. 9th St. & St. Marks Pl.) | 212-358-9282 | www.fleamarketcafe.com

A "buzzy" "neighborhood staple", this "unpretentious" East Villager plies "reliable" French bistro bites at a "reasonable cost" in "cheerful" digs filled with "kitschy" (and purchasable) bric-a-brac; it's a "steal" for brunch, but the "tight seating" fills up fast.

NEW Flex Mussels *Seafood*   22 | 17 | 19 | $46

E 80s | 174 E. 82nd St. (bet. Lexington & 3rd Aves.) | 212-717-7772 | www.flexmussels.com

Making a "powerful" debut on the UES, this Prince Edward Island-spawned "seafood shack" showcases 23 "enticing" preparations of "meaty mussels" in a "bright", "casual" space; even if the "service needs to be tweaked", "boisterous" bivalve buffs keep it "packed to the gills."

Flor de Mayo ● *Chinese/Peruvian*   21 | 10 | 17 | $23

W 80s | 484 Amsterdam Ave. (bet. 83rd & 84th Sts.) | 212-787-3388
W 100s | 2651 Broadway (bet. 100th & 101st Sts.) | 212-663-5520

"Mouthwatering" rotisserie chicken is the "trademark" of these "efficient", ever-"popular" Upper Westsiders slinging "low-cost" Chinese-Peruvian eats; "no-nonsense" service and "bare-bones" digs mean maybe they're "not the classiest", but "takeout" is always an option.

Flor de Sol 🅢 *Spanish*   22 | 22 | 20 | $48

TriBeCa | 361 Greenwich St. (bet. Franklin & Harrison Sts.) | 212-366-1640 | www.flordesolnyc.com

"Dark" and "romantic", this "old-style" TriBeCa Spaniard floors admirers with its "delicious" tapas, "awesome sangria" and overall "sexiness"; it's an "excellent date spot" if you're in the mood for "vibrant energy" that peaks on "live flamenco" nights.

NEW Flying Cow ● *Argentinean/Steak*   - | - | - | M

Williamsburg | 2 Hope St. (Roebling St.) | Brooklyn | 718-387-7111 | www.the-flyingcow.com

Its French predecessor, Gribouille, didn't fly, but this newcomer to a low-key Williamsburg block is betting on its own steak frites, among other "simple", beef-centric Argentine dishes; oversized Edison bulbs at the bar and a savvy soundtrack lend the lacy-curtained space some kick.

NEW Fonda *Mexican*   - | - | - | M

Park Slope | 434 Seventh Ave. (bet. 14th & 15th Sts.) | Brooklyn | 718-369-3144

Inhabiting the space that was previously Little D Eatery, this Park Slope arrival from a former Rosa Mexicano culinary director presents a punchy vibe free of sombreros and mariachi; its seasonal Nuevo

	FOOD	DECOR	SERVICE	COST

Mexican offerings are matched with an array of cocktails, best enjoyed out on the back patio.

Fornino *Pizza*
∇ 23 | 14 | 17 | $25

Williamsburg | 187 Bedford Ave. (bet. 6th & 7th Sts.) | Brooklyn | 718-384-6004

Even "pizza snobs" are "blown away" by this "cool" Williamsburg entry, whose "wood-burning" oven produces "wow-worthy" pies incorporating "just-right thin crusts", "knockout" toppings and "house-grown herbs"; it's a "sparse" setup, but "you'll want to go back for more."

44 & X Hell's Kitchen ◑ *American*
22 | 19 | 21 | $45

W 40s | 622 10th Ave. (44th St.) | 212-977-1170
44½ ◑ *American*
W 40s | 626 10th Ave. (bet. 44th & 45th Sts.) | 212-399-4450
www.44andX.com

"Updated American comfort food" (think "truffled mac 'n' cheese") delivered by "hunky" waiters is the lure at these "lively", "oh-so-gay" Hell's Kitchen Americans; the "sleek" setups get "noisy", especially when the "enticing bar scene" is at full tilt.

☒ Four Seasons ⧈ *American*
26 | 28 | 27 | $95

E 50s | 99 E. 52nd St. (bet. Lexington & Park Aves.) | 212-754-9494 | www.fourseasonsrestaurant.com

"Fifty years old and still going strong", this Philip Johnson–designed "classic" "defines upper-crust" New American dining in the Pool Room at night and "power-lunching" in the Grill Room by day; under the aegis of owner-hosts Alex von Bidder and Julian Niccolini, "everyone is made to feel rich and famous" – as long as they have "deep pockets" – and despite the loss of longtime chef Christian Albin, surveyors report that the food is "excellent as always."

Fragole *Italian*
23 | 16 | 20 | $34

Carroll Gardens | 394 Court St. (1st Pl.) | Brooklyn | 718-522-7133 | www.fragoleny.com

The "fantastic" "fresh pastas" deliver "real quality for the price" at this "small" Carroll Gardens Italian, where the "comforting" cooking and "warm service" heighten the "homey vibe"; by now it's a "neighborhood favorite", so "go early to avoid the wait."

Francisco's Centro Vasco *Spanish*
21 | 12 | 18 | $51

Chelsea | 159 W. 23rd St. (bet. 6th & 7th Aves.) | 212-645-6224 | www.centrovasco.ypguides.net

Take "a group of hungry people" and "chow down" on "monster lobsters" at this Chelsea Spanish "throwback", a "sure bet" for a "cheap", "messy" shellfish "fix" (just "add sangria"); the pace is "hectic" and the room needs "revamping", but somehow it's "always busy."

Frank ◑⌂ *Italian*
24 | 13 | 16 | $33

E Village | 88 Second Ave. (bet. 5th & 6th Sts.) | 212-420-0202 | www.frankrestaurant.com

"Like nonna's kitchen", this "cash-only" East Village "hole-in-the-wall" "never misses a beat", serving "scrumptious" "rustic Italian" at "yesterday's prices"; it's a "rushed", "no-frills" joint with "squished seating", but the "long lines" persist since "frankly" the food's "worth waiting for."

	FOOD	DECOR	SERVICE	COST

Frankie & Johnnie's Steakhouse ⊠ *Steak* | 22 | 15 | 20 | $65 |

Garment District | 32 W. 37th St. (bet. 5th & 6th Aves.) | 212-947-8940
W 40s | 269 W. 45th St., 2nd fl. (bet. B'way & 8th Ave.) | 212-997-9494 ◐
www.frankieandjohnnies.com

Expect "no surprises" from this "traditional" twosome, just "consistent" "high-quality beef" and "old-school" service from "tuxedoed waiters"; if the '20s-era "Broadway standby" near Times Square now seems "dated", its "clubby" Garment District offshoot is classier and "quieter."

Frankies Spuntino *Italian* | 24 | 19 | 21 | $38 |

LES | 17 Clinton St. (bet. Houston & Stanton Sts.) | 212-253-2303 ◐
Carroll Gardens | 457 Court St. (bet. 4th Pl. & Luquer St.) | Brooklyn | 718-403-0033 ⊜
www.frankiesspuntino.com

"Delectable" Italian small plates at "gentle prices" ensure this "cute" couple stays "crowded" to capacity; the Carroll Gardens original boasts a "pretty garden" while its just-"expanded" LES sibling now "accommodates more of the willing masses", but still the "waits" can be "painful."

Franny's *Pizza* | 24 | 16 | 20 | $38 |

Prospect Heights | 295 Flatbush Ave. (bet. Prospect Pl. & St. Marks Ave.) | Brooklyn | 718-230-0221 | www.frannysbrooklyn.com

"Always crowded", this small Prospect Heights "winner" is known mainly for "stellar" brick-oven pizzas crafted with "the freshest" "local and seasonal" ingredients, but don't overlook the "superior" starters and "sophisticated cocktails"; it's "a tad expensive", but the "artful" eats guarantee plenty of "action" and "noise."

Fratelli *Italian* | 21 | 17 | 21 | $38 |

Bronx | 2507 Eastchester Rd. (Mace Ave.) | 718-547-2489

"They aim to please" at this "friendly", "family-run" Bronx Italian, providing "plentiful" helpings of "solid" standards at an "affordable" price; the style's "simple" but "satisfying", so "if you find yourself" in the "neighborhood", "eat and enjoy."

Fraunces Tavern ⊠ *American* | 16 | 21 | 18 | $45 |

Financial District | 54 Pearl St. (Broad St.) | 212-968-1776 | www.frauncestavern.com

The "days of yore" endure at this Financial District "heirloom", the circa-1762 tavern where "Washington said farewell to his troops"; it's an "attraction" for "out-of-town guests" and "history buffs", despite "undistinguished" American fare that "should be better."

Fred's at Barneys NY *American/Italian* | 20 | 19 | 19 | $49 |

E 60s | Barneys NY | 660 Madison Ave., 9th fl. (60th St.) | 212-833-2200

Break from "the rigors of shopping" at this "chichi" Midtown "store canteen", where "fashionistas" toy with "dependable" Tuscan–New American fare that's as "expensive" as the "clothes downstairs"; while "mobbed" at lunch ("bring your Valium"), it's "a sleeper for dinner."

Freemans ◐ *American* | 21 | 23 | 17 | $47 |

LES | Freeman Alley (off Rivington St., bet. Bowery & Chrystie Sts.) | 212-420-0012 | www.freemansrestaurant.com

"Tucked at the end of an alley", this Lower East Side New American is "super-alluring" to "über-hip" types out to down "deluxe comfort food" in "high-end" "hunting lodge" digs decked with "wild game trophies"; its "too-cool-for-school" rep ensures "happening" vibes and "maddening waits."

French Roast ◗ *French* | 17 | 15 | 15 | $29 |

G Village | 78 W. 11th St. (bet. 5th & 6th Aves.) | 212-533-2233
W 80s | 2340 Broadway (85th St.) | 212-799-1533
www.frenchroastny.com

"Teeming" 24/7 "hangouts", these Greenwich Village–UWS "pseudo-French" cafes are "convenient" for "passable" "bistro"-style "basics" at a "decent price"; their "popularity" seems undiminished by "absentminded" service and "cramped", often "noisy" quarters.

Fresco by Scotto 🗷 *Italian* | 23 | 20 | 21 | $61 |

E 50s | 34 E. 52nd St. (bet. Madison & Park Aves.) | 212-935-3434
Fresco on the Go 🗷 *Italian*
E 50s | 40 E. 52nd St. (bet. Madison & Park Aves.) | 212-754-2700
Financial District | 114 Pearl St. (Hanover Sq.) | 212-635-5000
www.frescobyscotto.com

Being "welcomed like family" is a major appeal of this "pricey" Midtown Italian "oasis" that remains a "favorite" thanks to its "delicious" fare, "personal" service, "pretty room" and "attractive crowd" studded with "TV personalities"; those in a hurry hit the takeout branches.

Friend of a Farmer *American* | 18 | 17 | 17 | $32 |

Gramercy | 77 Irving Pl. (bet. 18th & 19th Sts.) | 212-477-2188 | www.friendofafarmernyc.com

Mimicking the "cozy" style of "a Vermont B&B", this "wholesome" "Gramercy mainstay" serves "well-prepared" American "home cookin'" at "reasonable prices" in an ever-so-"quaint" "country setting"; just beware of "slow" going and "endless lines" during weekend brunch.

Fuleen Seafood ◗ *Chinese/Seafood* | 23 | 7 | 15 | $29 |

Chinatown | 11 Division St. (Bowery) | 212-941-6888

Connoisseurs of "authentic" Hong Kong–style seafood lean on this Chinatown "dive" for "dazzling", "ultrafresh" fish at "affordable" rates; if the "language barrier" ("point to the menu photos") and "low-rent" surroundings detract, "top-notch" eating till 3 AM "makes it all worthwhile."

NEW Fulton *Seafood* | 22 | 18 | 21 | $63 |

E 70s | 205 E. 75th St. (bet. 2nd & 3rd Aves.) | 212-288-6600 | www.fultonnyc.com

Quick to "catch on" with the "affluent" Upper East Side set, this "sophisticated" new seafooder from the owners of Citarella is a "mature" milieu for "excellent" fin fare served by an "eager-to-please" crew; however, unlike its fish market namesake, there are "no wholesale prices here."

Fushimi *Japanese* | 24 | 23 | 20 | $45 |

Bay Ridge | 9316 Fourth Ave. (bet. 93rd & 94th Sts.) | Brooklyn | 718-833-7788
Staten Island | 2110 Richmond Rd. (Lincoln Ave.) | 718-980-5300
www.fushimi-us.com

Find "Manhattan-caliber" Japanese fare in the boroughs via this colorful Bay Ridge–SI twosome, which has the locals "hooked" on "lovingly prepared" sushi, "ultramodern" decor and "crazy" "nightlife"; it's "not cheap", but the "cheerful" scene is bound to "impress."

Gabriela's Mexican

FOOD	DECOR	SERVICE	COST
18	16	16	$35

W 90s | 688 Columbus Ave. (bet. 93rd & 94th Sts.) | 212-961-0574 | www.gabrielas.com

"Bright" and "bustling", this UWS "Mexican standby" "hits the spot" with "tasty" "staples" and "irresistible" margaritas in a "spacious" setting including a "pleasant" "front patio"; "service is lacking", but "fair prices" bring out families with *niños* in tow.

Gabriel's ☒ Italian

FOOD	DECOR	SERVICE	COST
22	18	22	$62

W 60s | 11 W. 60th St. (bet. B'way & Columbus Ave.) | 212-956-4600 | www.gabrielsbarandrest.com

"Convenience to Lincoln Center", "consistently fine" food and service, the chance to sit next to "broadcast types from nearby CNN and ABC" and the presence of "gracious" owner-host Gabriel Aiello cement this "pricey" Columbus Circle Tuscan's standing as a "NY institution"; go after 8 PM or for lunch so you won't have to "compete for attention."

Gahm Mi Oak ● Korean

FOOD	DECOR	SERVICE	COST
21	14	16	$22

Garment District | 43 W. 32nd St. (bet. B'way & 5th Ave.) | 212-695-4113

"A piping hot bowl" of "hearty" *sollongtang* beef soup "will cure most ailments" at this 24/7 Garment District Korean, "one of the most authentic" joints around for "traditional" specialties; given the "cheap" and "satisfying" chow, few fret over downscale decor.

Gallagher's Steak House ● Steak

FOOD	DECOR	SERVICE	COST
21	19	19	$67

W 50s | 228 W. 52nd St. (bet. B'way & 8th Ave.) | 212-245-5336 | www.gallaghersnysteakhouse.com

"Exactly what you'd expect" from an "old-time" Theater District cow palace, this circa-1927 "guys' place" recalls "the world of Damon Runyon" with its "gargantuan" steaks and "gruff" service; it may be looking "long in the tooth", but the prices are kept right up to date.

Gargiulo's Italian

FOOD	DECOR	SERVICE	COST
22	19	21	$46

Coney Island | 2911 W. 15th St. (bet. Mermaid & Surf Aves.) | Brooklyn | 718-266-4891 | www.gargiulos.com

"Time stands still" at this "cavernous" Coney Island "institution", a 1907-vintage "family favorite" for "homestyle" "Southern Italian classics" from a tux-clad staff "out of central casting"; before they "roll you out", see if "your number comes up" to "win the entire meal free."

☒ Gari Japanese

FOOD	DECOR	SERVICE	COST
27	15	21	$80

W 70s | 370 Columbus Ave. (bet. 77th & 78th Sts.) | 212-362-4816

☒ Sushi of Gari Japanese

E 70s | 402 E. 78th St. (bet. 1st & York Aves.) | 212-517-5340

☒ Sushi of Gari 46 Japanese

W 40s | 347 W. 46th St. (bet. 8th & 9th Aves.) | 212-957-0046 www.sushiofgari.com

Gari Sugio's "creative genius" has "sushiphiles" in "heaven" at his "top-tier" Japanese threesome, where the "exquisite", "super-fresh" preparations "tantalize" even in "spartan" surroundings; to really see "what the fuss is about", the "omakase blowout" is the sort of "outrageous" "splurge" that'll "change your life."

	FOOD	DECOR	SERVICE	COST

Gascogne *French*
21 19 20 $51

Chelsea | 158 Eighth Ave. (bet. 17th & 18th Sts.) | 212-675-6564 |
www.gascognenyc.com

"True to Gascony", this "very French" Chelsea bistro is a "longtime"
"best bet" for "moderately priced" "standards" served by "amiable"
sorts in an "intimate" space; throw in the "lovable garden out back"
and "it has all that you need" and more.

Gavroche *French*
18 16 19 $45

W Village | 212 W. 14th St. (bet. 7th & 8th Aves.) | 212-647-8553 |
www.gavroche-ny.com

Offering "French cooking for everyman", this "relaxed" West Villager
appeals to "neighborhood folks" with its "basic" but "enjoyable" bistro
fare and "warm" service; as the interior's somewhat "tired", the
"backyard garden" "oasis" is a "big plus."

Gazala Place *Mideastern*
23 8 17 $25

W 40s | 709 Ninth Ave. (bet. 48th & 49th Sts.) | 212-245-0709 |
www.gazalaplace.com

A "unique" purveyor of Mideastern Druse dishes, this Hell's Kitchen
"shoebox" is a "delight" for "expertly prepared" hummus, falafel and
pitas; despite a "cramped", "sparse" space, the low prices and BYO
policy make it a wallet "winner."

Geido *Japanese*
▽ 23 15 20 $32

Prospect Heights | 331 Flatbush Ave. (7th Ave.) | Brooklyn |
718-638-8866

"The neighborhood loves" this "welcoming" Prospect Heights
Japanese for its "consistent" "top-of-the-line sushi" and "efficient"
service; it's "affordable to boot", so the "funky, graffiti-decorated"
room is "justifiably" "jam-packed" at prime times.

Geisha 🆇 *Japanese*
22 21 19 $64

E 60s | 33 E. 61st St. (bet. Madison & Park Aves.) | 212-813-1113 |
www.geisharestaurant.com

"Sleek" and possibly "too chic", this UES Franco-Japanese strives to be
"as pleasing as its namesake", serving "nuanced" cuisine (including
"swanky sushi") to "beautiful people" who can easily cover the "expensive" tabs; it's "heavy on the scene" overall, but the "eye candy" is
especially on display in the "stylish bar."

Gemma ◗ *Italian*
19 21 19 $47

E Village | Bowery Hotel | 335 Bowery (bet. 2nd & 3rd Sts.) | 212-505-9100 |
www.theboweryhotel.com

Given its attachment to the "chic Bowery Hotel", this "little gem" is a
"surprisingly" "unpretentious" spot for "rustic" Italian fare in a
"warm", "candlelit" setting with an "old-world" feel; still, it's full of
"younger", "trendy" types who seem interested mostly in "seeing
and being seen."

General Greene *American*
▽ 20 19 20 $35

Fort Greene | 229 DeKalb Ave. (Clermont Ave.) | Brooklyn | 718-222-1510 |
www.thegeneralgreene.com

"Comfort food thrives" at this "funky" Fort Greene yearling, where the
"well-prepared", well-priced American menu focuses on "clever"

small plates with "fresh, local" leanings; a "helpful staff" oversees the "simple, attractive" space, and "excellent mixologists" abet the generally "lively" mood.

Gennaro ⊄ *Italian*

FOOD	DECOR	SERVICE	COST
24	14	18	$40

W 90s | 665 Amsterdam Ave. (bet. 92nd & 93rd Sts.) | 212-665-5348

"Loved by the locals", this plain UWS Italian is "packed every night" with enthusiasts "squeezing in" for "wonderful, down-to-earth" food at a "moderate" cost; just "beware" of "rushed service" and the "no-reservations/no-credit-cards" policy – and "expect to wait."

🆕 Get Fresh *Eclectic*

FOOD	DECOR	SERVICE	COST
-	-	-	M

Park Slope | 370 Fifth Ave. (bet. 5th & 6th Sts.) | Brooklyn | 718-360-8469 | www.getfreshnyc.com

Look for affordable Eclectic fare made from "quality" ingredients (some grown in the back garden) at this "sweet" Park Sloper; it's a market by day, but dim lights and atmospheric music disguise that fact at brunch and dinnertime – and there's also patio seating.

Ghenet *Ethiopian*

FOOD	DECOR	SERVICE	COST
▽ 20	16	17	$31

Park Slope | 348 Douglass St. (bet. 4th & 5th Aves.) | Brooklyn | 718-230-4476 | www.ghenet.com

"An adventure in eating" awaits at this Park Slope Ethiopian, which "stands out" with "savory" platters that patrons scoop up using "spongy" injera bread; "laid-back and atmospheric", it's an "unusual" but "satisfying experience."

Gigino Trattoria *Italian*

FOOD	DECOR	SERVICE	COST
21	20	19	$45

TriBeCa | 323 Greenwich St. (bet. Duane & Reade Sts.) | 212-431-1112 | www.gigino-trattoria.com

Gigino at Wagner Park *Italian*

Financial District | 20 Battery Pl. (West St.) | 212-528-2228 | www.gigino-wagnerpark.com

"Still going strong", this "inviting" TriBeCa "favorite" offers "delicious pizza" and other "solid" Italian basics in "comfortable" digs (the Greenwich Street original looks like a stage-set farmhouse); "take a non-NYer" to the Wagner Park offshoot, whose "terrific" terrace boasts a "majestic view of Lady Liberty" and the harbor.

🆉 Gilt 🅢🅜 *American*

FOOD	DECOR	SERVICE	COST
25	28	26	$116

E 50s | NY Palace Hotel | 455 Madison Ave. (bet. 50th & 51st Sts.) | 212-891-8100 | www.giltnewyork.com

To experience the height of 20th-century luxury, head for this "magnificent" Midtowner plying "impeccable", prix fixe–only New American fare within over-the-top "opulent" digs; factor in "amazing" wines and "fantastic" "formal" service, and you've got some of the "finest hotel dining in NY" – with price tags to match.

Giorgione *Italian*

FOOD	DECOR	SERVICE	COST
21	18	17	$55

SoHo | 307 Spring St. (bet. Greenwich & Hudson Sts.) | 212-352-2269 | www.giorgionenyc.com

Sited "off the beaten track" in West SoHo, this Italian "find" from Giorgio DeLuca (of Dean & DeLuca fame) "exceeds expectations" with "top-notch" pizza and pasta served by "amicable" staffers; it's favored by "hip" folks who tend to be "upbeat" but "noisy."

	FOOD	DECOR	SERVICE	COST

Giorgio's of Gramercy *American*   `21` `18` `22` `$47`

Flatiron | 27 E. 21st St. (bet. B'way & Park Ave. S.) | 212-477-0007 |
www.giorgiosofgramercy.com

It's "easy to miss", but this Flatiron "hideaway" is "a staple" in the
neighborhood for "well-executed", "well-priced" New American fare
and "gracious service" that makes everyone "feel like a regular"; followers "fall back on" its "quiet" consistency "again and again."

Giovanni Venticinque *Italian*   ▽ `22` `19` `21` `$60`

E 80s | 25 E. 83rd St. (bet. 5th & Madison Aves.) | 212-988-7300

"Convenient to the Met", this "soothing" UES Tuscan diverts museumgoers with "reliable" "old-world cuisine" in a "cozy", recently remodeled setting with a "touch of class"; well-to-do adults report it's "ready
to please" as long as you're ready to "open your wallet."

Gnocco Caffe ● *Italian*   `23` `17` `20` `$38`

E Village | 337 E. 10th St. (bet. Aves. A & B) | 212-677-1913 |
www.gnocco.com

"High marks for authenticity" go to this "cute little" East Village Italian,
a "no-attitude" source of "affordable" Emilian specialties like the
eponymous appetizer (a "must-try") and "amazing" pizza; the "convivial atmosphere" extends to a "charming garden out back."

Gobo *Vegan/Vegetarian*   `23` `18` `20` `$34`

E 80s | 1426 Third Ave. (81st St.) | 212-288-5099
G Village | 401 Sixth Ave. (bet. 8th St. & Waverly Pl.) | 212-255-3242
www.goborestaurant.com

"Who needs meat" when this Greenwich Village–Upper East Side
pair's "crave-worthy" vegan/vegetarian fare offers an "inspired" "surprise" ("don't fear seitan") at a "reasonable price"; with "very Zen"
setups where you just may "sit next to Tibetan monks", they're "the
place to convert carnivores."

Golden Unicorn *Chinese*   `20` `12` `14` `$27`

Chinatown | 18 E. Broadway, 2nd fl. (Catherine St.) | 212-941-0911 |
www.goldenunicornrestaurant.com

The carts "keep rolling on" at this "ginormous" Chinatown "dim sum
extravaganza", where you can sample a "large array" of "trustworthy"
morsels "on the cheap"; "chaotic" conditions and "haphazard" service
don't deter the "bustling crowds", so "be prepared to wait."

Gonzo *Italian/Pizza*   `21` `17` `18` `$44`

G Village | 140 W. 13th St. (bet. 6th & 7th Aves.) | 212-645-4606

A "pleasant surprise" for a "casual bite", this Village Italian specializes
in "crisp, satisfying pizza" with "imaginative toppings" and a signature
"grilled crust"; add a "personable" staff and "reasonable prices", and
it's a "true delight" – "except for the noise level."

good *American*   `21` `15` `17` `$37`

W Village | 89 Greenwich Ave. (bet. Bank & W. 12th Sts.) | 212-691-8080 |
www.goodrestaurantnyc.com

"Not bad" for a "neighborhood" joint, this West Village New American
"hits the spot" with "yummy" takes on "comfort food", "decent prices"
and service that's "fine if you aren't in a hurry"; the "knockout" brunch
is a "favorite" that attracts goodly "lines."

goodburger *Burgers*

	FOOD	DECOR	SERVICE	COST
	18	9	13	$14

E 40s | 800 Second Ave. (42nd St.) | 212-922-1700
E 50s | 636 Lexington Ave. (54th St.) | 212-838-6000
Flatiron | 870 Broadway (bet. 17th & 18th Sts.) | 212-529-9100
W 40s | 23 W. 45th St. (bet. 5th & 6th Aves.) | 212-354-0900
www.goodburgerny.com

"As the name says", this "back-to-basics" chainlet is a "no-brainer" for "honest", "properly cooked" burgers and "darn tasty" fries "on the go"; then again, it's no bargain for a "fast-food joint" – and "enough with the blaring music!"

Good Enough to Eat *American*

	FOOD	DECOR	SERVICE	COST
	21	15	17	$27

W 80s | 483 Amsterdam Ave. (bet. 83rd & 84th Sts.) | 212-496-0163 | www.goodenoughtoeat.com

The "wholesome" "home cookin'" at this "New Englandy" UWS American is "definitely good enough" for the "country-kitsch" fans "smooshed" into its "whimsical", "farmlike" digs; it's a "legend" for brunch, so expect "endless waits" and "bedlam" on weekends.

Good Fork Ⓜ *Eclectic*

	FOOD	DECOR	SERVICE	COST
	24	18	22	$43

Red Hook | 391 Van Brunt St. (bet. Coffey & Dikeman Sts.) | Brooklyn | 718-643-6636 | www.goodfork.com

An "original" in an "unlikely locale", this "outstanding", "thimble-size" Red Hook Eclectic offers some "inventive" Asian twists at "modest prices"; "personalized" service and "great cocktails" make it even more "worth the trek", but with the "secret out", "reservations are crucial."

Gordon Ramsay ⓈⓂ *French*

	FOOD	DECOR	SERVICE	COST
	24	24	24	$143

W 50s | London NYC Hotel | 151 W. 54th St. (bet. 6th & 7th Aves.) | 212-468-8888 | www.gordonramsay.com

"Screaming" "TV chef" Gordon Ramsay orchestrates a "class act from start to finish" at this prix fixe-only New French in Midtown's London NYC Hotel, where the cuisine's "fresh piquant flavors" are matched with "excellent wines", "elegant" "mirrored" atmosphere and "top-notch" service; however, there are those who believe "the hype outdoes" the actual experience – especially given the "sky-high" tabs.

Ⓩ Gotham Bar & Grill *American*

	FOOD	DECOR	SERVICE	COST
	27	25	26	$78

G Village | 12 E. 12th St. (bet. 5th Ave. & University Pl.) | 212-620-4020 | www.gothambarandgrill.com

Starting with the $25 prix fixe lunch "steal", this Village standby presided over by "masterful chef" Alfred Portale is always "a wonderful experience", from the "skyscraping" "haute" New American cuisine to the "breathtaking", "high-ceilinged" modern space and "unobtrusive-yet-attentive" service; sure, it's "pricey", but who'd expect the MoMA of modern American dining to come cheap – "holy great food, Batman!"

Gottino ❶ *Italian*

	FOOD	DECOR	SERVICE	COST
	21	20	19	$40

G Village | 52 Greenwich Ave. (bet. Charles & Perry Sts.) | 212-633-2590 | www.ilovegottino.com

Villagers are in their "comfort zone" at this "cozy and warm" enoteca, where a "hip" crowd lines the "white marble bar" noshing on "lovely"

Italian small plates paired with "excellent wines"; "tabs can add up quick", but for "quality and charm" it's worth getting to know.

	FOOD	DECOR	SERVICE	COST

Gradisca *Italian* ▽ 23 | 18 | 19 | $47

G Village | 126 W. 13th St. (bet. 6th Ave. & 7th Ave. S.) | 212-691-4886 | www.gradiscanyc.com

This "neighborly" little "haunt" "hidden" in the Village "deserves kudos" for "fresh"-made pasta and other "*buonissimo*" Italian fare delivered by a "sweet" staff; the "low lighting" and "friendly" feel are as comforting as the "reasonable prices."

Graffiti Ⓜ *Eclectic* ▽ 26 | 17 | 23 | $42

E Village | 224 E. 10th St. (bet. 1st & 2nd Aves.) | 212-677-0695 | www.graffitinyc.com

Pastry chef Jehangir Mehta's "minuscule" East Village Eclectic "will wow you" with "masterful", "Indian-inspired" small plates whose "unique and addictive combinations" "consistently surprise" at "not-bad" prices; the "shoebox" space and "communal table" are "half the fun", provided "you don't need privacy."

Ⓩ Gramercy Tavern *American* 28 | 26 | 27 | $112

Flatiron | 42 E. 20th St. (bet. B'way & Park Ave. S.) | 212-477-0777 | www.gramercytavern.com

High on the list of "NYC's gastronomic pleasures", Danny Meyer's Flatiron "crown jewel", voted the city's Most Popular, "shines" with chef Michael Anthony's "exquisite" New American cooking that "honors the ingredients", "upscale-rustic", New England tavern–inspired atmosphere and "flawless" "warm" service; for the full effect, eat in the "formal" prix fixe–only dining room, but a "more-casual", "less-expensive" meal can be had in the "buzzy", equally attractive front bar area.

Grand Sichuan *Chinese* 21 | 8 | 13 | $26

Chelsea | 229 Ninth Ave. (24th St.) | 212-620-5200 ☽
Chinatown | 125 Canal St. (Chrystie St.) | 212-625-9212 ⊕
E 50s | 1049 Second Ave. (bet. 55th & 56th Sts.) | 212-355-5855
E Village | 19-23 St. Marks Pl. (bet. 2nd & 3rd Aves.) | 212-529-4800
G Village | 15 Seventh Ave. S. (bet. Carmine & Leroy Sts.) | 212-645-0222
Murray Hill | 227 Lexington Ave. (bet. 33rd & 34th Sts.) | 212-679-9770
Rego Park | 98-108 Queens Blvd. (bet. 66th Rd. & 67th Ave.) | Queens | 718-268-8833
www.thegrandsichuan.com

The "four-alarm" heat will "light up your taste buds" at these "popular" Chinese purveyors of "satisfying Sichuan specialties" at "bargain" rates; if the "curt" service and "scruffy" decor don't quite "measure up", you can "get it delivered."

Ⓩ Gray's Papaya ☽⊕ *Hot Dogs* 20 | 4 | 13 | $6

Garment District | 539 Eighth Ave. (37th St.) | 212-904-1588
G Village | 402 Sixth Ave. (8th St.) | 212-260-3532
W 70s | 2090 Broadway (72nd St.) | 212-799-0243

"You haven't been to NY unless you've been" to one of these "stand-up counters" offering "recession-proof" meals of "snappy" dogs and "delish" fruit drinks at "a price anyone can afford"; the "unique experience" includes "rubbing elbows with the rich, poor" and possibly "people from other planets."

Great Jones Cafe ● *Cajun*

NoHo | 54 Great Jones St. (bet. Bowery & Lafayette St.) | 212-674-9304 | www.greatjones.com

Those "cravin' Cajun" hit this "very dressed-down" NoHo "standby" that's "dependable" for "Southern comfort classics" on the "cheap"; the "snug" space is easily "overrun", though, especially when "the whole neighborhood shows up" for the "dynamite brunch."

Great NY Noodle Town ●⇗ *Noodle Shop*

Chinatown | 28½ Bowery (Bayard St.) | 212-349-0923

Long a "no-frills" fixture, this "dirt-cheap" C-Towner remains a "favorite" for "salt-baked seafood" and "slurpalicious" noodle soups; the "gruff" staff and "bare-bones" digs can be "offputting", but those in-the-know "never tire of" those noodles.

Greenhouse Café *American*

Bay Ridge | 7717 Third Ave. (bet. 77th & 78th Sts.) | Brooklyn | 718-833-8200 | www.greenhousecafe.com

Its "many regulars" "count on" this "Bay Ridge staple" for standout New American standards in a "pleasant" space with a "glassed-in" rear greenhouse room; maybe it's "nothing new", but "you'll get your money's worth."

Greenwich Grill/
Sushi Azabu *Japanese/Mediterranean*

TriBeCa | 428 Greenwich St. (bet. Laight & Vestry Sts.) | 212-274-0428 | www.greenwichgrill.com

"Fusion that really works" sums up the "Japanese-infused" Med menu at this "tasteful" TriBeCan's ground-floor eatery, while its "sexy" basement sushi bar slices "silken" fish "flown in daily from Japan"; despite its "impeccable" hospitality and "not unreasonable" cost, somehow it remains "undiscovered."

Grifone ⊠ *Italian*

E 40s | 244 E. 46th St. (bet. 2nd & 3rd Aves.) | 212-490-7275 | www.grifonenyc.com

"Professional in all respects", this "quiet", "old-line" Northern Italian in the U.N. vicinity maintains "consistent quality" with its "superb" cuisine and service; however, some suggest "it's time" to bring the "'80s" decor in line with the "expense-account" prices.

Grimaldi's ⇗ *Pizza*

Dumbo | 19 Old Fulton St. (bet. Front & Water Sts.) | Brooklyn | 718-858-4300
NEW Douglaston | Douglaston Plaza | 242-02 61st Ave. (bet. Douglaston Pkwy. & 244th St.) | Queens | 718-819-2133 www.grimaldis.com

For "perfect", "blackened" thin-crust pizzas with the "freshest possible" toppings, it's hard to beat this "cash-only", "no-frills" Dumbo "classic" tucked "under the Brooklyn Bridge"; "believe the hype": the pies "really are that good" – and the weekend lines "really are that punishing"; N.B. Queens dwellers now have their own outlet in Douglaston.

	FOOD	DECOR	SERVICE	COST

☑ Grocery, The 🖼️Ⓜ️ *American*   `27` `17` `25` `$60`
Carroll Gardens | 288 Smith St. (bet. Sackett & Union Sts.) | Brooklyn |
718-596-3335 | www.thegroceryrestaurant.com
Carroll Gardens' "tiny Smith Street wonder" produces "impeccable"
"seasonal" New American cuisine that competes with Manhattan's
big-leaguers thanks to its "passionately engaged" husband-and-wife
owners; "friendly", "personal" service and a "magical backyard" temper complaints about an interior the size of "your living room."

Gruppo *Pizza*   `∇ 25` `15` `21` `$22`
E Village | 186 Ave. B (bet. 11th & 12th Sts.) | 212-995-2100 |
www.gruppothincrust.com
"Truly magic" for "thin-crust lovers", this "competent" East Village
cubbyhole loads its "quintessential" crisp pizza with "flavorful sauce",
"fresh mozz" and "high-end toppings"; given its "upbeat" attitude, the
"simple digs" are easily excused.

NEW Gus & Gabriel 🏷️ *American*   `-` `-` `-` `I`
W 70s | 222 W. 79th St. (bet. Amsterdam Ave. & B'way) | 212-362-7470 |
www.gusandgabriel.com
Chef Michael Psilakis has moved his successful UWS Greek taverna to
bigger digs, replacing it with this budget-friendly New American; the
tiny quarters have been done up with a vaguely nautical theme, and
the food tends toward rib-sticking comfort dishes.

Gus' Place 🅞 *Greek/Mediterranean*   `21` `14` `21` `$39`
G Village | 192 Bleecker St. (bet. MacDougal St. & 6th Ave.) | 212-777-1660 |
www.gusplacenyc.com
With "awesome homestyle" cooking and an "incredibly warm staff"
led by the eponymous owner himself, this Village Greek-Med "exudes
charm"; the "teeny" quarters are "a bit cramped", but local loyalists
consider it a gustatory "treat" where "the price is right."

Gusto 🅞 *Italian*   `21` `19` `20` `$55`
G Village | 60 Greenwich Ave. (Perry St.) | 212-924-8000 |
www.gustonyc.com
"Still going strong" after yet another "chef change", this "snazzy",
"never-boring" Villager delivers "refined" Italian fare via a "smiling"
staffe; regulars report it's "a little pricey", with the name reflected in
the "energy" and "decibel level."

Gyu-Kaku *Japanese*   `22` `19` `19` `$46`
E 40s | 805 Third Ave., 2nd fl. (50th St.) | 212-702-8816
E Village | 34 Cooper Sq. (bet. Astor Pl. & 4th St.) | 212-475-2989
www.gyu-kaku.com
"DIY BBQ" is the deal at these "festive" Japanese franchises, where
"helpful" staffers supply "high-quality" "raw materials" to "cook at
your own table" on "little hibachi grills"; the "trendy settings" are
"quite popular" in spite of tabs that have a way of adding up.

NEW Haakon's Hall 🅞 *American*   `-` `-` `-` `M`
W 100s | 1187 Amsterdam Ave. (bet. 118th & 119th Sts.) | 212-300-4166 |
www.haakonshallny.com
Named for the chef's son as well as a historic hall in Norway, this
Morningside Heights newcomer offers American childhood comforts

like PB&J, alphabet soup and 'TV dinners', tweaked for grown-up tastes; a publike vibe and easygoing prices make it a *velkom* arrival.

Hale & Hearty Soups *Sandwiches/Soup* | 19 | 7 | 13 | $12 |

Chelsea | Chelsea Mkt. | 75 Ninth Ave. (bet. 15th & 16th Sts.) | 212-255-2400

E 40s | 685 Third Ave. (43rd St.) | 212-681-6460 🗷

E 40s | Grand Central | lower level (42nd St. & Vanderbilt Ave.) | 212-983-2845

E 60s | 849 Lexington Ave. (bet. 64th & 65th Sts.) | 212-517-7600

Financial District | 55 Broad St. (Beaver St.) | 212-509-4100 🗷

Garment District | 462 Seventh Ave. (35th St.) | 212-971-0605 🗷

W 40s | 30 Rockefeller Plaza (49th St.) | 212-265-2117 🗷

W 40s | 49 W. 42nd St. (bet. 5th & 6th Aves.) | 212-575-9090 🗷

W 50s | 55 W. 56th St. (bet. 5th & 6th Aves.) | 212-245-9200 🗷

Brooklyn Heights | 32 Court St. (Remsen St.) | Brooklyn | 718-596-5600 🗷

www.haleandhearty.com

Additional locations throughout the NY area

"Variety" is the watchword at this "cafeteria-style" soup 'n' sandwich chain that's an "eat-and-run" staple in many a "lunchtime rotation"; despite "overcrowding", often "nowhere to sit" and "abrupt service", most find them a viable stop for "quick nutrition."

Hallo Berlin *German* | 19 | 9 | 12 | $21 |

W 40s | 626 10th Ave. (bet. 44th & 45th Sts.) | 212-977-1944 | www.halloberlinrestaurant.com

You "could do worse" "for a wurst" than the "simple", "affordable" German grub at this "basic" Hell's Kitchen "beer hall"; "massive" brews "from the fatherland" help patrons "forget the grumpy service" and "thrown-together" low-budget backdrop.

Hampton Chutney Co. *Indian* | 21 | 10 | 14 | $16 |

SoHo | 68 Prince St. (bet. Crosby & Lafayette Sts.) | 212-226-9996

W 80s | 464 Amsterdam Ave. (bet. 82nd & 83rd Sts.) | 212-362-5050

www.hamptonchutney.com

Crafting "wondrous dosas" with fusion "twists", these Indian "quick-bite" outlets offer an "addictive" "change of pace" whether in the "casual" SoHo original or the UWS "stroller central"; the food improves "body and soul", while the prices do likewise for the "budget."

NEW Hanci Turkish Cuisine *Turkish* | ▽ 24 | 16 | 21 | $32 |

W 50s | 854 10th Ave. (bet. 56th & 57th Sts.) | 212-707-8144 | www.hancituirkishnyc.com

A handy "neighborhood newcomer" in the West Midtown "boonies", this "friendly" "little" Turk supplies "top-notch" takes on meze and other "quality" faves; maybe the storefront space is "not much to look at", but at least the BYO policy helps keep tabs in line.

Hanco's ⊘ *Vietnamese* | ▽ 22 | 6 | 14 | $11 |

Boerum Hill | 85 Bergen St. (bet. Hoyt & Smith Sts.) | Brooklyn | 718-858-6818

NEW Park Slope | 350 Seventh Ave. (10th St.) | Brooklyn | 718-499-8081

If you're hanco-ring for "classic" *banh mi* sandwiches, this Boerum Hill Vietnamese nook and its new, "larger" Park Slope sibling distinguish themselves with a "cheap", "toothsome" lineup plus "great bubble teas"; as the decor "leaves everything to be desired", many "get it to go."

	FOOD	DECOR	SERVICE	COST

Ⓩ HanGawi *Korean* — 26 | 24 | 23 | $47

Murray Hill | 12 E. 32nd St. (bet. 5th & Madison Aves.) | 212-213-0077 | www.hangawirestaurant.com

At this Murray Hill Korean "retreat", you'll experience "bliss" with "amazing vegetarian" fare and "exquisite" service in a "Zen-like" "temple setting"; most diners are "serene" about the slightly "upmarket" cost given all the good things they get "for the money."

NEW Harbour Ⓢ *Seafood* — ▽ 21 | 26 | 24 | $62

SoHo | 290 Hudson St. (bet. Dominick & Spring Sts.) | 212-989-6410 | www.harbournyc.com

Deep-sea dining sails into way West SoHo via this "friendly" newcomer with a "beautiful" yachtlike design; the menu focuses on sustainable seafood and "wine bargains" (the list offers 20 bottles under $25), so the somewhat remote locale is the only sticking point.

Harrison, The *American* — 24 | 21 | 23 | $63

TriBeCa | 355 Greenwich St. (Harrison St.) | 212-274-9310 | www.theharrison.com

"Would that there were more gems in NYC like" this "perennial favorite", where Amanda Freitag's "exceptional" Med-inspired New American cooking comes in "elegant but relaxed", "Hamptons-in-TriBeCa" digs; "genuinely welcoming service" ices the cake for its "lively, hip crowd."

Harry Cipriani ◐ *Italian* — 21 | 21 | 21 | $96

E 50s | Sherry Netherland Hotel | 781 Fifth Ave. (bet. 59th & 60th Sts.) | 212-753-5566 | www.cipriani.com

The see-and-be-seen crowd "is what it's about" at this "clublike" Venetian in Midtown's Sherry Netherland, where the "patrician class" gathers to "dine and dish" over "not-bad" food and the "best Bellinis"; it has major "high-end" appeal, though many maintain the "pretentiousness" and "exorbitant" tabs are just "too much."

Harry's Cafe ◐Ⓢ *Eclectic* — 24 | 22 | 22 | $54

Financial District | 1 Hanover Sq. (bet. Pearl & Stone Sts.) | 212-785-9200

Harry's Steak Ⓢ *Steak*

Financial District | 97 Pearl St. (bet. Broad St. & Hanover Sq.) | 212-785-9200 www.harrysnyc.com

"Masters and mistresses of the universe" consider this duo in the Financial District's historic India House a Wall Street "landmark" that's worth the splurge; the underground meatery furnishes "sophisticated" steaks while the upstairs cafe is "the place to be" for Eclectic eats and a "bustling" bar – both have access to one of "NYC's best" wine cellars.

NEW Harry's Italian ◐ *Italian* — - | - | - | M

Financial District | 2 Gold St. (bet. Maiden Ln. & Platt St.) | 212-747-0797

Don't ask for a slice – they only serve whole pies, plus pastas and other Italian classics, at this Financial District arrival from the Harry's folks; the outdoor area is anchored by a giant Gustavo Bonevardi sculpture, while inside there's lots of communal seating, plus a bar with its own late-night menu.

Haru *Japanese* — 20 | 17 | 18 | $41

E 40s | 280 Park Ave. (enter on 48th St., bet. Madison & Park Aves.) | 212-490-9680

(continued)

Haru

E 70s | 1327 Third Ave. (76th St.) | 212-452-1028 ◑
E 70s | 1329 Third Ave. (76th St.) | 212-452-2230 ◑
Financial District | 1 Wall Street Ct. (bet. Beaver & Pearl Sts.) | 212-785-6850
Flatiron | 220 Park Ave. S. (18th St.) | 646-428-0989 ◑
W 40s | 205 W. 43rd St. (bet. B'way & 8th Ave.) | 212-398-9810 ◑
W 80s | 433 Amsterdam Ave. (bet. 80th & 81st Sts.) | 212-579-5655 ◑
www.harusushi.com

This "big-fish" Japanese chain is a "winning" "go-to" for "generous" cuts of "consistently fresh" sushi served "without much pretension" in "postmodern" digs; the "solid value" keeps them "super-busy", so count on "in-and-out" pacing and "high decibels."

Hasaki ◑ *Japanese*   24 | 15 | 19 | $48

E Village | 210 E. Ninth St. (bet. 2nd & 3rd Aves.) | 212-473-3327 | www.hasakinyc.com

For "superior sushi" and "excellent" cooked dishes "at a reasonable price", this "long-standing" East Village Japanese remains "a cut above" the "local" competition; predictably, the "cramped space" and no-reservations policy lead to "waits at peak times."

Hatsuhana ◙ *Japanese*   25 | 17 | 21 | $57

E 40s | 17 E. 48th St. (bet. 5th & Madison Aves.) | 212-355-3345
E 40s | 237 Park Ave. (46th St.) | 212-661-3400
www.hatsuhana.com

"Where it all started" for sushi in Midtown, this "old-guard" Japanese twosome still sates the "suits" with "pristine" fish and "well-seasoned" service "without a lot of fanfare"; but while the eating's "consistently" "first-class", the surroundings "feel a bit tired" given the prices.

◪ Havana Alma de Cuba *Cuban*   23 | 18 | 21 | $38

W Village | 94 Christopher St. (bet. Bedford & Bleecker Sts.) | 212-242-3800 | www.havananyc.com

"You won't want to go home" once this "bopping" Village Cuban brings on its "outstanding", "fairly priced" food and "upbeat" atmospherics; it can be a "jammed" "party" fueled by sangria and Latin bands, but the patio is "great for avoiding the noise."

Havana Central *Cuban*   17 | 16 | 16 | $32

Union Sq | 22 E. 17th St. (bet. B'way & 5th Ave.) | 212-414-4999
W 40s | 151 W. 46th St. (bet. 6th & 7th Aves.) | 212-398-7440
W 100s | 2911 Broadway (bet. 113th & 114th Sts.) | 212-662-8830
www.havanacentral.com

"The masses" mambo into these "high-volume" "tropical" triplets to enjoy "heaping portions" of "decent" Cuban eats, "fab drinks" and "festive" vibes at a "moderate" cost; however, the "noise level can be a distraction" and the servers are said to "run on Havana time."

Haveli ◑ *Indian*   22 | 17 | 20 | $34

E Village | 100 Second Ave. (bet. 5th & 6th Sts.) | 212-982-0533

A "real standout" among its Curry Row rivals, this East Village Indian vet "steadily" "satisfies" via "flavorful" dishes served "with a smile" in a "relaxing" setting ("no sitars, but that's ok"); it "costs a bit more" than the neighbors, but the "high quality" is "worth it."

	FOOD	DECOR	SERVICE	COST

Hearth *American/Italian*
25 | 20 | 23 | $64

E Village | 403 E. 12th St. (1st Ave.) | 646-602-1300 |
www.restauranthearth.com

Something "civilized" in the East Village, this "culinary delight" from
the "inventive" Marco Canora kindles admiration with "marvelous"
Tuscan-American cuisine served by a "spot-on" staff in rustically
"stylish" digs sporting a few "front-row seats" overlooking the kitchen;
naturally, this "class" act commands "high prices for the area."

Heartland Brewery *Pub Food*
14 | 14 | 15 | $29

Garment District | Empire State Bldg. | 350 Fifth Ave. (34th St.) |
212-563-3433
Seaport | 93 South St. (Fulton St.) | 646-572-2337
Union Sq | 35 Union Sq. W. (bet. 16th & 17th Sts.) | 212-645-3400
W 40s | 127 W. 43rd St. (bet. B'way & 6th Ave.) | 646-366-0235
W 50s | 1285 Sixth Ave. (51st St.) | 212-582-8244
www.heartlandbrewery.com

"Elegant it ain't", but this chain of "brash" brew barns "has you covered" for "adequate pub fare" and suds on tap "to wash it down"; less
heartening are the "formulaic" feel and hordes of "thirsty tourists";
N.B. the Theater District branch recently opened a next-door patty
place called HB Burger.

Heidelberg *German*
18 | 16 | 16 | $37

E 80s | 1648 Second Ave. (bet. 85th & 86th Sts.) | 212-628-2332

"Old-school" sorts say *danke schön* to this Yorkville standby for
"keeping alive" the brauhaus tradition with "waiters in lederhosen"
delivering "hearty" German fare and "huge steins of beer" amid *echt*
"Teutonic decor"; while "unapologetically" "kitschy", the Bavarian
oompah "merriment" is also "quite a hoot."

Hell's Kitchen *Mexican*
23 | 16 | 19 | $43

W 40s | 679 Ninth Ave. (bet. 46th & 47th Sts.) | 212-977-1588 |
www.hellskitchen-nyc.com

"Seems more like heaven" gush fans of this "lively" Clinton Nuevo
Mexicano, citing the "bold", "modern", "fairly priced" cuisine and
"killer" cocktails; it's "accommodating" and "well located for theatergoers", but as it gets "crowded", "come early."

Henry's End *American*
24 | 15 | 23 | $47

Brooklyn Heights | 44 Henry St. (bet. Cranberry & Middagh Sts.) |
Brooklyn | 718-834-1776 | www.henrysend.com

"Year after year", this "personable" Brooklyn Heights New American
endears "meat eaters" with "succulent" "exotic game" paired with "all-
American wines"; if the "tight" space has all "the intimacy of a phone
booth", "simpatico" service and "reasonable prices" fully compensate.

Hibino 🏛 *Japanese*
▽ 25 | 19 | 23 | $36

Cobble Hill | 333 Henry St. (Pacific St.) | Brooklyn | 718-260-8052 |
www.hibino-brooklyn.com

A "must-try" for its Kyoto-style "daily *obanzai*" (small plate) lineup,
this "super-cute" Cobble Hill Japanese also "keeps things exciting"
with "superior sushi" and "fresh, warm" "homemade tofu"; "gracious"
staffers tend the "minimalist" space, and "considering the high quality", the price is "excellent."

| | FOOD | DECOR | SERVICE | COST |

Hill Country *BBQ* — 21 | 16 | 14 | $33

Flatiron | 30 W. 26th St. (bet. B'way & 6th Ave.) | 212-255-4544 | www.hillcountryny.com

"Meat lovers" let out a "big yee-haw" for this "stompin'" Flatiron BBQ "barn", a "Texas roadhouse" "replica" where "lip-smacking" 'cue is ordered "by weight" over the counter and comes "wrapped in butcher paper"; critics beef about the "oddball" "self-serve" system, but food-wise it's the "real deal" – with Hill Country pricing to boot.

HK ◑ *American* — 17 | 18 | 17 | $34

Garment District | 523 Ninth Ave. (39th St.) | 212-947-4208 | www.hkhellskitchen.com

"Much needed" in the humdrum "Port Authority vicinity", this "cool" American "delivers" with its "decent", "all-purpose" menu and "sleek", "modern" looks; "spotty" service notwithstanding, it's an "affordable" local "anchor" with an especially "lively brunch scene."

Holy Basil ◑ *Thai* — 21 | 18 | 17 | $31

E Village | 149 Second Ave., 2nd fl. (bet. 9th & 10th Sts.) | 212-460-5557 | www.holybasilrestaurant.com

This "welcoming" East Village Thai is a "real rarity" serving up "crave-worthy" "classics" at prices "that won't upset" your budget; moreover, the "dim lighting" and "intimate" "second-floor" setting lend it "lots of character" for a "casual date."

Home *American* — 21 | 17 | 19 | $43

G Village | 20 Cornelia St. (bet. Bleecker & W. 4th Sts.) | 212-243-9579 | www.homerestaurantnyc.com

"True to its name", this "teeny" Village American is a "sweet" spot for "delightful" "home cooking" reflecting a "fresh, local" "twist" (insiders tout the "amazing brunch"); if the "squeezed" space requires "patience", the "pocket back garden" is a "pleasant alternative."

NEW Hotel Griffou ◑ *American* — ∇ 20 | 24 | 21 | $63

G Village | 21 W. Ninth St. (bet. 5th & 6th Aves.) | 212-358-0228

Formerly the notorious Marylou's, this "clubby" subterranean Villager is now a hipper-than-thou eatery from a team with links to Freemans, La Esquina and the Waverly Inn; expect retro-tinged New Americana served in a "stunning" setting comprising five "themed" rooms, but "start dialing" now – reservations are hard to come by for mere mortals.

House, The ◑ *Mediterranean* — 22 | 24 | 21 | $54

Gramercy | 121 E. 17th St. (bet. Irving Pl. & Park Ave. S.) | 212-353-2121 | www.thehousenyc.com

Take "that special someone" to this "elegant" "little" Gramercy "hide-away" lodged in a "quaint" 1854-vintage carriage house, where "warm" staffers present a Med menu starring "tasty" "tapas-style" plates; it's a "pricey" "treat", but the "cozy" vibe makes you "feel right at home."

Houston's *American* — 20 | 18 | 19 | $40
(aka Hillstone)

E 50s | Citigroup Ctr. | 153 E. 53rd St. (enter at 3rd Ave. & 54th St.) | 212-888-3828

(continued)

| | FOOD | DECOR | SERVICE | COST |

(continued)

Houston's

Murray Hill | NY Life Bldg. | 378 Park Ave. S. (27th St.) | 212-689-1090 | www.hillstone.com

So "enjoyable" "you forget it's a chain", these "comfy", "midpriced" Americans "have a great formula going" with their "flavorful" "staples" ("two words: spinach dip") and "lively" "boy-meets-girl" bars; they "pack 'em in", though, so "wait times can be ludicrous."

Hudson Cafeteria *American/Eclectic* `19` `22` `18` `$51`

W 50s | Hudson Hotel | 356 W. 58th St. (bet. 8th & 9th Aves.) | 212-554-6000 | www.morganshotelgroup.com

"It feels hip just to walk in" to this Hudson Hotel American-Eclectic, where the "dark", "dramatic", "high-ceilinged" space provides a "medieval" backdrop (à la "Harry Potter's dining hall") for the food's "modern flair"; it's "pricey" but "impressive", and come summer the terrace is a "green sanctuary."

Hudson River Café ❷ *American/Seafood* `19` `21` `18` `$52`

Harlem | 697 W. 133rd St. (12th Ave.) | 212-491-9111 | www.hudsonrivercafe.com

An "ambitious" "trailblazer" in "up-and-coming" West Harlem, this "inviting" New American focuses on "solid" (if "pricey") seafood in bi-level digs with ample "outdoor real estate" that "steals the show"; "service fluctuates", but the jazz-inflected "groove" comes as a "nice surprise."

Hummus Place ❷ *Israeli/Vegetarian* `23` `10` `16` `$16`

E Village | 109 St. Marks Pl. (bet. Ave. A & 1st Ave.) | 212-529-9198
G Village | 71 Seventh Ave. S. (bet. Barrow & Bleecker Sts.) | 212-924-2022
G Village | 99 MacDougal St. (bet. Bleecker & W. 3rd Sts.) | 212-533-3089
W 70s | 305 Amsterdam Ave. (bet. 74th & 75th Sts.) | 212-799-3335
NEW W 90s | 2608 Broadway (bet. 98th & 99th Sts.) | 212-222-5462
www.hummusplace.com

"Heavenly" "homemade hummus" makes this "one-trick-pony" chainlet "addicting" for "quick and easy" Israeli eats at a cost that's "too good to believe"; sure, the service and decor are "less than stellar", but "legions of followers" keep them humming nonetheless.

Hundred Acres ❷ *American* `19` `19` `20` `$48`

SoHo | 38 MacDougal St. (Prince St.) | 212-475-7500 | www.hundredacresnyc.com

The "low-pressure" "younger sibling of Five Points and Cookshop", this SoHo New American concocts "enticing", "farm-fresh" "comfort food" in a "homey" setting with an "atrium room" in back; however, though it's "upbeat" and "fair-priced", critics cite "just-ok" eats and high "noise levels."

Ici Ⓜ *American/French* `21` `19` `20` `$40`

Fort Greene | 246 DeKalb Ave. (bet. Clermont & Vanderbilt Aves.) | Brooklyn | 718-789-2778 | www.icirestaurant.com

To discover "the benefits of eating local" try this "pioneer" Fort Greene Franco-American's "well-prepared" "greenmarket" menu; the "welcoming staff", "neighborhoody" setting with an "inviting" patio and "affordable" tabs make it a "relaxing" "change of pace."

	FOOD	DECOR	SERVICE	COST

I Coppi *Italian*
23 | 22 | 22 | $47

E Village | 432 E. Ninth St. (bet. Ave. A & 1st Ave.) | 212-254-2263 | www.icoppinyc.com

You'll "forget the bustle of the city" ensconced in the "enchanting" "all-year" garden at this "cozy" East Village "old-style refuge" for "excellent" Tuscan cooking and regional wines; the "warm" service and "low-key" ambiance help explain why surveyors call it a "diamond in the rough."

Ideya *Caribbean*
▽ 21 | 16 | 19 | $36

SoHo | 349 W. Broadway (bet. Broome & Grand Sts.) | 212-625-1441 | www.ideya.net

This "laid-back" SoHo Caribbean "hits the spot" with "surprisingly good" grub served "with no fanfare" in "funky" surroundings; however, revelers report the "food takes a back seat" to the "mind-blowing" mojitos and "lively" atmosphere.

Il Bagatto ●Ⓜ *Italian*
24 | 17 | 18 | $40

E Village | 192 E. Second St. (bet. Aves. A & B) | 212-228-0977 | www.ilbagattonyc.com

"Big crowds" find "satisfaction" at this "homey" East Village trattoria thanks to its "fab" "fresh pastas" and other "Italian classics" at "modest prices"; service is "hit-or-miss" and the "cramped" quarters are "not that comfy", but "be prepared to wait" anyway.

Il Bambino *Italian*
▽ 25 | 17 | 22 | $18

Astoria | 34-08 31st Ave. (bet. 34th & 35th Sts.) | Queens | 718-626-0087 | www.ilbambinonyc.com

This "tiny" Astoria "panini paradise" is a "star of the neighborhood" thanks to its "awesome" pressed sandwiches and other "recession-proof" Italian bites; the "warm and cozy" cafe setting features a recently added back patio and "very friendly service."

Il Bastardo ● *Italian/Steak*
19 | 18 | 18 | $42

Chelsea | 191 Seventh Ave. (bet. 21st & 22nd Sts.) | 212-675-5980 | www.ilbastardonyc.com

"Unassuming" but hardly illegitimate, this Chelsea Tuscan steakhouse is a "reliable" "standby" that serves "uncomplicated" but "well-executed" meals "without breaking the bank"; its "dark", "comfortable" atmosphere extends to a next-door enoteca, Bar Baresco.

🄩 Il Buco ● *Italian/Mediterranean*
24 | 23 | 22 | $61

NoHo | 47 Bond St. (bet. Bowery & Lafayette St.) | 212-533-1932 | www.ilbuco.com

A "buzzy NYC" crowd collects at this NoHo "destination" for "exceptional" "rustic" Med-Italian fare "emphasizing local suppliers"; its "cool" "antiques-filled" "farmhouse" space boasts seriously *romantico* atmosphere (especially the "amazing wine cellar"), while "knowledgeable" service makes "pricey" tabs easy to stomach.

Il Cantinori *Italian*
23 | 21 | 23 | $63

G Village | 32 E. 10th St. (bet. B'way & University Pl.) | 212-673-6044 | www.ilcantinori.com

"Everything clicks" at this "long-running" Village Northern Italian, from the "terrific" "traditional" fare to the "pro service" and "elegant setting" garnished with "lovely" flowers; it's "pricey", but for "that special occasion" it's a "classic" that "will never go out of style."

Il Corallo Trattoria *Italian* 21 | 12 | 17 | $27

SoHo | 176 Prince St. (bet. Sullivan & Thompson Sts.) | 212-941-7119
If you're "low on cash" and "don't mind rubbing elbows", this "quaint little" SoHo Italian slings a "massive menu" of "hearty" pastas at "unbeatable" prices; otherwise it's "nothing special", but the return clientele and no-reservations rule keep it "crowded."

Il Cortile *Italian* 23 | 20 | 21 | $54

Little Italy | 125 Mulberry St. (bet. Canal & Hester Sts.) | 212-226-6060 | www.ilcortile.com
"Indulge yourself" with *abbondanza* at this Little Italy "mainstay" renowned for its "excellent" Italian fare and "courtly" service in an appealingly airy venue featuring a "wonderful atrium"; though "a bit costly", its "honest" cooking "will fill you up", so "what's not to love?"

Il Gattopardo ● *Italian* 24 | 19 | 24 | $62

W 50s | 33 W. 54th St. (bet. 5th & 6th Aves.) | 212-246-0412 | www.ilgattopardonyc.com
An "unsung" haven of "adult" dining right around the corner from MoMA, this "soothing" Midtowner radiates "sophistication" with its "first-class" Neapolitan fare and "courteous service"; partialists insist the "ungimmicky" flair is "well worth" the "platinum-card" pricing.

⚡ Il Giglio 🅢 *Italian* 26 | 20 | 25 | $76

TriBeCa | 81 Warren St. (bet. Greenwich St. & W. B'way) | 212-571-5555 | www.ilgigliorestaurant.com
Both "quality and quantity" are a "sure bet" at this "exceptional" TriBeCa Tuscan, which "always satisfies" as "black-tie" servers dish out "free tidbits" that give way to "fabulous old-world" cuisine; no surprise, the "VIP" treatment costs "big bucks."

ilili *Lebanese* 24 | 23 | 20 | $53

Chelsea | 236 Fifth Ave. (bet. 27th & 28th Sts.) | 212-683-2929 | www.ililinyc.com
"Traditional dishes" get a "modern" "kick" at this "high-end" Chelsea Lebanese specializing in "marvelous" small plates served "with panache"; a "striking", "huge" wood-paneled space with a "trendy music track" adds to the "convivial" feel, but it's "easy to run up a big bill."

⚡ Il Mulino 🅢 *Italian* 27 | 19 | 24 | $87

G Village | 86 W. Third St. (bet. Sullivan & Thompson Sts.) | 212-673-3783 | www.ilmulino.com
"Keep hitting the redial key" and "if you're lucky", you'll ultimately be "rewarded" with a reservation at what many consider the "il ultimo" when it comes to "classic Southern Italian" food; sure, it's "crowded and noisy", but that's because this Village standby "never misses"; P.S. "bring your appetite and someone else's credit card" – or go for the more accessible lunch, unless the presidents are there.

Il Palazzo *Italian* ∇ 23 | 19 | 22 | $44

Little Italy | 151 Mulberry St. (bet. Grand & Hester Sts.) | 212-343-7000
"One of the better Little Italy" options, this Italian "staple" is "dependable yet not too pricey" for a fix of "solid", seafood-centric cooking

served by an "attentive" team; regulars reveal that, seatingwise, the "indoor garden" "is the way to go."

Il Passatore ⌷ *Italian*

▽ 24 | 18 | 23 | $32

Williamsburg | 14 Bushwick Ave. (bet. Devoe St. & Metropolitan Ave.) | Brooklyn | 718-963-3100 | www.ilpassatorebrooklyn.com

"Tucked away" in East Williamsburg, this "low-profile" Italian nook is "definitely worth finding" to sample "melt-in-your-mouth" "homestyle" dishes from Emilia-Romagna at a "tremendous" "value"; a "casual", "cash-only" setup, it passes muster with "many a young and hip" local.

Il Postino ● *Italian*

23 | 18 | 20 | $70

E 40s | 337 E. 49th St. (bet. 1st & 2nd Aves.) | 212-688-0033 | www.ilpostinorestaurant.com

The "entertaining" waiters "announce so many specials" you'll need a "memory chip" at this "dependable", tranquil U.N.-area Italian choice for "*delizioso*" "old-school" dining; just beware that beyond "the spiel", the bill can "easily be astronomical."

NEW Il Punto *Italian*

▽ 20 | 18 | 22 | $50

Garment District | 507 Ninth Ave. (38th St.) | 212-244-0088 | www.ilpuntony.com

If you liked the old Osteria Gelsi, the brightly lit Garment District Italian tucked behind Port Authority, you'll like its new incarnation; though there's a different chef, just about everything else is the same, from the subdued vibe, white linen–topped tables and oak bar to the midpriced Puglian specialties.

Il Riccio ● *Italian*

20 | 16 | 21 | $53

E 70s | 152 E. 79th St. (bet. Lexington & 3rd Aves.) | 212-639-9111 | www.ilricciony.com

Well-known to "locals", this "welcoming" UES Southern Italian plies its "attractive clientele" with "zesty" fare in "cozy" quarters that "get tight" at "peak hours"; it "may not be innovative", but "lots of regulars" ("the mayor" among them) report "it's hard not to like."

☑ Il Tinello ⌷ *Italian*

25 | 20 | 25 | $72

W 50s | 16 W. 56th St. (bet. 5th & 6th Aves.) | 212-245-4388

A bastion of "old-world style and class", this "genteel" Midtown Italian caters to a "high-end" clientele with "outstanding food" from a "formal" staff that ensures "you're treated like a king"; it requires "lots of bucks", but big spenders swear the "premium" is more than "justified."

Inagiku *Japanese*

22 | 20 | 23 | $67

E 40s | Waldorf-Astoria | 111 E. 49th St. (bet. Lexington & Park Aves.) | 212-355-0440 | www.inagiku.com

"Elegant" and "totally old-fashioned" down to the "obi-sashed waitresses", this Japanese vet "embedded in the Waldorf-Astoria" is a "quiet" purveyor of "impeccable" sushi; its $38 lunch prix fixe is "a surprisingly good deal", but dinner's a "high-priced spread."

NEW Inakaya *Japanese*

▽ 22 | 21 | 23 | $71

W 40s | NY Times Bldg. | 231 W. 40th St. (bet. 7th & 8th Aves.) | 212-354-2195 | www.inakayany.com

Catch "the chef show" at this Japanese newcomer, which brings the Tokyo original's "infectious" routine to Midtown as cooks manning robata grills engage in "loud" call-and-response with the servers while preparing "simple", "flavorful" fare; it's "gimmicky" but "really fun", at least until the check comes.

NEW Inatteso Pizzabar Casano *Pizza* ▽ 21 | 19 | 19 | $35

Financial District | 28 West St. (1st Pl.) | 212-267-8000 | www.inattesopizzabar.com

Joining sibling Adrienne's Pizzabar in the Financial District, this pizzeria proves neighborhood-appropriate with its minimalist decor and ample bar space that's already filling up in the post-work hours; pies are the specialty, but there's also a full menu of other well-priced Italian classics.

Indochine ● *French/Vietnamese* 21 | 21 | 19 | $52

E Village | 430 Lafayette St. (bet. Astor Pl. & 4th St.) | 212-505-5111 | www.indochinenyc.com

"Still sexy" "after all these years", this "vibrant" Franco-Vietnamese across from the Public Theater "continues to deliver" with "excellent high-end" cuisine courtesy of a "model staff"; cynics shrug it "needs a revamp", but for most it's a "trusty standby" with "cool" "sheen" intact.

Indus Valley *Indian* 22 | 16 | 20 | $32

W 100s | 2636 Broadway (100th St.) | 212-222-9222 | www.indusvalleyusa.com

As a "go-to" for "quality" Indian, this UWS neighborhood "winner" induces loyalty with its "spot-on", "nicely spiced" cooking and "friendly, efficient service"; maybe it's slightly "pricier than the competition", but the $13 lunch buffet would be a "deal" in the Indus Valley.

'ino ● *Italian* 24 | 15 | 20 | $30

G Village | 21 Bedford St. (bet. Downing St. & 6th Ave.) | 212-989-5769 | www.cafeino.com

You "munch and sip" at this "sweet" Italian Village "cubbyhole" wine bar that's a "hipster" "favorite" for "super" vinos and panini at "fantastic-value" rates; you'll "have to squeeze" 'ino, but "that's part of the charm."

'inoteca ● *Italian* 23 | 18 | 19 | $40

LES | 98 Rivington St. (Ludlow St.) | 212-614-0473
NEW Murray Hill | 323 Third Ave. (24th St.) | 212-683-3035
www.inotecanyc.com

It's "quite the scene" at this "easygoing" LES wine bar, a "buzzy" "hangout" for "trendy" types "mingling" over "artful", midpriced "Italian tapas" and panini chased with "terrific" vinos; the new Murray Hill sibling in Bar Milano's former digs offers more of the same plus added "space."

NEW Inside Park at St. Bart's *American* 17 | 19 | 16 | $46

E 50s | 109 E. 50th St. (Park Ave.) | 212-593-3333 | www.insideparknyc.com
Set in the "grand" community hall at St. Bartholomew's church, this Midtown newcomer resembles an "elegant" "refectory" serving New American fare; a sprawling terrace adds "alfresco" appeal, but if it's "quiet", maybe that's due to "standard" food and "spotty" staffing.

Insieme *Italian* 23 | 20 | 22 | $71

W 50s | The Michelangelo Hotel | 777 Seventh Ave. (bet. 50th & 51st Sts.) | 212-582-1310 | www.restaurantinsieme.com
"Modern Italian meets traditional" under chef Marco Canora's "distinctive" aegis at this Times Square "beacon of sophistication", where

	FOOD	DECOR	SERVICE	COST

"refined" cuisine and "gracious" service validate the "high-end" pricing; while quibblers debate whether the "stark white decor" is "glamorous" or "off-putting", in truth it's "all about the food" here.

☑ Ippudo ◐ *Noodle Shop* · 25 · 20 · 19 · $27

E Village | 65 Fourth Ave. (bet. 9th & 10th Sts.) | 212-388-0088 |
www.ippudo.com/ny/

A "mecca" for "mouthwatering" "hand-pulled ramen" (including the "extra-flavorful" tonkotsu variety), this "groovy" East Village branch of a Japanese chain supplies "soul-warming" slurps for "light" tabs; just use your noodle and "get there early" because "extreme popularity" spells "absurd waits."

Irving Mill *American* · 20 · 21 · 19 · $53

Gramercy | 116 E. 16th St. (bet. Irving Pl. & Union Sq. E.) | 212-254-1600 |
www.irvingmill.com

"Warm" and "subdued", this Gramercy New American is an "inviting" "rustic" haven where the "adventurous", mainly "carnivorous" menu introduces "innovative riffs" via the "greenmarket"; despite chef changes and a rep as a "Gramercy Tavern wannabe", "it works" and prices are "not out of line."

Isabella's *American/Mediterranean* · 20 · 19 · 19 · $44

W 70s | 359 Columbus Ave. (77th St.) | 212-724-2100 |
www.brguestrestaurants.com

"Still going strong" "for a reason", Steve Hanson's "cheerful" "UWS staple" is "tried-and-true" for Med–New American eats and "aim-to-please" service "without any sticker shock"; it hosts a "go-to" brunch, and it's always "a treat" to snare an "alfresco" table and "watch the world go by" on Columbus Avenue.

Ise *Japanese* · 21 · 13 · 17 · $36

E 40s | 151 E. 49th St. (bet. Lexington & 3rd Aves.) | 212-319-6876
Financial District | 56 Pine St. (bet. Pearl & William Sts.) | 212-785-1600 |
www.iserestaurant.com ⑤
W 50s | 58 W. 56th St. (bet. 5th & 6th Aves.) | 212-707-8702

For a "straightforward sushi" fix, these "traditional" izakaya joints "outshine many" with "fresh" fish "done right" at a "reasonable cost"; the service and decor are "not high-tier", but they "fill a need" and get "busy during lunch" thanks to the "homestyle" specials.

Island Burgers & Shakes *Burgers* · 21 · 9 · 16 · $18

W 50s | 766 Ninth Ave. (bet. 51st & 52nd Sts.) | 212-307-7934 |
www.islandburgersny.com

With an "endless variety of toppings" embellishing its "fat, drippy burgers", this Hell's Kitchen "hole-in-the-wall" outdoes "Baskin-Robbins" with "almost too much choice"; "fabulous" shakes ice the cake, but it's still "a bummer" that "they don't do fries."

I Sodi ◐ *Italian* · ▽ 23 · 18 · 23 · $57

W Village | 105 Christopher St. (bet. Bleecker & Hudson Sts.) |
212-414-5774

Stowed in a "wee" West Village lair, this "chic" yearling "lovingly prepares" "tempting" "traditional Italian" dishes and fields an "informed" staff; "costly" but "worth every penny", it "fills up quickly" with admirers who only "wish it weren't so little."

	FOOD	DECOR	SERVICE	COST

Italianissimo *Italian*
▽ 23 | 19 | 24 | $50

E 80s | 307 E. 84th St. (bet. 1st & 2nd Aves.) | 212-628-8603 | www.italianissimonyc.net

"Though miniature", this UES Italian "amazes" with "splendid" cuisine, a "charming" setting and service that "makes you feel like family"; somewhat "pricey" tabs don't deter loyal locals who "jealously guard" the "secret" ("shhh, don't tell!").

Ithaka *Greek/Seafood*
21 | 18 | 21 | $47

E 80s | 308 E. 86th St. (bet. 1st & 2nd Aves.) | 212-628-9100 | www.ithakarestaurant.com

"Reliably fresh" fish grilled "just right" leads the lineup at this Yorkville Greek seafooder, a "Mykonos-like" neighborhood "taverna" known for its "congeniality" and "fair prices"; a "guitar player" adds to the "relaxed" mood, and "if you want to linger", "it's no problem."

I Tre Merli ● *Italian*
18 | 18 | 17 | $50

SoHo | 463 W. Broadway (bet. Houston & Prince Sts.) | 212-254-8699
W Village | 183 W. 10th St. (W. 4th St.) | 212-929-2221
www.itremerli.com

Having "seen hipper days", this "old SoHo favorite" remains a "durable" "hang" for "decent Italian" eats and "people-watching" in an "attractive" space that's "open to the street"; its West Village offshoot is "more intimate" albeit equally "expensive for what you get."

I Trulli *Italian*
23 | 21 | 21 | $59

Murray Hill | 122 E. 27th St. (bet. Lexington Ave. & Park Ave. S.) | 212-481-7372 | www.itrulli.com

Upholding a "well-deserved reputation", this "no-pretense" Murray Hill Italian enhances its "superb" Pugliese specialties with "caring service" and "fantastic" vinos from the "adjacent wine bar"; the "rustic" space "appeals in all seasons" with its "pretty garden" and "fabulous fireplace", though penny-pinchers protest it's "not cheap."

Itzocan ⊟ *Mexican*
23 | 11 | 18 | $34

E 100s | 1575 Lexington Ave. (101st St.) | 212-423-0255 | www.itzocanbistro.com
E Village | 438 E. Ninth St. (bet. Ave. A & 1st Ave.) | 212-677-5856 | www.itzocanrestaurant.com ●

The "enticing" food "doesn't rely on formula" at this "teeny-weeny" Mexican duo, with the East Village original turning out "gourmet" fare and the UES offshoot spinning "French fusion" twists; common to both are the "capable staff", "elbow-to-elbow seating" and "cash-only" policy.

Ivo & Lulu ⊟ *Caribbean/French*
▽ 20 | 12 | 16 | $30

SoHo | 558 Broome St. (bet. 6th Ave. & Varick St.) | 212-226-4399

A "serious" "taste sensation" in a "tiny package", this "out-of-the-way" SoHo French-Caribbean combines "boldly spiced" specialties with a "funky" milieu; the room gets "crowded" fast, but with a "rare BYO" policy abetting the "affordable" prices, it's "totally worth" any "wait."

Izakaya Ten ● *Japanese*
▽ 21 | 20 | 19 | $43

Chelsea | 207 10th Ave. (bet. 22nd & 23rd Sts.) | 212-627-7777

"Hip" neighbors find this way West Chelsea Japanese tenable for a "creative" variety of small plates served in "compact", "minimalist" digs; both the Nippon-style "pop" soundtrack and "extensive" sake selection factor into the "buzzing atmosphere."

Jack's Luxury Oyster Bar 🗷 Continental/French | ▽ 26 | 17 | 23 | $65

E Village | 101 Second Ave. (bet. 5th & 6th Sts.) | 212-979-1012

Though it's "under the radar" at this point, you're "in for a treat" at this pint-size East Villager where the "incredible" French-Continental seafood lives up to the "costly" tabs; if the "tight space" is less than luxurious, "excellent service compensates."

Jackson Diner ⊄ Indian | 22 | 8 | 13 | $24

Jackson Heights | 37-47 74th St. (bet. Roosevelt & 37th Aves.) | Queens | 718-672-1232 | www.jacksondiner.com

"Authentic levels of spice" make this Jackson Heights Indian a destination for "heavenly" eats at "darn cheap" prices, especially during the $10 buffet lunch; the "school cafeteria" ambiance detracts, but "close your eyes" and you'll know why it's a perennial "crowd-pleaser."

Jackson Hole American | 17 | 10 | 14 | $22

E 60s | 232 E. 64th St. (bet. 2nd & 3rd Aves.) | 212-371-7187 ●
E 80s | 1611 Second Ave. (bet. 83rd & 84th Sts.) | 212-737-8788 ●
E 90s | 1270 Madison Ave. (91st St.) | 212-427-2820
Murray Hill | 521 Third Ave. (35th St.) | 212-679-3264 ●
W 80s | 517 Columbus Ave. (85th St.) | 212-362-5177
Bayside | 35-01 Bell Blvd. (35th Ave.) | Queens | 718-281-0330 ●
Jackson Heights | 69-35 Astoria Blvd. (70th St.) | Queens | 718-204-7070 ●
www.jacksonholeburgers.com

"It's all about" the "colossal", "sloppy burgers" at this "all-American", "generic", "diner-esque" chainlet, a "legendary" source of "obscene portions" that "won't leave a hole in your wallet"; if the burgers don't "extinguish your hunger", maybe the "hordes of teens and kids" will.

Jack the Horse Tavern American | 24 | 21 | 20 | $45

Brooklyn Heights | 66 Hicks St. (Cranberry St.) | Brooklyn | 718-852-5084 | www.jackthehorse.com

More than a "favorite neighborhood" watering hole, this "inviting" Brooklyn Heights tavern ponies up "terrific" New American fare served by a "wonderful" staff; sited "on a sleepy corner", it's a refuge of "relaxed" "charm" and the regulars "hope it stays that way."

Jacques French | 20 | 19 | 18 | $44

E 80s | 206 E. 85th St. (bet. 2nd & 3rd Aves.) | 212-327-2272
NoLita | 20 Prince St. (bet. Elizabeth & Mott Sts.) | 212-966-8886
www.jacquesnyc.com

These "standby" brasseries are "solid" for "midpriced" bites like the "wonderful" moules frites, with the UES original cleaving "true French" while North African accents surface in NoLita; maybe the service "could be a bit friendlier", but you'll "feel like you're in Paris."

Jaiya Thai Thai | 21 | 11 | 14 | $30

Murray Hill | 396 Third Ave. (28th St.) | 212-889-1330 | www.jaiya.com

"They aren't kidding" about the "serious heat" at this real-deal Murray Hill Siamese, where the "excellent" chow escalates up to "sweat-inducing levels of spiciness"; the "bare-bones" "decor needs help", but most couldn't care less given the "budget" tabs.

	FOOD	DECOR	SERVICE	COST

Jake's Steakhouse *Steak* — 23 | 19 | 21 | $55

Bronx | 6031 Broadway (242nd St.) | 718-581-0182 | www.jakessteakhouse.com

"What a surprise!" cry carnivores at this Riverdale steakhouse, where "top-of-the-line", house-aged beef (courtesy of meat-wholesaler owners) is "served up with class"; there's a handsome upstairs space "overlooking Van Cortlandt Park", and it's a "good value" to boot.

James Ⓜ *American* — ▽ 23 | 21 | 21 | $48

Prospect Heights | 605 Carlton Ave. (St. Marks Ave.) | Brooklyn | 718-942-4255 | www.jamesrestaurantny.com

An "ambitious" "standout" in an "unassuming" Prospect Heights locale, this New American yearling produces "top-notch" seasonal fare and "amazingly crafted cocktails" in a "swanky" space run by a "wonderful staff"; it's an "unmitigated success" with "upscale" locals who "pack in regularly."

Jane *American* — 21 | 17 | 19 | $40

G Village | 100 W. Houston St. (bet. La Guardia Pl. & Thompson St.) | 212-254-7000 | www.janerestaurant.com

"Sweet" and "accessible", this "reliable" Village New American "goes down easy" with its "creative", "well-priced" "comfort" fare and "upbeat" service; it's favored by "young", "energetic" types who produce "ridiculous" "crowds" at its "blockbuster brunch."

Japonais Ⓢ *Japanese* — 20 | 23 | 18 | $55

Gramercy | 111 E. 18th St. (bet. Irving Pl. & Park Ave. S.) | 212-260-2020 | www.japonaisnewyork.com

"Not your usual" Japanese, this "trendy" Gramercy eyeful is out to "impress" by serving "fancy" cuisine with a "French twist" in "sultry" Asian surroundings that also host a "froufrou" "lounge scene"; some gripe about the price tag, "but what did you expect?"

Japonica *Japanese* — 23 | 15 | 20 | $48

G Village | 100 University Pl. (12th St.) | 212-243-7752 | www.japonicanyc.com

It's "nothing flashy", but this Village Japanese standby maintains a "fine reputation" for "consistently" "heavenly" sushi cut in "mega-portions" and matched with "gracious" service; though the "space needs an update", the "first-rate" eating makes the cost "easy to swallow."

Jean Claude Ⱞ *French* — 23 | 17 | 20 | $47

SoHo | 137 Sullivan St. (bet. Houston & Prince Sts.) | 212-475-9232 | www.jeanclauderestaurant.com

"Francophiles delight" at the "delish" Gallic "home cooking" that makes this petite SoHo bistro a "genuine" "find"; with an "attentive staff" and a backdrop "straight out of Paris", it's both "charming" and an "excellent value" – as long as "you don't mind paying cash."

Ⓩ Jean Georges Ⓢ *French* — 28 | 27 | 28 | $127

W 60s | Trump Int'l Hotel | 1 Central Park W. (bet. 60th & 61st Sts.) | 212-299-3900 | www.jean-georges.com

Led by the eponymous "creative genius", this Columbus Circle Nouveau French is "reason enough to live in or visit NY"; offering one of the city's "best" prix fixe lunch deals (two plates for $29), it "does everything right", from the "inventive" cuisine ("will heaven be this good?") and "courteous" pro service to the "high-ceilinged" space that's "elegance defined"; N.B. for a more casual meal, try the adjacent Nougatine.

⊡ Jean Georges' Nougatine French   27 | 24 | 26 | $64

W 60s | Trump Int'l Hotel | 1 Central Park W. (bet. 60th & 61st Sts.) | 212-299-3900 | www.jean-georges.com

"Elegance made to look easy" is the forte of the adjacent, "more-casual" counterpart to Jean Georges, whose "still-excellent" modern French cuisine, "stellar" setting and "courteous" service all offer plenty of the "wow" factor; best of all, its $26 lunch prix fixe is "among the most joyful bargains in NY"; N.B. it's a big "power breakfast" place too.

⊡ Jewel Bako ⊠ Japanese   25 | 21 | 23 | $79

E Village | 239 E. Fifth St. (bet. 2nd & 3rd Aves.) | 212-979-1012

A "manicured crowd" files into this "bite-size" East Village Japanese to "savor" "pristine" sushi and "impeccable service" in a "tranquil" space that's like "a world of its own"; overseen by "superb" owners Jack and Grace Lamb, it has "quite the following" despite prices that are "more than a little precious."

Jewel of India Indian   20 | 18 | 19 | $42

W 40s | 15 W. 44th St. (bet. 5th & 6th Aves.) | 212-869-5544 | www.jewelofindianyc.com

Holding "steady" in Midtown, this "relaxing" Indian duplex is "fre-quented by businesspeople" who vouch for the "palatable" food and "helpful" service; given "solid" buys like the $17 lunch buffet, few fuss if the decor is "a little dated."

J.G. Melon ●⊘ Pub Food   21 | 13 | 16 | $27

E 70s | 1291 Third Ave. (74th St.) | 212-744-0585

"Prepsters and gossip girls galore" "deluge" this long-running UES pub, a "justly popular" "staple" for "superior burgers" and cottage fries ("don't try anything else"); even with "irritable" service and the "no-credit-cards" "hassle", it's a "standard-bearer" for the "popped-collar" set.

Jimmy's No. 43 ● American   ▽ 20 | 16 | 18 | $35

E Village | 43 E. Seventh St., downstairs (bet. 2nd & 3rd Aves.) | 212-982-3006 | www.jimmysno43.com

There's no need to maintain a liquid diet at Jimmy Carbone's "no-attitude" East Village pub, which serves "remarkably" "tasty" American small plates in a subterranean "college rathskeller" lair; of course, there's also a "well-selected tap list" to wash down the grub.

Jing Fong Chinese   20 | 11 | 11 | $22

Chinatown | 20 Elizabeth St. (bet. Bayard & Canal Sts.) | 212-964-5256

Dim sum devotees "throng" this "vast" Hong Kong–style "spectacle" in Chinatown, where "rolling carts" proffer an "immense", "yummy" selection "for only a pittance"; it's a "garish", "hectic" show with a "Chinese-speaking" staff, so it helps to "be adventurous."

JJ's Asian Fusion Ⓜ Asian Fusion   ▽ 24 | 17 | 21 | $29

Astoria | 37-05 31st Ave. (bet. 37th & 38th Sts.) | Queens | 718-626-8888 | www.jjsfusion.com

Celebrated for its "awesome edamame potstickers", this "little" Astoria outpost also offers "fresh", "inventive" sushi and other "zingy"

Asian fusion fare; the "moderately priced" eats and "wonderful service" make for an "excellent neighborhood choice."

Joe Allen ● *American*   17 | 16 | 18 | $43
W 40s | 326 W. 46th St. (bet. 8th & 9th Aves.) | 212-581-6464 | www.joeallenrestaurant.com
This "pubby" "haunt" is a "perennial favorite" on Restaurant Row and "always buzzing" with theatergoers and Broadway show folk scarfing "straightforward" American fare; its "crowd-pleasing" act remains "on the mark" despite service that's "notoriously indifferent" unless "you're a casting agent."

Joe & Pat's *Italian/Pizza*   24 | 12 | 17 | $24
Staten Island | 1758 Victory Blvd. (Manor Rd.) | 718-981-0887
A Staten Island "pinnacle of pizza" since 1960, this "family-friendly" "joint" shows an "adept hand" crafting "superior" pies featuring the "thinnest crust" and "phenomenal" toppings; given the "good prices" and "addictive" eats, no wonder it's usually "busy."

Joe Doe *American*   ∇ 23 | 19 | 23 | $47
E Village | 45 E. First St. (bet. 1st & 2nd Aves.) | 212-780-0262 | www.chefjoedoe.com
"Small place, big heart" sums up this ultra-"cozy" East Villager, an "innovative" New American whose "tasty drinks" and "delicious" seasonal "spins on classic comfort food" are buoyed by "responsive service"; though "not cheap", it's so "endearing" you'll "forget about that."

Joe's Ginger ⇌ *Chinese*   20 | 9 | 13 | $23
Chinatown | 25 Pell St. (Doyers St.) | 212-285-0333 | www.joeginger.com
Serving "extra-tasty" soup dumplings and other "satisfying" "Shanghai grub", this C-towner is a "dependable" stop "without the wait" of its like-named local rivals; there's little ambiance and they "do rush you along", but then its jury-duty clientele is "not there to linger."

Joe's Pizza *Pizza*   22 | 6 | 12 | $10
G Village | 7 Carmine St. (bet. Bleecker St. & 6th Ave.) | 212-255-3946 ●
Midwood | 1621 Kings Hwy. (E. 16th St.) | Brooklyn | 718-339-4525 ⇌
Park Slope | 137 Seventh Ave. (bet. Carroll St. & Garfield Pl.) | Brooklyn | 718-398-9198
www.joespizza.com
Little "slices of heaven", these separately owned pie parlors purvey "out-of-this-world" "old-school" pizza ("delicate crust", "fresh toppings") for a "small price"; given the "no-frills" settings and "no-nonsense" staffers, they work best "on the go."

Joe's Shanghai *Chinese*   22 | 9 | 14 | $25
Chinatown | 9 Pell St. (bet. Bowery & Mott St.) | 212-233-8888 ⇌
W 50s | 24 W. 56th St. (bet. 5th & 6th Aves.) | 212-333-3868
Flushing | 136-21 37th Ave. (bet. Main & Union Sts.) | Queens | 718-539-3838 ⇌
www.joeshanghairestaurants.com
Those "scrumptious" soup dumplings are "all the rage" at this Shanghainese threesome, where the low-cost specialties are "oh-so-worth" the "communal seating", "brusque" service and "nonexistent" decor; they're "on the regular tourist route", so "expect to wait."

	FOOD	DECOR	SERVICE	COST

John's of 12th Street ⊉ *Italian*

20 | 13 | 17 | $34

E Village | 302 E. 12th St. (2nd Ave.) | 212-475-9531

As "old-line Italian" as it gets, this 1908-vintage East Village "fixture" still supplies "plentiful" plates of "red-sauce" "staples" via staffers who could be awaiting a "casting director"; though it's undeniably "dated", the time-tested "character" will "win you over."

☒ John's Pizzeria *Pizza*

22 | 13 | 16 | $24

E 60s | 408 E. 64th St. (bet. 1st & York Aves.) | 212-935-2895
G Village | 278 Bleecker St. (bet. 6th Ave. & 7th Ave. S.) | 212-243-1680 ◐⊉
W 40s | 260 W. 44th St. (bet. B'way & 8th Ave.) | 212-391-7560 ◐
www.johnspizzerianyc.com

This "then, now and forever" of NYC pizza has expanded Uptown and lots of loyal Johnists have followed; however, "if you want a true NY experience", "head to the grungy original on Bleecker", "brave the lines" and "cram into one of the little wooden booths" for what may well be "the best pizza ever" – straight out of the coal-fired brick oven.

☒ JoJo *French*

25 | 22 | 24 | $69

E 60s | 160 E. 64th St. (bet. Lexington & 3rd Aves.) | 212-223-5656 |
www.jean-georges.com

"Gallic charm abounds" at Jean-Georges Vongerichten's UES "haute bistro", where "mature", "well-dressed" types "relish" "delectable" French fare and "solicitous" service in a "quiet", "elegant" townhouse; it's "always a winner" "for a tête-à-tête", and especially for the $24 prix fixe lunch.

Jolie *French*

21 | 19 | 20 | $43

Boerum Hill | 320 Atlantic Ave. (bet. Hoyt & Smith Sts.) | Brooklyn |
718-488-0777 | www.jolierestaurant.com

Nestled in a "*très jolie*" setting, this "welcoming" Boerum Hill "neighborhood French" boîte "fills the bill" for "consistently" "solid" cooking; advocates add the shady back patio alone is "reason enough to go."

NEW Jo's ◐ *American*

- | - | - | M

NoLita | 264 Elizabeth St. (bet. Houston & Prince Sts.) | 212-966-9640 |
www.josnyc.com

Set in the former Tasting Room space, this NoLita newcomer already feels like a fixture thanks to its 1920s-inspired interior; the menu matches its easygoing vibe with spruced-up Traditional American dishes and classic cocktails, all at refreshingly modest prices.

Josephina ◑ *American*

18 | 17 | 18 | $48

W 60s | 1900 Broadway (bet. 63rd & 64th Sts.) | 212-799-1000 |
www.josephinanyc.com

"Super convenient" for "pre-show eats", this New American "standby" across from Lincoln Center supplies a "decent" menu and service primed to get you "out the door in time for act one"; "shoehorned" seating and "frenetic" pacing are the predictable snags.

NEW Joseph Leonard ◑Ⓜ *American*

- | - | - | M

G Village | 170 Waverly Pl. (Grove St.) | 646-429-8383 |
www.josephleonard.com

Restaurateur Gabe Stulman (ex Little Owl, Market Table) does it again with this bite-size Villager centered around a zinc bar and sporting a homey-but-hip look featuring lots of antiques; in the open kitchen, a Bouchon Bakery alum sends out well-priced, seasonal, bistro-ish New American fare three meals a day – keeping the 30-odd seats regularly full.

Josie's *Eclectic*
19 | 14 | 17 | $34

Murray Hill | 565 Third Ave. (37th St.) | 212-490-1558
W 70s | 300 Amsterdam Ave. (74th St.) | 212-769-1212
www.josiesnyc.com

"Herbivores" "delight" in this "organically influenced" UWS-Murray Hill Eclectic twosome, whose "breezy", "bustling" setups often feel like "chick city"; they're "convenient" and "won't break the bank", so never mind if the staff can "seem very green."

Joya ⊄ *Thai*
23 | 17 | 19 | $23

Cobble Hill | 215 Court St. (bet. Warren & Wyckoff Sts.) | Brooklyn | 718-222-3484

"Enjoyment" awaits at this "cheerful" Cobble Hill Thai, a "favorite" thanks to its "sensational" food at "super-cheap" prices; it's always "crazy busy" with "trendy" young things "rockin'" to "deafening music", but, joya joya, there's a "quieter garden" in back.

Jubilee *French*
22 | 16 | 20 | $51

E 50s | 347 E. 54th St. (bet. 1st & 2nd Aves.) | 212-888-3569 | www.jubileeny.net

For a "French fix" "without pretension", this "congenial" Sutton Place bistro caters to "local" "adults" with *magnifique* mussels leading a "well-prepared" lineup; still, the "close" space can get "jammed" and the decor "needs a face-lift – or some good makeup."

Jules ◑ *French*
18 | 16 | 16 | $42

E Village | 65 St. Marks Pl. (bet. 1st & 2nd Aves.) | 212-477-5560 | www.julesbistro.com

East Village "bon vivants" bop into this "cozy" bistro to enjoy "well-made" Gallic bites at a "reasonable price" and "film noir" vibes enhanced by nightly jazz combos; alas, "true to their French roots", the service can be "indifferent."

Juliette *French*
▽ 19 | 19 | 18 | $34

Williamsburg | 135 N. Fifth St. (bet. Bedford Ave. & Berry St.) | Brooklyn | 718-388-9222 | www.juliettewilliamsburg.com

"Charming" and "consistent", this Williamsburg "neighborhood bistro" sizes up "dependably" well for "honest" French fare in a "sunny" setting; in "good weather", the spacious "roof deck" is a prime "people-watching" perch.

Junior's *Diner*
17 | 12 | 16 | $26

E 40s | Grand Central | lower level (42nd St. & Vanderbilt Ave.) | 212-983-5257
W 40s | Shubert Alley | 1515 Broadway (enter on 45th St., bet. B'way & 8th Ave.) | 212-302-2000 ◑
Downtown Bklyn | 386 Flatbush Ave. Ext. (DeKalb Ave.) | Brooklyn | 718-852-5257 ◑
www.juniorscheesecake.com

Though best known for its original "Brooklyn landmark" Formica diner location and by-now "world-famous" cheesecake, this trio also vends

| | FOOD | DECOR | SERVICE | COST |

"decent" sandwiches, burgers and such; the Manhattan locations don't share the "history", but they're "quick" and budget-friendly.

Kabab Café ◨⇗ *Egyptian*
▽ 24 | 13 | 23 | $33

Astoria | 25-12 Steinway St. (25th Ave.) | Queens | 718-728-9858
It's "hard to outdo" "jovial" chef-owner Ali El Sayed and his "home"-style Egyptian "culinary delights" at this "teeny" Astorian, where insiders "ignore the menu" since there are "more specials than seats"; not only are the "memorable" meals "worth the schlep", but the BYO policy is a "cherry on top."

Kafana ⇗ *Serbian*
▽ 22 | 19 | 24 | $32

E Village | 116 Ave. C (bet. 7th & 8th Sts.) | 212-353-8000 | www.kafananyc.com
Offering a rare "chance to try" Serbian cuisine, this "welcoming" "little" East Villager tenders a "rich", "rib-sticking" menu that's particulary suited to "pork lovers"; the "warm, personal" service and "homey" backdrop help make the "authentic" encounter "very worthwhile."

Kai ◪◨ *Japanese*
▽ 26 | 24 | 24 | $79

E 60s | Ito En | 822 Madison Ave., 2nd fl. (bet. 68th & 69th Sts.) | 212-988-7277 | www.itoen.com
"Real class" takes a "distinctive Japanese" turn at this UES kaiseki specialist sited atop tea merchant Ito En, where the "exquisite" spread is "served with devoted attention" in "elegant", "peaceful" surroundings; yes, "you pay for it", but connoisseurs declare "damn the cost!"

NEW Kajitsu ◨ *Japanese/Vegetarian*
- | - | - | E

E Village | 414 E. Ninth St. (bet. Ave. A & 1st Ave.) | 212-228-4873 | www.kajitsunyc.com
Vegetarian Japanese fare gets "incredibly inventive" at this new East Villager, where the "amazing" kaiseki menus feature the "traditional", meatless *shojin* cuisine that originated in Buddhist monasteries; "serene", "austere" environs keep the focus on the "high-quality" food, at least until the bill arrives.

Kampuchea ◨ *Cambodian*
22 | 16 | 20 | $35

LES | 78 Rivington St. (Allen St.) | 212-529-3901 | www.kampucheanyc.com
With a "creative menu" starring "brothy" noodles and "memorable" sandwiches, this "laid-back" LES "staple" cooks up "Cambodian street food with panache"; fortunately, it's also "well priced" and "personable", but "go early" before the "cramped quarters" become "crowded" with happy kampers.

Kang Suh ● *Korean*
21 | 12 | 16 | $36

Garment District | 1250 Broadway (32nd St.) | 212-564-6845
"Whenever the mood strikes" for cook-your-own Korean BBQ, this 24/7 Garment District stalwart "satisfies" "without emptying your wallet"; a "first-rate" roster of other "authentic" dishes and a sushi bar also figure, distracting from the "hurried" service and "mediocre" decor.

◲ Kanoyama ● *Japanese*
26 | 15 | 20 | $54

E Village | 175 Second Ave. (11th St.) | 212-777-5266 | www.kanoyama.com
This "impressive" East Village Japanese contender stays a "slice above" the competition with an "exotic" selection of "exquisitely pre-

pared" sushi whose "surefire" quality "far surpasses the price paid"; the "tight", "spare" space gets "elbow-to-elbow crowded", but still afishionados advise "go for it."

Kati Roll Co. *Indian*   20 | 5 | 11 | $12

Garment District | 49 W. 39th St. (bet. 5th & 6th Aves.) | 212-730-4280
G Village | 99 MacDougal St. (bet. Bleecker & W. 3rd Sts.) | 212-420-6517 ◑
www.thekatirollcompany.com

Among "the tastiest street foods" going, the signature burrito-esque rolls at these Village–Garment District "hole-in-the-wall" Indians can grow "addictive", especially if "you're on a budget"; despite their "food-court" digs and "assembly-line" style, most only "wish there were more locations."

Katsu-Hama *Japanese*   21 | 10 | 15 | $26

E 40s | 11 E. 47th St. (bet. 5th & Madison Aves.) | 212-758-5909
NEW **W 50s** | 45 W. 55th St., 2nd fl. (bet. 5th & 6th Aves.) | 212-541-7145 ◑
www.katsuhama.com

A "good one-trick pony", this Midtown Japanese katsu "shrine" specializes in "crispy-on-the-outside", "juicy-on-the-inside" fried cutlets that "melt in your mouth"; "mediocre" digs to the contrary, it's a natural for lunch thanks to "economical" prices and "fast" service; N.B. the 55th Street branch opened post-Survey.

◪ Katz's Delicatessen *Deli*   23 | 9 | 12 | $23

LES | 205 E. Houston St. (Ludlow St.) | 212-254-2246 |
www.katzdeli.com

"You can't say you're truly a New Yorker" till you've eaten at this sprawling, white Formica LES "institution", on the scene since 1888; whether the city's "best old-time deli" or not, it's certainly "way up there" with "awesome sandwiches", "great dogs" and "real knishes" (as for decor and service, delis aren't supposed to have any); critics counter "heartburn alley", "for tourists only", a "used-to-be"; N.B. I'll have whatever Meg Ryan was having.

Keens Steakhouse *Steak*   24 | 23 | 23 | $69

Garment District | 72 W. 36th St. (bet. 5th & 6th Aves.) | 212-947-3636 |
www.keens.com

"One of the oldest" (circa 1885) and "best" NY steakhouses, this Garment District "museum" also boasts an extensive collection of Lincoln, Roosevelt and theater memorabilia – not to mention 88,000 "vintage clay pipes" hanging from the ceiling; although "always crowded", it's surprisingly "seldom talked about" despite "exceptionally great" mutton chops, desserts, scotches, wines and beer all served by "quick, pro waiters"; N.B. there's plenty of party space too.

Kefi *Greek*   22 | 16 | 18 | $38

W 80s | 505 Columbus Ave. (bet. 84th & 85th Sts.) | 212-873-0200 |
www.kefirestaurant.com

Back on the scene in a "larger" new UWS location, Michael Psilakis' "high-energy" Greek is drawing "throngs" with his "glorious" Hellenic "comfort food", "quickie" service and "bargain-basement" tabs; the fact that it "now accepts reservations and credit cards" gets a hardy "*opa!*" (ditto the generally "better" site), though it's still "crazy crowded" and "deafeningly loud."

Kellari Taverna ● *Greek*

FOOD	DECOR	SERVICE	COST
22	21	21	$52

W 40s | 19 W. 44th St. (bet. 5th & 6th Aves.) | 212-221-0144 | www.kellari.us

Kellari's Parea ● *Greek*

Flatiron | 36 E. 20th St. (bet. B'way & Park Ave. S.) | 212-777-8448 | www.kellari-parea.com

"Find your inner Zorba" at this "festive" Theater District Greek, a "comfortable", "pretty" spot where "outstanding grilled fish" and some of the "best spanakopita this side of the Aegean" are shuttled by an "eager-to-please" staff; its more "casual" Flatiron sibling shares the same "delightful" food as well as the same "Euro pricing."

NEW Keste Pizza e Vino *Pizza*

FOOD	DECOR	SERVICE	COST
∇ 21	13	18	$28

G Village | 271 Bleecker St. (bet. Cornelia & Jones Sts.) | 212-243-1500 | www.kestepizzeria.com

For a "pure pizza experience", check out this "real-deal" Village newcomer where the "masterful", "authentic" pies are prepared by a chef who also serves as president of the Italian Association of Neapolitan Pizza; fans say they're a "great addition to the pizzeria craze sweeping Manhattan."

Killmeyer's Old Bavaria Inn *German*

FOOD	DECOR	SERVICE	COST
∇ 18	20	20	$36

Staten Island | 4254 Arthur Kill Rd. (Sharrotts Rd.) | 718-984-1202 | www.killmeyers.com

An "extensive beer menu" is paired with "big portions" of hearty German grub at this "fun" Staten Islander in Charleston, the "perfect place to knock off a wurst"; "interesting 1930s decor", a "hopping" outdoor biergarten and staffers in "traditional outfits" jazz up this otherwise "no-frills" affair.

Kings' Carriage House *American*

FOOD	DECOR	SERVICE	COST
22	25	23	$72

E 80s | 251 E. 82nd St. (bet. 2nd & 3rd Aves.) | 212-734-5490 | www.kingscarriagehouse.com

Set in a "chintz and plaid"–laden townhouse, this "charming", "romantic" Upper Eastsider exudes the "warm glow" of a "country getaway"; the "delicious" New Americana on offer is available only via "expensive" prix fixe menus, but the overall effect is so "enchanting" that no one minds much.

Kingswood *Australian*

FOOD	DECOR	SERVICE	COST
19	21	17	$49

G Village | 121 W. 10th St. (bet. Greenwich & 6th Aves.) | 212-645-0018 | www.kingswoodnyc.com

"Good-looking twentysomethings" and "fashionista wannabes" pile into this "sceney" Villager where the "above-average", "Aussie-accented" American grub plays second fiddle to the "action" at the bar; "pretentious" service and a noise level akin to a "jet engine test facility" are the downsides.

Ki Sushi *Japanese*

FOOD	DECOR	SERVICE	COST
∇ 25	20	21	$36

Boerum Hill | 122 Smith St. (bet. Dean & Pacific Sts.) | Brooklyn | 718-935-0575 | www.ki-sushi.com

"Fastidious" preparation and presentation – "they know how to treat a fish" – sets this "original" Boerum Hill sushi supplier apart from the competition; "attentive" service and a "dimly lit", "adult ambiance" that's "appropriate for a Saturday night" add to its allure.

Kitchen Club *French/Japanese*
| | 23 | 21 | 23 | $47 |

NoLita | 30 Prince St. (Mott St.) | 212-274-0025 | www.thekitchenclub.com

Still rather "undiscovered" after 20 years, this "quirky" NoLita spot features "imaginative" French-Japanese fusion fare (and "to-die-for dumplings") via owner-chef Marja Samsom; fans applaud its "whimsical decor" and "good value", but note that it's the "resident pooch", Chibi, who "really owns the joint."

Kitchenette *Southern*
| | 19 | 15 | 16 | $25 |

Harlem | 1272 Amsterdam Ave. (bet. 122nd & 123rd Sts.) | 212-531-7600
TriBeCa | 156 Chambers St. (bet. Greenwich St. & W. B'way) | 212-267-6740
www.kitchenetterestaurant.com

"Bring your appetite" to this Southern duo dishing out "generous portions" of "stick-to-your-ribs" comfort chow for cheap; "crowded" conditions and "crazed" service prevail during the "zoo"-like weekend brunch that's a magnet for "homesick folks from Dixie."

Kittichai *Thai*
| | 22 | 26 | 20 | $57 |

SoHo | 60 Thompson Hotel | 60 Thompson St. (bet. Broome & Spring Sts.) | 212-219-2000 | www.kittichairestaurant.com

"Sleek" and "sexy", this SoHo "haute Thai" serves "creative" dishes (like those "addictive chocolate babyback ribs") in a "glitzy" room that features pools stocked with floating "orchids and candles"; "be prepared to spend a pretty penny" for the privilege, but then again you'll probably "impress your date."

Klee Brasserie *American/European*
| | 20 | 18 | 20 | $53 |

Chelsea | 200 Ninth Ave. (bet. 22nd & 23rd Sts.) | 212-633-8033 | www.kleebrasserie.com

This "under-the-radar" Chelsea Euro-American wants to be a "neighborhood drop-in place" and is "working hard" at it with "imaginative" cooking, "welcoming" staffers and a "charming" setting; yet even though the food is "far from run-of-the-mill", many say the "prices should be lower."

Klong ◐ *Thai*
| | 21 | 18 | 17 | $26 |

E Village | 7 St. Marks Pl. (bet. 2nd & 3rd Aves.) | 212-505-9955 | www.klongnyc.com

"Authentic" Bangkok street food lands on St. Marks Place via this "go-to" Thai that's "dark" and "sexy" – and "cheap" enough for "broke college students" on third dates; but since it's usually "frenetically busy", "be ready to wait" to get in and then be "rushed" as "speedy" servers try to turn tables.

Knickerbocker Bar & Grill ◐ *American*
| | 20 | 17 | 19 | $51 |

G Village | 33 University Pl. (9th St.) | 212-228-8490 | www.knickerbockerbarandgrill.com

"NYU professors, students and parents" alike frequent this circa-1977 Village "mainstay" known for "generous portions" of "tasty" Americana and "wonderful" weekend jazz; maybe the "clubby" interior "needs updating", but regulars say the "unpretentious", "old NY" mood is fine as is.

	FOOD	DECOR	SERVICE	COST

Knife + Fork Ⓜ European
∇ 21 | 18 | 19 | $53

E Village | 108 E. Fourth St. (bet. 1st & 2nd Aves.) | 212-228-4885 | www.knife-fork-nyc.com

"Creative" Modern European cooking served in a "sweet" storefront setting keeps the trade brisk at this "little" East Village "gem"; though it's a tad pricey à la carte, regulars say the "spectacular" $45 six-course tasting menu is the "way to go."

Koi Japanese
22 | 23 | 20 | $63

W 40s | Bryant Park Hotel | 40 W. 40th St. (bet. 5th & 6th Aves.) | 212-921-3330 | www.koirestaurant.com

"Young" types favor this "sceney" Bryant Park Hotel Japanese for its "superb sushi" and "Asian fusion done to perfection" served in a "beautiful" room; "snooty service" and "loud" crowds don't detract from the "fun", but given the "pricey" tabs, it's tastier on "someone else's dime."

Korzo ◑ European
∇ 20 | 18 | 20 | $31
(fka Eurotrip)

Park Slope | 667 Fifth Ave. (bet. 19th & 20th Sts.) | Brooklyn | 718-285-9425 | www.eurotripbrooklyn.com

Providing "culinary adventures" in the South Slope, this "laid-back", recently redubbed Central European offers "unusual" regional wines to match the "stick-to-your-ribs" fare; "postmodern" digs, "enthusiastic" service and "great beers on tap" complete the trip.

Kuma Inn Ⓜ⊟ Filipino/Thai
24 | 13 | 21 | $36

LES | 113 Ludlow St., 2nd fl. (bet. Delancey & Rivington Sts.) | 212-353-8866 | www.kumainn.com

"Hard to find, but easy to like", this "secretive", second-floor Lower Eastsider hidden up a flight of stairs provides "excellent" Filipino-Thai small plates in a "really little space"; "reasonable prices" and a "bonus BYO" policy offset the "weary" decor and "cash-only" rule.

Kum Gang San ◑ Korean
21 | 15 | 16 | $36

Garment District | 49 W. 32nd St. (bet. B'way & 5th Ave.) | 212-967-0909
Flushing | 138-28 Northern Blvd. (bet. Bowne & Union Sts.) | Queens | 718-461-0909
www.kumgangsan.net

There's "something for everyone" at these 24/7 Korean BBQ joints known for "tasty" menus and "rapid-fire" service that makes dining "feel like a race rather than a meal"; "wacky" decor elements including a "waterfall" and a "white baby grand piano" appeal to "kitsch" aficionados.

🅉 Kuruma Zushi Ⓢ Japanese
27 | 16 | 24 | $154

E 40s | 7 E. 47th St., 2nd fl. (bet. 5th & Madison Aves.) | 212-317-2802

At this Midtown mezzanine "hole-in-the-wall", "true master" Toshihiro Uezu is at work serving up the "freshest possible", most "lovingly prepared" fish to a necessarily well-heeled "alpha male scene"; although it's "very expensive", take out a second mortgage and "go omakase."

Kyotofu ◑Ⓜ Dessert/Japanese
21 | 19 | 19 | $31

W 40s | 705 Ninth Ave. (bet. 48th & 49th Sts.) | 212-974-6012 | www.kyotofu-nyc.com

For a guilt-free "alternative to traditional ice creams and cakes", check out this "interesting" Hell's Kitchen Japanese dessert specialist where the "exquisite" sweets are "built on a foundation of tofu"; "spaceship" decor and a "fun" vibe make for a "clever concept well executed", though critics say the savory offerings are "less consistent."

⊠ Kyo Ya ●M *Japanese*   27 | 23 | 26 | $91

E Village | 94 E. Seventh St., downstairs (1st Ave.) | 212-982-4140
"Very special" East Village kaiseki specialist whose "superb", "beautifully presented" multicourse meals served in stylishly "Zen surroundings" are considered one of the city's best-kept "secrets"; just brace yourself for a "glacial pace" and ultra-"high-end" tabs – although admirers insist that it's a "fraction of the price" of its better-known competitors.

La Baraka *French*   21 | 17 | 23 | $41

Little Neck | 255-09 Northern Blvd. (2 blocks e. of Little Neck Pkwy.) | Queens | 718-428-1461
After three decades, "it's still a pleasure" to dine at this "family-owned and -operated" Little Neck "blessing" thanks to its "solid", well-priced "French country" cooking with some Moroccan flair; "one-in-a-million hostess Lucette" is so "welcoming" that no one notices the "worn decor."

La Bergamote *Bakery/French*   25 | 14 | 15 | $14

Chelsea | 169 Ninth Ave. (20th St.) | 212-627-9010
W 50s | 515 W. 52nd St. (bet. 10th & 11th Aves.) | 212-586-2429
www.labergamotenyc.com
"Carrie Bradshaw" wannabes are "addicted" to these "irresistible" patisserie/cafes serving "sinful" baked goods plus French bites; the larger Hell's Kitchen branch offers outdoor seating and more savory options than the "cramped" Chelsea original, but both feel "like Paris" in terms of "attitude" and price.

La Boîte en Bois *French*   22 | 17 | 21 | $53

W 60s | 75 W. 68th St. (bet. Columbus Ave. & CPW) | 212-874-2705 | www.laboitenyc.com
An "old favorite" for diners with a "curtain to make", this 25-year-old French bistro near Lincoln Center offers "delicious" meals and "attentive" service in a "postage stamp"–size space; check out the $40 pre-theater prix fixe, a "terrific" deal.

La Bonne Soupe *French*   18 | 13 | 16 | $30

W 50s | 48 W. 55th St. (bet. 5th & 6th Aves.) | 212-586-7650 | www.labonnesoupe.com
A "coffee shop–like boîte" that's been a Midtown "institution" since 1973, this "dated but tasty" French bistro is famed for its "knock-your-beret-off onion soup" and "oh-so-affordable" tabs; back on the scene following a fire, it's "comforting to know it's still there."

L'Absinthe *French*   22 | 22 | 21 | $68

E 60s | 227 E. 67th St. (bet. 2nd & 3rd Aves.) | 212-794-4950 | www.labsinthe.com
"Almost Paris", this "posh" Upper East Side brasserie is home to a "classy", "well-heeled following", living up to its reputation as "Balthazar for the middle-aged"; *"très bien"* classic French fare, a "charming" art nouveau setting and "caring" service make the "expensive" tabs more palatable.

| | FOOD | DECOR | SERVICE | COST |

NEW La Carbonara *Italian* ▽ 22 | 19 | 19 | $34

W Village | 202 W. 14th St. (bet. 7th & 8th Aves.) | 212-255-2060 |
www.lacarbonaranyc.com

"Taking the mood of the times and combining it with really good food", this new West Village Italian sells "no entree over $15", leading some to say they "could get used to the recession"; it's already a "contender" that suggests "advance reservations."

Ⓩ Lady Mendl's *American* 22 | 26 | 23 | $45

Gramercy | Inn at Irving Pl. | 56 Irving Pl. (bet. 17th & 18th Sts.) |
212-533-4466 | www.ladymendls.com

Something "right out of Henry James", this ultra-"civilized" Gramercy Park tea salon makes "childhood dreams come true" with "finger-sandwiches-and-scones" cuisine served in a "lovely Victorian" setting; though you may need "smelling salts when you get the check", most agree such "turn-of-the-century elegance" is worth the modern-day cost.

La Esquina ● *Mexican* 21 | 22 | 17 | $44

Little Italy | 114 Kenmare St. (bet. Cleveland Pl. & Lafayette St.) |
646-613-7100 | www.esquinanyc.com

There are three ways to sample the "flavorful" fare at this way "hip" Little Italy Mexican: a 24-hour "taco stand", a "funky" sit-down cafe and a "totally fabulous" subterranean grotto accessed "beyond the bouncer", "through the kitchen and down the stairs" – "*if* you can get a reservation"; naturally, everyone prefers the latter since that's where the "beautiful girls" are.

La Flor Bakery & Cafe ⊄ *Bakery/Mexican* ▽ 23 | 13 | 17 | $28

Woodside | 53-02 Roosevelt Ave. (53rd St.) | Queens | 718-426-8023 |
www.laflorestaurant.com

Flor-ists find it "hard to believe" that such "adventurous" Mexican-Eclectic sweets and savories turn up in this tiny Woodside bakery/cafe parked in an "unpromising" location "in the shadow of the el train"; "friendly" service and "bargain" pricing compensate for "no decor" and no plastic.

NEW La Fonda del Sol *Spanish* 22 | 20 | 21 | $56

E 40s | MetLife Bldg. | 200 Park Ave. (enter at 44th St. & Vanderbilt Ave.) |
212-867-6767 | www.patinagroup.com

A legendary Swinging '60s eatery is reincarnated at this "colorful" split-level newcomer near Grand Central, where chef Josh DeChellis executes "excellent" Spanish fare, offering tapas in the "hopping" bar area and full plates in the "calmer" formal dining room; if "not as original as the original", it's still a "buzzy" hit.

Ⓩ La Grenouille Ⓢ *French* 27 | 28 | 27 | $107

E 50s | 3 E. 52nd St. (bet. 5th & Madison Aves.) | 212-752-1495 |
www.la-grenouille.com

The last of NY's "great classic French" restaurants, this "elegant", "flower-filled" Midtown standby helmed by perfectionist Charles Masson is a "feast for every sense", offering "excellent everything" while making you "feel like royalty" (i.e. possibly confusing you with your fellow patrons); if you haven't seen it yet, the upstairs dining atelier is "drop-dead charming" and ideal for less expensive lunches.

	FOOD	DECOR	SERVICE	COST

Lake Club *Continental/Eclectic* ▽ 20 | 23 | 22 | $49

Staten Island | 1150 Clove Rd. (Victory Blvd.) | 718-442-3600 |
www.lake-club.com

A "sylvan" Sunnyside setting – on a private island "overlooking Clove
Lake and the park" – is the hook at this Staten Island "gem" also known
for its "pleasing" Continental-Eclectic menu and "relaxed" ambiance;
some say the place is "more about the view than anything else", but
there's agreement that it fills the bill for "special-event" dining.

La Lanterna di Vittorio ❶ *Italian* 19 | 23 | 17 | $29

G Village | 129 MacDougal St. (bet. W. 3rd & 4th Sts.) | 212-529-5945 |
www.lalanternacaffe.com

Always a "safe bet" for "date night", this "discreet" Village Italian is an
"intimate" nexus for "affordable" pizzas, pastas and desserts served
beside a "blazing fireplace" or in the "covered garden"; "live jazz" in
the adjoining bar enhances the "quintessentially romantic" mood.

La Lunchonette *French* 21 | 14 | 18 | $47

Chelsea | 130 10th Ave. (enter on 18th St., bet. 10th & 11th Aves.) |
212-675-0342

This circa-1987 West Chelsea "pioneer" "used to be locationally challenged", but now finds itself in "trendy" High Line territory; look for
"well-executed French staples" like cassoulet and boeuf bourguignon
along with some "kooky" touches, i.e. that "singing accordion player."

La Mangeoire *French* 21 | 20 | 22 | $50

E 50s | 1008 Second Ave. (bet. 53rd & 54th Sts.) | 212-759-7086 |
www.lamangeoire.com

"Fresh flowers" and "wonderful smells" are hallmarks of this "uncom-
promisingly French" Midtown "throwback" where "satisfying"
Provençal fare is served in "rustic" environs; "economical" tabs and
"warm and fuzzy" service round out the "old-fashioned" experience.

La Masseria ❶ *Italian* 23 | 20 | 22 | $55

W 40s | 235 W. 48th St. (bet. B'way & 8th Ave.) | 212-582-2111 |
www.lamasserianyc.com

There's a "sure hand in the kitchen" of this Theater District Southern
Italian where the "down-to-earth" cooking is as much of a draw as
the "perfect location"; though a few find the "curtain-call rush"
too "noisy and frenetic", the staff "works like mad to get you to your
show on time."

La Mirabelle *French* 23 | 18 | 23 | $51

W 80s | 102 W. 86th St. (bet. Amsterdam & Columbus Aves.) |
212-496-0458 | www.lamirabelleny.com

Like eating at *grand-mère's*, this "family-run", "been-around-forever"
French bistro is an UWS "comfort zone" for folks in their "golden
years" who appreciate "homey" cooking at "not-so-terrible prices"; if
you're lucky, "you may hear the waitresses sing a little Edith Piaf."

Lan *Japanese* 23 | 17 | 20 | $53

E Village | 56 Third Ave. (bet. 10th & 11th Sts.) | 212-254-1959 |
www.lan-nyc.com

"Something for everyone" could be the motto of this East Village
Japanese serving "super-fresh sushi" and "tasty" cooked items, all

washed down with artisanal sakes; "Zen-like", candlelit digs and "pleasant" service lend "standby" status, and though "expensive, it's worth it."

Land Thai   22 | 16 | 19 | $29

E 80s | 1565 Second Ave. (bet. 81st & 82nd Sts.) | 212-439-1847
W 80s | 450 Amsterdam Ave. (bet. 81st & 82nd Sts.) | 212-501-8121
www.landthaikitchen.com

"Budget nights out" don't get much more cost-effective than at this "bustling" crosstown duo that supplies "outstanding" Thai standards with just the "right amount of spice" for just the right amount of dough; but "dinky" dimensions (think "a hallway with chairs") lead claustrophobes to opt for their "lightning-fast delivery."

L & B Spumoni Gardens Dessert/Pizza   23 | 10 | 15 | $22

Bensonhurst | 2725 86th St. (bet. W. 10th & 11th Sts.) | Brooklyn |
718-449-6921 | www.spumonigardens.com

This 71-year-old Italian "institution" is famed for "legendary" Sicilian squares "as thick as a Bensonhurst accent" and "perfectly creamy" spumoni; even if the 'gardens' are actually "picnic tables" on an "asphalt pavement", this "trip down memory lane" is worth it for the "classic Brooklyn people-watching" alone.

Landmarc ● French   20 | 19 | 19 | $48

TriBeCa | 179 W. Broadway (bet. Leonard & Worth Sts.) | 212-343-3883
W 60s | Time Warner Ctr. | 10 Columbus Circle, 3rd fl. (60th St. at B'way) |
212-823-6113
www.landmarc-restaurant.com

Marc Murphy's "casual", "family-friendly" restaurants are "bustling" destinations for "solid" French cooking and "extensive", "barely marked up" wine lists; the original "rustic" TriBeCa outpost is more "intimate" than its "urban bunker" Time Warner Center sibling, but both are "busy", and "no-reservations" policies portend a "wait" at prime times.

Landmark Tavern American/Irish   17 | 19 | 19 | $38

W 40s | 626 11th Ave. (46th St.) | 212-247-2562 |
www.thelandmarktavern.org

Folks seeking an "old NY experience" head for this "long-enduring" way West Side tavern where "not much has changed" since it opened in 1868; its "simple" American-Irish pub grub lies somewhere between "solid" and "so-so", so for most the "thrill here is the building itself."

Lanza Italian   18 | 16 | 19 | $43

E Village | 168 First Ave. (bet. 10th & 11th Sts.) | 212-674-7014

It's "throwback" time at this circa-1904 East Village Italian known for "quality red-sauce" cooking at "fair prices"; maybe the "tin-ceilinged" setting is a bit "faded" and the overall experience too "old-fashioned" for modernists, but a "filling" experience is guaranteed for all.

La Palapa ● Mexican   19 | 16 | 17 | $34

E Village | 77 St. Marks Pl. (bet. 1st & 2nd Aves.) | 212-777-2537
G Village | 359 Sixth Ave. (bet. Washington Pl. & W. 4th St.) | 212-243-6870
www.lapalapa.com

"Flavorful" south-of-the-border eats and "killer margaritas" provide the *uno-dos* "punch" at this "nothing-fancy" cross-Village Mexican duo; "party" atmospherics and "reasonable prices" work equally well for "large groups" or just a "casual" meal out.

	FOOD	DECOR	SERVICE	COST

La Petite Auberge *French*

20 17 22 $47

Murray Hill | 116 Lexington Ave. (bet. 27th & 28th Sts.) | 212-689-5003 | www.lapetiteaubergeny.com

"Time stands still – in the best possible way" – at this old Murray Hill bistro favored for its "butter-and-cream" French cooking "without hype or attitude"; *oui*, it may be "a little frayed around the edges", but "affordable" tabs and "treat-you-like-family" service make many glad that "it never changes."

La Pizza Fresca Ristorante *Italian*

23 16 18 $42

Flatiron | 31 E. 20th St. (bet. B'way & Park Ave. S.) | 212-598-0141 | www.lapizzafrescaristorante.com

"Interesting" brick-oven Neapolitan pizza and "top-notch" pastas accompanied by an "extensive wine list" make this "casual" yet "sophisticated" Flatiron Italian "better than expected"; while service can be "hit-or-miss", "when they're on, they're on."

NEW L'Artusi *Italian*

21 21 22 $56

W Village | 228 W. 10th St. (bet. Bleecker & Hudson Sts.) | 212-255-5757 | www.lartusi.com

From the dell'anima team comes this West Village "New Wave Italian" that's "more spacious" than its sibling but just as "loud" and "of the moment"; look for a "vibrant" menu that's "conducive to sharing", "eager-to-please" service and an "easy-on-the-eyes crowd", and don't miss the "beautiful wine cellar"–cum–private room.

La Rural *Argentinean/Steak*

∇ 21 17 20 $43

W 90s | 768 Amsterdam Ave. (bet. 97th & 98th Sts.) | 212-749-2929

They "really know how to grill meat" at this UWS Argentine where carnivores report "ample portions" of "really great" steak served in the former Pampa digs; "helpful", "heavily accented" staffers lend "authenticity", while "moderate prices" distract from the "noisy" atmosphere.

La Sirène ⊅ *French*

∇ 23 12 21 $45

SoHo | 558½ Broome St. (Varick St.) | 212-925-3061 | www.lasirenenyc.com

"Small and funky", this "bohemian" 25-seater in West SoHo pairs an "ambitious", seafood-heavy French menu with money-saving BYO and "cash-only" policies; the "lack of decor" and "tight" seating go unnoticed thanks to a "hoot" of an owner, who plays the "roles of chef, maitre d' and schmoozer."

Las Ramblas ● *Spanish*

24 18 23 $37

G Village | 170 W. Fourth St. (bet. Cornelia & Jones Sts.) | 646-415-7924 | www.lasramblasnyc.com

"Monumental" food at fair prices lands in the "teeny-tiny" room of this Village Spaniard where the tapas selection is so "transcendent" that some want to "order everything on the menu"; granted, there are "elbow-room" issues, but "energetic" owner Natalie Sanz is so "charming" that few mind.

La Superior ●⊅ *Mexican*

∇ 23 11 16 $17

Williamsburg | 295 Berry St. (bet. S. 2nd & 3rd Sts.) | Brooklyn | 718-388-5988 | www.lasuperiornyc.com

"Amazing" Mexican street food is the hook at this Williamsburg spot where the "small portions" deliver "big flavors", especially those "to-

"die-for" tiny tacos; despite a cash-only policy, "no booze" (as yet) and service and decor that "leave much to be desired", the waits to get in can be "longer than a flight to Mexico."

La Taqueria *Mexican*   20 | 14 | 16 | $17

Park Slope | 72 Seventh Ave. (bet. Berkeley & Lincoln Pls.) | Brooklyn | 718-398-4300

Rachel's Taqueria *Mexican*

Park Slope | 408 Fifth Ave. (bet. 7th & 8th Sts.) | Brooklyn | 718-788-1137 | www.rachelstaqueria.com

"Overstuffed burritos" – the "perfect greasy hangover cure" – and other "delish" Mexican standards draw fans to these el cheapo Park Slope taquerias; despite (or maybe because of) the "funky beach bar decor" and "laid-back", "Left Coast" vibe, many prefer them for "takeout."

La Taza de Oro 🗷🗷 *Puerto Rican*   ▽ 20 | 5 | 14 | $16

Chelsea | 96 Eighth Ave. (bet. 14th & 15th Sts.) | 212-243-9946

"No one leaves hungry" from this cash-only, "pre-gentrification" Chelsea coffee shop thanks to its "simple" but "wonderful" Puerto Rican comfort chow; while the digs are strictly "hole-in-the-wall", the portions are "large", the tabs "cheap" and the mood *"mi casa es su casa."*

🗷 L'Atelier de Joël Robuchon *French*   28 | 25 | 26 | $127

E 50s | Four Seasons Hotel | 57 E. 57th St. (bet. Madison & Park Aves.) | 212-829-3844 | www.fourseasons.com

Although there are a few tables, it's "most fun sitting at the counter" eating small plates of Joël Robuchon's "imaginative", Japanese-inflected French cuisine; as high ratings show, most consider this East Midtowner to be simply *"merveilleux"*, however, a few report that dining here is "deceivingly expensive" and wonder if the chef has "spread himself too thin."

Lattanzi ●🗷 *Italian*   22 | 19 | 21 | $55

W 40s | 361 W. 46th St. (bet. 8th & 9th Aves.) | 212-315-0980 | www.lattanzinyc.com

Sure, this "reliable" Restaurant Row Italian delivers "great performances" pre-theater, but insiders say it's "even better" after 8 when "authentic Roman-Jewish" dishes (including its "signature fried artichokes") are available; other pluses include a "pretty" garden and "smooth service"; as for the cost, "pricey is the word."

Laut 🗷 *Malaysian/Thai*   ▽ 24 | 18 | 23 | $31

Union Sq | 15 E. 17th St. (bet. B'way & 5th Ave.) | 212-206-8989 | www.lautnyc.com

From the owners of Mizu Sushi comes this Thai-Malaysian hybrid off Union Square offering a "delicately seasoned" array of Pan-Asian dishes that also work well for "takeout or delivery"; the place may be "small", but so are the tabs, hence its decidedly "young" following.

Lavagna *Italian*   23 | 17 | 21 | $47

E Village | 545 E. Fifth St. (bet. Aves. A & B) | 212-979-1005 | www.lavagnanyc.com

"Honest cooking" and a "well-chosen wine list" make this "unpretentious" Italian a bona fide Alphabet City "find", especially when you factor in "easy-on-the-pocket" pricing; romancers purr it's "perfect for a first date", although what's "intimate" to some is just plain "tight" to others.

La Villa Pizzeria *Pizza* | 21 | 16 | 18 | $28 |

Mill Basin | Key Food Shopping Ctr. | 6610 Ave. U (bet. 66th & 67th Sts.) | Brooklyn | 718-251-8030
Park Slope | 261 Fifth Ave. (bet. 1st St. & Garfield Pl.) | Brooklyn | 718-499-9888 | www.lavillaparkslope.com
Howard Bch | Lindenwood Shopping Ctr. | 82-07 153rd Ave. (82nd St.) | Queens | 718-641-8259

"Casual" outer-borough trio known for "addictive" brick-oven pizza and other "delicious", "red-sauce" standards that are a hit with its "big-hair-Ban-Lon-shirt" crowd; "moderate" tabs trump the "lackluster decor."

Lazzara's *Pizza* | ∇ 23 | 11 | 16 | $19 |

Garment District | 221 W. 38th St., 2nd fl. (bet. 7th & 8th Aves.) | 212-944-7792
NEW **W 40s** | 617 Ninth Ave. (bet. 43rd & 44th Sts.) | 212-245-4440 ☽ www.lazzaraspizza.com

"Fantastic thin-crust" square pies are the signature of these "un-celebrated" Midtown pizzerias; the Garment District original exudes a "speakeasy" vibe with a hidden, second-floor location, while its brand-new Hell's Kitchen sibling is more generic, but does offer single slices.

Le Barricou ☽ *French* | ∇ 23 | 20 | 19 | $31 |

Williamsburg | 533 Grand St. (bet. Lorimer St. & Union Ave.) | Brooklyn | 718-782-7372 | www.lebarricouny.com
Importing a bit of "France to Brooklyn", this "charming" East Williamsburg bistro serves a well-priced country French menu in "cozy", brick-walled quarters; regulars gathered around the "fireplace" in the "back wine room" wonder why it remains such a "best-kept secret."

Z Le Bernardin ☒ *French/Seafood* | 28 | 27 | 28 | $142 |

W 50s | 155 W. 51st St. (bet. 6th & 7th Aves.) | 212-554-1515 | www.le-bernardin.com
Back on top with the No. 1 rating for Food in this year's Survey, this hand-some wood-paneled French seafood specialist in Midtown, helmed by Maguy LeCoze and chef Eric Ripert, is "a world-class restaurant", "con-sistently wonderful" and consistently "civilized"; if you can afford it, let the chef do a tasting menu for you – if you can't, the $45 prix fixe lunch is one of "NYC's best bargains"; P.S. parties upstairs can be "very special."

Le Bilboquet *French* | 23 | 16 | 17 | $60 |

E 60s | 25 E. 63rd St. (bet. Madison & Park Aves.) | 212-751-3036
Very good French food notwithstanding, it's definitely "scene" over cuisine at this "loud" East Side bistro/"party spot" where the "pretty" "cosmopolitan" crowd prefers "air kissing" to eating; to bypass the staff's "attitude", it helps to "have a foreign accent" or "drive up in a Porsche Cayenne" "accompanied by photographers."

Le Boeuf à la Mode ☒ *French* | 21 | 19 | 22 | $58 |

E 80s | 539 E. 81st St. (bet. East End & York Aves.) | 212-249-1473 | www.leboeufalamode.net
A "pleasant time warp" set on the "extreme East Side", this circa-1962 French bistro is a "real survivor", where "just-right classics" are served in a "quiet", white-tablecloth setting with plenty of "room between tables";

it's frequented mainly by the "AARP set", and though fans say it's the epitome of "old-world charm", critics counter it's just plain "getting old."

☑ Le Cirque ☒ *French* | 24 | 26 | 24 | $127 |

E 50s | One Beacon Court | 151 E. 58th St. (bet. Lexington & 3rd Aves.) | 212-644-0202 | www.lecirque.com

Now in its third incarnation in a rich, 36-year history, Sirio Maccioni's Midtown French "classic" thrills its "elegant, celeb-sprinkled crowd" with "sublime" food, decor and service – even the wallpaper is interesting; while it continues to be a "quintessential NYC dining experience", some feel it's "slipped a bit", however, the prix fixe lunch and dinners are a "steal" and there's also a casual, less expensive cafe, presided over by two of Sirio's sons, Marco and Mauro.

L'Ecole *French* | 24 | 21 | 22 | $55 |

SoHo | Intl. Culinary Ctr. | 462 Broadway (Grand St.) | 212-219-3300 | www.frenchculinary.com

Since the staffers of this SoHo French lab/eatery are "culinary students" and the "bargain" prices are well below those of its competitors, surveyors cut it plenty of slack and would award the students "A's"; but tougher graders say the program is "hit-or-miss" and "needs more work."

Le Colonial *French/Vietnamese* | 20 | 23 | 20 | $55 |

E 50s | 149 E. 57th St. (bet. Lexington & 3rd Aves.) | 212-752-0808 | www.lecolonialnyc.com

Channeling "old Saigon", this "exotic" Midtowner offers "well-spiced" French-Vietnamese fusion fare in a "don-your-linen-suit" setting rife with "potted palms" and "whirring ceiling fans"; ok, it's "pricey" and may "lack the buzz it once enjoyed", but the "otherworldly" upstairs lounge is just as "transporting" as ever.

Leela Lounge ☒ *Indian* | ▽ 21 | 17 | 18 | $35 |

G Village | 1 W. Third St. (bet. B'way & Mercer St.) | 212-529-2059 | www.leelalounge.com

A "different", "healthy" menu featuring "cool twists on traditional Indian" dishes made without butter or heavy cream draws devotees to this inexpensive Villager; given the "fun" vibe and "friendly" (albeit "slow") service, some wonder why there's "always a table" available.

Le Gamin *French* | 18 | 17 | 17 | $26 |

E Village | 536 E. Fifth St. (bet. Aves. A & B) | 212-529-8933 ◗
Prospect Heights | 556 Vanderbilt Ave. (bet. Bergen & Dean Sts.) | Brooklyn | 718-789-5171
www.legamin.com

Though now down to two locations, this shrinking mini-chain still slings "basic" French bistro eats (and particularly "excellent crêpes") in "relaxed" settings with "prices to match"; still, the "Gallic charm" wears a bit thin when it comes to the "scattered service."

Le Gigot �M *French* | 23 | 18 | 22 | $56 |

G Village | 18 Cornelia St. (bet. Bleecker & W. 4th Sts.) | 212-627-3737 | www.legigotrestaurant.com

"If it were any more French you'd need a passport" at this "delightful" Village boîte where both the Provençal cooking and the service "couldn't be nicer"; despite "costly" tabs and seating that makes you "feel like a sardine", most report "eating like a king."

	FOOD	DECOR	SERVICE	COST

Le Jardin Bistro *French*
20 | 18 | 19 | $46

NoLita | 25 Cleveland Pl. (bet. Kenmare & Spring Sts.) | 212-343-9599 | www.lejardinbistro.com

It's all about the "beautiful" garden at this aptly named NoLita French bistro where the "serene" backyard is "shaded by real grapevines"; indeed, the "straightforward" Gallic offerings come at such *"bon marché"* tabs that admirers rate it a "charming" stop "year-round."

NEW Le Magnifique ● *French*
- | - | - | M

E 70s | 1022A Lexington Ave. (73rd St.) | 212-879-6190

Owners of the erstwhile Buzina Pop have swapped Brazilian fare for French bistro dishes at this reinvented Upper Eastsider, where the pricing is as relaxed as the setting; the duplex space features a casual bar downstairs, an airy dining room above and fair-weather sidewalk seats.

Le Marais *French/Steak*
22 | 16 | 17 | $53

W 40s | 150 W. 46th St. (bet. 6th & 7th Aves.) | 212-869-0900 | www.lemarais.net

Bringing "superb" steaks to the "heart of the Theater District", this kosher "keeper" serves a French-influenced menu; it's too bad "service has never been great here", but nevertheless, it's "always full" – and if you enjoy your dinner it's good to know there's an "attached butcher shop."

Le Monde *French*
18 | 18 | 17 | $34

W 100s | 2885 Broadway (bet. 112th & 113th Sts.) | 212-531-3939 | www.lemondenyc.com

Always "crowded" with "Columbia academics", this "solid" Morningside Heights bistro is a campus "mainstay" for "satisfying" French cooking focusing on the "cuisine of the Loire Valley"; "inconsistent" service goes unnoticed thanks to the "inexpensive" tabs, "relaxing" mood and "appealing" sidewalk seating.

Lemongrass Grill *Thai*
16 | 11 | 15 | $26

Financial District | 84 William St. (Maiden Ln.) | 212-809-8038 | www.lemongrassgrillnyc.com
Murray Hill | 138 E. 34th St. (bet. Lexington & 3rd Aves.) | 212-213-3317 | www.lemongrassgrill34thst.com
W 90s | 2534 Broadway (bet. 94th & 95th Sts.) | 212-666-0888 | www.lemongrassgrillbroadway.com
Cobble Hill | 156 Court St. (bet. Dean & Pacific Sts.) | Brooklyn | 718-522-9728
Park Slope | 61A Seventh Ave. (bet. Berkeley & Lincoln Pls.) | Brooklyn | 718-399-7100

"Ubiquitous" mini-chain slinging "generous portions" of "basic", "not spectacular" Thai chow for "cheap" tariffs; unless you "close your eyes" to the decor and service, you may wish to opt for takeout or "rapid-fire" delivery.

Lenny's *Sandwiches*
17 | 8 | 14 | $14

E 50s | 1024 Second Ave. (54th St.) | 212-355-5700
E 60s | 1269 First Ave. (68th St.) | 212-288-0852
E 70s | 1481 Second Ave. (77th St.) | 212-288-5288
Financial District | 108 John St. (bet. Cliff & Pearl Sts.) | 212-385-2828
Flatiron | 16 W. 23rd St. (5th Ave.) | 212-462-4433
G Village | 418 Sixth Ave. (9th St.) | 212-353-0300

(continued)

Lenny's

W 40s | 60 W. 48th St. (bet. 5th & 6th Aves.) | 212-997-1969
W 40s | 613 Ninth Ave. (43rd St.) | 212-957-7800
W 70s | 302 Columbus Ave. (74th St.) | 212-580-8300
W 80s | 489 Columbus Ave. (84th St.) | 212-787-9368
www.lennysnyc.com
Additional locations throughout the NY area

Credit an "assembly-line" process that "Henry Ford would be proud of" for the "quick", "fresh" sandwiches sold by this all-over-town chain; ok, there's "no atmosphere", but "affordable" tabs and a "smorgasbord of options" keep regulars regular.

Leo's Latticini 🗲Ⓜ Deli/Italian
(aka Mama's of Corona)

∇ 27 | 12 | 21 | $15

Corona | 46-02 104th St. (46th Ave.) | Queens | 718-898-6069

"Awesome" Italian heros and "delicious homemade mozzarella" are the draws at this "friendly", "family-owned" Corona deli that's been on the scene since 1920; while the setting's "nothing fancy", the place has "character", not to mention "can't-be-beat" prices.

Le Pain Quotidien Bakery/Belgian

19 | 15 | 14 | $23

E 60s | 833 Lexington Ave. (bet. 63rd & 64th Sts.) | 212-755-5810
E 70s | 252 E. 77th St. (bet. 2nd & 3rd Aves.) | 212-249-8600
E 80s | 1131 Madison Ave. (bet. 84th & 85th Sts.) | 212-327-4900
Flatiron | ABC Carpet & Home | 38 E. 19th St. (bet. B'way & Park Ave. S.) | 212-673-7900
G Village | 10 Fifth Ave. (8th St.) | 212-253-2324
G Village | 801 Broadway (11th St.) | 212-677-5277
SoHo | 100 Grand St. (bet. Greene & Mercer Sts.) | 212-625-9009
W 50s | 922 Seventh Ave. (58th St.) | 212-757-0775
W 60s | 60 W. 65th St. (bet. B'way & CPW) | 212-721-4001
W 70s | 50 W. 72nd St. (bet. Columbus Ave. & CPW) | 212-712-9700
www.painquotidien.com
Additional locations throughout the NY area

"Informal" Belgian bakery/cafe chain known for its "killer" baked goods and "reasonably healthy", mostly "organic" fare; the farmhouse-"rustic" interiors with "long communal tables" are conducive to "solo dining", so aside from "snail's-pace" service, most feel the "formula works."

Le Perigord French

24 | 21 | 25 | $78

E 50s | 405 E. 52nd St. (bet. FDR Dr. & 1st Ave.) | 212-755-6244 | www.leperigord.com

"Adults" who believe in "dressing for dinner" tout this Sutton Place "epitome of elegance", a "formal dining" "standard" since 1964 offering "sublime" haute French cuisine served by "tuxedoed" professionals overseen by "watchful" owner Georges Briguet; granted, it's "not inexpensive" but it is the "last of a vanishing breed" and "well worth" experiencing.

Le Petit Marché French

23 | 19 | 22 | $48

Brooklyn Heights | 46 Henry St. (bet. Cranberry & Middagh Sts.) | Brooklyn | 718-858-9605 | www.bkbistro.com

"First-class" Gallic fare, a "well-chosen wine list" and a "welcoming" mien keep Brooklyn Heights residents "coming back" to this "comfortable" French bistro; though the "prices are not exactly *petits*", they're perfectly "reasonable for the quality."

Le Refuge *French*

21 | 20 | 20 | $57

E 80s | 166 E. 82nd St. (bet. Lexington & 3rd Aves.) | 212-861-4505 | www.lerefugenyc.com

Living up to its name, this "long-lasting" (since 1980) Upper East Side bistro has been a sanctuary for "simple", "quality" French meals away from "the noise and hustle of the city"; admirers praise its "cozy", candlelit rooms and "lovely" back garden, and tolerate the rather "expensive" price tags.

NEW Le Relais de Venise
L'Entrecôte *Steak*

- | - | - | M

E 50s | 590 Lexington Ave. (52nd St.) | 212-758-3989 | www.relaisdevenise.com

Hoping to replicate its runaway success in Paris, London and Barcelona, this new East Midtown French steakhouse serves but one meal (a green salad plus steak frites) for one set price ($24); the no-reservations policy has also been imported, but so far there aren't the same lines as in Europe.

Le Rivage *French*

20 | 17 | 21 | $46

W 40s | 340 W. 46th St. (bet. 8th & 9th Aves.) | 212-765-7374 | www.lerivagenyc.com

Things "run like clockwork pre-theater" at this Restaurant Row "golden oldie" that's been dishing out "dependable" French *"cuisine bourgeoise"* since 1958; maybe the setting's getting "a little tired", but few mind given the "convenient location" and "bargain" $25 prix fixe served after 8 PM.

Les Enfants Terribles ☻ *African/French*

▽ 18 | 17 | 16 | $37

LES | 37 Canal St. (Ludlow St.) | 212-777-7518 | www.lesenfantsterriblesnyc.com

"Effortlessly cool", "hip and humming", this Lower Eastsider features an "interesting" French-African menu that comes at a "reasonable" price yet "doesn't taste as exotic as it sounds"; nonetheless, it's particularly "fun late night", drawing a "diverse", often "loud crowd."

Les Halles ☻ *French*

20 | 17 | 17 | $47

Financial District | 15 John St. (bet. B'way & Nassau St.) | 212-285-8585
Murray Hill | 411 Park Ave. S. (bet. 28th & 29th Sts.) | 212-679-4111
www.leshalles.net

Even if Anthony Bourdain "doesn't cook here anymore", he "left his mark" at these "atmospheric" French bistros via "sturdy" signature dishes like those "killer steak frites"; "upbeat" vibes and "affordable" tabs trump the "too-small tables" and "noise, noise and more noise."

Le Singe Vert ☻ *French*

18 | 15 | 17 | $40

Chelsea | 160 Seventh Ave. (bet. 19th & 20th Sts.) | 212-366-4100 | www.lesingevert.com

"Giving the 6th arrondissement a run for its money", this *"très authentique"* Chelsea bistro is a "fine ambassador" when it comes to "serviceable", "great-value" Gallic grub; critics who find the "knee-to-knee" dimensions too "tight" opt for "sidewalk" seats serving up swell "Seventh Avenue" sightseeing.

	FOOD	DECOR	SERVICE	COST

NEW Levant East *American/French*

	-	-	-	M

LES | The Hotel on Rivington | 107 Rivington St. (bet. Essex & Ludlow Sts.) | 212-796-8040

The latest settler in the dining room of the LES' Thor Hotel, this wannabe-trendy newcomer offers midpriced French bistro/American spa dishes in a high-ceilinged space that's little changed from its earlier incarnations; since it's overseen by nightlife maven Matt Levine (the Eldridge), expect more care lavished on the cocktails than the food.

L'Express ● *French*

17	15	14	$33

Flatiron | 249 Park Ave. S. (20th St.) | 212-254-5858 | www.lexpressnyc.com

"Open 24/7", this "useful" Flatiron bistro is a "late-night" "standby" featuring "casual", "French-for-beginners" eats that "won't break the bank"; true, "tables are close together", the service "so-so" and the noise level can be "killer", but "in the middle of the night, who cares?"

Le Zie 2000 ● *Italian*

22	15	18	$40

Chelsea | 172 Seventh Ave. (bet. 20th & 21st Sts.) | 212-206-8686 | www.lezie.com

Flaunting its "staying power", this "wildly popular" Chelsea Italian offers an "excellent" Venetian menu for "reasonable" dough (just be aware that the "price of the specials is way higher" than the standard entrees); regulars angle for a "table in the back room" to avoid the "deafening" decibels up front.

Liberty View *Chinese*

▽ 19	14	15	$28

Financial District | 21 South End Ave. (bet. 3rd Pl. & W. Thames St.) | 212-786-1888 | www.libertyviewrestaurant.com

"Lovely outside seating" with a "million-dollar view of the Statue of Liberty" is the raison d'être of this Battery Park City "white-tablecloth" Chinese; despite just "ok service", a "blah" interior and "nothing exotic" on the menu, the price is right – and it's a "safe" bet for "out-of-towners."

Liebman's *Deli*

21	9	18	$23

Bronx | 552 W. 235th St. (Johnson Ave.) | 718-548-4534 | www.liebmansdeli.com

An "authentic" representation of a "dying breed", this "old-fashioned", low-budget kosher deli in the Bronx "does all the standards well", from "wonderful knishes" to "delicious" overstuffed sandwiches; sure, the decor is "nothing to write home about", but that's a given for the genre.

Lil' Frankie's Pizza ●⇄ *Pizza*

23	15	17	$30

E Village | 19 First Ave. (bet. 1st & 2nd Sts.) | 212-420-4900 | www.lilfrankies.com

"Darn good" thin-crust Neapolitan pizza and other "dependable" Italian staples are slung at this East Village "hipster hangout" spun off from Frank; despite "crowded, cramped" digs and a "cash-only" rule, it's quite the "social destination", maybe because of the "very good value."

Lisca *Italian*

22	15	21	$40

W 90s | 660 Amsterdam Ave. (bet. 92nd & 93rd Sts.) | 212-799-3987 | www.liscanyc.com

"Sweet" and "low-key", this "family-run" Upper West Side Tuscan is just the ticket for "consistent" Italian cooking at moderate tabs;

it also "has customer service down" pat, making for a "lovely neighborhood dining experience."

Little Giant *American*

FOOD	DECOR	SERVICE	COST
22	17	19	$46

LES | 85 Orchard St. (Broome St.) | 212-226-5047 |
www.littlegiantnyc.com

"Giant tastes" arrive in a "little space" at this LES New American "gem" where the "farm-to-table" comfort food cooking makes for "lick-the-plate-clean" dining; for best results, "go early" or "be prepared to get very cozy with the table next to you"; P.S. "brunch is tops."

☒ Little Owl *American/Mediterranean*

FOOD	DECOR	SERVICE	COST
26	19	23	$54

W Village | 90 Bedford St. (Grove St.) | 212-741-4695 |
www.thelittleowlnyc.com

Chef Joey Campanaro's "soulfully executed", "attractively priced" Med–New American food is served in a "Cracker Jack box–size" space at this West Village "neighborhood scene"; given the "notoriously difficult reservations" and "cramped", "noisy" conditions, regulars report it is definitely "for the young and agile."

Lobo *Tex-Mex*

FOOD	DECOR	SERVICE	COST
▽ 15	16	18	$28

Cobble Hill | 218 Court St. (bet. Baltic & Warren Sts.) | Brooklyn |
718-858-7739 ⊟
Park Slope | 188 Fifth Ave. (Sackett St.) | Brooklyn |
718-636-8886 ◑
www.lobonyc.com

"Heaping portions" of "sturdy" Tex-Mex chow and "fantastic" margaritas provide the "double whammy" at this "funky" Brooklyn twosome; despite "predictable" menus and "mall food court" decor, fans say Cobble Hill's "newly renovated" back patio is a fine spot to "relax with friends."

Lobster Box ◑ *Seafood*

FOOD	DECOR	SERVICE	COST
19	15	17	$47

Bronx | 34 City Island Ave. (bet. Belden & Rochelle Sts.) | 718-885-1952 |
www.lobsterboxrestaurant.com

Ever since 1946, this City Island seafooder has dished up "excellent" examples of the namesake crustacean, though the views of Long Island Sound are really the "best thing" here; cynics say it "exists on its past glory", citing "disorganized" service and "tired" looks.

Locale *Italian*

FOOD	DECOR	SERVICE	COST
▽ 21	22	19	$32

Astoria | 33-02 34th Ave. (33rd St.) | Queens | 718-729-9080 |
www.localeastoria.com

"Manhattan comes to Astoria" via this "trendy" Queens Italian serving "hip patrons" an "ingenious" menu for "outer-borough prices"; given its "loungey" atmosphere, amusing "people-watching" and "solid brunch", most don't mind that "service isn't a priority."

☒NEW☒ Locanda Verde *Italian*

FOOD	DECOR	SERVICE	COST
22	22	20	$57

TriBeCa | Greenwich Hotel | 379 Greenwich St. (N. Moore St.) |
212-925-3797 | www.locandaverdenyc.com

Second time's a charm at this new haute-casual "neighborhood" spot in TriBeCa's Greenwich Hotel; ex A Voce chef Andrew Carmellini offers a "delicious" (if "not blow-your-mind") rustic Italian menu, backed up by "knowledgeable" service, "reasonable" pricing, a glowing, tavernesque setting and "lots of hustle and bustle."

	FOOD	DECOR	SERVICE	COST

Locanda Vini & Olii ⓜ *Italian* — ▽ 22 | 22 | 21 | $48

Clinton Hill | 129 Gates Ave. (bet. Cambridge Pl. & Grand Ave.) | Brooklyn | 718-622-9202 | www.locandany.com

"Urban renewal" turns up in Clinton Hill at this "old apothecary shop" that's been converted into a "creative", midpriced Tuscan eatery; "warm owners" and a most "charming" setting compensate for the "microscopic" portion sizes.

Lokal *Mediterranean* — ▽ 18 | 16 | 19 | $31

Greenpoint | 905 Lorimer St. (Bedford Ave.) | Brooklyn | 718-384-6777 | www.lokalbistro.com

Thanks to a lokation overlooking McCarren Park, this "cool", "relaxed" Greenpoint Med exudes a distinct "picnic" vibe when its huge doors open up in warm weather; the cooking's "better than expected", the service "friendly" and the tabs priced for "hipster" budgets.

Lombardi's ⊘ *Pizza* — 24 | 13 | 16 | $24

NoLita | 32 Spring St. (bet. Mott & Mulberry Sts.) | 212-941-7994 | www.firstpizza.com

"Still the king of coal-fired pizza", this "old-school" NoLita fixture serves up "slightly charred" "thin-crust" pies that are the "ultimate" for die-hard fans; it's "cash only" and can be kinda "touristy", but at least the "swift service" makes the "long lines flow fast."

Londel's Supper Club ⓜ *Southern* — ▽ 19 | 18 | 19 | $36

Harlem | 2620 Frederick Douglass Blvd. (bet. 139th & 140th Sts.) | 212-234-6114 | www.londelsrestaurant.com

With its "old-time elegance", "good food" and live weekend jazz, this "reliable" Southern belle on Harlem's Strivers' Row "transports" fans to "another era"; on Sundays, the "after-church crowd" sings the praises of the brunch buffet.

London Lennie's *Seafood* — 22 | 17 | 20 | $43

Rego Park | 63-88 Woodhaven Blvd. (bet. Fleet Ct. & Penelope Ave.) | Queens | 718-894-8084 | www.londonlennies.com

A "standby for umpteen years", this Rego Park "jewel in the boroughs" is always "jumping" with afishionados tucking into "wonderfully fresh" seafood; "don't expect fancy-schmancy" – the scene is "family-oriented" – and the pricing is "reasonable" to Manhattanites but "special occasion" for Queens.

Lorenzo's *Italian* — ▽ 19 | 22 | 21 | $49

Staten Island | Hilton Garden Inn | 1100 South Ave. (Lois Ln.) | 718-477-2400 | www.lorenzosdining.com

Sunday's jazz brunch may be the "best deal on Staten Island" at this "welcoming" Hilton Garden Inn Italian in Bloomfield that also hosts cabaret performers on weekends; the room's "pretty" and the service "excellent", but as for the menu, opinions range from "above-average" to "needs updating."

Los Dados *Mexican* — 16 | 18 | 16 | $44

Meatpacking | 73 Gansevoort St. (Washington St.) | 646-810-7290 | www.losdadosmexican.com

"Location" is the thing at this "funky", High Line–handy Meatpacking Mexican, not the "so-so" chow and "overpriced" cocktails; indeed, since chef Sue Torres' departure, the "food seems to be beside the point", though the "buzzing atmosphere" remains.

NEW Lot 2 Ⓜ American
- | - | - | M

Park Slope | 687 Sixth Ave. (bet. 19th & 20th Sts.) | Brooklyn | 718-499-5623 | www.lot2restaurant.com

A Gramercy Tavern alum turns out New Americana with a rustic Italian bent at this small, stripped-down arrival in the burgeoning South Slope; its succinct roster of moderately priced dishes, many featuring house-made charcuterie, is abetted by a smartly quirky wine-and-beer list.

Ⓩ Lucali ⏚ Pizza
26 | 16 | 19 | $24

Carroll Gardens | 575 Henry St. (bet. Carroll St. & 1st Pl.) | Brooklyn | 718-858-4086

"Get there early" since this cash-only Carroll Gardens pizzeria "has a line of people waiting before it even opens"; while it's impossible to reach agreement on who serves the "best pizza and calzone in the city", there's no question that this place is right up there "among the best."

NEW Lucas Steakhouse Ⓜ Steak
- | - | - | VE

Astoria | 34-55 32nd St. (35th Ave.) | Queens | 718-786-5200 | www.lucassteakhouse.com

From the Locale team comes this new Astoria chop shop near the American Museum of the Moving Image; rendered in exposed brick and tufted leather, the petite, 25-seat space mirrors the pared-down menu – but not the big-ticket tabs.

NEW Luce Italian
- | - | - | M

W 60s | 2014 Broadway (bet. 68th & 69th Sts.) | 212-724-1400 | www.lucenyc.com

Heaping bowls of fresh pasta and other hearty Italian classics attract both locals and Lincoln Center–goers to this midpriced UWS enoteca; ample sidewalk seating on Broadway augments the rustic Tuscan interior, complete with vaulted ceilings and wine racks built into the walls.

Lucien ◑ French
22 | 17 | 19 | $44

E Village | 14 First Ave. (1st St.) | 212-260-6481 | www.luciennyc.com

Bringing "Paris within reach", this "special" East Village French bistro attracts "beret-clad" locals and "expats" with "*délicieux*" dishes for "moderate" sums; "genial" owner Lucien Bahaj "makes everyone feel welcome" in the "cramped" quarters, though some of the waiters "have more tattoos than experience."

Lucky Strike ◑ French
16 | 17 | 15 | $34

SoHo | 59 Grand St. (bet. W. B'way & Wooster St.) | 212-941-0772 | www.luckystrikeny.com

"One of the last remnants of 'old' SoHo", Keith McNally's "chic but casual" survivor still dispenses a "real winner" of a burger plus assorted French bistro items into the "wee hours"; "fair prices" and "perfect faux-aged decor" offset the "dining room din" and "hit-or-miss" cooking.

NEW Lucy Browne's American
- | - | - | I

W Village | 225 Varick St. (Clarkson St.) | 212-463-7101 | www.lucybrownesny.com

The revolving-door West Village space most recently home to Steak Frites has been rejiggered into this neon-signed, all-American venue whose wide-ranging menu includes everything from burgers to po' boys to shrimp and grits; cheap tabs, loud music and lots of seats are drawing in younger types.

NEW Lugo Caffe ●☒ *Italian* ▽ 21 | 21 | 22 | $49

Garment District | 1 Penn Plaza (33rd St., bet. 7th & 8th Aves.) | 212-760-2700 | www.lugocaffe.com

Injecting a little dolce vita into the "barren" zone around MSG, this new Garment District Italian (in the former Tupelo Grill digs) combines midpriced, "tasty" food with a "metro" ambiance; insiders sidestep the "noisy bar crowd" by retreating to the "cavernous" back room.

Lumi ● *Italian* 18 | 19 | 21 | $56

E 70s | 963 Lexington Ave. (70th St.) | 212-570-2335 | www.lumirestaurant.com

"Unsung" yet "well-established", this longtime Italian serves "solid if not inspirational" Tuscan fare to a crowd right out of "Upper East Side central casting"; "lovely" atmospherics ("charming" fireplaces, "ever-changing artwork" and "attractive sidewalk seating") distract from the "pricey" tabs.

Lunetta Ⓜ *Italian* 21 | 17 | 18 | $42

Boerum Hill | 116 Smith St. (bet. Dean & Pacific Sts.) | Brooklyn | 718-488-6269 | www.lunetta-ny.com

A Flatiron offshoot faded into the sunset but the "cherished" Boerum Hill original remains, serving "deceptively simple" Italian small plates crafted from "seasonal ingredients"; the small 'kitchen bar' area with a view of the chef "rocks", ditto the "charming garden."

☒ Lupa ● *Italian* 25 | 18 | 21 | $54

G Village | 170 Thompson St. (bet. Bleecker & Houston Sts.) | 212-982-5089 | www.luparestaurant.com

"More affordable" than "other stars in the Mario Batali constellation", this "festive" Village trattoria (aka the "poor man's Babbo") is always "jumping" with "happy campers" who are "loopy" for its "robust" Roman repasts and "approachable wine list"; since it lacks *molto* space and reservations are "tough", regulars "go off-peak" to score a seat.

Lure Fishbar *Seafood* 23 | 23 | 21 | $58

SoHo | 142 Mercer St., downstairs (Prince St.) | 212-431-7676 | www.lurefishbar.com

As "swank and fashionable" as ever, this subterranean SoHo sea-fooder seduces surveyors with "terrific" fish and "exquisite" sushi served in "plush", "porthole-windowed" digs reminiscent of a "luxurious private yacht"; "anchors-aweigh" pricing is also part of the package, along with a "loud", "ahoy-matey!" bar scene.

Lusardi's *Italian* 23 | 18 | 22 | $62

E 70s | 1494 Second Ave. (bet. 77th & 78th Sts.) | 212-249-2020 | www.lusardis.com

A reminder of "what dinner out for grown-ups ought to be", this "wood-paneled", "old-world-mannered" UES "perennial" features "seriously good" Northern Italian food served by an "attentive" crew overseen by "affable" owner Mauro Lusardi; despite "high-end" pricing and a rather "staid" scene, its "loyal clientele" finds "comfort here in troubled times."

	FOOD	DECOR	SERVICE	COST

NEW Lusso *Italian* ▽ 17 | 17 | 19 | $46

SoHo | 331 W. Broadway (Grand St.) | 212-431-0131 | www.lussonyc.com

Situated at the end of SoHo's bustling Restaurant Row on West Broadway, this "warm" newcomer proffers a classic menu of Italian standards that's moderately priced; its small, "stylish" setting – a mix of weathered brick and dark oak – suggests a Tuscan wine bar.

Luz *Nuevo Latino* ▽ 24 | 18 | 20 | $36

Fort Greene | 177 Vanderbilt Ave. (bet. Myrtle Ave. & Willoughby St.) | Brooklyn | 718-246-4000 | www.luzrestaurant.com

"Inventive" Nuevo Latino cuisine meets "casual" atmospherics at this Fort Greene "neighborhood star" that may be "Brooklyn's best-kept secret"; "affordable" tabs and "friendly" service keep it "rightly busy every weekend", weekdays not so much.

Luzzo's *Pizza* 25 | 14 | 18 | $28

E Village | 211 First Ave. (bet. 12th & 13th Sts.) | 212-473-7447 | www.luzzomania.com

It's "all about the coal ovens" at this East Village pizzeria known for "sinful", "thin and crispy" pies made from "top-class" Italian ingredients; maybe the decor's "nondescript" and the pasta "hit-or-miss", but when it comes to the main event, "they sure know what they're doing."

NEW Macao Trading Co. ☻ *Chinese/Portuguese* 18 | 24 | 19 | $50

TriBeCa | 311 Church St. (bet. Lispenard & Walker Sts.) | 212-431-8750 | www.macaonyc.com

From the strange-bedfellows team of David Waltuck (Chanterelle) and some Employees Only employees comes this "hip" new TriBeCan celebrating Macao's melting-pot cuisine via family-style dishes in Portuguese or Chinese iterations; unfortunately, the 1940s "Indiana Jones"-ish design and "wonderful" cocktails "outshine the food."

Macelleria ☻ *Italian/Steak* ▽ 21 | 18 | 19 | $59

Meatpacking | 48 Gansevoort St. (bet. Greenwich & Washington Sts.) | 212-741-2555 | www.macelleriarestaurant.com

"In the heart of the trendy Meatpacking District", this untrendy if "pricey" Italian steakhouse offers "honest" "food with soul" in a "rustic" setting; even those who say it's "not remarkable" admit it's a "solid" option when "there's a wait everywhere else."

Macondo ☻ *Pan-Latin* - | - | - | M

LES | 157 E. Houston St. (bet. Allen & Eldridge Sts.) | 212-473-9900 | www.macondonyc.com

Latin street food from Spain and South America fills out the small plates–heavy menu of this LES sibling of Rayuela; the strikingly designed space may be pretty slick for funky Houston Street, but the pricing is as laid-back as the mood.

Madiba ☻ *African* ▽ 20 | 19 | 17 | $35

Fort Greene | 195 DeKalb Ave. (Carlton Ave.) | Brooklyn | 718-855-9190 | www.madibarestaurant.com

A "party atmosphere" prevails at this "colorful" Fort Greene "converted garage" where a "diverse young crowd" "grooves to the beat" of live world music while tucking into "unusual" South African cuisine; tabs are "cheap", service "easygoing" and the vibe suits the "Age of Obama."

	FOOD	DECOR	SERVICE	COST

Madison's *Italian*
▽ 20 | 17 | 19 | $44

Bronx | 5686 Riverdale Ave. (259th St.) | 718-543-3850
"Well-supported by the neighborhood", this "solid, steady" Italian in Riverdale's "culinary wasteland" delivers "dependable" dining in a "cozy, candlelit" setting; its rather "upscale" ambitions are reflected in costs that are "a bit pricey for the area", but the overall word is "what's not to like?"

Maggie Brown ⊅ *American/Eclectic*
▽ 19 | 19 | 19 | $27

Clinton Hill | 455 Myrtle Ave. (bet. Washington & Waverly Aves.) | Brooklyn | 718-643-7001 | www.maggiebrownrestaurant.com
Primarily known as a "neighborhood brunch joint", this Clinton Hill American-Eclectic serves "quality" food "modeled after grandma's cooking" for "value" tabs; a "delightful garden" adds to the "feel-at-home" vibe, ditto the "spot-on service."

Maison ● *French*
19 | 18 | 17 | $35

W 50s | 1700 Broadway (53rd St.) | 212-757-2233 | www.maisonnyc.com
"Traditional" French brasserie fare, "reasonably priced", satisfies "tourists" and "City Center" attendees at this "informal" cafe located just "north of Times Square"; its key selling points – a big "open-air" patio and a "24-hour" open-door policy – make up for service that lurches from "friendly" to "amateurish."

Malagueta Ⓜ *Brazilian*
▽ 25 | 14 | 22 | $36

Astoria | 25-35 36th Ave. (28th St.) | Queens | 718-937-4821 | www.malaguetany.com
An "unsung treasure" hidden away on an "unlikely" Astoria corner, this "low-key" Brazilian "family restaurant" serves "refined" dishes for "reasonable" sums in a decidedly "not-fancy" setting; the staff's "sincere desire to please" keeps the "repeat" trade brisk.

Malatesta Trattoria ●⊅ *Italian*
22 | 16 | 19 | $35

W Village | 649 Washington St. (Christopher St.) | 212-741-1207
"Sexy, stubbled" staffers serve "super-affordable pastas" at this "*autentico*" Northern Italian trattoria in the West Village; it's "*molto popolare*" in warm weather given the view of the "Christopher Street parade" from its sidewalk seats – the "only hassle" is the cash-only rule.

Maloney & Porcelli ● *Steak*
22 | 20 | 22 | $65

E 50s | 37 E. 50th St. (bet. Madison & Park Aves.) | 212-750-2233 | www.maloneyandporcelli.com
"Midtown money men" in their "Brooks Brothers best" tuck into the "justifiably famous" crackling pork shank at Alan Stillman's "big steak palace"; the vibe is "clubhouse without the golf course", the portions and the tabs "man-sized", and the upstairs party room and weekend wine deal are "must-trys."

Mamajuana Cafe ● *Dominican/Nuevo Latino*
▽ 23 | 22 | 20 | $42

Inwood | 247 Dyckman St. (bet. Payson & Seaman Aves.) | 212-304-0140 | www.mamajuana-cafe.com
"*The* happening place in Inwood", this "lively" venue serves up superior Dominican-Nuevo Latino dishes kicked up a notch by "knock-your-socks-off" mojitos; still, not everyone "goes back for the food alone – it's all about the crowd" and that "can't-be-beat" Spanish mission decor.

	FOOD	DECOR	SERVICE	COST

Mamá Mexico ● *Mexican*
20 | 17 | 19 | $37

E 40s | 214 E. 49th St. (bet. 2nd & 3rd Aves.) | 212-935-1316
W 100s | 2672 Broadway (102nd St.) | 212-864-2323
www.mamamexico.com

"Colorful", "cheerful" and "loud as hell", this "kitschy" Mexican duo is a "hoot" thanks to "tacky" decor and a "party-time" vibe fueled by a "blaring mariachi band" (that's a "love/hate relationship" for many); still, the food "rocks" and the margaritas are "mule-kickingly" strong.

Mama's Food Shop ⊄ *American*
▽ 20 | 9 | 14 | $16

E Village | 200 E. Third St. (bet. Aves. A & B) | 212-777-4425 |
www.mamasfoodshop.com

"Cheap, filling" American comfort chow "and plenty of it" is the recipe for success at this "basic", cash-only East Villager that appeals to the "pierced-eyebrow" set; most folks "don't even think of eating in" given the limited number of tables and "divey" atmosphere.

NEW Mañana ●▨ *Mexican*
▽ 21 | 18 | 19 | $60

E 60s | 27 E. 61st St. (bet. Madison & Park Aves.) | 212-752-8900 |
www.mananarestaurantnyc.com

More "sophisticated" than "your typical Mexican", this new Upper Eastsider from the Serafina group is housed in the former Lollipop space; look for "expensive" takes on "Americanized" classics served in sexy, scarlet-hued digs, with serious dining up front and equally serious partying in the "loud" back lounge.

Mancora ● *Peruvian*
▽ 20 | 13 | 17 | $30

E Village | 99 First Ave. (6th St.) | 212-253-1011

"Named after the South American surf town", this "authentic" East Village Peruvian comes across with "delicious rotisserie chicken" and "interesting ceviche" washed down with "sinfully good" pisco sours, all at "bargain" rates; however, it's hard to "enjoy the atmosphere" as they "need more lighting."

Mandarin Court *Chinese*
20 | 9 | 14 | $23

Chinatown | 61 Mott St. (bet. Bayard & Canal Sts.) | 212-608-3838

The "mother of dim sum places", this C-town vet allows you to compose a meal from "roll-around carts" stocked with "mysterious", "fabulous" tidbits; the food is "as good as the service is nonexistent" (ditto the decor), but at least the price is right; it's usually "packed on weekend mornings", so pay court "early."

Mandoo Bar *Korean*
21 | 11 | 16 | $21

Garment District | 2 W. 32nd St. (bet. B'way & 5th Ave.) |
212-279-3075

"Myriad variations" of "stellar" Korean dumplings (aka mandoo) are "freshly made by motherly hands" in the window of this Garment District "pit stop"; the "crowded", "minimally decorated" digs may be "uncomfortable", but the chow is "inexpensive" and "stomach-filling."

Manducatis *Italian*
22 | 13 | 20 | $46

LIC | 13-27 Jackson Ave. (47th Ave.) | Queens | 718-729-4602 |
www.manducatis.com

An example of "the way NY used to be", this "dark" LIC red-sauce Italian serves "old-school" food in a "time-warp" setting that "could be

| | FOOD | DECOR | SERVICE | COST |

1965"; regulars forgo the menu and "just tell them to bring it on" along with a bottle from the "killer wine list."

Manetta's 🅱 *Italian*
22 | 16 | 20 | $39

LIC | 10-76 Jackson Ave. (49th Ave.) | Queens | 718-786-6171

In "what's fast becoming a trendy neighborhood", this "old-fashioned" LIC Italian lures locals with "sublime brick-oven pizza" and "true trattoria-quality" cooking at "bargain" rates; fans "love eating outside in the summer" – and the fireplace is "charming in winter" too.

Mangia 🅱 *Mediterranean*
19 | 12 | 13 | $23

E 40s | 16 E. 48th St. (bet. 5th & Madison Aves.) | 212-754-7600
Flatiron | 22 W. 23rd St. (bet. 5th & 6th Aves.) | 212-647-0200
W 50s | 50 W. 57th St. (bet. 5th & 6th Aves.) | 212-582-5882
www.mangiatogo.com

Desk jockeys "on the run" tout this "bustling" Med trio for its "gourmet" "grab-and-go" offerings including a "cut-above" salad bar and sandwich board; ok, it's a bit "pricey for what it is", but "everything's fresh" and there are certainly "lots of choices."

Maoz Vegetarian *Mideastern/Veg.*
21 | 8 | 14 | $11

G Village | 59 E. Eighth St. (bet. B'way & University Pl.) | 212-420-5999
Union Sq | 38 Union Sq. E. (bet. 16th & 17th Sts.) | 212-260-1988
NEW **W 40s** | 558 Seventh Ave. (40th St.)
NEW **W 70s** | 2047A Broadway (enter on Amsterdam Ave., bet. 70th & 71st Sts.) | 212-362-2622 ◗
www.maozusa.com

These "Dutch imports" offer "superb" Middle Eastern–vegetarian chow via "fresh-tasting falafel" sandwiches or salads that are customizable at an "unlimited" toppings bar; they're hard to beat for "inexpensive", "guilt-free" grazing, but cramped settings may lead to takeout.

Mara's Homemade *Cajun*
23 | 12 | 21 | $36

E Village | 342 E. Sixth St. (bet. 1st & 2nd Aves.) | 212-598-1110 | www.marashomemade.com

"Bringing N'Awlins hospitality to NY", this "funky" East Villager turns out "unique" Cajun cooking (including an "authentic crawfish boil") that's "as good as you'll get outside of the Delta"; though the decor is "drab", the "atmosphere is as fun as the friendly owner" and the tabs are a "bargain."

Marc Forgione *American*
(fka Forge)
▽ 23 | 23 | 22 | $60

TriBeCa | 134 Reade St. (bet. Greenwich & Hudson Sts.) | 212-941-9401 | www.marcforgione.com

Eponymous chef-owner Marc Forgione (son of renowned toque Larry Forgione) does "inventive", "straight-off-the-farm" "greenmarket" cuisine at this TriBeCa New American, formerly known as Forge; the "spot-on service" plays well against a "stylish, rustic" setting that combines "candlelight and exposed brick" to "romantic" effect.

NEW Marea 🅱 *Italian/Seafood*
26 | 25 | 24 | $97

W 50s | 240 Central Park S. (bet. B'way & 7th Ave.) | 212-582-5100 | www.marea-nyc.com

Bucking the current trend of scaled-back menus and just-folks decor, this ultra-"luxe", ultra-"expensive" Italian seafooder in San

| | FOOD | DECOR | SERVICE | COST |

Domenico's former CPS digs comes from chef Michael White and restaurateur Chris Cannon, no strangers to *alta cucina* and *alta atmosfera*
(their other collaborations are Alto and Convivio); expect "inventive
interpretations" of global fin fare served in a "stunning", "contemporary" room fitted out with imported onyx, polished rosewood and
starched white tablecloths.

NEW Marfa *Southwestern*
| - | - | - | I |

E Village | 101 E. Second St. (bet. Ave. A & 1st Ave.) | 212-673-8908 |
www.marfanyc.com

Named after the West Texas artists' haven, this East Village hideaway
in the former Waikiki Wally's space slings dirt-cheap Southwestern
grub washed down with Lone Star beer; the bare-bones digs are split
into two narrow dining areas, manned by a spunky crew and energized
by a honky-tonk soundtrack.

Maria Pia *Italian*
| 19 | 17 | 19 | $38 |

W 50s | 319 W. 51st St. (bet. 8th & 9th Aves.) | 212-765-6463 |
www.mariapianyc.com

"Very popular" pre-curtain, this "no-frills" Theater District Italian
serves "solid", "traditional red-sauce" dishes at a good "bang-for-the-
buck" price; maybe the "noise" and "overzealous" service need work,
but at least there's "minimal tourist infestation" here.

Marina Cafe *Seafood*
| 19 | 23 | 20 | $43 |

Staten Island | 154 Mansion Ave. (Hillside Terr.) | 718-967-3077 |
www.marinacafegrand.com

The "beautiful views" of Great Kills Harbor are sure to "take your
breath away" but may overshadow the "tasty", "reasonably priced"
fare and "attentive" service at this longtime Staten Island seafooder;
a tiki bar deck and nightly live music also enhance its "special-
place" local rep.

Mario's M *Italian*
| 22 | 14 | 19 | $41 |

Bronx | 2342 Arthur Ave. (bet. 184th & 186th Sts.) | 718-584-1188 |
www.mariosrestarthurave.com

You almost "expect to bump into Frank Sinatra" at this circa-1919
Arthur Avenue "landmark" where a straight-"out-of-central-casting"
crew serves "delicious" Southern Italian food (including a "not-to-be-
missed" pizza); everything here is "vintage", including decor that's a
"throwback" to the "glorious '50s."

NEW Mari Vanna ● *Russian*
| - | - | - | E |

Flatiron | 41 E. 20th St. (bet. B'way & Park Ave. S.) | 212-777-1955 |
www.ginzaproject.ru

Traditional Russian cuisine (think blini with caviar served in nesting
matryoshka dolls) matched with an extensive vodka list turns up at this
new Flatiron arrival; the tchotchke-laden, grandma's-living-room setting has some of-the-moment touches – i.e. artfully peeling wallpaper –
while the czar-worthy pricing is similarly very modern day.

Market Table *American*
| 23 | 18 | 21 | $53 |

G Village | 54 Carmine St. (Bedford St.) | 212-255-2100 |
www.markettablenyc.com

"Fresh is the mantra" of this "relaxed" Villager where "locally sourced"
ingredients "come together in beautiful ways" on a "smart" New

American menu that also features a "broad selection" of seafood; given the "inviting", brick-lined space and winning staff, the "noisy" acoustics and "hard-to-get reservations" are forgivable.

MarkJoseph Steakhouse 🗷 *Steak*
24 | 18 | 22 | $73

Financial District | 261 Water St. (off Peck Slip) | 212-277-0020 | www.markjosephsteakhouse.com

"Near (but not like) the touristy Seaport", this "unpretentious" Financial District chophouse serves "decadent" steaks and sides to the "usual Wall Street types" who bring along "extra loot" to cover the "expensive" tabs; "if your arteries can handle it", the "bacon appetizer is a must."

Markt *Belgian*
20 | 17 | 17 | $42

Flatiron | 676 Sixth Ave. (21st St.) | 212-727-3314 | www.marktrestaurant.com

Reminiscent of a "little slice" of Flanders in the Flatiron, this "ersatz trip to Belgium" pairs "delicious mussels" with an "extensive selection" of Belgian ales; if the noise level is a "challenge", either learn "sign language" or "bring someone you don't want to listen to."

☑ Marlow & Sons ●Ⓜ *American*
26 | 21 | 21 | $41

Williamsburg | 81 Broadway (bet. Berry St. & Wythe Ave.) | Brooklyn | 718-384-1441 | www.marlowandsons.com

"One of the best in Williamsburg", this "foodies' date place" lures locals and "locavores" alike with a "limited menu" of "first-rate", market-driven American small plates; one part country store, one part bar/eatery, it's "always packed" given the "always delicious", "fairly priced" grub.

Marseille ● *French/Mediterranean*
21 | 19 | 20 | $48

W 40s | 630 Ninth Ave. (44th St.) | 212-333-3410 | www.marseillenyc.com

A "well-oiled pre-theater machine", this "better-than-average" Hell's Kitchen brasserie is as "charming as its namesake", turning out "delightful" French-Med fare in "roomy", "atmospheric" digs; "reasonable" pricing and "expert", "get-you-to-the-show-on-time" service burnishes its reputation.

Maruzzella ● *Italian*
21 | 17 | 22 | $44

E 70s | 1483 First Ave. (bet. 77th & 78th Sts.) | 212-988-8877 | www.maruzzellanyc.com

The "tasty" Northern Italiana is "lovingly prepared" at this longtime UES "neighborhood haunt" best known for its "welcoming", "aim-to-please" owners; the "intimate" setting and pricing that "won't max out your credit card" add to the overall "eat-good-feel-good" experience.

Mary Ann's *Tex-Mex*
16 | 11 | 14 | $28

Chelsea | 116 Eighth Ave. (16th St.) | 212-633-0877 ⊟
E Village | 80 Second Ave. (5th St.) | 212-475-5939 ⊟
TriBeCa | 107 W. Broadway (bet. Chambers & Reade Sts.) | 212-766-0911
www.maryannsmexican.com

A "step above fast food", these "generic" Tex-Mex standbys draw patrons because of their "as cheap as it gets" tabs ("hey, it's a recession"), not the "uninspired" chow; "poor service" and "greasy-spoon" settings help explain the popularity of their "knock-your-socks-off margaritas."

	FOOD	DECOR	SERVICE	COST

Mary's Fish Camp 🛇 *Seafood* | 24 | 13 | 18 | $43 |

W Village | 64 Charles St. (W. 4th St.) | 646-486-2185 |
www.marysfishcamp.com

It's all about the "famous lobster rolls" at this "unpretentious", no-reservations West Village fish shack that provides a "summers-in-Maine" experience but with "no sunburn"; "no squidding", the lines to get into the "shoehorn-tight" space are "long", yet most diners are still "happy as clams."

Z Mas ● *American* | 27 | 25 | 27 | $86 |

G Village | 39 Downing St. (bet. Bedford & Varick Sts.) | 212-255-1790 |
www.masfarmhouse.com

Every neighborhood should have a restaurant like this "cozy", "casual but elegant" Village New American where chef Galen Zamarra "cooks to the patron's taste" and "employees seem to have an advanced degree in 'nice'"; if it's still relatively "undiscovered", that's probably due to its "small" size and an "expensive" price point for this neck of the woods.

Z Masa 🛇Ⓜ *Japanese* | 26 | 24 | 25 | $520 |

W 60s | Time Warner Ctr. | 10 Columbus Circle, 4th fl. (60th St. at B'way) |
212-823-9800 | www.masanyc.com

Let's get the tough part out of the way – yes, the $400 prix fixe-only dinner menu makes this *the most expensive restaurant in NY*; however, committed foodies say "it's worth it" to enjoy the "freshest possible", "work-of-art" seafood served in "Zen perfection" by the "understated but personable" chef, Masayoshi Takayama, at this TWC Japanese; anyone who has paid for NBA playoff floor seats or center orchestra tickets at the Met will realize that this is a bargain – if you want the best.

Matilda 🗭 *Italian/Mexican* | ▽ 26 | 24 | 23 | $37 |

E Village | 647 E. 11th St. (bet. Aves. B & C) | 212-777-3355 |
www.matildarestaurant.com

"Original" to a fault, this colorful East Village "standout" fuses Tuscan and Mexican cuisine into an "adventurous", "creative concept done right"; "cool" mod decor and "bargain" pricing make up for the small-ish setting, though alfresco sidewalk seating eases the squeeze.

Matsugen *Japanese* | 22 | 21 | 21 | $67 |

TriBeCa | 241 Church St. (Leonard St.) | 212-925-0202 |
www.jean-georges.com

For the "Jean-Georges Vongerichten experience translated into Japanese", try this TriBeCa "adventure" offering a "dizzying" variety of "homemade soba" plus "standout" sushi and shabu-shabu in a "slick" (verging on "austere") setting; sure, it's "expensive" and the portions "small for the money", but the $35 "year-round prix fixe dinner" is an "outstanding buy."

Matsuri ● *Japanese* | 22 | 25 | 20 | $62 |

Chelsea | Maritime Hotel | 369 W. 16th St., downstairs (9th Ave.) |
212-243-6400 | www.themaritimehotel.com

"Atmosphere" is king at this "big, dramatic" space under Chelsea's Maritime Hotel where Tadashi Ono's "smooth-as-silk sushi" and a "long sake list" are nearly overwhelmed by the "epic decor"; whether this once-"trendy" spot is "still relevant", however, is a matter of debate: fans report it's "always hopping", foes reply "pricey" and "past its prime."

	FOOD	DECOR	SERVICE	COST

Max *Italian* — 22 | 16 | 16 | $32

E Village | 51 Ave. B (bet. 3rd & 4th Sts.) | 212-539-0111 ⊟
TriBeCa | 181 Duane St. (bet. Greenwich & Hudson Sts.) | 212-966-5939
www.max-ny.com

"Wonderful pastas" are the thing to order at these "hip" trattorias where you "won't max out your credit card"; "bored" staffers and "shabby-chic decor bordering on downright shabby" come with the territory.

Max Brenner ❷ *Dessert* — 18 | 18 | 15 | $26

G Village | 841 Broadway (bet. 13th & 14th Sts.) | 212-388-0030 | www.maxbrenner.com

Chocolate is a "way of life" at this "mass-market" Village dessert vendor where "tourists" and "herds of children" get a "sugar rush" from a sweets menu that's the "size of a telephone book"; "slower-than-molasses" service and an "overdone Willy Wonka theme" are the sour notes.

Max SoHa ❷⊟ *Italian* — 21 | 14 | 16 | $30

W 100s | 1274 Amsterdam Ave. (123rd St.) | 212-531-2221

Max Caffe ❷ *Italian*

W 100s | 1262 Amsterdam Ave. (122nd St.) | 212-531-1210
www.maxsoha.com

"Typically mobbed" with the "Columbia crowd" given their location, these "tiny" UWS Italians are best accessed during "summer school"; "perfecto pasta" and "excellent value" compensate for the "ridiculously cramped" quarters and "service lacking finesse."

Maya *Mexican* — 23 | 19 | 20 | $55

E 60s | 1191 First Ave. (bet. 64th & 65th Sts.) | 212-585-1818 | www.modernmexican.com

"Inventive" food meets "sexy margaritas" at this "fancy" UES Mexican where the "upscale" experience extends to the "mind-reader" service and "haute pricing"; while it skews "loud" during prime times, ultimately most report "perfection all the way" here.

Maze *French* — 25 | 22 | 22 | $71

W 50s | London NYC Hotel | 151 W. 54th St. (bet. 6th & 7th Aves.) | 212-468-8889 | www.gordonramsay.com

Those who "can't afford" Gordon Ramsay's "more formal" next-door "showcase" opt for this "a-maze-ing" adjunct in Midtown's London Hotel that specializes in "creative" New French small plates; but despite the "better price point", tabs can still "add up quickly."

Maz Mezcal *Mexican* — 19 | 17 | 19 | $38

E 80s | 316 E. 86th St. (bet. 1st & 2nd Aves.) | 212-472-1599 | www.mazmezcal.com

If the "trip to Cozumel is off", there's always this "venerable" UES Mexican serving "quality" cuisine and "perfectly balanced margaritas" for "honest prices"; "welcoming" owners enhance the "festive" mood – no wonder it's a "neighborhood mob scene."

McCormick & Schmick's *Seafood* — 20 | 18 | 20 | $53

W 50s | 1285 Sixth Ave. (enter on 52nd St., bet. 6th & 7th Aves.) | 212-459-1222 | www.mccormickandschmicks.com

"Upscale chain" fishmonger near Rockefeller Center vending "consistently good" seafood in a "pub-style" setting; fans call it a "good fall-

| | FOOD | DECOR | SERVICE | COST |

back" for "business dining", but foes counter it's too "predictable" and "formulaic in a town that cherishes originality."

Mediterraneo ❶ *Italian*   18 | 15 | 15 | $43

E 60s | 1260 Second Ave. (66th St.) | 212-734-7407 |
www.mediterraneonyc.com

"Beautiful people with foreign accents" populate this "always crowded" Upper East Side Italian where the "double-kiss" is de rigueur and "homemade black linguine" is the thing to order; to escape the "indifferent" service and "cacophony" during prime times, regulars retreat to the "outside seats."

Mee Noodle Shop *Noodle Shop*   18 | 5 | 13 | $16

E 40s | 922 Second Ave. (49th St.) | 212-888-0027
Murray Hill | 547 Second Ave. (bet. 30th & 31st Sts.) | 212-779-1596
W 50s | 795 Ninth Ave. (53rd St.) | 212-765-2929 |
www.meenoodleshopnyc.com

These separately owned "little slices of Chinatown" will never "be confused with gourmet experiences" but they sure sate noodle-soup "cravings" at "Depression-era prices"; hopefully you'll be "too busy" slurping to notice the "subway station–like decor" and "choppy service."

Megu *Japanese*   23 | 26 | 22 | $82

TriBeCa | 62 Thomas St. (bet. Church St. & W. B'way) |
212-964-7777

Megu Midtown *Japanese*

E 40s | Trump World Tower | 845 United Nations Plaza (1st Ave. &
47th St.) | 212-964-7777
www.megunyc.com

A "scene for the eyes and a treat for the palate", this "sexy, showy" Japanese twosome serves "inventive", "top-class" food in "dramatic" settings centered around a giant "ice Buddha"; "outstanding" service embellishes the "refined" mood, leaving the "Daddy Warbucks"-worthy pricing as the only discordant note.

Melt *American*   ▽ 21 | 17 | 20 | $35

Park Slope | 440 Bergen St. (bet. 5th St. & Flatbush Ave.) | Brooklyn |
718-230-5925 | www.meltnyc.com

"Chic and modern", this Park Slope New American is just the ticket for an "intimate dinner" or "kicking back with friends" over "terrific", "reasonably priced" dishes served by an "accommodating" crew; insiders say it's "best for brunch" – "they know their way around an egg."

Menchanko-tei *Noodle Shop*   20 | 11 | 15 | $21

E 40s | 131 E. 45th St. (bet. Lexington & 3rd Aves.) | 212-986-6805
W 50s | 43-45 W. 55th St. (bet. 5th & 6th Aves.) | 212-247-1585 ❶
www.menchankotei.com

"Rushed at lunch" but more "pleasant at dinnertime", these Midtown noodle shops dish out "authentic, satisfying" bowls of udon and ramen plus an "extensive selection of sake" to "throngs of salarymen"; "giveaway pricing" makes up for the "no-frills" decor and service.

Mercadito ❶ *Mexican*   22 | 15 | 18 | $38

E Village | 179 Ave. B (bet. 11th & 12th Sts.) | 212-529-6490

Mercadito Cantina ❶ *Mexican*

E Village | 172 Ave. B (bet. 10th & 11th Sts.) | 212-388-1750

(continued)

Mercadito Grove *Mexican*
W Village | 100 Seventh Ave. S. (bet. Bleecker & Grove Sts.) | 212-647-0830
www.mercaditorestaurants.com
The "portions are tiny" at this Mexican trio (ditto the "minuscule" settings), but the flavors are "amazing" (e.g. "tasty two-bite tacos", "boffo guacamole" samplers); though prices "aren't as cheap as they look on the menu" and can "add up fast", nobody pays much attention after a couple of margaritas.

Mercat *Spanish*
21 | 19 | 18 | $52
NoHo | 45 Bond St. (bet. Bowery & Lafayette St.) | 212-529-8600 |
www.mercatnyc.com
Much "more convenient than Barcelona", this bi-level NoHo Spaniard serves "delicious Catalan specialties" in a subway-tiled main room with an "open kitchen" or in a rustic, brick-walled basement; a charter member of the "burgeoning tapas scene", it features the requisite "artful plating", "noisy" acoustics and small-plate-"big-bill" pricing.

Mercer Kitchen ● *American/French*
21 | 22 | 19 | $57
SoHo | Mercer Hotel | 99 Prince St. (Mercer St.) | 212-966-5454 |
www.jean-georges.com
As "upscale basements" go, this "well-known" SoHo perennial via Jean-Georges Vongerichten still attracts "preciously cool", "dressed-to-kill" folk with "consistently delicious" French–New American food served in "dark", "stylish" digs; somewhat "snobby" service and "no-bargain" pricing are the sticking points.

Mermaid Inn *Seafood*
20 | 17 | 19 | $45
E Village | 96 Second Ave. (bet. 5th & 6th Sts.) | 212-674-5870
W 80s | 568 Amsterdam Ave. (bet. 87th & 88th Sts.) | 212-799-7400
www.themermaidnyc.com
"You can almost hear the foghorns" blare at these "rustic" "charmers" that channel "Cape Cod" with "scrumptious" "comfort seafood" menus showcasing an "amazing" lobster roll; bonus points go to the "vibrant" settings, "reasonable prices" and "free chocolate pudding for dessert."

NEW Mesa Coyoacan ● *Mexican*
- | - | - | M
Williamsburg | 372 Graham Ave. (bet. Conselyea St. & Skillman Ave.) |
Brooklyn | 718-782-8171 | www.mesacoyoacan.com
Regional Mexican specialties like Oaxacan tamales are plated at this Williamsburg newcomer whose open-air entrance, communal table and recession-friendly tabs are luring in locals; the traditional *comida* can be washed down with beer and sangria, though the lack of margaritas may be a minus for some.

☒ Mesa Grill *Southwestern*
23 | 19 | 21 | $57
Flatiron | 102 Fifth Ave. (bet. 15th & 16th Sts.) | 212-807-7400 |
www.mesagrill.com
TV's lothario chef, Bobby Flay, still puts out "great Southwestern meals" that have kept this high-ceilinged "utilitarian" place in the Flatiron full year after year; the margaritas and Sunday brunch are standouts, but some question whether this "oldie but goodie" maybe "needs some extra zest."

	FOOD	DECOR	SERVICE	COST

Meskerem *Ethiopian*

	21	9	15	$25

G Village | 124 MacDougal St. (bet. Bleecker & W. 3rd Sts.) | 212-777-8111

W 40s | 468 W. 47th St. (bet. 9th & 10th Aves.) | 212-664-0520

A "spicy" dining "adventure" awaits at this "literally finger-licking-good" Ethiopian duo where you handily scoop up "delicious stews" using "spongy" injera bread as a utensil; "cheap" tabs trump the "lackluster settings" and "inconsistent service."

Métisse *Brazilian/French*

	18	16	20	$44

W 100s | 239 W. 105th St. (bet. Amsterdam Ave. & B'way) | 212-666-8825 | www.metisserestaurant.com

"Affordable and affable", this "cozy" Columbia-area "favorite" refuels student bodies with a "delicious" combination of Brazilian and French bistro "classics"; maybe there are "no surprises", but overall it's a "neighborhood treat in a neighborhood with too few of them."

Metrazur ⑧ *American*

	21	21	19	$54

E 40s | Grand Central | East Balcony (42nd St. & Vanderbilt Ave.) | 212-687-4600 | www.charliepalmer.com

"Wave to the little people scurrying to their trains" from a "magnificent" balcony perch at this New American overlooking the Grand Central Concourse; Charlie Palmer's chow is "sophisticated" and if service ranges from "calm" to "perfunctory", such details are "incidental" given the "incredible" setting.

Metro Marché *French*

	19	14	19	$36

W 40s | Port Authority | 625 Eighth Ave. (41st St.) | 212-239-1010 | www.metromarche.com

Commuters and theatergoers seeking a "safe haven" in the wilds of Port Authority tout this "bus station" brasserie offering "surprisingly good" traditional Parisian fare at "value" prices; it's "better than you'd expect", though the location splits surveyors: "handy-dandy" vs. "chaotic."

Mexicana Mama Ⓜ⇄ *Mexican*

	22	13	18	$34

G Village | 47 E. 12th St. (bet. B'way & University Pl.) | 212-253-7594

W Village | 525 Hudson St. (bet. Charles & W. 10th Sts.) | 212-924-4119

"Long waits" and "cheek-by-jowl" dining are part of the package at this "tiny" West Village "hot spot" that draws droves with "pleasingly complex" Mexican chow that's a "decent value"; the 12th Street model is somewhat larger but just as "unprepossessing" as its sibling, with the same "cash-only" policy.

Mezzaluna ◑ *Italian*

	21	14	18	$43

E 70s | 1295 Third Ave. (bet. 74th & 75th Sts.) | 212-535-9600 | www.mezzalunany.com

Pizza Mezzaluna ⇄ *Pizza*

NEW **G Village** | 146 W. Houston St. (MacDougal St.) | 212-533-1242

"Socializing" is the thing at this "little" UES Italian "canteen", a longtime "neighborhood favorite" beloved for its "delicious" pasta and "delectable" wood-fired pizza, not the "cramped, noisy" conditions; the even tinier new Village outlet is primarily a take-out venue.

	FOOD	DECOR	SERVICE	COST

Mezzogiorno *Italian* | 21 | 17 | 19 | $43 |

SoHo | 195 Spring St. (Sullivan St.) | 212-334-2112 | www.mezzogiorno.com
Although the crowd is "very Euro", this circa-1987 SoHo standby is
"thoroughly New York", offering "consistently excellent" food and "attentive service" in chic but "comfortable" digs; "everything's right with
the world" when an "outdoor" sidewalk seat is available.

Mia Dona *Italian* | 21 | 17 | 19 | $53 |

E 50s | 206 E. 58th St. (bet. 2nd & 3rd Aves.) | 212-750-8170 |
www.miadona.com
"Another success story" for Donatella Arpaia, this Italian yearling near
Bloomie's offers "splendid" cooking in a chic, "style"-is-everything
setting; though surveyors debate the cost – "well priced" vs.
"overpriced" – and the service – "enthusiastic" vs. "snobbish" – there's
agreement on the overall "comforting vibe"; N.B. the departure of chef
Michael Psilakis puts its Food score in question.

Michael Jordan's The Steak House NYC *Steak* | 20 | 20 | 19 | $66 |

E 40s | Grand Central | Northwest Balcony (43rd St. & Vanderbilt Ave.) |
212-655-2300 | www.theglaziergroup.com
Score a "courtside view" of the "milling crowds" under Grand Central's
"constellational canopy" at this "heady" steakhouse with a "lively bar
scene"; some say you may need a "size 15 wallet to pay the bill", but
there's always the $24 lunch prix fixe for bargain-hunters.

Michael's ☒ *Californian* | 20 | 20 | 21 | $68 |

W 50s | 24 W. 55th St. (bet. 5th & 6th Aves.) | 212-767-0555 |
www.michaelsnewyork.com
"Table-hopping is always on the menu" at this Midtown "power lunch"
(and breakfast) nexus where "entertainment and media" moguls
come to "eat and be seen"; the "consistent" Californian fare is "not inexpensive" and may "taste better the better known you are."

Mill Basin Kosher Deli *Deli* | 22 | 15 | 18 | $24 |

Mill Basin | 5823 Ave. T (59th St.) | Brooklyn | 718-241-4910 |
www.millbasindeli.com
The "authentically Jewish" sandwiches are "stuffed – and you'll be
too" – at this "quality" kosher deli "holdout" in Mill Basin; it also doubles as a quasi-"art museum" with works by Erté, Lichtenstein and
Chagall on display that are definitely not "chopped liver."

☑ Milos, Estiatorio ● *Greek/Seafood* | 27 | 23 | 23 | $82 |

W 50s | 125 W. 55th St. (bet. 6th & 7th Aves.) | 212-245-7400 | www.milos.ca
"Reliable" for "fish as fresh as it gets" served by "friendly", "informative" staffers, this all-white modern Midtown Greek "seafood palace"
is "always buzzing"; for best financial results, "stick to the starters"
since the per-pound prices of the main-course fish can be "an issue."

Minca ●⇥ *Noodle Shop* | ▽ 22 | 11 | 18 | $20 |

E Village | 536 E. Fifth St. (bet. Aves. A & B) | 212-505-8001
A "low-key" contender in the "East Village ramen wars", this cash-only
"neighborhood" Japanese noodle shop specializes in "cheap and filling" repasts; however, given the "teeny-tiny" dimensions and lack of
decor, you probably won't want to "linger too long."

	FOOD	DECOR	SERVICE	COST

Z NEW Minetta Tavern ● *French* — 20 | 21 | 21 | $56

G Village | 113 MacDougal St. (bet. Bleecker & W. 3rd Sts.) | 212-475-3850

Proving what a "creative, disciplined" restaurateur can do, Keith McNally (Balthazar, Pastis, et al.) has spruced up this circa-1937 Village old-timer and added "very good" French bistro fare served by a "well-trained, customer-oriented staff"; "loud and noisy and full of beautiful people", it's a bona fide "swiveling-head" "scene" that's "worth the headache of trying to get a reservation."

Mingala Burmese *Burmese* — 20 | 11 | 18 | $27

E 70s | 1393B Second Ave. (bet. 72nd & 73rd Sts.) | 212-744-8008
E Village | 21-23 E. Seventh St. (bet. 2nd & 3rd Aves.) | 212-529-3656

Folks seeking "change-of-pace Asian" dining tout the "tangy" Burmese chow at these "penny-pincher paradises"; rather "grim" settings are offset by the "healthy, unusual" offerings and "pleasant" service.

Mint *Indian* — ▽ 21 | 20 | 18 | $45

E 50s | San Carlos Hotel | 150 E. 50th St. (bet. Lexington & 3rd Aves.) | 212-644-8888 | www.mintny.com

"Cool and sleek . . . and green", this "upscale" Midtown Indian is a "refreshing change" when you're "craving a little style" along with "well-prepared" subcontinental fare; though it's a bit "sleepy" and "caters mostly to tourists", the food is "tasty" and "well worth the higher prices."

Miranda *Italian/Pan-Latin* — ▽ 21 | 22 | 27 | $36

Williamsburg | 80 Berry St. (N. 9th St.) | Brooklyn | 718-387-0711 | www.mirandarestaurant.com

"Personable owners" "ensure a delightful visit" at this Williamsburg spot featuring "delicious" dishes fusing Pan-Latin and Italian flavors; the "charming" setting is a mix of exposed-brick walls and a concrete floor.

Miriam *Israeli/Mediterranean* — 21 | 18 | 20 | $33

Park Slope | 79 Fifth Ave. (Prospect Pl.) | Brooklyn | 718-622-2250 | www.miriamrestaurant.com

"Not your typical" Park Slope venue, this "comfortable" spot features "lovingly made", nicely priced Israeli-Med cuisine served by a "terrific" staff; brunch is "outstanding" – and "well worth" the inevitable wait.

Mishima *Japanese* — 24 | 14 | 21 | $36

Murray Hill | 164 Lexington Ave. (bet. 30th & 31st Sts.) | 212-532-9596 | www.mishimany.com

Murray Hill "sleeper sushi" destination known for its "high value", low prices and relative "best-kept-secret" status; the level of "quality control" extends from the "very fresh" fish to the "gentle", "eager-to-please" service, but unfortunately not to the "bland decor."

Miss Mamie's *Soul Food/Southern* — ▽ 21 | 11 | 15 | $24

Harlem | 366 W. 110th St. (bet. Columbus & Manhattan Aves.) | 212-865-6744

Miss Maude's *Soul Food/Southern*

Harlem | 547 Lenox Ave. (bet. 137th & 138th Sts.) | 212-690-3100 www.spoonbreadinc.com

You'll feel like you "died and went to Dixie" at these "casual" Harlem soul food siblings where fans derive "enormous pleasure" from the "dangerously delicious" North Carolina cooking; the pricing is "great" and the service "friendly" but "painfully slow."

Mizu Sushi ⊠ *Japanese* · 23 · 14 · 17 · $38

Flatiron | 29 E. 20th St. (bet. B'way & Park Ave. S.) | 212-505-6688
"Twentysomething professionals" pile into this Flatiron Japanese "scene" that lures "pretty young things" with a combination of "sake bombs", "slammin'" sushi and "blaring pop music" heavy on the "Justin Timberlake"; oldsters retreat to the bar area – it's "less deafening" there.

Mo-Bay *Caribbean/Soul Food* · ▽ 20 · 18 · 17 · $36

Harlem | 17 W. 125th St. (bet. 5th & Lenox Aves.) | 212-876-9300 | www.mobayuptownnyc.com
"Southern flair" is alive and well at this "popular" Harlem eatery that fuses a "fine" Caribbean–soul food menu with nightly "live music"; it can get "loud" and the setting's "small", but the overall "vibe is good" and the price is right.

⊠ Modern, The ⊠ *American/French* · 26 · 26 · 25 · $114

W 50s | Museum of Modern Art | 9 W. 53rd St. (bet. 5th & 6th Aves.) | 212-333-1220 | www.themodernnyc.com
"Raising museum dining to a new level", this Danny Meyer French–New American on MoMA's ground floor is "always a treat" thanks to Gabriel Kreuther's "work-of-art" food, "friendly", "well-informed service" and a choice of two "superb" dining areas: a "lovely" formal room in back overlooking the museum's sculpture garden, and a "more casual, less expensive" bar-cafe up front with a leafy, wall-length photomural by German artist Thomas Demand.

Moim Ⓜ *Korean* · 24 · 23 · 21 · $39

Park Slope | 206 Garfield Pl. (bet. 7th & 8th Aves.) | Brooklyn | 718-499-8092 | www.moimrestaurant.com
There's "more than the usual kimchi" on offer at this Park Slope Korean where the "modern" menu showcases "unusual twists" on classic dishes with "lots of Seoul"; the "beautifully designed" space is equal parts "Zen" and "trendy", but despite the "fancy" ambiance, the pricing "won't break the bank."

Molyvos ● *Greek* · 22 · 19 · 21 · $56

W 50s | 871 Seventh Ave. (bet. 55th & 56th Sts.) | 212-582-7500 | www.molyvos.com
"Carnegie Hall is not the only place in the neighborhood that sings" – this nearby "chic Greek" is a "wonderful" "cradle of civilization" offering "superior" cooking paired with "upbeat" service; sure, all those "Aegean delicacies" (including all-day meze) can "add up" pricewise, but the $37 pre-theater prix fixe is a "fine bargain."

NEW Momofuku Bakery & Milk Bar ● *Bakery* · 21 · 12 · 15 · $16

E Village | 207 Second Ave. (enter on 13th St. bet. 2nd & 3rd Aves.) | 212-475-7899 | www.momofuku.com
David Chang's new pint-size adjunct to his Momofuku Ssäm Bar churns out "sinful" baked goods, "heavenly" soft-serve ice cream and those infamous pork buns in a "crowded", "standing-room-only" space; while "slow" counter service and "double-digit tabs" detract, most of the East Village "hipster population" is on board.

	FOOD	DECOR	SERVICE	COST

☑ **Momofuku Ko** *American* `27` `18` `23` `$130`
E Village | 163 First Ave. (bet. 10th & 11th Sts.) | 212-475-7899 |
www.momofuku.com
If you live long enough to get into this "closet-size" 12-stooler in the
East Village, David Chang and his team will deliver an Asian-accented
American "multicourse foodie experience" that's "as exciting as dining gets"; those who don't understand "what all the shouting is about"
say the "rock 'n' roll f*** you attitude doesn't play", given the "$100 prix
fixe–only tab.

Momofuku Noodle Bar *American* `23` `15` `18` `$33`
E Village | 171 First Ave. (bet. 10th & 11th Sts.) | 212-777-7773 |
www.momofuku.com
The first entry in David Chang's East Village empire, this "House that
Pork Built" dishes out "delicious" Japanese-inflected American chow
(including "melt-in-your-mouth" pork buns and "amazing" ramen)
from a "cool open kitchen" staffed by "constantly yelling cooks"; given
the "bargain" tabs and a rep as one of the "best noodle shops around",
it's always "packed at prime times."

☑ **Momofuku Ssäm Bar** ● *American* `25` `16` `19` `$46`
E Village | 207 Second Ave. (13th St.) | 212-254-3500 | www.momofuku.com
"Fabulous fatty" pork buns, "bold", burritolike *ssäms* and other
"knockout" Asian-inflected New American dishes draw "loud" crowds
to David Chang's "no-frills" East Villager; though the "constantly
transforming menu" is "as good as advertised", the "austere", "uncomfortable" setting leaves some seeking "ssäm more elbow room",
and "chairs with backs."

Momoya *Japanese* `23` `20` `20` `$40`
Chelsea | 185 Seventh Ave. (21st St.) | 212-989-4466
W 80s | 427 Amsterdam Ave. (bet. 80th & 81st Sts.) | 212-580-0007
www.themomoya.com
For "tasty", "beautifully presented" sushi "without pretense", check
out this "calm" Japanese duo in Chelsea and the UWS; "efficient",
"no-rush" service prevails inside the "sleek", "modern" settings, and
as a bonus, the "quality" rolls come "without high price tags."

NEW **Monkey Bar** ●⊠ *American* `18` `22` `20` `$61`
E 50s | Elysée Hotel | 60 E. 54th St. (bet. Madison & Park Aves.) |
212-308-2950
Another successful restaurant revival for *Vanity Fair* editor Graydon
Carter, this longtime Midtowner is now a "fantastic, celebrity-packed
experience" offering a retro-tinged American menu via chef Larry
Forgione served in a "glamorous" nightclub-ish space decorated with
"beautiful" murals by Edward Sorel; reservations can only be re-
quested by e-mail (reservations@monkeybarnewyork.com), unless
you're a "F.O.G. – friend of Graydon."

Monster Sushi *Japanese* `18` `11` `16` `$32`
Chelsea | 158 W. 23rd St. (bet. 6th & 7th Aves.) | 212-620-9131 ●
W 40s | 22 W. 46th St. (bet. 5th & 6th Aves.) | 212-398-7707
www.monstersushi.com
"Monster appetites" are a prerequisite at this "affordable", "blue-
collar" Japanese twosome where gluttons can "barely get their

mouths around" the "giant" portions; "spartan" surroundings and "rushed" service don't matter if you're looking to "eat till you bust."

NEW Montenapo *Italian*   - | - | - | E

W 40s | NY Times Bldg. | 250 W. 41st St. (bet. 7th & 8th Aves.) | 212-764-7663 | www.montenaporestaurant.com

Overlooking the garden atrium of the New York Times building, this sprawling new Italian exudes contemporary chic, with glass walls, soaring ceilings and an overall la dolce vita vibe; the tasty, multiregional menu seems priced for headier times, but both the service and the crowd are snappy.

Morandi ● *Italian*   22 | 20 | 19 | $52

G Village | 211 Waverly Pl. (Charles St.) | 212-627-7575 | www.morandiny.com

A "bustling scene" with "drinks clinking" and necks craning when "boldface names" enter, Keith McNally's "homey" Villager "makes you wonder where the recession is"; "flavorful" Italian cooking, "welcoming" service and a "farmhouse-chic" setting keep devotees "full, happy and wanting to come back for more."

Moran's Chelsea *American*   18 | 20 | 21 | $46

Chelsea | 146 10th Ave. (19th St.) | 212-627-3030 | www.moranschelsea.com

"Time stands still" at this "been-there-forever" Chelsea American that lays on the charm with a "warm" pub setting replete with a "crackling fire" and a "beautiful" display of Waterford crystal; "solid, high-value" eats and "friendly" staffers make for truly "comfortable" dining here.

Morgan, The Ⓜ *American*   20 | 23 | 20 | $43

Murray Hill | The Morgan Library & Museum | 225 Madison Ave. (bet. 36th & 37th Sts.) | 212-683-2130 | www.themorgan.org

"It doesn't get much classier" than this lunch-only option in Murray Hill's Morgan Library, where "tasty" New American bites are offered either in the "serene" atrium cafe or the "elegant" chamber that was once J. Pierpont's dining room; for best results, "wear pearls" and "bring your bankbook."

ⓩ Morimoto *Japanese*   25 | 26 | 23 | $81

Chelsea | 88 10th Ave. (bet. 15th & 16th Sts.) | 212-989-8883 | www.morimotonyc.com

Iron Chef Masaharu Morimoto "lives up to the hype" at this "over-the-top" West Chelsea Japanese where "exquisite" dishes are served by "attentive" staffers in a "wonderfully modern", "all-white" duplex setting (don't miss the "high-tech toilets"); since "money is no object here", you might as well "spare no expense" and spring for the "omagod omakase."

Morrell Wine Bar & Cafe *American*   18 | 16 | 18 | $49

W 40s | 1 Rockefeller Plaza (49th St., bet. 5th & 6th Aves.) | 212-262-7700 | www.morrellwinebar.com

"Smack dab in the middle" of Rockefeller Center, this "dependable" New American wine bar/cafe delivers "solid" grub, "fantastic" vinos and some mighty "good people-watching" from its outdoor patio; even better, its "unpretentious" vibe is "satisfying" for both tourists and locals alike.

	FOOD	DECOR	SERVICE	COST

Morton's The Steakhouse *Steak* | 24 | 20 | 23 | $77 |

E 40s | 551 Fifth Ave. (45th St.) | 212-972-3315
NEW **Downtown Bklyn** | NY Marriott Brooklyn | 339 Adams St.
(bet. Tillary & Willoughby Sts.) | Brooklyn | 718-596-2700
www.mortons.com

"Superb steaks" and "birdbath-size martinis" complement each other at
these clublike chain chophouses where the beef presentation starts the
"show" but the "presentation of the bill" may come as a "shock"; still, the
"first-rate" food is "consistent from location to location", ditto the "reliable" service and "wood-paneled", "testosterone"-charged ambiance.

Motorino ⏺ *Pizza* | 22 | 17 | 18 | $29 |

NEW **E Village** | 349 E. 12th St. (bet. 1st & 2nd Aves.) | 212-777-2644
Williamsburg | 319 Graham Ave. (Devoe St.) | Brooklyn | 718-599-8899
www.motorinopizza.com

Top-notch Neapolitan "wood-fired brick-oven pizzas" with "fresh toppings" and "smoky-good" crusts draw piesani to this "funky" East
Williamsburg pizzeria; "friendly" servers, "attention to detail" and affordable prices make for an overall "pleasant" experience; N.B. the
East Village spin-off opened post-Survey.

NEW **Mott, The** *American* | - | - | - | M |

Little Italy | 173 Mott St. (Broome St.) | 212-966-1411

With its nondescript facade and stylish whitewashed interior, it feels
like SoHo in Little Italy at this loungey newcomer serving moderately
priced New Americana made from local, seasonal ingredients; the abbreviated space matches the abbreviated menu.

Moustache *Mideastern* | 21 | 12 | 16 | $25 |

NEW **E 100s** | 1621 Lexington Ave. (102nd St.) | 212-828-0030 ⏺
E Village | 265 E. 10th St. (bet. Ave. A & 1st Ave.) | 212-228-2022 ⊕
W Village | 90 Bedford St. (bet. Barrow & Grove Sts.) | 212-229-2220 ⏺⊕
www.moustachepitza.com

"Holy hummus", the tabs sure are "cheap" at this Middle Eastern trio
turning out "garlic-forward dips", "pillowy pitas" and "tasty" specialty
'pitzas'; regulars ignore the "beyond-slow" service and "tiny", "yurt"-
like settings: the "bread makes it all worthwhile" here.

Mr. Chow ⏺ *Chinese* | 21 | 21 | 18 | $78 |

E 50s | 324 E. 57th St. (bet. 1st & 2nd Aves.) | 212-751-9030
Mr. Chow Tribeca ⏺ *Chinese*
TriBeCa | 121 Hudson St. (N. Moore St.) | 212-965-9500
www.mrchow.com

Either "too sexy for words" or "a parody of itself", Michael Chow's
eponymous Chinese duo divides voters: partisans praise the "outstanding" chow and "chic" digs, but cynics nix the "don't-ask-don't-
tell" menuless ordering wherein "pushy" waiters "choose the meal for
you" – often at an "astronomical" cost.

Mr. K's *Chinese* | 22 | 23 | 23 | $60 |

E 50s | 570 Lexington Ave. (51st St.) | 212-583-1668 | www.mrks.com

"Over-the-top" art deco design replete with "pink booths" and "Erté"-
style etched glass lends a "regal" aura to this "delicious" Midtown
"haute Chinese"; ok, it "may be cheaper to fly to China than to eat
here", but at least the $28 "prix fixe lunch is a bargain."

	FOOD	DECOR	SERVICE	COST

Mughlai *Indian*
20 | 14 | 19 | $37

W 70s | 320 Columbus Ave. (75th St.) | 212-724-6363

The food may not be "fancy", but this longtime UWS Indian remains a "neighborhood staple" for "tasty", "delicately spiced" dishes and "welcoming" service that encourage you to "tuck in and enjoy"; "fair prices" make the "neglected" decor more bearable.

My Moon *Mediterranean*
▽ 19 | 25 | 19 | $41

Williamsburg | 184 N. 10th St. (bet. Bedford & Driggs Aves.) | Brooklyn | 718-599-7007 | www.mymoonnyc.com

For a "slice of the *Arabian Nights*" in Williamsburg, "romantics" head to this "cavernous", "dimly lit" Mediterranean with an "amazing" outdoor patio; even though the "food doesn't measure up to the visuals", it's "solid" enough, ditto the service.

Nam *Vietnamese*
21 | 17 | 19 | $40

TriBeCa | 110 Reade St. (W. B'way) | 212-267-1777 | www.namnyc.com

Devotees deem this "out-of-the-way" TriBeCan "well worth" a trip for "friendly" service and "subtly flavored" Vietnamese fare; the "upscale", "white-tablecloth" space is either "pretty" or "boring", but at least the tabs won't "hurt your wallet."

Nanni 🏿 *Italian*
24 | 15 | 22 | $59

E 40s | 146 E. 46th St. (bet. Lexington & 3rd Aves.) | 212-697-4161 | www.nannirestaurant.com

"As old-school as it gets", this circa-1968 Northern Italian "time warp" near Grand Central remains a "standby" for "tastes-like-home" classics ferried by "ancient waiters" with "thick accents"; though pricey tabs and "drab" digs detract, admirers still "wouldn't change a thing."

Nanoosh *Mediterranean*
19 | 14 | 15 | $19

NEW **E 60s** | 1273 First Ave. (bet. 68th & 69th Sts.) | 917-677-7575
W 60s | 2012 Broadway (bet. 68th & 69th Sts.) | 212-362-7922
www.nanoosh.com

"Creative takes on hummus" fill out the menus of these "high concept" crosstown Meds set in "laid-back", "minimalist" rooms; "excellent wraps" and "freshly baked pita" at "inexpensive" tabs compensate for the lack of atmosphere and service.

Naples 45 🏿 *Italian*
17 | 14 | 16 | $36

E 40s | MetLife Bldg. | 200 Park Ave. (45th St.) | 212-972-7001 | www.patinagroup.com

"Folks in transit" commend the "consistently good" wood-fired pizza at this "cacophonous" Italian just north of Grand Central; despite "rushed" service and "antiseptic" looks, it works well for "fast biz" lunches or a "quick" bite "before catching a train"; N.B. closed weekends.

NEW Naya *Lebanese*
▽ 21 | 22 | 21 | $43

E 50s | 1057 Second Ave. (bet. 55th & 56th Sts.) | 212-319-7777 | www.nayarestaurants.com

A "feast for the eyes", this new Midtown Lebanese is "cleverly designed" in a "modernist", "space-age" style that makes its "narrow" setting seem more "open" and inviting; "friendly" staffers proffer "delicious" meze as well as some "unusual dishes" that should meet any budget.

	FOOD	DECOR	SERVICE	COST

Neary's ● Irish
16 | 15 | 20 | $44

E 50s | 358 E. 57th St. (1st Ave.) | 212-751-1434
"Charming host" Jimmy Neary "makes you feel at home" at this "cozy" Midtowner where a "seasoned staff" right out of "central casting" ferries "hearty" Irish pub food; the "clubby", "older" crowd usually includes some "local politicos", but it's the kind of place where "everyone knows everyone" moments after walking in.

Negril ⓜ Caribbean/Jamaican
21 | 19 | 18 | $36

G Village | 70 W. Third St. (bet. La Guardia Pl. & Thompson St.) | 212-477-2804 | www.negrilvillage.com
For a "taste of the Caribbean" in Greenwich Village, check out this "loungey" Villager known for "authentically spicy" Jamaican dishes and "strong" tropical drinks; "pulsating reggae" rhythms lend an "energetic" vibe that doesn't extend to the "island-time" service; N.B. the Chelsea original has shuttered.

Nëo Sushi ● Japanese
21 | 18 | 21 | $61

W 80s | 2298 Broadway (83rd St.) | 212-769-1003 | www.neosushi.com
This UWS Japanese has "Nobu-like ambitions", offering "tantalizing" sushi "so beautiful that you hesitate to eat it" served by a "knowledgeable" crew; however, the "investment-banker pricing" is so "shocking" to some that it "mars" the overall experience.

New Bo-Ky ⊄ Noodle Shop
▽ 22 | 5 | 11 | $13

Chinatown | 80 Bayard St. (bet. Mott & Mulberry Sts.) | 212-406-2292
Ultra-"cheap" tabs allow folks to "eat themselves silly" at this 25-year-old C-town "hole-in-the-wall" beloved for its "gigantic bowls" of "really tasty" Chinese and Vietnamese noodle soups; "bright lights", "mandatory table sharing" and "halfhearted service" are the downsides.

New French American
▽ 21 | 15 | 18 | $39

W Village | 522 Hudson St. (bet. Charles & 10th Sts.) | 212-807-7357
No longer new and definitely "not French", this "low-key" West Village yearling offers a "limited menu" of American bistro items served in a "simple", "diner-ish" setting; it "came out of nowhere" and suddenly got "quite popular", maybe because of its "reasonable" tabs and "whimsical" mood.

New Leaf Cafe ⓜ American
21 | 23 | 20 | $45

Washington Heights | Fort Tryon Park | 1 Margaret Corbin Dr. (190th St.) | 212-568-5323 | www.nyrp.org
"Lush" Fort Tryon Park is the backdrop for this "bucolic" spot near the Cloisters where Scott Campbell's "creative" New American cooking "matches the setting"; an "enchanting" terrace and "genuinely helpful" staff add to the "lovely" experience, and many send "kudos to Bette Midler", whose green-minded nonprofit runs this "picturesque" place.

New Yeah Shanghai Deluxe ⊄ Chinese
▽ 24 | 10 | 15 | $23

Chinatown | 65 Bayard St. (Mott St.) | 212-566-4884
A secret no longer, this "friendly", cash-only Shanghainese lures "crowds" to Chinatown with an "overwhelming" menu of "intriguing" options, including "incredible" juicy dumplings and pork shoulders; yeah, the setting's "no-frills", but no one cares given the "unbelievably affordable" tabs.

	FOOD	DECOR	SERVICE	COST

New York Burger Co. *Burgers* 17 | 9 | 13 | $15
Flatiron | 678 Sixth Ave. (bet. 21st & 22nd Sts.) | 212-229-1404
Murray Hill | 303 Park Ave. S. (bet. 23rd & 24th Sts.) | 212-254-2727
www.newyorkburgerco.com
For "made-to-order burgers" you can "sink your teeth into", these
patty palaces are "better-than-average" alternatives to the nearby
"Shake Shack lines"; still, "fast-food-joint" decor and "amateur service"
leave some "skeptical."

Nha Trang *Vietnamese* 22 | 7 | 14 | $19
Chinatown | 148 Centre St. (bet. Walker & White Sts.) | 212-941-9292
Chinatown | 87 Baxter St. (bet. Bayard & Canal Sts.) | 212-233-5948
"Law-and-order types" from nearby courthouses tout these C-town
twins for their "tasty noodle soups" and other "terrific", "seriously
cheap" Vietnamese vittles ("you have to work hard to spend $20 a person
here"); "nonexistent" decor and "erratic" service are the downsides.

Nice Green Bo ⊅ *Chinese* 23 | 5 | 11 | $19
Chinatown | 66 Bayard St. (bet. Elizabeth & Mott Sts.) | 212-625-2359
At this "tiny, busy" Chinatown storefront, "succulent" soup dumplings
and other "hot-mess" Shanghainese specialties arrive at "cramped"
communal tables; dirt-"cheap" tabs trump the "laughable" decor and
"throw-the-food-at-you" service.

Nice Matin *French/Mediterranean* 20 | 18 | 18 | $47
W 70s | 201 W. 79th St. (Amsterdam Ave.) | 212-873-6423 |
www.nicematinnyc.com
An all-around "feel-good experience", this UWS approximation of the
"south of France" plies "vibrant" French-Med favorites in "stylish",
"chick flick"–worthy digs; though "crowds" can beget "haphazard"
service, there are kudos for the "fabulous" brunch, "lovely" sidewalk
tables and "reasonable prices."

Niche *American* ▽ 24 | 17 | 23 | $43
E 80s | 1593 Second Ave. (bet. 82nd & 83rd Sts.) | 212-734-5500 |
www.nichebarnyc.com
"Trendy" yearling from the owners of Etats-Unis blending "simple",
"surprisingly good" New Americana with "attentive" service; the
"small" setting, equipped with a single, marble-topped communal
table, is a magnet for "cliques of women", hence its rep as an Upper
East Side "pickup" joint.

Nick & Stef's Steakhouse ⊠ *Steak* 20 | 18 | 19 | $61
Garment District | 9 Penn Plaza (enter on 33rd St., bet. 7th & 8th Aves.) |
212-563-4444 | www.patinagroup.com
In a part of town with "few standouts", this "viable" Midtown steakhouse
"convenient" to MSG and Penn Station scores with "tender",
"aged beef" and "fast, friendly" service; sure, it's a "splurge", but its
"secret door into the Garden" is "worth the extra bucks."

Nick & Toni's Cafe *Mediterranean* 19 | 16 | 18 | $50
W 60s | 100 W. 67th St. (bet. B'way & Columbus Ave.) | 212-496-4000 |
www.nickandtoniscafe.com
Though a "diluted version" of the Hamptons original, this "cozy" Med
"handy" to Lincoln Center still draws a "sophisticated crowd" (heavy

on ABC "TV execs") with "smart", wood-fired pizzas and seafood; both the "spotty" service and "modest" interior could stand a "refresher."

Nick's *Pizza*
23 | 13 | 18 | $26

E 90s | 1814 Second Ave. (94th St.) | 212-987-5700 | www.nicksnyc.com

Forest Hills | 108-26 Ascan Ave. (bet. Austin & Burns Sts.) | Queens | 718-263-1126 ⇄

"Thin-crusted perfection" emerges from the brick ovens of these "no-frills" pizzerias where the "new-school" pies are "mouthwatering", though service can be "hit-or-miss"; the UES satellite needs your "support" as it "endures the Second Avenue subway construction" out front.

ⓩ Nicky's Vietnamese Sandwiches ⇄ *Sandwiches*
22 | 5 | 15 | $10

E Village | 150 E. Second St. (Ave. A) | 212-388-1088

Boerum Hill | 311 Atlantic Ave. (bet. Hoyt & Smith Sts.) | Brooklyn | 718-855-8838

www.nickyssandwiches.com

Banh-vivants relish the "crunchy", "savory" *banh mi* sandwiches "made to order" at this East Village/Boerum Hill twosome; the lines go on "forever" and there's "no atmosphere", but "no one ever complains" what with the "incredibly cheap" tabs and the "excellent" pho at the Brooklyn branch.

Nicola's ◐ *Italian*
22 | 16 | 20 | $61

E 80s | 146 E. 84th St. (bet. Lexington & 3rd Aves.) | 212-249-9850

An "'in' crowd" of UES "neighborhood" types lauds this "amiable" trattoria for its "outstanding" Italian entrees served by an "aim-to-please" crew; but "walk-ins" who get "seated in Siberia" grumble about "attitude" and prices that seem French.

99 Miles to Philly ◐⇄ *Cheesesteaks*
19 | 9 | 14 | $13

E Village | 94 Third Ave. (bet. 12th & 13th Sts.) | 212-253-2700 | www.99milestophilly.net

"Get your fix" of "greasy cheesesteak goodness" – "with or without the Cheez Whiz" – at this East Village "dive" considered "as good as it gets in NYC" for "true-Philly" sandwiches; "there's no decor", but no one's griping given the "recession-appropriate" prices; P.S. "know the lingo before ordering."

Ninja *Japanese*
∇ 16 | 25 | 22 | $73

TriBeCa | 25 Hudson St. (bet. Duane & Reade Sts.) | 212-274-8500 | www.ninjanewyork.com

"Kids" get a kick out of this "one-of-a-kind" TriBeCa Japanese "theme park" set in a "replica of a Ninja village" and staffed by "cheeky" waiter/magicians who supply the "camp factor"; most agree that the "acceptable" eats are way "overpriced" – but then again "you're paying for the atmosphere."

Nino's ◐ *Italian*
21 | 19 | 21 | $56

E 70s | 1354 First Ave. (bet. 72nd & 73rd Sts.) | 212-988-0002 | www.ninosnyc.com

Nino's Bellissima Pizza *Italian*

E 40s | 890 Second Ave. (bet. 47th & 48th Sts.) | 212-355-5540 | www.ninospositano.com

(continued)

Nino's Positano *Italian*
E 40s | 890 Second Ave. (bet. 47th & 48th Sts.) | 212-355-5540 |
www.ninospositano.com

Nino's Tuscany *Italian*
W 50s | 117 W. 58th St. (bet. 6th & 7th Aves.) | 212-757-8630 |
www.ninostuscany.com

Nino's 208 *Italian*
NEW **E 50s** | 208 E. 58th St. (bet. 2nd & 3rd Aves.) | 212-750-7766 |
www.ninosnyc.com

At these "upbeat" Italian "institutions", "consummate host" Nino
Selimaj "makes everyone feel welcome" while supplying *"bellissimo"*
(albeit "pricey") classic *cucina*; most of the branches skew "elegant",
but the more "casual" Positano boasts an adjacent pizzeria with "excellent" brick-oven pies.

NEW **Nios** *American*   - | - | - | E
W 40s | Muse Hotel | 130 W. 46th St. (bet. 6th & 7th Aves.) |
212-485-2999 | www.niosrestaurant.com

"Inviting" new Times Square wine bar/eatery in the Muse Hotel
with a mostly American menu that also throws tempura and pizza
into the mix; the "noisy" front area is fitted out with a long marble bartop and flat-screen virtual fireplace, while the "dark" back room is
more conversation friendly.

Nizza ☉ *French/Italian*   21 | 17 | 20 | $38
W 40s | 630 Ninth Ave. (bet. 44th & 45th Sts.) | 212-956-1800 |
www.nizzanyc.com

The Côte d'Azur alights in Hell's Kitchen via this "sleek", "inviting"
French-Italian whose "inventive" Niçoise menu "spikes the taste buds"
and comes at "fiscally responsible" tabs; "efficient" staffers and a variety of "ambitious gluten-free" items add allure.

Z Nobu *Japanese*   27 | 23 | 23 | $83
TriBeCa | 105 Hudson St. (Franklin St.) | 212-219-0500
Z Nobu 57 ☉ *Japanese*
W 50s | 40 W. 57th St. (bet. 5th & 6th Aves.) | 212-757-3000
Z Nobu, Next Door *Japanese*
TriBeCa | 105 Hudson St. (bet. Franklin & N. Moore Sts.) |
212-334-4445
www.noburestaurants.com

The recession notwithstanding, even three locations can barely contain the crowds flocking to this "popular" Japanese-Peruvian trio that
combines "great", "inventive" food with "cool, sexy" atmospherics
and "high energy"; while "far from cheap", no one complains since this
is one of those rare experiences that's "even better than promised" –
something like "angels dancing in your mouth."

Nocello *Italian*   21 | 17 | 19 | $51
W 50s | 257 W. 55th St. (bet. B'way & 8th Ave.) | 212-713-0224 |
www.nocello.net

Regulars "come hungry" to this "swello" Theater District Tuscan turning out "oversized plates" of "well-executed" grub at tabs that "won't
break the bank"; a location "convenient" to both Carnegie Hall and
City Center compensates for the sometimes "slow" service.

	FOOD	DECOR	SERVICE	COST

Noche Mexicana *Mexican*

∇ 25 | 9 | 18 | $20

W 100s | 852 Amsterdam Ave. (bet. 101st & 102nd Sts.) | 212-662-6900 | www.noche-mexicana.com

It's "easy to overeat" and "hard to overspend" at this UWS Mexican "standout" where regulars rhapsodize over the "best tamales north of the border" and "burritos like God intended"; since staffers "struggle" with English and the "drab" digs are a "downer", "great delivery" saves the day.

NoHo Star ● *American*

18 | 15 | 16 | $35

NoHo | 330 Lafayette St. (Bleecker St.) | 212-925-0070 | www.nohostar.com

"NoHo way" are locals tired of this "neighborhoody", 25-year-old New American vet known for "upscale coffee-shop eats" and "surprisingly good" Chinese chow; if the "dated" decor and "wavering" service aren't exactly stellar, its "funky charm" and "decent prices" still shine.

Nomad *African*

∇ 20 | 15 | 18 | $34

E Village | 78 Second Ave. (4th St.) | 212-253-5410 | www.nomadny.com

East Village nomads wander into this "narrow passageway" to explore its "excellent" North African specialties (e.g. "delightful tagines") and "tasty" regional wines; "friendly" staffers and "bargain" $20 prix fixe dinners make for "affordable, romantic" repasts.

Nonna *Italian*

18 | 14 | 17 | $35

W 80s | 520 Columbus Ave. (85th St.) | 212-579-3194 | www.nonnarestaurant.com

Dining at this "solid" UWS Italian is "like going to grandma's for pasta night", assuming she also served "meal-in-itself" antipasti and "well-priced" wines; maybe the "uninspired" interior and "bland" service need work, but the "good-bang-for-the-buck" pricing is fine as is.

Noodle Bar ⊅ *Pan-Asian*

∇ 20 | 11 | 17 | $21

G Village | 26 Carmine St. (bet. Bedford & Bleecker Sts.) | 212-524-6800
LES | 172 Orchard St. (Stanton St.) | 212-228-9833
www.noodlebarnyc.com

"Minimalist" is putting it mildly at these "cash-only" Downtown Pan-Asians offering "fast, tasty" chow that's more than "affordable"; they work for a "time-crunched lunch" or on-the-fly dinner, though the newer, larger LES satellite is preferable to the "tiny" NYU-area original.

Noodle Pudding ⓂⒹ *Italian*

25 | 17 | 21 | $41

Brooklyn Heights | 38 Henry St. (bet. Cranberry & Middagh Sts.) | Brooklyn | 718-625-3737

"Don't be put off by the name" of this "amazing" Brooklyn Heights Italian famed for "upscale" food, "downscale", cash-only prices and "always packed" conditions; though it's "super kid-friendly" – read: lots of "clatter and chatter" – "no reservations" translates into "ridiculous" waits.

Nook ⊅ *Eclectic*

∇ 19 | 9 | 16 | $33

W 50s | 746 Ninth Ave. (bet. 50th & 51st Sts.) | 212-247-5500

"Keep your elbows in" at this "teeny" Hell's Kitchen 24-seater that's more than "true to its name" dimensionswise; payoffs include "tasty" Eclectic eats, "bargain" tabs and an "icing-on-the-cake" BYO policy, but there are some deficits: "brusque" service and below "basic" decor.

Norma's American

FOOD	DECOR	SERVICE	COST
25	19	20	$41

W 50s | Le Parker Meridien Hotel | 119 W. 56th St. (bet. 6th & 7th Aves.) | 212-708-7460 | www.normasnyc.com

"Conspicuous consumption" doesn't get much more "decadent" than the $1,000 caviar omelet at this "over-the-top" Midtown American known for its "power" breakfasts and "blissful" brunches; the prices notwithstanding, this place can turn waffles into a "special occasion."

Northeast Kingdom American

FOOD	DECOR	SERVICE	COST
-	-	-	M

Bushwick | 18 Wyckoff Ave. (Troutman St.) | Brooklyn | 718-386-3864 | www.north-eastkingdom.com

Named after a remote region of Vermont, this modestly priced mom-and-pop New American "hidden" on a bleak Bushwick corner is set in a rustic room fitted out with salvaged wood that complements its "creative", down-home menu (e.g. organic chicken pot pie, Berkshire pork loin); a "basic" brunch is offered on weekends.

North Square American

FOOD	DECOR	SERVICE	COST
23	19	22	$47

G Village | Washington Square Hotel | 103 Waverly Pl. (MacDougal St.) | 212-254-1200 | www.northsquareny.com

"Easily overlooked" but "worth finding", this "locals' favorite" near NYU offers "approachable" New American food, "moderate costs" and "unhurried" service; "grown-ups" appreciate "having a real conversation" at this "sleeper keeper."

NEW No. 7 ◐ American

FOOD	DECOR	SERVICE	COST
∇ 23	23	22	$41

Fort Greene | 7 Greene Ave. (bet. Cumberland & Fulton Sts.) | Brooklyn | 718-522-6370 | www.no7restaurant.com

Fort Greeners feel lucky to have this pint-size "new star" featuring "spot-on" American chow ferried by "knowledgeable" servers; despite a "chaotic bar scene", the whitewashed, art deco–inflected dining room has a "relaxed" feel, making it an "appealing" choice pre- or post-BAM.

Novecento ◑ Argentinean/Steak

FOOD	DECOR	SERVICE	COST
∇ 22	19	20	$44

SoHo | 343 W. Broadway (bet. Broome & Grand Sts.) | 212-925-4706 | www.novecento.com

Carnivores who "can't make it to Buenos Aires" settle for this SoHo Argentine steakhouse, a "popular" nexus for "melt-in-your-mouth" beef, "great empanadas" and "lively soccer games" on the tube; "friendly price tags" and "excellent people-watching" compensate for the "high volume" and "long waits, even with a reservation."

Novitá Italian

FOOD	DECOR	SERVICE	COST
24	18	22	$56

Gramercy | 102 E. 22nd St. (bet. Lexington Ave. & Park Ave. S.) | 212-677-2222 | www.novitanyc.com

While there's "nothing glitzy" about this Gramercy "gem", it still dazzles with "superb" Tuscan specialties (e.g. "divine" truffled ravioli) served by "smiling waiters"; although the "intimate" setting is usually "tightly packed", most maintain the end "reward" is "worth the discomfort."

Nurnberger Bierhaus German

FOOD	DECOR	SERVICE	COST
∇ 20	17	19	$32

Staten Island | 817 Castleton Ave. (bet. Davis & Pelton Aves.) | 718-816-7461 | www.nurnbergerbierhaus.com

"Bring your appetite – as well as someone else's" – to this "old-fashioned" SI beer hall in West Brighton vending big portions of "authentic" Germanica washed down with a "fantastic" selection of Bavarian brews; "reasonable" tabs and a "laid-back" vibe also draw applause, though some "could do without the waitresses' 'Helga' costumes."

Nyonya ⌀ *Malaysian*   23 | 12 | 14 | $24

Little Italy | 194 Grand St. (bet. Mott & Mulberry Sts.) | 212-334-3669 ●
Bensonhurst | 2322 86th St. (bet. 23rd & 24th Aves.) | Brooklyn | 718-265-0888
Sunset Park | 5323 Eighth Ave. (54th St.) | Brooklyn | 718-633-0808 ●
www.penangusa.com

Known for "heaping plates" of "amazing noodles chock-full of seafood", these "cash-only" Malaysians are just the thing when you "can't afford a ticket to Kuala Lumpur"; despite "expressionless" service and "dumpy" decor, the "unbeatable combo" of "good and cheap" keeps regulars "streaming in."

NEW Oak Room *American*   18 | 25 | 21 | $76

W 50s | Plaza Hotel | 10 Central Park S. (bet. 5th & 6th Aves.) |
212-758-7777 | www.oakroomny.com

Back on the scene following a three-year "face-lift", this Plaza Hotel "landmark" has been "polished" up and its oak-lined, turn-of-the-last-century "gentlemen's club" setting is as "magnificent" as ever; unfortunately, the New American "fine-dining" menu (and "robber-baron" price tags) still need "more work."

Z NEW Oceana *American/Seafood*   - | - | - | E

W 40s | McGraw Hill Bldg. | 1221 Sixth Ave. (enter on 49th St. bet. 6th & 7th Aves.) | 212-759-5941 | www.oceanarestaurant.com

Recently transplanted to a sprawling new setting in Midtown's McGraw Hill building, this "polished" New American seafooder still offers the same "melt-in-your-mouth" menu, "doting" service and "well-spaced" tables; the tabs remain as "expensive" as ever, though the prix fixe-only policy of the past is no more – everything's à la carte now.

Ocean Grill *Seafood*   23 | 20 | 21 | $55

W 70s | 384 Columbus Ave. (bet. 78th & 79th Sts.) | 212-579-2300 |
www.brguestrestaurants.com

"Ocean-to-table fresh" seafood "prepared with flair" and served "knowledgeably" is the hook at Steve Hanson's "upscale" UWS poisson palace that also boasts a "wonderful raw bar"; the "spacious" interior can be "louder than a ship's engine room", however, so conversationalists "get there early" for an outdoor table.

Odeon, The ● *American/French*   19 | 18 | 18 | $49

TriBeCa | 145 W. Broadway (bet. Duane & Thomas Sts.) | 212-233-0507 |
www.theodeonrestaurant.com

"Now older than most of its diners", this TriBeCa bistro remains a "breezy" boîte where "accommodating" staffers sling "uncomplicated" Franco-American basics; "still relevant", particularly "late night", it's as "comfortable and classy" as an "old pair of Gucci loafers."

Olana ☒ *American*   23 | 23 | 22 | $61

Murray Hill | 72 Madison Ave. (bet. 27th & 28th Sts.) | 212-725-4900 |
www.olananyc.com

"Deluxe in all the right ways", this New American yearling near Madison Square serves "delicious, innovative" food including a popular "'make-your-own' tasting menu"; "plush red velvet" furniture and "panoramic pastoral murals" set the scene for "adult conversation", fostered by "hands-on" owners and a "pro" team.

Old Homestead *Steak* | 24 | 17 | 21 | $72 |

Meatpacking | 56 Ninth Ave. (bet. 14th & 15th Sts.) | 212-242-9040 | www.theoldhomesteadsteakhouse.com

"Alpha males" dig this 1868 "landmark" for its "tender steaks and tough waiters" – specifically, those "juicy" chops proffered in "William Howard Taft–like portions" by staffers "who've been around since the Meatpacking District was for meatpacking"; despite a recent revamp, the space still "feels like the set of an old gangster movie", though the "mammoth checks" are more up to date.

Olea *Mediterranean* | ▽ 23 | 21 | 21 | $33 |

Fort Greene | 171 Lafayette Ave. (Adelphi St.) | Brooklyn | 718-643-7003 | www.oleabrooklyn.com

"Laid-back and friendly", this Fort Greene Mediterranean near BAM has rejiggered its menu to feature "more tapas" than before, with "terrific" results; the "rustic" setting remains "inviting" (maybe even "romantic"), though fans wish it had "a little more space" and "a little less noise."

Olives *Mediterranean* | 22 | 21 | 21 | $58 |

Union Sq | W Union Sq. Hotel | 201 Park Ave. S. (17th St.) | 212-353-8345 | www.toddenglish.com

Todd English's modern Mediterranean in the W Union Square turns out "imaginative, just plain delicious food" abetted by "informative" service and "tasteful" decor; the only drawback is the crowd in the "hopping" bar area.

Ollie's *Chinese* | 15 | 9 | 13 | $24 |

W 40s | 411 W. 42nd St. (bet. 9th & 10th Aves.) | 212-868-6588
W 60s | 1991 Broadway (bet. 67th & 68th Sts.) | 212-595-8181 ●
W 80s | 2315 Broadway (84th St.) | 212-362-3111 ●
W 100s | 2957 Broadway (116th St.) | 212-932-3300 ●

"No-frills" is putting it mildly at this West Side mini-chain vending "serviceable", "affordable" Chinese food dished up "so fast you're out the door before you finish chewing"; the "madhouse" milieu persuades plenty to opt for "lightning-quick delivery" instead.

Omai *Vietnamese* | 22 | 16 | 19 | $42 |

Chelsea | 158 Ninth Ave. (bet. 19th & 20th Sts.) | 212-633-0550 | www.omainyc.com

"Don't blink" or you might miss this "small" Chelsea Vietnamese with "no sign", serving "creative", "clean-tasting" cuisine in an "unpretentious" room with a "soothing" vibe; when you're this "close to the Joyce", it's "hard to do better for the price."

Omen ● *Japanese* | ▽ 25 | 19 | 22 | $59 |

SoHo | 113 Thompson St. (bet. Prince & Spring Sts.) | 212-925-8923

To "feel Zen", try this Kyoto-style SoHo standby offering "superior sashimi" and noodles "served in the traditional way", but no sushi; there's "no scene" either and it's certainly "not cheap", but "the experience is theater" for die-hard "Japanese country food" fans.

	FOOD	DECOR	SERVICE	COST

Omonia Cafe ◑ *Greek*
18 | 15 | 14 | $22

Bay Ridge | 7612-14 Third Ave. (bet. 76th & 77th Sts.) | Brooklyn | 718-491-1435

Astoria | 32-20 Broadway (33rd St.) | Queens | 718-274-6650

"Definitive" baklava and other sweets draw devotees to these "pleasant" Greek coffeehouses in Astoria and Bay Ridge; given their sidewalk seats and late-night closings, it's easy to "sit for hours" – especially since the staff "doesn't seem to care if you're there or not."

NEW Onda ◑ *South American*
▽ 22 | 22 | 24 | $44

Seaport | 229 Front St. (bet. Beekman St. & Peck Slip) | 212-513-0770 | www.ondanyc.com

Tucked into a "charming" space on the Seaport's burgeoning Front Street, this loungey small-plates purveyor lives up to its name ('vibe' in Spanish); the "surprisingly good" South American nibbles bear "recession-friendly" price tags, complemented by "interesting" wines.

O'Neals' ◑ *American*
17 | 17 | 19 | $44

W 60s | 49 W. 64th St. (bet. B'way & CPW) | 212-787-4663 | www.onealsny.com

"Convivial" and "super-convenient to Lincoln Center", this "spacious" saloon serving "consistent" all-American comfort chow remains an "old faithful" for those who need to "get to the performance on time"; late-nighters cram in to bend an elbow at the "always-crowded bar."

1 Dominick ◑ *Italian*
23 | 18 | 21 | $44

SoHo | 1 Dominick St. (bet. 6th Ave. & Varick St.) | 212-647-0202 | www.1dominick.com

Conveniently set next to SoHo's "avant-garde theater", the Here Arts Center, this "funky" nook delivers "delicious", "comforting" Italian sandwiches and small plates at a moderate price; a "modern", unpretentious setup and "friendly" staff have most calling it a "fun dining experience."

One 83 *Italian*
19 | 20 | 21 | $51

E 80s | 1608 First Ave. (bet. 83rd & 84th Sts.) | 212-327-4700 | www.one83restaurant.com

"Civilized" dining is alive and well in Yorkville at this "under-the-radar" Northern Italian where "tasty" Tuscan food is served by a "caring" crew in a "big, open" space; occasional "live jazz" and a "wonderful garden" enhance the "enjoyable" mood.

☑ One if by Land, Two if by Sea *American*
24 | 26 | 24 | $101

G Village | 17 Barrow St. (bet. 7th Ave. S. & W. 4th St.) | 212-228-0822 | www.oneifbyland.com

With flowers, firelight, piano music, "royal-treatment" service and "better-than-ever" American food, Aaron Burr's 18th-century carriage house is "hands-down the most romantic dining spot in town" – but only if price is no object; indeed, if this Village "landmark" doesn't get her to say yes, nothing will.

101 *American/Italian*
21 | 19 | 20 | $43

Bay Ridge | 10018 Fourth Ave. (101st St.) | Brooklyn | 718-833-1313 | www.101nyc.com

"Tasty, large" portions of Italian-American favorites, an "enjoyable" scene and a "view of the Verrazano" ensure that this "comfortable, social" Bay Ridge bastion remains a "neighborhood standby"; the "wise guy wannabe" contingent adds to its "Brooklyn attitude."

NEW Opus ● *Italian* ∇ 23 | 18 | 22 | $46

E 80s | 1574 Second Ave. (bet. 81st & 82nd Sts.) | 212-772-2220 | www.opusnyc.com

An extensive selection of "excellent gluten-free" dishes is the hook at the new Yorkville Italian that also hopes to lure in locals with its "outstanding" pizza; brought to you by chef Giuseppe Lentini (ex Tini's, Lentini's), it's a "first-class operation" if "not a magnum opus."

Orchard, The Ⓜ *American* 23 | 22 | 22 | $54

LES | 162 Orchard St. (bet. Rivington & Stanton Sts.) | 212-353-3570 | www.theorchardny.com

"Everyone looks gorgeous" at this "chic" LES New American lit with a "mellow-yellow glow"; the "creative" menu is famed for its selection of "flat-out fabulous" flatbreads, and if the place is "pricier than its neighbors", it's worth it for a "perfect first date."

◪ Oriental Garden *Chinese/Seafood* 23 | 11 | 15 | $34

Chinatown | 14 Elizabeth St. (bet. Bayard & Canal Sts.) | 212-619-0085

Offering the "best Cantonese seafood in NY", this 25-year-old Chinatown vet features the freshest possible fish "taken live from the tanks up front" as well as a wide variety of dim sum; sure, it's "crowded and noisy", the white Formica decor is pretty "basic" and not all the waiters speak English, but most agree "no one does it better."

Orsay *French* 18 | 20 | 17 | $59

E 70s | 1057 Lexington Ave. (75th St.) | 212-517-6400 | www.orsayrestaurant.com

"They have the bistro thing down pat" at this "ebullient" UES French cafe, a "ladies-who-lunch" magnet with "reliable" cooking and an "ooh-la-la" setting that deftly replicates "Paris in Manhattan"; for best results, "an accent is de rigueur", as is "knowing the maitre d'."

Orso ● *Italian* 22 | 18 | 22 | $54

W 40s | 322 W. 46th St. (bet. 8th & 9th Aves.) | 212-489-7212 | www.orsorestaurant.com

Still a Theater District "class act", this "stylish" Tuscan dishes out "always-on-the-mark" *cucina* via staffers whose "performance art" ensures "you won't miss the curtain"; famous among "rubberneckers" as a post-show "celeb canteen", it's usually "sold out" way in advance.

NEW Ortine *European* - | - | - | I

Prospect Heights | 622 Washington Ave. (bet. Dean & Pacific Sts.) | Brooklyn | 718-622-0026 | www.ortine.com

Everything from Belgian waffles to lasagna turns up on the menu of this "cute" new Prospect Heights "neighborhood cafe" whose European lineup skews mostly Italian; bottomless cups of coffee, a cozy, living room–like setting and almost-cheaper-than-home tabs draw the locals.

Osso Buco *Italian* 17 | 14 | 17 | $39

E 90s | 1662 Third Ave. (93rd St.) | 212-426-5422

(continued)

(continued)

Osso Buco

G Village | 88 University Pl. (bet. 11th & 12th Sts.) | 212-645-4525
www.ossobuco2go.com

"Middle-of-the-pack" Uptown/Downtown Italians known for "family-style" platters "piled high" with "solid" red-sauce chow (regulars dub them "Carmine's without the tourists"); sure, they're "far from glamorous" and picky eaters sigh "osso mediocre", but there are no complaints about the pricing.

Osteria al Doge ◑ *Italian*   20 | 17 | 20 | $48

W 40s | 142 W. 44th St. (bet. B'way & 6th Ave.) | 212-944-3643 |
www.osteria-doge.com

Although a "stone's throw from Times Square", this "reasonably priced", "quick-turnaround" Italian "doesn't feel like a tourist trap" thanks to "earthy" Venetian fare and a duplex setting that's a "bit more elegant" than the norm; regulars recommend "sitting in the balcony" to "avoid the din" below.

Osteria del Circo ◑ *Italian*   22 | 23 | 21 | $63

W 50s | 120 W. 55th St. (bet. 6th & 7th Aves.) | 212-265-3636 |
www.osteriadelcirco.com

The Maccioni sons are the ringmasters at this "three-ring extravaganza" near City Center known for "amusing" decor and "seriously good" Northern Italiana prepared with "flair"; a breezy ambiance makes this tent "more open than pop's" Le Cirque, yet the "professionalism" and trapeze-"high" pricing are similar.

Osteria Laguna ◑ *Italian*   19 | 17 | 18 | $48

E 40s | 209 E. 42nd St. (bet. 2nd & 3rd Aves.) | 212-557-0001 |
www.osteria-laguna.com

"Classy", "consistent" Venetian victuals and a "moderately priced" Italian wine list pair well at this "upbeat", "comfortable" East Midtowner; "convenient" to both Grand Central and the U.N., it's "crowded and noisy" during weekday lunch but a "true neighborhood place on weekends."

Otto ◑ *Pizza*   23 | 19 | 18 | $40

G Village | 1 Fifth Ave. (enter on 8th St., bet. 5th Ave. & University Pl.) |
212-995-9559 | www.ottopizzeria.com

"High-end" "designer" pizzas, "perfect pastas" and a wine list "as long as a phone book" are the lures at this Village enoteca/pizzeria from the Batali-Bastianich team; "accessible" pricing helps mitigate "insane" waits, "erratic" service and a faux train-station setting that can be "louder than a Kiss concert."

Z Ouest *American*   24 | 22 | 23 | $64

W 80s | 2315 Broadway (bet. 83rd & 84th Sts.) | 212-580-8700 |
www.ouestny.com

A leader in the UWS culinary "renaissance", Tom Valenti offers an American "haute comfort" menu that's "adventuresome but never outlandish" and "just gets better" over time; add in "good-value" pricing, "always attentive" service and an "attractive" setting with "comfortable" red-leather banquettes, and it's easy to see why its smart clientele considers this venue to be "tried-and-true."

Our Place *Chinese*   20 | 14 | 19 | $36

E 50s | 141 E. 55th St. (bet. Lexington & 3rd Aves.) | 212-753-3900 |
www.ourplace-teagarden.com
E 80s | 1444 Third Ave. (82nd St.) | 212-288-4888 |
www.ourplaceuptown.com

Thanks to "well-prepared" Shanghainese dishes in Midtown and "don't-miss" dim sum on the UES, these separately owned Chinese "make a game effort" for a place among their more renowned competitors; prices skew "upscale", but "good value" makes them "worth every penny."

Outback Steakhouse *Steak*   14 | 12 | 16 | $35

E 50s | 919 Third Ave. (enter on 56th St., bet. 2nd & 3rd Aves.) | 212-935-6400
Flatiron | 60 W. 23rd St. (bet. 5th & 6th Aves.) | 212-989-3122
Dyker Heights | 1475 86th St. (15th Ave.) | Brooklyn | 718-837-7200
Bayside | Bay Terrace | 23-48 Bell Blvd. (26th Ave.) | Queens | 718-819-0908
Elmhurst | Queens Pl. | 88-01 Queens Blvd. (56th Ave.) | Queens |
718-760-7200
Staten Island | 280 Marsh Ave. (Platinum Ave.) | 718-761-3907
www.outback.com

"Crikey", that signature bloomin' onion is a "bloomin' must" at this "cheap" chophouse chain that's "more buck than bang" given the "pedestrian" steaks, "homogenized" mien and "indefatigably cheerful" service; though it "impresses the kids", grown-ups find it all too "ersatz."

☒ Oyster Bar ☒ *Seafood*   22 | 18 | 17 | $49

E 40s | Grand Central | lower level (42nd St. & Vanderbilt Ave.) |
212-490-6650 | www.oysterbarny.com

"Right-off-the-boat" seafood, an "unparalleled" selection of bivalves and a super white wine list are the hooks at this "durable", circa-1913 fishmonger, a "historic" staple in the "bowels of Grand Central" known for its glorious "vaulted ceilings"; ok, it's "noisy", has "brusque" service and you'll definitely "shell out" to eat here, yet most consider it the "one and only" – particularly if you "sit at the counter for the full experience" and order the oyster pan roast.

Pacificana *Chinese*   ▽ 24 | 17 | 21 | $27

Sunset Park | 813 55th St., 2nd fl. (8th Ave.) | Brooklyn | 718-871-2880
The "carts keep rolling by" hawking a virtual "galaxy" of "tasty", Hong Kong–style dim sum at this "big" Sunset Park Cantonese; the service is often "fast and furious", but given those "great prices" it's still a "wonderful way to spend an afternoon."

Padre Figlio ☒ *Italian*   ▽ 20 | 16 | 22 | $58

E 40s | 310 E. 44th St. (bet. 1st & 2nd Aves.) | 212-286-4310 |
www.padrefiglio.com

"Excellent" Piedmontese steaks inject some "testosterone" into the otherwise "quiet" scene at this Italian yearling set on an "obscure" block near the U.N.; yes, it's "expensive", but a $35 dinner prix fixe and "attentive" service from a "friendly" father-son team compensate.

Paladar *Nuevo Latino*   ▽ 22 | 17 | 20 | $37

LES | 161 Ludlow St. (bet. Houston & Stanton Sts.) | 212-473-3535 |
www.paladarrestaurant.com

"Young" cats on the LES "party" prowl pop up at this "hip" Nuevo Latino for chef Aarón Sanchez's "inventive" cooking chased with "awesome",

	FOOD	DECOR	SERVICE	COST

"sneak-up-on-you" mojitos; "reasonable" tabs and "accommodating" staffers keep things "loud" and "fun" till the wee hours.

☑ Palm, The *Steak* | 24 | 18 | 22 | $73 |

E 40s | 837 Second Ave. (bet. 44th & 45th Sts.) | 212-687-2953 🟤
E 40s | 840 Second Ave. (bet. 44th & 45th Sts.) | 212-697-5198
NEW TriBeCa | 206 West St. (bet. Chambers & Warren Sts.) | 646-395-6391
W 50s | 250 W. 50th St. (bet. B'way & 8th Ave.) | 212-333-7256
www.thepalm.com

"Although the original [837 Second Avenue] location is best", all four local branches of this national chain are "consistent crowd-pleasers" thanks to "top-quality" steaks, lobsters and sides; toss in "friendly" (if occasionally "gruff") waiters, theatrical speakeasy decor and a choice of "lower-cost daily specials" and it's no wonder that this has been a NYC "favorite" since 1926.

Palma ◑ *Italian/Mediterranean* | ▽ 23 | 20 | 20 | $44 |

G Village | 28 Cornelia St. (bet. Bleecker St. & 6th Ave.) | 212-691-2223 | www.palmanyc.com

It's all about the "laid-back" "Mediterranean feel" at this "charming" "neighborhood" Villager vaunted for its "excellent" Sicilian fare, "personalized service" and "unbeatable" outdoor patio; there's also a separate "farmhouse dining room" that's just the ticket for "private events."

Palo Santo *Pan-Latin* | 23 | 23 | 22 | $42 |

Park Slope | 652 Union St. (bet. 4th & 5th Aves.) | Brooklyn | 718-636-6311 | www.palosanto.us

"One of the more interesting" Park Slope options, this "inviting" if somewhat "out-of-the-way" Pan-Latin plies a "sophisticated", "market-driven" menu via a "charismatic" chef/proprietor; modest prices and a "gorgeous" space that resembles an art installation add to its allure.

Pampano *Mexican/Seafood* | 24 | 22 | 21 | $58 |

E 40s | 209 E. 49th St. (bet. 2nd & 3rd Aves.) | 212-751-4545 | www.modernmexican.com

Chef Richard Sandoval and tenor Plácido Domingo make a "*fantástico*" team at this "dazzling" Midtown Mexican where the fish-centric menu is as "phenomenal" as its "classy" townhouse setting; of course, it all comes at a rather "high" price, but for a "quicker", more affordable fix, try their lunch taqueria around the corner.

Pamplona ☒ *Spanish* | 22 | 15 | 21 | $50 |

Murray Hill | 37 E. 28th St. (bet. Madison Ave. & Park Ave. S.) | 212-213-2328 | www.pamplonanyc.com

Alex Ureña's "fine", "upmarket" Murray Hill homage to Northern Spanish cuisine is built around a "wonderful" selection of "bold" tapas; "attentive" service and sangria that "goes straight to your head" make it easy to forget the "bland" interior and "lousy" location.

Pam Real Thai Food ⇌ *Thai* | 22 | 9 | 17 | $23 |

W 40s | 402 W. 47th St. (bet. 9th & 10th Aves.) | 212-315-4441 Ⓜ
W 40s | 404 W. 49th St. (bet. 9th & 10th Aves.) | 212-333-7500
www.pamrealthai.com

"Savory" Siamese cooking that's "big on spice" – that means "hot" – yet "light on the wallet" summarizes the appeal of these "super-authentic" Hell's Kitchen Thais; given that most "leave satisfied every time", the "no-frills" atmosphere and no-credit-cards policy are evidently no big deal.

Paola's *Italian*

23 | 19 | 22 | $57

E 80s | 1295 Madison Ave. (92nd St.) | 212-794-1890 | www.paolasrestaurant.com

There may be "more crowds and noise" at its new Carnegie Hill setting, but the "same excellent food" and "always-smiling" namesake host remain at this "longtime", recently transplanted Italian "favorite"; also unchanged – yet more aptly described following the move – are the "Madison Avenue prices."

Papaya King *Hot Dogs*

20 | 4 | 12 | $8

E 80s | 179 E. 86th St. (3rd Ave.) | 212-369-0648 ●⇪
Harlem | 121 W. 125th St. (bet. Lenox & 7th Aves.) | 212-678-4268 🅂⇪
W Village | 200 W. 14th St. (7th Ave. S.) | 212-367-8090
www.papayaking.com

"As vital to NYC as the subway", these "guilty pleasure" hot dog dens are renowned for "crispy-skinned" franks and "wacky tropical" drinks that supply "super-value" sustenance "on the fly"; since there are "no seats" and the "service is nothing to brag about", "eat and go" is the preferred approach.

Pappardella ● *Italian*

19 | 16 | 19 | $41

W 70s | 316 Columbus Ave. (75th St.) | 212-595-7996

"Decently priced" Italian dishes "prepared well" and served with an "amiable" touch "packs them in" at this "casual" UWS "neighborhood spot"; for more legroom and better "people-watching" opportunities, regulars "sit outside when it's nice."

Paradou ● *French*

21 | 18 | 19 | $46

Meatpacking | 8 Little W. 12th St. (bet. Greenwich & Washington Sts.) | 212-463-8345 | www.paradounyc.com

A "cheery tonic to tough times", this "hype"-free Meatpacking District bistro serves "excellent" French fare with a "touch of flair" at a "good price"; it's best known for its "lovely" back garden and "can't-be-beat" brunch that includes unlimited champagne cocktails.

Paris Commune *French*

19 | 19 | 19 | $45

W Village | 99 Bank St. (Greenwich St.) | 212-929-0509 | www.pariscommune.net

"Eating well at a good price" may not be revolutionary, but it's pleasing for partisans of this "not trendy" French bistro parked in the "ever more trendy West Village"; an "almost Parisian setting" is buttressed by a "great brunch" and "cool wine bar downstairs."

Park, The ● *Mediterranean*

16 | 22 | 15 | $42

Chelsea | 118 10th Ave. (bet. 17th & 18th Sts.) | 212-352-3313 | www.theparknyc.com

"Spacious" is an understatement at this multilevel, multifloor, garden-equipped Chelsea juggernaut with a "vibrant" "club atmosphere" that's "good for groups" and drop-ins from the nearby High Line; still, many shrug it's "all scene", citing "nonmemorable" Med eats and "rude" service; N.B. check out the hot tub on the roof.

	FOOD	DECOR	SERVICE	COST

Park Avenue . . . *American*

24 | 26 | 23 | $73

E 60s | 100 E. 63rd St. (bet. Lexington & Park Aves.) | 212-644-1900 |
www.parkavenyc.com

Truly a "restaurant for all seasons", this UES "winner" "switches its
name, menu and decor" quarterly "according to Mother Nature", but is
a "great choice anytime" thanks to "totally pleasing" New Americana,
"casually luxurious" looks and "top-rate" service; year-round, it draws
a "refined" crowd willing to spring for the "pricey" experience.

Park Avenue Bistro ⑤ *French*

22 | 18 | 20 | $57

Murray Hill | 377 Park Ave. S. (bet. 26th & 27th Sts.) | 212-689-1360 |
www.parkavenuebistronyc.com

A "stark white" room with rotating selections of "modern art" is the setting for this Murray Hill bistro where both the traditional French fare and
pricing have been "kicked up a notch"; whether the new decor is an improvement over its earlier, "more traditional" incarnation is debatable.

Park Side ❶ *Italian*

24 | 19 | 21 | $46

Corona | 107-01 Corona Ave. (51st Ave.) | Queens | 718-271-9321 |
www.parksiderestaurant.com

"Frequent fliers" get the "Tony Soprano treatment" at this Corona
"red-sauce" institution where the "to-die-for" Italian food comes at
"prices you can live with"; it's usually "mobbed" on weekends, but still
earns a thumbs-up for "old-school" accoutrements like "tuxedoed"
service, "white tablecloths" and "valet parking."

Parlor Steakhouse *Steak*

21 | 20 | 21 | $59

E 90s | 1600 Third Ave. (90th St.) | 212-423-5888 |
www.parlorsteakhouse.com

The UES finally has an "upscale" steakhouse that proffers "classic"
chops and a "generous seafood selection" in "casual", bi-level digs
overseen by "welcoming" hosts; critics see "nothing spectacular"
aside from the "Midtown prices", but locals laud it for a "civilized
meal" and a "good stiff drink."

Parma ❶ *Italian*

22 | 15 | 21 | $60

E 70s | 1404 Third Ave. (bet. 79th & 80th Sts.) | 212-535-3520

"Sinatra-era standards" are plated at this UES Northern Italian "war-
horse" on the scene since 1977 and a "favorite" among well-heeled
neighbors like "Robert Rubin"; though it's certainly "dependable", the
"unappealing decor" makes it the kind of place to "bring your family,
not your girlfriend."

Pars Grill House & Bar *Persian*

∇ 20 | 13 | 16 | $34

Chelsea | 249 W. 26th St. (bet. 7th & 8th Aves.) | 212-929-9860 |
www.parsgrillhouse.com

All signs suggest that this Chelsea Persian with lots of "savory
dishes", weekend belly dancing and "Farsi being spoken" is a bona
fide "real deal"; "reasonable" tabs offset iffy service and "not
particularly comfortable" digs.

Pascalou *French*

21 | 14 | 19 | $42

E 90s | 1308 Madison Ave. (bet. 92nd & 93rd Sts.) | 212-534-7522

"Sardines aren't as close in the tin as you'll be" at this Carnegie Hill
micro-bistro where a "New York City–size kitchen" puts out an "ex-

	FOOD	DECOR	SERVICE	COST

tensive" selection of Gallic "standards"; a "bargain" early-bird and free "eavesdropping" at the "elbow-to-elbow" tables make it a "neighborhood favorite."

Pasha Turkish
| 20 | 18 | 20 | $42 |

W 70s | 70 W. 71st St. (bet. Columbus Ave. & CPW) | 212-579-8751 | www.pashanewyork.com

At this UWS stand-in for "exotic Istanbul", "tasty" Turkish cuisine is served by a "courteous" crew in a "low-lit", "rich-red" setting made for "intimate" repasts; just a "short hop" from Lincoln Center, it's also a hit with pre-theatergoers who tout the "bargain" prix fixe.

Pasquale's Rigoletto Italian
| 21 | 16 | 19 | $43 |

Bronx | 2311 Arthur Ave. (Crescent Ave.) | 718-365-6644

"Satisfying" red-sauce favorites, "friendly" service and "free parking" hit the "Bronx trifecta" at this "quintessential" Arthur Avenue "taste of Italy"; it's a "standout in a neighborhood of great Italian restaurants", even if the "decor looks like it hasn't been redone since it opened."

Pastis ● French
| 21 | 21 | 17 | $49 |

Meatpacking | 9 Ninth Ave. (Little W. 12th St.) | 212-929-4844 | www.pastisny.com

It's all "bustle", "all the time" at Keith McNally's "people-watching pleasure dome", a "fashionable" fragment of "Paris by way of the Meatpacking District" where the French bistro cooking is almost as "fabulous" as the "poseur" crowd; "long lines", "a lot of noise" and "passive-aggressive" service come with the territory, but regulars say it's best at the "unheralded" breakfast hour.

Pastrami Queen Deli
| 20 | 5 | 13 | $25 |

E 70s | 1125 Lexington Ave. (bet. 78th & 79th Sts.) | 212-734-1500 | www.pastramiqueen.com

"Forget about cholesterol" and literally "eat your heart out" at this "tip-top" UES kosher deli known for sandwiches "stacked high" with "spicy, tender" pastrami along with other examples of "Jewish soul food"; what with the "tired" decor and "tiny seating area", you probably "won't want to eat in."

Patricia's Italian
| ▽ 24 | 14 | 20 | $31 |

Bronx | 1080-1082 Morris Park Ave. (bet. Haight & Lurting Aves.) | 718-409-9069 | www.patriciasmorrispark.com
Bronx | 3883 E. Tremont Ave. (Cross Bronx Expwy.) | 718-918-1800 | www.patriciasoftremont.com

If "a lot of a good thing" for a modest price appeals, "bring an appetite" to these "always packed", separately owned Bronx Italians celebrated for their "great pizzas and pastas"; the "unpretentious" ambiance extends down to the house music, i.e. "clanking dishes."

Patroon 🅩 American
| 21 | 20 | 20 | $67 |

E 40s | 160 E. 46th St. (bet. Lexington & 3rd Aves.) | 212-883-7373 | www.patroonrestaurant.com

Ken Aretsky's "posh" Midtowner is a "masters-of-the-universe" magnet, where "bankers" with "unlimited expense accounts" tuck into "refined" New Americana in a "very male" room decorated with Old New York photographs; the "wonderful roof deck" is the place to be on warm summer nights.

	FOOD	DECOR	SERVICE	COST

Patsy's *Italian*

21 | **17** | **20** | **$53**

W 50s | 236 W. 56th St. (bet. B'way & 8th Ave.) | 212-247-3491 | www.patsys.com

"First-rate" red gravy and "starched white tablecloths" set the "retro-land" mood at this circa-1944 Southern Italian near Carnegie Hall best known as a haunt of "Ol' Blue Eyes" (some think they're "still holding a table" for him); granted, "it'll cost ya" and may even be a bit "ordinary", but ultimately "you can't argue with tradition."

Patsy's Pizzeria *Pizza*

20 | **11** | **15** | **$26**

Chelsea | 318 W. 23rd St. (bet. 8th & 9th Aves.) | 646-486-7400
E 60s | 1312 Second Ave. (69th St.) | 212-639-1000
E 60s | 206 E. 60th St. (bet. 2nd & 3rd Aves.) | 212-688-9707
G Village | 67 University Pl. (bet. 10th & 11th Sts.) | 212-533-3500
Harlem | 2287-91 First Ave. (bet. 117th & 118th Sts.) | 212-534-9783
Murray Hill | 509 Third Ave. (bet. 34th & 35th Sts.) | 212-689-7500
W 70s | 61 W. 74th St. (bet. Columbus Ave. & CPW) | 212-579-3000
www.patsyspizzeriany.com

"Crispy" thin-crusts, "savory" sauces and "real mozzarella" unite in brick-ovened harmony at these "noisy", "no-frills" pizzerias; the separately owned Harlem original "merits a detour" for purists seeking the "real deal", but the other locales work well for anyone "on the go, low on dough or with kids in tow."

Peaches Ⓜ *Southern*

- | **-** | **-** | **I**

Bed-Stuy | 393 Lewis Ave. (bet. Decatur & MacDonough Sts.) | Brooklyn | 718-942-4162 | www.peachesbrooklyn.com

Feeding Bed-Stuy's growing "hunger for additions to its restaurant scene", this "casual" Southerner earns a "thumbs-up" for "decently priced" comfort food with an organic pedigree, served with "Southern charm"; the "no-fuss" setting includes a breezy garden patio.

Peanut Butter & Co. *Sandwiches*

21 | **13** | **17** | **$14**

G Village | 240 Sullivan St. (bet. Bleecker & W. 3rd Sts.) | 212-677-3995 | www.ilovepeanutbutter.com

The "name speaks for itself" at this "sticky" Village "niche restaurant" where "yummy" peanut butter appears in "every imaginable" sandwich iteration to the delight of "kids" and "brown-bag" cuisine connoisseurs; still, those opposed to "gimmicks" observe "you could make it at home for a fraction of the price."

Ⓩ Pearl Oyster Bar Ⓢ *Seafood*

26 | **15** | **19** | **$46**

G Village | 18 Cornelia St. (bet. Bleecker & W. 4th Sts.) | 212-691-8211 | www.pearloysterbar.com

"You can almost smell the ocean" at Rebecca Charles' Village porthole-in-the-wall where "mouthwatering" lobster rolls and other "simply prepared", "none-fresher" fish dishes feel like an "ode to New England"; yarr, the "reel deal" "isn't cheap", but it's yours "if you can bear the wait" to get in.

Pearl Room *Seafood*

20 | **19** | **20** | **$52**

Bay Ridge | 8201 Third Ave. (82nd St.) | Brooklyn | 718-833-6666 | www.thepearlroom.com

A "special night out" takes an "old-school" turn at this "Bay Ridge scene" cherished for its "appealingly presented" seafood, "caring

| | FOOD | DECOR | SERVICE | COST |

staff" and "comfortable" setting that includes an "always-busy bar"; however, some report kitchen "inconsistencies" that sharpen the "pricey" tabs' pinch.

Peasant ☒ *Italian* | 24 | 22 | 20 | $58 |

NoLita | 194 Elizabeth St. (bet. Prince & Spring Sts.) | 212-965-9511 | www.peasantnyc.com

"Homey" Italian fare pulled from a "blazing brick oven" makes for "magnificent" meals at this "rustic" NoLita eatery, done up in a "spartan" but somehow "romantic" style with an open kitchen and basement wine bar; it's no longer a "trial to order" now that *il menu* carries an English translation, though the same "lordly" prices still apply.

Peep ◑ *Thai* | 18 | 19 | 19 | $30 |

SoHo | 177 Prince St. (bet. Sullivan & Thompson Sts.) | 212-254-7337 | www.peepsoho.net

At this "boisterous" SoHo Thai, "affordable" "food with flair" plays second fiddle to the "surreal", "bright pink" setting (kind of a "futuristic" "hair salon") and "do-not-miss" restrooms; "great lunch specials" have many eyeing a daytime visit.

Peking Duck House *Chinese* | 23 | 15 | 17 | $41 |

Chinatown | 28 Mott St. (bet. Mosco & Pell Sts.) | 212-227-1810
E 50s | 236 E. 53rd St. (bet. 2nd & 3rd Aves.) | 212-759-8260
www.pekingduckhousenyc.com

"Duck is what they do best" at this Chinese duo where the "fabulous" featured fowl is "expertly carved" tableside; mallard mavens maintain the rest of the menu is "just ordinary" (ditto the settings and service), though the BYO C-town outpost is a better value.

Pellegrino's *Italian* | 23 | 19 | 22 | $45 |

Little Italy | 138 Mulberry St. (bet. Grand & Hester Sts.) | 212-226-3177

"Dependably good" Italian cooking and "pro" service set this Little Italy "standby" a "cut above" the neighborhood norm, convincing even "nontourists" to become "regulars"; come summer, sightseers of all stripes "sit outside for the main attraction": Mulberry Street people-watching.

Penelope *American* | 22 | 19 | 19 | $25 |

Murray Hill | 159 Lexington Ave. (30th St.) | 212-481-3800 | www.penelopenyc.com

"Elevated comfort food" in a "country kitsch" setting simulates a "trip to New England minus the long drive" at this Murray Hill American decorated like an "Anthropologie store"; true, the brunch lines are as "long" as ever, but there is some good news: "they now accept credit cards."

Pepe Giallo To Go *Italian* | 22 | 13 | 17 | $22 |

Chelsea | 253 10th Ave. (bet. 24th & 25th Sts.) | 212-242-6055
Pepe Rosso Caffe *Italian*
E 40s | Grand Central | lower level (42nd St. & Vanderbilt Ave.) | 212-867-6054
E Village | 127 Ave. C (8th St.) | 212-529-7747
Pepe Rosso Osteria *Italian*
W 50s | 346 W. 52nd St. (bet. 8th & 9th Aves.) | 212-245-4585
Pepe Rosso To Go *Italian*
SoHo | 149 Sullivan St. (bet. Houston & Prince Sts.) | 212-677-4555

(continued)

(continued)

Pepe Verde To Go *Italian*

W Village | 559 Hudson St. (bet. Perry & W. 11th Sts.) | 212-255-2221
www.peperossotogo.com

"Quick", "quality pasta for a pittance" is the trademark of this "reliable"
Italian mini-"empire" prized for its "large selection" of fill-your-belly
favorites; just "don't go for the atmosphere" – depending on the location,
the "no-pretenses" dining area can be "about the size of a twin bed."

Z Pepolino *Italian* | 26 | 18 | 22 | $54 |

TriBeCa | 281 W. Broadway (bet. Canal & Lispenard Sts.) | 212-966-9983 |
www.pepolino.com

"Outstanding" TriBeCa trattoria presenting a "real taste" of Tuscany in
a "relaxed", bi-level setting tended by an "informed" crew; fans "don't
understand why it isn't more popular" – maybe the "off-the-beaten-
track" address and "sobering" tabs have something to do with it.

Pera *Mediterranean* | 21 | 21 | 21 | $51 |

E 40s | 303 Madison Ave. (bet. 41st & 42nd Sts.) | 212-878-6301 |
www.peranyc.com

"Something different in the Grand Central neighborhood", this "elegant"
Med attracts the "biz-lunch" bunch via "delightful" dishes "carefully
crafted" with a Turkish accent; the room oozes "sophistication", ditto the
service, but no surprise, the experience comes with a "high price tag."

Perbacco *Italian* | 23 | 16 | 20 | $49 |

E Village | 234 E. Fourth St. (bet. Aves. A & B) | 212-253-2038

"Inspired" Italian cooking earns accolades at this "avant-garde" East
Villager whose offerings now incorporate "molecular gastronomy"
thanks to an "innovative" new chef; staffers are "helpful" and the pricing
"reasonable", leaving the "small, tight" setting as the only drawback.

Peri Ela *Turkish* | 20 | 16 | 19 | $43 |

E 90s | 1361 Lexington Ave. (bet. 90th & 91st Sts.) | 212-410-4300 |
www.periela.com

Folks "headed to the 92nd Street Y" tout this "welcoming" Carnegie
Hill Turk as a "convenient" pre- or post-event stop for "fresh, traditional cooking" at "good prices"; the space may be "smallish", but in a
neighborhood "barren" of diversity, it's "far better than it has to be."

Perilla *American* | 25 | 21 | 23 | $55 |

G Village | 9 Jones St. (bet. Bleecker & W. 4th Sts.) | 212-929-6868 |
www.perillanyc.com

"Neighborly" environs and "dignified" staffers direct the focus to
"where it should be" at this "standout" Villager: on *Top Chef* champ
Harold Dieterle's "imaginative", "ever-revolving" New American
menu; in short, it's an "absolutely enjoyable" exercise in "simple elegance", so long as your credit is good.

Periyali *Greek* | 24 | 20 | 22 | $58 |

Flatiron | 35 W. 20th St. (bet. 5th & 6th Aves.) | 212-463-7890 |
www.periyali.com

"One of the first" of its kind and still "one of the best", this Flatiron
"doyen" of "upscale" Greek dining gratifies fans with its "outstanding"
food, "accommodating" service and "civilized", "sailcloth-ceilinged"

room; though this "elegant" splash in the "Aegean" is a definite "splurge", no one is complaining.

	FOOD	DECOR	SERVICE	COST

NEW Perle French

▽ 18 | 19 | 18 | $40

Financial District | 62 Pearl St. (bet. Broad St. & Coenties Slip) | 212-248-4848 | www.perle-nyc.com

The "Wall Street hordes" have discovered this new Financial District French brasserie, an atmospheric "neighborhood find" situated above a basement wine bar; regulars say the food's "tasty" albeit "inconsistent" ("stay with the basics"), but there's no argument about those "good prices."

Per Lei ● Italian

20 | 17 | 18 | $52

E 70s | 1347 Second Ave. (71st St.) | 212-439-9200 | www.perleinyc.com

One part Italian restaurant, one part "Eurotrash" lounge, this "sceney" Upper Eastsider (and Baraonda sibling) is usually "packed" with "young" things nibbling on "fab food" ferried by "handsome staffers"; there's "refreshing" alfresco seating come summer, but year-round prepare for an "expensive" out-*lei*.

NEW Permanent Brunch ● American

- | - | - | I

E Village | 95 First Ave. (bet. 5th & 6th Sts.) | 212-533-3315 | www.permanentbrunch.com

Brunch at dinnertime is the odd concept at this gimmicky new East Villager offering the usual midday Americana with a Southern twist; the price is right, the compact digs smartly designed with custom-made subway tiles and the freewheeling mood even allows patrons to play DJ via their iPods.

Perry Street ● French

25 | 24 | 23 | $67

W Village | 176 Perry St. (West St.) | 212-352-1900 | www.jean-georges.com

"Highly civilized" sums up the scene at Jean-Georges Vongerichten's West Village "gem" where "sublime" Asian-tinged French cuisine, "well-controlled sound levels" and a "minimalist" setting recalling an "airport lounge in Geneva" make for "positively serene" dining; yes, it's "expensive", so bargain-hunters go for the $24 prix fixe lunch and "save a bunch."

☑ Per Se American/French

28 | 28 | 28 | $303

W 60s | Time Warner Ctr. | 10 Columbus Circle, 4th fl. (60th St. at B'way) | 212-823-9335 | www.perseny.com

Apart from the $275 prix fixe dinner cost, this Time Warner Center aerie overlooking Columbus Circle is deemed "perfect in every way", with the ambiance, French–New American food and (No. 1-rated) service all "sublime"; even if you need a "Centurion card" and at least three hours to enjoy the meal, fans believe that Thomas Keller's "edible art" is simply "the best in America" – unless his French Laundry does it better; N.B. à la carte small plates are now available in the salon area.

Persephone Greek

22 | 18 | 21 | $60

E 60s | 115 E. 60th St. (bet. Lexington & Park Aves.) | 212-339-8363 | www.persephoneny.com

"Beautifully prepared fish" is a given at this Bloomie's-area "cousin" of Periyali, a similarly "upscale" practitioner of "refined" Hellenic cuisine served by "responsive" staffers; "high prices" have also made the transfer uptown, perhaps why it's "never busy."

Persepolis *Persian*

| 21 | 16 | 19 | $40 |

E 70s | 1407 Second Ave. (bet. 73rd & 74th Sts.) | 212-535-1100 | www.persepolisnyc.com

Folks tout this UES Persian for its "different but delicious" dishes, especially its "excellent" signature dish, sour cherry rice; the "aroma-filled" room may be "simple" verging on "spare", but "unobtrusive service" and "moderate" pricing open a window onto a neglected cuisine.

Pershing Square *American*

| 16 | 16 | 16 | $37 |

E 40s | 90 E. 42nd St. (Park Ave.) | 212-286-9600 | www.pershingsquare.com

"Location" is everything at this "cavernous" American brasserie nestled beneath the "Park Avenue overpass" opposite Grand Central; while the food and service "don't dazzle", it's still a magnet for business "meeting-and-eating" types as well as "commuters" grabbing "cocktails on the way to the train."

Petaluma *Italian*

| 19 | 17 | 19 | $46 |

E 70s | 1356 First Ave. (73rd St.) | 212-772-8800

A "real survivor", this circa-1986 UES Italian keeps on keeping on with a "consistent", fairly fared, "something-for-everyone" menu, "friendly" service and "comfortable" digs; though "nothing fancy", it attracts everyone from "neighborhood moms" to Sotheby's "beautiful people."

☑ Peter Luger Steak House ⊅ *Steak*

| 27 | 15 | 19 | $76 |

Williamsburg | 178 Broadway (Driggs Ave.) | Brooklyn | 718-387-7400 | www.peterluger.com

Now in its 26th consecutive year as our surveyors' "favorite" steakhouse, this Williamsburg porterhouse specialist "lives up to the hype" as a "quintessential NY experience", with lots of imitators but "none that compare" to the "real thing"; despite prime prices, theatrically "grumpy service" and an "inconvenient" no-credit-card policy, it's worth the trek for what fans call the "best steak in the world - period."

Pete's Downtown Ⓜ *Italian*

| ▽ 19 | 17 | 20 | $43 |

Dumbo | 2 Water St. (Old Fulton St.) | Brooklyn | 718-858-3510 | www.petesdowntown.com

"Splendid views of lower Manhattan" are the calling card of this otherwise "nothing-out-of-the-ordinary" Dumbo Italian where the "red-sauce" cuisine is "old-fashioned" but "affordable"; still, if you "can't spring for River Café", it's a "decent" fallback.

Pete's Tavern ❶ *Pub Food*

| ▽ 16 | 16 | 16 | $33 |

Gramercy | 129 E. 18th St. (Irving Pl.) | 212-473-7676 | www.petestavern.com

"Old-time ambiance" oozes from the bar and booths of this "19th-century landmark" Gramercy pub renowned as an "O. Henry" haunt; "killer burgers" excepted, the "true NY flavor" doesn't translate to the grub, thus most "go for the history, not the food."

Petite Abeille *Belgian*

| 17 | 14 | 15 | $30 |

Flatiron | 44 W. 17th St. (bet. 5th & 6th Aves.) | 212-727-2989
Gramercy | 401 E. 20th St. (1st Ave.) | 212-727-1505
TriBeCa | 134 W. Broadway (Duane St.) | 212-791-1360

(continued)

Petite Abeille

W Village | 466 Hudson St. (Barrow St.) | 212-741-6479 ☏
www.petiteabeille.com

"Terrific" moule frites and "lots of different beers" are the "Belgium 101" course highlights of this "frugal" Flemish mini-chain; "sweet" Tintin-themed decor trumps the "cramped" dimensions and "rushed, move-that-table" service.

Petite Crevette ☏ *Seafood* ▽ 25 | 19 | 21 | $36

Carroll Gardens | 144 Union St. (enter on Hicks St., bet. President & Union Sts.) | Brooklyn | 718-855-2632

"Unpretentious" is putting it mildly at this "tiny" Carroll Gardens sea-fooder where the "menu is handwritten on the wall" and the "bargain" tabs are abetted by "BYO" and "cash-only" policies; bottom line, it "delivers the goods", although trade-offs include "funky" atmospher-ics and "cheek-by-jowl" seating.

Petit Oven Ⓜ *American/French* - | - | - | M

Bay Ridge | 276 Bay Ridge Ave. (bet. Ridge Blvd. & 3rd Ave.) | Brooklyn | 718-833-3443 | www.petit-oven.com

Two Bay Ridge gals, chef "Kat" Ploszaj and manager Nicole Brown, have turned a tiny neighborhood hole-in-the-wall into a satisfying French-American bistro, and its midpriced, mostly organic offerings have been drawing quite a local following; though the à la carte menu can seem a bit pricey, the $35 three-course prix fixe is a bargain.

Petrossian *Continental/French* 24 | 24 | 24 | $77

W 50s | 182 W. 58th St. (7th Ave.) | 212-245-2214 | www.petrossian.com

"Russian nobles" would feel at home at this French-Continental "gold standard" near Carnegie Hall, an art deco "enchanter" specializing in the "ultimate in conspicuous consumption" – "fine" caviar and champagne – ministered by "seamless" servers; "great value" prix fixes (and a nearby cafe) allow the same "high-life" experience at a lower cost.

Philippe ⬤ *Chinese* 24 | 20 | 20 | $69

E 60s | 33 E. 60th St. (bet. Madison & Park Aves.) | 212-644-8885 | www.philippechow.com

Philippe Chow Express ⬤ *Chinese*

NEW **G Village** | 469 Sixth Ave. (bet. 11th & 12th Sts.) | 212-929-8949 | www.philippechowexpress.com

Like its rival, Mr. Chow, this "dark" and "sexy" East Side Chinese is a "trendoid" and "celeb" magnet offering first-rate fare along with the delicious "feeling that you're in on something"; still, many wonder if the "food is flown from the mainland" given the "ridiculously expen-sive" tabs; N.B. the tiny Village satellite opened post-Survey.

Philoxenia Ⓜ *Greek* ▽ 24 | 20 | 22 | $37

Astoria | 32-07 34th Ave. (bet. 32nd & 33rd Sts.) | Queens | 718-626-2000 | www.philoxeniarestaurant.com

"Hearty" Hellenic cooking that soars "above and beyond" typical taverna treatments is the forte of this "special", modestly priced Queens Greek; figure in "pleasant" service and a brick-lined, "rustic village" setting and it's easy to understand why it's considered one of "Astoria's best."

	FOOD	DECOR	SERVICE	COST

Pho Bang ⍻ *Vietnamese* — 20 | 5 | 11 | $15

Little Italy | 157 Mott St. (bet. Broome & Grand Sts.) | 212-966-3797
Elmhurst | 82-90 Broadway (Elmhurst Ave.) | Queens | 718-205-1500
Flushing | 41-07 Kissena Blvd. (Main St.) | Queens | 718-939-5520

Pho phans bang the drum for the "hit-the-spot" signature soups at this Vietnamese trio; they're utterly "utilitarian" affairs, with "cheap" tabs and "lightning-fast" ladling offsetting the "divey" decor and "emotionless" service.

Phoenix Garden ⍻ *Chinese* — 23 | 8 | 13 | $31

E 40s | 242 E. 40th St. (bet. 2nd & 3rd Aves.) | 212-983-6666 | www.thephoenixgarden.com

Despite "pushy" service and a "remarkable lack of concern for decor", this East Midtown Chinese still thrills with "first-class Cantonese" cooking (many say its "signature" salt and pepper shrimp may be "the best anywhere"); it's cash-only, but "super-cheap" with a BYO policy.

Pho Pasteur *Vietnamese* — ∇ 21 | 7 | 14 | $20

Chinatown | 85 Baxter St. (bet. Bayard & Canal Sts.) | 212-608-3656

There's "no business like pho business" at this "cheap" C-town Vietnamese that summons "jury-duty" lunchers for "filling" noodle soups and other Saigon "standards" on the quick; since there's "no decor" and not much service, most adopt an "eat-and-run" approach.

Pho Viet Huong *Vietnamese* — ∇ 22 | 10 | 14 | $22

Chinatown | 73 Mulberry St. (bet. Bayard & Canal Sts.) | 212-233-8988 | www.phoviethuongnyc.com

A natural "when on jury duty", this "consistently good" Chinatown Vietnamese near the courts does justice to a "large variety" of dishes, with a pho-cus on noodle soups; for most, the "bargain" rates render the "unfancy" setting and "so-so" service not worth litigating.

Piadina ●⍻ *Italian* — ∇ 22 | 17 | 19 | $41

G Village | 57 W. 10th St., downstairs (bet. 5th & 6th Aves.) | 212-460-8017 | www.piadinanyc.com

Channeling a "small town restaurant in Italy", this "homey" Village "grotto" serves a "simple", "hearty" menu in a "darkly lit" setting with "romantic" appeal to spare; it draws a "young" following thanks to "budget" tabs, though the "no-credit-card" policy is a source of "frustration."

Piano Due ⌧ *Italian* — 24 | 24 | 23 | $72

W 50s | Equitable Center Arcade | 151 W. 51st St., 2nd fl. (bet. 6th & 7th Aves.) | 212-399-9400 | www.pianoduenyc.net

"Quiet and sophisticated", this "posh" second-floor "oasis" hidden off a Midtown breezeway may be "hard to find" but is worth seeking out for "master" chef Michael Cetrulo's "decadent" Italian cooking; the "very formal space" comes at a "very formal cost", so many reserve it for a "special-occasion splurge"; P.S. have a drink first at Palio Bar, the downstairs watering hole decorated with a "magnificent" Sandro Chia mural.

Piccola Venezia *Italian* — 25 | 16 | 23 | $57

Astoria | 42-01 28th Ave. (42nd St.) | Queens | 718-721-8470 | www.piccola-venezia.com

"It's an offer you can't refuse": they'll "make whatever you want" just "like you're family" at this perennial Astoria Italian where the red gravy "can make a grown man cry"; despite "tacky red" decor and "expensive-for-Queens" tariffs, it remains an "old-time favorite."

Piccolo Angolo Ⓜ Italian
25 | 13 | 22 | $43

W Village | 621 Hudson St. (Jane St.) | 212-229-9177 | www.piccoloangolo.com

"Shirt-sleeves Italian" cooking "done right" served in portions sized "large and larger" helps explain the popularity of this "hard-to-get-into" West Villager; "endearing" owner Renato Migliorini's "Gatling-gun-speed recitation of the specials" adds to the "charm", though some find the "manic" room too "claustrophobic" and "noisy."

ⓩ Picholine ⓈⓂ French/Mediterranean
27 | 25 | 26 | $120

W 60s | 35 W. 64th St. (bet. B'way & CPW) | 212-724-8585 | www.picholinenyc.com

With chef Terry Brennan playing "at the top of his game", this Lincoln Center-area French-Med has become "one of the best restaurants in town", offering "refined", "always delicious" food and "impeccable" service; admittedly, it "can get pricey" but it has risen to "perennial favorite" status thanks to its "excellent" wines, "sensational" cheeses and "warm" ambiance.

Picket Fence American
▽ 19 | 16 | 19 | $29

Ditmas Park | 1310 Cortelyou Rd. (bet. Argyle & Rugby Rds.) | Brooklyn | 718-282-6661 | www.picketfencebrooklyn.com

The food is as "comfortable" as the setting at this "friendly" Ditmas Parker where free "starter bowls of popcorn" are followed by "copious" plates of "affordable" Americana; it's popular with "neighborhood" types since "lollygagging is well tolerated", and there's a "lovely patio" to boot.

PicNic Market & Café Deli/French
▽ 20 | 15 | 19 | $38

W 100s | 2665 Broadway (bet. 101st & 102nd Sts.) | 212-222-8222 | www.picnicmarket.com

"Inspiring" Gallic "comfort food" with a market-"fresh" spin finds favor with UWS locals at this "low-key" French bistro that also vends a limited selection of artisanal cheeses and charcuterie; expect a "spare", "unassuming" setting, but at least there are "no ants."

Pietrasanta Italian
19 | 14 | 18 | $38

W 40s | 683 Ninth Ave. (47th St.) | 212-265-9471 | www.pietrasantarestaurant.com

"Pre-theater" types get "in and out quick" at this "reliable" Hell's Kitchen "stalwart", though regulars find it more "memorable after the Broadway crowd has left"; you "can't beat the price" given the "always satisfying" homemade pastas, though some find the cooking's merely "competent" here.

Pietro's Ⓢ Italian/Steak
24 | 16 | 23 | $66

E 40s | 232 E. 43rd St. (bet. 2nd & 3rd Aves.) | 212-682-9760 | www.pietros.com

Both the staffers and the patrons of this "vintage"-1932 Italian steakhouse near Grand Central seem to have "been there since day one", tucking into "excellent" chops and pastas; sure, the pricing's "not cheap" and the "Levittown decor" "not exactly inspiring", but the fact that it "never changes" is exactly why fans like it.

	FOOD	DECOR	SERVICE	COST

Pigalle ❷ *French* **18 | 18 | 19 | $38**

W 40s | Hilton Garden Inn Hotel | 790 Eighth Ave. (48th St.) | 212-489-2233 | www.pigallenyc.com

"Unpretentious and affordable", this Hell's Kitchen French brasserie is a "handy" fallback for both show-goers and "tourist bus" passengers; though some dismiss it as a "glorified diner", proponents praise its "well-prepared" grub and credible "streets-of-Paris" ambiance.

Pig Heaven ❷ *Chinese* **19 | 13 | 18 | $34**

E 80s | 1540 Second Ave. (bet. 80th & 81st Sts.) | 212-744-4333 | www.pigheaven.biz

Swine dining fans go "hog wild" over the "tasty" Chinese dishes on offer at this UES "old faithful" overseen by "hostess with the mostest" Nancy Lee; some say it's "inconsistent" and the porcine decor is getting "long in the tooth", but it is "inexpensive" and particularly "kid-friendly."

Pinche Taqueria *Mexican* **▽ 22 | 13 | 17 | $16**

NEW **NoHo** | 333 Lafayette St. (Bleecker St.) | 212-343-9977
NoLita | 227 Mott St. (bet. Prince & Spring Sts.) | 212-625-0090
www.pinchetaqueria.us

Imported from Tijuana, these Downtown taqueria twins bring "authentic" West Coast Mexicana to NY via "unbelievable fish tacos" and other "satisfying", "well-seasoned" eats; "hole-in-the-wall" settings are tempered by "quick" service and "extremely affordable" tabs.

Ping's Seafood *Chinese/Seafood* **21 | 11 | 14 | $28**

Chinatown | 22 Mott St. (bet. Bayard & Pell Sts.) | 212-602-9988 ❷
Elmhurst | 83-02 Queens Blvd. (Goldsmith St.) | Queens | 718-396-1238

"Fine Hong Kong–style" seafood and "inspired" dim sum are dispensed at "bargain" rates by this "hectic" twosome where the crowd is "packed in like sardines" and the staff "avoids English at all costs"; novices are advised to "share a table and see what others are eating."

Pink Tea Cup ❷☕ *Soul Food/Southern* **22 | 12 | 17 | $24**

W Village | 42 Grove St. (bet. Bedford & Bleecker Sts.) | 212-807-6755 | www.thepinkteacup.com

Providing equal parts of "grease and eccentricity", this "campy" West Villager dishes out "down-home" soul food of the "artery-hardening", "guilty-pleasure" variety; the prices are "great", the digs "tiny" and the service "mamalike" – as in "you'd better eat your greens, honey."

Pinocchio Ⓜ *Italian* **▽ 22 | 16 | 23 | $48**

E 90s | 1748 First Ave. (bet. 90th & 91st Sts.) | 212-828-5810

"Tiny" though it may be, this UES Italian has "devoted local followers" who squeeze in for "old-school" meals "like grandma made" (or wished she could); midlevel tabs and "terrific" service from a "mom-and-pop" team make for one "great neighborhood" resource.

Pintaile's Pizza *Pizza* **19 | 6 | 13 | $17**

E 80s | 1573 York Ave. (bet. 83rd & 84th Sts.) | 212-396-3479
E 90s | 26 E. 91st St. (bet. 5th & Madison Aves.) | 212-722-1967

"Healthy", "politically correct" pizzas with whole wheat thin crusts and "innovative" veggie toppings lure "fancy" folks to this UES duo; though the pies are "unusual", the tiny, "nondescript" digs are typical for the genre, so many reserve them "for takeout only."

	FOOD	DECOR	SERVICE	COST

Piola *Pizza* ▽ 19 | 16 | 19 | $25

G Village | 48 E. 12th St. (bet. B'way & University Pl.) | 212-777-7781 | www.piola.it

An "endless list" of "flashy" toppings with some "Brazilian twists" adorn the "crisp, light" pizzas popping out of the brick oven at this "buzzing" Village pie palace; "attractive staffers", "robust" drinks and "frequently changing artwork" distinguish it from the competition.

Pio Pio *Peruvian* 22 | 13 | 16 | $24

E 90s | 1746 First Ave. (bet. 90th & 91st Sts.) | 212-426-5800
Murray Hill | 210 E. 34th St. (bet. 2nd & 3rd Aves.) | 212-481-0034
W 90s | 702 Amsterdam Ave. (94th St.) | 212-665-3000
Bronx | 264 Cypress Ave. (bet. 138th & 139th Sts.) | 718-401-3300
Jackson Heights | 84-13 Northern Blvd. (bet. 84th & 85th Sts.) | Queens | 718-426-1010
Rego Park | 62-30 Woodhaven Blvd. (63rd Ave.) | Queens | 718-458-0606 ⊄
www.piopionyc.com

"Succulent" rotisserie chicken slathered in "habit-forming" "spicy green sauce" makes these "festive" Peruvians perennially "popular" pit stops for "plentiful" portions at "pittance" prices; "cacophonous" crowds and "hallway" settings lead many to go the "take-out" route.

Pipa *Spanish* 20 | 23 | 16 | $42

Flatiron | ABC Carpet & Home | 38 E. 19th St. (bet. B'way & Park Ave. S.) | 212-677-2233

"Chandelier showroom" decor lends a *Phantom of the Opera* feel to this "cool" Flatiron Spaniard; *picante* tapas and *potente* sangria distract from "inattentive" service and "adds-up-fast" pricing.

Pisticci *Italian* 24 | 19 | 20 | $33

W 100s | 125 La Salle St. (B'way) | 212-932-3500 | www.pisticcinyc.com

Populated by "brainy Columbia" types, this "adorable, affordable" Italian "in the shadow of Grant's Tomb" is "deservedly popular" thanks to "flavorful" cooking "prepared with TLC"; "roomy" dimensions, "friendly" service and "free jazz" Sunday nights ice the cake.

Pizza 33 ◐ *Pizza* 19 | 8 | 11 | $11

Chelsea | 268 W. 23rd St. (8th Ave.) | 212-206-0999
G Village | 527 Sixth Ave. (14th St.) | 212-255-6333
Murray Hill | 489 Third Ave. (33rd St.) | 212-545-9191
www.pizza33nyc.com

To "curb your appetite" after a "long night", there's always this "dependable" pizzeria trio dispensing "basic" thin-crust pies into the wee hours; seating is "limited" and so is the service, but they're "convenient" stops for those in need of low-budget "hangover recovery."

P.J. Clarke's ◐ *Pub Food* 17 | 15 | 16 | $36

E 50s | 915 Third Ave. (55th St.) | 212-317-1616
P.J. Clarke's at Lincoln Square ◐ *Pub Food*
W 60s | 44 W. 63rd St. (Columbus Ave.) | 212-957-9700
P.J. Clarke's on the Hudson *Pub Food*
Financial District | 4 World Financial Ctr. (Vesey St.) | 212-285-1500
www.pjclarkes.com

"Old NY" can be sampled "on a hamburger bun" at this "legendary" Midtown saloon that's a genuine "time machine back to 1884", and equally renowned for its "pub food of a high order"; the spin-offs' lack of history is paid back in "convenience" for Lincoln Center–goers and "terrific" harbor views for FiDi diners.

Place, The *American/Mediterranean* ▽ 19 | 22 | 18 | $47

W Village | 310 W. Fourth St. (bet. Bank & 12th Sts.) | 212-924-2711 | www.theplaceny.com

"Dark" and "dreamy", this "cozy" West Village boîte is just the place to "take your sweetie" for "first-rate" Med-New American cooking and bonus canoodling beside the "fireplace"; though seating's a touch "tight", the "unhurried" pace and "friendly" service enhance the "romancing."

Planethailand 212 ◑ *Japanese/Thai* 19 | 17 | 15 | $28

Flatiron | 30 W. 24th St. (bet. 5th & 6th Aves.) | 212-727-7026 | www.pt212.com

Look for an "expansive" menu of "above-average" chow at this "boho-chic" Flatiron Thai-Japanese (its "big-box" Williamsburg cousin has closed); expect "Walmart prices" and "spaced-out service."

Pó *Italian* 25 | 17 | 22 | $51

G Village | 31 Cornelia St. (bet. Bleecker & W. 4th Sts.) | 212-645-2189
Carroll Gardens | 276 Smith St. (bet. Degraw & Sackett Sts.) | Brooklyn | 718-875-1980
www.porestaurant.com

Still "going strong", this Village "nook" (and its equally "well-oiled" Carroll Gardens outPóst) is famed for "first-rate" "gourmet Italian" cooking that's most accessible via the $52 "bargain" tasting menu; "not much elbow room" is offset by the overall "welcoming" mood.

Poke ⊠⇱ *Japanese* 25 | 14 | 17 | $40

E 80s | 343 E. 85th St. (bet. 1st & 2nd Aves.) | 212-249-0569

"Standout sushi" and "fantastic rolls" make for "Zen-like" meals at this "popular" UES Japanese set in "absolutely un-Zen-like" digs; while the "BYO" and "cash-only" policies help "keep prices down", the "no-reservations" rule leads to "long lines" that are a "big drag."

Pomaire *Chilean* 20 | 17 | 22 | $46

W 40s | 371 W. 46th St. (bet. 8th & 9th Aves.) | 212-956-3056 | www.pomairenyc.com

"Intensely flavored" Chilean cuisine comes as a "delightful surprise" at this "cozy" Restaurant Row venue, ditto the "wallop" packed by its "sublime" pisco sours; the digs are "homey" verging on plain-Jane, but a "cordial" host and "focused staff" add some polish.

Pomme de Terre *French* 22 | 18 | 20 | $40

Ditmas Park | 1301 Newkirk Ave. (Argyle Rd.) | Brooklyn | 718-284-0005 | www.pdtny.com

"Up-and-coming" Ditmas Park gets a boost via this "likable little" bistro from the minds behind Farm on Adderley; expect "creative" takes on "simple" French favorites, along with "thoughtful" service, "tight quarters" and maybe even "a wait" now that the "word's gotten out."

Pomodoro Rosso *Italian* 21 | 16 | 20 | $43

W 70s | 229 Columbus Ave. (bet. 70th & 71st Sts.) | 212-721-3009

"Well-above-average" Lincoln Center–area Italian turning out "huge bowls" of midpriced "red-sauce" standards in "quaint", "fittingly

	FOOD	DECOR	SERVICE	COST

cheesy" environs; regulars "get there early" to avoid the crush caused by the "no-reservations" policy.

Pongal *Indian/Vegetarian* | 22 | 14 | 16 | $25 |

Murray Hill | 110 Lexington Ave. (bet. 27th & 28th Sts.) | 212-696-9458 | www.pongalnyc.com

The "delicious" dosas "rock" at this Curry Hill Southern Indian known for "light", "high-quality" kosher vegetarian fare; "penny-pincher prices" compensate for the "graceless" service and "elbow-to-elbow" seating; P.S. the recently shuttered First Avenue branch is "truly missed."

Pongsri Thai *Thai* | 20 | 12 | 16 | $28 |

Chelsea | 165 W. 23rd St. (bet. 6th & 7th Aves.) | 212-645-8808
Chinatown | 106 Bayard St. (Baxter St.) | 212-349-3132
W 40s | 244 W. 48th St. (bet. B'way & 8th Ave.) | 212-582-3392
www.pongsri.com

"Foreign flavor" fans favor the "tempting array" of "savory" Thai dishes at these "dependable", "bargain"-priced Siamese triplets; given the "cold service" and "sparse" verging on "shabby" settings, many reserve them as "dine-and-dash" options.

Ponticello *Italian* | ▽ 24 | 19 | 23 | $47 |

Astoria | 46-11 Broadway (bet. 46th & 47th Sts.) | Queens | 718-278-4514 | www.ponticelloristorante.com

"Hearty" Northern Italian cooking satisfies the "high expectations" at this "inviting" Astorian where an "accommodating" staff lets you "have it your way"; "pinky-ringed" regulars admit the "prices are high for Queens" but "worth it", especially when you reserve the "private wine-cellar room."

Pop Burger ● *Burgers* | 18 | 14 | 13 | $19 |

E 50s | 14 E. 58th St. (bet. 5th & Madison Aves.) | 212-991-6644
Meatpacking | 58-60 Ninth Ave. (bet. 14th & 15th Sts.) | 212-414-8686
www.popburger.com

Perfect antidotes for the "late-night munchies" (or après the Apple Store), this Meatpacking-Midtown duo dispatches "deelish" "White Castle"–size burgers into the wee hours; "blasting music" and "indifferent service" lend a "club feel" that's accentuated by their "lounge areas."

Popover Cafe *American* | 18 | 13 | 17 | $27 |

W 80s | 551 Amsterdam Ave. (bet. 86th & 87th Sts.) | 212-595-8555 | www.popovercafe.com

"Poofy popovers" are the draw at this longtime UWS "happy place", but the "homey" American comfort-food menu "holds its own" too; despite "distracted" service and "tatty", "teddy-bears-all-over" decor, "stroller"-pushing "droves" make it a "madhouse on weekends."

NEW Porchetta *Italian* | 24 | 9 | 16 | $16 |

E Village | 110 E. Seventh St. (bet. Ave. A & 1st Ave.) | 212-777-2151 | www.porchettanyc.com

The "swine is divine" and the price is fine at Sara Jenkins' "stellar" new East Village Italian that "focuses on one thing": "sinfully good" herb-roasted pork offered either as a sandwich or on a platter alongside beans and veggies; unless you can nab one of the six stools in the "cubicle"-size space, "plan on takeout."

	FOOD	DECOR	SERVICE	COST

Porter House New York *Steak*
| 24 | 25 | 23 | $74 |

W 60s | Time Warner Ctr. | 10 Columbus Circle, 4th fl. (60th St. at B'way) | 212-823-9500 | www.porterhousenewyork.com

"Classy" but "not snobby", Michael Lomonaco's "civilized" Time Warner Center steakhouse offers "skillfully prepared" chops and "excellent sides" abetted by "genial", "textbook service" and a "beautifully appointed" room with "million-dollar" Central Park views; naturally, all this "luxe" is "reflected in the bill", but it's fully in keeping with a "wonderful dining experience."

Portofino *Italian/Seafood*
| ▽ 19 | 19 | 18 | $51 |

Bronx | 555 City Island Ave. (Cross St.) | 718-885-1220 | www.portofinocityisland.com

"Lovely waterfront views" and "steady quality" make this "convivial" City Island Italian seafooder a year-round "staple"; maybe the interior could use "updating", but service is "on the money" as are tabs priced to "keep the riffraff out."

Post House *Steak*
| 24 | 21 | 22 | $77 |

E 60s | Lowell Hotel | 28 E. 63rd St. (bet. Madison & Park Aves.) | 212-935-2888 | www.theposthouse.com

Not as "glitzy" as some of its upstart rivals, this "refined" East Side steakhouse lures the "Brooks Brothers" crowd with "classic" chops, "proper", "female-friendly" service and an "old-style", Americana-decorated setting; of course, such "fine dining" comes at a "hefty" price, but most leave "satisfied and well fed."

Posto *Pizza*
| 24 | 15 | 19 | $28 |

Gramercy | 310 Second Ave. (18th St.) | 212-716-1200 | www.postothincrust.com

"Paper-thin crusts" and "terrific toppings" make for one "superior" pizza at this "tiny", "under-the-radar" Gramercy "perennial"; it's usually "packed", but "quick" service and warm-weather outdoor seating ease the crush.

NEW Pranna ●☒ *Asian*
| ▽ 20 | 25 | 20 | $53 |

Murray Hill | 79 Madison Ave. (bet. 28th & 29th Sts.) | 212-696-5700 | www.prannarestaurant.com

"Massive" is the word on this "chic" new Southeast Asian near Madison Park (the former Scopa) that provides "tasty", midpriced fare and "conscientious service" in a "splashy", "oversized" setting; still, the "loud DJ", "exotic" drinks and "be-seen" vibe suggest to some it's as much "club" as restaurant.

Prem-on Thai *Thai*
| ▽ 21 | 16 | 17 | $32 |

G Village | 138 W. Houston St. (bet. MacDougal & Sullivan Sts.) | 212-353-2338 | www.prem-on.com

"Solid" Thai food with some "new twists" served in a "modern", "highly stylized" setting wins fans for this "sexy" (if rather "secret") Greenwich Villager; "reasonable" pricing helps offset the occasionally "rush-rush" service.

Press 195 *Sandwiches*
| 21 | 14 | 15 | $20 |

Park Slope | 195 Fifth Ave. (bet. Berkeley Pl. & Union St.) | Brooklyn | 718-857-1950

(continued)

Press 195

Bayside | 40-11 Bell Blvd. (bet. 40th & 41st Aves.) | Queens | 718-281-1950 | www.press195.com

An "eye-poppingly extensive" selection of "excellent" panini fills out the menu of these "easy" Bayside/Park Slope sandwich shops; even though "everything takes forever to come out of the kitchen", few mind since the "light fare" is equally "light on the wallet."

Primavera ● *Italian*　24 | 20 | 24 | $74

E 80s | 1578 First Ave. (82nd St.) | 212-861-8608 | www.primaveranyc.com

"Longstanding" patrons tout this UES Northern Italian where the "excellent" food and "elegant" mood are overseen by a "focused" crew led by "welcoming" host Nicola Civetta; it's a "diamond in an area of rhinestones" with a justified touch of "snob appeal", hence the "high costs."

Prime Grill *Steak*　22 | 19 | 18 | $70

E 40s | 60 E. 49th St. (bet. Madison & Park Aves.) | 212-692-9292 | www.theprimegrill.com

Think "Peter Luger for the observant" to get the gist of this Midtown kosher steakhouse dispensing "terrific" cuts of beef and "shockingly good sushi" with "no fussiness"; maybe the "deli"-quality service and "off-the-charts" pricing "could be improved", but overall it's a "great place to celebrate life's *simchas*."

Primehouse New York *Steak*　24 | 23 | 23 | $70

Murray Hill | 381 Park Ave. S. (27th St.) | 212-824-2600 | www.brguestrestaurants.com

"Not your typical steakhouse", Steve Hanson's "chic" Murray Hill carnivorium is "more modern and trendy" than the norm, with "Vegas"-like looks and "well-trained" staffers; "juicy, flavorful" chops and a "fantastic" Caesar salad made tableside help detract from the one major beef: those "Park Avenue prices."

NEW Prime Meats ●⇄ *American/German*　∇ 19 | 23 | 20 | $36

Carroll Gardens | 465 Court St. (Luquer St.) | Brooklyn | 718-254-0327 | www.frankspm.com

Spun off from Frankies Spuntino down the block, this new, cash-only Carroll Gardens German-American offers an abbreviated selection of charcuterie and small plates for reasonable dough; the wood-lined throwback of a setting is fitted out with a long bar and smattering of booths and tables, though plans for further expansion are in the works.

Primola *Italian*　22 | 15 | 20 | $63

E 60s | 1226 Second Ave. (bet. 64th & 65th Sts.) | 212-758-1775

"Where you sit is as important as what you eat" at this UES "heavy-hitter" magnet where the "tasty" Italian grub at times plays second fiddle to the "kiss-ass" scene; despite "expensive" pricing, "there's no recession here."

Provence en Boite *Bakery/French*　20 | 18 | 19 | $36

Carroll Gardens | 263 Smith St. (Degraw St.) | Brooklyn | 718-797-0707 | www.provenceenboite.com

There's "a bit of Provence" in Carroll Gardens at this "genuine" French bakery/cafe where a "husband-and-wife team" dispense "dreamy crêpes" and "bistro classics" along with "amazing bread"; a "welcoming" mood and "great-deal" pricing add to its allure.

NEW Provini ❶ *Italian*

-	-	-	I

Park Slope | 1302 Eighth Ave. (13th St.) | Brooklyn | 718-369-2154
To a part of Park Slope light on dining options comes this corner cafe from the owner of Bar Toto, whose tiny, tin-ceilinged, bistro-like digs are lined in mirrors and dominated by a full dark-wood bar; the brief, nicely priced menu of pastas and other Italian crowd-pleasers is designed to go well with the *vini* on offer.

Prune *American*

24	16	21	$49

E Village | 54 E. First St. (bet. 1st & 2nd Aves.) | 212-677-6221 | www.prunerestaurant.com
"Stellar" chef Gabrielle Hamilton does some "fancy footwork in the kitchen" at this "tiny" East Village "foodie's paradise", offering an "adventurous", well-"thought-through" New American menu led by "wonderful bone marrow"; despite "squished seating" and an inevitable "wait" to get in, it's a "cult favorite" for its "decadent brunch" alone.

PT ❶≠ *Italian*

-	-	-	M

Williamsburg | 331 Bedford Ave. (bet. S. 2nd & 3rd Sts.) | Brooklyn | 718-388-7438
Communal seating adds to the "casual" mood at this "charming", mid-priced Williamsburg wine bar offering hearty Italian fare and a strong vino list; service is "lovely" if a "little green", ditto the "cute garden."

Public *Eclectic*

22	25	19	$56

NoLita | 210 Elizabeth St. (bet. Prince & Spring Sts.) | 212-343-7011 | www.public-nyc.com
Done up in "ironic retro-schoolhouse" style, this "hip" NoLita Eclectic represents "quintessential Downtown dining" with its "inspired", Australian-accented global fare, "interesting aesthetics" and overall "antipodean cool"; even if the "space outperforms the food" (and the food outperforms the service), it's ever the "fashionable" experience.

Pukk *Thai/Vegetarian*

∇ 23	16	18	$21

E Village | 71 First Ave. (bet. 4th & 5th Sts.) | 212-253-2742 | www.pukknyc.com
"Quick and quirky", this East Village Thai purveys a "varied" vegetarian roster for prices "so cheap you'll think you're actually in Thailand"; the mod "futuro" setting, heavy on the "tiny white tiles", draws mixed response, though there's agreement the loos are "the coolest."

Pump Energy Food *Health Food*

17	7	13	$15

E 50s | Crystal Pavilion | 805 Third Ave. (50th St.) | 212-421-3055 🖪
Financial District | 80 Pine St. (Pearl St.) | 212-785-1110
Flatiron | 31 E. 21st St. (bet. B'way & Park Ave. S.) | 212-253-7676
Garment District | 112 W. 38th St. (bet. B'way & 6th Ave.) | 212-764-2100 🖪
Murray Hill | 275 Madison Ave. (bet. 39th & 40th Sts.) | 212-697-7867 🖪
W 50s | 40 W. 55th St. (bet. 5th & 6th Aves.) | 212-246-6844
www.thepumpenergyfood.com
"Guiltless", "sensible" eating geared toward keeping your "New Year's resolutions" is the idea behind this health food mini-chain with bare-bones settings and service; those who find the "dull" offerings

about "as interesting as brown rice" suggest "smothering everything in hot sauce."

Pure Food & Wine *Vegan/Vegetarian* | 21 | 20 | 21 | $55 |

Gramercy | 54 Irving Pl. (bet. 17th & 18th Sts.) | 212-477-1010 | www.purefoodandwine.com

Novices should bring an "open mind" to this "tranquil" Gramercy Parker known for its "ingenious" raw vegan menu and "gorgeous garden"; but while fans of "ethical" dining can't get enough of its "no-guilt" offerings, critics say it's way too "expensive" for just "salads in disguise."

Puttanesca *Italian* | 19 | 16 | 17 | $40 |

W 50s | 859 Ninth Ave. (56th St.) | 212-581-4177 | www.puttanesca.com

One of those "neighborhood places" where you can count on a "comforting", "mop-up-the-red-sauce" meal, this "boisterous" Hell's Kitchen Italian near Lincoln Center is a "reliable pre-theater option"; "chatty servers" and "good value" are also part of the package.

Pylos ◑ *Greek* | 25 | 23 | 21 | $48 |

E Village | 128 E. Seventh St. (bet. Ave. A & 1st Ave.) | 212-473-0220 | www.pylosrestaurant.com

"Clay pots line the ceiling" and "hearty, rustic" food fills the plates at this "modern" East Village Hellenic that really "captures the spirit of dining in Greece"; regulars tout the "nice buzz", "prompt service" and "real-people" pricing, and advise you make a "meal of the appetizers and everyone will be happy."

NEW Qoo Robata Bar ◑ *Japanese* | - | - | - | M |

Williamsburg | 367 Metropolitan Ave. (Havemeyer St.) | Brooklyn | 718-384-9493

Going beyond Williamsburg's typical quick-fix sushi options, this new midpriced Japanese izakaya near the BQE is centered around a U-shaped bar where diners can watch the chefs grilling skewered meats and fish; a rooftop patio is in the works for starlit sake sipping.

Q Thai Bistro *Thai* | 21 | 18 | 18 | $37 |

Forest Hills | 108-25 Ascan Ave. (bet. Austin & Burns Sts.) | Queens | 718-261-6599 | www.qthaibistrony.com

A "slightly exotic" setting and "intimate" air tempt diners to "linger" at this Queens "find" that's "one of the few places you can take a date in Forest Hills"; expect "quality" Thai cooking with a French accent, at tabs that are a tad "pricey" for the neighborhood.

Quaint *American*   ∇ | 23 | 20 | 23 | $36 |

Sunnyside | 46-10 Skillman Ave. (bet. 46th & 47th Sts.) | Queens | 917-779-9220 | www.quaintnyc.com

Set near the "historic Sunnyside Gardens district", this "relaxed" New American bistro provides a "succinct menu" of "delicious dishes" embellished with "lovely organic touches"; fans call it a "wonderful neighborhood" resource, citing its "convivial" air and "lovely back garden."

Quality Meats ◑ *American/Steak* | 24 | 22 | 22 | $73 |

W 50s | 57 W. 58th St. (bet. 5th & 6th Aves.) | 212-371-7777 | www.qualitymeatsnyc.com

The "staid steakhouse" scene gets a "trendy" spin at this "hip" Midtown cow palace where the chops "live up to the name" and the "neo-industrial" decor channels a "Gansevoort Street" butcher shop; pundits plug the "top-notch" service and "terrific homemade ice cream" and easily tolerate the "heady" pricing.

Quantum Leap Health Food/Vegetarian

`20` `12` `18` `$23`

E Village | 203 First Ave. (bet. 12th & 13th Sts.) | 212-673-9848
G Village | 226 Thompson St. (bet. Bleecker & W. 3rd Sts.) |
212-677-8050 | www.quantumleapwestvillage.com
Flushing | 65-64 Fresh Meadow Ln. (67th Ave.) | Queens | 718-461-1307
"Healthy tastes great" at this "pleasant" vegetarian trio where "students" and the "Birkenstock set" dig into "basic", "meatless" fare along with a few fish dishes; the service is "attentive", the price point "inexpensive" and the decor strictly "no-frills."

Quartino ⊅ Italian

`▽ 20` `18` `21` `$40`

NoHo | 11 Bleecker St. (Elizabeth St.) | 212-529-5133
"Fresh, organic ingredients" are the basis of this "intimate" NoHo Italian whose "simple menu" bears a vegetarian focus as well as some Ligurian twists; the "excellent" wine list similarly reflects the sustainable ethos, while a "quaint" patio delights fresh-air fanatics.

Quatorze Bis French

`20` `19` `20` `$58`

E 70s | 323 E. 79th St. (bet. 1st & 2nd Aves.) | 212-535-1414
Very "French in a NY kind of way", this longtime UES bistro pleases its "older crowd" with "genuine", "uncomplicated" cooking in a "charming", "Paris-without-the-Parisians" setting; regulars like the "clubby" air and "unobtrusive" service, not the "somewhat pricey" tariffs.

Quattro Gatti Italian

`22` `17` `22` `$49`

E 80s | 205 E. 81st St. (bet. 2nd & 3rd Aves.) | 212-570-1073
"Traditional" is the word for this 25-year-old UES trattoria, a "tried-and-true" "staple" with four lives left whose "satisfying" cooking and "decent" pricing "never go out of style"; the "unflustered staff" will even provide a "lesson on Italian pronunciation" on the side.

Queen Italian

`24` `14` `20` `$44`

Brooklyn Heights | 84 Court St. (bet. Livingston & Schermerhorn Sts.) |
Brooklyn | 718-596-5955 | www.queenrestaurant.com
"Old-fashioned" and proud of it, this "longtime" "heart-of-Brooklyn-Heights" Italian has been serving a "classic red-sauce" menu to "lawyers", jurors and "politicians" since 1958; similarly "old-school service" is a crowning touch, and as for the "tired" decor, loyal subjects suggest "get over it already."

Queen of Sheba ● Ethiopian

`21` `14` `15` `$27`

W 40s | 650 10th Ave. (bet. 45th & 46th Sts.) | 212-397-0610 |
www.shebanyc.com
"Pungent odors" set the "exotic" mood at this Hell's Kitchen Ethiopian where "eating with your hands" "adds to the experience"; the "solid", low-budget menu includes "lots of vegetarian choices", but the "run-down" digs and "mute" service "leave something to be desired."

Quercy French

`22` `15` `20` `$42`

Cobble Hill | 242 Court St. (bet. Baltic & Kane Sts.) | Brooklyn | 718-243-2151
"Honest" "rural French" fare coaxes Cobble Hillers into this "quaint" spin-off of La Lunchonette that "nobody seems to know about"; prices

are "moderate", the setting quite "comfortable" and the staff always "glad to see you", so many query why it "isn't packed every night."

NEW Quinto Quarto *Italian* | - | - | - | M |

G Village | 14 Bedford St. (bet. Downing & Houston Sts.) | 212-675-9080 | www.quintoquarto.com

Importing a "quintessential osteria" to Greenwich Village, this rustic newcomer serves traditional Roman fare at "surprisingly affordable" rates; exposed brick and weathered wood beams burnish the "intimate" vibe, though some say the "charming" staffers are "more entertaining than the food."

Rack & Soul *BBQ/Southern* | 19 | 10 | 16 | $26 |

W 100s | 258 W. 109th St. (B'way) | 212-222-4800 | www.rackandsoul.com

Now ensconced in new digs, this Columbia-area Southerner still doles out "tender" BBQ and other "terrific", "gut-busting" soul food for "fair prices"; the staff is "efficient", but finger-lickers not into the "generic", "luncheonette" setting say "takeout is better."

Radegast Hall ● *European* | ▽ 16 | 21 | 14 | $24 |

Williamsburg | 113 N. Third St. (Berry St.) | Brooklyn | 718-963-3973 | www.radegasthall.com

"Bohemian as all heck", this "rowdy" Williamsburg beer hall is populated with "big fellas" draining steins and scarfing down "good-value" European eats with an Austrian accent; ok, it's probably "more bar than restaurant" with "almost nonexistent" service, but that "vast", picnic-tabled space topped by a retractable roof is really "awesome."

Rai Rai Ken ●⊟ *Noodle Shop* | 21 | 10 | 16 | $15 |

E Village | 214 E. 10th St. (bet. 1st & 2nd Aves.) | 212-477-7030

"Ritual-worthy" ramen floating in "deeply flavored broths" "hits the spot" at this "bare-bones" East Village noodle shop where the "cheap college food" comes "fast" thanks to "no-nonsense", "just-like-Tokyo" service; better be prepared to "wait for a seat", since the space is about the "size of a janitor's closet."

Ramen Setagaya *Noodle Shop* | 19 | 10 | 15 | $18 |

E Village | 141 First Ave. (bet. 9th St. & St. Marks Pl.) | 212-529-2740 ⊟
NEW E Village | 34A St. Marks Pl. (bet. 2nd & 3rd Aves.) | 212-387-7959 ●⊟
NEW G Village | 90 University Pl. | (bet. 11th & 12th Sts.) ●
NEW Flushing | 37-02 Prince St. (37th Ave.) | Queens | 718-321-0290 ●

"Slurp-slurp" seekers savor the "simple satisfaction" supplied by "subtly simmered" ramen and broths at this burgeoning noodle shop mini-chain; it's "fast food in spirit if not in taste", and good enough that there's "no need to wait in line" at its "Momo-something" competitors.

Rao's ⊠⊟ *Italian* | 23 | 16 | 21 | $72 |

Harlem | 455 E. 114th St. (Pleasant Ave.) | 212-722-6709 | www.raos.com

Frank Pellegrino's "legendary" East Harlem Italian may be the "toughest reservation on the planet", but lucky insiders vow it's "one helluva experience" what with the "quality" "old-style" cooking and "exclusive" crowd of "connected" types and "movie stars"; wannasees settle for the "Vegas outlet", the "cookbook" or a "jar of Rao's sauce from the supermarket."

	FOOD	DECOR	SERVICE	COST

Raoul's ● *French*

24 | 20 | 21 | $60

SoHo | 180 Prince St. (bet. Sullivan & Thompson Sts.) | 212-966-3518 | www.raouls.com

"Reliably cool" for 35 years, this "timeless" SoHo "ace in the hole" is a "treat for all the senses" with "stellar" French bistro standards, "splendid service" and a "sexy" back garden; it's usually jammed with "terminally hip" young types and "nostalgic gray-hairs" who hope this "perfect spot" stays "forever unchanged."

Rare Bar & Grill *Burgers*

21 | 14 | 16 | $31

G Village | 228 Bleecker St. (bet. Carmine St. & 6th Ave.) | 212-691-7273

Murray Hill | Shelburne Murray Hill Hotel | 303 Lexington Ave. (37th St.) | 212-481-1999

www.rarebarandgrill.com

"Burgers are a work of art" at these "rare finds" where the "tasty" patties come with "delectable" toppings along with a "must-try fries sampler"; maybe the service and decor are "underdone", but ambiancewise they're "vibrant scenes", especially at Murray Hill's "rooftop bar."

Rasputin ●Ⓜ *Continental*

∇ 20 | 20 | 17 | $89

Sheepshead Bay | 2670 Coney Island Ave. (Ave. X) | Brooklyn | 718-332-8111 | www.rasputinny.com

"Vodka-fueled fun" continues into the wee hours at this "over-the-top", Vegas-on-the-Volga Continental cabaret in Sheepshead Bay; the ultrapricey Russian-inflected eats are "beautifully presented" in "enormous" quantities, assuming you can take your eyes off the "half-clad" showgirls long enough to focus on the food.

Ravagh *Persian*

∇ 20 | 12 | 18 | $30

E 60s | 1237 First Ave. (bet. 66th & 67th Sts.) | 212-861-7900

Murray Hill | 11 E. 30th St. (bet. 5th & Madison Aves.) | 212-696-0300

"Authentic" kebabs and cherry rice are among the "close-to-home-cooked" Persian specialties offered at this "cozy" East Side duo showcasing an "under-represented" cuisine; what they "lack in ambiance" they make up for with "excellent value"; N.B. the UES branch is BYO.

Rayuela *Pan-Latin*

22 | 24 | 20 | $54

LES | 165 Allen St. (bet. Rivington & Stanton Sts.) | 212-253-8840 | www.rayuelanyc.com

"Small plates are the name of the game" at this "sexy" LES Pan-Latin where the "freestyle" fare is "outta sight", particularly after a few "brilliantly engineered cocktails"; "hip" young things tout the "gorgeous" duplex setting built around a live "olive tree", but think it's time to "revisit the prices."

⚠️NEW Recipe *American*

- | - | - | M

W 80s | 452 Amsterdam Ave. (bet. 81st & 82nd Sts.) | 212-501-7755 | www.recipenyc.com

A focus on local ingredients arrives on the UWS via this 26-seat New American whose rustic menu keeps things simple, and moderately priced; the homey interior feels more downtown than up, decorated in a very-of-the-moment style with lots of salvaged wood, bare brick and filament light bulbs.

	FOOD	DECOR	SERVICE	COST

Red Cat *American/Mediterranean* | 23 | 19 | 22 | $57 |

Chelsea | 227 10th Ave. (bet. 23rd & 24th Sts.) | 212-242-1122 |
www.theredcat.com

Gallery-goers, "hep cats" and a "sea of regulars" think this "crazy
busy" West Chelsea "standout" is the "cat's meow", from the "first-
rate" Med–New American cooking to the "upbeat staff" and "refreshingly unpretentious" mood; sure, it can be "a bit spendy", but it's hard
to put a price on something so "purr-fect."

Red Egg *Chinese/Peruvian* | ▽ 20 | 17 | 20 | $32 |

Little Italy | 202 Centre St. (Howard St.) | 212-966-1123 |
www.redeggnyc.com

Set in the "no-man's-land" between Chinatown and Little Italy, this
Chinese yearling plies "tasty" "all-day" dim sum jazzed up with some
"Peruvian fusion" dishes, all for "cheap" sums; "no carts", "no table
sharing" and "loungelike", space-age decor separate it from the pack.

Redeye Grill ☻ *American/Seafood* | 20 | 19 | 20 | $56 |

W 50s | 890 Seventh Ave. (56th St.) | 212-541-9000 | www.redeyegrill.com

"Big, brassy" and "touristy", Shelly Fireman's "boisterous" New
American seafooder remains a "crowd-pleaser" dispensing "tasty"
chow at a "cost fair to the experience"; the "eye-popping" space is
decked out with murals and revolving shrimp sculptures, while an "on-
the-ball staff" tends to those bound for Carnegie Hall across the street.

Redhead, The ☻Ⓩ *American* | 21 | 15 | 19 | $40 |

E Village | 349 E. 13th St. (bet. 1st & 2nd Aves.) | 212-533-6212 |
www.theredheadnyc.com

New American "comfort food made with love" (and a Southern accent)
is the draw at this "ultimate local restaurant" in the East Village; "barlike"
looks and a "no-reservations" policy to the contrary, it's acclaimed for
its "casually humorous" staffers, "value" pricing and "stiff cocktails."

Regency *American* | ▽ 18 | 22 | 22 | $64 |

E 60s | Loews Regency Hotel | 540 Park Ave. (61st St.) | 212-339-4050 |
www.loewshotels.com

"De rigueur for NY hot shots", this Regency Hotel room is the place for
"power breakfasts" with pols and plutocrats closing deals before
9 AM; otherwise, you can expect "tranquil" New American lunches
and, come evening, a shift to "supper-club" mode when it becomes
Feinstein's, offering "solid" fare and "generous drinks."

Relish ☻ *American* | ▽ 20 | 18 | 17 | $30 |

Williamsburg | 225 Wythe Ave. (bet. Metropolitan Ave. & N. 3rd St.) |
Brooklyn | 718-963-4546 | www.relish.com

A "classic 1950s diner" is the streamlined setting for this "nostalgic"
American comfort-food dispenser in Williamsburg, and its "hipper-
than-thou" followers report "consistent" chow served in a "sexy", film
noir–ish room; fresh-air fiends tout the "awesome" garden.

Remi *Italian* | 22 | 23 | 21 | $62 |

W 50s | 145 W. 53rd St. (bet. 6th & 7th Aves.) | 212-581-4242 |
www.remi-ny.com

"Subtle, satisfying" Venetian cuisine is "served with grace" at this 20-
year-old Midtowner whose "eye-catching space" is adorned with

"lovely" murals of the Grand Canal; the decidedly "upscale prices" don't seem to faze "heavy-hitters doing deals over lunch" or theatergoers bent on a "romantic night out."

Republic *Pan-Asian*

18 | 13 | 15 | $24

Union Sq | 37 Union Sq. W. (bet. 16th & 17th Sts.) | 212-627-7172 | www.thinknoodles.com

It's best to be "young at heart" at this "boisterous", "cafeteria"-style Union Square Pan-Asian where "notable" noodles and other "nourishing" eats come "cheap" and "fast"; mature types put off by "communal tables", "hard bench seating" and an "overwhelming" racket vote for "takeout."

Re Sette ● *Italian*

21 | 17 | 20 | $53

W 40s | 7 W. 45th St. (bet. 5th & 6th Aves.) | 212-221-7530 | www.resette.com

"Unusual" Barese regional specialties, a "mellow" mood and an "out-of-the-way" locale just a "short walk from Times Square" make this Midtown Italian a "terrific" option for pre-theater repasts or "business lunching"; service is "helpful", while the King's Table upstairs lets you "re-set" royally in private.

Resto ● *Belgian*

20 | 15 | 17 | $41

Murray Hill | 111 E. 29th St. (bet. Lexington Ave. & Park Ave. S.) | 212-685-5585 | www.restonyc.com

An "unparalleled beer menu" paired with a "signature burger" and "must-have moules" draws an "energetic" crowd to this "trendy" Murray Hill Belgian gastropub; no question, it's "lively" and "fun", even if the "jet-engine" noise levels make "conversation impossible."

Rhong-Tiam *Thai*

∇ 22 | 15 | 17 | $32

G Village | 541 La Guardia Pl. (bet. Bleecker & W. 3rd Sts.) | 212-477-0600 | www.rhong-tiam.com

"Authentic", "burn-your-tongue" Thai cooking turns up the heat at this "unique" NYU-area Siamese that fans deem "more interesting" than the norm and well-priced to boot; still, some find "nothing memorable" going on, citing an "uneven" kitchen and "sterile" setting.

Rice ⊟ *Eclectic*

19 | 15 | 18 | $22

Murray Hill | 115 Lexington Ave. (28th St.) | 212-686-5400
NoHo | 292 Elizabeth St. (bet. Bleecker & Houston Sts.) | 212-226-5775 ●
Dumbo | 81 Washington St. (bet. Front & York Sts.) | Brooklyn | 718-222-9880
Fort Greene | 166 DeKalb Ave. (Cumberland St.) | Brooklyn | 718-858-2700
www.riceny.com

It's "clear why rice is a staple of many diets" after a visit to these "low-key", "cash-only" Eclectics offering different varieties of the grain prepared in "inventive ways"; its "crunchy crowd" lauds the "conscientious" staff, "super-cheap" rates and plethora of "vegetarian choices."

Rice 'n' Beans ● *Brazilian*

20 | 9 | 16 | $27

W 50s | 744 Ninth Ave. (bet. 50th & 51st Sts.) | 212-265-4444

"Cheap and cheerful", this "super-tiny" Hell's Kitchen Brazilian doles out "huge amounts" of "hearty", "done-to-perfection" grub at a "perfect price point"; alright, it's a "genuine hole-in-the-wall", with "no room for your knees", but fans (and theatergoers) still "love it for what it is."

Rickshaw Dumpling Bar *Chinese*

FOOD	DECOR	SERVICE	COST
17	10	14	$15

Flatiron | 61 W. 23rd St. (bet. 5th & 6th Aves.) | 212-924-9220 | www.rickshawdumplings.com

"Inventive" takes on the "humble dumpling" paired with soup or salad make for "surprisingly filling" meals at Anita Lo's "fast-food" Flatiron Chinese; it's "popular with the work-lunch crowd", despite a "sterile" setting, "assembly-line" service and what some call a "conspicuously ordinary" product.

Riingo *American/Japanese*

21	20	18	$54

E 40s | Alex Hotel | 205 E. 45th St. (bet. 2nd & 3rd Aves.) | 212-867-4200 | www.riingo.com

Marcus Samuelsson's "underappreciated" New American–Japanese in Midtown's Alex Hotel turns out "tantalizing" fusion fare in a "serene" setting that's "minimalist" to some, "lacking in imagination" to others; though prices skew "upscale" and service can be "indifferent", it's good enough to "show off to out-of-towners."

Risotteria *Italian*

22	12	17	$27

G Village | 270 Bleecker St. (Morton St.) | 212-924-6664 | www.risotteria.com

"Allergic gourmands" tout the "enlightened gluten-free options" at this Village Italian where "they know risotto" in all its "delicious", "customized" permutations; the "shoebox" setting and "slack service" are easily overlooked given the "low-budget" tabs and "high yummy factor."

NEW Ritz Asia ☻ *Pan-Asian*

-	-	-	M

G Village | 189 Bleecker St. (bet. MacDougal St. & 6th Ave.) | 212-228-3366 | www.ritzasia.com

"Creative" cooked Pan-Asian dishes and a wide selection of sushi and sashimi fill out the menu of this Village newcomer boasting slick, Tao-esque atmospherics; yet even though it's been "billed as a budget Nobu", some shrug it's "just another neighborhood joint" with an "inexpensive" price point.

Z River Café *American*

26	28	26	$127

Dumbo | 1 Water St. (bet. Furman & Old Fulton Sts.) | Brooklyn | 718-522-5200 | www.rivercafe.com

A "beauty inside and out" with "food as good" as its "magical harbor view", Buzzy O'Keeffe's "amazing" New American on the Dumbo side of the Brooklyn Bridge is one of those "not-to-be-missed" NY experiences – just bear in mind that jackets are required and dinner is $98 prix fixe only; with a table overlooking the water "watching Manhattan light up at sunset", that special someone will be hard-pressed not to say 'yes.'

River Room ⓜ *Southern*

∇ 20	24	18	$48

Harlem | Riverbank State Park | W. 145th St. (Riverside Dr.) | 212-491-1500 | www.theriverroomofharlem.com

"Pleasant", "down-home" Southern vittles are "served proudly" at this "remote" waterside venue in Harlem's Riverbank State Park; weekend jazz, a "summer terrace" and "unsurpassed" Hudson River views through windowed walls distract from any "service kinks."

	FOOD	DECOR	SERVICE	COST

Riverview *American*
∇ 21 | 22 | 22 | $52

LIC | 2-01 50th Ave. (East River & 49th Ave.) | Queens | 718-392-5000 |
www.riverviewny.com

If your companion doesn't inspire, you can always "fall in love with the
Manhattan skyline" at this "romantic" LIC New American with a
"can't-go-wrong" riverbank setting; it's got "special occasion" written
all over it thanks to "excellent food" and "kind" service.

Roberta's ●⊅ *Pizza*
∇ 22 | 15 | 18 | $26

Bushwick | 261 Moore St. (Bogart St.) | Brooklyn | 718-417-1118 |
www.robertaspizza.com

"Delicious" "designer pies" turn up at this year-old, cash-only "gem of
a pizza joint" in "up-and-coming" Bushwick; a "painfully hip crowd"
frequents the "funky" space and swears it's "worth the trek."

☑ Roberto ☒ *Italian*
26 | 18 | 21 | $52

Bronx | 603 Crescent Ave. (Hughes Ave.) | 718-733-9503 |
www.roberto089.com

"Excellent Italian food" "prepared using fresh ingredients from the local Arthur Avenue shops" justifies a trip to this "warm", "friendly"
Bronx standout and explains "the crowds and long waits"; for best results, let Roberto choose your meal for you at half the price this quality
would cost in Manhattan.

Roberto Passon ● *Italian*
21 | 16 | 18 | $44

W 50s | 741 Ninth Ave. (50th St.) | 212-582-5599 |
www.robertopasson.com

"Deservedly popular" and "convenient to Broadway", this Hell's
Kitchen Italian produces "bold-flavored" Venetian dishes that distract from its "bland decor"; service is "speedy" and tabs are "fair"
(especially the $14 prix fixe lunch), but watch out for "price surprises"
on the specials.

Roc ● *Italian*
22 | 19 | 20 | $50

TriBeCa | 190A Duane St. (Greenwich St.) | 212-625-3333 |
www.rocrestaurant.com

An "exuberant owner" and "sweetheart" waiters inject some "person-
ality" into this "charming" TriBeCa Italian where the "sophisticated"
cuisine echoes the overall feel of "relaxed elegance"; maybe it's
"pricier than other neighborhood spots", but worth it for the "fun
outside seating" alone.

Rocking Horse Cafe *Mexican*
20 | 16 | 17 | $40

Chelsea | 182 Eighth Ave. (bet. 19th & 20th Sts.) | 212-463-9511 |
www.rockinghorsecafe.com

There's "electricity" in the air at this "colorful" Chelsea "mainstay"
known for its "creative", "higher-end" Mexican food, "deadly" margaritas and "festive" following; service may be "hit-or-miss" and "earplugs" essential, but overall it's a "rockin' good time."

Rock-n-Sake ☒ *Japanese*
∇ 23 | 19 | 19 | $43

Chelsea | 138 W. 25th St. (bet. 6th & 7th Aves.) | 212-255-7253 |
www.rocknsakeny.com

The "unassuming" streetside presence doesn't hint at the "surprisingly upscale", nightclub-ish interior of this Chelsea Japanese where

| | FOOD | DECOR | SERVICE | COST |

the – believe it or not – "really good" Cajun-inflected eats reflect its New Orleans roots; "reasonable" tabs offset the "loud music" and "strange location."

Rolf's *German*

| 14 | 21 | 16 | $41 |

Gramercy | 281 Third Ave. (22nd St.) | 212-477-4750

"Zany" says it best about this Gramercy Park German "relic" vending a "frozen-in-time" menu of "unmemorable" Bavarian dishes (*achtung* if you're watching your weight"); still, it's worth a Christmastime visit when it's festooned with more "sparkly" ornaments than the "tree at Rockefeller Center."

Roll-n-Roaster ◑ *Sandwiches*

| 20 | 9 | 12 | $16 |

Sheepshead Bay | 2901 Emmons Ave. (bet. E. 29th St. & Nostrand Ave.) | Brooklyn | 718-769-5831 | www.rollnroaster.com

"Inhalable" roast beef sandwiches and "cheez on anything you pleez" make this Sheepshead Bay fast-food "legend" just the thing for a "no-frills quick bite" or "late-night" nosh; there might be "not much atmosphere" or service, but "you'll sure feel like you're in Brooklyn."

Room Service *Thai*

| 18 | 18 | 16 | $29 |

Chelsea | 166 Eighth Ave. (bet. 18th & 19th Sts.) | 212-691-0299 | www.roomservicerestaurant.com
NEW **W 40s** | 690 Ninth Ave. (bet. 47th & 48th Sts.) | 212-582-0999 | www.orderroomservicenyc.com ◑

"Trendy and cool", these "high-design Thai places" offer "inexpensive", "consistently good" food in "lively" settings that are "nothing like the Waldorf" but much more like a "disco"; "minimal" service and "way-loud" acoustics are part of the package.

Rosa Mexicano ◑ *Mexican*

| 22 | 20 | 20 | $49 |

E 50s | 1063 First Ave. (58th St.) | 212-753-7407
Flatiron | 9 E. 18th St. (bet. B'way & 5th Ave.) | 212-533-3350
W 60s | 61 Columbus Ave. (62nd St.) | 212-977-7700
www.rosamexicano.com

"Haute Mexican isn't an oxymoron" at this "high-energy" trio, famed for "fancy" food and "irresistible guacamole" made tableside by an "obliging" crew; the digs are "swanky", the mood "party" and the bills will set you back, but "wicked" pomegranate margaritas "ease the pain."

Rosanjin ◪ *Japanese*

| ▽ 24 | 21 | 25 | $140 |

TriBeCa | 141 Duane St. (bet. Church St. & W. B'way) | 212-346-0664 | www.rosanjintribeca.com

It's a "treat for all the senses" at this "elegant" TriBeCa Japanese where the "impeccable", "genuine kaiseki" repasts are "graciously" served in serene, "simply decorated" surroundings; the "unforgettable experience" comes with an equally memorable price tag, though now there are more "affordable" à la carte options available.

Rose Water *American*

| 26 | 18 | 23 | $45 |

Park Slope | 787 Union St. (6th Ave.) | Brooklyn | 718-783-3800 | www.rosewaterrestaurant.com

Aka the "Blue Hill of Brooklyn", this "refined" Park Sloper proffers a "fantastic" New American menu built around "sustainable", "locally sourced" ingredients; fans find "no thorns" here, save for the too-"small" setting and long "lines" for the "big-draw brunch."

	FOOD	DECOR	SERVICE	COST

Rossini's *Italian* — 23 | 19 | 24 | $60

Murray Hill | 108 E. 38th St. (bet. Lexington & Park Aves.) | 212-683-0135 | www.rossinisrestaurant.com

If you're in the mood for "throwback" dining, this Murray Hill Northern Italian "standby" blends "excellent" food and "tuxedoed", "treat-you-like-a-king" service with "live piano" during the week and Saturday night "opera singers"; sure, it's "high priced" and "may seem old to some – but so does a 1982 Latour."

Rothmann's *Steak* — 22 | 20 | 23 | $72

E 50s | 3 E. 54th St. (bet. 5th & Madison Aves.) | 212-319-5500 | www.rothmannssteakhouse.com

A "polished operation" with "no pretense", this East Midtown steakhouse "skips the gruff" shtick and provides "solicitous service" along with "outstanding" beef and sides; spacious, "understated" surroundings suit the "manly men" in the crowd who fleetingly "feel like investment bankers" when the "hefty" check arrives.

NEW Rouge Tomate ⊠ *American* — 22 | 26 | 22 | $64

E 60s | 10 E. 60th St. (bet. 5th & Madison Aves.) | 646-237-8977 | www.rougetomatenyc.com

Some of the "finest health-conscious cuisine in town" turns up at this "green" Midtown New American where the "attention to detail" extends from the "willowy" servers to the "stunning" duplex setting complete with "simulated rainforest views"; the "haute health food" thrills its "fashionista" following, the "high prices for small portions" not so much.

Royal Siam *Thai* — ∇ 21 | 13 | 19 | $29

Chelsea | 240 Eighth Ave. (bet. 22nd & 23rd Sts.) | 212-741-1732

"Tried-and-true" Thai comfort food keeps this "well-located" neighborhood spot a longtime Chelsea "standby"; even if the decor "leaves something to be desired", it's "friendly", "quiet and calm" for "when you want to talk" and, not incidentally, the "price is right."

RUB BBQ *BBQ* — 20 | 10 | 16 | $30

Chelsea | 208 W. 23rd St. (bet. 7th & 8th Aves.) | 212-524-4300 | www.rubbbq.net

The "way a BBQ joint should be", this "old-school" Chelsea pit stop offers "succulent" Kansas City–style 'cue in a "stripped-down" setting that doesn't encourage lingering – "unless you love Formica"; the main "rub" is that they "frequently run out" of favorite dishes, so regulars "go early" to snag those "legendary burnt ends."

Ruby Foo's ● *Pan-Asian* — 18 | 20 | 18 | $43

W 40s | 1626 Broadway (49th St.) | 212-489-5600 | www.brguestrestaurants.com

Sure, it's a "mass-market" "tourist destination" that can be a "zoo", but even locals admit that this Times Square Pan-Asian "theme park" offers "perfectly good" (if "predictable") chow and "wonderfully garish" "mahjong palace" decor; many add it's "too bad the UWS location closed."

Rue 57 ● *French* — 18 | 17 | 16 | $48

W 50s | 60 W. 57th St. (6th Ave.) | 212-307-5656 | www.rue57.com

Constantly "packed to the gills", this "easily accessed" Midtown brasserie teams "traditional" French dishes with an "unexpected" sushi bar lineup; "spotty" service, "shoehorn" seating and overall "hustle bustle" (boosted by "background music in the foreground") come with the *territoire*.

Rughetta ⧄ *Italian* 　　22 | 17 | 21 | $48

E 80s | 347 E. 85th St. (bet. 1st & 2nd Aves.) | 212-517-3118 | www.rughetta.com

There's "no artifice", just "delish", "moderately priced" Roman cuisine (including a few dishes "you don't see everywhere") at this "hidden" Yorkville "sleeper"; although a recent expansion eased the "tight" quarters, it remains as "cozy" as ever, perhaps because of the "warm", "hospitable" staff.

Russian Samovar ◑ *Continental* 　　20 | 18 | 19 | $51

W 50s | 256 W. 52nd St. (bet. B'way & 8th Ave.) | 212-757-0168 | www.russiansamovar.com

"Countless varieties" of infused vodkas keep things "festive" at this Theater District Continental where it helps to bring along a "designated driver"; the food and service are "better than in the motherland", but things come to a boil "late, when the music starts" and the expats begin to "sing and dance."

Russian Tea Room *Continental* 　　19 | 24 | 21 | $73

W 50s | 150 W. 57th St. (bet. 6th & 7th Aves.) | 212-581-7100 | www.russiantearoomnyc.com

"Tourists outnumber locals" at this longtime Midtown Continental "landmark" next to Carnegie Hall where the "tasty" Russian-accented cooking plays second balalaika to the "glitzy", "over-the-top" setting; nyet-sayers complain it's "lost its mystique" and regret paying "big bucks" for "nostalgia."

Ruth's Chris Steak House *Steak* 　　23 | 20 | 22 | $70

W 50s | 148 W. 51st St. (bet. 6th & 7th Aves.) | 212-245-9600 | www.ruthschris.com

A "pound of beef" meets a "stick of butter" at this Theater District link of the New Orleans–based steakhouse chain known for its "sizzling cholesterol" and "tongue-twister name"; look for "exceptional" chops, "courteous" service, "clubby" environs and "dent-in-the-wallet" prices.

NEW Rye ◑ *American* 　　- | - | - | E

Williamsburg | 247 S. First St. (bet. Havemeyer & Roebling Sts.) | Brooklyn | 718-218-8047 | www.ryerestaurant.com

No signage and speakeasy-chic decor suggest the trendy leanings of this new Williamsburg arrival hidden away on sleepy South First Street; look for seasonal New Americana, vintage cocktails poured at a massive mahogany bar and price tags geared more toward condo owners than starving hipsters.

Sacred Chow *Vegan/Vegetarian* 　　▽ 20 | 15 | 16 | $23

G Village | 227 Sullivan St. (bet. Bleecker & 3rd Sts.) | 212-337-0863 | www.sacredchow.com

"Fresh, homemade" kosher vegan food pulls in the Birkenstock set at this "casual" Village health-fooder where "delicious" eats and "won't-break-the-bank" tabs make folks feel "virtuous"; skeptics find it "not as cute as its name", with "uncomfortable seating" to boot.

	FOOD	DECOR	SERVICE	COST

Safran ● *French/Vietnamese*
▽ 20 | 17 | 18 | $40

Chelsea | 88 Seventh Ave. (bet. 15th & 16th Sts.) | 212-929-1778 |
www.safran88.com

"Unusual combinations" work well on the menu of this "sweet" French-Vietnamese in Chelsea known for its slick, modern mien and "relaxing" repasts; fans say it's "great for the price" whether you "graze on appetizers" or pull out all the stops and "eat hearty."

Sahara ● *Turkish*
21 | 14 | 16 | $30

Gravesend | 2337 Coney Island Ave. (bet. Aves. T & U) | Brooklyn |
718-376-8594 | www.saharapalace.com

"Big crowds" convene at this "huge" Gravesend Turk to dive into "tender grilled meats" and other "aromatic", "flavorful" dishes plated in portions "humongous" enough to share; service and decor are merely "adequate", but the "affordable" costs keep it "packed on a daily basis."

Saigon Grill ● *Vietnamese*
20 | 12 | 14 | $26

G Village | 91-93 University Pl. (bet. 11th & 12th Sts.) | 212-982-3691
W 90s | 620 Amsterdam Ave. (90th St.) | 212-875-9072

"Quality" Vietnamese food "as good as it is plentiful" lures hordes to this "no-nonsense", "high-turnover" duo; "pittance" prices make it easy to forgive digs "lacking charm" and "hurried", "eat-it-and-beat-it" service.

Sakagura ● *Japanese*
25 | 21 | 21 | $54

E 40s | 211 E. 43rd St., downstairs (bet. 2nd & 3rd Aves.) | 212-953-7253 |
www.sakagura.com

"Squirreled away" in the basement of a "nondescript office building" near Grand Central, this semi-"secret" Japanese izakaya purveys "delicious" small plates paired with "top-of-the-line" sakes; it's "cheaper than flying to Japan", but the dinner tabs add up, so bargain-hunters opt for lunch.

Sala *Spanish*
22 | 19 | 20 | $39

Flatiron | 35 W. 19th St. (bet. 5th & 6th Aves.) | 212-229-2300
NoHo | 344 Bowery (Great Jones St.) | 212-979-6606
www.salanyc.com

"Sensual" NoHo-Flatiron Spaniards wooing a "young crowd" with "tantalizing" tapas, "solid" sangria and "dark", "romantic" settings; "tiny tables" and "loud celebrations" don't dampen their "popularity", and tabs are "reasonable" enough – unless you find it "hard to stop ordering."

Salaam Bombay *Indian*
▽ 21 | 17 | 18 | $36

TriBeCa | 317 Greenwich St. (bet. Duane & Reade Sts.) | 212-226-9400 |
www.salaambombay.com

While it's the $14 lunch buffet you're likely to remember, this "quality" TriBeCa Indian also serves as a "pleasant" dinner destination after the "worker bees" head home; a "peaceful" setting and "good service" make it a "refined alternative to Curry Row."

Sala Thai *Thai*
22 | 14 | 19 | $30

E 80s | 1718 Second Ave. (bet. 89th & 90th Sts.) | 212-410-5557

"Not fancy but always good", this "venerable" UES Thai has become a "neighborhood institution" thanks to "affordable" dishes brimming with "good heat and fresh flavors"; "low-key" atmospherics, "friendly" service and a "recent remodel" burnish its enduring appeal.

	FOOD	DECOR	SERVICE	COST
Salt *American*	23	19	20	$45

SoHo | 58 MacDougal St. (bet. Houston & Prince Sts.) | 212-674-4968
Salt Bar ⬤Ⓜ⤴ *American*
LES | 29A Clinton St. (bet. Houston & Stanton Sts.) | 212-979-8471
www.saltnyc.com

"Wonders" emerge from the "small kitchen" of this "tiny" SoHo New American fitted out with "cozy" communal tables; its more bar-centric LES sibling rolls out a "simpler" menu geared more to "nibbling and drinking", but both branches offer heightened flavors.

	FOOD	DECOR	SERVICE	COST
NEW **Salumeria Rosi Parmacotto** *Italian*	23	18	20	$39

W 70s | 283 Amsterdam Ave. (bet. 73rd & 74th Sts.) | 212-877-4800 | www.salumeriarosi.com

Terrific tapas Italian-style illuminate this "tiny" new UWS salumeria/enoteca from Cesare Casella offering mini-plates with mega-tastes; the "amazing array of cured meats" from its retail counter, "knowledgeable" staff and upbeat vibe trump the "nano"-size quarters.

	FOOD	DECOR	SERVICE	COST
Salute! *Italian*	18	18	17	$51

Murray Hill | 270 Madison Ave. (39th St.) | 212-213-3440 | www.salutenyc.com

"Business lunch" is the thing to do at this pseudo-"sophisticated" Murray Hill Italian where "suits" and "over-perfumed" types show up to flex their "expense accounts"; the "solid" food comes at "Maserati" prices, and service can be "condescending", but at least the food and the staff are "very attractive."

	FOOD	DECOR	SERVICE	COST
Sambuca *Italian*	20	16	19	$38

W 70s | 20 W. 72nd St. (bet. Columbus Ave. & CPW) | 212-787-5656 | www.sambucanyc.com

"Old-style" Southern Italian food arrives "by the truckload" at this "affordable", "family-style" UWS joint that phrasemakers dub "Carmine's without the tourists"; other bonuses include an "excellent" gluten-free menu and a "smiling" staff that's "tolerant of pediatric diners."

	FOOD	DECOR	SERVICE	COST
Sammy's Roumanian *Jewish*	20	10	18	$56

LES | 157 Chrystie St. (Delancey St.) | 212-673-0330

Literally "not for the faint of heart" – unless "vodka dissolves cholesterol" – this "only-in-NY" LES "schmaltz palace" dishes out "traditional" Jewish cooking to a "crazy", bar mitzvah-style crowd alternately "singing and plotzing"; sure, it's a "corny" "Catskills throwback", but *oy vey*, it's "a hoot" at least "once in a lifetime" – which may be all you can handle.

	FOOD	DECOR	SERVICE	COST
Sandro's ⬤ *Italian*	25	15	20	$59

E 80s | 306 E. 81st St. (bet. 1st & 2nd Aves.) | 212-288-7374

An "artist in the kitchen" (and a "real character" in the dining room), longtime chef Sandro Fioriti offers "heavenly" Roman fare full of "flavors as expansive as he is" at his eponymous UES trattoria; fans say he "deserves a better space", skeptics counter "beware the pricey specials."

	FOOD	DECOR	SERVICE	COST
NEW **San Marzano** ⬤ *Pizza*	-	-	-	I

LES | 71 Clinton St. (Rivington St.) | 212-228-5060 | www.smarzano.com
It's all about the petite pizzas and giant calzones at this new, low-budget LES pie palace famed for a wood-fired brick oven that cooks

most dishes in under two minutes; slightly upscale decor helps distinguish it from the pack, ditto the namesake imported tomatoes.

☑ San Pietro ☒ *Italian*   26 | 22 | 25 | $82

E 50s | 18 E. 54th St. (bet. 5th & Madison Aves.) | 212-753-9015 | www.sanpietro.net

Cover subjects for "*Forbes* and the *WSJ*" do lunch at this Midtown "CEO" magnet where "first-rate" Italiana is ferried by "class-act" staffers "falling over themselves" to please; come suppertime, it's "quieter", though at any time of day, expect to "pay like a power broker."

Sant Ambroeus *Italian*   22 | 20 | 20 | $60

E 70s | 1000 Madison Ave. (bet. 77th & 78th Sts.) | 212-570-2211
W Village | 259 W. Fourth St. (Perry St.) | 212-604-9254
www.santambroeus.com

"Rubbing elbows with celebs" and the "ladies who lunch" comes with the territory at these "ever sceney" Italians whose "gorgeous" Milanese offerings are ferried by a "congenial" crew; "casually luxurious" decor and a "*ciao-bella*" mood make the checks easier to digest.

Sapori D'Ischia ☒ *Italian*   24 | 15 | 19 | $49

Woodside | 55-15 37th Ave. (56th St.) | Queens | 718-446-1500

"Hidden among the warehouses" of Woodside, this "destination hideaway" transforms nightly from an "Italian gourmet market" to a "rustic" Neapolitan eatery offering "imaginative" dishes; it's a "unique concept", with "live opera" singers on Thursday "adding to the delight."

Sapphire Indian *Indian*   21 | 18 | 19 | $42

W 60s | 1845 Broadway (bet. 60th & 61st Sts.) | 212-245-4444 | www.sapphireny.com

"Upmarket" Indian dining comes in a "genteel" setting at this "appealing" Upper Westsider convenient to both Lincoln Center and Columbus Circle; though the "top-notch" regional cuisine may be "on the expensive side" for the genre, the $14 lunch buffet is a "savory bargain."

Sapporo East ● *Japanese*   ∇ 18 | 9 | 15 | $27

E Village | 164 First Ave. (10th St.) | 212-260-1330

"Still going strong", this "rock-steady" East Village Japanese has been churning out "no-frills sushi" and "authentic ramen" since 1982; regulars report prime-time "long lines" despite "nonexistent" decor and service.

Sarabeth's *American*   20 | 17 | 18 | $36

Chelsea | Chelsea Mkt. | 75 Ninth Ave. (bet. 15th & 16th Sts.) | 212-989-2424 | www.sarabeth.com
E 70s | Whitney Museum | 945 Madison Ave. (75th St.) | 212-570-3670 | www.sarabeth.com ☒
E 90s | 1295 Madison Ave. (bet. 92nd & 93rd Sts.) | 212-410-7335 | www.sarabeth.com
NEW Garment District | Lord & Taylor | 424 Fifth Ave., 5th fl. (bet. 38th & 39th Sts.) | 212-391-3344 | www.sarabeth.com
W 50s | 40 Central Park S. (bet. 5th & 6th Aves.) | 212-826-5959 | www.sarabethscps.com
W 80s | 423 Amsterdam Ave. (bet. 80th & 81st Sts.) | 212-496-6280 | www.sarabeth.com

"Good old American comfort food" served in "tearoom" settings speaks to the "girls meeting for lunch" at this "preppy" mini-chain; it can be "crazy busy" for breakfast and brunch, when the "spread-thin" service adds to the "daunting waits", but gets markedly "quieter at dinner."

NEW Saraghina ⇗ Pizza

-	-	-	M

Bed-Stuy | 435 Halsey St. (Lewis Ave.) | Brooklyn | 718-574-0010
With a charmingly rustic space, this cash-only BYO pizzeria looks like it's been in Bed-Stuy forever, but it's actually a recent entry into the late-'00s Great Neapolitan Pizza Wars; topping options are scant, if classic, but daily seafood specials help round out the menu.

Saravanaas Indian

24	10	13	$22

Murray Hill | 81 Lexington Ave. (26th St.) | 212-679-0204
"Delicious dosas" and other "straight-ahead" vegetarian dishes fill out the menu of this Murray Hill Indian offering "a breather" from the standard "curry this-and-that"; "good-value" pricing makes the "brusque service" and "fluorescent-lit", "bare-bones" setting more bearable.

Sardi's Ⓜ Continental

18	22	20	$55

W 40s | 234 W. 44th St. (bet. B'way & 8th Ave.) | 212-221-8440 | www.sardis.com
"Showbiz caricatures" on the walls meet "showbiz characters" in the seats at this Theater District "chuck wagon to the stars" since 1921, where the Continental food "could be better" and waiters are "straight out of central casting"; snobs say it's a "shell of its former self" but fans still "love it if only for the history."

Sarge's Deli ◐ Deli

20	9	16	$26

Murray Hill | 548 Third Ave. (bet. 36th & 37th Sts.) | 212-679-0442
On the Murray Hill scene since 1964, this "down 'n' dirty" deli doles out the obligatory "overstuffed sandwiches" on a 24/7 basis; the "decor hasn't aged well" and "service is indifferent on a good day", but the eats are "worth every clogged artery" and at least the "prices won't kill you."

Ⓩ Sasabune ⓈⓂ Japanese

28	11	22	$95

E 70s | 401 E. 73rd St. (bet. 1st & York Aves.) | 212-249-8583
It's "omakase only" at Kenji Takahashi's UES Japanese "temple" where "go-with-the-flow" types eat "whatever the chef says", with "pristine", "dreamy" results; sushi fanatics find the experience is so "life-changing" that the "tiny" setting and prime pricing don't detract.

Saul American

26	19	24	$65

Boerum Hill | 140 Smith St. (bet. Bergen & Dean Sts.) | Brooklyn | 718-935-9844 | www.saulrestaurant.com
There's a "real buzz" in the air at Saul Bolton's "classy" Boerum Hill New American where the "sublime fine dining" includes "seriously good" food matched with "impeccable" service; maximalists wish the "understated" storefront space had "more character" and penny-pinchers cite "Manhattan prices", but overall this one's a "real winner."

Savann French/Mediterranean

21	15	20	$41

W 70s | 414 Amsterdam Ave. (bet. 79th & 80th Sts.) | 212-580-0202 | www.savann.com
"Civilized" says it all about this "low-key" UWS French-Med stalwart set in a "blessedly quiet room" where you can actually "hear others talking to you"; given the "satisfying" chow, "good value" and "attentive" service, many feel it's "never as crowded as it deserves to be."

	FOOD	DECOR	SERVICE	COST

Savoia *Pizza* — 21 | 18 | 20 | $35

Carroll Gardens | 277 Smith St. (bet. Degraw & Sackett Sts.) | Brooklyn | 718-797-2727

"Fancy" Neapolitan-style pizza straight out of a "wood-burning oven" is the thing to order at this "casual" Carroll Gardens Italian; "low tabs", service that's "there when needed" and "sidewalk tables" offering "good people-watching" make it a bona fide "neighborhood standby."

SavorNY ☒ *Eclectic* — ▽ 20 | 18 | 21 | $40

LES | 63 Clinton St. (bet. Rivington & Stanton Sts.) | 212-358-7125 | www.savornyrestaurant.com

"Small plates" with "big tastes" sum up this under-the-radar LES Eclectic turning out tapas-style dishes from "all over the world" paired with "reasonably priced wines"; an air of "genuine hospitality" warms the ultra-"intimate", 26-seat setting.

Savoy *American/Mediterranean* — 24 | 20 | 22 | $61

SoHo | 70 Prince St. (Crosby St.) | 212-219-8570 | www.savoynyc.com

"Greenmarket cuisine pioneer" Peter Hoffman crafts "memorable" Med-New American meals from the "freshest local produce" at this "original" SoHo duplex, now in its 20th year; a "crackerjack staff" and dual fireplaces keep the mood "warm", but for all-out "romance", lovebirds flock "upstairs."

NEW Sazon *Puerto Rican* — - | - | - | M

TriBeCa | 105 Reade St. (bet. Church St. & W. B'way) | 212-406-1900 | www.sazonnyc.com

Bringing Puerto Rican vittles to TriBeCa, this Sofrito sibling occupies a vividly painted bi-level setting with a bar area nearly as big as its dining room; the dance lounge downstairs suggests that its focus may be as much about meeting as eating.

Scaletta *Italian* — 22 | 20 | 23 | $54

W 70s | 50 W. 77th St. (bet. Columbus Ave. & CPW) | 212-769-9191 | www.scalettaristorante.com

"Soft lighting" sets the "decorous" tone at this longtime UWS Northern Italian where the "old-world" cooking is on par with the "courteous" service; its "sophisticated", "mature" clientele touts its "generous table spacing" and sound level perfect for "quiet conversation."

☒ Scalinatella ● *Italian* — 26 | 18 | 22 | $83

E 60s | 201 E. 61st St., downstairs (3rd Ave.) | 212-207-8280

Set in a "cavelike" Upper East Side basement, this "cozy" Italian is known for its "outstanding" Capri-style cuisine and soigné, "moneyed" crowd; while service may be debatable, there's agreement on the "steep" tabs - especially the "unpriced specials" that may leave the uninitiated "very surprised."

☒ Scalini Fedeli ☒ *Italian* — 26 | 24 | 25 | $87

TriBeCa | 165 Duane St. (bet. Greenwich & Hudson Sts.) | 212-528-0400 | www.scalinifedeli.com

Located in the "beautiful", "barrel-vaulted" space that housed the original Bouley, this TriBeCa Northern Italian from chef Michael Cetrulo provides "excellent" food and "pro service"; "expensive", yes, but "for a terrific meal it's absolutely worth it"; "le scalini che ti porto al cielo."

	FOOD	DECOR	SERVICE	COST

Scalino *Italian* ▽ 24 | 13 | 23 | $38

Park Slope | 347 Seventh Ave. (10th St.) | Brooklyn | 718-840-5738
The space is "small", but the quality's "high" at this "unassuming"
Park Slope Italian offering a "limited menu" of "hearty country" cooking; aside from a "chalkboard menu", there's "zero decor" in the
"spare" setting, but "great value" and "concerned" service make up for it.

Scarlatto ● *Italian* 21 | 18 | 20 | $47

W 40s | 250 W. 47th St. (bet. B'way & 8th Ave.) | 212-730-4535 |
www.scarlattonyc.com
A "well-oiled" machine in the "heart of the Theater District", this
"popular" Northern Italian offers "pleasing", "fairly priced" meals and
"steady-hand", show-sensitive service; the "pretty" space (adorned
with *Roman Holiday* film stills) is "often noisy", so insiders avoid the
"chaos" and "dine upstairs."

☒ Scarpetta *Italian* 26 | 22 | 23 | $71

Chelsea | 355 W. 14th St. (bet. 8th & 9th Aves.) | 212-691-0555 |
www.scarpettanyc.com
Even "jaded NYers" get "weak in the knees" over the "transcendent"
Italian cooking at Scott Conant's "wonder on 14th Street", where his
signature spaghetti can "transport you to Rome a lot faster than Alitalia";
expect suitably "airborne" pricing, a "stylish", "skylit" setting and,
naturally, "hard-to-get" reservations.

Schiller's ● *Eclectic* 18 | 19 | 17 | $40

LES | 131 Rivington St. (Norfolk St.) | 212-260-4555 | www.schillersny.com
Keith McNally's "gritty cousin" to Pastis, Balthazar and Minetta
Tavern, this "zippy" LES Eclectic dispenses "simple food done well" to
"hip" young types in a "vintage" bistro setting oozing "funky charm"
(check out that "coed bathroom"); sure, things can get "chaotic", but
few care since the "price is right."

ᴺᴱᵂ Schnipper's Quality Kitchen ☒ *American* ▽ 17 | 14 | 16 | $18

W 40s | NY Times Bldg. | 620 Eighth Ave. (41st St.) | 212-921-2400 |
www.schnippers.com
This "diner-type" "fast-food joint" in the new NY Times building looks
like a "bright, shiny" "Topeka bus station" and dishes out a "comfort-
food-galore" American menu; glass walls make it easy to "watch the
passing parade" to and from the Port Authority across the street.

Scottadito Osteria Toscana *Italian* ▽ 20 | 18 | 18 | $36

Park Slope | 788A Union St. (bet. 6th & 7th Aves.) | Brooklyn | 718-636-4800
Credit "hearty" Tuscan cooking, a "charming farmhouse" setting and
"welcoming" service for the "pleasant all-around experience" at this
Park Slope Italian; the "top-quality brunch" is a neighborhood "favorite", while relatively "low prices" and a bonus fireplace ice the cake.

ᴺᴱᵂ Scuderia ● *Italian* ▽ 18 | 17 | 16 | $45

G Village | 257 Sixth Ave. (bet. Bleecker & Houston Sts.) | 212-206-9111 |
www.scuderianyc.com
Spun off from Village hot spot Da Silvano across the street, this more
affordable new Italian is overseen by Silvano Marchetto's daughter
and offers "casual" eats in "cool" digs decorated with "classic rock al-

	FOOD	DECOR	SERVICE	COST

"bum covers"; "stingy" portions and "mediocre" service don't faze the "sceney" crowd having "one big party."

SEA *Thai* `22` `23` `18` `$27`

E Village | 75 Second Ave. (bet. 4th & 5th Sts.) | 212-228-5505
NEW Meatpacking | 835 Washington St. (Little W. 12th St.) | 212-243-3339 ●
Williamsburg | 114 N. Sixth St. (Berry St.) | Brooklyn | 718-384-8850 | www.seathairestaurant.com ●

"Sinus-clearing" chow "comes out fast and hot" at this "trendy Thai" trio touted for their terrifically "low prices"; the "tiny" East Village original is less "clublike" than the "huge", "kick-ass" Williamsburg branch or the "happening" new Meatpacking outpost, both complete with "thumping music", "indoor ponds" and "giant Buddhas."

Sea Grill ☒ *Seafood* `24` `24` `23` `$68`

W 40s | Rockefeller Ctr. | 19 W. 49th St. (bet. 5th & 6th Aves.) | 212-332-7610 | www.theseagrillnyc.com

Never mind that it's "tourist central", you'll find "first-rate" seafood and "impeccable service" at this "elegant" Rock Center "room with a view"; indeed, a "window table" overlooking the "beautiful Christmas tree" and "falling skaters on the ice rink" will make up for what you'll be spending.

NEW Seasonal ● *Austrian* ∇ `25` `21` `23` `$64`

W 50s | 132 W. 58th St. (bet. 6th & 7th Aves.) | 212-957-5550 | www.seasonalnyc.com

"Inventive takes" on Austrian food are yours at this "understated" new Midtown boîte with "high standards" and more than a few "modern twists"; "novel wines" and "fit-for-a-king" service explain the "big" price tags, though bargain-hunters say the $64 tasting menu is a "no-brainer."

2nd Ave Deli ● *Deli* `22` `12` `16` `$28`

Murray Hill | 162 E. 33rd St. (bet. Lexington & 3rd Aves.) | 212-689-9000 | www.2ndavedeli.com

It "ain't on Second Avenue" anymore, but this "busy" Murray Hill "re-creation" of the "legendary" East Village original lures longtime loyalists with its "towering", "overstuffed" sandwiches and other Jewish noshes; deli decor (i.e. not much), "high prices" and "surly" waiters don't make a dent in the "long lines"; N.B. an UES spin-off is in the works.

NEW Sel de Mer ●♥ *Mediterranean/Seafood* `–` `–` `–` `M`

Williamsburg | 374 Graham Ave. (bet. Conselyea St. & Skillman Ave.) | Brooklyn | 718-387-4181

An eclectic approach to seafood – think mussels Roquefort and fish-cake sliders – informs the Mediterranean menu of this young salt in Williamsburg that also acknowledges landlubbers with T-bone steaks and burgers; pricing is as modest as the decor, a mix of pressed tin wainscoting and brown paper–tablecloths.

Seo *Japanese* ∇ `24` `18` `21` `$50`

E 40s | 249 E. 49th St. (bet. 2nd & 3rd Aves.) | 212-355-7722

Giving its Japanese rivals "a run for their money", this "hidden" Midtowner near the U.N. offers an "international" crowd "exquisite" cooked dishes and "excellent traditional sushi"; the "bland" interior is offset by "good value" and a back room overlooking a "Zen-like" garden.

	FOOD	DECOR	SERVICE	COST

Serafina ● *Italian*

| | 18 | 16 | 16 | $42 |

E 50s | 38 E. 58th St. (bet. Madison & Park Aves.) | 212-832-8888 🖂
E 60s | 29 E. 61st St. (bet. Madison & Park Aves.) | 212-702-9898
E 70s | 1022 Madison Ave., 2nd fl. (79th St.) | 212-734-2676
W 40s | Time Hotel | 224. W. 49th St. (bet. B'way & 8th Ave.) |
212-247-1000
W 50s | Dream Hotel | 210 W. 55th St. (B'way) | 212-315-1700
www.serafinarestaurant.com

"Upbeat" Italians dispensing "better-than-average" eats (think "designer pizzas" and salads) with a "side order of packed and noisy"; they're "chic" and "affordable", so long as you can stomach "indifferent" service and a crowd of people far prettier than you.

Serendipity 3 ● *Dessert*

| | 18 | 19 | 15 | $31 |

E 60s | 225 E. 60th St. (bet. 2nd & 3rd Aves.) | 212-838-3531 |
www.serendipity3.com

"Everest-like sundaes" and other "sumptuous desserts" supply the "brain freeze" at this "sugary" East Side ice cream parlor–cum–gift shop–cum–playland; sure, it's "knee-deep with kids" and "tourists", the waits can be "ridiculous" and the staff "surly", but that's all forgiven once its "legendary" frozen hot chocolate and way-long hot dogs arrive.

Sette *Italian*

| | ∇ 20 | 19 | 20 | $37 |

Park Slope | 207 Seventh Ave. (3rd St.) | Brooklyn | 718-499-7767 |
www.setteparkslope.com

"Pleasant" says it all about this "low-lit" Park Slope Italian with a rustic seasonal menu that's "dependably good", ditto the "enthusiastic" service; "nifty values" and an "all-seasons" tented patio complete the "enjoyable" picture.

Sette Mezzo ⊖ *Italian*

| | 22 | 16 | 20 | $68 |

E 70s | 969 Lexington Ave. (bet. 70th & 71st Sts.) | 212-472-0400

It's "very social" at this UES Italian "neighborhood place – if your neighborhood is Park Avenue" – where regulars have "charge accounts" and outsiders pay cash; "solid" food, "money-is-no-object" pricing and a "private-club" feel come with the territory; N.B. a post-Survey renovation puts its Decor score in question.

Seven 🖂 *American*

| | 19 | 17 | 18 | $45 |

Chelsea | 350 Seventh Ave. (bet. 29th & 30th Sts.) | 212-967-1919 |
www.sevenbarandgrill.com

"Better-than-average" New Americana is served for "average" sums at this "crowded" nexus in the restaurant "no-man's-land" around MSG and Penn Station; the "bar controls the scene" here, so regulars in the mood for conversation "eat upstairs" where it's "less noisy."

718 *French*

| | 21 | 20 | 20 | $40 |

Astoria | 35-01 Ditmars Blvd. (35th St.) | Queens | 718-204-5553 |
www.718restaurant.com

"Sophisticated enough to be called 212", this "intimate" Astoria "favorite" keeps the locals coming with its "chic" "Euro" vibe and "wonderful" French food with "Spanish flair"; there are grumbles about "high prices" "for Queens", but "attentive" service and a "killer" weekend brunch deal add value.

	FOOD	DECOR	SERVICE	COST

Sevilla ● *Spanish*
22 | 15 | 21 | $40

W Village | 62 Charles St. (W. 4th St.) | 212-929-3189 |
www.sevillarestaurantandbar.com

"Garlic and sangria" collide at this "old-as-the-hills" Village "paella palace" where the "hearty" Spanish cooking and "dangerous" wine punches have "withstood the test of time" for nearly 70 years; maybe the decor could use a "spiff up", but the "old-school" service is fine as is.

Sezz Medi' *Mediterranean/Pizza*
20 | 15 | 17 | $33

W 100s | 1260 Amsterdam Ave. (122nd St.) | 212-932-2901 |
www.sezzmedi.com

A "giant wood-fired oven" churns out "crisp" thin-crust pizza and "solid" roasted items at this Morningside Heights Med; "prompt" service and Columbia student-friendly prices please fans, who bypass the "nondescript" interior in favor of the "street terrace" seating.

Sfoglia *Italian*
25 | 19 | 22 | $63

E 90s | 1402 Lexington Ave. (92nd St.) | 212-831-1402 |
www.sfogliarestaurant.com

"High class but low-key", this Carnegie Hill Italian enjoys a "cultlike following" of "neighborhood" types and "92nd Street Y" attendees; the "distinctive" food is "simply scrumptious", the setting "shabby-chic" and the service "well informed" – so despite "stiff" tabs, "landing a reservation here is like winning Lotto."

Shabu-Shabu 70 *Japanese*
21 | 13 | 20 | $42

E 70s | 314 E. 70th St. (bet. 1st & 2nd Aves.) | 212-861-5635

Cook-it-yourself types tout the "authentic" eponymous dish at this "been-around-forever" UES Japanese that also vends "simple", "fresh" sushi; it's "well priced" and the staff is "friendly", so "loyal regulars" willingly overlook the "shabby-shabby" surroundings.

Shabu-Tatsu *Japanese*
23 | 13 | 18 | $37

E Village | 216 E. 10th St. (bet. 1st & 2nd Aves.) | 212-477-2972

It's alright to "play with your food" at this "tiny" East Village Japanese shabu-shabu/sukiyaki specialist where "hands-on" cooks do it themselves in hot pots or on the BBQ grill; though the "tight" interior is "devoid of charm", the tabs are "cheap" and it's "fun for the whole gang."

ⓏShake Shack *Burgers*
23 | 12 | 14 | $15

Flatiron | Madison Square Park | 23rd St. (Madison Ave.) | 212-889-6600
NEW **W 70s** | 366 Columbus Ave. (77th St.) | 646-747-8770
NEW **Flushing** | Citi Field | 126th St. & Roosevelt Ave. | Queens
www.shakeshack.com

"Fast food has become slow food" at this counter-service mini-chain that has "converted impatient NYers into Zen, line-loving foodies" eager to sample those "good-value" gourmet burgers and St. Louis frozen custards; the Flatiron original is alfresco, the UWS version has indoor seats and the Citi Field outpost is a window behind the scoreboard.

Shalizar ● *Persian*
▽ 21 | 19 | 21 | $35

E 80s | 1420 Third Ave. (bet. 80th & 81st Sts.) | 212-288-0012 |
www.shalizarnyc.com

A "bit more upscale" than its nearby sibling, Persepolis, this "authentic" UES yearling presents Persian fare with a "tasty zing" served in a "peaceful", brick-walled setting; "sweet" service and "modest" prices add to the "quality" feel, but be careful – those pomegranate mojitos can become a "vice."

NEW Shang Chinese
23 | 22 | 21 | $67

LES | Thompson LES Hotel | 187 Orchard St. (bet. Houston & Stanton Sts.) | 212-260-7900 | www.shangrestaurant.com
"Toronto wunderkind" Susur Lee makes his NYC debut at this "chic" LES newcomer where the "revelatory" Chinese fusion dishes (like the signature "zillion-ingredient" Singapore slaw) are meant to be shared – and charged to an "expense account"; insiders use the Allen Street "hotel lobby" entrance to avoid the steep staircase on Orchard.

Shanghai Café ⊟ Chinese
∇ 23 | 9 | 11 | $18

Little Italy | 100 Mott St. (bet. Canal & Hester Sts.) | 212-966-3988
The soup dumplings are a "sheer delight" at this "no-frills" Little Italy Chinese that churns them out "fast" and "cheap", along with other Shanghainese eats; a "helter-skelter" vibe and a staff that seemingly "can't wait for you to leave" are the downsides.

Shanghai Pavilion Chinese
22 | 17 | 20 | $40

E 70s | 1378 Third Ave. (bet. 78th & 79th Sts.) | 212-585-3388
"Tranquil" and "civilized", this Upper East Side Chinese "sleeper" purveys "fine-quality" Shanghai-style eats that are "as good as C-town" at "affordable" rates; amazingly, it's "more than a cut above the norm on the decor front" and the staffers "don't throw the food at you – they serve it."

Sharz Cafe & Wine Bar Mediterranean
20 | 14 | 19 | $43

E 80s | 435 E. 86th St. (bet. 1st & York Aves.) | 212-876-7282
"Unassuming" and "relaxed", this "low-volume" Yorkville Med is a bona fide "neighborhood hangout" with "zesty" cooking and an "extensive" wine list; sure, the dimensions are "tight" and the decor tends to be "dreary", but "mom-and-pop pricing" saves the day.

Sheep Station ◑⊟ Australian
∇ 18 | 16 | 17 | $28

Park Slope | 149 Fourth Ave. (Douglass St.) | Brooklyn | 718-857-4337 | www.sheepstation.net
There's a "touch of cool" to this "casual" Park Slope Australian where "expats" and "burly rugby guys" tuck into "quality bar food" and chug kiwi brews; with its corrugated-tin decor, "happy" staffers and "inexpensive", "cash-only" tabs, habitués "never want to leave."

Shelly's New York ◑ ⊠ Italian
∇ 19 | 19 | 19 | $55

W 50s | 41 W. 57th St. (bet. 5th & 6th Aves.) | 212-245-2422 | www.shellysnewyork.com
Though it's best known for "very fresh seafood", Shelly Fireman's Midtown Italian also serves "satisfying" pastas in an "attractive" triplex setting; devotees wish the menu weren't "always changing", but allow it works well for a "client lunch" or "pre-Carnegie Hall."

Shorty's ◑ Cheesesteaks
∇ 22 | 9 | 15 | $18

W 40s | 576 Ninth Ave. (bet. 41st & 42nd Sts.) | 212-967-3055 | www.shortysnyc.com
"Heavenly cheesesteaks" arrive with a little "Philly attitude" at this "raucous" spot behind the Port Authority whose low-budget fixin's are

"shipped in daily from the homeland"; the "frat-house" setting is often so "noisy and crowded" that it's hard to hear the "sound of your arteries slamming shut."

Shorty's.32 *American* | 23 | 17 | 22 | $49 |

SoHo | 199 Prince St. (bet. MacDougal & Sullivan Sts.) | 212-375-8275 | www.shortys32.com

"Long on flavor" if short on space, this SoHo 32-seater packs them in with "top-notch" American comfort food at a "good price"; the "no-reservations" policy makes for prime-time queues, so regulars "go early" or join the off-duty "chefs and night owls" after hours.

NEW SHO Shaun Hergatt ⑤ *French* | ▽ 29 | 29 | 29 | $95 |

Financial District | 40 Broad St., 2nd fl. (Exchange Pl.) | 212-809-3993 | www.shoshaunhergatt.com

Luxury dining is alive and well at this "spectacular", "sprawling" new Financial District space whose main room overlooks a "glass-walled open kitchen"; the few voters who have sampled chef Shaun Hergatt's "superb" Asian-accented French cooking report it sho is pricey (dinner is prix fixe only), but if money *is* an object, there are breakfast and lunch options as well.

Shula's Steak House *Steak* | 21 | 19 | 20 | $70 |

W 40s | Westin Times Sq. Hotel | 270 W. 43rd St. (bet. B'way & 8th Ave.) | 212-201-2776 | www.donshula.com

Coach Don Shula's "quiet" Times Square steakhouse plates "pricey", "flavorful" cuts in "linebacker"-size portions amid a collection of Miami Dolphins memorabilia; still, referees rule it "second string", noting that the "gimmicky menu-on-a-pigskin" "works in Peoria, not NY."

Shun Lee Cafe ❷ *Chinese* | 21 | 17 | 19 | $42 |

W 60s | 43 W. 65th St. (bet. Columbus Ave. & CPW) | 212-769-3888 | www.shunleewest.com

Often a "first act" for Lincoln Center-goers, this "venerable" Upper West Side Chinese provides "tasty" vittles and "perfectly prepared dim sum" via "speedy" staffers; "modest" rates make it a "savvy alternative" to its pricier "brother next door", provided you can overlook the checkerboard decor.

Shun Lee Palace ❷ *Chinese* | 23 | 20 | 22 | $57 |

E 50s | 155 E. 55th St. (bet. Lexington & 3rd Aves.) | 212-371-8844 | www.shunleepalace.com

Michael Tong has "been doing it right for decades" at this "posh", circa-1971 Midtown Chinese where the "high-quality" cuisine is "served with style" by "waiters in tuxedos"; the "fancy", "white-tablecloth" decor hints at the "premium" prices, but then again, "you get what you pay for" – and then some here.

Shun Lee West ❷ *Chinese* | 22 | 21 | 21 | $55 |

W 60s | 43 W. 65th St. (bet. Columbus Ave. & CPW) | 212-595-8895 | www.shunleewest.com

Chinese dining doesn't get fancier than at this "polished" Lincoln Center-area "benchmark" known for "marvelous" meals and "invisible" "white-glove service"; the "dramatic", black-lacquer-and-gold-dragon decor remains an "iconic" backdrop to this "first-rate" experience.

	FOOD	DECOR	SERVICE	COST

Siam Square 🅜 *Thai*
▽ 23 | 17 | 22 | $35

Bronx | 564 Kappock St. (Henry Hudson Pkwy.) | 718-432-8200 |
www.siamsq.com

A "step up from the usual", this "neighborhood" Riverdale Thai in an "unlikely location" offers "delicious" food; forget the "dingy exterior": inside, you'll find a "relaxing atmosphere" and "well-below-Manhattan prices."

NEW Sinigual *Mexican*
▽ 22 | 21 | 20 | $44

E 40s | 640 Third Ave. (41st St.) | 212-286-0250 |
www.sinigualrestaurants.com

"Tropical" atmospherics set an exotic tone at this "spacious" newcomer near Grand Central serving an "upscale" yet midpriced "contemporary" Mexican menu; "solicitous service" makes it "conducive to business lunches", while "expertly made drinks" fuel the "after-work" scene.

Sip Sak *Turkish*
19 | 12 | 16 | $33

E 40s | 928 Second Ave. (bet. 49th & 50th Sts.) | 212-583-1900 |
www.sip-sak.com

Despite the "strange name", this U.N.-area Turk has a "well-deserved following" thanks to its "knock-your-fez-off" mezes and other "Istanbul"-quality standards; fans don't mind the "ordinary" ambiance and "brusque owner – the "economical" tabs are that good.

🇿 Sistina *Italian*
26 | 20 | 24 | $78

E 80s | 1555 Second Ave. (bet. 80th & 81st Sts.) | 212-861-7660

Seemingly an "UES neighbors' secret", this Northern Italian "standout" deserves to be better known given its "absolutely delicious", "authentic" cuisine, extensive wine cellar and "personal", "attentive" service presided over by owner Giuseppe Bruno; sure, it's on the "expensive" side but those "unbelievable specials" are worth it.

67 Burger *Burgers*
21 | 12 | 16 | $18

Fort Greene | 67 Lafayette Ave. (Fulton St.) | Brooklyn | 718-797-7150 |
www.67burger.com

Fort Greene's "nice little" burger joint proffers "juicy" patties, fries in "huge portions" and above-average "tap beers"; the "futuristic-McDonald's" decor is "basic" and the "cafeteria-style" ordering gets chaotic, but a BAM-rrific location makes it a "flippin' winner."

S'MAC *American*
21 | 10 | 14 | $16

E Village | 345 E. 12th St. (bet. 1st & 2nd Aves.) | 212-358-7912 |
www.smacnyc.com
Pinch & S'MAC *American/Pizza*
W 80s | 474 Columbus Ave. (bet. 82nd & 83rd Sts.) | 212-686-5222 |
www.pinchandsmac.com

"Gooey" and "gimmicky", this East Village mac 'n' cheese specialist cranks out a "dizzying number" of "clever" variations (even "gluten free"), all for "affordable" dough; the UWS outpost adds burgers, fries and "pizza by the inch" to the "habit-forming" mix.

NEW Smile, The *Mediterranean*
- | - | - | I

NoHo | 26 Bond St., downstairs (bet. Bowery & Lafayette St.) | 646-329-5836 |
www.thesmilenyc.com

A multitasker's delight, this new NoHo underground cafe/general store serves a limited Mediterranean menu of salads and sandwiches in rustic digs heavy on reclaimed wood and Edison light bulbs; the sundries for sale range from clothing to candles, but the pièce de résistance is an on-premises tattoo parlor for those who really want to remember the experience.

Smith, The ● *Pub Food*

| 19 | 16 | 18 | $35 |

E Village | 55 Third Ave. (bet. 10th & 11th Sts.) | 212-420-9800 | www.thesmithnyc.com

"Boisterous" is putting it mildly at this "college-oriented" East Villager that's a "trendy" magnet for the "under-30" set who tout its "upscale" American pub grub and "recession-buster" tabs; "impossible crowds" and "curt service" don't dampen the overall "cheerful" mood.

Smith & Wollensky *Steak*

| 23 | 19 | 21 | $73 |

E 40s | 797 Third Ave. (49th St.) | 212-753-1530 | www.smithandwollensky.com

"Mucho macho" Midtown meathouse "standard-bearer" where "darn good slabs of beef" are served to "power suits" by "chummy", "old-time" waiters; though wags tag it "Smith and Expensky", the "huge" duplex quarters seldom seem to have many empty seats.

Smoke Joint *BBQ*

| 21 | 11 | 15 | $23 |

Fort Greene | 87 S. Elliott Pl. (Lafayette Ave.) | Brooklyn | 718-797-1011 | www.thesmokejoint.com

"Fancy it ain't", but this Fort Greene "hole-in-the-wall" comes across with "tangy", "finger-lickin'" BBQ and "fixin's done right"; it's just the ticket for a "quick", "cheap" fill-up "before BAM", though the new bar "extension" may have "overstretched the service" a bit.

Smorgas Chef *Scandinavian*

| 18 | 14 | 17 | $36 |

Financial District | 53 Stone St. (William St.) | 212-422-3500
NEW **Murray Hill** | Scandinavia Hse. | 58 Park Ave. (bet. 37th & 38th Sts.) | 212-847-9745
W Village | 283 W. 12th St. (4th St.) | 212-243-7073 ●
www.smorgaschef.com

"Excellent" Swedish meatballs are the lure at this Scandinavian mini-chain where the "interesting" offerings are as "affordable as the Ikea cafeteria" but "more refined"; though "bare-bones" is the general design principle, Stone Street has outdoor seats, while the new Park Avenue outpost sports a live tree.

Snack *Greek*

| 24 | 13 | 19 | $27 |

SoHo | 105 Thompson St. (bet. Prince & Spring Sts.) | 212-925-1040

"Fantastic", "home-cooked" Greek fare "revamped" for modern tastes has crowds wedging into this truly "tiny" SoHo Hellenic that's "perfect for a first date" – if you want to get close fast; given its "excellent" bang for the buck, regulars go "off-peak" to avoid the "interminable waits."

Snack Taverna *Greek*

| 21 | 16 | 19 | $41 |

W Village | 63 Bedford St. (Morton St.) | 212-929-3499

Snack's "busy", "more spacious" offspring set on a "picturesque" West Village corner offers "upmarket", "lick-the-plate-clean" takes on traditional Greek recipes; though the "low-key" setting verges on "non-descript", moderate pricing makes it a "weekday go-to" for locals.

	FOOD	DECOR	SERVICE	COST

Soba Nippon *Noodle Shop*
22 | 17 | 19 | $39

W 50s | 19 W. 52nd St. (bet. 5th & 6th Aves.) | 212-489-2525 |
www.sobanippon.com

"Serious soba" supporters say this "serene" Midtown Japanese takes buckwheat noodles grown on their own farm, then "dresses them up" with "minimal adjustments for Anglo tastes"; the tabs may seem "a little expensive", but not after you factor in the "heavenly quality."

Soba-ya *Noodle Shop*
24 | 16 | 18 | $32

E Village | 229 E. Ninth St. (bet. 2nd & 3rd Aves.) | 212-533-6966 |
www.sobaya-nyc.com

The "tranquil" setting complements the "hits-the-spot" soba "hand cut to perfection" at this East Village noodle shop; it's a no-brainer for a "cheap", heartwarming date, though its "recent college grad customer base" warns of "lines out the door" at prime times.

Socarrat Paella Bar *Spanish*
24 | 17 | 20 | $44

Chelsea | 259 W. 19th St. (bet. 7th & 8th Aves.) | 212-462-1000 |
www.socarratpaellabar.com

In a "league of its own", this "tiny" Chelsea Spaniard approaches "paella perfection" with "amazing" renditions enhanced with bits of crunchy crust "scraped from the pan"; it's "already outgrown" the "cramped" setting (furnished with one "long communal table"), though "bowled-over" fans declare the "long waits" totally worth it.

Sofia ● *Greek*
▽ 23 | 14 | 21 | $37

(fka S'Agapo)

Astoria | 34-21 34th Ave. (35th St.) | Queens | 718-626-0303

"Regional specialties from the isle of Crete" are the thing at this Astoria Greek (formerly known as S'Agapo) where regulars "dress casually and bring a big appetite"; it "doesn't look like much", but "reasonable" tabs and a "homey", "welcoming" vibe make up for it.

Sofrito ● *Puerto Rican*
21 | 19 | 19 | $42

E 50s | 400 E. 57th St. (bet. 1st Ave. & Sutton Pl.) | 212-754-5999 |
www.sofritony.com

"Celebration" central, this "loungey" Sutton Place "hot spot" dispenses "wonderful" Puerto Rican cuisine and "killer mojitos" for "moderate" sums; "dark, sexy" digs distract from the slightly "slow" service, though the "teeth-chattering din" – it's "always someone's birthday" – can be harder to ignore.

NEW Sojourn ● *Eclectic*
▽ 24 | 21 | 24 | $41

E 70s | 244 E. 79th St. (bet. 2nd & 3rd Aves.) | 212-537-7745 |
www.sojournrestaurant.com

An "inspired" list of Eclectic small plates provides "incredible nibbles" for the "diverse crowd" convening at this UES newcomer; though the vibe is decidedly "downtown cool", a few feel the "cocktail bar" setting and "blaring music" "don't match the high-quality cuisine."

Solera ⌧ *Spanish*
20 | 18 | 21 | $57

E 50s | 216 E. 53rd St. (bet. 2nd & 3rd Aves.) | 212-644-1166 |
www.solerany.com

"Charmingly low-key", this "quiet" Midtown Spaniard is a "steady" source for "upscale" tapas, paella and "tasty" Iberian fare; "old-school" service, "comfortable" environs and a "great sherry selection" help make the "pricey" tabs easier to swallow.

Solo *Mediterranean* ▽ 22 | 22 | 20 | $71

E 50s | 550 Madison Ave. (bet. 55th & 56th Sts.) | 212-833-7800 | www.solonyc.com

Glatt kosher cooking gets an "upscale" spin at this Midtown Med where the "remarkably good" food is on a par with the "cool", modern setting; though you'll need "lots of shekels" to cover the "yikes"-inducing bill, the faithful still dub it the "non-dairy cream of the crop."

Son Cubano *Cuban* 21 | 20 | 17 | $47

Meatpacking | 405 W. 14th St. (bet. 9th Ave. & Washington St.) | 212-366-1640 | www.soncubanonyc.com

Brace yourself for *"la vida loca"* at this "clubby" Meatpacking District Cuban where "gorgeous young" things nibble on "authentically spicy" chow and swill "powerful" mojitos; "sign language" is the usual mode of communication given the "earsplitting decibels."

Song ⭙ *Thai* 23 | 16 | 18 | $24

Park Slope | 295 Fifth Ave. (bet. 1st & 2nd Sts.) | Brooklyn | 718-965-1108

"Delectable" Thai grub at "wonderfully cheap" tabs "packs a punch" at this cash-only Park Sloper, the "nearly identical" sibling of Cobble Hill's Joya with the same "concrete-box" decor and "hurried" service; too bad the noise level is so "close to painful" that many seek refuge in the "calmer" back garden.

NEW Sonia Rose Ⓜ *French* ▽ 21 | 20 | 21 | $40

LES | 74 Orchard St. (bet. Broome & Grand Sts.) | 212-260-5317 | www.soniarosenyc.com

This reincarnation of a former Murray Hill French bistro brings some "intimate charm" to the LES via a "romantic" setting enhanced by "wonderful" cooking and "moderate" pricing (the prix fixes "will steal your heart"); despite solid scores, skeptics still wonder if it will ever "measure up to the original."

Sookk *Thai* ▽ 22 | 18 | 18 | $27

W 100s | 2686 Broadway (bet. 102nd & 103rd Sts.) | 212-870-0253

A "cheerfully decorated" little "candy box" of a place, this "cozy" UWS Thai turns out the kind of "original", "exotic" street eats that you'd find on Bangkok's Yaowarat Road; it's "affordable" and "tasty" enough to be often "booked solid", "awkward service" to the contrary.

NEW Sora Lella ◑ *Italian* ▽ 19 | 18 | 19 | $59

SoHo | 300 Spring St. (bet. Greenwich & Hudson Sts.) | 212-366-4749 | www.soralellanyc.com

Spun off from a famed trattoria in Italy, this "refined" West SoHo newcomer purveys "authentic", old-fashioned Roman cooking in a high-ceilinged, whitewashed-brick setting; pricing is also on the high side, while the "well-intentioned" service is "still finding its footing."

NEW Sorella ◑Ⓜ *Italian* - | - | - | M

LES | 95 Allen St. (bet. Broome & Delancey Sts.) | 212-274-9595 | www.sorellanyc.com

Piedmont comes to the LES at this "charming" new Italian with a "smart menu" of midpriced small plates; the spare, brick-walled digs seem clearly influenced by the Momofuku empire, right down to the communal seating and classic rock soundtrack.

Sosa Borella ● *Argentinean/Italian* | 19 | 17 | 19 | $43 |

W 50s | 832 Eighth Ave. (50th St.) | 212-262-7774 | www.sosaborella.com
Its "delightful blend of Italian and Argentine" dishes makes this "casual", price-sensitive Hell's Kitchen double-decker "different from the usual" Theaterland options; it's expectedly "busy before shows", so insiders drop by after 8 to "schmooze with friends" and loosen up on its "lovely rooftop" deck.

Soto ●☒ *Japanese* | ▽ 28 | 22 | 22 | $85 |

G Village | 357 Sixth Ave. (bet. 4th St. & Washington Pl.) | 212-414-3088
There's "nothing so-so" about Sotohiro Kosugi's "special-occasion" Village Japanese frequented by "independently wealthy" "connoisseurs" seeking "pristine", "work-of-art" sushi and "superbly executed" cooked items; the "serene" mood is only disturbed when the bill arrives.

South Fin Grill *Seafood/Steak* | 19 | 23 | 18 | $52 |

Staten Island | 300 Father Capodanno Blvd. (Sand Ln.) | 718-447-7679 | www.southfingrill.com
"Dazzling views" of the bay and the Verrazano Bridge add to the "true seaside experience" at this "pretty" Staten Island surf 'n' turfer located "right on the boardwalk" in South Beach; maybe the service has "a way to go", but it's still great for a midpriced date.

South Gate *American* | 24 | 25 | 24 | $75 |

W 50s | Jumeirah Essex Hse. | 154 Central Park S. (bet. 6th & 7th Aves.) | 212-484-5120 | www.154southgate.com
Diners are "nothing but impressed" by this CPS New American where chef "Kerry Heffernan is in his element" working "wonders" in an "ultramodern" setting enhanced by "meticulous service"; true, it's "expensive", but "well-heeled" well-wishers say it "deserves a bigger following."

☒ Sparks Steak House ☒ *Steak* | 25 | 20 | 22 | $77 |

E 40s | 210 E. 46th St. (bet. 2nd & 3rd Aves.) | 212-687-4855 | www.sparkssteakhouse.com
Ever at "the apex" of Midtown steakhouses, this longstanding "testosterone fest" matches "to-die-for" chops and sides with an "unbelievable wine list" and good "old-fashioned" service "straight out of Damon Runyon"; it's a bada-"big-time" favorite, but bring along plenty of "cash to burn" and prepare to "cool your heels" before being seated.

Spice *Thai* | 21 | 16 | 17 | $26 |

Chelsea | 199 Eighth Ave. (bet. 19th & 20th Sts.) | 212-989-1116
E 70s | 1411 Second Ave. (bet. 73rd & 74th Sts.) | 212-988-5348
E Village | 104 Second Ave. (6th St.) | 212-533-8900
NEW E Village | 77 E. 10th St. (4th Ave.) | 212-388-9006
NEW G Village | 39 E. 13th St. (bet. B'way & University Pl.) | 212-982-3758
www.spicethainyc.com
"Frugal" folks find this "commercial Thai" quintet a "total deal" for "tasty" (if "predictable") Siamese standards that "don't skimp on the house's namesake"; regulars reckon it's worth abiding the "crowded conditions" and "hit-or-miss service" – "can thousands of NYU students be wrong?"

	FOOD	DECOR	SERVICE	COST

☑ Spice Market ● *SE Asian* | 23 | 26 | 20 | $60 |

Meatpacking | 403 W. 13th St. (9th Ave.) | 212-675-2322 |
www.jean-georges.com

"Taking Southeast Asian street food to a new level", this "spectacular" Meatpacking District duplex demonstrates Jean-Georges Vongerichten's "multifaceted genius"; "excellent family-style" dishes, "sexy" underdressed servers, "delicious fun drinks" and a "spot-cool" setting combine to make this a "great place for a special night with friends or family" – especially in a private room downstairs.

Spicy & Tasty ⇗ *Chinese* | 23 | 10 | 14 | $26 |

Flushing | 39-07 Prince St. (39th Ave.) | Queens | 718-359-1601

"As advertised", the "quality" Sichuan specialties at this Flushing Chinese turn on enough "vibrant" flavor and heat to "make you feel alive"; "plain decor" and "no-nonsense" service may detract, but aficionados aver this is "as authentic as it gets", and tabs are too.

Spiga *Italian* | 23 | 19 | 21 | $50 |

W 80s | 200 W. 84th St. (bet. Amsterdam Ave. & B'way) | 212-362-5506 |
www.spiganyc.com

Fans feel this "small" UWS "neighborhood" Italian "should get more recognition" given its "rich", "intriguing" dishes and "congenial" service; though there's some debate about the price – "reasonable" vs. "expensive" – the "unrushed" pace and "rustic" air are fine as is.

Spigolo *Italian* | 25 | 16 | 23 | $61 |

E 80s | 1561 Second Ave. (81st St.) | 212-744-1100

"Gracious hosts" Scott and Heather Fratangelo display a "magic touch" at their UES "vest-pocket gem", where the Italian cooking is as "superior" as the setting is "minuscule"; while "you can spend a lot really fast here", its "popularity" makes reservations "difficult" – though they're "easier in summer" when sidewalk seating "doubles its size."

Spitzer's Corner ● *American* | 20 | 19 | 18 | $31 |

LES | 101 Rivington St. (Ludlow St.) | 212-228-0027 | www.spitzerscorner.com

A "good-time spot" that corners a "youthful" clientele, this LES gastropub pairs "satiating" New American grub with a "mind-blowing" beer list that's "longer than the menu"; despite "hunting-shack" decor, "picnic-table" seating and "not-great" service, it's "always packed."

Spotted Pig ● *European* | 23 | 18 | 17 | $47 |

W Village | 314 W. 11th St. (Greenwich St.) | 212-620-0393 |
www.thespottedpig.com

"Throngs" of A-listers hog the tables at this "too popular" Village gastropub-cum-"madhouse", all vying for a snoutful of April Bloomfield's "killer" Modern European fare ("gnudi, gnudi, gnudi!"); the "brouhaha" to get in translates into "mind-numbing" waits and strained service, but insiders note there's "virtually no crowd at lunch."

NEW Spunto *Pizza* | ▽ 22 | 12 | 17 | $21 |

G Village | 65 Carmine St. (7th Ave. S.) | 212-242-1200

As a "welcome" addition to the Gruppo/Posto/Vezzo family, this new Village pizzeria honors its roots with "well-executed" "super-thin-crust" pies at "affordable" prices; the brick-walled digs "may not ooze character", but for a spontaneous nosh it's a "no-brainer."

Square Meal ☒ *American* | 23 | 18 | 23 | $49 |

E 90s | 30 E. 92nd St. (bet. 5th & Madison Aves.) | 212-860-9872 | www.squaremealnyc.com

Yura Mohr's "splendid menu" of "imaginative" comfort food squares well with the "neighborly" setting at this "accomplished" Carnegie Hill American; its "mature" following, citing the "warm service" and BYO-friendly policy, doesn't mind that it's "not the trendiest spot" around.

☑ Sripraphai ⇗ *Thai* | 27 | 13 | 16 | $26 |

Woodside | 64-13 39th Ave. (bet. 64th & 65th Sts.) | Queens | 718-899-9599 | www.sripraphairestaurant.com

"Only an epicurean adventure to Bangkok can match a trip" to this "casual", "cash-only" Woodside Siamese boasting reliably "fresh", "flavorful" food for minimal dough; it's again voted Top Thai in this Survey, so you'll need to "get there early to beat the crowds."

Stage Deli ◑ *Deli* | 20 | 10 | 14 | $30 |

W 50s | 834 Seventh Ave. (bet. 53rd & 54th Sts.) | 212-245-7850 | www.stagedeli.com

"Excess is something to be admired" at this "fast-paced" Midtown deli where "ginormous sandwiches", "nonexistent" decor and "grouchy" "old-timer" servers are all part of an ongoing "tradition" since 1937; it's also known for "jowl-to-jowl hordes" of "out-of-towners" who come to learn the difference between the bagel and the lox.

Stamatis ◑ *Greek* | 22 | 12 | 18 | $35 |

Astoria | 29-09 23rd Ave. (bet. 29th & 31st Sts.) | Queens | 718-932-8596

"Traditional Greek" dishes "just like your *yiayia* would make" draw crowds to this "steady" Astoria Hellenic, home to "hearty" "peasant" preparations served at a cost that "can't be beat"; the setting may be "spartan", but "lines form on the weekends" regardless.

Stand ◑ *Burgers* | 19 | 14 | 15 | $22 |

G Village | 24 E. 12th St. (bet. 5th Ave. & University Pl.) | 212-488-5900 | www.standburger.com

"Fun variations" on a "damn good burger" and "heavenly" booze-enhanced shakes make this "high-quality" Villager a standby for NYU types; since it's more than "easy on the wallet", most ignore the "lax" service, "cafeteria" ambiance and "pounding music."

NEW Standard Grill ◑ *American* | ▽ 22 | 24 | 22 | $59 |

Meatpacking | Standard Hotel | 846 Washington St. (bet. Little W. 12th & 13th Sts.) | 212-645-4100 | www.thestandardgrill.com

A "wonderful addition" to the Meatpacking District, this "happening" newcomer offers "excellent" American standards from ex Lever House chef Dan Silverman to a "beautiful" crowd of fashionistas, hotel guests and "High-Liners"; whether you wind up on sidewalk seats along Washington Street, in the "high-volume" front cafe or the more "comfortable" main dining room, you should expect some "commotion."

Stanton Social ◑ *Eclectic* | 23 | 21 | 18 | $53 |

LES | 99 Stanton St. (bet. Ludlow & Orchard Sts.) | 212-995-0099 | www.thestantonsocial.com

"Stylish small plates" suit the "twentysomething" following at this "nightclubish" LES Eclectic where "delish" "finger food" meant to be

	FOOD	DECOR	SERVICE	COST

shared works well with the "*Gossip-Girl*-trendy" scene; "fun drinks" help blot out pricing and acoustics that tend to be "on the high side."

STK *Steak*
| | 21 | 23 | 19 | $76 |

Meatpacking | 26 Little W. 12th St. (bet. 9th Ave. & Washington St.) | 646-624-2444 | www.stkhouse.com

A "true meat market", this "sexy" Meatpacking District chop shop draws "energetic" "party" people with "quality" beef and "strong drinks" served in a "slick", "Vegas nightclub" setting; "hefty prices", "loud" acoustics and "pushy service" to the contrary, it's still "quite the scene."

Stone Park Café *American*
| | 25 | 20 | 22 | $50 |

Park Slope | 324 Fifth Ave. (3rd St.) | Brooklyn | 718-369-0082 | www.stoneparkcafe.com

"Personal care" enhances the "all-around solid" dining at this Park Slope "neighborhood keeper" where an "attentive" crew serves midpriced, "supremely satisfying" New Americana; the "neo-farmhouse" quarters are apt to be "packed", especially during the "scrumptious brunch."

Strip House ● *Steak*
| | 25 | 23 | 22 | $74 |

G Village | 13 E. 12th St. (bet. 5th Ave. & University Pl.) | 212-328-0000 | www.striphouse.com

One part "suave", one part "sultry", this Village chop shop serves "superior steaks" and "heavenly" sides in a "burlesque-show" milieu defined by a "rich red" palette, "low" lighting and naughty "framed pinups"; "top-dollar" tabs and "invariably tardy seating" come with the territory.

Sueños Ⓜ *Mexican*
| | 22 | 18 | 19 | $47 |

Chelsea | 311 W. 17th St. (bet. 8th & 9th Aves.) | 212-243-1333 | www.suenosnyc.com

Chef-owner Sue Torres sure "knows her stuff" as evidenced by this Chelsea "gourmet Mexican" where her "imaginative" cooking is the "real thing" and the service is always "inviting"; tabs can be "a bit pricey", but after a few "fabulous margaritas", no one minds.

Ⓩ Sugiyama ●ⓈⓂ *Japanese*
| | 27 | 20 | 27 | $105 |

W 50s | 251 W. 55th St. (bet. B'way & 8th Ave.) | 212-956-0670 | www.sugiyama-nyc.com

This "pleasant, if basic" West Midtown Japanese is not well enough known given that it's "*the place*" to have a "real kaiseki dinner" in NYC, right down to the time you get the bill; "you'll think you're in Tokyo" while enjoying the "unique", "inventive" multicourse meals turned out by the always amiable Nao Sugiyama.

Superfine Ⓜ *Mediterranean*
| | 20 | 19 | 17 | $33 |

Dumbo | 126 Front St. (bet. Jay & Pearl Sts.) | Brooklyn | 718-243-9005

"Always busy", this "epicenter of the Dumbo community" purveys "fine but not super" Med eats for bargain tabs in a cavernous, "warehouse-chic" setting; just "don't expect much quiet conversation" given the "busy" bar scene, free pool table and Sunday "bluegrass brunch."

Supper ●⌀ *Italian*
| | 24 | 18 | 18 | $37 |

E Village | 156 E. Second St. (bet. Aves. A & B) | 212-477-7600 | www.supperrestaurant.com

"Love goes into every dish" at this "jumping", "cash-only" East Village "rough gem" serving rustic Italian grub (with notably "zesty" pastas) in a

| | FOOD | DECOR | SERVICE | COST |

"communal-seating" setting; "great value" and a "no-reservations" policy keep the "hipsters" lined up on the street.

Surya *Indian* ▽ 21 | 16 | 19 | $37

W Village | 302 Bleecker St. (bet. Grove St. & 7th Ave. S.) | 212-807-7770 | www.suryany.com

"Quiet" and "consistent", this "sophisticated" West Village Indian offers "above-average" contempo cuisine and "novel" drinks; if the "simple, spare" interior doesn't appeal, there's always that "remarkable garden."

SushiAnn 🖫 *Japanese* 25 | 17 | 22 | $67

E 50s | 38 E. 51st St. (bet. Madison & Park Aves.) | 212-755-1780 | www.sushiann.com

Midtown corporate types take "valued clients" to this "steadfast" Japanese for "delicate sushi" that's "very close to what you get in Japan", "served with style" by a "long-tenured staff"; it's always "busy at lunch", despite the "lack of ambiance" and those "big-investment" price tags.

Sushiden *Japanese* 23 | 16 | 21 | $58

E 40s | 19 E. 49th St. (bet. 5th & Madison Aves.) | 212-758-2700
W 40s | 123 W. 49th St. (bet. 6th & 7th Aves.) | 212-398-2800 🖫
www.sushiden.com

"Traditionalists" tout this "intimate" Midtown Japanese twosome for "reliable" sushi that's so "fresh it's almost alive"; the surroundings are "spare" and tabs "can skyrocket", but the nearly "invisible" "soft-spoken", kimono-clad staff may be its most memorable feature.

Sushi Hana ● *Japanese* 20 | 17 | 19 | $37

E 70s | 1501 Second Ave. (78th St.) | 212-327-0582
W 80s | 466 Amsterdam Ave. (bet. 82nd & 83rd Sts.) | 212-874-0369
Handy for "locals", these separately owned Japanese joints slice "generous portions" of "good basic" sushi accompanied by an array of "interesting rolls"; while both are "friendly" and "reasonably priced", the UES site ups the ante with a stand-alone sake bar.

SushiSamba ● *Brazilian/Japanese* 21 | 20 | 17 | $51

Flatiron | 245 Park Ave. S. (bet. 19th & 20th Sts.) | 212-475-9377
W Village | 87 Seventh Ave. S. (Barrow St.) | 212-691-7885
www.sushisamba.com

"Free-spirited" pair featuring an "original" Japanese-Brazilian "hybrid" menu, "party"-hearty atmospherics and "open-air" seating on the Village outlet's "beautiful roof"; although service skews "slow", the staff is always "quick with the check."

⛨ Sushi Seki ●🖫 *Japanese* 26 | 13 | 21 | $75

E 60s | 1143 First Ave. (bet. 62nd & 63rd Sts.) | 212-371-0238
Sushi aficionados may debate which raw fish is NYC's best, but chef Seki's omakase platters "have no peer" – and it serves until 2:30 AM weeknights; despite "poor decor", "you'll never regret" eating at this Eastsider, especially if "you're on an expense account."

⛨ Sushi Sen-nin *Japanese* 26 | 17 | 21 | $55

Murray Hill | 30 E. 33rd St. (bet. Madison Ave. & Park Ave. S.) | 212-889-2208 | www.sushisennin.com
The "freshest fish around" makes this Murray Hill Japanese an area "winner" for "hearty portions" of "top-drawer" sushi (including "some

truly unique rolls") and "courteous" service; if it still seems "undiscovered", that could be due to the price tag.

	FOOD	DECOR	SERVICE	COST

Sushiya *Japanese*
20 | 14 | 19 | $34

W 50s | 28 W. 56th St. (bet. 5th & 6th Aves.) | 212-247-5760
It's all about "bang for the buck" at this old-fangled Midtown Japanese proffering "respectable sushi" at decidedly "gentle prices"; trade-offs include "dreary" digs and occasionally "rushed" service, but it still "gets crowded" midday when desk jockeys show up for a "three-sake lunch."

☑ Sushi Yasuda ☒ *Japanese*
28 | 21 | 24 | $84

E 40s | 204 E. 43rd St. (bet. 2nd & 3rd Aves.) | 212-972-1001 | www.sushiyasuda.com
This "understated", "blond wood-paneled" sushi purveyor near Grand Central is "as good as it gets outside of Japan"; being served by Naomichi Yasuda at the bar is an "experience not to be missed", with "exotic fish saved for those with the palate – and wallet – to appreciate them"; for price-sensitive clients, the $23 dinner prix fixe is "one of the best deals in town."

Sushi Zen ☒ *Japanese*
25 | 20 | 23 | $63

W 40s | 108 W. 44th St. (bet. B'way & 6th Ave.) | 212-302-0707 | www.sushizen-ny.com
"Small" and "somewhat under the radar", this Theater District Japanese "teases the palate" with "exquisite sushi prepared by "expert" slicers in an oh-so-"tranquil setting"; after such an "elegant" performance, it's easier to "maintain a Zen attitude" when the "high-end" check arrives.

Swagat Indian Cuisine *Indian*
21 | 12 | 19 | $25

W 70s | 411A Amsterdam Ave. (bet. 79th & 80th Sts.) | 212-362-1400 | www.swagatupperwestside.com
Particularly "adept" at spicing, this UWS Indian is a "solid" neighborhood resource, thanks to its "solicitous service" and "bang-on" prices; to sidestep the "cramped", "hole-in-the-wall" setting, loyalists keep their delivery number "on autodial."

NEW Sweet Emily's *American*
∇ 18 | 16 | 22 | $36

W 50s | 321 W. 51st St. (bet. 8th & 9th Aves.) | 212-957-9338 | www.sweetemilysnyc.com
There's "plenty to choose from" at this new Hell's Kitchen arrival offering a big menu of New American "variations on comfort food" with Latin and Southern accents; while the setting (formerly René Pujol) is strictly plain-Jane, the "reasonable" pricing compensates.

NEW Sweetiepie ●Ⓜ *American/Dessert*
∇ 14 | 22 | 18 | $30

G Village | 19 Greenwich Ave. (bet. Christopher & W. 10th Sts.) | 212-337-3333 | www.sweetiepierestaurant.com
Aka "Sweet Tooth" Central, this "kid-friendly" new Villager serves American chow and a variety of desserts in an "over-the-top" setting that's a cross between Rumplemayer's and "Barbie's Dream House"; still, critics say the food's "mediocre" and "overpriced."

Sweet Melissa *Dessert/Sandwiches*
21 | 17 | 17 | $20

Cobble Hill | 276 Court St. (bet. Butler & Douglass Sts.) | Brooklyn | 718-855-3410

(continued)

Sweet Melissa

Park Slope | 175 Seventh Ave. (bet. 1st & 2nd Sts.) | Brooklyn | 718-502-9153
www.sweetmelissapatisserie.com

Besides "pretty-as-a-picture pastries", these "attractive" Brooklyn patisseries also offer "moms" a "moment of peace" to chat over coffee, a "casual lunch" or afternoon tea; "cute" gardens sweeten the deal, though a few sourpusses cite "costly" goods and "spaced-out service."

Sweetwater ● *American*

▽ 21 | 20 | 20 | $35

Williamsburg | 105 N. Sixth St. (bet. Berry St. & Wythe Ave.) |
Brooklyn | 718-963-0608 | www.sweetwaterny.com

Folks seeking something "kind of classy" in Williamsburg recommend this "charming" little bistro that tenders "delicious" New American comfort food in an "old-style", garden-equipped setting; even better, the Brooklyn-priced grub is "served with a smile."

Swifty's ● *American*

18 | 17 | 18 | $63

E 70s | 1007 Lexington Ave. (bet. 72nd & 73rd Sts.) | 212-535-6000 |
www.swiftysny.com

"Society doyennes hold court" at this UES "Wasp clubhouse" where the "back room" is the place to sit and "a vodka and a salad" the typical order; sure, you'll pay "top dollar" for the American food and service is "not too swifty", but it's the perfect stopover for those traveling between Palm Beach and the Hamptons by way of Park Avenue.

Sylvia's *Soul Food*

19 | 14 | 18 | $33

Harlem | 328 Lenox Ave. (bet. 126th & 127th Sts.) | 212-996-0660 |
www.sylviassoulfood.com

A Harlem "landmark" since 1962, this soul food "mecca" is famed for its "rib-sticking" Southern grub and Sunday gospel brunches; "impersonal service" and "tour-bus" hordes lead some to fret it's "coasting", but fans insist it's still an "experience" worth having.

Symposium *Greek*

19 | 14 | 19 | $27

W 100s | 544 W. 113th St. (bet. Amsterdam Ave. & B'way) | 212-865-1011

Ever the "popular Columbia haunt", this Morningside Heights Greek "perennial" endures thanks to "satisfying" food ("gotta get the flaming saganaki"), "bohemian" vibes and notable "value"; maybe the "nothing-fancy" space "never changes", but, then again, "if it ain't broke . . ."

Szechuan Gourmet *Chinese*

22 | 11 | 15 | $27

Garment District | 21 W. 39th St. (bet. 5th & 6th Aves.) | 212-921-0233 |
www.szechuangourmetnyc.com

NEW **W 50s** | 242 W. 56th St. (bet. B'way & 8th Ave.) | 212-265-2226
Flushing | 135-15 37th Ave. (bet. Main & Prince Sts.) | Queens |
718-888-9388

"Adventurous" folks who "like it hot" head for this simple Sichuan trio offering "fabulous" "fiery" fare for "cut-rate" tabs; indeed, the Flushing original's "vast selection" is so "authentic" and "extravagantly spiced" that "they should stamp your passport on the way in."

☒ Tabla *Indian*

25 | 25 | 24 | $77

Flatiron | 11 Madison Ave. (25th St.) | 212-889-0667 | www.tablany.com

"Better than ever", this "upscale but casual" second-floor dining room off Madison Square Park offers chef Floyd Cardoz's "creative" take on

Indian food that's "a bit Mumbai, a bit NY", but more than a bit "delicious"; while this "unique" place is "not cheap", the "staff is so friendly you feel like staying all day", and there's also the ground-floor Bread Bar for a "quicker, less expensive" experience.

Table d'Hôte *French*

20 | 16 | 20 | $49

E 90s | 44 E. 92nd St. (bet. Madison & Park Aves.) | 212-348-8125
The seating's so "tight" you may have to "synchronize" knives with your neighbor, but a "loyal following" still turns up at this "petite" Carnegie Hill vet known for its "tasty" French bistro cooking and "charming" service; "convenient" to the 92nd Street Y, it's also "one of the better values" hereabouts.

NEW Table 8 *Californian*

▽ 15 | 20 | 13 | $57

E Village | Cooper Sq. Hotel | 25 Cooper Sq. (bet 5th & 6th Sts.) | 212-475-3400 | www.coopersquarehotel.com
Celeb toque Govind Armstrong transplants his LA franchise to the Bowery via this "trendy" new Californian in the Cooper Square Hotel, where the "average", small plate–heavy menu includes house-cured meats and fish from its signature salt bar; still, "clueless" service, "deafening" noise and "overpriced, minuscule" portions lead many to label it a "disappointing" experience.

Taboon *Mediterranean/Mideastern*

23 | 19 | 20 | $53

W 50s | 773 10th Ave. (52nd St.) | 212-713-0271
One good "reason to venture" into way West Hell's Kitchen, this "welcoming" Med–Middle Eastern boasts an "amazing" lineup of "to-die-for" breads from its taboon oven, along with "imaginative meze" and other "quality" eats; "engaging service" and an "upbeat" vibe complete the picture, but count on company since the "secret's out."

Taci's Beyti *Mediterranean/Turkish*

▽ 22 | 9 | 16 | $25

Midwood | 1955 Coney Island Ave. (bet. Ave. P & Kings Hwy.) | Brooklyn | 718-627-5750
Med mavens are "hooked" on this Midwood BYO Turk and its "satisfying portions" of "fine" classic dishes, especially those "delicious" kebabs; the "plain setting" may sport the "brightest lights this side of Broadway", but "you'll smile when you pay the bill."

Tailor Ⓜ *Dessert/Eclectic*

▽ 22 | 21 | 23 | $63

SoHo | 525 Broome St. (bet. Sullivan & Thompson Sts.) | 212-334-5182 | www.tailornyc.com
"Mad genius" chef Sam Mason "does wonders" fashioning "utterly bespoke" entrees and desserts at this "groundbreaking" SoHo Eclectic; the "quirkiness" – and cost – "takes some getting used to", but the "challenging" cuisine, "crazy cocktails" and "chill", shabby-chic quarters add up to some of the "most interesting dining" around.

Taïm ⇪ *Israeli*

▽ 25 | 9 | 16 | $14

W Village | 222 Waverly Pl. (bet. W. 11th & Perry Sts.) | 212-691-1287 | www.taimfalafel.com
Aptly named (after the "Hebrew word for 'tasty'"), this cash-only Village Israeli "hole-in-the-wall" aïms to please with "phenomenal", all-veggie falafels slung "quick" and "cheap", and paired with "superb smoothies"; since the "tiny" space sports "just a few stools", "takeout" is a given.

	FOOD	DECOR	SERVICE	COST

Takahachi *Japanese*
25 | 16 | 22 | $39

E Village | 85 Ave. A (bet. 5th & 6th Sts.) | 212-505-6524 ●
TriBeCa | 145 Duane St. (bet. Church St. & W. B'way) | 212-571-1830
www.takahachi.net

"Standbys" for "succulent" sushi, these Downtown Japanese are also lauded for "inventive rolls" and "wonderful" daily specials; though they're "simply decorated", the "caring" staffers and "down-to-earth prices" are enough to retain "lots of regulars."

Taksim *Turkish*
20 | 10 | 18 | $29

E 50s | 1030 Second Ave. (bet. 54th & 55th Sts.) | 212-421-3004 | www.taksim.us

This "congenial" Midtown Turk is an "easy", "everyday" option for "generous" helpings of "tasty" standards from a relatively "short menu"; but while the food and that "good value" sure "hit the spot", the "unspectacular" setting leads most to tak out.

Talay ● *Pan-Latin/Thai*
∇ 21 | 24 | 18 | $43

Harlem | 701 W. 135th St. (12th Ave.) | 212-491-8300 | www.talayrestaurant.com

With its "excellent" Thai-Latino small plates and designer drinks, this "classy" Harlem "hot spot" "reinvents the fusion scene" for the "up-and-coming ViVa" area; "sexy", Tao-esque decor and high-"volume" nightlife antics hint at why it's pretty "pricey for this neck of the woods."

☒ Tamarind ● *Indian*
25 | 22 | 23 | $54

Flatiron | 41-43 E. 22nd St. (bet. B'way & Park Ave. S.) | 212-674-7400 | www.tamarinde22.com

"Elegant and grown-up", this "transporting" Flatiron Indian oozes "sophistication" with "dream-worthy" cooking (rated No. 1 in its genre) served by a "gracious" team in a "special occasion"–worthy space; predictably, the "prices are in orbit", though the tabs are more down to earth at the $24 prix fixe lunch or in the adjacent Tea Room.

Tang Pavilion *Chinese*
20 | 17 | 20 | $38

W 50s | 65 W. 55th St. (bet. 5th & 6th Aves.) | 212-956-6888

This "trustworthy" Midtown Chinese remains "a cut above" for "classic" Shanghai-style cuisine and "fast service" in "roomy" digs; since it "won't break the bank", it's become a "favorite" in the "Radio City vicinity."

☒ Tanoreen Ⓜ *Mediterranean/Mideastern*
26 | 10 | 21 | $31

Bay Ridge | 7523 Third Ave. (76th St.) | Brooklyn | 718-748-5600 | www.tanoreen.com

Med-Mideastern cooking rises to a "whole new level" at Rawia Bishara's Bay Ridge "pacesetter" where "fantastic spices" yield "out-of-this-world" food for "moderate" tabs; the staffers are "helpful", and following a recent "move to bigger digs", there's now better "luck getting a table."

☒ Tao ● *Pan-Asian*
21 | 26 | 19 | $59

E 50s | 42 E. 58th St. (bet. Madison & Park Aves.) | 212-888-2288 | www.taorestaurant.com

The "young and restless" flock to this "über-cool" Midtown Pan-Asian featuring a "mega-size" Buddha, "pulsing music" and "obstacle-course" seating; the "expensive", "spot-on" chow may be "secondary to the scenery", but overall this 10-year-old still "impresses."

	FOOD	DECOR	SERVICE	COST

Tarallucci e Vino *Italian* | 21 | 18 | 18 | $34 |

E Village | 163 First Ave. (10th St.) | 212-388-1190
Flatiron | 15 E. 18th St. (bet. B'way & 5th Ave.) | 212-228-5400
www.taralluccievino.net

"Just right" for an "unpretentious" bite, this "casual" Flatiron Italian serves "first-rate" small plates and "quality wines" in a "cute and cozy" venue that offers takeout up front; the East Village original's counter-service cafe is "better for pastries and cappuccinos."

Tartine ⊄ *French* | 22 | 15 | 18 | $33 |

W Village | 253 W. 11th St. (4th St.) | 212-229-2611

For "comfort food with a French accent", this cash-only, BYO-friendly West Villager matches "terrific" bistro dishes with "snug" dimensions and "unbeatable prices"; just be sure to "dress for the weather on weekends" since you'll be standing in the "asphalt waiting room."

Taverna Kyclades *Greek/Seafood* | 25 | 12 | 18 | $36 |

Astoria | 33-07 Ditmars Blvd. (bet. 33rd & 35th Sts.) | Queens | 718-545-8666 | www.tavernakyclades.com

Hellenists brave "fierce lines" at this "real-thing" Astoria Greek for "generous portions" of "fantastic", "ultrafresh seafood" served at "affordable" rates; the "strictly no-frills" space is typically "packed" like "the 4 train at rush hour", so "get there early."

Tavern on the Green *American* | 15 | 25 | 18 | $66 |

W 60s | Central Park W. (bet. 66th & 67th Sts.) | 212-873-3200 | www.tavernonthegreen.com

That "storybook" setting is "everything you could ask for" at this "glitzy" Central Park "landmark", from the "splashy" interiors worthy of "Liberace" to the garden "wonderland"; sure, the "pedestrian" American fare and "so-so service" come at "princely prices", but "let's face it" – "you're paying for the locale", period; N.B. it has recently changed ownership.

T-Bar Steak & Lounge *Steak* | 22 | 19 | 21 | $61 |

E 70s | 1278 Third Ave. (bet. 73rd & 74th Sts.) | 212-772-0404 | www.tbarnyc.com

For a "change from the traditional", Tony Fortuna's UES steakhouse re-sets the bar with "outstanding" meats and "accommodating" service in "upscale" digs complete with a "busy" lounge; the "sophisticated", "over-35 locals" who can afford it consider it their "native habitat."

Tea & Sympathy *British* | 21 | 18 | 19 | $28 |

W Village | 108 Greenwich Ave. (bet. 12th & 13th Sts.) | 212-807-8329 | www.teaandsympathynewyork.com

"Teleport to England" via this "jolly olde" West Village teahouse for "smashing" Britannic bites or a "proper pot" during the "traditional afternoon tea"; the "wee" space entails "waits" and the expat staffers insist on "lots of rules", but "you'll feel like you're in Blighty" – "cheers, luv!"

Ⓩ Telepan *American* | 26 | 21 | 24 | $71 |

W 60s | 72 W. 69th St. (bet. Columbus Ave. & CPW) | 212-580-4300 | www.telepan-ny.com

Led by "master-of-the-greenmarket" Bill Telepan, this New American is a "deeply satisfying adult restaurant" that draws UWS regulars with "dependably delicious" food, "unobtrusive service", "convenience to Lincoln Center" and "soothing" (some say "dull") decor; fans tout Sunday's brunch as "the best in town."

Telly's Taverna ● *Greek/Seafood*

| 23 | 14 | 18 | $39 |

Astoria | 28-13 23rd Ave. (bet. 28th & 29th Sts.) | Queens | 718-728-9056 | www.tellystaverna.com

"Pristine fish right off the grill" is the lure at this 20-year-old Astoria Greek, a straightforward choice for "solid" seafood and meze on a "recession budget"; the functional decor is "not spectacular", so in warmer weather the "outside seating" is more atmospheric.

NEW 10 Downing ● *American*

| 21 | 21 | 20 | $56 |

G Village | 10 Downing St. (6th Ave.) | 212-255-0300 | www.10downingnyc.com

No, "you won't find the prime minister here", but you may feel you're paying in pounds at this "sunny", "noisy-but-fun" Villager where "hip" locals down "sophisticated" New American cuisine; "fantastic" fine art and "people-watching"–friendly front windows ensure there's plenty to please the eye.

Tenzen *Japanese*

| 22 | 15 | 19 | $33 |

E 50s | 988 Second Ave. (bet. 52nd & 53rd Sts.) | 212-980-5900 ●
E 80s | 1714 Second Ave. (89th St.) | 212-369-3600 ●
W 70s | 285 Columbus Ave. (73rd St.) | 212-580-7300 ●
Bensonhurst | 7116 18th Ave. (71st St.) | Brooklyn | 718-621-3238
www.tenzanrestaurants.com

"Right-off-the-boat" sushi served "with a smile" qualify these "convenient" cross-borough Japanese as "sure bets", especially given the "gigantic" pieces and "miniature" prices; the "spare settings" are "not for a romantic interlude", hence their "tops-for-takeout" rep.

Teodora *Italian*

| 20 | 15 | 19 | $52 |

E 50s | 141 E. 57th St. (bet. Lexington & 3rd Aves.) | 212-826-7101 | www.teodorarestaurant.com

A "haven from the bustle" of Midtown, this "traditional" Northern Italian is *molto bene* for "ample portions" of "homemade pastas" and other "honest" fare; maybe the "plain surroundings" could use a "face-lift", but at least the "peaceful" vibes make "conversation" easy.

Teresa's *Diner*

| 19 | 11 | 15 | $23 |

Brooklyn Heights | 80 Montague St. (Hicks St.) | Brooklyn | 718-797-3996

"Standard diner fare" comes with a "Polish accent" at this "Brooklyn Heights standby" set in a "simple", coffee shop–like storefront; the "can't-be-bothered" staff is "renowned for its surliness", but the place is so "easy on the budget" that nobody cares.

Terrace in the Sky Ⓜ *French/Mediterranean*

| 22 | 24 | 22 | $71 |

W 100s | 400 W. 119th St. (bet. Amsterdam Ave. & Morningside Dr.) | 212-666-9490 | www.terraceinthesky.com

Made for "romance and special occasions", this "classy" Morningside Heights French-Med rooftop aerie offers "magnificent" "360-degree views" of the city, "top-flight food" and "at-your-command" service; so even if prices are also "in the sky", there are "few places better" when it's time to "celebrate."

	FOOD	DECOR	SERVICE	COST

NEW Terrazza Toscana ⏺ *Italian* — | – | – | M

W 50s | 742 Ninth Ave. (50th St.) | 212-315-9191 |
www.terrazzatoscana.com

Show-goers applaud this midpriced Theater District newcomer that
plies a tempting Tuscan menu abetted by a 400-label wine list and a
tastefully ornate interior outfitted with wrought iron and chandeliers;
it lives up to its name with a swell rooftop terrace.

Tevere *Italian* ▽ 24 | 19 | 21 | $63

E 80s | 155 E. 84th St. (bet. Lexington & 3rd Aves.) | 212-744-0210 |
www.teverenyc.com

It's "strictly kosher", but "you wouldn't know it" given how "tasty" the
"authentic Roman" specialties are at this "been-there-for-ages" UES
Italian; as a bonus, the "cozy" "old-world" quarters exude enough "romance" to make the prices easier to digest.

Thai Pavilion *Thai* ▽ 24 | 15 | 23 | $23

NEW Astoria | 23-92 21st St. (bet. 23rd Terrace & 24th Ave.) |
Queens | 718-274-2088
Astoria | 37-10 30th Ave. (37th St.) | Queens | 718-777-5546
www.thaipavilionny.com

For an "unassuming neighborhood Thai", this "long-standing" Astorian
supplies surprisingly "excellent quality" via a "diverse" menu served
by a "most efficient" staff; a "low-key", "family-run" affair, its "no-
frills" decor is offset by come-hither tabs; N.B. the 21st Street branch
opened post-Survey.

Thalassa ⌧ *Greek/Seafood* 24 | 25 | 23 | $66

TriBeCa | 179 Franklin St. (bet. Greenwich & Hudson Sts.) | 212-941-7661 |
www.thalassanyc.com

"Greece's gift to TriBeCa", this "classy" Hellene offers seafood "cooked
to perfection" and "elegantly served" in an "airy" space where the "only
thing missing is the smell of the ocean"; while the pricing is on the
"splurgey" side, the "standout" performance justifies the cost for most.

Thalia ⏺ *American* 19 | 19 | 18 | $48

W 50s | 828 Eighth Ave. (50th St.) | 212-399-4444 |
www.restaurantthalia.com

"Broadway show"-goers tout this Hell's Kitchen New American as "totally reliable" for "quality" chow, "reasonable costs" and "cheerful"
service "keyed to curtain time"; pre-theater may be "clamorous", but
the "tourist buses" idling outside provide "great people-watching."

Thomas Beisl ⏺ *Austrian* 17 | 14 | 16 | $40

Fort Greene | 25 Lafayette Ave. (Ashland Pl.) | Brooklyn | 718-222-5800
"Just across from BAM", this "low-key" Fort Greene Viennese serves
"mammoth portions" of "midpriced" Austrian fare washed down with a
"thoughtfully stocked" list of European beers and wines; though foes
grumble "inconsistent", it's "handy" when "running for the curtain."

Tía Pol *Spanish* 25 | 15 | 18 | $41

Chelsea | 205 10th Ave. (bet. 22nd & 23rd Sts.) | 212-675-8805 |
www.tiapol.com

They're "packing them in for a reason" at this "tiny", *muy* "authentic"
Chelsea Spaniard that "hits the spot" with an all-tapas menu that in-

| | FOOD | DECOR | SERVICE | COST |

cludes "specials that are actually special"; the "imaginative morsels" ease the pain of "tabs that run up fast" and the "hassle to get in."

Tierras Colombianas ⊭ *Colombian*
∇ 19 | 13 | 17 | $27

Astoria | 33-01 Broadway (33rd St.) | Queens | 718-956-3012
You'd better "come hungry" to this Astoria "greasy spoon" that serves "king-size portions" of "better-than-average" Colombian grub that's as "authentic" as a "trip to Bogota"; ok, "it's not fancy" and takes "no credit cards", but "good prices" "keep the place busy."

Tiffin Wallah *Indian*
∇ 24 | 14 | 18 | $21

Murray Hill | 127 E. 28th St. (bet. Lexington & Park Aves.) | 212-685-7301 | www.tiffinwallah.us
Neophytes at this Murray Hill Southern Indian (and Chennai Garden sibling) "never dreamed" that kosher vegetarian street food "could taste so good", especially that "quite-a-deal" $7 lunch buffet; true, the setting is "simple", but at these prices "who cares?"

Tio Pepe ● *Mexican/Spanish*
∇ 20 | 15 | 19 | $37

G Village | 168 W. Fourth St. (bet. Cornelia & Jones Sts.) | 212-242-9338 | www.tiopepenyc.com
"Lively" Village vet on the scene since 1970 plating up "plentiful" portions of "traditional" Mexican-Spanish grub in a "loud" room (the enclosed garden is more subdued); skeptics cite "unremarkable" eating, but overall it's "dependable for the money."

Tiramisu *Italian*
20 | 15 | 18 | $39

E 80s | 1410 Third Ave. (80th St.) | 212-988-9780
Offering "something for all ages", this "family-friendly" Italian is an UES source for "comforting" pastas and pizza; the setting and service may be "nothing special", but the "bustling", "noisy" scene speaks for itself.

∅ Tocqueville ⊠ *American/French*
26 | 26 | 25 | $78

Union Sq | 1 E. 15th St. (bet. 5th Ave. & Union Sq. W.) | 212-647-1515 | www.tocquevillerestaurant.com
For a "very civilized" "special treat", this Union Square-area French-New American "deserves greater recognition", offering a "jewel-box" dining room with a "relaxing, sophisticated" ambiance, "spectacular service" and, most importantly, chef Marco Moreira's "original", "to-die-for" cooking; fans say they "would eat here every day" if they could just afford it – fortunately, there is a $44 pre-theater prix fixe.

Toloache *Mexican*
23 | 18 | 20 | $45

W 50s | 251 W. 50th St. (bet. B'way & 8th Ave.) | 212-581-1818 | www.toloachenyc.com
"Quite the surprise", this "modern" Theater District duplex turns out "novel twists" on "hard-to-find" Nuevo Mexicano dishes, as well as a "great guacamole selection" and "sinful margaritas" concocted from a 100-strong tequila list; though it's "a tad pricey", that's not keeping the "crowds" – and the resultant "high" decibels – away.

Tommaso *Italian*
23 | 19 | 21 | $49

Dyker Heights | 1464 86th St. (bet. 14th & 15th Aves.) | Brooklyn | 718-236-9883 | www.tommasoinbrooklyn.com
"Old-world" all the way, this circa-1969 Dyker Heights Italian offers "classic red-sauce" cooking so "delicious" that a glance at the "patrons'

| | FOOD | DECOR | SERVICE | COST |

waistlines" indicates "how popular the pasta is"; "if you're lucky", "singing owner" Thomas Verdillo will supply a "side of live opera."

☑ Tomoe Sushi *Japanese*
26 | 8 | 16 | $43

G Village | 172 Thompson St. (bet. Bleecker & Houston Sts.) | 212-777-9346

As "tiny" and "unassuming" as ever, this "best-value" Tokyo-style Village sushi joint is still packing them in after almost 30 years; "get there early" (or "pay an NYU student to stand in line for you") and you'll "never think of a California roll in quite the same way" – "only the fish aren't happy to be here."

Tom's ☒⇆ *Diner*
20 | 15 | 23 | $17

Prospect Heights | 782 Washington Ave. (Sterling Pl.) | Brooklyn | 718-636-9738

"Step back in time" at this '30s-era Prospect Heights "hangover joint", a "kitschy", counter-service cafe where the "friendliest people in the world" serve "reliable" diner fare (and egg creams) for "ridiculously cheap" sums; Saturday brunch is a neighborhood "ritual", so brace yourself for "lines around the block."

NEW Tonda Ⓜ *Pizza*
- | - | - | I

E Village | 235 E. Fourth St. (bet. Aves. A & B) | 212-254-2900 | www.tondapzza.com

At this sunny new Alphabet City pizzeria, whitewashed brick and rows of wine bottles serve as decor; despite a much vaunted, $30,000 wood-fired oven, the affordable menu has no item priced over $15.

Tony's Di Napoli *Italian*
19 | 15 | 18 | $39

E 80s | 1606 Second Ave. (83rd St.) | 212-861-8686
W 40s | 147 W. 43rd St. (bet. B'way & 6th Ave.) | 212-221-0100 ◑
www.tonysnyc.com

This "Carmine's-style" duo specializes in "family-style" platters of Italian chow "large enough to feed a small army"; yes, "it's a zoo" and the food can be "ordinary", but the mood's "celebratory" and God knows, "no one leaves hungry" or broke.

Topaz Thai *Thai*
21 | 12 | 16 | $28

W 50s | 127 W. 56th St. (bet. 6th & 7th Aves.) | 212-957-8020

"Handy" to Carnegie Hall, this "simple", "small" Siamese slings "super" standards at a "lightning-fast", "here's-the-food-here's-the-check" pace; despite "drab decor" and "no elbow room", it's "always packed" thanks to "bargain" tabs.

Tosca Café ◐ *Italian*
▽ 21 | 22 | 19 | $33

Bronx | 4038 E. Tremont Ave. (bet. Miles & Sampson Aves.) | 718-239-3300 | www.toscanyc.com

"Trendy nightclub" meets "popular" restaurant at this "easy-on-the-eye" Throgs Neck Italian that serves everything from pasta to sushi and turns into "quite a scene" after dark; "service can be sporadic", but "there aren't many places in the Bronx" that host both a "hopping bar" and a "fantastic" brunch.

Totonno's Pizzeria Napolitano *Pizza*
22 | 10 | 14 | $23

E 80s | 1544 Second Ave. (bet. 80th & 81st Sts.) | 212-327-2800
Murray Hill | 462 Second Ave. (26th St.) | 212-213-8800

(continued)

Totonno's Pizzeria Napolitano

Coney Island | 1524 Neptune Ave. (bet. W. 15th & 16th Sts.) | Brooklyn | 718-372-8606 Ⓜ🖭
www.totonnos.com

With the "landmark" Coney Island original back in business following a fire, its East Side satellites are no longer the only outlets for its "real-deal", "perfectly crisped" brick-oven pizza; though both the digs and the service are strictly "no-frills", the "fail-safe" pies are to-totally "worth it."

FOOD	DECOR	SERVICE	COST

Tournesol *French* | 24 | 15 | 18 | $42

LIC | 50-12 Vernon Blvd. (bet. 50th & 51st Aves.) | Queens | 718-472-4355 |
www.tournesolnyc.com

"Paris" alights on the "Ile de la Cité de Long Island" at this "hipster French bistro", a "LIC highlight" thanks to its "superior" cooking and "reasonable" tabs; it oozes "Gallic authenticity" right down to the "expat" staff, but it's "no secret anymore" so the "tight" space is apt to be "jammed."

Trata *Greek/Seafood* | 22 | 18 | 19 | $61

E 70s | 1331 Second Ave. (bet. 70th & 71st Sts.) | 212-535-3800 |
www.trata.com

The seafood all but "leaps off the boat onto your plate" at this "up-scale" UES Greek, serving "delicately prepared" fish in an "attractive" modern setting manned by an "accommodating" crew; those put off by the "pricey" by-the-pound tabs tout the $25 prix fixe lunch.

Trattoria Dell'Arte ❶ *Italian* | 22 | 20 | 20 | $57

W 50s | 900 Seventh Ave. (bet. 56th & 57th Sts.) | 212-245-9800 |
www.trattoriadellarte.com

A "hospitable crowd-pleaser" opposite Carnegie Hall, this Northern Italian "beehive" dishes out "mouthwatering" antipasti and "fantastic thin pizza" in a room decorated with "amusing" anatomical sculpture ("sit under the boob"); it's "somewhat pricey" and "hectic", but this is "where the action is."

☒ Trattoria L'incontro Ⓜ *Italian* | 27 | 20 | 25 | $54

Astoria | 21-76 31st St. (Ditmars Blvd.) | Queens | 718-721-3532 |
www.trattorialincontro.com

"As good as anything in Manhattan", this mega-"popular" Astoria Italian offers a "fantastic" menu (rated No. 1 in its genre) served by "charming" waiters who will "rattle off" an "endless list of tempting specials" (bring a "tape recorder"); "hunky chef" Rocco Sacramone will "treat you like a *paisan*", while the "wine bar next door" eases the inevitable "wait."

Trattoria Pesce & Pasta *Italian/Seafood* | 19 | 15 | 18 | $36

E 50s | 1079 First Ave. (59th St.) | 212-888-7884
G Village | 262 Bleecker St. (bet. 6th Ave. & 7th Ave. S.) | 212-645-2993 ❶
W 90s | 625 Columbus Ave. (bet. 90th & 91st Sts.) | 212-579-7970
www.pescepasta.com

"It is what it says", so expect "plenty of fish and pasta" at these "neighborly" Italians that are "reliable" resources for "satisfying" food at "fair prices"; they're "not much to look at" and the "garlicky" menus hold "no surprises", but you'll "walk out full and happy."

	FOOD	DECOR	SERVICE	COST

Trattoria Romana *Italian*   24 | 15 | 22 | $44

Staten Island | 1476 Hylan Blvd. (Benton Ave.) | 718-980-3113 |
www.trattoriaromana.com

They "go out of their way" to please at this "spirited" Staten Islander,
a "local" Dongan Hills "favorite" with "delicious" "homemade" Italian
dishes served in an "old-school" setting; its "squished-in tables" are
often "packed", so "be prepared to wait."

Trattoria Trecolori *Italian*   21 | 19 | 22 | $42

W 40s | 254 W. 47th St. (bet. B'way & 8th Ave.) | 212-997-4540 |
www.trattoriatrecolori.com

"Convenient" for the Broadway bound, this "unsung" Theater District
Italian serves "well-executed" standards ferried by an "enthusiastic"
crew that "gets you out on time" for the curtain; though "not intimate",
it's a "charming" act and the "price is right."

Tre *Italian*   ∇ 19 | 17 | 18 | $48

LES | 173 Ludlow St. (bet. Houston & Stanton Sts.) | 212-353-3353 |
www.trenewyork.com

Italian gets "hip" at this neo-rustic LES yearling offering an "inventive",
pasta-centric menu for a "respectable price" in "cozy", "whitewashed"
digs; "portions are a bit small", but it remains a "solid date spot" that's
just "waiting to be discovered."

tre dici ⊠ *Italian*   21 | 18 | 20 | $51

Chelsea | 128 W. 26th St. (bet. 6th & 7th Aves.) | 212-243-8183
tre dici steak ⊠ *Steak*
Chelsea | 128 W. 26th St., 2nd fl. (bet. 6th & 7th Aves.) | 212-243-2085
www.tredicinyc.com

An "unexpected find" on an "odd" block, this Chelsea double-decker
puts some "killer" twists on familiar Italian items in an "attractive"
modern space overseen by a "spot-on" staff; the upstairs steakhouse
is done up like a "sexy" "speakeasy" and serves "impressive" pastas
and red meat.

Tree ◐ *French*   19 | 17 | 18 | $42

E Village | 190 First Ave. (bet. 11th & 12th Sts.) | 212-358-7171 |
www.treenyc.com

East Village Francophiles root for this "casual" French bistro's "tasty"
comfort food, "capable service" and "good value"; if the "minuscule"
space seems overly "intimate", the "charming" all-weather garden is
a sizable "bonus."

Trestle on Tenth *American*   19 | 17 | 20 | $49

Chelsea | 242 10th Ave. (24th St.) | 212-645-5659 | www.trestleontenth.com

"Everything seems to work" at this "relaxed" Chelsea New American that
earns "buzzworthiness" thanks to "adventurous" Swiss-influenced
cooking and a "creative wine list" at "economy-appropriate" prices;
the "comfy" setting is enhanced by a "wonderful" garden out back.

Triangolo ◐ *Italian*   20 | 14 | 20 | $43

E 80s | 345 E. 83rd St. (bet. 1st & 2nd Aves.) | 212-472-4488 |
www.triangolorestaurant.com

"Local" folks angling for "reasonably priced" Italian "classics" turn to this
"sweet" UES "standby", a "no-fuss" option for "solid pastas" and "warm"

service; the "small" setup may be "nothing to write home about", but "repeat customers" don't mind if it stays "under the radar."

Tribeca Grill *American* 22 | 21 | 22 | $61

TriBeCa | 375 Greenwich St. (Franklin St.) | 212-941-3900 | www.tribecagrill.com

A 20-year-old "anchor" in TriBeCa, this "upscale but not uptight" New American from Drew Nieporent and Robert De Niro "hasn't lost its touch" for "well-executed" food and "top-notch" service; it's built a "reputation" as a "relaxed scene" with an "interesting crowd" that doesn't think twice about the tab.

Trinity Place *Eclectic* ∇ 19 | 23 | 19 | $43

Financial District | 115 Broadway (enter on Cedar St., bet. B'way & Trinity Pl.) | 212-964-0939 | www.trinityplacenyc.com

Financial District denizens tout this relatively "undiscovered" Eclectic lodged in a "former bank vault", where the "upscale menu" holds some "nice surprises"; after work, the "crowded bar" scene can get "loud", so regulars hit the back room for "conversation."

Triomphe *French* 24 | 22 | 23 | $67

W 40s | Iroquois Hotel | 49 W. 44th St. (bet. 5th & 6th Aves.) | 212-453-4233 | www.triompheny.com

"Out-of-the-way" and relatively "unknown", this "tasteful" Midtown "gem" is an "oasis of tranquility" where "cosseting" staffers serve "superb" French fare in "quiet", "civilized" surroundings; "high prices" come with the territory, but it's a "refined" find, "especially for pre-theater."

Tsampa ❶ *Tibetan* ∇ 21 | 19 | 20 | $29

E Village | 212 E. Ninth St. (bet. 2nd & 3rd Aves.) | 212-614-3226

"One of the few" spots to tsample Tibetan cooking, this "affordable" East Villager offers a "tasty" ohm-nivorous menu with "great vegetarian options" served by a "friendly" crew; low-lit and "low-key", it's a "serene change of pace" for its "young-folks" following.

Tse Yang *Chinese* 24 | 23 | 24 | $63

E 50s | 34 E. 51st St. (bet. Madison & Park Aves.) | 212-688-5447 | www.tseyangnyc.com

Furnishing "haute Chinese for the carriage trade", this East Midtowner plies "fabulous" cuisine (notably an "incomparable" Peking duck) with "skill and pride" in luxe digs bedecked with "fancy" wall hangings and aquariums; it's the kind of place to "judge others by", even if the "dear prices" make it "best for business."

Turkish Cuisine ❶ *Turkish* 19 | 15 | 19 | $34

W 40s | 631 Ninth Ave. (bet. 44th & 45th Sts.) | 212-397-9650 | www.turkishcuisinenyc.com

The "name might be bland, but the food isn't" at this "quick and easy" Hell's Kitchen Turk that "tries hard to please" with "satisfying" standards at "reasonable prices"; though "nothing fancy" lookswise, it's still a "staple" for the "theater crowd."

Turkish Grill *Turkish* ∇ 23 | 14 | 18 | $29

Sunnyside | 42-03 Queens Blvd. (42nd St.) | Queens | 718-392-3838

For a "real taste" of Turkey, this Sunnyside "neighborhood" joint "fills the bill" with "great" grub "served up simple" in portions large enough to "allow for sharing"; the storefront setup is "a bit drab", but "good pricing" and a "friendly" mood keep it "busy."

☒ Turkish Kitchen *Turkish*

23 **18** **19** **$42**

Murray Hill | 386 Third Ave. (bet. 27th & 28th Sts.) | 212-679-6633 | www.turkishkitchen.com

"Skip the trip to Istanbul" and let this Murray Hill "standout" stand in for it via a menu of "distinctive Turkish delights" (including a "best-bet" brunch buffet) served in a fez-tive, "deep-red" setting; "helpful" staffers and "inventive cocktails" boost its rep as a "consistent keeper."

Turks & Frogs *Turkish*

19 **19** **19** **$41**

TriBeCa | 458 Greenwich St. (bet. Desbrosses & Watts Sts.) | 212-966-4774 | www.turksandfrogs.com

An "affordable" TriBeCa "find", this "underappreciated" Turk delivers "well-executed" eats (with notably "excellent" meze) and "attentive" service in "attractive", antiques-enhanced digs; "dim lighting" and a "lack of crowds" lend "seductive" "date-night" appeal.

Turkuaz *Turkish*

19 **19** **19** **$36**

W 100s | 2637 Broadway (100th St.) | 212-665-9541 | www.turkuazrestaurant.com

"Definitely a mood-setter", this "quirky" UWS Turk is done up in a "silken" "bazaar" guise that's "just exotic enough" for a fantasy "Arabian night" date (complete with "Bedouin-chic" weekend belly dancing); in addition, it offers "tasty", "well-served" basics and a "bountiful", "real-value" brunch.

Turquoise *Seafood*

21 **17** **19** **$57**

E 80s | 240 E. 81st St. (bet. 2nd & 3rd Aves.) | 212-988-8222 | www.turquoisenyc.com

Observant observers note that this "understated" UES seafooder is "now kosher", while still specializing in a "surprisingly good" (if "limited") lineup of the "freshest" fish; but despite its "potential", a few feel blue over service "kinks" and "expensive" tabs.

Tuscany Grill *Italian*

24 **19** **21** **$50**

Bay Ridge | 8620 Third Ave. (bet. 86th & 87th Sts.) | Brooklyn | 718-921-5633

"Locals" rely on this "quaint", "neighborhoody" Bay Ridge fixture for "delicious" contemporary Tuscan food at "midrange" prices; a "sweet, capable" staff "maintains its quality", probably why the regulars always "look very happy."

12th St. Bar & Grill *American*

21 **19** **21** **$38**

Park Slope | 1123 Eighth Ave. (12th St.) | Brooklyn | 718-965-9526 | www.12thstreetbarandgrill.com

Situated "slightly off the beaten Park Slope path", this "old standby" offers its "simple", "flavorful" New American fare in "pleasant" environs; "value" pricing and "solicitous" service keep 'em coming; N.B. its "more casual" round-the-corner bar serves the same menu.

12 Chairs *American/Mideastern*

19 **14** **16** **$28**

SoHo | 56 MacDougal St. (bet. Houston & Prince Sts.) | 212-254-8640 | www.12chairs.lbu.com

"College students" and other budget-minded sorts make a beeline for this "bohemian" SoHo cafe beloved for its "homey" American–Middle

Eastern basics, "chill atmosphere" and "low prices"; service is "marginal" and the dimensions "small" – though FYI, "they do have more than 12 chairs."

☑ 21 Club 🄯 American
FOOD	DECOR	SERVICE	COST
22	24	24	$73

W 50s | 21 W. 52nd St. (bet. 5th & 6th Aves.) | 212-582-7200 | www.21club.com

"A NYC icon", this "memorabilia-filled", circa-1929 Midtown speak-easy is "a place to enjoy the past" – i.e. "the time when we dressed for dinner"; besides coming to eat, you get to "watch famous writers, actors and business" folk chowing down on "true-blue American cooking", e.g. $30 burgers; P.S. it's most accessible at the $24 prix fixe lunch, and upstairs its private rooms are "perfect" for parties.

26 Seats 🄼 French
FOOD	DECOR	SERVICE	COST
21	16	19	$38

E Village | 168 Ave. B (bet. 10th & 11th Sts.) | 212-677-4787

"The name doesn't lie" about how "tiny" this "cozy" French "neighborhood performer"/"date spot" in the East Village really is, but the fact that you "eat well" at bistro prices just makes the place "more charming" – likewise the staff that's "sweet" but sometimes "slow."

Two Boots Pizza
FOOD	DECOR	SERVICE	COST
19	10	14	$16

E 40s | Grand Central | lower level (42nd St. & Vanderbilt Ave.) | 212-557-7992 | www.twoboots.com
NEW E 80s | 1617 Second Ave. (84th St.) | 212-734-0317 | www.twoboots.com ●
E Village | 42 Ave. A (3rd St.) | 212-254-1919 | www.twoboots.com ●
LES | 384 Grand St. (bet. Norfolk & Suffolk Sts.) | 212-228-8685 | www.twoboots.com
NoHo | 74 Bleecker St. (B'way) | 212-777-1033 | www.twoboots.com ●
NEW W 40s | 625 Ninth Ave. (bet. 44th & 45th Sts.) | 212-956-2668 | www.twoboots.com ●
W Village | 201 W. 11th St. (7th Ave. S.) | 212-633-9096 | www.twoboots.com ●
Park Slope | 514 Second St. (bet. 7th & 8th Aves.) | Brooklyn | 718-499-3253 | www.twobootsbrooklyn.com

Pizzaphiles "love the kick" of this "offbeat" chain's "assertively spiced" pies, whose "sturdy" cornmeal crusts, "snazzy" toppings and "crazy names" distract from the outlets' minimal looks and service; the separately owned Park Slope satellite is a "rambunctious" family "favorite" where moppets "can be as loud as they want."

212 ● American
FOOD	DECOR	SERVICE	COST
18	17	17	$47

E 60s | 133 E. 65th St. (bet. Lexington & Park Aves.) | 212-249-6565 | www.212restaurant.com

"Younger" "Euros" and other "trendy" types dial "the area code" – i.e. this "lively", "noisy" Bloomie's-area eatery/vodka bar – when seeking a "sexy" scene; if the New American fare is "so-so" and priced "a bit high", never mind – you come for the "meet market" and the "people-watching."

202 Cafe Mediterranean
FOOD	DECOR	SERVICE	COST
20	20	18	$37

Chelsea | Chelsea Mkt. | 75 Ninth Ave. (bet. 15th & 16th Sts.) | 646-638-1173

Get your "food and retail therapy" in the same "cool space" at this Med "brunch favorite" right "in the middle of" Nicole Farhi's "chic" Chelsea

Market boutique; maybe you "can't afford" the clothes, but its "tasty, simple" fare "isn't pricey" – though be prepared for "weak service."

2 West *Steak*

FOOD	DECOR	SERVICE	COST
22	22	23	$62

Financial District | Ritz-Carlton Battery Park | 2 West St. (Battery Pl.) | 917-790-2525 | www.ritzcarlton.com

No-surprises "upscale dining" is the deal at this "classy" steakhouse inside the Ritz-Carlton Battery Park; a room "quiet enough to have a conversation" and "excellent" service means it fills the bill for "business lunches" – especially considering the expense account–worthy tabs.

NEW Txikito Ⓜ *Spanish*

FOOD	DECOR	SERVICE	COST
23	15	20	$47

Chelsea | 240 Ninth Ave. (bet. 24th & 25th Sts.) | 212-242-4730 | www.txikitonyc.com

Unlike saying its name (pronounced 'chi-kee-toe'), your tongue will "welcome" this Chelsea newcomer's "authentic" Basque "twist on tapas" merged with "informed" service in a "woody" cubbyhole setting; the cost "adds up quickly", but it's already "crowded" with converts heading "back for more."

Umberto's Clam House *Italian/Seafood*

FOOD	DECOR	SERVICE	COST
18	13	17	$41

Little Italy | 386 Broome St. (Mulberry St.) | 212-343-2053 | www.umbertosclamhouse.com ●
Bronx | 2356 Arthur Ave. (186th St.) | 718-220-2526 | www.umbertosclamhousebronx.com

Dubbed "Clam Sauce Central", these Italian "throwbacks" "still ring true" for "typical" pastas served with "no surprises"; the Little Italy original's "splashy", *Godfather*-esque past is a magnet for "out-of-towners", while the Arthur Avenue spin-off is "not as touristy."

NEW Umi Nom Ⓩ⳨ *Filipino/Thai*

FOOD	DECOR	SERVICE	COST
-	-	-	M

Clinton Hill | 433 DeKalb Ave. (Classon Ave.) | Brooklyn | 718-789-8806 | www.uminom.com

Spun off from the popular LES spot Kuma Inn, this new Clinton Hill Filipino offers a Thai-accented small-plates menu similar to its parent's; set in a former Laundromat, the now-sleek, still narrow setting includes a skylight, open kitchen and long sake bar.

Uncle Jack's Steakhouse *Steak*

FOOD	DECOR	SERVICE	COST
23	19	22	$71

Garment District | 440 Ninth Ave. (bet. 34th & 35th Sts.) | 212-244-0005
W 50s | 44 W. 56th St. (bet. 5th & 6th Aves.) | 212-245-1550
Bayside | 39-40 Bell Blvd. (40th Ave.) | Queens | 718-229-1100
www.unclejacks.com

To "satisfy a steak craving" with "no pomp" and "no pretense", try this "traditional" trio that tenders "on-point" beef ferried by a "winning staff"; they're "popular" enough to be "players" in the chop wars, even if some cry uncle at their "steep" tabs.

Uncle Nick's *Greek*

FOOD	DECOR	SERVICE	COST
20	12	17	$34

Chelsea | 382 Eighth Ave. (29th St.) | 212-609-0500
W 50s | 747 Ninth Ave. (bet. 50th & 51st Sts.) | 212-245-7992
www.unclenicksgreekrestaurant.com

A "festive" "Greek fix" awaits at this "affable", "moderately priced" taverna twosome that serves "classic" dishes ranging from seafood to cheese flambé; the Hell's Kitchen original features a "fun" next-door *ouzaria,* while the Chelsea spin-off is more "spacious" than its sire.

	FOOD	DECOR	SERVICE	COST

Ⓩ Union Square Cafe *American* | 27 | 23 | 26 | $69 |

Union Sq | 21 E. 16th St. (bet. 5th Ave. & Union Sq. W.) | 212-243-4020 | www.unionsquarecafe.com

Now 25 years old, Danny Meyer's original restaurant "remains at the top of its form" thanks to "lovingly prepared" American food, a "tremendous wine list", "warm, welcoming" service, "charming" environs and, most important these days, "good value"; it has become a "NY landmark", and having the Union Square Greenmarket around the corner insures its ingredients are high quality.

Ushiwakamaru Ⓩ *Japanese* | ▽ 26 | 16 | 20 | $72 |

G Village | 136 W. Houston St. (bet. MacDougal & Sullivan Sts.) | 212-228-4181

There are "few others as authentic" as this "tiny" Village Japanese where "real sushi eaters" hit the bar and shell out for "awesome" omakase; maybe the decor is a bit "lacking", but followers who "care about the fish, not the frills" consider it their "secret" – and "hope it stays that way."

Uskudar *Turkish* | 19 | 10 | 17 | $37 |

E 70s | 1405 Second Ave. (bet. 73rd & 74th Sts.) | 212-988-2641 | www.uskudarnyc.com

"Tiny and terrific", this UES Turkish "hole-in-the-wall" is "dependable" for "surprisingly fine" staples that taste "homemade"; despite the "close quarters", "cheery" service and "moderate" tabs make it "tough to complain."

Utsav ❶ *Indian* | 20 | 18 | 18 | $40 |

W 40s | 1185 Sixth Ave., 2nd fl. (bet. 46th & 47th Sts.) | 212-575-2525 | www.utsavny.com

"Spacious" and "calm", this Midtown mezzanine "oasis" "gets it right" with "well-flavored" Indian dishes served in a "modern setting" that's particularly "enjoyable before a show"; come lunchtime, the $18 buffet is a "crowd-puller" that's "hard to beat."

Uva ❶ *Italian* | 21 | 21 | 19 | $41 |

E 70s | 1486 Second Ave. (bet. 77th & 78th Sts.) | 212-472-4552 | www.uvawinebarnewyork.com

"Date central" for the "twenty- to thirtysomething" set, this "buzzing" UES Italian entices with "addicting" light bites, "winning" wines, "affordability" and "eye candy" galore ("both staff and customers"); if the "cozy" interior gets too "noisy", try the "year-round garden."

Vai ❶ *Mediterranean* | 22 | 18 | 20 | $45 |

W 70s | 225 W. 77th St. (bet. Amsterdam Ave. & B'way) | 212-362-4500 | www.vairestaurant.com

UWS "trendy" types have a "new favorite" in this "charming", enoteca-ish eatery that matches "excellent" Med plates with "interesting" wines and "warm" "hospitality" in a "sweet" but "tight space"; fans deem it "promising" save for one downside: the "noise level."

Valbella Ⓩ *Italian* | 25 | 25 | 25 | $77 |

Meatpacking | 421 W. 13th St. (bet. 9th Ave. & Washington St.) | 212-645-7777 | www.valbellany.com

For "adult" dining in the Meatpacking District, this Northern Italian "class act" is a "sharp" looker with "fabulous" cuisine and a "superb wine list" that's "longer than *Harry Potter*"; it's on the "high end" price-wise, but the payoff is "treat-you-like-a-king" service.

V&T ● *Italian/Pizza* | 18 | 9 | 14 | $23 |

W 100s | 1024 Amsterdam Ave. (bet. 110th & 111th Sts.) | 212-666-8051
"Time seems to have stopped" at this Columbia-area "relic", a "red-gravy", budget-friendly Italian famed for its "primo" pizza and "college-kid" crowd; "nondescript decor" and "cartoonishly surly" waiters just "add to the charm."

Vatan Ⓜ *Indian* | 22 | 21 | 21 | $40 |

Murray Hill | 409 Third Ave. (29th St.) | 212-689-5666 | www.vatanny.com
With "nifty" new decor and a more "spacious layout", this recently re-opened "Indian village" mockup in Murray Hill remains a "vegetarian paradise", offering a $31 unlimited spread of "superior" meatless fare; "eager" service enables the "delightful pig-out."

NEW Veloce Pizzeria ●Ⓩ *Pizza* | - | - | - | M |

E Village | 103 First Ave. (bet. 6th & 7th Sts.) | 212-777-6677 | www.velocepizzeria.com
Sara Jenkins (Porchetta) and the Bar Veloce crew enter NYC's pizza fray at this roomy new East Villager serving Sicilian-style square pies; aside from the old-school checkered tablecloths, the digs are spiffier than the genre norm, ditto the well-curated Southern Italian wine list.

Vento *Italian* | 19 | 18 | 17 | $47 |

Meatpacking | 675 Hudson St. (14th St.) | 212-699-2400 | www.brguestrestaurants.com
Holding "steady" amid the "Meatpacking hubbub", Steve Hanson's "unpretentious" double-decker Italian is a "popular" fallback for "reasonable" eating and "cheerful" (if "uneven") service; the "young" ones on "outside seats" report that the "people-watching is half the fun."

Ⓩ Veritas *American* | 26 | 22 | 25 | $111 |

Flatiron | 43 E. 20th St. (bet. B'way & Park Ave. S.) | 212-353-3700 | www.veritas-nyc.com
"Nirvana for oenophiles" thanks to its "showstopping wine list", this otherwise "muted" Flatiron New American is also a "gourmand's dream" distinguished by new chef Grégory Pugin's "exceptional" skills and "top-of-the-line service"; the $85 prix fixe–only menu is an "indulgence" that's truly "worth saving up for."

Vermicelli *Vietnamese* | 20 | 16 | 19 | $33 |

E 70s | 1492 Second Ave. (bet. 77th & 78th Sts.) | 212-288-8868 | www.vermicellirestaurant.com
Forget the "misleading name": this "little" UES "neighborhood" nexus honestly boasts a "big variety" of "well-prepared", "well-priced" Vietnamese staples, enhanced by "sweet service"; its lunch-box special is a "local favorite" for "taste and value."

Veselka *Ukrainian* | 19 | 12 | 15 | $22 |

E Village | 144 Second Ave. (9th St.) | 212-228-9682 ●
E Village | First Park | 75 E. First St. (1st Ave.) | 347-907-3317 ⊯
www.veselka.com
Whether for a "no-nonsense" brunch or "late-night munchies", this 24/7 East Village "stalwart" slings "substantial" helpings of Ukrainian

"cheap eats" that sure "hit the spot"; despite "moody" service and "informal" digs, it's often a "full house"; N.B. East First Street's 'Little Veselka' stand plies a condensed version of the menu.

Vespa *Italian*

19 | 18 | 19 | $43

E 80s | 1625 Second Ave. (bet. 84th & 85th Sts.) | 212-472-2050 | www.vesparestaurant.com

"Once you've squeezed in", this "accommodating" UES "shoebox" "will win you over" with its "character" and "tasty", "fair-priced" Italiana (especially the "homemade pastas"); in "warm weather", the "buzzy" atmospherics extend to a "charming garden."

NEW Vesta *Italian*

∇ 25 | 21 | 26 | $29

Astoria | 21-02 30th Ave. (21st St.) | Queens | 718-545-5550 | www.vestavino.com

Locals "can't stop raving about" this Astoria newcomer that blends "locally grown" ingredients into "fabulous" pizzas and Italian plates served in a rustic "neighborhood" setting; add "welcoming service", well-priced wines and a "wonderful brunch", and it "exceeds expectations" all around.

Vezzo *Pizza*

23 | 14 | 16 | $24

Murray Hill | 178 Lexington Ave. (31st St.) | 212-839-8300 | www.vezzothincrust.com

"Marvelous pizza" is the métier of this "casual" Murray Hill Italian that puts out "super thin–crust" pies loaded with "generous" toppings at "easily affordable" rates; "close quarters" to the contrary, the "low-lit" room and "cheap wines" make it an "enjoyable" enough "joint."

Via Brasil *Brazilian/Steak*

20 | 15 | 18 | $40

W 40s | 34 W. 46th St. (bet. 5th & 6th Aves.) | 212-997-1158 | www.viabrasilrestaurant.com

There's always "a lot of meat" for the money at this Theater District Brazilian steakhouse where the "solid" specialties are augmented by "great caipirinhas" and "live jazz" piano on weekends; the digs may be "blah", but it's a "happening" scene "before or after the theater."

NEW Via dei Mille ● *Italian*

∇ 24 | 24 | 22 | $53

SoHo | 357 W. Broadway (bet. Broome & Grand Sts.) | 212-431-0080 | www.viadeimilleny.com

Traditional tastes meet SoHo-style "fashion" at this Northern Italian newcomer where trendy touches like a DJ keep the "beautiful people" coming; though the "nightclub" airs and posh prices are "distracting", early visitors report a "vibrant" scene.

Via Emilia ⊠⇗ *Italian*

22 | 16 | 18 | $38

Flatiron | 47 E. 21st St. (bet. B'way & Park Ave. S.) | 212-505-3072 | www.viaemilia.us

"Unpretentious" and "easy", this Flatiron Italian "sleeper" plies pastaphiles with "rich" "homemade" dishes from the Emilia-Romagna region accompanied by "impressive" regional wines; lira-pinchers note it's an "amazing value", though that no-plastic policy is a "bummer."

Viand *Coffee Shop*

17 | 8 | 17 | $22

E 60s | 673 Madison Ave. (bet. 61st & 62nd Sts.) | 212-751-6622 ⇗
(continued)

(continued)

Viand

E 70s | 1011 Madison Ave. (78th St.) | 212-249-8250
E 80s | 300 E. 86th St. (2nd Ave.) | 212-879-9425 ⏺
W 70s | 2130 Broadway (75th St.) | 212-877-2888 |
www.viandnyc.com ⏺

An "extensive menu" of "reliable" "luncheonette" vittles (including some of the "best turkey sandwiches anywhere") served "quick" keeps this "typical" coffee shop quartet "humming"; there's "no atmosphere" and "sardine-can" seating, but at least the "prices won't make you cringe."

Via Quadronno *Italian*   22 | 16 | 17 | $44

E 70s | 25 E. 73rd St. (bet. 5th & Madison Aves.) | 212-650-9880

Via Quadronno Cafe 🗷 *Italian*

E 50s | GM Bldg. | 767 Fifth Ave. (59th St.) | 212-421-5300
www.viaquadronno.com

Favored by "tailored blonds" and "Euros with money", this "*molto autentico*" UES Milanese is "quick-bite" central when you're in the mood for a "fabulous" panini-and-gelato fix; the "snug" setting, "confused" service and "wildly expensive" tabs don't faze its "snooty-patooty" crowd; N.B. the cafe in the GM building offers counter service only.

ViceVersa 🗷 *Italian*   22 | 21 | 22 | $54

W 50s | 325 W. 51st St. (bet. 8th & 9th Aves.) | 212-399-9291 |
www.viceversarestaurant.com

"Stylish" but "not stuffy", this Theater District "keeper" is a "convenient oasis" for "top-notch" Italian fare and "smooth" service in a "contemporary" setting enhanced by a "peaceful" patio; admirers applaud it as a "stress-free" experience that's always "well worth the price."

Vico ⏺ *Italian*   20 | 15 | 21 | $65

E 90s | 1302 Madison Ave. (bet. 92nd & 93rd Sts.) | 212-876-2222

"Clubby but reliable", this Carnegie Hill Italian is a sanctum of "upscale attitude" where "insiders" can count on "satisfying" food and "civil" service; outsiders report "not much charm" and "outrageous prices", but there is some good news: it now accepts credit cards.

Victor's Cafe ⏺ *Cuban*   21 | 19 | 20 | $52

W 50s | 236 W. 52nd St. (bet. B'way & 8th Ave.) | 212-586-7714 |
www.victorscafe.com

"Viva Victor!": this "tried-and-true" Theater District Cuban is "still *caliente*" for "flavorful" dishes both "traditional and modern" chased with potent, "leave-your-car-keys-at-home" mojitos; the "tropical energy" and "solicitous" service make for an always "upbeat" pre-theater prelude.

View, The 🅼 *American*   16 | 25 | 19 | $90

W 40s | Marriott Marquis Hotel | 1535 Broadway, 47th fl. (bet. 45th & 46th Sts.) | 212-704-8900 | www.nymarriottmarquis.com

Set in the Marriott's "revolving rooftop" overlooking Times Square's "bright lights", this 25-year-old New American restaurant-cum-"tourist's delight" boasts the "view of a lifetime", though the prix fixe menu is a lot "less spectacular"; just try not to get "dizzy" "when you see the prices."

	FOOD	DECOR	SERVICE	COST

Villa Mosconi 🗷 *Italian*
22 | 18 | 23 | $48

G Village | 69 MacDougal St. (bet. Bleecker & Houston Sts.) | 212-673-0390 | www.villamosconi.com

"Old-fashioned" Italian dining is "alive and well" at this '70s-vintage Villager that "can't be beat" for "real-deal favorites" (i.e. that "stand-out homemade" pasta) and "warm" service; maybe it's "a bit creaky", but once you're here "you're part of the family."

Vincent's ◐ *Italian*
21 | 13 | 18 | $36

Little Italy | 119 Mott St. (Hester St.) | 212-226-8133 | www.originalvincents.com

It's all about the signature hot sauce spicing up the "old-world" Italian "standards" at this Little Italy "mainstay", on the scene since 1904; its "vintage" neighborhood "character" remains intact, though nowadays the tables are more likely to be "crowded with tourists."

NEW Vinegar Hill House *American*
∇ 24 | 22 | 21 | $42

Vinegar Hill | 72 Hudson Ave. (bet. Front & Water Sts.) | Brooklyn | 718-522-1018 | www.vinegarhillhouse.com

Although "tucked away" in a "no-signage" space in Vinegar Hill, this "tiny" tyro is creating quite a "buzz" with its "brief menu" of "superb", "fairly priced" New Americana; fitted out with "salvaged" furnishings, the "rustic" room is already "ridiculously packed."

Virgil's Real Barbecue ◐ *BBQ*
19 | 14 | 16 | $35

W 40s | 152 W. 44th St. (bet. B'way & 6th Ave.) | 212-921-9494 | www.virgilsbbq.com

There's "no dieting allowed" at this "huge" Times Square "hoedown" that "pleases the masses" with "heaping plates" of "serious", "sloppy" barbecue; though "overcrowded" and "tourist-centric", it's a low-budget "fix" so long as you can abide "dazed" staffers and "sticky fingers."

Vong *French/Thai*
22 | 23 | 21 | $65

E 50s | 200 E. 54th St. (3rd Ave.) | 212-486-9592 | www.jean-georges.com

This "high-end" Midtowner from Jean-Georges Vongerichten "still impresses" with an "enticing" French-Thai menu that "leaves the palate tingling", served by a "gracious" crew in a "stylish" Siamese setting; though it's definitely "not cheap", the $24 lunch prix fixe is a "bargain."

NEW Vutera ◐ *Mediterranean*
- | - | - | M

Williamsburg | 345 Grand St., downstairs (bet. Havemeyer St. & Marcy Ave.) | Brooklyn | 718-388-8451

Set below Williamsburg's Rose Live Music nightclub, this new subterranean Mediterranean exudes rustic romance with candlelight, low beamed ceilings and an overall wine-cellar feel; the smallish, midpriced menu is equally inviting, and there's a bonus garden for nature lovers.

Waldy's Wood Fired Pizza *Pizza*
22 | 10 | 15 | $18

Chelsea | 800 Sixth Ave. (bet. 27th & 28th Sts.) | 212-213-5042 | www.waldyspizza.com

"Inspired" "crispy" pies emerge from the wood oven at Waldy Malouf's anchovy-sized Chelsea pizzeria, and "terrific", "imaginative" toppings add "zest"; "delivery" seems to be the best option, what with the "no-frills" space and "lack of seating."

	FOOD	DECOR	SERVICE	COST

Walker's ● *Pub Food*
17 | 14 | 17 | $31

TriBeCa | 16 N. Moore St. (Varick St.) | 212-941-0142

A "rare bird" in "overly trendy" TriBeCa, this "affordable" "neighborhood haunt" is an "old faithful" for "decent", "dolled-up pub grub" and "relaxed good times"; "after all these years" it still exudes "casual charm", and regulars "wouldn't change it a bit."

Wallsé *Austrian*
25 | 22 | 24 | $71

W Village | 344 W. 11th St. (Washington St.) | 212-352-2300 | www.kg-ny.com

Kurt Gutenbrunner's "creative takes" on Austrian cuisine are nothing less than a "revelation" at this "intimate" West Villager that blends "sophisticated" dishes, "excellent" wines and "impeccable service" with "tastefully designed" digs lined with Julian Schnabel art; just "bring a lot of schillings" when you "waltz in."

NEW Walter Foods ● *American*
▽ 23 | 22 | 22 | $44

Williamsburg | 253 Grand St. (Roebling St.) | Brooklyn | 718-387-8783 | www.walterfoods.com

Williamsburg's "adult" denizens deem this American debut a "perfect fit" thanks to "well-executed" eats and "solid" cocktails, served by "pros" in a handsome, saloon-style setting; simultaneously "classy" and "lively", it "already feels like it's been there forever."

Wasabi Lobby ● *Japanese*
19 | 13 | 18 | $32

E 80s | 1584 Second Ave. (82nd St.) | 212-988-8882 | www.wasabilobbynyc.com

Granted, the name may be "too cute for its own good", but lobbyists still plug this UES Japanese for its "inventive sushi" and "friendly" service; if the atmosphere's "lacking", the "well-priced" edibles are enough to satisfactorily "stimulate the senses."

Watawa *Japanese*
▽ 25 | 19 | 23 | $32

Astoria | 33-10 Ditmars Blvd. (bet. 33rd & 35th Sts.) | Queens | 718-545-9596

The "sushi gods are smiling on Astoria" at this "little Japanese treasure" where "phenomenal", "super-fresh" fish is prepared with "care" and served by an "excellent" team; given the "crazy good value", the "simple" surroundings are oftentimes "buzzing."

Water Club *American*
21 | 25 | 23 | $68

Murray Hill | East River at 30th St. (enter on 23rd St.) | 212-683-3333 | www.thewaterclub.com

"Hard-to-top" waterfront views set the "calming" mood at this "classy" American set on an East River barge, where the "wonderful food" and "pro service" are just the ticket for a "romantic evening" or "special occasion"; folks on a budget bypass the "big-bucks" bills via the "delightful" $39 Sunday brunch buffet.

⊠ Water's Edge ⊠ *American/Seafood*
22 | 26 | 23 | $64

LIC | East River & 44th Dr. (Vernon Blvd.) | Queens | 718-482-0033 | www.watersedgenyc.com

Thanks to "priceless" views of the Midtown skyline, this LIC New American has been a "favorite" for the "romantically" inclined for the past 25 years; the "top-notch" seafood, "excellent" staffers and free water taxi service from Manhattan take the edge off the "high" cost; P.S. it now boasts "new owners, a new chef" and "spruced-up surroundings."

NEW Watty & Meg *American*

-	-	-	M

Cobble Hill | 248 Court St. (Kane St.) | Brooklyn | 718-643-0007 | www.wattyandmeg.com

The affordable American menu at this Cobble Hill newcomer also includes some Southern-accented dishes like shrimp and grits; the interior is a funky-chic mix of repurposed items including Harlem church pews, a Colonial-style chandelier and salvaged tiles from City Hall.

Waverly Inn & Garden ● *American*

19	22	19	$72

W Village | 16 Bank St. (Waverly Pl.)

A "stargazer's" delight, this "private club"-like West Village tavern owned by *Vanity Fair* honcho Graydon Carter is a charming "celebrity haunt" where the "happy few" tuck into "gourmet American comfort food" while the "paparazzi lurk outside"; phone reservations aren't accepted, but walk-in requests are possible provided you're willing to dine "early or late."

wd-50 ●Ⓜ *American/Eclectic*

24	19	23	$92

LES | 50 Clinton St. (bet. Rivington & Stanton Sts.) | 212-477-2900 | www.wd-50.com

"Adventurous" types "leave their culinary inhibitions at the door" at this "LES wonder", where chef Wylie Dufresne's kitchen-cum-lab "never ceases to amaze" with its "fanciful" New American–Eclectic "creations"; for those with a taste for the "avant-garde", it's a "cool" (albeit "pricey") experience – even if "some of the experiments don't work."

West Bank Cafe *American*

19	16	19	$45

W 40s | Manhattan Plaza | 407 W. 42nd St. (bet. 9th & 10th Aves.) | 212-695-6909 | www.westbankcafe.com

"Handy" to the "off-Broadway theaters", this Hell's Kitchen New American is an "old standby" for "agreeable" grazing at "fair prices"; though decidedly "low-key", it's a "showbiz hangout" where "familiar faces" may appear and it's usually "thronged" before the curtain goes up.

NEW West Branch *American*

19	17	18	$48

W 70s | 2178 Broadway (77th St.) | 212-777-6764 | www.thewestbranchnyc.com

"Tom Valenti has hit the bull's-eye" at this "bustling" UWS newcomer, a "more casual" cousin of Ouest that branches out into "well-rendered", "well-priced" American bistro classics; with a "true-to-form" traditional setting and "helpful service", it's "very promising" – but "way too noisy."

Westville *American*

22	12	18	$25

W Village | 210 W. 10th St. (bet. Bleecker & W. 4th Sts.) | 212-741-7971

Westville East *American*

E Village | 173 Ave. A (11th St.) | 212-677-2033 | www.westvillenyc.com

"Vegetarians and carnivores alike" dig the "delish home cooking" at these cross-Village American "bohemian havens" known for their "farm-fresh veggies" and "dirt-cheap" prices; the "small", "spartan" spaces "fill up fast", so brace yourself for "crowds and noise."

	FOOD	DECOR	SERVICE	COST

NEW White Slab Palace ◐ *Scandinavian*
| | - | - | - | M |

LES | 77 Delancey St. (Allen St.) | 212-334-0913

Rapidly gentrifying Allen Street is home to this new Scandinavian from the Good World team offering Nordic fare to Lower Eastsiders in need of a cheap feed; the amply windowed corner setting feels like an old saloon, with a taxidermy-and-distressed-wood look that's considered the height of hip design these days.

Whym *American*
| | 19 | 17 | 19 | $42 |

W 50s | 889 Ninth Ave. (bet. 57th & 58th Sts.) | 212-315-0088 | www.whymnyc.com

Expect "no pretense" at this "worthy" Hell's Kitchen New American that gives "innovative spins" to comfort food at "prices that aren't over the top"; the "recently expanded space" is now "more open and airy" for dining "pre-show" – or just "on a whim."

'wichcraft *Sandwiches*
| | 20 | 11 | 14 | $16 |

Chelsea | 269 11th Ave. (bet. 27th & 28th Sts.) | 212-780-0577 🛇
E 40s | 245 Park Ave. (47th St.) | 212-780-0577 🛇
E 40s | 555 Fifth Ave. (46th St.) | 212-780-0577 🛇
Flatiron | 11 E. 20th St. (bet. B'way & 5th Ave.) | 212-780-0577
G Village | 60 E. Eighth St. (Mercer St.) | 212-780-0577
Murray Hill | Equinox | 1 Park Ave. (33rd St.) | 212-780-0577
SoHo | Equinox | 106 Crosby St. (Prince St.) | 212-780-0577
TriBeCa | 397 Greenwich St. (Beach St.) | 212-780-0577
W 40s | Bryant Park | Sixth Ave. (bet. 40th & 42nd Sts.) | 212-780-0577
W 50s | 1 Rockefeller Plaza (on 50th St., bet. 5th & 6th Aves.) | 212-780-0577
www.wichcraftnyc.com
Additional locations throughout the NY area

"Tom Colicchio's wizardry" lies behind this "crafty" local chain that conjures up "upper-crust sandwiches" made from "inventive combos" of "fresh" ingredients; despite "long" prime-time lines and "hefty price tags", legions of lunchers are "under their spell."

Wildwood Barbeque *BBQ*
| | 17 | 17 | 17 | $39 |

Flatiron | 225 Park Ave. S. (bet. 18th & 19th Sts.) | 212-533-2500 | www.brguestrestaurants.com

The "Steve Hanson formula" draws "youngish" "urban chic" types to this Flatiron "hog heaven" for "full-flavored" BBQ and "good ol' times" in "big, loud" digs; critics contend the 'cue "falls short for the price", but overall it's still "decent for NYC."

Wo Hop ◐⇄ *Chinese*
| | 21 | 5 | 12 | $20 |

Chinatown | 17 Mott St., downstairs (Canal St.) | 212-267-2536

This "old-time" Chinatown "fixture" (since 1938) obliges the "budget-minded" with "killer" Cantonese chow served into the "wee hours"; although it's a "dinky" basement "hovel" with "grudging service", "there's a reason" for those "lines" in the stairwell.

⊠ Wolfgang's Steakhouse *Steak*
| | 25 | 20 | 22 | $77 |

Murray Hill | 4 Park Ave. (33rd St.) | 212-889-3369
TriBeCa | 409 Greenwich St. (bet. Beach & Hubert Sts.) | 212-925-0350
www.wolfgangssteakhouse.com

Cleaving to the "upscale" steakhouse template, these Peter Luger "xeroxes" serve "quality" chops in "old-fashioned style" to a "noisy",

	FOOD	DECOR	SERVICE	COST

expense-account clientele; they do "pack them in" and "reservation times are frequently disregarded", so "count on waiting."

Wollensky's Grill ● *Steak* — 23 | 17 | 20 | $57

E 40s | 201 E. 49th St. (3rd Ave.) | 212-753-0444 | www.smithandwollensky.com

For the "casual side of Smith & Wollensky", try its "less expensive" next-door annex, a "lively" alternative for a "quick", "flavorful" steak break (or "excellent burger") in an "old-school" barroom setting; its "late" hours allow "night owls" to alight until 2 AM.

Wombat ●⇱ *Australian* — ▽ 23 | 18 | 23 | $33

Williamsburg | 613 Grand St. (bet. Leonard & Lorimer Sts.) | Brooklyn | 718-218-7077 | www.thewombatbar.com

As "authentically Australian" as it gets, this "fun little" Williamsburg bar/eatery enthralls fans with "pretty awesome" Ozzie pub grub and "friendly", "well-oiled" service; specials like Tuesday's $13 lobster deal are "worth venturing out for", mate.

Wondee Siam *Thai* — 22 | 9 | 16 | $23

W 40s | 641 10th Ave. (bet. 45th & 46th Sts.) | 212-245-4601 | www.wondeesiam3.com
W 50s | 792 Ninth Ave. (bet. 52nd & 53rd Sts.) | 212-459-9057 ⇱
W 50s | 813 Ninth Ave. (bet. 53rd & 54th Sts.) | 917-286-1726 | www.wondeesiam2.com
NEW **W 100s** | 969 Amsterdam Ave. (bet. 107th & 108th Sts.) | 212-531-1788 | www.wondeesiamv.com

"Cheap eats" lure "serious Thai" junkies to this "authentic" Hell's Kitchen triad (and their new UWS sibling) for a "swift" fix of "fabulous food" from "the Land of Smiles"; sure, there's "not much ambiance" or service, but at these prices "who can complain?"

Woo Lae Oak *Korean* — 21 | 21 | 19 | $51

SoHo | 148 Mercer St. (bet. Houston & Prince Sts.) | 212-925-8200 | www.woolaeoaksoho.com

Fans of "hands-on" dining tout this "snazzy" SoHo Korean specialist in cook-it-yourself BBQ; though "pricey" and "not so authentic", it's "trendier than 32nd Street" and the "model-type waiters" don't hurt either.

Wu Liang Ye *Chinese* — 22 | 11 | 15 | $33

E 80s | 215 E. 86th St. (bet. 2nd & 3rd Aves.) | 212-534-8899
Murray Hill | 338 Lexington Ave. (bet. 39th & 40th Sts.) | 212-370-9648 | www.wuliangyeny.com
W 40s | 36 W. 48th St. (bet. 5th & 6th Aves.) | 212-398-2308

A "fire extinguisher" comes in handy at this Chinese trio, where the "hot spices" suffusing the "well-crafted" Sichuan fare will "bring tears to your eyes"; despite "lackluster" looks and "brusque" service, their "authenticity" and modest prices make them neighborhood "favorites."

X.O. *Chinese* — 20 | 13 | 15 | $31

Chinatown | 96 Walker St. (bet. Centre & Lafayette Sts.) | 212-343-8339
Little Italy | 148 Hester St. (bet. Bowery & Elizabeth St.) | 212-965-8645 ⇱

There's a "huge variety" of Hong Kong-style dim sum available at "dirt-cheap" prices at this "fast-paced" Chinatown-Little Italy pair, whose "reliable food" includes many "adventurous" choices; just know that the digs are "nothing special, and neither is the service."

	FOOD	DECOR	SERVICE	COST

Xunta ● *Spanish* | 21 | 14 | 16 | $32

E Village | 174 First Ave. (bet. 10th & 11th Sts.) | 212-614-0620 |
www.xuntatapasbar.com

"Carefree" twentysomethings "sit around barrels" and "rub elbows"
over "yummy tapas" and "strong sangria" at this "casual" East Village
Spaniard; sure, it gets "loud and crowded", and you'll "never get the
waitress' attention", but at least the prices won't beat your budget.

Yakitori Totto ● *Japanese* | 25 | 17 | 20 | $46

W 50s | 251 W. 55th St., 2nd fl. (bet. B'way & 8th Ave.) | 212-245-4555 |
www.torysnyc.com

Proving there's "more than sushi" to Japanese cuisine, this "real-deal"
Midtown yakitori grill offers an "exotic menu" with "choices aplenty",
but is best known for its "addictive" skewered meats and veggies; on the
downside, the tabs "sure add up" and the house is "always packed."

Yama ⌧ *Japanese* | 24 | 13 | 17 | $41

E 40s | 308 E. 49th St. (bet. 1st & 2nd Aves.) | 212-355-3370
Gramercy | 122 E. 17th St. (Irving Pl.) | 212-475-0969
G Village | 38-40 Carmine St. (bet. Bedford & Bleecker Sts.) | 212-989-9330
www.yamarestaurant.com

Celebrated for "sumo"-size slabs of "super-fresh fish", these "no-
nonsense" Japanese "favorites" proffer a "first-rate" "fix for any sushi
craving" for "decent" dough; their "tight quarters" are regularly
"mobbed", but "have patience – it's worth the wait."

Yerba Buena *Pan-Latin* | 24 | 21 | 23 | $47

E Village | 23 Ave. A (bet. Houston & 2nd Sts.) | 212-529-2919
NEW **G Village** | 1 Perry St. (Greenwich Ave.) | 212-620-0808 ●
www.ybnyc.com

Pan-Latin cooking benefits from a "fresh approach" at this "sexy" East
Village yearling where chef Julian Medina's "nuevo spins" yield "terrific
flavors" enhanced by "warm" service and "carefully crafted cocktails";
boosters see a "real gem" whose rising "popularity" is "well deserved";
N.B. the Perry Street branch opened post-Survey.

York Grill *American* | 21 | 20 | 22 | $52

E 80s | 1690 York Ave. (bet. 88th & 89th Sts.) | 212-772-0261
For "adult dining" in "out-of-the-way" Yorkville, this "clublike" New
American provides "sensible meals" and "accommodating" service; it's
"not cheap" for the area, but keeps the locals "feeling well taken care of."

Yuca Bar ● *Pan-Latin* | 21 | 15 | 16 | $32

E Village | 111 Ave. A (7th St.) | 212-982-9533 | www.yucabarnyc.com
"Boisterous" young folk jam into this "colorful" East Villager in pursuit
of "tasty", "well-priced" Pan-Latin nibbles chased with "tropical cocktails" and "dangerous sangria"; the "people-watching" is primo "if
that's your thing", but "don't expect a quiet meal."

Yuka *Japanese* | 21 | 10 | 17 | $31

E 80s | 1557 Second Ave. (bet. 80th & 81st Sts.) | 212-772-9675
"One of the best values" for "quality sushi" Uptown, this Yorkville
Japanese "hole-in-the-wall" draws crowds with its "amazing" $21 all-
you-can-eat offer; though "cramped" and "not much to look at", it's
"hard to beat" – for best results, "go hungry."

	FOOD	DECOR	SERVICE	COST

Yuki Sushi ◐ *Japanese*
21 | 15 | 21 | $32

W 90s | 656 Amsterdam Ave. (92nd St.) | 212-787-8200

A knack for "well-crafted", "decently priced" sushi and courteous service qualify this UWS Japanese as a "neighborhood go-to" even if the lineup is "not very exciting"; though the "casual" setting is "not glamorous", "delivery is super-fast."

Yuva *Indian*
23 | 18 | 20 | $42

E 50s | 230 E. 58th St. (bet. 2nd & 3rd Aves.) | 212-339-0090 | www.yuvanyc.com

"Familiarity and inventiveness" come together at this East Midtown Indian that "goes beyond the usual" with "refined variations" on well-known standards served by a "sweet, helpful" crew; "affordable" tabs (notably the $14 buffet lunch) offset the "nondescript decor."

Zabar's Cafe *Deli*
19 | 7 | 11 | $19

W 80s | 2245 Broadway (80th St.) | 212-787-2000 | www.zabars.com

For a "low-priced" "quick munch", this "rough-and-ready" UWS "institution" dishes out "appetizing" deli favorites (bagels, nova, etc.) from a "fast-paced counter"; the "surly" service, "bare" backdrop and "hectic" crowds are nothing short of a "true NY experience."

Zaitzeff *Burgers*
∇ 22 | 12 | 16 | $21

E Village | 18 Ave. B (bet. 2nd & 3rd Sts.) | 212-477-7137 ◑
Financial District | 72 Nassau St. (John St.) | 212-571-7272
www.zaitzeffnyc.com

Grab a glamburger at these "unpretentious" Downtown joints where the "flavorful" roster includes patties made of sirloin, Kobe beef, turkey or veggies, supplemented by "excellent fries"; they're "really a cut above", though paupers ponder if they're really "worth the price."

Zarela *Mexican*
20 | 16 | 17 | $44

E 50s | 953 Second Ave. (bet. 50th & 51st Sts.) | 212-644-6740 | www.zarela.com

"Still going strong", Zarela Martinez's "fast-paced" East Midtown duplex remains a "consistent winner" for "bold" Mexican chow and a "hopping" nightlife scene at the "deafening" street-level bar; just "beware" of margaritas so "lethal" that "you might forget to eat."

Zaytoons *Mideastern*
21 | 13 | 17 | $21

Carroll Gardens | 283 Smith St. (Sackett St.) | Brooklyn | 718-875-1880
Fort Greene | 472 Myrtle Ave. (bet. Hall St. & Washington Ave.) | Brooklyn | 718-623-5522
Prospect Heights | 594 Vanderbilt Ave. (St. Marks Ave.) | Brooklyn | 718-230-3200 ⊟
www.zaytoonsrestaurant.com

Like a "second kitchen" for locals, these "convenient" Brooklynites are "steady" suppliers of "solid" "homemade" Mideastern grub; though they're certainly "nothing fancy", the cost is very "easy to swallow" – especially at the BYO outposts in Carroll Gardens and Fort Greene.

Za Za *Italian*
20 | 14 | 20 | $40

E 60s | 1207 First Ave. (bet. 65th & 66th Sts.) | 212-772-9997 | www.zazanyc.com

"Locals" favor this "unassuming" East Side "standby" for "fine", "freshly made" Florentine cuisine "served with a smile" for "reasonable"

| | FOOD | DECOR | SERVICE | COST |

dough; though the interior is "dull", the "back garden" is a "big attraction" in clement weather.

Zebú Grill *Brazilian* | 20 | 16 | 20 | $38 |

E 90s | 305 E. 92nd St. (bet. 1st & 2nd Aves.) | 212-426-7500 | www.zebugrill.com

Slightly "off the beaten track", this "cozy" UES Brazilian "passes muster" with a variety of "authentic", "moderately priced" churrasco knocked back with "knockout caipirinhas"; it's always "welcoming" and "never too loud or too full."

🆕 Ze Café *French/Italian* | ▽ 21 | 23 | 21 | $53 |

E 50s | 398 E. 52nd St. (bet. FDR Dr. & 1st Ave.) | 212-758-1944

Occupying the "former shop" of fancy florist Zezé, this "adorable" Sutton Place newcomer is an "instant hit" thanks to its "elegant" Franco-Italian offerings and "lovely" floral displays; it's a "breath of scented air" for "society" gals and other "upper-crust" types, though some find ze prices "too precious."

☒ Zenkichi Ⓜ *Japanese* | 25 | 27 | 25 | $55 |

Williamsburg | 77 N. Sixth St. (Wythe Ave.) | Brooklyn | 718-388-8985 | www.zenkichi.com

Perfect for an "intimate" tryst with "your secret flame", this Williamsburg izakaya is hidden behind a "nondescript exterior" concealing a "dark" triplex setting lined with "mirrors and bamboo"; diners summon the "spot-on" staffers with "buzzers" to order "refined" Japanese small plates, and though it's "a splurge", it's sure to "make a big impression."

Zen Palate *Vegetarian* | 18 | 14 | 17 | $31 |

W 40s | 663 Ninth Ave. (46th St.) | 212-582-1669 | www.zenpalate.com

A former chain that's been "downsized" to a single site in Hell's Kitchen, this "dependable" BYO features "inspired vegetarian cooking" so "refreshing" "you won't miss the meat"; granted, the atmosphere is "ho-hum", but both the "healthful" chow and "modest prices" leave fans feeling "virtuous."

Zero Otto Nove Ⓜ *Pizza* | 25 | 23 | 21 | $43 |

Bronx | 2357 Arthur Ave. (186th St.) | 718-220-1027 | www.roberto089.com

A "less costly" spin-off of Arthur Avenue favorite Roberto, this "terrific" pizzeria honors its "pedigree" with "magnificent" brick-oven pies and other "old-country" Italiana served by a "friendly" team; decorated with a trompe l'oeil Salerno streetscape, the "delightful surroundings" are typically "lively", so "bring earplugs."

Zest Ⓜ *American* | ▽ 23 | 21 | 21 | $57 |

Staten Island | 977 Bay St. (Willow Ave.) | 718-390-8477 | www.zestsiny.com

Living up to its name, this "Manhattan-like" New American "brings zest" to a "lonely stretch" of Staten Island's Rosebank with "top-notch" French-inspired fare and "attentive service"; it's "pricey" but "totally charming", notably in the back courtyard that recalls a "European cafe."

	FOOD	DECOR	SERVICE	COST

Zoë *American*

| 20 | 17 | 19 | $50 |

SoHo | 90 Prince St. (bet. B'way & Mercer St.) | 212-966-6722 |
www.zoerestaurant.com

A "longtime backup" for brunchers and shopaholics, this "relaxed"
SoHo New American "works fine" for "well-prepared" food served by
a "caring" staff; a few fret it's "nothing special" given its price point,
but it "keeps on tickin'" for a crowd of "steady" regulars.

Zoma *Ethiopian*

| ∇ 23 | 20 | 19 | $30 |

Harlem | 2084 Frederick Douglass Blvd. (bet. 112th & 113th Sts.) |
212-662-0620 | www.zomanyc.com

For a "more upscale" Ethiopian experience, this "sleek" Harlem spot
specializes in "well-spiced" platters of "rich, earthy" stews meant to
be scooped up with "scrumptious" injera bread; it's particularly fun for
"newbies", but everyone "leaves stuffed" for a "good price."

Zorzi ●🅱 *Italian*

| ∇ 21 | 22 | 18 | $64 |

Murray Hill | 1 E. 35th St. (bet. 5th & Madison Aves.) | 212-213-9167 |
www.zorzi-nyc.it

A "welcome addition" to an underserved part of Murray Hill, this
Northern Italian offers "comfort food" with "high-end" contemporary
accents in a "posh", bi-level space; early word calls it "surprisingly
good", but brace yourself for a steep tab.

Zum Schneider 🚫 *German*

| 19 | 17 | 18 | $30 |

E Village | 107 Ave. C (7th St.) | 212-598-1098 | www.zumschneider.com
East Villagers "raise their mugs" to this "rowdy" "Bavarian beer hall",
a "convivial" retreat for zum "rib-sticking" Deutschlandia washed
down with brews "by the liter", all at "attractive prices"; it's usually
"full to the rafters", but if you're up for "revelry", look no further.

Zum Stammtisch *German*

| 22 | 19 | 20 | $39 |

Glendale | 69-46 Myrtle Ave. (bet. 69th Pl. & 70th St.) | Queens |
718-386-3014 | www.zumstammtisch.com

"Ach du lieber!", this "old-school" Glendale German is the "real deal"
for "heaping" helpings of "awesome" Teutonic favorites served by
"charming fräuleins" in "full dress"; a "schmaltzy" echt-Bavarian
setting, "wonderful beer selection" and fair prices all bolster the
"good-hearted atmosphere."

Zutto *Japanese*

| ∇ 23 | 18 | 21 | $39 |

TriBeCa | 77 Hudson St. (Harrison St.) | 212-233-3287 | www.sushizutto.com
"TriBeCa locals" swear this "friendly little" Japanese "sleeper" will
amaze you with its "winning combination" of "fantastic sushi" and
"reasonable" tabs; since it's relatively "unknown and unappreciated",
it's an excellent "low-key" alternative "when you can't get into Nobu."

INDEXES

LOCATION MAPS

Cuisines

Includes restaurant names, locations and Food ratings.

AFGHAN

Afghan Kebab	**multi.**	19

AFRICAN

abistro	**Ft Greene**	25
Les Enfants	**LES**	18

AMERICAN (NEW)

Abigail	**Prospect Hts**	20
Alchemy	**Park Slope**	19
Allen/Delancey	**LES**	23
NEW André	**E 50s**	-
Annisa	**G Vill**	27
Apiary	**E Vill**	22
☑ applewood	**Park Slope**	26
☑ Asiate	**W 60s**	24
NEW Aureole	**W 40s**	29
Back Forty	**E Vill**	21
☑ Bar Americain	**W 50s**	23
Bar Blanc	**G Vill**	22
barmarché	**NoLita**	18
Battery Gdns.	**Financial**	18
Beacon	**W 50s**	23
Bistro Ten 18	**W 100s**	19
Black Duck	**Murray Hill**	20
BLT Market	**W 50s**	23
☑ Blue Hill	**G Vill**	27
Blue Ribbon	**multi.**	24
Blue Ribbon Bakery	**G Vill**	24
Boathouse	**E 70s**	17
Bobo	**W Vill**	22
Bouchon Bakery	**W 60s**	23
NEW Braeburn	**W Vill**	21
Brasserie 44	**W 40s**	20
NEW Brasserie 1605	**W 40s**	-
Bridge Cafe	**Financial**	21
Broadway East	**LES**	22
Brown Café	**LES**	23
Bruckner B&G	**Bronx**	-
NEW Bussaco	**Park Slope**	22
Butter	**E Vill**	20
NEW Buttermilk	**Carroll Gdns**	23
CamaJe	**G Vill**	20
Casellula	**W 50s**	25
Caviar Russe	**E 50s**	25
NEW Charles	**W Vill**	18
Chestnut	**Carroll Gdns**	24
Cibo	**E 40s**	20
☑ Clinton St. Baking	**LES**	25
Commerce	**W Vill**	22
Community Food	**W 100s**	21
Compass	**W 70s**	22

Cornelia St. Cafe	**G Vill**	19
Country	**Murray Hill**	21
☑ Craft	**Flatiron**	25
Craftbar	**Flatiron**	22
David Burke Townhse.	**E 60s**	25
Delicatessen	**NoLita**	18
Diner	**W'burg**	24
Ditch Plains	**G Vill**	18
☑ Dovetail	**W 70s**	26
Dressler	**W'burg**	25
Duane Park	**TriBeCa**	23
DuMont	**W'burg**	22
Eatery	**W 50s**	20
eighty one	**W 80s**	25
elmo	**Chelsea**	16
Essex	**LES**	18
Etats-Unis	**E 80s**	23
Farm/Adderley	**Ditmas Pk**	22
5 Front	**Dumbo**	19
NEW Five Leaves	**W'burg**	23
5 9th	**Meatpacking**	19
5 Points	**NoHo**	22
Flatbush Farm	**Park Slope**	20
44/44½	**W 40s**	22
☑ Four Seasons	**E 50s**	26
Fred's at Barneys	**E 60s**	20
Freemans	**LES**	21
NEW Fulton	**E 70s**	22
Gen. Greene	**Ft Greene**	20
☑ Gilt	**E 50s**	25
Giorgio's	**Flatiron**	21
good	**W Vill**	21
☑ Gotham B&G	**G Vill**	27
☑ Gramercy Tavern	**Flatiron**	28
Greenhouse	**Bay Ridge**	21
☑ Grocery	**Carroll Gdns**	27
NEW Gus/Gabriel	**W 70s**	-
NEW Haakon's Hall	**W 100s**	-
Harrison	**TriBeCa**	24
Hearth	**E Vill**	25
Henry's End	**Bklyn Hts**	24
NEW Hotel Griffou	**G Vill**	20
Hudson River	**Harlem**	19
Hundred Acres	**SoHo**	19
Ici	**Ft Greene**	21
NEW Inside Park	**E 50s**	17
Irving Mill	**Gramercy**	20
Isabella's	**W 70s**	20
Jack Horse	**Bklyn Hts**	24
James	**Prospect Hts**	23
Jane	**G Vill**	21

Jimmy's | **E Vill**	20
Joe Doe | **E Vill**	23
Josephina | **W 60s**	18
NEW Joseph Leonard | **G Vill**	-
Kings' Carriage | **E 80s**	22
Kingswood | **G Vill**	19
Klee Brass. | **Chelsea**	20
Knickerbocker | **G Vill**	20
Z Lady Mendl's | **Gramercy**	22
NEW Levant East | **LES**	-
Little Giant | **LES**	22
Z Little Owl | **W Vill**	26
NEW Lot 2 | **Park Slope**	-
Maggie Brown | **Clinton Hill**	19
Marc Forgione | **TriBeCa**	23
Market Table | **G Vill**	23
Z Marlow/Sons | **W'burg**	26
Z Mas | **G Vill**	27
Melt | **Park Slope**	21
Mercer Kitchen | **SoHo**	21
Metrazur | **E 40s**	21
Z Modern | **W 50s**	26
NEW Momofuku Bakery | **E Vill**	21
Z Momofuku Ko | **E Vill**	27
Momofuku Noodle | **E Vill**	23
Z Momofuku Ssäm | **E Vill**	25
Z NEW Monkey Bar | **E 50s**	18
Morgan | **Murray Hill**	20
Morrell Wine | **W 40s**	18
NEW Mott | **L Italy**	-
New French | **W Vill**	21
New Leaf | **Wash. Hts**	21
Niche | **E 80s**	24
NEW Nios | **W 40s**	-
NoHo Star | **NoHo**	18
Norma's | **W 50s**	25
Northeast Kingdom | **Bushwick**	-
North Sq. | **G Vill**	23
NEW No. 7 | **Ft Greene**	23
NEW Oak Room | **W 50s**	18
Z NEW Oceana | **W 40s**	-
Olana | **Murray Hill**	23
Z One if by Land | **G Vill**	24
101 | **Bay Ridge**	21
Orchard | **LES**	23
Z Ouest | **W 80s**	24
Park Ave. | **E 60s**	24
Patroon | **E 40s**	21
Perilla | **G Vill**	25
Z Per Se | **W 60s**	28
Petit Oven | **Bay Ridge**	-
Picket Fence | **Ditmas Pk**	19
Place | **W Vill**	19
Pop Burger | **multi.**	18
NEW Prime Meat | **Carroll Gdns**	19

Prune | **E Vill**	24
Quaint | **Sunnyside**	23
Quality Meats | **W 50s**	24
NEW Recipe | **W 80s**	-
Red Cat | **Chelsea**	23
Redeye Grill | **W 50s**	20
Redhead | **E Vill**	21
Regency | **E 60s**	18
Relish | **W'burg**	20
Riingo | **E 40s**	21
Z River Café | **Dumbo**	26
Riverview | **LIC**	21
Rose Water | **Park Slope**	26
NEW Rouge Tomate | **E 60s**	22
NEW Rye | **W'burg**	-
Salt | **multi.**	23
Saul | **Boerum Hill**	26
Savoy | **SoHo**	24
Seven | **Chelsea**	19
Shorty's.32 | **SoHo**	23
Smith | **E Vill**	19
South Gate | **W 50s**	24
Spitzer's | **LES**	20
NEW Standard Grill | **Meatpacking**	22
Stone Park | **Park Slope**	25
NEW Sweet Emily's | **W 50s**	18
Sweetwater | **W'burg**	21
Z Telepan | **W 60s**	26
NEW 10 Downing | **G Vill**	21
Thalia | **W 50s**	19
Z Tocqueville | **Union Sq**	26
Trestle on 10th | **Chelsea**	19
Tribeca Grill | **TriBeCa**	22
12th St. B&G | **Park Slope**	21
212 | **E 60s**	18
Z Union Sq. Cafe | **Union Sq**	27
Z Veritas | **Flatiron**	26
View | **W 40s**	16
NEW Vinegar Hill Hse. | **Vinegar Hill**	24
NEW Walter Foods | **W'burg**	23
Z Water's Edge | **LIC**	22
NEW Watty/Meg | **Cobble Hill**	-
wd-50 | **LES**	24
West Bank Cafe | **W 40s**	19
NEW West Branch | **W 70s**	19
Whym | **W 50s**	19
York Grill | **E 80s**	21
Zest | **SI**	23
Zoë | **SoHo**	20

AMERICAN (TRADITIONAL)

Algonquin | **W 40s**	17
Alias | **LES**	21

Angus McIndoe	**W 40s**	17
NEW Barberry	**W'burg**	-
Barking Dog	**multi.**	15
Brooklyn Diner	**multi.**	17
Bryant Park	**W 40s**	17
Bubba Gump	**W 40s**	14
Bubby's	**multi.**	18
Cafe Cluny	**W Vill**	21
Cafeteria	**Chelsea**	18
Chadwick's	**Bay Ridge**	22
Coffee Shop	**Union Sq**	15
Cookshop	**Chelsea**	22
NEW Cornelius	**Prospect Hts**	18
Corner Bistro	**W Vill**	22
Dirty Bird	**W Vill**	18
Dylan Prime	**TriBeCa**	24
E.A.T.	**E 80s**	19
EJ's Luncheon.	**multi.**	16
Elaine's	**E 80s**	13
Fairway Cafe	**multi.**	18
NEW Fat Hippo	**LES**	20
Fatty's Cafe	**Astoria**	22
Fraunces Tavern	**Financial**	16
Friend/Farmer	**Gramercy**	18
Good Enough/Eat	**W 80s**	21
Heartland	**multi.**	14
HK	**Garment**	17
Home	**G Vill**	21
Houston's	**multi.**	20
Hudson Cafeteria	**W 50s**	19
Jackson Hole	**multi.**	17
Joe Allen	**W 40s**	17
NEW Jo's	**NoLita**	-
Landmark Tavern	**W 40s**	17
NEW Lucy Browne	**W Vill**	-
Mama's Food	**E Vill**	20
Angelo/Maxie's	**Flatiron**	22
Moran's	**Chelsea**	18
Odeon	**TriBeCa**	19
O'Neal's	**W 60s**	17
Penelope	**Murray Hill**	22
NEW Permanent Brunch	**E Vill**	-
Pershing Sq.	**E 40s**	16
Popover Cafe	**W 80s**	18
Sarabeth's	**multi.**	20
NEW Schnipper's	**W 40s**	17
S'MAC/Pinch	**multi.**	21
Square Meal	**E 90s**	23
NEW Sweetiepie	**G Vill**	14
Swifty's	**E 70s**	18
Tavern on Green	**W 60s**	15
T-Bar Steak	**E 70s**	22
12 Chairs	**SoHo**	19
Z 21 Club	**W 50s**	22

Walker's	**TriBeCa**	17
Water Club	**Murray Hill**	21
Waverly Inn	**W Vill**	19
Westville	**multi.**	22

ARGENTINEAN

Azul Bistro	**LES**	22
Buenos Aires	**E Vill**	22
Chimichurri Grill	**W 40s**	22
NEW El Almacén	**W'burg**	-
NEW Flying Cow	**W'burg**	-
La Rural	**W 90s**	21
Novecento	**SoHo**	22
Sosa Borella	**W 50s**	19

ASIAN

Z Asia de Cuba	**Murray Hill**	22
Z Asiate	**W 60s**	24
Z Buddakan	**Chelsea**	23
China Grill	**W 50s**	22
Citrus B&G	**W 70s**	20

ASIAN FUSION

Ajna Bar	**Meatpacking**	19
Chinese Mirch	**multi.**	19
Chow Bar	**W Vill**	20
JJ's Asian Fusion	**Astoria**	24

AUSTRALIAN

Bondi Rd.	**LES**	18
8 Mile Creek	**NoLita**	20
NEW Five Leaves	**W'burg**	23
Kingswood	**G Vill**	19
Sheep Sta.	**Park Slope**	18
Wombat	**W'burg**	23

AUSTRIAN

Blaue Gans	**TriBeCa**	21
Café Katja	**LES**	23
Café Sabarsky	**E 80s**	22
Cafe Steinhof	**Park Slope**	18
NEW Seasonal	**W 50s**	25
Thomas Beisl	**Ft Greene**	17
Wallsé	**W Vill**	25

BAKERIES

Amy's Bread	**multi.**	24
Blue Ribbon Bakery	**G Vill**	24
Bouchon Bakery	**W 60s**	23
City Bakery	**Flatiron**	22
Z Clinton St. Baking	**LES**	25
La Bergamote	**multi.**	25
La Flor Bakery	**Woodside**	23
Le Pain Q.	**multi.**	19
NEW Momofuku Bakery	**E Vill**	21
Provence/Boite	**Carroll Gdns**	20

BARBECUE

☑ Blue Smoke	multi.	21
Brother Jimmy	multi.	16
NEW Chimney	E 100s	-
Daisy May's	W 40s	23
Dallas BBQ	multi.	15
Dinosaur BBQ	Harlem	22
☑ Fette Sau	W'burg	25
Hill Country	Flatiron	21
Rack & Soul	W 100s	19
RUB BBQ	Chelsea	20
Smoke Joint	Ft Greene	21
Virgil's BBQ	W 40s	19
Wildwood BBQ	Flatiron	17

BELGIAN

B. Café	multi.	21
BXL	multi.	20
Café de Bruxelles	W Vill	21
Le Pain Q.	multi.	19
Markt	Flatiron	20
Petite Abeille	multi.	17
Resto	Murray Hill	20

BRAZILIAN

NEW Bossa Nova	W 50s	21
Cafe Colonial	NoLita	19
Churrascaria	multi.	23
Circus	E 60s	20
Coffee Shop	Union Sq	15
NEW Favela Cubana	G Vill	-
Malagueta	Astoria	25
Métisse	W 100s	18
Rice 'n' Beans	W 50s	20
SushiSamba	multi.	21
Via Brasil	W 40s	20
Zebú Grill	E 90s	20

BRITISH

ChipShop	multi.	19
NEW Clerkenwell	LES	-
Tea & Sympathy	W Vill	21

BURGERS

Big Nick's	W 70s	17
Black Iron	E Vill	21
BLT Burger	G Vill	20
brgr	Chelsea	19
Burger Heaven	multi.	16
☑ burger joint	W 50s	24
Corner Bistro	W Vill	22
☑ db Bistro Moderne	W 40s	24
DuMont	W'burg	22
Five Guys	multi.	20
5 Napkin Burger	W 40s	21
goodburger	multi.	18

Island Burgers	W 50s	21
Jackson Hole	multi.	17
J.G. Melon	E 70s	21
NY Burger	multi.	17
P.J. Clarke's	multi.	17
Pop Burger	multi.	18
Rare B&G	multi.	21
☑ Shake Shack	multi.	23
67 Burger	Ft Greene	21
Stand	G Vill	19
Zaitzeff	multi.	22

BURMESE

Mingala Burmese	multi.	20

CAJUN

Bayou	SI	22
Bourbon St. Café	Bayside	18
Delta Grill	W 40s	20
Great Jones Cafe	NoHo	20
Mara's	E Vill	23

CALIFORNIAN

Michael's	W 50s	20
NEW Table 8	E Vill	15

CAMBODIAN

Kampuchea	LES	22

CARIBBEAN

NEW Arcane	E Vill	-
NEW Crudo	Garment	-
Don Pedro's	E 90s	21
Ideya	SoHo	21
Ivo & Lulu	SoHo	20
Mo-Bay	Harlem	20

CAVIAR

Caviar Russe	E 50s	25
Petrossian	W 50s	24

CHEESE SPECIALISTS

☑ Adour	E 50s	26
Allen/Delancey	LES	23
☑ applewood	Park Slope	26
☑ Artisanal	Murray Hill	23
☑ Babbo	G Vill	27
NEW Bar Artisanal	TriBeCa	21
☑ Bar Boulud	W 60s	23
BLT Market	W 50s	23
Casellula	W 50s	25
☑ Chanterelle	TriBeCa	28
☑ Craft	Flatiron	25
☑ Daniel	E 60s	28
☑ db Bistro Moderne	W 40s	24
☑ Eleven Madison	Flatiron	27
Gordon Ramsay	W 50s	24

☑ Gramercy Tavern | **Flatiron**	28
'inoteca | **multi.**	23
☑ Jean Georges | **W 60s**	28
☑ La Grenouille | **E 50s**	27
☑ Modern | **W 50s**	26
Otto | **G Vill**	23
☑ Per Se | **W 60s**	28
☑ Picholine | **W 60s**	27
Savoy | **SoHo**	24

CHEESESTEAKS

Carl's Steaks | **multi.**	21
99 Mi. to Philly | **E Vill**	19
Shorty's | **W 40s**	22

CHILEAN

Pomaire | **W 40s**	20

CHINESE

(* dim sum specialist)

Amazing 66 | **Chinatown**	22
Big Wong | **Chinatown**	22
Café Evergreen* | **E 60s**	18
Chef Ho's | **E 80s**	23
Chiam | **E 40s**	21
China Fun* | **multi.**	15
China 1 | **E Vill**	17
Chinatown Brass.* | **NoHo**	21
Chin Chin | **E 40s**	23
Dim Sum Go Go* | **Chinatown**	21
Dumpling Hse. | **LES**	22
Dumpling Man | **E Vill**	19
East Manor* | **Flushing**	19
Empire Szechuan | **multi.**	15
Excellent Dumpling* | **Chinatown**	20
Flor/Mayo | **multi.**	21
Fuleen | **Chinatown**	23
Golden Unicorn* | **Chinatown**	20
Grand Sichuan | **multi.**	21
Jing Fong* | **Chinatown**	20
Joe's Shanghai | **multi.**	22
Joe's | **Chinatown**	20
Liberty View | **Financial**	19
NEW Macao Trading | **TriBeCa**	18
Mandarin Court* | **Chinatown**	20
Mee Noodle | **multi.**	18
Mr. Chow | **multi.**	21
Mr. K's | **E 50s**	22
New Bo-Ky | **Chinatown**	22
New Yeah | **Chinatown**	24
Nice Green Bo | **Chinatown**	23
NoHo Star | **NoHo**	18
Ollie's | **multi.**	15
☑ Oriental Gdn.* | **Chinatown**	23
Our Place* | **multi.**	20

Pacificana* | **Sunset Pk**	24
Peking Duck | **multi.**	23
Philippe | **multi.**	24
Phoenix Gdn. | **E 40s**	23
Pig Heaven | **E 80s**	19
Ping's Sea.* | **multi.**	21
Red Egg* | **L Italy**	20
Rickshaw Dumpling | **Flatiron**	17
NEW Shang | **LES**	23
Shanghai Café | **L Italy**	23
Shanghai Pavilion | **E 70s**	22
Shun Lee Cafe* | **W 60s**	21
Shun Lee Palace | **E 50s**	23
Shun Lee West | **W 60s**	22
Spicy & Tasty | **Flushing**	23
Szechuan Gourmet | **multi.**	22
Tang Pavilion | **W 50s**	20
Tse Yang | **E 50s**	24
Wo Hop | **Chinatown**	21
Wu Liang Ye | **multi.**	22
X.O.* | **multi.**	20

COFFEE SHOPS/ DINERS

Brooklyn Diner | **multi.**	17
Burger Heaven | **multi.**	16
Diner | **W'burg**	24
Edison | **W 40s**	16
EJ's Luncheon. | **multi.**	16
Empire Diner | **Chelsea**	15
Junior's | **multi.**	17
La Taza de Oro | **Chelsea**	20
Relish | **W'burg**	20
NEW Schnipper's | **W 40s**	17
Teresa's | **Bklyn Hts**	19
Tom's | **Prospect Hts**	20
Viand | **multi.**	17

COLOMBIAN

Tierras | **Astoria**	19

CONTINENTAL

Battery Gdns. | **Financial**	18
Cole's Dock | **SI**	20
Jack's Lux. | **E Vill**	26
Lake Club | **SI**	20
Petrossian | **W 50s**	24
Rasputin | **Sheepshead**	20
Russian Samovar | **W 50s**	20
Russian Tea | **W 50s**	19
Sardi's | **W 40s**	18

CREOLE

Bayou | **SI**	22
Delta Grill | **W 40s**	20

CUBAN

Amor Cubano	**Harlem**	22
🛂 Asia de Cuba	**Murray Hill**	22
Cafecito	**E Vill**	23
Cafe Con Leche	**multi.**	18
Café Habana/Outpost	**multi.**	23
Cuba	**G Vill**	22
Cuba Cafe	**Chelsea**	18
Cubana Café	**multi.**	21
NEW Favela Cubana	**G Vill**	-
🛂 Havana Alma	**W Vill**	23
Havana Central	**multi.**	17
Son Cubano	**Meatpacking**	21
Victor's Cafe	**W 50s**	21

DELIS

Artie's Deli	**W 80s**	18
🛂 Barney Greengrass	**W 80s**	23
Ben's Kosher	**multi.**	18
🛂 Carnegie Deli	**W 50s**	22
Ess-a-Bagel	**multi.**	23
🛂 Katz's Deli	**LES**	23
Lenny's	**E 50s**	17
Leo's Latticini	**Corona**	27
Liebman's	**Bronx**	21
Mill Basin Deli	**Mill Basin**	22
Pastrami Queen	**E 70s**	20
Sarge's Deli	**Murray Hill**	20
2nd Ave Deli	**Murray Hill**	22
Stage Deli	**W 50s**	20
Zabar's Cafe	**W 80s**	19

DESSERT

Bouchon Bakery	**W 60s**	23
Café Sabarsky	**E 80s**	22
ChikaLicious	**E Vill**	25
🛂 Chocolate Room	**multi.**	25
Junior's	**multi.**	17
Kyotofu	**W 40s**	21
La Bergamote	**multi.**	25
🛂 Lady Mendl's	**Gramercy**	22
L & B Spumoni	**Bensonhurst**	23
Max Brenner	**G Vill**	18
NEW Momofuku Bakery	**E Vill**	21
Omonia	**multi.**	18
Serendipity 3	**E 60s**	18
NEW Sweetiepie	**G Vill**	14
Sweet Melissa	**multi.**	21
Tailor	**SoHo**	22

DOMINICAN

Cafe Con Leche	**multi.**	18
El Malecon	**multi.**	21
Mamajuana	**Inwood**	23

EASTERN EUROPEAN

Sammy's	**LES**	20

ECLECTIC

Abigael's	**Garment**	20
NEW Bistrouge	**E Vill**	24
NEW Bizaare Ave.	**Astoria**	-
🛂 Bouley Upstairs	**TriBeCa**	26
Carol's	**SI**	25
NEW Chimney	**E 100s**	-
NEW Double Crown	**NoHo**	20
Elizabeth	**NoLita**	19
Fatty's Cafe	**Astoria**	22
NEW Get Fresh	**Park Slope**	-
Good Fork	**Red Hook**	24
Graffiti	**E Vill**	26
Harry's	**Financial**	24
Hudson Cafeteria	**W 50s**	19
Josie's	**multi.**	19
La Flor Bakery	**Woodside**	23
Lake Club	**SI**	20
Maggie Brown	**Clinton Hill**	19
Nook	**W 50s**	19
Public	**NoLita**	22
Rice	**multi.**	19
SavorNY	**LES**	20
Schiller's	**LES**	18
NEW Sojourn	**E 70s**	24
Stanton Social	**LES**	23
Tailor	**SoHo**	22
Trinity Pl.	**Financial**	19
wd-50	**LES**	24

EGYPTIAN

NEW Casa La Femme	**W Vill**	20
Kabab Café	**Astoria**	24

ETHIOPIAN

Awash	**multi.**	22
NEW Bati	**Ft Greene**	-
Ghenet	**Park Slope**	20
Meskerem	**multi.**	21
Queen of Sheba	**W 40s**	21
Zoma	**Harlem**	23

EUROPEAN

August	**W Vill**	22
Belcourt	**E Vill**	20
NEW Bistrouge	**E Vill**	24
🛂 Cru	**G Vill**	26
NEW Crudo	**Garment**	-
🛂 Danny Brown	**Forest Hills**	26
Don Pedro's	**E 90s**	21
Employees Only	**W Vill**	18
Klee Brass.	**Chelsea**	20
Knife + Fork	**E Vill**	21
Korzo	**Park Slope**	20
NEW Ortine	**Prospect Hts**	-
Radegast	**W'burg**	16
Spotted Pig	**W Vill**	23

FILIPINO

Kuma Inn | **LES**	24
NEW Umi Nom | **Clinton Hill**	-

FRENCH

☑ Adour | **E 50s**	26
Allegretti | **Flatiron**	24
NEW André | **E 50s**	-
NEW Arcane | **E Vill**	-
Bagatelle | **Meatpacking**	19
NEW BarBao | **W 80s**	21
Barbès | **Murray Hill**	20
Bistro 33 | **Astoria**	23
Bouchon Bakery | **W 60s**	23
☑ Bouley | **TriBeCa**	28
Breeze | **W 40s**	21
Brick Cafe | **Astoria**	21
☑ Café Boulud | **E 70s**	27
Café du Soleil | **W 100s**	18
Cafe Gitane | **NoLita**	20
Café Henri | **multi.**	21
☑ Carlyle | **E 70s**	23
☑ Chanterelle | **TriBeCa**	28
☑ Corton | **TriBeCa**	27
Danal | **G Vill**	20
☑ Daniel | **E 60s**	28
☑ Degustation | **E Vill**	26
Elephant | **E Vill**	20
☑ Eleven Madison | **Flatiron**	27
Geisha | **E 60s**	22
Gordon Ramsay | **W 50s**	24
Ici | **Ft Greene**	21
Indochine | **E Vill**	21
Ivo & Lulu | **SoHo**	20
Jack's Lux. | **E Vill**	26
☑ Jean Georges | **W 60s**	28
☑ Jean Georges Noug. | **W 60s**	27
Jolie | **Boerum Hill**	21
Kitchen Club | **NoLita**	23
La Baraka | **Little Neck**	21
La Bergamote | **multi.**	25
La Boîte en Bois | **W 60s**	22
☑ La Grenouille | **E 50s**	27
☑ L'Atelier/Robuchon | **E 50s**	28
☑ Le Bernardin | **W 50s**	28
☑ Le Cirque | **E 50s**	24
L'Ecole | **SoHo**	24
Le Colonial | **E 50s**	20
Le Marais | **W 40s**	22
Le Perigord | **E 50s**	24
Le Rivage | **W 40s**	20
Les Enfants | **LES**	18
Maze | **W 50s**	25
Mercer Kitchen | **SoHo**	21
☑ Modern | **W 50s**	26
Nizza | **W 40s**	21

Perry St. | **W Vill**	25
☑ Per Se | **W 60s**	28
Petit Oven | **Bay Ridge**	-
Petrossian | **W 50s**	24
☑ Picholine | **W 60s**	27
PicNic Market | **W 100s**	20
Safran | **Chelsea**	20
Savann | **W 70s**	21
718 | **Astoria**	21
NEW SHO Shaun Hergatt | **Financial**	29
Terrace in Sky | **W 100s**	22
☑ Tocqueville | **Union Sq**	26
Triomphe | **W 40s**	24
26 Seats | **E Vill**	21
Vong | **E 50s**	22
NEW Ze Café | **E 50s**	21

FRENCH (BISTRO)

NEW Almond | **Flatiron**	20
Alouette | **W 90s**	20
A.O.C. | **multi.**	20
Bacchus | **Boerum Hill**	23
NEW Bar Artisanal | **TriBeCa**	21
☑ Bar Boulud | **W 60s**	23
Belleville | **Park Slope**	19
Benoit | **W 50s**	19
Bistro Cassis | **W 70s**	20
Bistro Chat Noir | **E 60s**	18
Bistro Citron | **W 80s**	20
Bistro du Nord | **E 90s**	18
Bistro Les Amis | **SoHo**	21
Bistro 61 | **E 60s**	20
Cafe Cluny | **W Vill**	21
Cafe Joul | **E 50s**	18
Cafe Loup | **G Vill**	19
Cafe Luluc | **Cobble Hill**	19
Cafe Luxembourg | **W 70s**	20
Cafe Moutarde | **Park Slope**	19
Cafe Un Deux/Le Petit | **W 40s**	16
CamaJe | **G Vill**	20
Canaille | **Park Slope**	22
Capsouto Frères | **TriBeCa**	23
Casimir | **E Vill**	19
Chez Jacqueline | **G Vill**	21
Chez Josephine | **W 40s**	20
Chez Napoléon | **W 50s**	20
Chez Oskar | **Ft Greene**	17
Cornelia St. Cafe | **G Vill**	19
Cosette | **Murray Hill**	20
☑ db Bistro Moderne | **W 40s**	24
Demarchelier | **E 80s**	16
Deux Amis | **E 50s**	20
Félix | **SoHo**	16
Flea Mkt. Cafe | **E Vill**	21
French Roast | **multi.**	17

Gascogne | **Chelsea**	21
Gavroche | **W Vill**	18
Jean Claude | **SoHo**	23
Z JoJo | **E 60s**	25
Jubilee | **E 50s**	22
Jules | **E Vill**	18
Juliette | **W'burg**	19
La Bonne Soupe | **W 50s**	18
La Lunchonette | **Chelsea**	21
La Mangeoire | **E 50s**	21
La Mirabelle | **W 80s**	23
Landmarc | **multi.**	20
La Petite Aub. | **Murray Hill**	20
La Sirène | **SoHo**	23
Le Barricou | **W'burg**	23
Le Bilboquet | **E 60s**	23
Le Boeuf/Mode | **E 80s**	21
Le Gamin | **multi.**	18
Le Gigot | **G Vill**	23
Le Jardin | **NoLita**	20
NEW Le Magnifique | **E 70s**	-
Le Monde | **W 100s**	18
Le Petit Marché | **Bklyn Hts**	23
Le Refuge | **E 80s**	21
Les Halles | **multi.**	20
Le Singe Vert | **Chelsea**	18
NEW Levant East | **LES**	-
L'Express | **Flatiron**	17
Lucien | **E Vill**	22
Lucky Strike | **SoHo**	16
Métisse | **W 100s**	18
Z NEW Minetta | **G Vill**	20
Nice Matin | **W 70s**	20
Odeon | **TriBeCa**	19
Paradou | **Meatpacking**	21
Paris Commune | **W Vill**	19
Park Ave. Bistro | **Murray Hill**	22
Pascalou | **E 90s**	21
Pastis | **Meatpacking**	21
Pomme/Terre | **Ditmas Pk**	22
Provence/Boite | **Carroll Gdns**	20
Quatorze Bis | **E 70s**	20
Quercy | **Cobble Hill**	22
Raoul's | **SoHo**	24
NEW Sonia Rose | **LES**	21
Sweetwater | **W'burg**	21
Table d'Hôte | **E 90s**	20
Tartine | **W Vill**	22
Tournesol | **LIC**	24
Tree | **E Vill**	19

FRENCH (BRASSERIE)

Z Artisanal | **Murray Hill**	23
Z Balthazar | **SoHo**	23
NEW Bar Breton | **Chelsea**	18
Brasserie | **E 50s**	20
Brasserie Cognac | **W 50s**	18
Brasserie 8½ | **W 50s**	21
Brasserie Julien | **E 80s**	18
Brass. Ruhlmann | **W 50s**	18
Café d'Alsace | **E 80s**	21
Cercle Rouge | **TriBeCa**	19
Z NEW DBGB | **E Vill**	23
Jacques | **multi.**	20
L'Absinthe | **E 60s**	22
Maison | **W 50s**	19
Marseille | **W 40s**	21
Metro Marché | **W 40s**	19
Orsay | **E 70s**	18
NEW Perle | **Financial**	18
Pigalle | **W 40s**	18
Rue 57 | **W 50s**	18

GASTROPUB

Alchemy | Amer. | **Park Slope**	19
NEW Clerkenwell | British | **LES**	-
NEW Cornelius | Amer. | **Prospect Hts**	18
Kingswood | Australian | **G Vill**	19
Resto | Belgian | **Murray Hill**	20
Spitzer's | Amer. | **LES**	20
Spotted Pig | Euro. | **W Vill**	23

GERMAN

Blaue Gans | **TriBeCa**	21
Hallo Berlin | **W 40s**	19
Heidelberg | **E 80s**	18
Killmeyer | **SI**	18
Nurnberger | **SI**	20
NEW Prime Meat | **Carroll Gdns**	19
Rolf's | **Gramercy**	14
Zum Schneider | **E Vill**	19
Zum Stammtisch | **Glendale**	22

GREEK

Agnanti | **multi.**	23
Ammos | **E 40s**	21
Anthos | **W 50s**	25
Avra | **E 40s**	25
Cafe Bar | **Astoria**	18
Cávo | **Astoria**	21
Eliá | **Bay Ridge**	26
Elias Corner | **Astoria**	23
Ethos | **multi.**	22
Gus' Place | **G Vill**	21
Ithaka | **E 80s**	21
Kefi | **W 80s**	22
Kellari Tav./Parea | **multi.**	22
Z Milos | **W 50s**	27
Molyvos | **W 50s**	22

Omonia	**multi.**	18
Periyali	**Flatiron**	24
Persephone	**E 60s**	22
Philoxenia	**Astoria**	24
Pylos	**E Vill**	25
Snack	**SoHo**	24
Snack Taverna	**W Vill**	21
Sofia	**Astoria**	23
Stamatis	**Astoria**	22
Symposium	**W 100s**	19
Taverna Kyclades	**Astoria**	25
Telly's Taverna	**Astoria**	23
Thalassa	**TriBeCa**	24
Trata	**E 70s**	22
Uncle Nick's	**multi.**	20

HEALTH FOOD

(See also Vegetarian)

Energy Kitchen	**multi.**	17
Pump Energy	**multi.**	17

HOT DOGS

NEW Bark Hot Dogs	**Park Slope**	–
Z Gray's Papaya	**multi.**	20
Papaya King	**multi.**	20
Z Shake Shack	**multi.**	23

ICE CREAM PARLORS

L & B Spumoni	**Bensonhurst**	23
Serendipity 3	**E 60s**	18

INDIAN

Amma	**E 50s**	24
NEW At Vermilion	**E 40s**	18
Baluchi's	**multi.**	17
Banjara	**E Vill**	23
Bay Leaf	**W 50s**	21
Bombay Palace	**W 50s**	20
Bombay Talkie	**Chelsea**	20
Brick Ln. Curry	**multi.**	21
Bukhara Grill	**E 40s**	22
Cafe Spice	**multi.**	18
Chennai Gdn.	**Murray Hill**	21
Chola	**E 50s**	23
Curry Leaf	**Murray Hill**	20
Darbar	**multi.**	21
Dawat	**E 50s**	23
Delhi Palace	**Jackson Hts**	22
dévi	**Flatiron**	23
NEW Dhaba	**Murray Hill**	22
Earthen Oven	**W 70s**	21
Hampton Chutney	**multi.**	21
Haveli	**E Vill**	22
Indus Valley	**W 100s**	22
Jackson Diner	**Jackson Hts**	22
Jewel of India	**W 40s**	20

Kati Roll	**multi.**	20
Leela Lounge	**G Vill**	21
Mint	**E 50s**	21
Mughlai	**W 70s**	20
Pongal	**Murray Hill**	22
Salaam Bombay	**TriBeCa**	21
Sapphire	**W 60s**	21
Saravanaas	**Murray Hill**	24
Surya	**W Vill**	21
Swagat Indian	**W 70s**	21
Z Tabla	**Flatiron**	25
Z Tamarind	**Flatiron**	25
Tiffin Wallah	**Murray Hill**	24
Utsav	**W 40s**	20
Vatan	**Murray Hill**	22
Yuva	**E 50s**	23

IRISH

Landmark Tavern	**W 40s**	17
Neary's	**E 50s**	16

ISRAELI

Z Azuri Cafe	**W 50s**	24
Hummus Pl.	**multi.**	23
Miriam	**Park Slope**	21
Taïm	**W Vill**	25

ITALIAN

(N=Northern; S=Southern)

Abboccato	**W 50s**	21
Acappella	N	**TriBeCa**	25
Accademia/Vino	**E 60s**	19
Acqua	S	**W 90s**	18
Acqua/Peck Slip	**Seaport**	21
Alberto	N	**Forest Hills**	23
Z Al Di La	N	**Park Slope**	26
Aleo	**Flatiron**	19
Alfredo of Rome	S	**W 40s**	18
Aliseo Osteria	**Prospect Hts**	23
Alloro	**E 70s**	22
Z Alto	N	**E 50s**	26
Amorina	**Prospect Hts**	25
NEW Anella	**Greenpt**	–
Angelina's	**SI**	21
Angelo's/Mulberry	S	**L Italy**	23
Angelo's Pizza	**multi.**	21
Antica Venezia	**W Vill**	23
Antonucci	**E 80s**	21
NEW Aperitivo	**E 40s**	20
ápizz	**LES**	24
Areo	**Bay Ridge**	23
NEW Armani Rist.	N	**E 50s**	23
Arno	N	**Garment**	20
Aroma	**NoHo**	24
Arqua	N	**TriBeCa**	22
Arté	N	**G Vill**	18

Arté Café | W 70s	18
Arturo's | G Vill	22
Aurora | multi.	25
A Voce | multi.	24
☑ Babbo | G Vill	27
Baci/Abbracci | W'burg	21
Bamonte's | W'burg	23
Baraonda | E 70s	18
Barbetta | N | W 40s	21
Barbone | E Vill	24
Barbuto | W Vill	22
Barolo | SoHo	18
Barosa | multi.	23
Bar Pitti | G Vill	23
Bar Stuzz. | S | Flatiron	19
Bar Toto | Park Slope	18
Bar Vetro | E 50s	20
Basilica | N | W 40s	20
Basso56 | S | W 50s	22
Basta Pasta | Flatiron	23
☑ Becco | W 40s	22
Beccofino | Bronx	22
Bella Blu | N | E 70s	20
Bella Via | LIC	22
Bellavitae | G Vill	23
Bellini | W 80s	18
Bello | W 50s	21
Beppe | N | Flatiron	23
Bettola | W 70s	21
Bianca | N | NoHo	24
Bice | N | E 50s	21
Bocca | S | Flatiron	21
Bocca di Bacco | N | W 50s	21
Bocca Lupo | Cobble Hill	24
Bocelli | SI	26
Bond 45 | W 40s	20
Borgo Antico | G Vill	18
Bottega/Vino | E 50s	22
Bottino | N | Chelsea	18
Bravo Gianni | N | E 60s	22
Bread | TriBeCa	19
Bricco | W 50s	20
Brick Cafe | N | Astoria	21
Brio | E 60s	18
Brioso | SI	24
Cacio e Pepe | S | E Vill	20
Cacio e Vino | S | E Vill	21
Cafe Fiorello | W 60s	20
Caffe Cielo | N | W 50s	20
Caffe Grazie | E 80s	19
Campagnola | E 70s	23
Campo | W 100s	18
Canaletto | N | E 60s	21
Cara Mia | W 40s	20
ⓝⓔⓦ Caravaggio | E 70s	-

Carmine's | S | multi.	20
Cascina | W 40s	19
Celeste | S | W 80s	23
Cellini | N | E 50s	22
Centolire | N | E 80s	21
Centro Vinoteca | W Vill	20
'Cesca | S | W 70s	22
Chianti | Bay Ridge	22
Ciaobella | E 80s	21
Cibo | N | E 40s	20
Cipriani Dolci | E 40s	20
Cipriani D'twn | SoHo	20
ⓝⓔⓦ Civetta | NoLita	19
☑ Convivio | S | E 40s	26
Coppola's | multi.	20
Cortina | N | E 70s	16
Covo | Harlem	23
Crispo | N | W Vill	23
Da Andrea | N | G Vill	23
Da Ciro | Murray Hill	21
Da Filippo | N | E 60s	21
Da Nico | L Italy	21
Da Noi | N | SI	23
Da Silvana | Forest Hills	20
Da Silvano | N | G Vill	20
Da Tommaso | N | W 50s	20
Da Umberto | N | Chelsea	24
Dean's | multi.	17
Defonte's | multi.	24
DeGrezia | E 50s	23
dell'anima | W Vill	25
☑ Del Posto | Chelsea	26
ⓝⓔⓦ de Santos | G Vill	21
Destino | E 50s	19
Dieci | E Vill	22
Dominick's | Bronx	23
Don Peppe | Ozone Pk	24
ⓝⓔⓦ Ducale | W 70s	16
Due | N | E 70s	21
Ecco | TriBeCa	23
Elaine's | E 80s	13
☑ Elio's | E 80s	24
ⓝⓔⓦ Emporio | NoLita	22
Ennio/Michael | G Vill	21
Enoteca Maria | SI	23
Enzo's | Bronx	23
Erminia | S | E 80s	25
☑ Esca | S | W 40s	25
etc. etc. | W 40s	20
Fabio Piccolo | E 40s	21
Falai | multi.	23
F & J Pine | Bronx	22
Felice | E 60s	20
☑ Felidia | E 50s	26
Filippo's | SI	24

F.illi Ponte | **TriBeCa**	23	
Fiorentino's | S | **Gravesend**	19	
Fiorini | S | **E 50s**	20	
Firenze | N | **E 80s**	20	
NEW 508 | **SoHo**	19	
Fragole | **Carroll Gdns**	23	
Frank | **E Vill**	24	
Frankies | **multi.**	24	
Franny's | **Prospect Hts**	24	
Fratelli | **Bronx**	21	
Fred's at Barneys | N | **E 60s**	20	
Fresco | N | **multi.**	23	
Gabriel's | N | **W 60s**	22	
Gargiulo's | S | **Coney Is**	22	
Gemma | **E Vill**	19	
Gennaro | **W 90s**	24	
Gigino | **multi.**	21	
Giorgione | **SoHo**	21	
Giovanni | N | **E 80s**	22	
Gnocco Caffe | N | **E Vill**	23	
Gonzo | **G Vill**	21	
Gottino | **G Vill**	21	
Gradisca | **G Vill**	23	
Grifone | N | **E 40s**	25	
Gusto | **G Vill**	21	
Harry Cipriani | N | **E 50s**	21	
NEW Harry's Italian | **Financial**	-	
Hearth | N | **E Vill**	25	
I Coppi | N | **E Vill**	23	
Il Bagatto | **E Vill**	24	
Il Bambino | **Astoria**	25	
Il Bastardo | N | **Chelsea**	19	
Z Il Buco | **NoHo**	24	
Il Cantinori | N | **G Vill**	23	
Il Corallo | **SoHo**	21	
Il Cortile | **L Italy**	23	
Il Gattopardo | S | **W 50s**	24	
Z Il Giglio | N | **TriBeCa**	26	
Z Il Mulino | S | **G Vill**	27	
Il Palazzo | **L Italy**	23	
Il Passatore | **W'burg**	24	
Il Postino | **E 40s**	23	
NEW Il Punto | **Garment**	20	
Il Riccio | S | **E 70s**	20	
Z Il Tinello | N | **W 50s**	25	
NEW Inatteso | **Financial**	21	
'ino | **G Vill**	24	
'inoteca | **multi.**	23	
Insieme | **W 50s**	23	
I Sodi | **W Vill**	23	
Italianissimo | **E 80s**	23	
I Tre Merli | N | **multi.**	18	
I Trulli | **Murray Hill**	23	
Joe & Pat's | **SI**	24	
John's/12th St. | **E Vill**	20	

NEW La Carbonara | S | **W Vill**	22	
La Lanterna | **G Vill**	19	
La Masseria | S | **W 40s**	23	
L & B Spumoni | **Bensonhurst**	23	
Lanza | S | **E Vill**	18	
La Pizza Fresca | **Flatiron**	23	
NEW L'Artusi | **W Vill**	21	
Lattanzi | S | **W 40s**	22	
Lavagna | **E Vill**	23	
La Villa Pizzeria | **multi.**	21	
Leo's Latticini | **Corona**	27	
Le Zie 2000 | N | **Chelsea**	22	
Lil' Frankie | **E Vill**	23	
Lisca | N | **W 90s**	22	
Locale | **Astoria**	21	
NEW Locanda Verde | **TriBeCa**	22	
Locanda Vini | N | **Clinton Hill**	22	
Lorenzo's | **SI**	19	
NEW Luce | **W 60s**	-	
NEW Lugo Caffe | **Garment**	21	
Lumi | N | **E 70s**	18	
Lunetta | **Boerum Hill**	21	
Z Lupa | S | **G Vill**	25	
Lusardi's | N | **E 70s**	23	
NEW Lusso | **SoHo**	17	
Luzzo's | S | **E Vill**	25	
Macelleria | N | **Meatpacking**	21	
Madison's | **Bronx**	20	
Malatesta | N | **W Vill**	22	
Manducatis | **LIC**	22	
Manetta's | **LIC**	22	
NEW Marea | **W 50s**	26	
Maria Pia | **W 50s**	19	
Mario's | S | **Bronx**	22	
Maruzzella | N | **E 70s**	21	
Matilda | N | **E Vill**	26	
Max | **multi.**	22	
Max SoHa/Caffe | **W 100s**	21	
Mediterraneo | N | **E 60s**	18	
Mezzaluna/Pizza | **E 70s**	21	
Mezzogiorno | N | **SoHo**	21	
Mia Dona | **E 50s**	21	
Miranda | **W'burg**	21	
NEW Montenapo | **W 40s**	-	
Morandi | **G Vill**	22	
Nanni | N | **E 40s**	24	
Naples 45 | S | **E 40s**	17	
Nicola's | **E 80s**	22	
Nino's | N | **multi.**	21	
Nizza | **W 40s**	21	
Nocello | N | **W 50s**	21	
Nonna | **W 80s**	18	
Noodle Pudding | **Bklyn Hts**	25	
Novità | N | **Gramercy**	24	
1 Dominick | S | **SoHo**	23	

Restaurant	Score
One 83 | N | **E 80s**	19
101 | **Bay Ridge**	21
NEW Opus | **E 80s**	23
Orso | N | **W 40s**	22
Osso Buco | **multi.**	17
Osteria al Doge | N | **W 40s**	20
Osteria del Circo | N | **W 50s**	22
Osteria Laguna | **E 40s**	19
Otto | **G Vill**	23
Padre Figlio | **E 40s**	20
Palma | S | **G Vill**	23
Paola's | **E 80s**	23
Pappardella | **W 70s**	19
Park Side | **Corona**	24
Parma | N | **E 70s**	22
Pasquale's | **Bronx**	21
Patricia's | **Bronx**	24
Patsy's | S | **W 50s**	21
Peasant | **NoLita**	24
Pellegrino's | **L Italy**	23
Pepe | **multi.**	22
Z Pepolino | N | **TriBeCa**	26
Perbacco | **E Vill**	23
Per Lei | **E 70s**	20
Petaluma | **E 70s**	19
Pete's D'town | **Dumbo**	19
Piadina | **G Vill**	22
Piano Due | **W 50s**	24
Piccola Venezia | **Astoria**	25
Piccolo Angolo | **W Vill**	25
Pietrasanta | **W 40s**	19
Pietro's | **E 40s**	24
Pinocchio | **E 90s**	22
Pisticci | S | **W 100s**	24
Pó | **multi.**	25
Pomodoro Rosso | **W 70s**	21
Ponticello | N | **Astoria**	24
NEW Porchetta | **E Vill**	24
Portofino | **Bronx**	19
Primavera | N | **E 80s**	24
Primola | **E 60s**	22
NEW Provini | **Park Slope**	-
PT | **W'burg**	-
Puttanesca | **W 50s**	19
Quartino | N | **NoHo**	20
Quattro Gatti | **E 80s**	22
Queen | **Bklyn Hts**	24
NEW Quinto Quarto | S | **G Vill**	-
Rao's | S | **Harlem**	23
Remi | **W 50s**	22
Re Sette | **W 40s**	21
Risotteria | **G Vill**	22
Z Roberto | **Bronx**	26
Roberto Passon | N | **W 50s**	21
Roc | **TriBeCa**	22

Restaurant	Score
Rossini's | N | **Murray Hill**	23
Rughetta | S | **E 80s**	22
NEW Salumeria Rosi | **W 70s**	23
Salute! | **Murray Hill**	18
Sambuca | S | **W 70s**	20
Sandro's | **E 80s**	25
Z San Pietro | S | **E 50s**	26
Sant Ambroeus | N | **multi.**	22
Sapori D'Ischia | **Woodside**	24
NEW Saraghina | **Bed-Stuy**	-
Savoia | **Carroll Gdns**	21
Scaletta | N | **W 70s**	22
Z Scalinatella | **E 60s**	26
Z Scalini Fedeli | N | **TriBeCa**	26
Scalino | **Park Slope**	24
Scarlatto | N | **W 40s**	21
Z Scarpetta | **Chelsea**	26
Scottadito | N | **Park Slope**	20
NEW Scuderia | **G Vill**	18
Serafina | **multi.**	18
Sette | S | **Park Slope**	20
Sette Mezzo | **E 70s**	22
Sfoglia | N | **E 90s**	25
Shelly's NY | **W 50s**	19
Z Sistina | N | **E 80s**	26
NEW Sora Lella | S | **SoHo**	19
NEW Sorella | **LES**	-
Sosa Borella | **W 50s**	19
Spiga | **W 80s**	23
Spigolo | **E 80s**	25
Supper | N | **E Vill**	24
Tarallucci | **multi.**	21
Teodora | N | **E 50s**	20
NEW Terrazza Toscana | N | **W 50s**	-
Tevere | S | **E 80s**	24
Tiramisu | **E 80s**	20
Tommaso | **Dyker Hts**	23
Tony's Di Napoli | S | **multi.**	19
Tosca Café | **Bronx**	21
Tratt. Dell'Arte | N | **W 50s**	22
Z Tratt. L'incontro | **Astoria**	27
Tratt. Pesce | **multi.**	19
Tratt. Romana | **SI**	24
Trattoria Trecolori | **W 40s**	21
Tre | **LES**	19
tre dici | **Chelsea**	21
Triangolo | **E 80s**	20
Tuscany Grill | N | **Bay Ridge**	24
Umberto's | **multi.**	18
Uva | **E 70s**	21
Valbella | N | **Meatpacking**	25
V&T | **W 100s**	18
Vento | **Meatpacking**	19
Vespa | **E 80s**	19

NEW Vesta | **Astoria**	25	Katsu-Hama | **multi.**	21
Vezzo | **Murray Hill**	23	Ki Sushi* | **Boerum Hill**	25
NEW Via dei Mille | N | **SoHo**	24	Kitchen Club | **NoLita**	23
Via Emilia | N | **Flatiron**	22	Koi* | **W 40s**	22
Via Quadronno | N | **multi.**	22	Z Kuruma Zushi* | **E 40s**	27
ViceVersa | **W 50s**	22	Kyotofu | **W 40s**	21
Vico | **E 90s**	20	Z Kyo Ya | **E Vill**	27
Villa Mosconi | **G Vill**	22	Lan* | **E Vill**	23
Vincent's | **L Italy**	21	Z Masa* | **W 60s**	26
Za Za | N | **E 60s**	20	Matsugen | **TriBeCa**	22
NEW Ze Café | **E 50s**	21	Matsuri* | **Chelsea**	22
Zero Otto | S | **Bronx**	25	Megu | **multi.**	23
Zorzi | N | **Murray Hill**	21	Menchanko-tei | **multi.**	20

JAMAICAN

Negril \| **G Vill** 21

JAPANESE

(* sushi specialist)

Aburiya Kinnosuke | **E 40s**	24	Minca | **E Vill**	22
Aji Sushi* | **Murray Hill**	21	Mishima* | **Murray Hill**	24
Aki* | **G Vill**	24	Mizu Sushi* | **Flatiron**	23
Arirang Hibachi | **multi.**	20	Momoya* | **multi.**	23
Z Bar Masa* | **W 60s**	26	Monster Sushi* | **multi.**	18
Bistro 33 | **Astoria**	23	Z Morimoto | **Chelsea**	25
Blue Ginger* | **Chelsea**	21	Nëo Sushi* | **W 80s**	21
Z Blue Ribbon Sushi* | **multi.**	26	Ninja | **TriBeCa**	16
Blue Ribbon Sushi B&G* | **W 50s**	24	Z Nobu* | **multi.**	27
Bond St.* | **NoHo**	25	Omen | **SoHo**	25
Chiyono | **E Vill**	25	Planet Thai | **Flatiron**	19
Cube 63 | **multi.**	22	Poke* | **E 80s**	25
Donguri | **E 80s**	26	NEW Qoo Robata | **W'burg**	-
EN Japanese | **W Vill**	23	Rai Rai Ken | **E Vill**	21
Z 15 East* | **Union Sq**	26	Ramen Setagaya | **multi.**	19
Fushimi* | **multi.**	24	Riingo | **E 40s**	21
Z Gari/Sushi* | **multi.**	27	Rock-n-Sake | **Chelsea**	23
Geido* | **Prospect Hts**	23	Rosanjin | **TriBeCa**	24
Geisha | **E 60s**	22	Sakagura | **E 40s**	25
Greenwich Grill/Sushi Azabu* | **TriBeCa**	26	Sapporo East* | **E Vill**	18
Gyu-Kaku | **multi.**	22	Z Sasabune* | **E 70s**	28
Haru* | **multi.**	20	Seo* | **E 40s**	24
Hasaki* | **E Vill**	24	Shabu-Shabu 70* | **E 70s**	21
Hatsuhana* | **E 40s**	25	Shabu-Tatsu | **E Vill**	23
Hibino* | **Cobble Hill**	25	Soba Nippon | **W 50s**	22
Inagiku* | **E 40s**	22	Soba-ya | **E Vill**	24
NEW Inakaya | **W 40s**	22	Soto* | **G Vill**	28
Z Ippudo | **E Vill**	25	Z Sugiyama | **W 50s**	27
Ise* | **multi.**	21	SushiAnn* | **E 50s**	25
Izakaya 10 | **Chelsea**	21	Sushiden* | **multi.**	23
Japonais | **Gramercy**	20	Sushi Hana* | **multi.**	20
Japonica* | **G Vill**	23	SushiSamba* | **multi.**	21
Z Jewel Bako* | **E Vill**	25	Z Sushi Seki* | **E 60s**	26
Kai | **E 60s**	26	Z Sushi Sen-nin* | **Murray Hill**	26
NEW Kajitsu | **E Vill**	-	Sushiya* | **W 50s**	20
Z Kanoyama* | **E Vill**	26	Z Sushi Yasuda* | **E 40s**	28
		Sushi Zen* | **W 40s**	25
		Takahachi* | **multi.**	25
		Tenzan* | **multi.**	22
		Z Tomoe Sushi* | **G Vill**	26
		Ushiwakamaru* | **G Vill**	26
		Wasabi Lobby* | **E 80s**	19

Watawa* | **Astoria**	25
Yakitori Totto | **W 50s**	25
Yama* | **multi.**	24
Yuka* | **E 80s**	21
Yuki Sushi* | **W 90s**	21
Z Zenkichi | **W'burg**	25
Zutto* | **TriBeCa**	23

JEWISH

Artie's Deli | **W 80s**	18
Z Barney Greengrass | **W 80s**	23
Ben's Kosher | **multi.**	18
Z Carnegie Deli | **W 50s**	22
Edison | **W 40s**	16
Z Katz's Deli | **LES**	23
Lattanzi | **W 40s**	22
Liebman's | **Bronx**	21
Mill Basin Deli | **Mill Basin**	22
Pastrami Queen | **E 70s**	20
Sammy's | **LES**	20
Sarge's Deli | **Murray Hill**	20
2nd Ave Deli | **Murray Hill**	22
Stage Deli | **W 50s**	20

KOREAN

(* barbecue specialist)

Bann | **W 50s**	21
NEW b-bap | **W 50s**	-
NEW Boka | **E Vill**	23
Cho Dang Gol* | **Garment**	23
Do Hwa* | **G Vill**	22
Dok Suni's | **E Vill**	22
Gahm Mi Oak | **Garment**	21
Z HanGawi | **Murray Hill**	26
Kang Suh* | **Garment**	21
Kum Gang San* | **multi.**	21
Mandoo Bar | **Garment**	21
Moim | **Park Slope**	24
Woo Lae Oak* | **SoHo**	21

KOSHER/ KOSHER-STYLE

Abigael's | **Garment**	20
Z Azuri Cafe | **W 50s**	24
Ben's Kosher | **multi.**	18
Caravan/Dreams | **E Vill**	20
Chennai Gdn. | **Murray Hill**	21
Le Marais | **W 40s**	22
Liebman's | **Bronx**	21
Mill Basin Deli | **Mill Basin**	22
Pastrami Queen | **E 70s**	20
Pongal | **Murray Hill**	22
Prime Grill | **E 40s**	22
Sacred Chow | **G Vill**	20
2nd Ave Deli | **Murray Hill**	22
Solo | **E 50s**	22

Tevere | **E 80s**	24
Turquoise | **E 80s**	21

LEBANESE

ilili | **Chelsea**	24
NEW Naya | **E 50s**	21

MALAYSIAN

Fatty Crab | **multi.**	22
Laut | **Union Sq**	24
Nyonya | **multi.**	23

MEDITERRANEAN

Aleo | **Flatiron**	19
Alta | **G Vill**	24
Amaranth | **E 60s**	18
NEW Barberry | **W'burg**	-
Barbounia | **Flatiron**	21
Beast | **Prospect Hts**	21
Bello Sguardo | **W 70s**	20
Bodrum | **W 80s**	19
Cafe Bar | **Astoria**	18
Cafe Centro | **E 40s**	20
Café du Soleil | **W 100s**	18
Cafe Ronda | **W 70s**	19
NEW Charles | **W Vill**	18
NEW City Winery | **SoHo**	18
NEW Civetta | **NoLita**	19
Conviv. Osteria | **Park Slope**	25
Danal | **G Vill**	20
NEW Dardanel | **E 50s**	18
Dee's Pizza | **Forest Hills**	21
Dervish | **W 40s**	18
Epices/Traiteur | **W 70s**	20
Extra Virgin | **W Vill**	22
Fig & Olive | **multi.**	20
NEW 508 | **SoHo**	19
5 Points | **NoHo**	22
Greenwich Grill/Sushi Azabu | **TriBeCa**	26
Gus' Place | **G Vill**	21
House | **Gramercy**	22
Z Il Buco | **NoHo**	24
Isabella's | **W 70s**	20
Z Little Owl | **W Vill**	26
Lokal | **Greenpt**	18
Mangia | **multi.**	19
Marseille | **W 40s**	21
Miriam | **Park Slope**	21
My Moon | **W'burg**	19
Nanoosh | **multi.**	19
Nice Matin | **W 70s**	20
Nick & Toni | **W 60s**	19
Olea | **Ft Greene**	23
Olives | **Union Sq**	22
Palma | **G Vill**	23

Park | **Chelsea**	16
Pera | **E 40s**	21
☑ Picholine | **W 60s**	27
Place | **W Vill**	19
Red Cat | **Chelsea**	23
Sahara | **Gravesend**	21
Savann | **W 70s**	21
Savoy | **SoHo**	24
NEW Sel de Mer | **W'burg**	-
Sezz Medi' | **W 100s**	20
Sharz Cafe | **E 80s**	20
NEW Smile | **NoHo**	-
Solo | **E 50s**	22
Superfine | **Dumbo**	20
Taboon | **W 50s**	23
Taci's Beyti | **Midwood**	22
☑ Tanoreen | **Bay Ridge**	26
Terrace in Sky | **W 100s**	22
202 Cafe | **Chelsea**	20
Vai | **W 70s**	22
NEW Vutera | **W'burg**	-

MEXICAN

Alma | **Carroll Gdns**	20
Barrio | **Park Slope**	17
Blockhead Burrito | **multi.**	16
Cabrito | **G Vill**	18
Café Frida | **W 70s**	19
Café Habana/Outpost | **multi.**	23
NEW Calexico | **Carroll Gdns**	-
Centrico | **TriBeCa**	20
Chipotle | **multi.**	18
Crema | **Chelsea**	21
Dos Caminos | **multi.**	20
El Parador Cafe | **Murray Hill**	21
El Paso Taqueria | **multi.**	23
NEW Fonda | **Park Slope**	-
Gabriela's | **W 90s**	18
Hell's Kitchen | **W 40s**	23
Itzocan | **multi.**	23
La Esquina | **L Italy**	21
La Flor Bakery | **Woodside**	23
La Palapa | **multi.**	19
La Superior | **W'burg**	23
La Taqueria/Rachel | **Park Slope**	20
Los Dados | **Meatpacking**	16
Mamá Mexico | **multi.**	20
NEW Mañana | **E 60s**	21
Matilda | **E Vill**	26
Maya | **E 60s**	23
Maz Mezcal | **E 80s**	19
Mercadito | **multi.**	22
NEW Mesa Coyoacan | **W'burg**	-
Mexicana Mama | **multi.**	22
Noche Mex. | **W 100s**	25
Pampano | **E 40s**	24

Pinche Taqueria | **multi.**	22
Rocking Horse | **Chelsea**	20
Rosa Mexicano | **multi.**	22
NEW Sinigual | **E 40s**	22
Sueños | **Chelsea**	22
Tio Pepe | **G Vill**	20
Toloache | **W 50s**	23
Zarela | **E 50s**	20

MIDDLE EASTERN

Chickpea | **multi.**	18
Gazala Place | **W 40s**	23
Maoz Veg. | **multi.**	21
Moustache | **multi.**	21
Taboon | **W 50s**	23
☑ Tanoreen | **Bay Ridge**	26
12 Chairs | **SoHo**	19
Zaytoons | **multi.**	21

MOROCCAN

Barbès | **Murray Hill**	20
Cafe Gitane | **NoLita**	20
Cafe Mogador | **E Vill**	21

NEW ENGLAND

Ed's Lobster | **NoLita**	21
Mermaid Inn | **multi.**	20
☑ Pearl Oyster | **G Vill**	26

NOODLE SHOPS

Bao Noodles | **Gramercy**	19
Donguri | **E 80s**	26
Great NY Noodle | **Chinatown**	22
☑ Ippudo | **E Vill**	25
Kampuchea | **LES**	22
Matsugen | **TriBeCa**	22
Mee Noodle | **multi.**	18
Menchanko-tei | **multi.**	20
Minca | **E Vill**	22
Momofuku Noodle | **E Vill**	23
New Bo-Ky | **Chinatown**	22
Noodle Bar | **multi.**	20
Pho Bang | **multi.**	20
Pho Pasteur | **Chinatown**	21
Pho Viet Huong | **Chinatown**	22
Rai Rai Ken | **E Vill**	21
Ramen Setagaya | **multi.**	19
Republic | **Union Sq**	18
Soba Nippon | **W 50s**	22
Soba-ya | **E Vill**	24

NORTH AFRICAN

Nomad | **E Vill**	20

NUEVO LATINO

NEW At Vermilion | **E 40s**	18
Cabana | **multi.**	21

Calle Ocho | W 80s — 21
Citrus B&G | W 70s — 20
Luz | Ft Greene — 24
Mamajuana | Inwood — 23
Paladar | LES — 22

PAN-ASIAN

Abigael's | Garment — 20
Aja | E 50s — 20
Amber | multi. — 20
Aquamarine | Murray Hill — 21
bluechili | W 50s — 20
Blue Ginger | Chelsea — 21
Chance | Boerum Hill — 22
NEW Double Crown | NoHo — 20
Noodle Bar | multi. — 20
Republic | Union Sq — 18
NEW Ritz Asia | G Vill — -
Ruby Foo's | W 40s — 18
Z Tao | E 50s — 21

PAN-LATIN

A Casa Fox | LES — 20
NEW Agua Dulce | W 50s — -
Boca Chica | E Vill — 19
Bogota | Park Slope — 20
Macondo | LES — -
Miranda | W'burg — 21
Palo Santo | Park Slope — 23
Rayuela | LES — 22
Talay | Harlem — 21
Yerba Buena | multi. — 24
Yuca Bar | E Vill — 21

PERSIAN

Pars Grill | Chelsea — 20
Persepolis | E 70s — 21
Ravagh | multi. — 20
Shalizar | E 80s — 21

PERUVIAN

Chimu | W'burg — 22
Coco Roco | multi. — 20
Flor/Mayo | multi. — 21
Mancora | E Vill — 20
Z Nobu | multi. — 27
Pio Pio | multi. — 22
Red Egg | L Italy — 20

PIZZA

Acqua | W 90s — 18
Adrienne's | Financial — 23
Amorina | Prospect Hts — 25
NEW Anella | Greenpt — -
Angelo's Pizza | multi. — 21
NEW Anselmo's | Red Hook — 16
NEW Aperitivo | E 40s — 20

ápizz | LES — 24
Artichoke Basille | E Vill — 23
Arturo's | G Vill — 22
Baci/Abbracci | W'burg — 21
Bella Blu | E 70s — 20
Bella Via | LIC — 22
Bettola | W 70s — 21
Big Nick's | W 70s — 17
Bricco | W 50s — 20
Brio | E 60s — 18
Cacio e Vino | E Vill — 21
Cafe Fiorello | W 60s — 20
NEW Co. | Chelsea — 22
Coals | Bronx — 25
Covo | Harlem — 23
Da Ciro | Murray Hill — 21
Dean's | multi. — 17
Dee's Pizza | Forest Hills — 21
Denino | SI — 25
Z Di Fara | Midwood — 27
Fornino | W'burg — 23
Franny's | Prospect Hts — 24
Gigino | multi. — 21
Gonzo | G Vill — 21
Grimaldi's | multi. — 25
Gruppo | E Vill — 25
NEW Harry's Italian | Financial — -
NEW Inatteso | Financial — 21
Joe & Pat's | SI — 24
Joe's Pizza | multi. — 22
Z John's Pizzeria | multi. — 22
NEW Keste Pizza | G Vill — 21
L & B Spumoni | Bensonhurst — 23
La Pizza Fresca | Flatiron — 23
La Villa Pizzeria | multi. — 21
Lazzara's | multi. — 23
Lil' Frankie | E Vill — 23
Lombardi's | NoLita — 24
Z Lucali | Carroll Gdns — 26
Luzzo's | E Vill — 25
Mediterraneo | E 60s — 18
Mezzaluna/Pizza | multi. — 21
Motorino | multi. — 22
Naples 45 | E 40s — 17
Nick's | multi. — 23
Nino's | E 40s — 21
NEW Nios | W 40s — -
NEW Opus | E 80s — 23
Otto | G Vill — 23
Patsy's Pizzeria | multi. — 20
Pintaile's Pizza | multi. — 19
Piola | G Vill — 19
Pizza 33 | multi. — 19
Posto | Gramercy — 24
Roberta's | Bushwick — 22

NEW San Marzano	LES	–
NEW Saraghina	Bed-Stuy	–
Savoia	Carroll Gdns	21
Sezz Medi'	W 100s	20
S'MAC/Pinch	W 80s	21
NEW Spunto	G Vill	22
Tiramisu	E 80s	20
NEW Tonda	E Vill	–
Totonno Pizza	multi.	22
Two Boots	multi.	19
V&T	W 100s	18
NEW Veloce Pizzeria	E Vill	–
NEW Vesta	Astoria	25
Vezzo	Murray Hill	23
Waldy's Pizza	Chelsea	22
Zero Otto	Bronx	25

POLISH

Teresa's	Bklyn Hts	19

PORTUGUESE

NEW Aldea	Flatiron	26
NEW Macao Trading	TriBeCa	18

PUB FOOD

Elephant & Castle	G Vill	17
Heartland	multi.	14
J.G. Melon	E 70s	21
Landmark Tavern	W 40s	17
Neary's	E 50s	16
Pete's Tavern	Gramercy	16
P.J. Clarke's	multi.	17
Smith	E Vill	19
Walker's	TriBeCa	17

PUERTO RICAN

La Taza de Oro	Chelsea	20
NEW Sazon	TriBeCa	–
Sofrito	E 50s	21

RUSSIAN

FireBird	W 40s	19
NEW Mari Vanna	Flatiron	–
Russian Samovar	W 50s	20
Russian Tea	W 50s	19

SANDWICHES

Amy's Bread	multi.	24
NEW An Choi	LES	21
NEW Baoguette	multi.	22
Z Barney Greengrass	W 80s	23
Bôi	E 40s	20
Bouchon Bakery	W 60s	23
Bread	NoLita	19
Brennan	Sheepshead	21
Così	multi.	16
Defonte's	multi.	24

Dishes	multi.	22
DuMont	W'burg	22
E.A.T.	E 80s	19
Ess-a-Bagel	multi.	23
Hale/Hearty	multi.	19
Hanco's	multi.	22
Il Bambino	Astoria	25
Kampuchea	LES	22
Z Katz's Deli	LES	23
Lenny's	multi.	17
Mangia	multi.	19
Z Nicky's	multi.	22
1 Dominick	SoHo	23
Pastrami Queen	E 70s	20
Peanut Butter Co.	G Vill	21
NEW Porchetta	E Vill	24
Press 195	multi.	20
Roll-n-Roaster	Sheepshead	20
Sarge's Deli	Murray Hill	20
2nd Ave Deli	Murray Hill	22
Stage Deli	W 50s	20
Sweet Melissa	multi.	21
'wichcraft	multi.	20
Zabar's Cafe	W 80s	19
Zaitzeff	multi.	22

SCANDINAVIAN

NEW AQ Kafé	W 50s	19
Z Aquavit	E 50s	25
Smorgas Chef	multi.	18
NEW White Slab	LES	–

SEAFOOD

Ammos	E 40s	21
Z Aquagrill	SoHo	26
Z Atlantic Grill	E 70s	23
Avra	E 40s	25
Black Duck	Murray Hill	20
BLT Fish	Flatiron	23
Blue Fin	W 40s	22
Z Blue Water	Union Sq	23
Bocelli	SI	26
Brooklyn Fish	Park Slope	22
Bubba Gump	W 40s	14
NEW Butcher Bay	E Vill	14
City Crab	Flatiron	18
City Hall	TriBeCa	21
City Is. Lobster	Bronx	19
City Lobster	W 40s	19
Cole's Dock	SI	20
Cowgirl	Seaport	16
Ditch Plains	G Vill	18
Docks Oyster	E 40s	19
Ed's Lobster	NoLita	21
Elias Corner	Astoria	23
Z Esca	W 40s	25

Fish | **G Vill**	22
NEW Fishtail | **E 60s**	23
NEW Flex Mussels | **E 80s**	22
Francisco's | **Chelsea**	21
Fuleen | **Chinatown**	23
NEW Fulton | **E 70s**	22
NEW Harbour | **SoHo**	21
Hudson River | **Harlem**	19
Ithaka | **E 80s**	21
Jack's Lux. | **E Vill**	26
Kellari Tav./Parea | **multi.**	22
Z Le Bernardin | **W 50s**	28
Lobster Box | **Bronx**	19
London Lennie | **Rego Pk**	22
Lure Fishbar | **SoHo**	23
NEW Marea | **W 50s**	26
Marina Cafe | **SI**	19
Mary's Fish | **W Vill**	24
McCormick/Schmick | **W 50s**	20
Mermaid Inn | **multi.**	20
Z Milos | **W 50s**	27
Z NEW Oceana | **W 40s**	-
Ocean Grill | **W 70s**	23
Z Oriental Gdn. | **Chinatown**	23
Z Oyster Bar | **E 40s**	22
Pampano | **E 40s**	24
Parlor Steak | **E 90s**	21
Z Pearl Oyster | **G Vill**	26
Pearl Room | **Bay Ridge**	20
Petite Crev. | **Carroll Gdns**	25
Ping's Sea. | **multi.**	21
Portofino | **Bronx**	19
Redeye Grill | **W 50s**	20
Sea Grill | **W 40s**	24
NEW Sel de Mer | **W'burg**	-
Shelly's NY | **W 50s**	19
South Fin | **SI**	19
Taverna Kyclades | **Astoria**	25
Telly's Taverna | **Astoria**	23
Thalassa | **TriBeCa**	24
Trata | **E 70s**	22
Tratt. Pesce | **multi.**	19
Turquoise | **E 80s**	21
Umberto's | **multi.**	18
Z Water's Edge | **LIC**	22

SERBIAN

Kafana | **E Vill**	22

SMALL PLATES

(See also Spanish tapas specialist)

Alta | Med. | **G Vill**	24
NEW Bar Breton | French | **Chelsea**	18
Bar Stuzz. | Italian | **Flatiron**	19
Beast | Med. | **Prospect Hts**	21
Bellavitae | Italian | **G Vill**	23
Bello Sguardo | Med. | **W 70s**	20
Beyoglu | Turkish | **E 80s**	21
NEW Bizaare Ave. | Eclectic | **Astoria**	-
Bocca Lupo | Italian | **Cobble Hill**	24
Bún | Viet. | **SoHo**	20
Casellula | Amer. | **W 50s**	25
Centro Vinoteca | Italian | **W Vill**	20
NEW City Winery | Med. | **SoHo**	18
Z Degustation | French/Spanish | **E Vill**	26
Dieci | Italian | **E Vill**	22
EN Japanese | Japanese | **W Vill**	23
Enoteca Maria | Italian | **SI**	23
Fig & Olive | Med. | **multi.**	20
NEW 508 | Med. | **SoHo**	19
Frankies | Italian | **multi.**	24
Gen. Greene | Amer. | **Ft Greene**	20
Gottino | Italian | **G Vill**	21
Graffiti | Eclectic | **E Vill**	26
House | Med. | **Gramercy**	22
ilili | Lebanese | **Chelsea**	24
'inoteca | Italian | **multi.**	23
Izakaya 10 | Japanese | **Chelsea**	21
Jimmy's | Amer. | **E Vill**	20
Kuma Inn | SE Asian | **LES**	24
Z L'Atelier/Robuchon | French | **E 50s**	28
Lunetta | Italian | **Boerum Hill**	21
Macondo | Pan-Latin | **LES**	-
Z Marlow/Sons | Amer. | **W'burg**	26
Maze | French | **W 50s**	25
Mercadito | Mex. | **multi.**	22
Olea | Med. | **Ft Greene**	23
NEW Onda | S Amer. | **Seaport**	22
Perbacco | Italian | **E Vill**	23
NEW Prime Meat | Amer./German | **Carroll Gdns**	19
Sakagura | Japanese | **E 40s**	25
NEW Salumeria Rosi | Italian | **W 70s**	23
SavorNY | Eclectic | **LES**	20
NEW Sojourn | Eclectic | **E 70s**	24
NEW Sorella | Italian | **LES**	-
Stanton Social | Eclectic | **LES**	23
Talay | Pan-Latin/Thai | **Harlem**	21
Tarallucci | Italian | **multi.**	21
NEW Umi Nom | Pan-Asian | **Clinton Hill**	-
Z Zenkichi | Japanese | **W'burg**	25

SOUL FOOD

Amy Ruth's | **Harlem**	22
Londel's | **Harlem**	19
Miss Mamie/Maude | **Harlem**	21
Mo-Bay | **Harlem**	20

Pink Tea Cup	**W Vill**	22
Sylvia's	**Harlem**	19

SOUP

Hale/Hearty	**multi.**	19
La Bonne Soupe	**W 50s**	18

SOUTH AFRICAN

Braai	**W 50s**	19
Madiba	**Ft Greene**	20

SOUTH AMERICAN

Cafe Ronda	**W 70s**	19
Empanada Mama	**W 50s**	22
NEW Onda	**Seaport**	22

SOUTHEAST ASIAN

Cafe Asean	**G Vill**	20
NEW Pranna	**Murray Hill**	20
Z Spice Market	**Meatpacking**	23

SOUTHERN

Amy Ruth's	**Harlem**	22
Bourbon St. Café	**Bayside**	18
NEW Brooklyn Star	**W'burg**	-
B. Smith's	**W 40s**	19
NEW Char No. 4	**Cobble Hill**	23
Egg	**W'burg**	23
Kitchenette	**multi.**	19
Londel's	**Harlem**	19
Miss Mamie/Maude	**Harlem**	21
Peaches	**Bed-Stuy**	-
NEW Permanent Brunch	**E Vill**	-
Pink Tea Cup	**W Vill**	22
Rack & Soul	**W 100s**	19
River Room	**Harlem**	20
Sylvia's	**Harlem**	19

SOUTHWESTERN

Agave	**W Vill**	18
Canyon Road	**E 70s**	21
Cilantro	**multi.**	17
Cowgirl	**multi.**	16
NEW Marfa	**E Vill**	-
Z Mesa Grill	**Flatiron**	23

SPANISH

(* tapas specialist)

Bar Carrera*	**multi.**	22
Boqueria*	**multi.**	22
Cafe Español	**G Vill**	20
Casa Mono*	**Gramercy**	25
Z Degustation	**E Vill**	26
El Boqueron*	**Astoria**	23
El Charro	**G Vill**	22
El Faro*	**W Vill**	22
El Quijote	**Chelsea**	20

El Quinto Pino*	**Chelsea**	21
Euzkadi*	**E Vill**	21
Flor/Sol*	**TriBeCa**	22
Francisco's	**Chelsea**	21
NEW La Fonda/Sol	**E 40s**	22
Las Ramblas*	**G Vill**	24
Mercat*	**NoHo**	21
Pamplona*	**Murray Hill**	22
Pipa*	**Flatiron**	20
Sala*	**multi.**	22
Sevilla	**W Vill**	22
Socarrat	**Chelsea**	24
Solera*	**E 50s**	20
Tía Pol*	**Chelsea**	25
Tio Pepe	**G Vill**	20
NEW Txikito*	**Chelsea**	23
Xunta*	**E Vill**	21

STEAKHOUSES

A.J. Maxwell's	**W 40s**	22
Angelo/Maxie's	**Flatiron**	22
Arirang Hibachi	**multi.**	20
Austin's Steak	**Bay Ridge**	19
Azul Bistro	**LES**	22
Ben & Jack's	**multi.**	23
Ben Benson's	**W 50s**	23
Benjamin Steak	**E 40s**	24
BLT Prime	**Gramercy**	25
Z BLT Steak	**E 50s**	25
Bobby Van's	**multi.**	22
Buenos Aires	**E Vill**	22
Bull & Bear	**E 40s**	20
Capital Grille	**multi.**	23
Chimichurri Grill	**W 40s**	22
Christos	**Astoria**	23
Churrascaria	**multi.**	23
Circus	**E 60s**	20
City Hall	**TriBeCa**	21
Club A Steak	**E 50s**	25
Craftsteak	**Chelsea**	24
Z Del Frisco's	**W 40s**	25
Delmonico's	**Financial**	23
DeStefano	**W'burg**	23
Dylan Prime	**TriBeCa**	24
Embers	**Bay Ridge**	21
Erawan	**Bayside**	23
Fairway Cafe	**W 70s**	18
NEW Flying Cow	**W'burg**	-
Frankie/Johnnie	**multi.**	22
Gallagher's	**W 50s**	21
Harry's	**Financial**	24
Il Bastardo	**Chelsea**	19
Jake's	**Bronx**	23
Keens	**Garment**	24
La Rural	**W 90s**	21

CUISINES

Le Marais	**W 40s**	22
NEW Le Relais/Venise	**E 50s**	–
Les Halles	**multi.**	20
NEW Lucas Steak	**Astoria**	–
Macelleria	**Meatpacking**	21
Maloney/Porcelli	**E 50s**	22
MarkJoseph	**Financial**	24
Michael Jordan	**E 40s**	20
Morton's	**multi.**	24
Nick & Stef	**Garment**	20
Novecento	**SoHo**	22
Old Homestead	**Meatpacking**	24
Outback	**multi.**	14
Z Palm	**multi.**	24
Parlor Steak	**E 90s**	21
Z Peter Luger	**W'burg**	27
Pietro's	**E 40s**	24
Porter House	**W 60s**	24
Post House	**E 60s**	24
Prime Grill	**E 40s**	22
Primehouse	**Murray Hill**	24
Quality Meats	**W 50s**	24
Rothmann's	**E 50s**	22
Ruth's Chris	**W 50s**	23
Shula's	**W 40s**	21
Smith/Wollensky	**E 40s**	23
South Fin	**SI**	19
Z Sparks	**E 40s**	25
STK	**Meatpacking**	21
Strip House	**G Vill**	25
T-Bar Steak	**E 70s**	22
tre dici	**Chelsea**	21
2 West	**Financial**	22
Uncle Jack's	**multi.**	23
Via Brasil	**W 40s**	20
Z Wolfgang's	**multi.**	25
Wollensky's	**E 40s**	23

SWISS

| **NEW** Café Select | **SoHo** | 21 |

TEAROOMS

Z Lady Mendl's	**Gramercy**	22
Sweet Melissa	**multi.**	21
Tea & Sympathy	**W Vill**	21

TEX-MEX

El Rio Grande	**Murray Hill**	18
Lobo	**multi.**	15
Mary Ann's	**multi.**	16

THAI

Bann Thai	**Forest Hills**	20
Breeze	**W 40s**	21
Elephant	**E Vill**	20
Erawan	**Bayside**	23

Holy Basil	**E Vill**	21
Jaiya Thai	**Murray Hill**	21
Joya	**Cobble Hill**	23
Kittichai	**SoHo**	22
Klong	**E Vill**	21
Kuma Inn	**LES**	24
Land	**multi.**	22
Laut	**Union Sq**	24
Lemongrass	**multi.**	16
Pam Real Thai	**W 40s**	22
Peep	**SoHo**	18
Planet Thai	**Flatiron**	19
Pongsri Thai	**multi.**	20
Prem-on Thai	**G Vill**	21
Pukk	**E Vill**	23
Q Thai Bistro	**Forest Hills**	21
Rhong-Tiam	**G Vill**	22
Room Service	**multi.**	18
Royal Siam	**Chelsea**	21
Sala Thai	**E 80s**	22
SEA	**multi.**	22
Siam Sq.	**Bronx**	23
Song	**Park Slope**	23
Sookk	**W 100s**	22
Spice	**multi.**	21
Z Sripraphai	**Woodside**	27
Talay	**Harlem**	21
Thai Pavilion	**Astoria**	24
Topaz Thai	**W 50s**	21
NEW Umi Nom	**Clinton Hill**	–
Vong	**E 50s**	22
Wondee Siam	**multi.**	22

TIBETAN

| Tsampa | **E Vill** | 21 |

TUNISIAN

| Epices/Traiteur | **W 70s** | 20 |

TURKISH

Akdeniz	**W 40s**	21
A La Turka	**E 70s**	19
Ali Baba	**multi.**	21
Bereket	**LES**	21
Beyoglu	**E 80s**	21
Bodrum	**W 80s**	19
NEW Hanci	**W 50s**	24
Pasha	**W 70s**	20
Pera	**E 40s**	21
Peri Ela	**E 90s**	20
Sahara	**Gravesend**	21
Sip Sak	**E 40s**	19
Taci's Beyti	**Midwood**	22
Taksim	**E 50s**	20
Turkish Cuisine	**W 40s**	19
Turkish Grill	**Sunnyside**	23

Z Turkish Kitchen | **Murray Hill**	23
Turks & Frogs | **TriBeCa**	19
Turkuaz | **W 100s**	19
Uskudar | **E 70s**	19

UKRAINIAN

Veselka | **E Vill**	19

VEGETARIAN

(* vegan)

Angelica Kit.* | **E Vill**	21
Blossom* | **multi.**	23
Candle Cafe* | **E 70s**	22
Candle 79* | **E 70s**	23
Caravan/Dreams* | **E Vill**	20
Chennai Gdn. | **Murray Hill**	21
Counter* | **E Vill**	20
NEW Dirt Candy | **E Vill**	23
Gobo* | **multi.**	23
Z HanGawi | **Murray Hill**	26
Hummus Pl. | **multi.**	23
NEW Kajitsu | **E Vill**	-
Maoz Veg. | **multi.**	21
Pongal | **Murray Hill**	22
Pukk | **E Vill**	23
Pure Food/Wine* | **Gramercy**	21
Quantum Leap | **multi.**	20
Quartino | **NoHo**	20
Sacred Chow* | **G Vill**	20
Saravanaas | **Murray Hill**	24

Taïm | **W Vill**	25
Tiffin Wallah | **Murray Hill**	24
Vatan | **Murray Hill**	22
Zen Palate | **W 40s**	18

VENEZUELAN

Z Caracas | **multi.**	24

VIETNAMESE

NEW An Choi | **LES**	21
NEW Baoguette | **multi.**	22
Bao Noodles | **Gramercy**	19
NEW BarBao | **W 80s**	21
Bôi | **E 40s**	20
Bún | **SoHo**	20
Hanco's | **multi.**	22
Indochine | **E Vill**	21
Le Colonial | **E 50s**	20
Nam | **TriBeCa**	21
New Bo-Ky | **Chinatown**	22
Nha Trang | **Chinatown**	22
Z Nicky's | **multi.**	22
Omai | **Chelsea**	22
Pho Bang | **multi.**	20
Pho Pasteur | **Chinatown**	21
Pho Viet Huong | **Chinatown**	22
Safran | **Chelsea**	20
Saigon Grill | **multi.**	20
Vermicelli | **E 70s**	20

Morningside
Heights

MORNINGSIDE
PARK

Cathedral Pkwy.

Harlem

East
Harlem

E. 110th St.

West
100s

W. 100th St.

East
100s

E. 100th St.

West
90s

W. 90th St.

East
90s

E. 90th St.

West
80s

W. 80th St.

CENTRAL
PARK

East
80s

E. 80th St.

CARL
SCHURZ
PARK

West
70s

W. 70th St.

East
70s

E. 70th St.

West
60s

W. 60th St.

East
60s

E. 60th St.

East
River

E. 59th St.

West
50s

W. 50th St.

East
50s

E. 50th St.

West
40s

TIMES
SQUARE

W. 40th St.

BRYANT
PARK

East
40s

E. 42nd St.

W. 42nd St.

E. 40th St.

Garment
District

W. 30th St.

Murray
Hill

W. 26th St.

MADISON
SQUARE
PARK

E. 23rd St.

Chelsea

Flatiron

Gramercy
Park

W. 14th St.

Union Sq.

E. 14th St.

Meatpacking
District

Greenwich
Village

WASHINGTON
SQ. PARK

East
Village

TOMPKINS
SQ. PARK

West
Village

W. Houston St.

E. 4th St.

NoHo

E. Houston St.

Lower
East Side

SoHo

NoLita

Canal St.

Little
Italy

Delancey St.

Hudson
River

TriBeCa

Worth St.

Chinatown

Pearl St.

Murray St.

CITY
HALL

Financial
District

South Street
Seaport

Wall St.

East
River

BATTERY
PARK

0   1/2 mi

RIVERSIDE PARK

MAPS

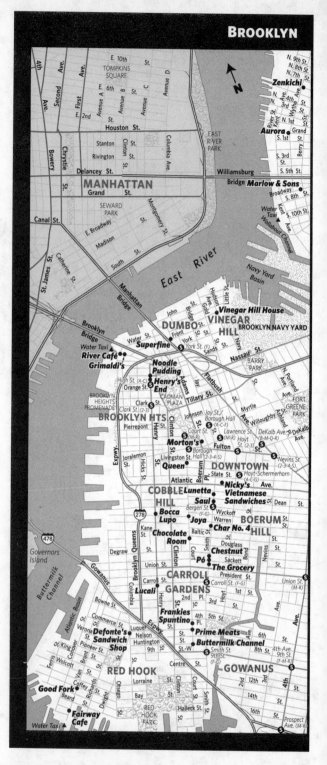

4th Ave.

Second Ave.

First Ave.

E. 10th St.

TOMPKINS
SQUARE

E. 6th St.

Avenue A

Avenue B

Avenue C

Avenue D

E. 2nd

Houston St.

Bowery

Chrystie St.

Stanton St.

Rivington St.

Clinton St.

Columbia Ave.

EAST
RIVER
PARK

Delancey St.

MANHATTAN

Grand St.

SEWARD
PARK

Canal St.

E. Broadway

Madison St.

Montgomery St.

St. James Pl.

Catherine St.

South St.

N. 9th St.

N. 8th St.

N. 7th St.

Zenkichi

N. 4th St.

Wythe

N. 3rd St.

N. 1st St.

River

Kent

Aurora Grand

S. 1st St.

Berry

S. 3rd St.

S. 5th St.

Williamsburg

Williamsburg
Bridge *Marlow & Sons*

Broadway

S. 8th St.

Water
Taxi

Kent

S. 10th St.

Wallabout Channel

East River

Manhattan
Bridge

Navy Yard
Basin

BROOKLYN NAVY YARD

John St.

Hudson St.

Gold St.

Little St.

Vinegar Hill House

DUMBO

**VINEGAR
HILL**

Front St.

York St.

Sands St.

Nassau St.

BARRY
PARK

N. Portland Ave.

Brooklyn
Bridge

Water St.

Superfine

York St. (F)

Water Taxi

River Café

Grimaldi's

*Noodle
Pudding*

Flatbush Ave.

Myrtle Ave.

FORT
GREENE
PARK

High St. (A–C)

Orange St.

*Henry's
End*

Adams St.

Jay St.

Willoughby St.

Willoughby Ave.

Clark St. (2–3)

BROOKLYN
HEIGHTS
PROMENADE

Clark St.

CADMAN
PLAZA

Tillary St.

DeKalb Ave. (B–M–Q–R)

DeKalb Ave.

BROOKLYN HTS.

Pierrepont St.

Henry St.

Clinton St.

Johnson St.

Jay St.,
Borough Hall
(A–C–F)

Lawrence St. (M–R)

Court St. (M–R)

Fulton St.

Hoyt St. (2–3)

Nevins St. (2–3–4–5)

Joralemon
St.

Morton's

Hicks St.

Borough
Hall (2–3–4–5)

Livingston St.

Queen

DOWNTOWN

State St.

Hoyt-Schermerhorn
(A–C–G)

Atlantic Ave.

Boerum Pl.

Nicky's

**COBBLE
HILL**

Lunetta

*Vietnamese
Sandwiches*

Dean St.

Expwy.

Saul

Bergen St. (F–G)

Wyckoff St.

**BOERUM
HILL**

*Bocca
Lupo*

Joya

Warren St.

Char No. 4

Kane St.

*Chocolate
Room*

Baltic St.

Smith St.

Douglass St.

Bond St.

Nevins St.

Degraw St.

Brooklyn Queens

Clinton St.

Court St.

Chestnut

Sackett St.

Union St.

P6

The Grocery

President St.

Union St. (M–R)

Carroll St.

Carroll St. (F–G)

1st St.

Columbia St.

Henry St.

**CARROLL
GARDENS**

2nd Pl.

3rd St.

2nd St.

Lucali

Bowne St.

4th Pl.

4th St.

5th St.

6th St.

*Frankies
Spuntino*

Espwy.

Luquer St.

Nelson St.

Huntington St.

9th St.

Prime Meats

Buttermilk Channel

Smith-
9th St.
(F–G)

4th Ave.
9th St.
(F–M–R)

Commerce St.

Centre St.

*Defonte's
Sandwich Shop*

Verona St.

Visitation Pl.

Van Brunt St.

Pioneer St.

King St.

Coffey St.

Ferris St.

Wolcott St.

Dwight St.

Richards St.

RED HOOK

Lorraine St.

RED
HOOK
PARK

Bay St.

Halleck St.

GOWANUS

Clinton St.

Court St.

Smith St.

2nd St.

12th St.

3rd Ave.

4th Ave.

14th St.

16th St.

Prospect
Ave. (M–R)

Good Fork

Beard St.

Otsego St.

*Fairway
Cafe*

Water Taxi

Governors
Island

Buttermilk
Channel

Atlantic Basin

Gowanus Expwy.

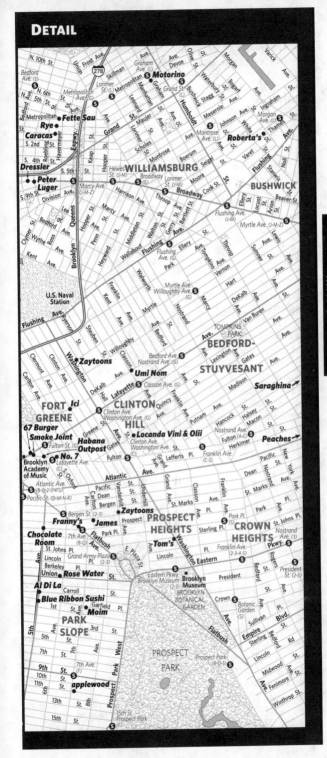

Locations

Includes names, street locations and Food ratings. Abbreviations key:
(a=Avenue, s=Street, e.g. 1a/116s=First Ave. at 116th St.;
3a/82-83s=Third Ave. between 82nd & 83rd Sts.)

Manhattan

CHELSEA

(26th to 30th Sts., west of 5th;
14th to 26th Sts., west of 6th)

Amy's Bread	9a/15-16s	24
NEW Bar Breton	5a/28-29s	18
Blossom	9a/21-22s	23
Blue Ginger	8a/15-16s	21
Bombay Talkie	9a/21-22s	20
Bottino	10a/24-25s	18
brgr	7a/26-27s	19
Z Buddakan	9a/16s	23
Cafeteria	7a/17s	18
NEW Co.	9a/24s	22
Cookshop	10a/20s	22
Craftsteak	10a/15-16s	24
Crema	17s/6-7a	21
Cuba Cafe	8a/20-21s	18
Dallas BBQ	8a/23s	15
Da Umberto	17s/6-7a	24
Z Del Posto	10a/16s	26
elmo	7a/19-20s	16
El Quijote	23s/7-8a	20
El Quinto Pino	24s/9-10a	21
Empire Diner	10a/22s	15
Energy Kitchen	17s/8-9a	17
Francisco's	23s/6-7a	21
Gascogne	8a/17-18s	21
Grand Sichuan	9a/24s	21
Hale/Hearty	9a/15-16s	19
Il Bastardo	7a/21-22s	19
ilili	5a/27-28s	24
Izakaya 10	10a/22-23s	21
Klee Brass.	9a/22-23s	20
La Bergamote	9a/20s	25
La Lunchonette	10a/18s	21
La Taza de Oro	8a/14-15s	20
Le Singe Vert	7a/19-20s	18
Le Zie 2000	7a/20-21s	22
Mary Ann's	8a/16s	16
Matsuri	16s/9a	22
Momoya	7a/21s	23
Monster Sushi	23s/6-7a	18
Moran's	10a/19s	18
Z Morimoto	10a/15-16s	25
Omai	9a/19-20s	22
Park	10a/17-18s	16
Pars Grill	26s/7-8a	20

Patsy's Pizzeria	23s/8-9a	20
Pepe	10a/24-25s	22
Pizza 33	23s/8a	19
Pongsri Thai	23s/6-7a	20
Red Cat	10a/23-24s	23
Rocking Horse	8a/19-20s	20
Rock-n-Sake	25s/6-7a	23
Room Service	8a/18-19s	18
Royal Siam	8a/22-23s	21
RUB BBQ	23s/7-8a	20
Safran	7a/15-16s	20
Sarabeth's	9a/15-16s	20
Z Scarpetta	14s/8-9a	26
Seven	7a/29-30s	19
Socarrat	19s/7-8a	24
Spice	8a/19-20s	21
Sueños	17s/8-9a	22
Tía Pol	10a/22-23s	25
tre dici	26s/6-7a	21
Trestle on 10th	10a/24s	19
202 Cafe	9a/15-16s	20
NEW Txikito	9a/24-25s	23
Uncle Nick's	8a/29s	20
Waldy's Pizza	6a/27-28s	22
'wichcraft	11a/27-28s	20

CHINATOWN

(Canal to Pearl Sts., east of B'way)

Amazing 66	Mott/Canal	22
Big Wong	Mott/Canal	22
Dim Sum Go Go	E Bway/Chatham	21
Excellent Dumpling	Lafayette/Canal	20
Fuleen	Division/Bowery	23
Golden Unicorn	E Bway/Catherine	20
Grand Sichuan	Canal/Chrystie	21
Great NY Noodle	Bowery/Bayard	22
Jing Fong	Elizabeth/Canal	20
Joe's Shanghai	Pell/Bowery	22
Joe's	Pell/Doyers	20
Mandarin Court	Mott/Canal	20
New Bo-Ky	Bayard/Mott	22
New Yeah	Bayard/Mott	24
Nha Trang	multi.	22
Nice Green Bo	Bayard/Elizabeth	23
Z Oriental Gdn.	Elizabeth/Canal	23
Peking Duck	Mott/Mosco-Pell	23
Pho Pasteur	Baxter/Canal	21
Pho Viet Huong	Mulberry/Canal	22

Ping's Sea. | *Mott/Bayard-Pell* 21
Pongsri Thai | *Bayard/Baxter* 20
Wo Hop | *Mott/Canal* 21
X.O. | *Walker/Centre-Lafayette* 20

EAST 40s

Aburiya Kinnosuke | *45s/2-3a* 24
Ali Baba | *2a/46s* 21
Ammos | *Vanderbilt/44-45s* 21
NEW Aperitivo | *3a/48s* 20
NEW At Vermilion | *Lex/46s* 18
Avra | *48s/Lex-3a* 25
Ben & Jack's | *44s/2-3a* 23
Benjamin Steak | *41s/Mad-Park* 24
Bobby Van's | *Park/46s* 22
Bôi | *multi.* 20
Brother Jimmy | *42s/Vanderbilt* 16
Bukhara Grill | *49s/2-3a* 22
Bull & Bear | *Lex/49s* 20
Burger Heaven | *multi.* 16
Cafe Centro | *Park/45s* 20
Cafe Spice | *42s/Vanderbilt* 18
Capital Grille | *42s/Lex-3a* 23
Chiam | *48s/Lex-3a* 21
Chin Chin | *49s/2-3a* 23
Chipotle | *44s/Lex-3a* 18
Cibo | *2a/41s* 20
Cipriani Dolci | *42s/Vanderbilt* 20
Z Convivio | *42s/1-2a* 26
Così | *45s/Mad-Vanderbilt* 16
Darbar | *46s/Lex-3a* 21
Dean's | *2a/42-43s* 17
Dishes | *multi.* 22
Docks Oyster | *3a/40s* 19
Energy Kitchen | *41s/2a* 17
Fabio Piccolo | *44s/2-3a* 21
goodburger | *2a/42s* 18
Grifone | *46s/2-3a* 25
Gyu-Kaku | *3a/50s* 22
Hale/Hearty | *multi.* 19
Haru | *Park/48s* 20
Hatsuhana | *multi.* 25
Il Postino | *49s/1-2a* 23
Inagiku | *49s/Lex-Park* 22
Ise | *49s/Lex-3a* 21
Junior's | *42s/Vanderbilt* 17
Katsu-Hama | *47s/5a-Mad* 21
Z Kuruma Zushi | *47s/5a-Mad* 27
NEW La Fonda/Sol | *Park/44s* 22
Mamá Mexico | *49s/2-3a* 20
Mangia | *48s/5a-Mad* 19
Mee Noodle | *2a/49s* 18
Megu | *1a/47s* 23
Menchanko-tei | *45s/Lex-3a* 20
Metrazur | *42s/Vanderbilt* 21

Michael Jordan | *43s/Vanderbilt* 20
Morton's | *5a/45s* 24
Nanni | *46s/Lex-3a* 24
Naples 45 | *Park/45s* 17
Nino's | *2a/47-48s* 21
Osteria Laguna | *42s/2-3a* 19
Z Oyster Bar | *42s/Vanderbilt* 22
Padre Figlio | *44s/1-2a* 20
Z Palm | *2a/44-45s* 24
Pampano | *49s/2-3a* 24
Patroon | *46s/Lex-3a* 21
Pepe | *42s/Vanderbilt* 22
Pera | *Mad/41-42s* 21
Pershing Sq. | *42s/Park* 16
Phoenix Gdn. | *40s/2-3a* 23
Pietro's | *43s/2-3a* 24
Prime Grill | *49s/Mad-Park* 22
Riingo | *45s/2-3a* 21
Sakagura | *43s/2-3a* 25
Seo | *49s/2-3a* 24
NEW Sinigual | *3a/41s* 22
Sip Sak | *2a/49-50s* 19
Smith/Wollensky | *3a/49s* 23
Z Sparks | *46s/2-3a* 25
Sushiden | *49s/5a-Mad* 23
Z Sushi Yasuda | *43s/2-3a* 28
Two Boots | *42s/Vanderbilt* 19
'wichcraft | *multi.* 20
Wollensky's | *49s/3a* 23
Yama | *49s/1-2a* 24

EAST 50s

Z Adour | *55s/5a-Mad* 26
Aja | *1a/58s* 20
Z Alto | *53s/5a-Mad* 26
Amma | *51s/2-3a* 24
NEW André | *57s/Lex-Park* -
Angelo's Pizza | *2a/55s* 21
Z Aquavit | *55s/Mad-Park* 25
NEW Armani Rist. | *5a/56s* 23
Baluchi's | *53s/2-3a* 17
Bar Vetro | *58s/2-3a* 20
Bice | *54s/5a-Mad* 21
Blockhead Burrito | *2a/50-51s* 16
Z BLT Steak | *57s/Lex-Park* 25
Bobby Van's | *54s/Lex-Park* 22
Bottega/Vino | *59s/5a-Mad* 22
Brasserie | *53s/Lex-Park* 20
Brick Ln. Curry | *53s/2-3a* 21
Burger Heaven | *multi.* 16
BXL | *51s/2-3a* 20
Cafe Joul | *1a/58-59s* 18
Caviar Russe | *Mad/54-55s* 25
Cellini | *54s/Mad-Park* 22
Chipotle | *52s/Lex-3a* 18

Restaurant	Rating
Chola	58s/2-3a	23
Club A Steak	58s/2-3a	25
Così	56s/Mad-Park	16
Darbar	55s/Lex-3a	21
NEW Dardanel	1a/58-59s	18
Dawat	58s/2-3a	23
DeGrezia	50s/2-3a	23
Destino	1a/50s	19
Deux Amis	51s/1-2a	20
Dishes	Park/53s	22
Dos Caminos	3a/50-51s	20
Energy Kitchen	2a/57-58s	17
Ess-a-Bagel	3a/50-51s	23
Ethos	1a/51s	22
Z Felidia	58s/2-3a	26
Fig & Olive	52s/5a-Mad	20
Fiorini	56s/2-3a	20
Z Four Seasons	52s/Lex-Park	26
Fresco	52s/Mad-Park	23
Z Gilt	Mad/50-51s	25
goodburger	Lex/54s	18
Grand Sichuan	2a/55-56s	21
Harry Cipriani	5a/59-60s	21
Houston's	3a/54s	20
NEW Inside Park	50s/Park	17
Jubilee	54s/1-2a	22
Z La Grenouille	52s/5a-Mad	27
La Mangeoire	2a/53-54s	21
Z L'Atelier/Robuchon	57s/Mad	28
Z Le Cirque	58s/Lex-3a	24
Le Colonial	57s/Lex-3a	20
Lenny's	2a/54s	17
Le Perigord	52s/FDR-1a	24
NEW Le Relais/Venise	Lex/52s	–
Maloney/Porcelli	50s/Mad	22
Mia Dona	58s/2-3a	21
Mint	50s/Lex-3a	21
Z NEW Monkey Bar	54s/Mad	18
Mr. Chow	57s/1-2a	21
Mr. K's	Lex/51s	22
NEW Naya	2a/55-56s	21
Neary's	57s/1a	16
Nino's	58s/2-3a	21
Our Place	55s/Lex-3a	20
Outback	56s/2-3a	14
Peking Duck	53s/2-3a	23
P.J. Clarke's	3a/55s	17
Pop Burger	58s/5a-Mad	18
Pump Energy	3a/50s	17
Rosa Mexicano	1a/58s	22
Rothmann's	54s/5a-Mad	22
Z San Pietro	54s/5a-Mad	26
Serafina	58s/Mad-Park	18
Shun Lee Palace	55s/Lex-3a	23
Sofrito	57s/1a-Sutton	21
Solera	53s/2-3a	20
Solo	Mad/55-56s	22
SushiAnn	51s/Mad-Park	25
Taksim	2a/54-55s	20
Z Tao	58s/Mad-Park	21
Tenzan	2a/52-53a	22
Teodora	57s/Lex-3a	20
Tratt. Pesce	1a/59s	19
Tse Yang	51s/Mad-Park	24
Via Quadronno	5a/59s	22
Vong	54s/3a	22
Yuva	58s/2-3a	23
Zarela	2a/50-51s	20
NEW Ze Café	52s/FDR-1a	21

EAST 60s

Restaurant	Rating
Accademia/Vino	3a/63-64s	19
Amaranth	62s/5a-Mad	18
Bistro Chat Noir	66s/5a-Mad	18
Bistro 61	1a/61s	20
Bravo Gianni	63s/2-3a	22
Brio	61s/Lex	18
Burger Heaven	Lex/62s	16
Cabana	3a/60-61s	21
Café Evergreen	1a/69-70s	18
Canaletto	60s/2-3a	21
China Fun	2a/64s	15
Circus	61s/Lex-Park	20
Da Filippo	2a/69-70s	21
Z Daniel	65s/Mad-Park	28
David Burke Townhse.	61s/Lex	25
Felice	1a/64s	20
Fig & Olive	Lex/62-63s	20
NEW Fishtail	62s/Lex-Park	23
Fred's at Barneys	Mad/60s	20
Geisha	61s/Mad-Park	22
Hale/Hearty	Lex/64-65s	19
Jackson Hole	64s/2-3a	17
Z John's Pizzeria	64s/1a-York	22
Z JoJo	64s/Lex-3a	25
Kai	Mad/68-69s	26
L'Absinthe	67s/2-3a	22
Le Bilboquet	63s/Mad-Park	23
Lenny's	1a/68s	17
Le Pain Q.	Lex/63-64s	19
NEW Mañana	61s/Mad-Park	21
Maya	1a/64-65s	23
Mediterraneo	2a/66s	18
Nanoosh	1a/68-69s	19
Park Ave.	63s/Lex	24
Patsy's Pizzeria	multi.	20
Persephone	60s/Lex	22
Philippe	60s/Mad-Park	24
Post House	63s/Mad-Park	24
Primola	2a/64-65s	22

Ravagh | *1a/66-67s*	20
Regency | *Park/61s*	18
NEW Rouge Tomate | *60s/5a*	22
Z Scalinatella | *61s/3a*	26
Serafina | *61s/Mad-Park*	18
Serendipity 3 | *60s/2-3a*	18
Z Sushi Seki | *1a/62-63s*	26
212 | *65s/Lex-Park*	18
Viand | *Mad/61-62s*	17
Za Za | *1a/65-66s*	20

EAST 70s

Afghan Kebab | *2a/70-71s*	19
A La Turka | *2a/74s*	19
Alloro | *77s/1-2a*	22
Z Atlantic Grill | *3a/76-77s*	23
Baraonda | *2a/75s*	18
Barking Dog | *York/77s*	15
B. Café | *75s/2-3a*	21
Bella Blu | *Lex/70-71s*	20
Boathouse | *Central Pk dr/72s*	17
Brother Jimmy | *2a/77-78s*	16
Z Café Boulud | *76s/5a-Mad*	27
Campagnola | *1a/73-74s*	23
Candle Cafe | *3a/74-75s*	22
Candle 79 | *79s/Lex-3a*	23
Canyon Road | *1a/76-77s*	21
NEW Caravaggio | *74s/5a-Mad*	–
Z Carlyle | *76s/Mad*	23
Cilantro | *1a/71s*	17
Cortina | *2a/75-76s*	16
Dallas BBQ | *3a/72-73s*	15
Due | *3a/79-80s*	21
EJ's Luncheon. | *3a/73s*	16
NEW Fulton | *75s/2-3a*	22
Z Gari/Sushi | *78s/1a-York*	27
Haru | *3a/76s*	20
Il Riccio | *79s/Lex-3a*	20
J.G. Melon | *3a/74s*	21
NEW Le Magnifique | *Lex/73s*	–
Lenny's | *2a/77s*	17
Le Pain Q. | *77s/2-3a*	19
Lumi | *Lex/70s*	18
Lusardi's | *2a/77-78s*	23
Maruzzella | *1a/77-78s*	21
Mezzaluna/Pizza | *3a/74-75s*	21
Mingala Burmese | *2a/72-73s*	20
Nino's | *1a/72-73s*	21
Orsay | *Lex/75s*	18
Parma | *3a/79-80s*	22
Pastrami Queen | *Lex/78-79s*	20
Per Lei | *2a/71s*	20
Persepolis | *2a/73-74s*	21
Petaluma | *1a/73s*	19
Quatorze Bis | *79s/1-2a*	20

Sant Ambroeus | *Mad/77-78s*	22
Sarabeth's | *Mad/75s*	20
Z Sasabune | *73s/1a-York*	28
Serafina | *Mad/79s*	18
Sette Mezzo | *Lex/70-71s*	22
Shabu-Shabu 70 | *70s/1-2a*	21
Shanghai Pavilion | *3a/78-79s*	22
NEW Sojourn | *79s/2-3a*	24
Spice | *2a/73-74s*	21
Sushi Hana | *2a/78s*	20
Swifty's | *Lex/72-73s*	18
T-Bar Steak | *3a/73-74s*	22
Trata | *2a/70-71s*	22
Uskudar | *2a/73-74s*	19
Uva | *2a/77-78s*	21
Vermicelli | *2a/77-78s*	20
Viand | *Mad/78s*	17
Via Quadronno | *73s/5a-Mad*	22

EAST 80s

Amber | *3a/80s*	20
Antonucci | *81s/Lex-3a*	21
Baluchi's | *2a/89-90s*	17
Beyoglu | *3a/81s*	21
Blockhead Burrito | *2a/81-82s*	16
Brasserie Julien | *3a/80-81s*	18
Burger Heaven | *3a/86-87s*	16
Café d'Alsace | *2a/88s*	21
Café Sabarsky | *5a/86s*	22
Caffe Grazie | *84s/5a-Mad*	19
Centolire | *Mad/85-86s*	21
Chef Ho's | *2a/89-90s*	23
Ciaobella | *2a/85s*	21
Cilantro | *2a/88-89s*	17
Demarchelier | *86s/Mad-Park*	16
Donguri | *83s/1-2a*	26
E.A.T. | *Mad/80-81s*	19
Elaine's | *2a/88-89s*	13
Z Elio's | *2a/84-85s*	24
Energy Kitchen | *2a/84-85s*	17
Erminia | *83s/2-3a*	25
Etats-Unis | *81s/2-3a*	23
Firenze | *2a/82-83s*	20
NEW Flex Mussels | *82s/Lex-3a*	22
Giovanni | *83s/5a-Mad*	22
Gobo | *3a/81s*	23
Heidelberg | *2a/85-86s*	18
Italianissimo | *84s/1-2a*	23
Ithaka | *86s/1-2a*	21
Jackson Hole | *2a/83-84s*	17
Jacques | *85s/2-3a*	20
Kings' Carriage | *82s/2-3a*	22
Land | *2a/81-82s*	22
Le Boeuf/Mode | *81s/E End*	21
Le Pain Q. | *Mad/84-85s*	19

LOCATIONS

Le Refuge	*82s/Lex-3a*	21
Maz Mezcal	*86s/1-2a*	19
Niche	*2a/82-83s*	24
Nicola's	*84s/Lex-3a*	22
One 83	*1a/83-84s*	19
NEW Opus	*2a/81-82s*	23
Our Place	*3a/82s*	20
Paola's	*Mad/92s*	23
Papaya King	*86s/3a*	20
Pig Heaven	*2a/80-81s*	19
Pintaile's Pizza	*York/83-84s*	19
Poke	*85s/1-2a*	25
Primavera	*1a/82s*	24
Quattro Gatti	*81s/2-3a*	22
Rughetta	*85s/1-2a*	22
Sala Thai	*2a/89-90s*	22
Sandro's	*81s/1-2a*	25
Shalizar	*3a/80-81s*	21
Sharz Cafe	*86s/1a-York*	20
Z Sistina	*2a/80-81s*	26
Spigolo	*2a/81s*	25
Tenzan	*2a/89s*	22
Tevere	*84s/Lex-3a*	24
Tiramisu	*3a/80s*	20
Tony's Di Napoli	*2a/83s*	19
Totonno Pizza	*2a/80-81s*	22
Triangolo	*83s/1-2a*	20
Turquoise	*81s/2-3a*	21
Two Boots	*2a/84s*	19
Vespa	*2a/84-85s*	19
Viand	*86s/2a*	17
Wasabi Lobby	*2a/82s*	19
Wu Liang Ye	*86s/2-3a*	22
York Grill	*York/88-89s*	21
Yuka	*2a/80-81s*	21

EAST 90s & 100s

(90th to 110th Sts.)

Barking Dog	*3a/94s*	15
Bistro du Nord	*Mad/93s*	18
Brother Jimmy	*3a/92s*	16
NEW Chimney	*2a/105-106s*	-
Chinese Mirch	*2a/94-95s*	19
Don Pedro's	*2a/96s*	21
El Paso Taqueria	*multi.*	23
Itzocan	*Lex/101s*	23
Jackson Hole	*Mad/91s*	17
Moustache	*Lex/102s*	21
Nick's	*2a/94s*	23
Osso Buco	*3a/93s*	17
Parlor Steak	*3a/90s*	21
Pascalou	*Mad/92-93s*	21
Peri Ela	*Lex/90-91s*	20
Pinocchio	*1a/90-91s*	22
Pintaile's Pizza	*91s/5a-Mad*	19

Pio Pio	*1a/90-91s*	22
Sarabeth's	*Mad/92-93s*	20
Sfoglia	*Lex/92s*	25
Square Meal	*92s/5a-Mad*	23
Table d'Hôte	*92s/Mad-Park*	20
Vico	*Mad/92-93s*	20
Zebú Grill	*92s/1-2a*	20

EAST VILLAGE

(14th to Houston Sts., east of B'way, excluding NoHo)

Angelica Kit.	*12s/1-2a*	21
Apiary	*3a/10-11s*	22
NEW Arcane	*Ave C/7-8s*	-
Artichoke Basille	*14s/1-2a*	23
Awash	*6s/1-2a*	22
Back Forty	*Ave B/11-12s*	21
Banjara	*1a/6s*	23
NEW Baoguette	*St Marks/2a*	22
Barbone	*Ave B/11-12s*	24
Bar Carrera	*2a/11-12s*	22
Belcourt	*4s/2a*	20
NEW Bistrouge	*13s/Ave A-1a*	24
Black Iron	*5s/Aves A-B*	21
Boca Chica	*1a/1s*	19
NEW Boka	*St Marks/2-3a*	23
Brick Ln. Curry	*6s/1-2a*	21
Buenos Aires	*6s/Aves A-B*	22
NEW Butcher Bay	*5s/Aves A-B*	14
Butter	*Lafayette/Astor-4s*	20
Cacio e Pepe	*2a/11-12s*	20
Cacio e Vino	*2a/4-5s*	21
Cafecito	*Ave C/11-12s*	23
Cafe Mogador	*St Marks/Ave A*	21
Z Caracas	*multi.*	24
Caravan/Dreams	*6s/1a*	20
Casimir	*Ave B/6-7s*	19
Chickpea	*14s/2-3a*	18
ChikaLicious	*10s/1-2a*	25
China 1	*Ave B/3-4s*	17
Chipotle	*St Marks/2-3a*	18
Chiyono	*6s/1-2a*	25
Counter	*1a/6-7s*	20
Dallas BBQ	*2a/St Marks*	15
Z **NEW** DBGB	*Bowery/Houston*	23
Z Degustation	*5s/2-3a*	26
Dieci	*10s/1-2a*	22
NEW Dirt Candy	*9s/Ave A-1a*	23
Dok Suni's	*1a/St Marks-7s*	22
Dumpling Man	*St Marks/Ave A*	19
Elephant	*1s/1-2a*	20
Euzkadi	*4s/1-2a*	21
Flea Mkt. Cafe	*Ave A/9s*	21
Frank	*2a/5-6s*	24
Gemma	*Bowery/2-3s*	19
Gnocco Caffe	*10s/Aves A-B*	23

Menus, photos, voting and more – free at ZAGAT.com

Graffiti | *10s/1-2a*	26
Grand Sichuan | *St Marks/2-3a*	21
Gruppo | *Ave B/11-12s*	25
Gyu-Kaku | *Cooper/Astor-4s*	22
Hasaki | *9s/2-3a*	24
Haveli | *2a/5-6s*	22
Hearth | *12s/1a*	25
Holy Basil | *2a/9-10s*	21
Hummus Pl. | *St Marks/Ave A*	23
I Coppi | *9s/Ave A-1a*	23
Il Bagatto | *2s/Aves A-B*	24
Indochine | *Lafayette/Astor-4s*	21
☑ Ippudo | *4a/9-10s*	25
Itzocan | *9s/Ave A-1a*	23
Jack's Lux. | *2a/5-6s*	26
☑ Jewel Bako | *5s/2-3a*	25
Jimmy's | *7s/2-3a*	20
Joe Doe | *1s/1-2a*	23
John's/12th St. | *12s/2a*	20
Jules | *St Marks/1-2a*	18
Kafana | *Ave C/7-8s*	22
🆕 Kajitsu | *9s/Ave A-1a*	-
☑ Kanoyama | *2a/11s*	26
Klong | *St Marks/2-3a*	21
Knife + Fork | *4s/1-2a*	21
☑ Kyo Ya | *7s/1a*	27
Lan | *3a/10-11s*	23
Lanza | *1a/10-11s*	18
La Palapa | *St Marks/1-2a*	19
Lavagna | *5s/Aves A-B*	23
Le Gamin | *5s/Aves A-B*	18
Lil' Frankie | *1a/1-2s*	23
Lucien | *1a/1s*	22
Luzzo's | *1a/12-13s*	25
Mama's Food | *3s/Aves A-B*	20
Mancora | *1a/6s*	20
Mara's | *6s/1-2a*	23
🆕 Marfa | *2s/Ave A-1a*	-
Mary Ann's | *2a/5s*	16
Matilda | *11s/Aves B-C*	26
Max | *Ave B/3-4s*	22
Mercadito | *multi.*	22
Mermaid Inn | *2a/5-6s*	20
Minca | *5s/Aves A-B*	22
Mingala Burmese | *7s/2-3a*	20
🆕 Momofuku Bakery | *2a/13s*	21
☑ Momofuku Ko | *1a/10s*	27
Momofuku Noodle | *1a/10s*	23
☑ Momofuku Ssäm | *2a/13s*	25
Motorino | *12s/1-2a*	22
Moustache | *10s/Ave A-1a*	21
☑ Nicky's | *2s/Ave A*	22
99 Mi. to Philly | *3a/12-13s*	19
Nomad | *2a/4s*	20
Pepe | *Ave C/8s*	22

Perbacco | *4s/Aves A-B*	23
🆕 Permanent Brunch | *1a/5-6s*	-
🆕 Porchetta | *7s/Ave A-1a*	24
Prune | *1s/1-2a*	24
Pukk | *1a/4-5s*	23
Pylos | *7s/Ave A-1a*	25
Quantum Leap | *1a/12-13s*	20
Rai Rai Ken | *10s/1-2a*	21
Ramen Setagaya | *multi.*	19
Redhead | *13s/1-2a*	21
Sapporo East | *1a/10s*	18
SEA | *2a/4-5s*	22
Shabu-Tatsu | *10s/1-2a*	23
S'MAC/Pinch | *12s/1-2a*	21
Smith | *3a/10-11s*	19
Soba-ya | *9s/2-3a*	24
Spice | *multi.*	21
Supper | *2s/Aves A-B*	24
🆕 Table 8 | *Cooper/5-6s*	15
Takahachi | *Ave A/5-6s*	25
Tarallucci | *1a/10s*	21
🆕 Tonda | *4s/Aves A-B*	-
Tree | *1a/11-12s*	19
Tsampa | *9s/2-3a*	21
26 Seats | *Ave B/10-11s*	21
Two Boots | *Ave A/3s*	19
🆕 Veloce Pizzeria | *1a/6-7s*	-
Veselka | *multi.*	19
Westville | *Ave A/11s*	22
Xunta | *1a/10-11s*	21
Yerba Buena | *Ave A/Houston*	24
Yuca Bar | *Ave A/7s*	21
Zaitzeff | *Ave B/2-3s*	22
Zum Schneider | *Ave C/7s*	19

FINANCIAL DISTRICT

(South of Murray St.)

Adrienne's | *Pearl/Coenties*	23
Battery Gdns. | *Battery Pk*	18
Blockhead Burrito | *North/Vesey*	16
Bobby Van's | *Broad/Exchange*	22
Bridge Cafe | *Water/Dover*	21
Chipotle | *Bway/Stone*	18
Così | *Vesey/West*	16
Delmonico's | *Beaver/William*	23
Energy Kitchen | *Nassau/Fulton*	17
Fraunces Tavern | *Pearl/Broad*	16
Fresco | *Pearl/Hanover*	23
Gigino | *Battery/West*	21
Hale/Hearty | *Broad/Beaver*	19
Harry's | *multi.*	24
🆕 Harry's Italian | *Gold/Maiden-Platt*	-
Haru | *Wall/Beaver-Pearl*	20
🆕 Inatteso | *West/1pl*	21

Ise | *Pine/Pearl-William*	21
Lemongrass | *William/Maiden*	16
Lenny's | *John/Cliff-Pearl*	17
Les Halles | *John/Bway-Nassau*	20
Liberty View | *S End/3pl-Thames*	19
MarkJoseph | *Water/Peck*	24
NEW Perle | *Pearl/Broad-Coenties*	18
P.J. Clarke's | *World Fin/Vesey*	17
Pump Energy | *Pine/Pearl*	17
NEW SHO Shaun Hergatt | *Broad/Exchange*	29
Smorgas Chef | *Stone/William*	18
Trinity Pl. | *Cedar/Bway-Trinity*	19
2 West | *West/Battery*	22
Zaitzeff | *Nassau/John*	22

FLATIRON DISTRICT

(14th to 26th Sts., 6th Ave. to
Park Ave. S., excluding Union Sq.)

NEW Aldea | *17s/5-6a*	26
Aleo | *20s/5-6a*	19
Allegretti | *22s/5-6a*	24
NEW Almond | *22s/Bway-Park*	20
Angelo/Maxie's | *Park/19s*	22
A Voce | *Mad/26s*	24
Barbounia | *Park/20s*	21
Bar Stuzz. | *Bway/21-22s*	19
Basta Pasta | *17s/5-6a*	23
Beppe | *22s/Bway-Park*	23
BLT Fish | *17s/5-6a*	23
Bocca | *19s/Bway-Park*	21
Boqueria | *19s/5-6a*	22
Chickpea | *6a/21-22s*	18
Chipotle | *6a/21-22s*	18
City Bakery | *18s/5-6a*	22
City Crab | *Park/19s*	18
Così | *6a/22-23s*	16
Z Craft | *19s/Bway-Park*	25
Craftbar | *Bway/19-20s*	22
dévi | *18s/Bway-5a*	23
Z Eleven Madison | *Mad/24s*	27
Energy Kitchen	17
Giorgio's | *21s/Bway-Park*	21
goodburger | *Bway/17-18s*	18
Z Gramercy Tavern | *20s/Bway*	28
Haru | *Park/18s*	20
Hill Country | *26s/Bway-6a*	21
Kellari Tav./Parea | *20s/Bway*	22
La Pizza Fresca | *20s/Bway-Park*	23
Lenny's | *23s/5a*	17
Le Pain Q. | *19s/Bway-Park*	19
L'Express | *Park/20s*	17
Mangia | *23s/5-6a*	19
NEW Mari Vanna | *20s/Bway-Park*	-
Markt | *6a/21s*	20

Z Mesa Grill | *5a/15-16s*	23
Mizu Sushi | *20s/Bway-Park*	23
NY Burger | *6a/21-2s*	17
Outback | *23s/5-6a*	14
Periyali | *20s/5-6a*	24
Petite Abeille | *17s/5-6a*	17
Pipa | *19s/Bway-Park*	20
Planet Thai | *24s/5-6a*	19
Pump Energy | *21s/Bway-Park*	17
Rickshaw Dumpling | *23s/5-6a*	17
Rosa Mexicano | *18s/Bway*	22
Sala | *19s/5-6a*	22
Z Shake Shack | *23s/Mad sq*	23
SushiSamba | *Park/19-20s*	21
Z Tabla | *Mad/25s*	25
Z Tamarind | *22s/Bway-Park*	25
Tarallucci | *18s/Bway-5a*	21
Z Veritas | *20s/Bway-Park*	26
Via Emilia | *21s/Bway-Park*	22
'wichcraft | *20s/Bway-5a*	20
Wildwood BBQ | *Park/18-19s*	17

GARMENT DISTRICT

(30th to 40th Sts., west of 5th)

Abigael's | *Bway/38-39s*	20
Arno | *38s/Bway-7a*	20
Ben's Kosher | *38s/7-8a*	18
Brother Jimmy | *8a/31s*	16
Chipotle | *multi.*	18
Cho Dang Gol | *35s/5-6a*	23
NEW Crudo | *35s/7-8a*	-
Frankie/Johnnie | *37s/5-6a*	22
Gahm Mi Oak | *32s/Bway-5a*	21
Z Gray's Papaya | *8a/37s*	20
Hale/Hearty | *7a/35s*	19
Heartland | *5a/34s*	14
HK | *9a/39s*	17
NEW Il Punto | *9a/38s*	20
Kang Suh | *Bway/32s*	21
Kati Roll | *39s/5-6a*	20
Keens | *36s/5-6a*	24
Kum Gang San | *32s/Bway-5a*	21
Lazzara's | *38s/7-8a*	23
NEW Lugo Caffe | *33s/7-8a*	21
Mandoo Bar | *32s/Bway-5a*	21
Nick & Stef | *33s/7-8a*	20
Pump Energy | *38s/Bway-6a*	17
Sarabeth's | *5a/38-39s*	20
Szechuan Gourmet | *39s/5-6a*	22
Uncle Jack's | *9a/34-35s*	23

GRAMERCY PARK

(14th to 23rd Sts., east of Park Ave. S.)

Bao Noodles | *2a/22-23s*	19
BLT Prime | *22s/Lex-Park*	25
Casa Mono | *Irving/17s*	25

Defonte's | *3a/21s* 24
Ess-a-Bagel | *1a/21s* 23
Friend/Farmer | *Irving/18-19s* 18
House | *17s/Irving-Park* 22
Irving Mill | *16s/Irving* 20
Japonais | *18s/Irving-Park* 20
Ƶ Lady Mendl's | *Irving/17-18s* 22
Novitá | *22s/Lex-Park* 24
Pete's Tavern | *18s/Irving* 16
Petite Abeille | *20s/1a* 17
Posto | *2a/18s* 24
Pure Food/Wine | *Irving/17s* 21
Rolf's | *3a/22s* 14
Yama | *17s/Irving* 24

GREENWICH VILLAGE

(Houston to 14th Sts., west of
B'way, east of 7th Ave. S.)

Aki | *4s/Barrow-Jones* 24
Alta | *10s/5-6a* 24
Amber | *6a/9-10s* 20
Amy's Bread | *Blkr/Leroy* 24
Annisa | *Barrow/7a-4s* 27
Arté | *9s/5a-Uni* 18
Arturo's | *Houston/Thompson* 22
Ƶ Babbo | *Waverly/MacDougal* 27
Baluchi's | *multi.* 17
Bar Blanc | *10s/Greenwich a* 22
Bar Carrera | 22
  Houston/MacDougal
Bar Pitti | *6a/Blkr-Houston* 23
Bellavitae | *Minetta/MacDougal* 23
BLT Burger | *6a/11-12s* 20
Ƶ Blue Hill | *Wash pl/MacDougal* 27
Blue Ribbon Bakery | 24
  Downing/Bedford
Borgo Antico | *13s/5a-Uni* 18
Cabrito | *Carmine/Bedford-Blkr* 18
Cafe Asean | *10s/6a* 20
Cafe Español | *multi.* 20
Café Henri | *Bedford/Downing* 21
Cafe Loup | *13s/6-7a* 19
Cafe Spice | *Uni/10-11s* 18
CamaJe | *MacDougal/Blkr* 20
Chez Jacqueline | *MacDougal/Blkr* 21
Cornelia St. Cafe | *Cornelia/4s* 19
Così | *multi.* 16
Ƶ Cru | *5a/9-10s* 26
Cuba | *Thompson/Blkr-3s* 22
Cubana Café | *Thompson/Prince* 21
Da Andrea | *13s/5-6a* 23
Danal | *5a/12-13s* 20
Da Silvano | *6a/Blkr* 20
NEW de Santos | *10s/Greenwich a* 21
Ditch Plains | *Bedford/Downing* 18
Do Hwa | *Carmine/Bedford* 22

El Charro | *Charles/Waverly* 22
Elephant & Castle | 17
  Greenwich a/Perry
Empire Szechuan | *multi.* 15
Ennio/Michael | *La Guardia/3s* 21
NEW Favela Cubana | –
  La Guardia/3s
Fish | *Blkr/Jones* 22
Five Guys | *La Guardia/Blkr* 20
French Roast | *11s/5-6a* 17
Gobo | *6a/8s-Waverly* 23
Gonzo | *13s/6-7a* 21
Ƶ Gotham B&G | *12s/5a-Uni* 27
Gottino | *Greenwich a/Charles* 21
Gradisca | *13s/6-7a* 23
Grand Sichuan | *7a/Carmine* 21
Ƶ Gray's Papaya | *6a/8s* 20
Gus' Place | *Blkr/MacDougal-6a* 21
Gusto | *Greenwich a/Perry* 21
Home | *Cornelia/Blkr-4s* 21
NEW Hotel Griffou | *9s/5-6a* 20
Hummus Pl. | *multi.* 23
Il Cantinori | *10s/Bway-Uni* 23
Il Mulino | *3s/Sullivan* 27
'ino | *Bedford/Downing-6a* 24
Jane | *Houston/La Guardia* 21
Japonica | *Uni/12s* 23
Joe's Pizza | *Carmine/Blkr-6a* 22
Ƶ John's Pizzeria | *Blkr/6-7a* 22
NEW Joseph Leonard | –
  Waverly/Grove
Kati Roll | *MacDougal/Blkr-3s* 20
NEW Keste Pizza | *Blkr/Cornelia* 20
Kingswood | *10s/6a* 19
Knickerbocker | *Uni/9s* 20
La Lanterna | *MacDougal/3-4s* 19
La Palapa | *6a/Wash pl-4s* 19
Las Ramblas | *4s/Cornelia-Jones* 24
Leela Lounge | *3s/Bway-Mercer* 21
Le Gigot | *Cornelia/Blkr-4s* 23
Lenny's | *6a/9s* 17
Le Pain Q. | *multi.* 19
Ƶ Lupa | *Thompson/Blkr* 25
Maoz Veg. | *8s/Bway-Uni* 21
Market Table | *Carmine/Bedford* 23
Ƶ Mas | *Downing/Bedford* 27
Max Brenner | *Bway/13-14s* 18
Meskerem | *MacDougal/Blkr-3s* 21
Mexicana Mama | *12s/Bway* 22
Mezzaluna/Pizza | 21
  Houston/MacDougal
Ƶ NEW Minetta | 20
  MacDougal/Blkr-3s
Morandi | *Waverly/Charles* 22
Negril | *3s/La Guardia* 21
Noodle Bar | *Carmine/Bedford* 20

North Sq.	*Waverly/MacDougal*	23
☑ One if by Land	*Barrow/7a*	24
Osso Buco	*Uni/11-12s*	17
Otto	*8s/5a-Uni*	23
Palma	*Cornelia/Blkr-6a*	23
Patsy's Pizzeria	*Uni/10-11s*	20
Peanut Butter Co.	*Sullivan/3s*	21
☑ Pearl Oyster	*Cornelia/Blkr*	26
Perilla	*Jones/Blkr-4s*	25
Philippe	*6a/11-12s*	24
Piadina	*10s/5-6a*	22
Piola	*12s/Bway-Uni*	19
Pizza 33	*6a/14s*	19
Pó	*Cornelia/Blkr-4s*	25
Prem-on Thai	*Houston/MacDougal*	21
Quantum Leap	*Thompson/3s*	20
NEW Quinto Quarto	*Bedford/Houston*	-
Ramen Setagaya	*Uni/11-12s*	19
Rare B&G	*Blkr/Carmine-6a*	21
Rhong-Tiam	*La Guardia/3s*	22
Risotteria	*Blkr/Morton*	22
NEW Ritz Asia	*Blkr/MacDougal*	-
Sacred Chow	*Sullivan/Blkr-3s*	20
Saigon Grill	*Uni/11-12s*	20
NEW Scuderia	*6a/Houston*	18
Soto	*6a/Wash-4s*	28
Spice	*13s/Bway-Uni*	21
NEW Spunto	*Carmine/7a*	22
Stand	*12s/5a-Uni*	19
Strip House	*12s/5a-Uni*	25
NEW Sweetiepie	*Greenwich a/10s*	14
NEW 10 Downing	*Downing/6a*	21
Tio Pepe	*4s/Cornelia-Jones*	20
☑ Tomoe Sushi	*Thompson/Blkr*	26
Tratt. Pesce	*Blkr/6-7a*	19
Ushiwakamaru	*Houston/MacDougal*	26
Villa Mosconi	*MacDougal/Blkr*	22
'wichcraft	*8s/Mercer*	20
Yama	*Carmine/Bedford-Blkr*	24
Yerba Buena	*Perry/Greenwich a*	24

HARLEM/
EAST HARLEM

(110th to 157th Sts., excluding
Columbia U. area)

Amor Cubano	*3a/111s*	22
Amy Ruth's	*116s/Lenox-7a*	22
Covo	*135s/12a*	23
Dinosaur BBQ	*131s/12a*	22
El Paso Taqueria	*116s/3a*	23
Hudson River	*133s/12a*	19
Kitchenette	*Amst/122-123s*	19
Londel's	*Douglass/139-140s*	19

Miss Mamie/Maude	*multi.*	21
Mo-Bay	*125s/5a-Lenox*	20
Papaya King	*125s/Lenox-7a*	20
Patsy's Pizzeria	*1a/117-118s*	20
Rao's	*114s/Pleasant*	23
River Room	*145s/Riverside*	20
Sylvia's	*Lenox/126-127s*	19
Talay	*135s/12a*	21
Zoma	*Douglass/112-113s*	23

LITTLE ITALY

(Canal to Kenmare Sts.,
Bowery to Lafayette St.)

Angelo's/Mulberry	*Mulberry/Grand*	23
Da Nico	*Mulberry/Broome*	21
Il Cortile	*Mulberry/Canal*	23
Il Palazzo	*Mulberry/Grand*	23
La Esquina	*Kenmare/Cleveland*	21
NEW Mott	*Mott/Broome*	-
Nyonya	*Grand/Mott-Mulberry*	23
Pellegrino's	*Mulberry/Grand*	23
Pho Bang	*Mott/Broome-Grand*	20
Red Egg	*Centre/Howard*	20
Shanghai Café	*Mott/Canal*	23
Umberto's	*Broome/Mulberry*	18
Vincent's	*Mott/Hester*	21
X.O.	*Hester/Bowery-Elizabeth*	20

LOWER EAST SIDE

(Houston to Canal Sts., east of
Bowery)

A Casa Fox	*Orchard/Stanton*	20
Alias	*Clinton/Riv*	21
Allen/Delancey	*Allen/Delancey*	23
NEW An Choi	*Orchard/Broome*	21
ápizz	*Eldridge/Riv-Stanton*	24
Azul Bistro	*Stanton/Suffolk*	22
Bereket	*Houston/Orchard*	21
Bondi Rd.	*Riv/Clinton-Suffolk*	18
Broadway East	*Bway/Jefferson*	22
Brown Café	*Hester/Essex*	23
Café Katja	*Orchard/Broome*	23
Chickpea	*Houston/Eldridge*	18
NEW Clerkenwell	*Clinton/Riv*	-
☑ Clinton St. Baking	*Clinton/Houston*	25
Cube 63	*Clinton/Riv-Stanton*	22
Dumpling Hse.	*Eldridge/Broome*	22
Essex	*Essex/Riv*	18
Falai	*multi.*	23
NEW Fat Hippo	*Clinton/Riv*	20
Frankies	*Clinton/Houston*	24
Freemans	*Riv/Bowery-Chrystie*	21
'inoteca	*Riv/Ludlow*	23
Kampuchea	*Riv/Allen*	22
☑ Katz's Deli	*Houston/Ludlow*	23

Kuma Inn	Ludlow/Delancey	24
Les Enfants	Canal/Ludlow	18
NEW Levant East	Riv/Essex	-
Little Giant	Orchard/Broome	22
Macondo	Houston/Allen	-
Noodle Bar	Orchard/Stanton	20
Orchard	Orchard/Riv	23
Paladar	Ludlow/Houston	22
Rayuela	Allen/Riv-Stanton	22
Salt	Clinton/Houston	23
Sammy's	Chrystie/Delancey	20
NEW San Marzano	Clinton/Riv	-
SavorNY	Clinton/Riv-Stanton	20
Schiller's	Riv/Norfolk	18
NEW Shang	Orchard/Houston	23
NEW Sonia Rose	Orchard/Broome	21
NEW Sorella	Allen/Broome	-
Spitzer's	Riv/Ludlow	20
Stanton Social	Stanton/Ludlow	23
Tre	Ludlow/Houston	19
Two Boots	Grand/Norfolk	19
wd-50	Clinton/Riv-Stanton	24
NEW White Slab	Delancey/Allen	-

MEATPACKING DISTRICT

(Gansevoort to 15th Sts., west of 9th Ave.)

Ajna Bar	Little W 12s/9a	19
Bagatelle	13s/9a-Wash	19
Fig & Olive	13s/9a-Wash	20
5 9th	9a/Gansevoort	19
Los Dados	Gansevoort/Wash	16
Macelleria	Gansevoort/Greenwich s	21
Old Homestead	9a/14-15s	24
Paradou	Little W 12s/Greenwich s	21
Pastis	9a/Little W 12s	21
Pop Burger	9a/14-15s	18
SEA	Wash/Little W 12s	22
Son Cubano	14s/9a-Wash	21
Z Spice Market	13s/9a	23
NEW Standard Grill	Wash/Little W 12s	22
STK	Little W 12s/9a-Wash	21
Valbella	13s/9a-Wash	25
Vento	Hudson/14s	19

MURRAY HILL

(26th to 40th Sts., east of 5th; 23rd to 26th Sts., east of Park Ave. S.)

Aji Sushi	3a/34-35s	21
Ali Baba	34s/2-3a	21
Amber	3a/27-28s	20
Aquamarine	2a/38-39s	21
Z Artisanal	32s/Mad-Park	23

Z Asia de Cuba	Mad/37-38s	22
Baluchi's	3a/24-25s	17
NEW Baoguette	Lex/25-26s	22
Barbès	36s/5a-Mad	20
Barking Dog	34s/Lex-3a	15
Ben & Jack's	5a/28-29s	23
Black Duck	28s/Lex-Park	20
Blockhead Burrito	3a/33-34s	16
Z Blue Smoke	27s/Lex-Park	21
Brother Jimmy	Lex/31s	16
Carl's Steaks	3a/34s	21
Chennai Gdn.	27s/Park	21
Chinese Mirch	Lex/28s	19
Coppola's	3a/27-28s	20
Cosette	33s/Lex-3a	20
Così		16
Country	Mad/29s	21
Curry Leaf	Lex/27s	20
Da Ciro	Lex/33-34s	21
NEW Dhaba	Lex/27-28s	22
Dos Caminos	Park/26-27s	20
El Parador Cafe	34s/1-2a	21
El Rio Grande	38s/Lex-3a	18
Ethos	3a/33-34s	22
Grand Sichuan	Lex/33-34s	21
Z HanGawi	32s/5a-Mad	26
Houston's	Park/27s	20
'inoteca	3a/24s	23
I Trulli	27s/Lex-Park	23
Jackson Hole	3a/35s	17
Jaiya Thai	3a/28s	21
Josie's	3a/37s	19
La Petite Aub.	Lex/27-28s	20
Lemongrass	34s/Lex-3a	16
Les Halles	Park/28-29s	20
Mee Noodle	2a/30-31s	18
Mishima	Lex/30-31s	24
Morgan	Mad/36-37s	20
NY Burger	Park/23-4s	17
Olana	Mad/27-28s	23
Pamplona	28s/Mad-Park	22
Park Ave. Bistro	Park/26-27s	22
Patsy's Pizzeria	3a/34-35s	20
Penelope	Lex/30s	22
Pio Pio	34s/2-3a	22
Pizza 33	3a/33s	19
Pongal	Lex/27-28s	22
NEW Pranna	Mad/28-29s	20
Primehouse	Park/27s	24
Pump Energy	Mad/39-40s	17
Rare B&G	Lex/37s	21
Ravagh	30s/5a-Mad	20
Resto	29s/Lex-Park	20
Rice	Lex/28s	19
Rossini's	38s/Lex-Park	23

LOCATIONS

Salute!	*Mad/39s*	18
Saravanaas	*Lex/26s*	24
Sarge's Deli	*3a/36-37s*	20
2nd Ave Deli	*33s/Lex-3a*	22
Smorgas Chef	*Park/37-38s*	18
☑ Sushi Sen-nin	*33s/Mad*	26
Tiffin Wallah	*28s/Lex-Park*	24
Totonno Pizza	*2a/26s*	22
☑ Turkish Kitchen	*3a/27-28s*	23
Vatan	*3a/29s*	22
Vezzo	*Lex/31s*	23
Water Club	*E River/23s*	21
'wichcraft	*Park/33s*	20
☑ Wolfgang's	*Park/33s*	25
Wu Liang Ye	*Lex/39-40s*	22
Zorzi	*35s/5a-Mad*	21

NOHO

(Houston to 4th Sts.,
Bowery to B'way)

Aroma	*4s/Bowery-Lafayette*	24
Bianca	*Blkr/Bowery-Elizabeth*	24
Bond St.	*Bond/Bway-Lafayette*	25
Chinatown Brass.	*Lafayette/Gr Jones*	21
NEW Double Crown	*Bowery/Blkr*	20
5 Points	*Gr Jones/Bowery*	22
Great Jones Cafe	*Gr Jones/Bowery*	20
☑ Il Buco	*Bond/Bowery-Lafayette*	24
Mercat	*Bond/Bowery-Lafayette*	21
NoHo Star	*Lafayette/Blkr*	18
Pinche Taqueria	*Lafayette/Blkr*	22
Quartino	*Blkr/Elizabeth*	20
Rice	*Elizabeth/Blkr-Houston*	19
Sala	*Bowery/Gr Jones*	22
NEW Smile	*Bond/Bowery*	–
Two Boots	*Blkr/Bway*	19

NOLITA

(Houston to Kenmare Sts.,
Bowery to Lafayette St.)

barmarché	*Spring/Elizabeth*	18
Bread	*Spring/Elizabeth-Mott*	19
Cafe Colonial	*Elizabeth/Houston*	19
Cafe Gitane	*Mott/Prince*	20
Café Habana/Outpost	*Prince/Elizabeth*	23
NEW Civetta	*Kenmare/Lafayette*	19
Delicatessen	*Prince/Lafayette*	18
Ed's Lobster	*Lafayette/Spring*	21
8 Mile Creek	*Mulberry/Prince*	20
Elizabeth	*Elizabeth/Houston*	19
NEW Emporio	*Mott/Prince*	22
Jacques	*Prince/Elizabeth-Mott*	20

NEW Jo's	*Elizabeth/Houston*	–
Kitchen Club	*Prince/Mott*	23
Le Jardin	*Cleveland/Kenmare*	20
Lombardi's	*Spring/Mott*	24
Peasant	*Elizabeth/Prince*	24
Pinche Taqueria	*Mott/Prince*	22
Public	*Elizabeth/Prince*	22

SOHO

(Canal to Houston Sts., west of
Lafayette St.)

☑ Aquagrill	*Spring/6a*	26
Aurora	*Broome/Thompson*	25
☑ Balthazar	*Spring/Bway*	23
Baluchi's	*Spring/Sullivan*	17
Barolo	*W Bway/Broome-Spring*	18
Bistro Les Amis	*Spring/Thompson*	21
Blue Ribbon	*Sullivan/Prince*	24
☑ Blue Ribbon Sushi	*Sullivan/Prince*	26
Boqueria	*Spring/Thompson*	22
Bún	*Grand/Crosby*	20
NEW Café Select	*Lafayette/Broome*	21
Chipotle	*Varick/Houston-King*	18
Cipriani D'twn	*W Bway/Broome*	20
NEW City Winery	*Varick/Vandam*	18
Dos Caminos	*W Bway/Houston*	20
Falai	*Lafayette/Prince*	23
Félix	*W Bway/Grand*	16
NEW 508	*Greenwich s/Canal*	19
Giorgione	*Spring/Greenwich s*	21
Hampton Chutney	*Prince/Crosby*	21
NEW Harbour	*Hudson/Spring*	21
Hundred Acres	*MacDougal/Prince*	19
Ideya	*W Bway/Broome-Grand*	21
Il Corallo	*Prince/Sullivan*	21
I Tre Merli	*W Bway/Houston*	18
Ivo & Lulu	*Broome/6a-Varick*	20
Jean Claude	*Sullivan/Houston*	23
Kittichai	*Thompson/Broome*	22
La Sirène	*Broome/Varick*	23
L'Ecole	*Bway/Grand*	24
Le Pain Q.	*Grand/Greene*	19
Lucky Strike	*Grand/W Bway*	16
Lure Fishbar	*Mercer/Prince*	23
NEW Lusso	*W Bway/Grand*	17
Mercer Kitchen	*Prince/Mercer*	21
Mezzogiorno	*Spring/Sullivan*	21
Novecento	*W Bway/Broome*	22
Omen	*Thompson/Prince*	25
1 Dominick	*Dominick/6a*	23
Peep	*Prince/Sullivan*	18
Pepe	*Sullivan/Houston*	22

Raoul's | *Prince/Sullivan* 24

Salt | *MacDougal/Prince* 23

Savoy | *Prince/Crosby* 24

Shorty's.32 | *Prince/MacDougal* 23

Snack | *Thompson/Prince* 24

NEW Sora Lella | 19
Spring/Greenwich s

Tailor | *Broome/Sullivan* 22

12 Chairs | *MacDougal/Prince* 19

NEW Via dei Mille | 24
W Bway/Broome

'wichcraft | *Crosby/Prince* 20

Woo Lae Oak | *Mercer/Houston* 21

Zoë | *Prince/Bway-Mercer* 20

SOUTH STREET SEAPORT

Acqua/Peck Slip | *Peck/Water* 21

Cabana | *South/Fulton* 21

Cowgirl | *Front/Dover* 16

Heartland | *South/Fulton* 14

NEW Onda | *Front/Beekman* 22

TRIBECA

(Canal to Murray Sts.,
west of B'way)

Acappella | *Hudson/Chambers* 25

Arqua | *Church/White* 22

Baluchi's | *Greenwich s/Warren* 17

NEW Bar Artisanal | *W Bway/6a* 21

Blaue Gans | *Duane/Church* 21

Z Bouley | *Duane/Hudson* 28

Z Bouley Upstairs | 26
W Bway/Duane

Bread | *Church/Walker* 19

Bubby's | *Hudson/N Moore* 18

Capsouto Frères | *Wash/Watts* 23

Carl's Steaks | *Chambers/Bway* 21

Centrico | *W Bway/Franklin* 20

Cercle Rouge | *W Bway/N Moore* 19

Z Chanterelle | *Harrison/Hudson* 28

Churrascaria | *W Bway/Franklin* 23

City Hall | *Duane/Church* 21

Z Corton | *W Bway/Walker* 27

Dean's | *Greenwich s/Harrison* 17

Duane Park | *Duane/Hudson* 23

Dylan Prime | *Laight/Greenwich s* 24

Ecco | *Chambers/Church* 23

F.illi Ponte | *Desbrosses/Wash* 23

Flor/Sol | *Greenwich s/Franklin* 22

Gigino | *Greenwich s/Duane* 21

Greenwich Grill/Sushi Azabu | 26
Greenwich s/Laight

Harrison | *Greenwich s/Harrison* 24

Z Il Giglio | *Warren/Greenwich s* 26

Kitchenette | 19
Chambers/Greenwich s

Landmarc | *W Bway/Leonard* 20

NEW Locanda Verde | 22
Greenwich s/N Moore

NEW Macao Trading | 18
Church/Lispenard

Marc Forgione | 23
Reade/Greenwich s

Mary Ann's | *W Bway/Chambers* 16

Matsugen | *Church/Leonard* 22

Max | *Duane/Greenwich s* 22

Megu | *Thomas/Church-W Bway* 23

Mr. Chow | *Hudson/N Moore* 21

Nam | *Reade/W Bway* 21

Ninja | *Hudson/Duane-Reade* 16

Z Nobu | *multi.* 27

Odeon | *W Bway/Duane* 19

Z Palm | *West/Chambers* 24

Z Pepolino | *W Bway/Canal* 26

Petite Abeille | *W Bway/Duane* 17

Roc | *Duane/Greenwich s* 22

Rosanjin | *Duane/Church* 24

Salaam Bombay | 21
Greenwich s/Duane-Reade

NEW Sazon | *Reade/Church* -

Z Scalini Fedeli | 26
Duane/Greenwich s

Takahachi | *Duane/Church* 25

Thalassa | *Franklin/Greenwich s* 24

Tribeca Grill | 22
Greenwich s/Franklin

Turks & Frogs | 19
Greenwich s/Desbrosses

Walker's | *N Moore/Varick* 17

'wichcraft | *Greenwich s/Beach* 20

Z Wolfgang's | 25
Greenwich s/Beach

Zutto | *Hudson/Harrison* 23

UNION SQUARE

(14th to 17th Sts., 5th Ave. to
Union Sq. E.)

Z Blue Water | *Union Sq/16s* 23

Coffee Shop | *Union Sq/16s* 15

Z 15 East | *15s/5a-Union Sq* 26

Havana Central | *17s/Bway-5a* 17

Heartland | *Union Sq/16-17s* 14

Laut | *17s/Bway-5a* 24

Maoz Veg. | *Union Sq/16-17s* 21

Olives | *Park/17s* 22

Republic | *Union Sq/16-17s* 18

Z Tocqueville | *15s/5a-Union Sq* 26

Z Union Sq. Cafe | *16s/5a* 27

WASHINGTON HTS./ INWOOD

(North of W. 157th St.)

Dallas BBQ | *Bway/165-166s* 15

El Malecon | *Bway/175s* 21

LOCATIONS

Empire Szechuan	*Bway/170s*	15
Mamajuana	*Dyckman/Payson*	23
New Leaf	*Corbin/190s*	21

WEST 40s

A.J. Maxwell's	*48s/5-6a*	22
Akdeniz	*46s/5-6a*	21
Alfredo of Rome	*49s/5-6a*	18
Algonquin	*44s/5-6a*	17
Amy's Bread	*9a/46-47s*	24
Angus McIndoe	*44s/Bway-8a*	17
NEW Aureole	*42s/Bway-6a*	29
Barbetta	*46s/8-9a*	21
Basilica	*9a/46-47s*	20
Z Becco	*46s/8-9a*	22
Blue Fin	*Bway/47s*	22
Bond 45	*45s/6-7a*	20
Brasserie 44	*44s/5-6a*	20
NEW Brasserie 1605	*Bway/48s*	-
Breeze	*9a/45-46s*	21
Brooklyn Diner	*43s/Bway-6a*	17
Bryant Park	*40s/5-6a*	17
B. Smith's	*46s/8-9a*	19
Bubba Gump	*Bway/43-44s*	14
BXL	*43s/Bway-6a*	20
Cafe Un Deux/Le Petit	*multi.*	16
Cara Mia	*9a/45-46s*	20
Carmine's	*44s/Bway-8a*	20
Cascina	*9a/45-46s*	19
Chez Josephine	*42s/9-10a*	20
Chimichurri Grill	*9a/43-44s*	22
Chipotle	*42s/5-6a*	18
Churrascaria	*49s/8-9a*	23
City Lobster	*49s/6a*	19
Così	*42s/5-6a*	16
Daisy May's	*11a/46s*	23
Dallas BBQ	*42s/7-8a*	15
Z db Bistro Moderne	*44s/5a*	24
Z Del Frisco's	*6a/48-49s*	25
Delta Grill	*9a/48s*	20
Dervish	*47s/6-7a*	18
Edison	*47s/Bway-8a*	16
Energy Kitchen	*47s/9-10a*	17
Z Esca	*43s/9a*	25
etc. etc.	*44s/8-9a*	20
FireBird	*46s/8-9a*	19
5 Napkin Burger	*9a/45s*	21
44/44½	*multi.*	22
Frankie/Johnnie	*45s/Bway-8a*	22
Z Gari/Sushi	*46s/8-9a*	27
Gazala Place	*9a/48-49s*	23
goodburger	*45s/5-6a*	18
Hale/Hearty	*multi.*	19
Hallo Berlin	*10a/44-45s*	19
Haru	*43s/Bway-8a*	20
Havana Central	*46s/6-7a*	17
Heartland	*43s/Bway-6a*	14
Hell's Kitchen	*9a/46-47s*	23
NEW Inakaya	*40s/7-8a*	22
Jewel of India	*44s/5-6a*	20
Joe Allen	*46s/8-9a*	17
Z John's Pizzeria	*44s/Bway*	22
Junior's	*45s/Bway-8a*	17
Kellari Tav./Parea	*44s/5-6a*	22
Koi	*40s/5-6a*	22
Kyotofu	*9a/48-49s*	21
La Masseria	*48s/Bway-8a*	23
Landmark Tavern	*11a/46s*	17
Lattanzi	*46s/8-9a*	22
Lazzara's	*9a/43-44s*	23
Le Marais	*46s/6-7a*	22
Lenny's	*multi.*	17
Le Rivage	*46s/8-9a*	20
Maoz Veg.	*7a/40s*	21
Marseille	*9a/44s*	21
Meskerem	*47s/9-10a*	21
Metro Marché	*8a/41s*	19
Monster Sushi	*46s/5-6a*	18
NEW Montenapo	*41s/7-8a*	-
Morrell Wine	*49s/5-6a*	18
NEW Nios	*46s/6-7a*	-
Nizza	*9a/44-45s*	21
Z NEW Oceana	*6a/49s*	-
Ollie's	*42s/9-10a*	15
Orso	*46s/8-9a*	22
Osteria al Doge	*44s/Bway-6a*	20
Pam Real Thai	*multi.*	22
Pietrasanta	*9a/47s*	19
Pigalle	*8a/48s*	18
Pomaire	*46s/8-9a*	20
Pongsri Thai	*48s/Bway-8a*	20
Queen of Sheba	*10a/45-46s*	21
Re Sette	*45s/5-6a*	21
Room Service	*9a/47-48s*	18
Ruby Foo's	*Bway/49s*	18
Sardi's	*44s/Bway-8a*	18
Scarlatto	*47s/Bway-8a*	21
NEW Schnipper's	*8a/41s*	17
Sea Grill	*49s/5-6a*	24
Serafina	*49s/Bway-8a*	18
Shorty's	*9a/41-42s*	22
Shula's	*43s/Bway-8a*	21
Sushiden	*49s/6-7a*	23
Sushi Zen	*44s/Bway-6a*	25
Tony's Di Napoli	*43s/Bway-6a*	19
Trattoria Trecolori	*47s/Bway*	21
Triomphe	*44s/5-6a*	24
Turkish Cuisine	*9a/44-45s*	19
Two Boots	*9a/44-45s*	19
Utsav	*6a/46-47s*	20

Via Brasil	46s/5-6a	20
View	Bway/45-46s	16
Virgil's BBQ	44s/Bway-6a	19
West Bank Cafe	42s/9-10a	19
'wichcraft	6a/40-42s	20
Wondee Siam	10a/45-46s	22
Wu Liang Ye	48s/5-6a	22
Zen Palate	9a/46s	18

WEST 50s

Abboccato	55s/6-7a	21
Afghan Kebab	9a/51-52s	19
NEW Agua Dulce	9a/53-54s	-
Angelo's Pizza	multi.	21
Anthos	52s/5-6a	25
NEW AQ Kafé	Bway/CPS-58s	19
☑ Azuri Cafe	51s/9-10a	24
Baluchi's	56s/Bway-8a	17
Bann	50s/8-9a	21
☑ Bar Americain	52s/6-7a	23
Basso56	56s/Bway-8a	22
Bay Leaf	56s/5-6a	21
NEW b-bap	9a/54-55s	-
Beacon	56s/5-6a	23
Bello	9a/56s	21
Ben Benson's	52s/6-7a	23
Benoit	55s/5-6a	19
Blockhead Burrito	50s/8-9a	16
BLT Market	6a/CPS	23
bluechili	51s/Bway-8a	20
Blue Ribbon Sushi B&G	58s/8a	24
Bobby Van's	50s/6-7a	22
Bocca di Bacco	9a/54-55s	21
Bombay Palace	52s/5-6a	20
NEW Bossa Nova	9a/51-52s	21
Braai	51s/8-9a	19
Brasserie Cognac	Bway/55s	18
Brasserie 8½	57s/5-6a	21
Brass. Ruhlmann	50s/5-6a	18
Bricco	56s/8-9a	20
Brooklyn Diner	57s/Bway-7a	17
☑ burger joint	56s/6-7a	24
Caffe Cielo	8a/52-53s	20
Capital Grille	51s/6-7a	23
☑ Carnegie Deli	7a/55s	22
Casellula	52s/9-10a	25
Chez Napoléon	50s/8-9a	20
China Grill	53s/5-6a	22
Così	Bway/50s	16
Da Tommaso	8a/53-54s	20
Eatery	9a/53s	20
Empanada Mama	9a/51-52s	22
Five Guys	55s/5-6a	20
Gallagher's	52s/Bway-8a	21
Gordon Ramsay	54s/6-7a	24

Hale/Hearty	56s/5-6a	19
NEW Hanci	10a/56-57s	24
Heartland	6a/51s	14
Hudson Cafeteria	58s/8-9a	19
Il Gattopardo	54s/5-6a	24
☑ Il Tinello	56s/5-6a	25
Insieme	7a/50-51s	23
Ise	56s/5-6a	21
Island Burgers	9a/51-52s	21
Joe's Shanghai	56s/5-6a	22
Katsu-Hama	55s/5-6a	21
La Bergamote	52s/10-11a	25
La Bonne Soupe	55s/5-6a	18
☑ Le Bernardin	51s/6-7a	28
Le Pain Q.	7a/58s	19
Maison	Bway/53s	19
Mangia	57s/5-6a	19
NEW Marea	CPS/Bway-7a	26
Maria Pia	51s/8-9a	19
Maze	54s/6-7a	25
McCormick/Schmick	52s/6a	20
Mee Noodle	9a/53s	18
Menchanko-tei	55s/5-6a	20
Michael's	55s/5-6a	20
☑ Milos	55s/6-7a	27
☑ Modern	53s/5-6a	26
Molyvos	7a/55-56s	22
Nino's	58s/6-7a	21
☑ Nobu	57s/5-6a	27
Nocello	55s/Bway-8a	21
Nook	9a/50-51s	19
Norma's	56s/6-7a	25
NEW Oak Room	CPS/5-6a	18
Osteria del Circo	55s/6-7a	22
☑ Palm	50s/Bway-8a	24
Patsy's	56s/Bway-8a	21
Pepe	52s/8-9a	22
Petrossian	58s/7a	24
Piano Due	51s/6-7a	24
Pump Energy	55s/5-6a	17
Puttanesca	9a/56s	19
Quality Meats	58s/5-6a	24
Redeye Grill	7a/56s	20
Remi	53s/6-7a	22
Rice 'n' Beans	9a/50-51s	20
Roberto Passon	9a/50s	21
Rue 57	57s/6a	18
Russian Samovar	52s/Bway	20
Russian Tea	57s/6-7a	19
Ruth's Chris	51s/6-7a	23
Sarabeth's	CPS/5-6a	20
NEW Seasonal	58s/6-7a	25
Serafina	55s/Bway	18
Shelly's NY	57s/5-6a	19
Soba Nippon	52s/5-6a	22

Sosa Borella	*8a/50s*	19
South Gate	*CPS/6-7a*	24
Stage Deli	*7a/53-54s*	20
Z Sugiyama	*55s/Bway-8a*	27
Sushiya	*56s/5-6a*	20
NEW Sweet Emily's	*51s/8-9a*	18
Szechuan Gourmet	*56s/8a*	22
Taboon	*10a/52s*	23
Tang Pavilion	*55s/5-6a*	20
NEW Terrazza Toscana	*9a/50s*	–
Thalia	*8a/50s*	19
Toloache	*50s/Bway-8a*	23
Topaz Thai	*56s/6-7a*	21
Tratt. Dell'Arte	*7a/56-57s*	22
Z 21 Club	*52s/5-6a*	22
Uncle Jack's	*56s/5-6a*	23
Uncle Nick's	*9a/50-51s*	20
ViceVersa	*51s/8-9a*	22
Victor's Cafe	*52s/Bway-8a*	21
Whym	*9a/57-58s*	19
'wichcraft	*50s/5-6a*	20
Wondee Siam	*multi.*	22
Yakitori Totto	*55s/Bway-8a*	25

WEST 60s

Z Asiate	*60s/Bway*	24
A Voce	*60s/Bway*	24
Z Bar Boulud	*Bway/63-64s*	23
Z Bar Masa	*60s/Bway*	26
Bouchon Bakery	*60s/Bway*	23
Cafe Fiorello	*Bway/63-64s*	20
Empire Szechuan	*Colum/68s*	15
Gabriel's	*60s/Bway-Colum*	22
Z Jean Georges	*CPW/60-61s*	28
Z Jean Georges Noug.	*CPW/60-61s*	27
Josephina	*Bway/63-64s*	18
La Boîte en Bois	*68s/Colum*	22
Landmarc	*60s/Bway*	20
Le Pain Q.	*65s/Bway-CPW*	19
NEW Luce	*Bway/68-69s*	–
Z Masa	*60s/Bway*	26
Nanoosh	*Bway/68-69s*	19
Nick & Toni	*67s/Bway*	19
Ollie's	*Bway/67-68s*	15
O'Neals'	*64s/Bway-CPW*	17
Z Per Se	*60s/Bway*	28
Z Picholine	*64s/Bway-CPW*	27
P.J. Clarke's	*63s/Colum*	17
Porter House	*60s/Bway*	24
Rosa Mexicano	*Colum/62s*	22
Sapphire	*Bway/60-61s*	21
Shun Lee Cafe	*65s/Colum*	21
Shun Lee West	*65s/Colum*	22
Tavern on Green	*CPW/66-67s*	15
Z Telepan	*69s/Colum*	26

WEST 70s

Amber	*Colum/70s*	20
Arté Café	*73s/Amst-Colum*	18
Bello Sguardo	*Amst/79-80s*	20
Bettola	*Amst/79-80s*	21
Big Nick's	*multi.*	17
Bistro Cassis	*Colum/70-71s*	20
Café Frida	*Colum/77-78s*	19
Cafe Luxembourg	*70s/Amst*	20
Cafe Ronda	*Colum/71-72s*	19
'Cesca	*75s/Amst*	23
China Fun	*Colum/71-72s*	15
Citrus B&G	*Amst/75s*	20
Compass	*70s/Amst-W End*	22
Coppola's	*79s/Amst-Bway*	20
Così	*Bway/76-77s*	16
Dallas BBQ	*72s/Colum-CPW*	15
Z Dovetail	*77s/Colum*	26
NEW Ducale	*Colum/79s*	16
Earthen Oven	*72s/Colum-CPW*	21
Epices/Traiteur	*70s/Colum*	20
Fairway Cafe	*Bway/74s*	18
Fatty Crab	*Bway/77s*	22
Z Gari/Sushi	*Colum/77-78s*	27
Z Gray's Papaya	*Bway/72s*	20
NEW Gus/Gabriel	*79s/Bway*	–
Hummus Pl.	*Amst/74-75s*	23
Isabella's	*Colum/77s*	20
Josie's	*Amst/74s*	19
Lenny's	*Colum/74s*	17
Le Pain Q.	*72s/Colum-CPW*	19
Maoz Veg.	*Amst/70-71s*	21
Mughlai	*Colum/75s*	20
Nice Matin	*79s/Amst*	20
Ocean Grill	*Colum/78-79s*	23
Pappardella	*Colum/75s*	19
Pasha	*71s/Colum-CPW*	20
Patsy's Pizzeria	*74s/Colum*	20
Pomodoro Rosso	*Colum/70s*	21
NEW Salumeria Rosi	*Amst/73-74s*	23
Sambuca	*72s/Colum-CPW*	20
Savann	*Amst/79-80s*	21
Scaletta	*77s/Colum-CPW*	22
Z Shake Shack	*Colum/77s*	23
Swagat Indian	*Amst/79-80s*	21
Tenzan	*Colum/73s*	22
Vai	*77s/Amst-Bway*	22
Viand	*Bway/75s*	17
NEW West Branch	*Bway/77s*	19

WEST 80s

Artie's Deli	*Bway/82-83s*	18
NEW BarBao	*82s/Amst-Colum*	21

Menus, photos, voting and more – free at ZAGAT.com

Z Barney Greengrass | *Amst/86s*	23

B. Café \| *Amst/87-88s* 21
Bellini \| *Colum/83-84s* 18
Bistro Citron \| *Colum/82-83s* 20
Blossom \| *Colum/82-83s* 23
Bodrum \| *Amst/88-89s* 19
Brother Jimmy \| *Amst/80-81s* 16
Cafe Con Leche \| *Amst/80-81s* 18
Calle Ocho \| *Colum/81-82s* 21
Celeste \| *Amst/84-85s* 23
Cilantro \| *Colum/83-84s* 17
Dean's \| *85s/Amst-Bway* 17
eighty one \| *81s/Colum* 25
EJ's Luncheon. \| *Amst/81-82s* 16
Flor/Mayo \| *Amst/83-84s* 21
French Roast \| *Bway/85s* 17
Good Enough/Eat \| *Amst/83s* 21
Hampton Chutney \| *Amst/82s* 21
Haru \| *Amst/80-81s* 20
Jackson Hole \| *Colum/85s* 17
Kefi \| *Colum/84-85s* 22
La Mirabelle \| *86s/Amst-Colum* 23
Land \| *Amst/81-82s* 22
Lenny's \| *Colum/84s* 17
Mermaid Inn \| *Amst/87-88s* 20
Momoya \| *Amst/80-81s* 23
Nëo Sushi \| *Bway/83s* 21
Nonna \| *Colum/85s* 18
Ollie's \| *Bway/84s* 15
Z Ouest \| *Bway/83-84s* 24
Popover Cafe \| *Amst/86-87s* 18
NEW Recipe \| *Amst/81-82s* -
Sarabeth's \| *Amst/80-81s* 20
S'MAC/Pinch \| *Colum/82-83s* 21
Spiga \| *84s/Amst-Bway* 23
Sushi Hana \| *Amst/82-83s* 20
Zabar's Cafe \| *Bway/80s* 19

WEST 90s

Acqua \| *Amst/95s* 18
Alouette \| *Bway/97-98s* 20
Cafe Con Leche \| *Amst/95-96s* 18
Carmine's \| *Bway/90-91s* 20
El Malecon \| *Amst/97-98s* 21
Gabriela's \| *Colum/93-94s* 18
Gennaro \| *Amst/92-93s* 24
Hummus Pl. \| *Bway/98-99s* 23
La Rural \| *Amst/97-98s* 21
Lemongrass \| *Bway/94-95s* 16
Lisca \| *Amst/92-93s* 22
Pio Pio \| *Amst/94s* 22
Saigon Grill \| *Amst/90s* 20
Tratt. Pesce \| *Colum/90-91s* 19
Yuki Sushi \| *Amst/92s* 21

WEST 100s

(See also Harlem/East Harlem)
Awash \| *Amst/106-107s* 22
Bistro Ten 18 \| *Amst/110s* 19
Blockhead Burrito \| *Amst/106s* 16
Café du Soleil \| *Bway/104s* 18
Campo \| *Bway/112-113s* 18
Community Food \| *Bway/112-113s* 21
Empire Szechuan \| *Bway/100s* 15
Flor/Mayo \| *Bway/100-101s* 21
NEW Haakon's Hall \| *Amst/118-119s* -
Havana Central \| *Bway/113s* 17
Indus Valley \| *Bway/100s* 22
Le Monde \| *Bway/112-113s* 18
Mamá Mexico \| *Bway/102s* 20
Max SoHa/Caffe \| *multi.* 21
Métisse \| *105s/Amst-Bway* 18
Noche Mex. \| *Amst/101-102s* 25
Ollie's \| *Bway/116s* 15
PicNic Market \| *Bway/101s* 20
Pisticci \| *La Salle/Bway* 24
Rack & Soul \| *109s/Bway* 19
Sezz Medi' \| *Amst/122s* 20
Sookk \| *Bway/102-103s* 22
Symposium \| *113s/Amst-Bway* 19
Terrace in Sky \| *119s/Amst* 22
Turkuaz \| *Bway/100s* 19
V&T \| *Amst/110-111s* 18
Wondee Siam \| *Amst/107-108s* 22

WEST VILLAGE

(Houston to 14th Sts., west of 7th Ave. S., excluding Meatpacking District)
Agave \| *7a/Charles-10s* 18
Antica Venezia \| *West/10s* 23
A.O.C. \| *Blkr/Grove* 20
August \| *Blkr/Charles-10s* 22
NEW Baoguette \| *Christopher/Bedford* 22
Barbuto \| *Wash/Jane-12s* 22
Bobo \| *10s/7a* 22
NEW Braeburn \| *Perry/Greenwich s* 21
Cafe Cluny \| *12s/4s* 21
Café de Bruxelles \| *Greenwich a/13s* 21
NEW Casa La Femme \| *Charles/Wash* 20
Centro Vinoteca \| *7a/Barrow* 20
NEW Charles \| *4s/10s* 18
Chow Bar \| *4s/10s* 20
Commerce \| *Commerce/Barrow* 22
Corner Bistro \| *4s/Jane* 22
Cowgirl \| *Hudson/10s* 16

LOCATIONS

Crispo	*14s/7-8a*	23
dell'anima	*8a/Jane*	25
Dirty Bird	*14s/7a*	18
El Faro	*Greenwich s/Horatio*	22
Employees Only	*Hudson/Christopher*	18
Energy Kitchen	*Christopher/7a*	17
EN Japanese	*Hudson/Leroy*	23
Extra Virgin	*4s/Charles-Perry*	22
Fatty Crab	*Hudson/Gansevoort*	22
Five Guys	*Blkr/7a*	20
Gavroche	*14s/7-8a*	18
good	*Greenwich a/Bank-12s*	21
☑ Havana Alma	*Christopher/Bedford*	23
I Sodi	*Christopher/Blkr*	23
I Tre Merli	*10s/4s*	18
NEW La Carbonara	*14s/7-8a*	22
NEW L'Artusi	*10s/Blkr*	21
☑ Little Owl	*Bedford/Grove*	26
NEW Lucy Browne	*Varick/Clarkson*	-
Malatesta	*Wash/Christopher*	22
Mary's Fish	*Charles/4s*	24
Mercadito	*7a/Blkr-Grove*	22
Mexicana Mama	*Hudson/Charles*	22
Moustache	*Bedford/Barrow*	21
New French	*Hudson/Charles*	21
Papaya King	*14s/7a*	20
Paris Commune	*Bank/Greenwich s*	19
Pepe	*Hudson/Perry-11s*	22
Perry St.	*Perry/West*	25
Petite Abeille	*Hudson/Barrow*	17
Piccolo Angolo	*Hudson/Jane*	25
Pink Tea Cup	*Grove/Bedford*	22
Place	*4s/Bank-12s*	19
Sant Ambroeus	*4s/Perry*	22
Sevilla	*Charles/4s*	22
Smorgas Chef	*12s/4s*	18
Snack Taverna	*Bedford/Morton*	21
Spotted Pig	*11s/Greenwich s*	23
Surya	*Blkr/Grove-7a*	21
SushiSamba	*7a/Barrow*	21
Taïm	*Waverky/11s-Perry*	25
Tartine	*11s/4s*	22
Tea & Sympathy	*Greenwich a/12-13s*	21
Two Boots	*11s/7a*	19
Wallsé	*11s/Wash*	25
Waverly Inn	*Bank/Waverly*	19
Westville	*10s/Blkr-4s*	22

Bronx

Beccofino	*Mosholu/Fieldston*	22
Bruckner B&G	*Bruckner/3a*	-
City Is. Lobster	*Bridge/City Is*	19

Coals	*Eastchester/Morris Pk*	25
Dallas BBQ	*Fordham/Deegan*	15
Dominick's	*Arthur/Crescent*	23
El Malecon	*Bway/231s*	21
Enzo's	*multi.*	23
F & J Pine	*Bronxdale/Matthews*	22
Fratelli	*Eastchester/Mace*	21
Jake's	*Bway/242s*	23
Liebman's	*235s/Johnson*	21
Lobster Box	*City Is/Belden*	19
Madison's	*Riverdale/259s*	20
Mario's	*Arthur/184-186s*	22
Pasquale's	*Arthur/Crescent*	21
Patricia's	*multi.*	24
Pio Pio	*Cypress/138-139s*	22
Portofino	*City Is/Cross*	19
☑ Roberto	*Crescent/Hughes*	26
Siam Sq.	*Kappock/Henry*	23
Tosca Café	*Tremont/Miles*	21
Umberto's	*Arthur/186s*	18
Zero Otto	*Arthur/186s*	25

Brooklyn

BAY RIDGE

Agnanti	*5a/78s*	23
Areo	*3a/84-85s*	23
Arirang Hibachi	*4a/88-89s*	20
Austin's Steak	*5a/90s*	19
Chadwick's	*3a/89s*	22
Chianti	*3a/85-86s*	22
Eliá	*3a/86-87s*	26
Embers	*3a/95-96s*	21
Five Guys	*5a/85-86s*	20
Fushimi	*4a/93-94s*	24
Greenhouse	*3a/77-78s*	21
Omonia	*3a/76-77s*	18
101	*4a/101s*	21
Pearl Room	*3a/82s*	20
Petit Oven	*Bay Ridge/3a*	-
☑ Tanoreen	*3a/76s*	26
Tuscany Grill	*3a/86-87s*	24

BEDFORD-STUYVESANT

Peaches	*Lewis/Decatur*	-
NEW Saraghina	*Halsey/Lewis*	-

BENSONHURST

L & B Spumoni	*86s/10-11s*	23
Nyonya	*86s/23-24a*	23
Tenzan	*18a/71s*	22

BOERUM HILL

Bacchus	*Atlantic/Bond-Nevins*	23
Chance	*Smith/Butler*	22

Hanco's | *Bergen/Hoyt-Smith* 22
Jolie | *Atlantic/Hoyt-Smith* 21
Ki Sushi | *Smith/Dean-Pacific* 25
Lunetta | *Smith/Dean-Pacific* 21
Z Nicky's | *Atlantic/Hoyt-Smith* 22
Saul | *Smith/Bergen-Dean* 26

BROOKLYN HEIGHTS

Chipotle | *Montague/Clinton* 18
ChipShop | *Atlantic/Henry* 19
Five Guys | *Montague/Clinton* 20
Hale/Hearty | *Court/Remsen* 19
Henry's End | *Henry/Cranberry* 24
Jack Horse | *Hicks/Cranberry* 24
Le Petit Marché | *Henry/Cranberry* 23
Noodle Pudding | *Henry/Cranberry* 25
Queen | *Court/Livingston* 24
Teresa's | *Montague/Hicks* 19

BUSHWICK

Northeast Kingdom | -
Wyckoff/Troutman
Roberta's | *Moore/Bogart* 22

CARROLL GARDENS

Alma | *Columbia/Degraw* 20
NEW Buttermilk | 23
Court/Huntington
NEW Calexico | *Union/Hicks* -
Chestnut | *Smith/Degraw* 24
Cubana Café | *Smith/Degraw* 21
Fragole | *Court/1pl* 23
Frankies | *Court/4pl* 24
Z Grocery | *Smith/Sackett* 27
Z Lucali | *Henry/Carroll-1pl* 26
Petite Crev. | *Union/Hicks* 25
Pó | *Smith/Degraw-Sackett* 25
NEW Prime Meat | *Court/Luquer* 19
Provence/Boite | *Smith/Degraw* 20
Savoia | *Smith/Degraw-Sackett* 21
Zaytoons | *Smith/Sackett* 21

CLINTON HILL

Locanda Vini | *Gates/Cambridge* 22
Maggie Brown | *Myrtle/Wash* 19
NEW Umi Nom | *DeKalb/Classon* -

COBBLE HILL

Bocca Lupo | *Henry/Warren* 24
Cafe Luluc | *Smith/Baltic* 19
NEW Char No. 4 | *Smith/Baltic* 23
Z Chocolate Room | *Court/Butler* 25
Coco Roco | *Smith/Bergen-Dean* 20
Cube 63 | *Court/Baltic-Warren* 22
Hibino | *Henry/Pacific* 25
Joya | *Court/Warren* 23
Lemongrass | *Court/Dean* 16

Lobo | *Court/Baltic-Warren* 15
Quercy | *Court/Baltic-Kane* 22
Sweet Melissa | *Court/Butler* 21
NEW Watty/Meg | *Court/Kane* -

CONEY ISLAND

Gargiulo's | *15s/Mermaid-Surf* 22
Totonno Pizza | *Neptune/15-16s* 22

DITMAS PARK

Farm/Adderley | 22
Cortelyou/Stratford
Picket Fence | *Cortelyou/Argyle* 19
Pomme/Terre | *Newkirk/Argyle* 22

DOWNTOWN

Dallas BBQ | *Livingston/Hoyt* 15
Junior's | *Flatbush/DeKalb* 17
Morton's | *Adams/Tillary* 24

DUMBO

Bubby's | *Main/Plymouth-Water* 18
5 Front | *Front/Old Fulton* 19
Grimaldi's | *Old Fulton/Front* 25
Pete's D'town | *Water/Old Fulton* 19
Rice | *Wash/Front-York* 19
Z River Café | *Water/Furman* 26
Superfine | *Front/Jay-Pearl* 20

DYKER HEIGHTS

Outback | *86s/15a* 14
Tommaso | *86s/14-15a* 23

FORT GREENE

abistro | *Carlton/Myrtle* 25
NEW Bati | *Fulton/Elliott* -
Café Habana/Outpost | 23
Fulton/Portland
Chez Oskar | *DeKalb/Adelphi* 17
Gen. Greene | *DeKalb/Clermont* 20
Ici | *DeKalb/Clermont* 21
Luz | *Vanderbilt/Myrtle* 24
Madiba | *DeKalb/Carlton* 20
NEW No. 7 | *Greene/Fulton* 23
Olea | *Lafayette/Adelphi* 23
Rice | *DeKalb/Cumberland* 19
67 Burger | *Lafayette/Fulton* 21
Smoke Joint | *Elliott/Lafayette* 21
Thomas Beisl | *Lafayette/Ashland* 17
Zaytoons | *Myrtle/Hall-Wash* 21

GRAVESEND

Fiorentino's | *Ave U/McDonald* 19
Sahara | *Coney Is/Aves T-U* 21

GREENPOINT

NEW Anella | *Franklin/Green* -
Lokal | *Lorimer/Bedford* 18

MIDWOOD

⊠ Di Fara | *Ave J/15s*	27
Joe's Pizza | *Kings/16s*	22
Taci's Beyti | *Coney Is/Ave P*	22

MILL BASIN

La Villa Pizzeria | *Ave U/66-67s*	21
Mill Basin Deli | *Ave T/59s*	22

PARK SLOPE

Alchemy | *5a/Bergen-St Marks*	19
⊠ Al Di La | *5a/Carroll*	26
A.O.C. | *5a/Garfield*	20
⊠ applewood | *11s/7-8a*	26
Baluchi's | *5a/2-3s*	17
NEW Bark Hot Dogs | *Bergen/5-6a*	-
Barrio | *7a/3s*	17
Bar Toto | *11s/6a*	18
Belleville | *5a/5s*	19
Blue Ribbon | *5a/1s-Garfield*	24
⊠ Blue Ribbon Sushi | *5a/1s*	26
Bogota | *5a/Lincoln-St Johns*	20
Brooklyn Fish | *5a/Degraw*	22
NEW Bussaco | *Union/6-7a*	22
Cafe Moutarde | *5a/Carroll*	19
Cafe Steinhof | *7a/14s*	18
Canaille | *5a/Prospect*	22
ChipShop | *5a/6-7s*	19
⊠ Chocolate Room | *5a/Propsect*	25
Coco Roco | *5a/6-7s*	20
Conviv. Osteria | *5a/Bergen*	25
Five Guys | *7a/6-7s*	20
Flatbush Farm | *St Marks/Flatbush*	20
NEW Fonda | *7a/14-15s*	-
NEW Get Fresh | *5a/5-6s*	-
Ghenet | *Douglass/4-5a*	20
Hanco's | *7a/10s*	22
Joe's Pizza | *7a/Carroll-Garfield*	22
Korzo | *5a/19-20s*	20
La Taqueria/Rachel | *multi.*	20
La Villa Pizzeria | *5a/1s-Garfield*	21
Lemongrass | *7a/Berkeley*	16
Lobo | *5a/Lincoln*	15
NEW Lot 2 | *6a/19-20s*	-
Melt | *Bergen/5s-Flatbush*	21
Miriam | *5a/Prospect*	21
Moim | *Garfield/7-8a*	24
Palo Santo | *Union/4-5a*	23
Press 195 | *5a/Berkeley-Union*	21
NEW Provini | *8a/13s*	-
Rose Water | *Union/6a*	26
Scalino | *7a/10s*	24
Scottadito | *Union/6-7a*	20
Sette | *7a/3s*	20
Sheep Sta. | *4a/Douglass*	18

Song | *5a/1-2s*	23
Stone Park | *5a/3s*	25
Sweet Melissa | *7a/1-2s*	21
12th St. B&G | *8a/12s*	21
Two Boots | *2s/7-8a*	19

PROSPECT HEIGHTS

Abigail | *Classon/St Johns*	20
Aliseo Osteria | *Vanderbilt/Park*	23
Amorina | *Vanderbilt/Prospect*	25
Beast | *Bergen/Vanderbilt*	21
NEW Cornelius | *Vanderbilt/Pacific*	18
Franny's | *Flatbush/Prospect*	24
Geido | *Flatbush/7a*	23
James | *Carlton/St Marks*	23
Le Gamin | *Vanderbilt/Bergen*	18
NEW Ortine | *Wash/Dean*	-
Tom's | *Wash/Sterling*	20
Zaytoons | *Vanderbilt/St Marks*	21

RED HOOK

NEW Anselmo's | *Van Brunt/Sullivan*	16
Defonte's | *Columbia/Luquer*	24
Fairway Cafe | *Van Brunt/Reed*	18
Good Fork | *Van Brunt/Coffey*	24

SHEEPSHEAD BAY

Brennan | *Nostrand/Ave U*	21
Rasputin | *Coney Island/Ave X*	20
Roll-n-Roaster | *Emmons/29s*	20

SUNSET PARK

Nyonya | *8a/54s*	23
Pacificana | *55s/8a*	24

VINEGAR HILL

NEW Vinegar Hill Hse. | *Hudson/Front*	24

WILLIAMSBURG

Aurora | *Grand/Wythe*	25
Baci/Abbracci | *Grand/Bedford*	21
Bamonte's | *Withers/Lorimer*	23
NEW Barberry | *Metro/Berry*	-
Barosa | *Graham/Ainslie*	23
NEW Brooklyn Star | *Havemeyer/N 7-8s*	-
⊠ Caracas | *Grand/Havemeyer*	24
Chimu | *Union/Meeker*	22
DeStefano | *Conselyea/Leonard*	23
Diner | *Bway/Berry*	24
Dressler | *Bway/Bedford-Driggs*	25
DuMont | *multi.*	22
Egg | *N 5s/Bedford-Berry*	23
NEW El Almacén | *Driggs/N 6-7s*	-
⊠ Fette Sau | *Metro/Havemeyer*	25

NEW Five Leaves | *Bedford/Lorimer*	23
NEW Flying Cow | *Hope/Roebling*	-
Fornino | *Bedford/6-7s*	23
Il Passatore | *Bushwick/Devoe*	24
Juliette | *N 5s/Bedford-Berry*	19
La Superior | *Berry/S 2-3s*	23
Le Barricou | *Grand/Lorimer*	23
Z Marlow/Sons | *Bway/Berry*	26
NEW Mesa Coyoacan | *Graham/Skillman*	-
Miranda | *Berry/N 9s*	21
Motorino | *Graham/Devoe*	22
My Moon | *N 10s/Bedford-Driggs*	19
Z Peter Luger | *Bway/Driggs*	27
PT | *Bedford/S 2-3s*	-
NEW Qoo Robata | *Metro/Havemeyer*	-
Radegast | *N 3s/Berry*	16
Relish | *Wythe/Metro-N 3s*	20
NEW Rye | *S 1s/Havemeyer*	-
SEA | *N 6s/Berry*	22
NEW Sel de Mer | *Graham/Skillman*	-
Sweetwater | *N 6s/Berry-Wythe*	21
NEW Vutera | *Grand/Havemeyer*	-
NEW Walter Foods | *Grand/Roebling*	23
Wombat | *Grand/Lorimer*	23
Z Zenkichi | *N 6s/Wythe*	25

Queens

ASTORIA

Afghan Kebab | *Steinway/28a*	19
Agnanti | *Ditmars/19s*	23
Bistro 33 | *Ditmars/21s*	23
NEW Bizaare Ave. | *36s/35a*	-
Brick Cafe | *33s/31a*	21
Cafe Bar | *36s/34a*	18
Cávo | *31a/42-43s*	21
Christos | *23a/41s*	23
El Boqueron | *34a/31s*	23
Elias Corner | *31s/24a*	23
Fatty's Cafe | *Ditmars/Crescent*	22
Il Bambino | *31a/34-35s*	25
JJ's Asian Fusion | *31a/37-38s*	24
Kabab Café | *Steinway/25a*	24
Locale | *34a/33s*	21
NEW Lucas Steak | *32s/35a*	-
Malagueta | *36a/28s*	25
Omonia | *Bway/33s*	18
Philoxenia | *34a/32-33s*	24
Piccola Venezia | *28a/42s*	25
Ponticello | *Bway/46-47s*	24
718 | *Ditmars/35s*	21

Sofia | *34a/35s*	23
Stamatis | *23a/29-31s*	22
Taverna Kyclades | *Ditmars/35s*	25
Telly's Taverna | *23a/28-29s*	23
Thai Pavilion | *multi.*	24
Tierras | *Bway/33s*	19
Z Tratt. L'incontro | *31s/Ditmars*	27
NEW Vesta | *30a/21s*	25
Watawa | *Ditmars/33r-35s*	25

BAYSIDE

Ben's Kosher | *26a/211s*	18
Bourbon St. Café | *Bell/40-41a*	18
Erawan | *multi.*	23
Jackson Hole | *Bell/35a*	17
Outback | *Bell/26a*	14
Press 195 | *Bell/40-41a*	21
Uncle Jack's | *Bell/40a*	23

COLLEGE POINT

Five Guys | *14a/132s*	20

CORONA

Leo's Latticini | *104s/46a*	27
Park Side | *Corona/51a*	24

DOUGLASTON

Grimaldi's | *61a/244s*	25

ELMHURST

Outback | *Queens/56a*	14
Pho Bang | *Bway/Elmhurst*	20
Ping's Sea. | *Queens/Goldsmith*	21

FLUSHING

Z Blue Smoke | *126s/Roosevelt*	21
East Manor | *Kissena/Kalmia*	19
Joe's Shanghai | *37a/Main*	22
Kum Gang San | *Northern/Bowne*	21
Pho Bang | *Kissena/Main*	20
Quantum Leap | *Fresh Meadow/67a*	20
Ramen Setagaya | *Prince/37a*	19
Z Shake Shack | *126s/Roosevelt*	23
Spicy & Tasty | *Prince/39a*	23
Szechuan Gourmet | *37a/Main*	22

FOREST HILLS

Alberto | *Metro/69-70a*	23
Baluchi's | *Queens/76a-76r*	17
Bann Thai | *Austin/Yellowstone*	20
Cabana | *70r/Austin-Queens*	21
Z Danny Brown | *Metro/71dr*	26
Da Silvana | *Yellowstone/Clyde*	20
Dee's Pizza | *Metro/74a*	21
Nick's | *Ascan/Austin*	23
Q Thai Bistro | *Ascan/Austin*	21

GLENDALE

Five Guys | *Woodhaven/74a* 20
Zum Stammtisch | *Myrtle/69pl* 22

HOWARD BEACH

La Villa Pizzeria | *153a/82s* 21

JACKSON HEIGHTS

Afghan Kebab | *37a/74-75s* 19
Delhi Palace | *74s/37a-37r* 22
Jackson Diner | *74s/Roosevelt* 22
Jackson Hole | *Astoria/70s* 17
Pio Pio | *Northern/84-85s* 22

JAMAICA

Bobby Van's | *American Airlines* 22

LITTLE NECK

La Baraka | *Northern/Little Neck* 21

LONG ISLAND CITY

Bella Via | *Vernon/48a* 22
Café Henri | *50a/Jackson* 21
Manducatis | *Jackson/47a* 22
Manetta's | *Jackson/49a* 22
Riverview | *50a/E River-49a* 21
Tournesol | *Vernon/50-51a* 24
🛿 Water's Edge | *E River/44dr* 22

OZONE PARK

Don Peppe | *Lefferts/135-149a* 24

REGO PARK

Barosa | *Woodhaven/62r* 23
Grand Sichuan | *Queens/66r* 21
London Lennie | *Woodhaven/Fleet* 22
Pio Pio | *Woodhaven/63a* 22

SUNNYSIDE

Quaint | *Skillman/46-47s* 23
Turkish Grill | *Queens/42s* 23

WOODSIDE

La Flor Bakery | *Roosevelt/53s* 23
Sapori D'Ischia | *37a/56s* 24
🛿 Sripraphai | *39a/64-65s* 27

Staten Island

Angelina's | *Ellis/Arthur Kill* 21
Arirang Hibachi | *Nelson/Locust* 20
Bayou | *Bay/Chestnut* 22
Bocelli | *Hylan/Clove-Old Town* 26
Brioso | *New Dorp/9s* 24
Carol's | *Richmond/Four Corners* 25
Cole's Dock | *Cleveland/Hylan* 20
Da Noi | *multi.* 23
Denino | *Port Richmond/Hooker* 25
Enoteca Maria | *Hyatt/Central* 23
Filippo's | *Richmond/Buel* 24
Fushimi | *Richmond/Lincoln* 24
Joe & Pat's | *Victory/Manor* 24
Killmeyer | *Arthur Kill/Sharrotts* 18
Lake Club | *Clove/Victory* 20
Lorenzo's | *South/Lois* 19
Marina Cafe | *Mansion/Hillside* 19
Nurnberger | *Castleton/Davis* 20
Outback | *Marsh/Platinum* 14
South Fin | *Capodanno/Sand* 19
Tratt. Romana | *Hylan/Benton* 24
Zest | *Bay/Willow* 23

Menus, photos, voting and more – free at ZAGAT.com

Special Features

Listings cover the best in each category and include names, locations and Food ratings. Multi-location restaurants' features may vary by branch.

BREAKFAST

(See also Hotel Dining)

NEW AQ Kafé | **W 50s**	19
Z Balthazar | **SoHo**	23
Z Barney Greengrass | **W 80s**	23
Brasserie | **E 50s**	20
Brooklyn Diner | **multi.**	17
Bubby's | **TriBeCa**	18
Cafe Colonial | **NoLita**	19
Cafe Con Leche | **W 80s**	18
Cafe Luxembourg | **W 70s**	20
Cafe Mogador | **E Vill**	21
Café Sabarsky | **E 80s**	22
Z Carnegie Deli | **W 50s**	22
City Bakery | **Flatiron**	22
City Hall | **TriBeCa**	21
Z Clinton St. Baking | **LES**	25
E.A.T. | **E 80s**	19
Egg | **W'burg**	23
EJ's Luncheon. | **multi.**	16
Good Enough/Eat | **W 80s**	21
HK | **Garment**	17
Z Jean Georges Noug. | **W 60s**	27
Z Katz's Deli | **LES**	23
Kitchenette | **multi.**	19
Landmarc | **W 60s**	20
Le Pain Q. | **multi.**	19
NEW Locanda Verde | **TriBeCa**	22
Michael's | **W 50s**	20
Morandi | **G Vill**	22
Naples 45 | **E 40s**	17
Nice Matin | **W 70s**	20
NoHo Star | **NoHo**	18
Norma's | **W 50s**	25
Pastis | **Meatpacking**	21
Patroon | **E 40s**	21
Penelope | **Murray Hill**	22
Pershing Sq. | **E 40s**	16
Popover Cafe | **W 80s**	18
NEW Prime Meat | **Carroll Gdns**	19
Regency | **E 60s**	18
Rue 57 | **W 50s**	18
Sant Ambroeus | **multi.**	22
Sarabeth's | **multi.**	20
NEW Smile | **NoHo**	-
Tartine | **W Vill**	22
Teresa's | **Bklyn Hts**	19
Veselka | **E Vill**	19

BRUNCH

Abigail | **Prospect Hts**	20
Alias | **LES**	21
Amy Ruth's | **Harlem**	22
A.O.C. | **W Vill**	20
Z applewood | **Park Slope**	26
Z Aquagrill | **SoHo**	26
Z Aquavit | **E 50s**	25
Z Artisanal | **Murray Hill**	23
Z Atlantic Grill | **E 70s**	23
Bagatelle | **Meatpacking**	19
Z Balthazar | **SoHo**	23
NEW Bar Artisanal | **TriBeCa**	21
Beacon | **W 50s**	23
Beast | **Prospect Hts**	21
Belcourt | **E Vill**	20
Blue Ribbon Bakery | **G Vill**	24
Z Blue Water | **Union Sq**	23
Bocca Lupo | **Cobble Hill**	24
NEW Braeburn | **W Vill**	21
Bubby's | **multi.**	18
Cafe Cluny | **W Vill**	21
Cafe Colonial | **NoLita**	19
Café de Bruxelles | **W Vill**	21
Cafe Loup | **G Vill**	19
Cafe Luxembourg | **W 70s**	20
Cafe Mogador | **E Vill**	21
Cafe Ronda | **W 70s**	19
Cafeteria | **Chelsea**	18
Caffe Cielo | **W 50s**	20
Capsouto Frères | **TriBeCa**	23
Z Carlyle | **E 70s**	23
Carmine's | **W 40s**	20
Celeste | **W 80s**	23
NEW City Winery | **SoHo**	18
NEW Clerkenwell | **LES**	-
Z Clinton St. Baking | **LES**	25
Cookshop | **Chelsea**	22
Cornelia St. Cafe | **G Vill**	19
Danal | **G Vill**	20
David Burke Townhse. | **E 60s**	25
dell'anima | **W Vill**	25
Delta Grill | **W 40s**	20
Diner | **W'burg**	24
E.A.T. | **E 80s**	19
Eatery | **W 50s**	20
Elephant & Castle | **G Vill**	17
elmo | **Chelsea**	16
Employees Only | **W Vill**	18
Essex | **LES**	18

Extra Virgin | **W Vill**	22
Fatty Crab | **multi.**	22
Félix | **SoHo**	16
5 Points | **NoHo**	22
Flea Mkt. Cafe | **E Vill**	21
Friend/Farmer | **Gramercy**	18
good | **W Vill**	21
Good Enough/Eat | **W 80s**	21
Great Jones Cafe | **NoHo**	20
HK | **Garment**	17
Home | **G Vill**	21
Isabella's | **W 70s**	20
Jane | **G Vill**	21
Joe Doe | **E Vill**	23
JoJo | **E 60s**	25
Kitchenette | **multi.**	19
Le Gigot | **G Vill**	23
Les Halles | **multi.**	20
L'Express | **Flatiron**	17
Little Giant | **LES**	22
Locale | **Astoria**	21
Macao Trading | **TriBeCa**	18
Maggie Brown | **Clinton Hill**	19
Mercadito | **multi.**	22
Mesa Grill | **Flatiron**	23
Miriam | **Park Slope**	21
Miss Mamie/Maude | **Harlem**	21
Nice Matin | **W 70s**	20
Norma's | **W 50s**	25
No. 7 | **Ft Greene**	23
Ocean Grill | **W 70s**	23
Odeon | **TriBeCa**	19
Olea | **Ft Greene**	23
Ouest | **W 80s**	24
Paradou | **Meatpacking**	21
Paris Commune | **W Vill**	19
Pastis | **Meatpacking**	21
Penelope | **Murray Hill**	22
Permanent Brunch | **E Vill**	-
Petrossian | **W 50s**	24
Pietrasanta | **W 40s**	19
Pink Tea Cup | **W Vill**	22
Pipa | **Flatiron**	20
Popover Cafe | **W 80s**	18
Prune | **E Vill**	24
Public | **NoLita**	22
River Café | **Dumbo**	26
Rose Water | **Park Slope**	26
Sarabeth's | **multi.**	20
Schiller's | **LES**	18
718 | **Astoria**	21
Spotted Pig | **W Vill**	23
Square Meal | **E 90s**	23
Stanton Social | **LES**	23
Stone Park | **Park Slope**	25

Sylvia's | **Harlem**	19
Tartine | **W Vill**	22
Telepan | **W 60s**	26
Tom's | **Prospect Hts**	20
Tribeca Grill | **TriBeCa**	22
Turkish Kitchen | **Murray Hill**	23
202 Cafe | **Chelsea**	20
Wallsé | **W Vill**	25
Water Club | **Murray Hill**	21
West Branch | **W 70s**	19
Zoë | **SoHo**	20

BUFFET

(Check availability)

Aquavit | **E 50s**	25
Bay Leaf | **W 50s**	21
Beacon | **W 50s**	23
Bizaare Ave. | **Astoria**	-
Bombay Palace | **W 50s**	20
Brasserie 8½ | **W 50s**	21
Brick Ln. Curry | **E Vill**	21
Bukhara Grill | **E 40s**	22
Carlyle | **E 70s**	23
Chennai Gdn. | **Murray Hill**	21
Chola | **E 50s**	23
Darbar | **multi.**	21
Delhi Palace | **Jackson Hts**	22
Dhaba | **Murray Hill**	22
Earthen Oven | **W 70s**	21
Jackson Diner | **Jackson Hts**	22
Jewel of India | **W 40s**	20
La Baraka | **Little Neck**	21
Lake Club | **SI**	20
Lorenzo's | **SI**	19
Mamajuana | **Inwood**	23
Oak Room | **W 50s**	18
One if by Land | **G Vill**	24
Persephone | **E 60s**	22
Salaam Bombay | **TriBeCa**	21
Sapphire | **W 60s**	21
South Fin | **SI**	19
South Gate | **W 50s**	24
Talay | **Harlem**	21
Tiffin Wallah | **Murray Hill**	24
Turkish Kitchen | **Murray Hill**	23
Turkuaz | **W 100s**	19
2 West | **Financial**	22
Utsav | **W 40s**	20
Water Club | **Murray Hill**	21
Yuva | **E 50s**	23

BYO

abistro | **Ft Greene**	25
Afghan Kebab | **multi.**	19
Amy Ruth's | **Harlem**	22
Angelica Kit. | **E Vill**	21

Baluchi's | **Murray Hill**	17
NEW Bati | **Ft Greene**	-
Bellini | **W 80s**	18
Bereket | **LES**	21
Brick Ln. Curry | **E 50s**	21
NEW Calexico | **Carroll Gdns**	-
Cube 63 | **LES**	22
Gazala Place | **W 40s**	23
NEW Get Fresh | **Park Slope**	-
NEW Hanci | **W 50s**	24
Ivo & Lulu | **SoHo**	20
Kabab Café | **Astoria**	24
Kuma Inn | **LES**	24
La Sirène | **SoHo**	23
☑ Lucali | **Carroll Gdns**	26
Mama's Food | **E Vill**	20
Mezzaluna/Pizza | **G Vill**	21
New Yeah | **Chinatown**	24
Noodle Bar | **LES**	20
Nook | **W 50s**	19
Peking Duck | **Chinatown**	23
Petite Crev. | **Carroll Gdns**	25
Pho Bang | **L Italy**	20
Phoenix Gdn. | **E 40s**	23
Poke | **E 80s**	25
Quantum Leap | **multi.**	20
Ravagh | **E 60s**	20
Room Service | **W 40s**	18
Spice | **E Vill**	21
Sweet Melissa | **Cobble Hill**	21
Taci's Beyti | **Midwood**	22
Tartine | **W Vill**	22
Tea & Sympathy | **W Vill**	21
Wondee Siam | **multi.**	22
Zaytoons | **multi.**	21
Zen Palate | **W 40s**	18

Fresco | **E 50s**	23
Gallagher's | **W 50s**	21
☑ Gotham B&G | **G Vill**	27
Home | **G Vill**	21
☑ La Grenouille | **E 50s**	27
☑ Le Bernardin | **W 50s**	28
☑ Le Cirque | **E 50s**	24
NEW Marea | **W 50s**	26
☑ Mas | **G Vill**	27
Matsuri | **Chelsea**	22
Megu | **TriBeCa**	23
Mercer Kitchen | **SoHo**	21
☑ Modern | **W 50s**	26
Molyvos | **W 50s**	22
☑ Nobu | **W 50s**	27
Olives | **Union Sq**	22
☑ One if by Land | **G Vill**	24
☑ Ouest | **W 80s**	24
☑ Palm | **multi.**	24
☑ Peter Luger | **W'burg**	27
Petrossian | **W 50s**	24
Raoul's | **SoHo**	24
Redeye Grill | **W 50s**	20
☑ River Café | **Dumbo**	26
River Room | **Harlem**	20
Rosa Mexicano | **multi.**	22
Ruby Foo's | **W 40s**	18
☑ Scarpetta | **Chelsea**	26
Sea Grill | **W 40s**	24
NEW SHO Shaun Hergatt | **Financial**	29
Tavern on Green | **W 60s**	15
Terrace in Sky | **W 100s**	22
Tratt. Dell'Arte | **W 50s**	22
View | **W 40s**	16
Water Club | **Murray Hill**	21
☑ Water's Edge | **LIC**	22

CELEBRATIONS

(Special prix fixe meals offered at major holidays)

☑ Adour | **E 50s**	26
Allegretti | **Flatiron**	24
NEW Aureole | **W 40s**	29
Beacon | **W 50s**	23
BLT Fish | **Flatiron**	23
BLT Prime | **Gramercy**	25
Bond 45 | **W 40s**	20
☑ Bouley | **TriBeCa**	28
☑ Buddakan | **Chelsea**	23
'Cesca | **W 70s**	23
☑ Cru | **G Vill**	26
☑ Daniel | **E 60s**	28
Duane Park | **TriBeCa**	23
eighty one | **W 80s**	25
FireBird | **W 40s**	19
☑ Four Seasons | **E 50s**	26

CELEBRITY CHEFS

Dan Barber
☑ Blue Hill | **G Vill**	27

Lidia Bastianich
☑ Del Posto | **Chelsea**	26
☑ Felidia | **E 50s**	26

Mario Batali
☑ Babbo | **G Vill**	27
Casa Mono | **Gramercy**	25
☑ Del Posto | **Chelsea**	26
☑ Esca | **W 40s**	25
☑ Lupa | **G Vill**	25
Otto | **G Vill**	23

April Bloomfield
Spotted Pig | **W Vill**	23

Saul Bolton
Saul | **Boerum Hill**	26

David Bouley		
Ⓩ Bouley | **TriBeCa**	28	
Ⓩ Bouley Upstairs | **TriBeCa**	26	
Daniel Boulud		
Ⓩ Bar Boulud | **W 60s**	23	
Ⓩ Café Boulud | **E 70s**	27	
Ⓩ Daniel | **E 60s**	28	
Ⓩ db Bistro Moderne | **W 40s**	24	
Ⓩ NEW DBGB | **E Vill**	23	
Antoine Bouterin		
Le Perigord | **E 50s**	24	
Jimmy Bradley		
Red Cat | **Chelsea**	23	
Terrance Brennan		
Ⓩ Artisanal | **Murray Hill**	23	
NEW Bar Artisanal | **TriBeCa**	21	
Ⓩ Picholine | **W 60s**	27	
Scott Bryan		
Apiary | **E Vill**	22	
David Burke		
David Burke Townhse. | **E 60s**	25	
NEW Fishtail | **E 60s**	23	
Marco Canora		
Hearth | **E Vill**	25	
Insieme | **W 50s**	23	
Floyd Cardoz		
Ⓩ Tabla | **Flatiron**	25	
Andrew Carmellini		
NEW Locanda Verde | **TriBeCa**	22	
Michael Cetrulo		
Piano Due | **W 50s**	24	
Ⓩ Scalini Fedeli | **TriBeCa**	26	
David Chang		
NEW Momofuku Bakery | **E Vill**	21	
Ⓩ Momofuku Ko | **E Vill**	27	
Momofuku Noodle | **E Vill**	23	
Ⓩ Momofuku Ssäm | **E Vill**	25	
Rebecca Charles		
Ⓩ Pearl Oyster | **G Vill**	26	
Tom Colicchio		
Ⓩ Craft | **Flatiron**	25	
Craftbar | **Flatiron**	22	
Craftsteak | **Chelsea**	24	
'wichcraft | **multi.**	20	
Scott Conant		
Ⓩ Scarpetta | **Chelsea**	26	
Josh de Chellis		
NEW La Fonda/Sol | **E 40s**	22	
Alain Ducasse		
Ⓩ Adour | **E 50s**	26	
Benoit | **W 50s**	19	
Wylie Dufresne		
wd-50 | **LES**	24	
Todd English		
Olives | **Union Sq**	22	

Sandro Fioriti		
Sandro's | **E 80s**	25	
Bobby Flay		
Ⓩ Bar Americain | **W 50s**	23	
Ⓩ Mesa Grill | **Flatiron**	23	
Amanda Freitag		
Harrison | **TriBeCa**	24	
Kurt Gutenbrunner		
Blaue Gans | **TriBeCa**	21	
Café Sabarsky | **E 80s**	22	
Wallsé | **W Vill**	25	
Gabrielle Hamilton		
Prune | **E Vill**	24	
Shaun Hergatt		
NEW SHO Shaun Hergatt | **Financial**	29	
Peter Hoffman		
Back Forty | **E Vill**	21	
Savoy | **SoHo**	24	
Daniel Humm		
Ⓩ Eleven Madison | **Flatiron**	27	
Michael Huynh		
NEW Baoguette | **multi.**	22	
NEW BarBao | **W 80s**	21	
Sara Jenkins		
NEW Porchetta | **E Vill**	24	
NEW Veloce Pizzeria | **E Vill**	–	
Thomas Keller		
Bouchon Bakery | **W 60s**	23	
Ⓩ Per Se | **W 60s**	28	
Gabriel Kreuther		
Ⓩ Modern | **W 50s**	26	
Susur Lee		
NEW Shang | **LES**	23	
Paul Liebrandt		
Ⓩ Corton | **TriBeCa**	27	
Anita Lo		
Annisa | **G Vill**	27	
Rickshaw Dumpling | **Flatiron**	17	
Michael Lomonaco		
Porter House | **W 60s**	24	
Pino Luongo		
Centolire | **E 80s**	21	
Waldy Malouf		
Beacon | **W 50s**	23	
Waldy's Pizza | **Chelsea**	22	
David Pasternack		
Ⓩ Esca | **W 40s**	25	
Zarela Martinez		
Zarela | **E 50s**	20	
Sam Mason		
Tailor | **SoHo**	22	
Nobu Matsuhisa		
Ⓩ Nobu | **multi.**	27	

Menus, photos, voting and more - free at ZAGAT.com

Marco Moreira
- ☑ 15 East | **Union Sq** — 26
- ☑ Tocqueville | **Union Sq** — 26

Masaharu Morimoto
- ☑ Morimoto | **Chelsea** — 25

Tadashi Ono
- Matsuri | **Chelsea** — 22

Charlie Palmer
- **NEW** Aureole | **W 40s** — 29
- Metrazur | **E 40s** — 21

David Pasternack
- ☑ Esca | **W 40s** — 25

Zak Pelaccio
- Fatty Crab | **multi.** — 22

Alfred Portale
- ☑ Gotham B&G | **G Vill** — 27

Michael Psilakis
- Anthos | **W 50s** — 25
- **NEW** Gus/Gabriel | **W 70s** — -
- Kefi | **W 80s** — 22

Gordon Ramsay
- Gordon Ramsay | **W 50s** — 24
- Maze | **W 50s** — 25

Mary Redding
- Brooklyn Fish | **Park Slope** — 22
- Mary's Fish | **W Vill** — 24

Eric Ripert
- ☑ Le Bernardin | **W 50s** — 28

Missy Robbins
- A Voce | **multi.** — 24

Joël Robuchon
- ☑ L'Atelier/Robuchon | **E 50s** — 28

Marcus Samuelsson
- ☑ Aquavit | **E 50s** — 25
- Riingo | **E 40s** — 21

Suvir Saran & Hemant Mathur
- dévi | **Flatiron** — 23

Gari Sugio
- ☑ Gari/Sushi | **multi.** — 27

Nao Sugiyama
- ☑ Sugiyama | **W 50s** — 27

Masayoshi Takayama
- ☑ Bar Masa | **W 60s** — 26
- ☑ Masa | **W 60s** — 26

Bill Telepan
- ☑ Telepan | **W 60s** — 26

Sue Torres
- Sueños | **Chelsea** — 22

Laurent Tourondel
- BLT Burger | **G Vill** — 20
- BLT Fish | **Flatiron** — 23
- BLT Market | **W 50s** — 23
- BLT Prime | **Gramercy** — 25
- ☑ BLT Steak | **E 50s** — 25

Alex Ureña
- Pamplona | **Murray Hill** — 22

Tom Valenti
- ☑ Ouest | **W 80s** — 24
- **NEW** West Branch | **W 70s** — 19

Jean-Georges Vongerichten
- ☑ Jean Georges | **W 60s** — 28
- ☑ JoJo | **E 60s** — 25
- Matsugen | **TriBeCa** — 22
- Mercer Kitchen | **SoHo** — 21
- Perry St. | **W Vill** — 25
- ☑ Spice Market | **Meatpacking** — 23
- Vong | **E 50s** — 22

David Waltuck
- ☑ Chanterelle | **TriBeCa** — 28

Jonathan Waxman
- Barbuto | **W Vill** — 22

Michael White
- ☑ Alto | **E 50s** — 26
- ☑ Convivio | **E 40s** — 26
- **NEW** Marea | **W 50s** — 26

Naomichi Yasuda
- ☑ Sushi Yasuda | **E 40s** — 28

Galen Zamarra
- ☑ Mas | **G Vill** — 27

CHEF'S TABLE

- Acappella | **TriBeCa** — 25
- **NEW** Aldea | **Flatiron** — 26
- ☑ Aquavit | **E 50s** — 25
- Avra | **E 40s** — 25
- ☑ Bar Boulud | **W 60s** — 23
- Barbuto | **W Vill** — 22
- Gordon Ramsay | **W 50s** — 24
- Hearth | **E Vill** — 25
- House | **Gramercy** — 22
- ☑ Il Buco | **NoHo** — 24
- Kai | **E 60s** — 26
- ☑ Kyo Ya | **E Vill** — 27
- Maloney/Porcelli | **E 50s** — 22
- Megu | **TriBeCa** — 23
- Mercadito | **E Vill** — 22
- **NEW** Montenapo | **W 40s** — -
- ☑**NEW** Oceana | **W 40s** — -
- Olives | **Union Sq** — 22
- Palma | **G Vill** — 23
- Park Ave. | **E 60s** — 24
- Remi | **W 50s** — 22
- Smith/Wollensky | **E 40s** — 23
- **NEW** Sojourn | **E 70s** — 24
- Valbella | **Meatpacking** — 25
- Yuva | **E 50s** — 23

CHILD-FRIENDLY

(See also Theme Restaurants;
* children's menu available)

- Amy Ruth's* | **Harlem** — 22
- Arirang Hibachi* | **multi.** — 20

Artie's Deli* | **W 80s**	18	Two Boots* | **multi.**	19
Bamonte's | **W'burg**	23	View* | **W 40s**	16
Barking Dog* | **multi.**	15	Virgil's BBQ* | **W 40s**	19
Barrio* | **Park Slope**	17	Zero Otto | **Bronx**	25
Bar Toto | **Park Slope**	18	Zum Stammtisch* | **Glendale**	22
Belleville* | **Park Slope**	19		
BLT Burger* | **G Vill**	20		

COMMUTER OASES

Grand Central	
Ammos | **E 40s**	21
Bobby Van's | **E 40s**	22
Brother Jimmy | **E 40s**	16
Burger Heaven | **E 40s**	16
Cafe Centro | **E 40s**	20
Cafe Spice | **E 40s**	18
Capital Grille | **E 40s**	23
Cipriani Dolci | **E 40s**	20
Dishes | **E 40s**	22
Docks Oyster | **E 40s**	19
Hale/Hearty | **E 40s**	19
Hatsuhana | **E 40s**	25
Junior's | **E 40s**	17
🆕 La Fonda/Sol | **E 40s**	22
Menchanko-tei | **E 40s**	20
Metrazur | **E 40s**	21
Michael Jordan | **E 40s**	20
Morton's | **E 40s**	24
Nanni | **E 40s**	24
🅩 Oyster Bar | **E 40s**	22
Patroon | **E 40s**	21
Pepe | **E 40s**	22
Pershing Sq. | **E 40s**	16
🅩 Sushi Yasuda | **E 40s**	28
Two Boots | **E 40s**	19
Penn Station	
Chipotle | **Garment**	18
🅩 Gray's Papaya | **Garment**	20
Nick & Stef | **Garment**	20
Uncle Jack's | **Garment**	23
Port Authority	
Angus McIndoe | **W 40s**	17
Chez Josephine | **W 40s**	20
Chimichurri Grill | **W 40s**	22
Dallas BBQ | **W 40s**	15
🅩 Esca | **W 40s**	25
etc. etc. | **W 40s**	20
HK | **Garment**	17
🅩 John's Pizzeria | **W 40s**	22
Marseille | **W 40s**	21
Metro Marché | **W 40s**	19
🆕 Montenapo | **W 40s**	-
🆕 Schnipper´s | **W 40s**	17
Shorty's | **W 40s**	22
Shula's | **W 40s**	21
West Bank Cafe | **W 40s**	19

🅩 Blue Smoke* | **Murray Hill**	21
Boathouse* | **E 70s**	17
Bocca Lupo* | **Cobble Hill**	24
Brennan | **Sheepshead**	21
Bubba Gump* | **W 40s**	14
Bubby's* | **multi.**	18
🆕 Buttermilk | **Carroll Gdns**	23
Café Habana/Outpost | **Ft Greene**	23
Cafe Un Deux/Le Petit* | **W 40s**	16
Carmine's | **W 40s**	20
Cowgirl* | **W Vill**	16
Dallas BBQ | **multi.**	15
Dean's | **multi.**	17
EJ's Luncheon.* | **multi.**	16
Farm/Adderley* | **Ditmas Pk**	22
Friend/Farmer* | **Gramercy**	18
Gargiulo's | **Coney Is**	22
Good Enough/Eat* | **W 80s**	21
Jackson Hole* | **multi.**	17
Junior's* | **multi.**	17
L & B Spumoni* | **Bensonhurst**	23
Landmarc* | **multi.**	20
La Villa Pizzeria | **multi.**	21
London Lennie* | **Rego Pk**	22
Max* | **multi.**	22
Max Brenner* | **G Vill**	18
Miss Mamie/Maude* | **Harlem**	21
Nick's | **multi.**	23
Ninja | **TriBeCa**	16
Noodle Pudding | **Bklyn Hts**	25
Otto | **G Vill**	23
Peanut Butter Co. | **G Vill**	21
Petite Abeille* | **multi.**	17
Picket Fence* | **Ditmas Pk**	19
Pig Heaven | **E 80s**	19
Pinche Taqueria | **NoHo**	22
Rack & Soul* | **W 100s**	19
Ruby Foo's* | **W 40s**	18
Sarabeth's | **multi.**	20
Serendipity 3 | **E 60s**	18
🅩 Shake Shack | **multi.**	23
S'MAC/Pinch* | **W 80s**	21
🆕 Sweetiepie* | **G Vill**	14
Sylvia's* | **Harlem**	19
Tavern on Green* | **W 60s**	15
Tony's Di Napoli | **multi.**	19

CRITIC-PROOF

(Gets lots of business despite so-so food)

Barking Dog	multi.	15
Blockhead Burrito	multi.	16
Brother Jimmy	multi.	16
Bubba Gump	W 40s	14
Burger Heaven	multi.	16
Cafe Un Deux/Le Petit	W 40s	16
China Fun	multi.	15
Coffee Shop	Union Sq	15
Così	multi.	16
Cowgirl	multi.	16
Dallas BBQ	multi.	15
Demarchelier	E 80s	16
Edison	W 40s	16
EJ's Luncheon.	multi.	16
Elaine's	E 80s	13
elmo	Chelsea	16
Empire Diner	Chelsea	15
Empire Szechuan	multi.	15
Fraunces Tavern	Financial	16
Heartland	multi.	14
Lemongrass	multi.	16
Mary Ann's	multi.	16
Ollie's	multi.	15
Outback	multi.	14
Pershing Sq.	E 40s	16
Tavern on Green	W 60s	15

DANCING

Cávo	Astoria	21
Rasputin	Sheepshead	20
River Room	Harlem	20
Sofrito	E 50s	21
Son Cubano	Meatpacking	21
Tavern on Green	W 60s	15

ENTERTAINMENT

(Call for days and times of performances)

Algonquin	varies	W 40s	17
Bacchus	live music	Boerum Hill	23
Blue Fin	jazz	W 40s	22
◪ Blue Smoke	jazz	Murray Hill	21
◪ Blue Water	jazz	Union Sq	23
Cafe Steinhof	varies	Park Slope	18
Chez Josephine	piano	W 40s	20
Cornelia St. Cafe	varies	G Vill	19
Delta Grill	live music	W 40s	20
NEW Favela Cubana	live music	G Vill	-
Flor/Sol	flamenco dance	TriBeCa	22
Ideya	jazz	SoHo	21
Jules	jazz	E Vill	18
Knickerbocker	jazz	G Vill	20
La Lanterna	jazz	G Vill	19
La Lunchonette	varies	Chelsea	21
Londel's	jazz	Harlem	19
◪ River Café	piano	Dumbo	26
Son Cubano	varies	Meatpacking	21
Sylvia's	gospel	Harlem	19
Tavern on Green	live music	W 60s	15
Tommaso	piano & vocalist	Dyker Hts	23
Walker's	jazz	TriBeCa	17

FIREPLACES

A Casa Fox	LES	20
Alberto	Forest Hills	23
Ali Baba	Murray Hill	21
Allegretti	Flatiron	24
Alta	G Vill	24
Antica Venezia	W Vill	23
◪ applewood	Park Slope	26
Arté	G Vill	18
Barosa	W'burg	23
Battery Gdns.	Financial	18
Benjamin Steak	E 40s	24
Beppe	Flatiron	23
Bistro Ten 18	W 100s	19
Black Duck	Murray Hill	20
Boathouse	E 70s	17
◪ Bouley	TriBeCa	28
◪ Bouley Upstairs	TriBeCa	26
Bourbon St. Café	Bayside	18
Brasserie 44	W 40s	20
Bruckner B&G	Bronx	-
NEW Casa La Femme	W Vill	20
Christos	Astoria	23
NEW Civetta	NoLita	19
Cornelia St. Cafe	G Vill	19
Dee's Pizza	Forest Hills	21
Delta Grill	W 40s	20
Elizabeth	NoLita	19
Employees Only	W Vill	18
F & J Pine	Bronx	22
Fatty's Cafe	Astoria	22
FireBird	W 40s	19
5 9th	Meatpacking	19
Frankie/Johnnie	Garment	22
Fraunces Tavern	Financial	16
Friend/Farmer	Gramercy	18
Geisha	E 60s	22

Giorgione | **SoHo**	21
Greenhouse | **Bay Ridge**	21
House | **Gramercy**	22
Ici | **Ft Greene**	21
I Trulli | **Murray Hill**	23
Keens | **Garment**	24
☑ Lady Mendl's | **Gramercy**	22
Lake Club | **SI**	20
La Lanterna | **G Vill**	19
Lattanzi | **W 40s**	22
Le Barricou | **W'burg**	23
Lobster Box | **Bronx**	19
Lorenzo's | **SI**	19
Lumi | **E 70s**	18
Manducatis | **LIC**	22
Manetta's | **LIC**	22
Moran's | **Chelsea**	18
Nino's | **E 50s**	21
Nurnberger | **SI**	20
Olana | **Murray Hill**	23
☑ One if by Land | **G Vill**	24
Paola's | **E 80s**	23
Park | **Chelsea**	16
Pearl Room | **Bay Ridge**	20
☑ Per Se | **W 60s**	28
Piccola Venezia | **Astoria**	25
Place | **W Vill**	19
Public | **NoLita**	22
Quality Meats | **W 50s**	24
Quartino | **NoHo**	20
Savoy | **SoHo**	24
Scottadito | **Park Slope**	20
Sheep Sta. | **Park Slope**	18
South Gate | **W 50s**	24
STK | **Meatpacking**	21
Telly's Taverna | **Astoria**	23
Terrace in Sky | **W 100s**	22
Triomphe | **W 40s**	24
☑ 21 Club | **W 50s**	22
Water Club | **Murray Hill**	21
☑ Water's Edge | **LIC**	22
Waverly Inn | **W Vill**	19
wd-50 | **LES**	24

GRACIOUS HOSTS

Angus McIndoe | Angus McIndoe | **W 40s**	17
Anthos | Donatella Arpaia | **W 50s**	25
Barbetta | Laura Maioglio | **W 40s**	21
☑ Blue Hill | Franco Serafin | **G Vill**	27
Bricco | Nino Cituogno | **W 50s**	20
☑ Chanterelle | Karen Waltuck | **TriBeCa**	28
Chez Josephine | Jean-Claude Baker | **W 40s**	20

Chin Chin | James Chin | **E 40s**	23
☑ Degustation | Grace & Jack Lamb | **E Vill**	26
Deux Amis | Bucky Yahiaoui | **E 50s**	20
Due | Ernesto Cavalli | **E 70s**	21
Eliá | Christina & Pete Lekkas | **Bay Ridge**	26
☑ Four Seasons | Julian Niccolini, Alex von Bidder | **E 50s**	26
Fresco | Marion Scotto | **E 50s**	23
☑ Jean Georges | Philippe Vongerichten | **W 60s**	28
☑ Jewel Bako | Grace & Jack Lamb | **E Vill**	25
Kitchen Club | Marja Samsom | **NoLita**	23
Klee Brass. | Lori Mason | **Chelsea**	20
La Baraka | Lucette Sonigo | **Little Neck**	21
☑ La Grenouille | Charles Masson | **E 50s**	27
La Mirabelle | Annick Le Douaron | **W 80s**	23
Las Ramblas | Natalie Sanz | **G Vill**	24
☑ Le Cirque | Sirio Maccioni | **E 50s**	24
Le Perigord | Georges Briguet | **E 50s**	24
Le Zie 2000 | Claudio Bonotto | **Chelsea**	22
Neary's | Jimmy Neary | **E 50s**	16
Nino's | Nino Selimaj | **E 70s**	21
Paola's | Paola Marracino | **E 80s**	23
Patroon | Ken Aretsky | **E 40s**	21
Piccolo Angolo | R. Migliorini | **W Vill**	25
Pig Heaven | Nancy Lee | **E 80s**	19
Primavera | Nicola Civetta | **E 80s**	24
Rao's | Frank Pellegrino | **Harlem**	23
☑ San Pietro | Gerardo Bruno | **E 50s**	26
☑ Sistina | Giuseppe Bruno | **E 80s**	26
Spigolo | Heather Fratangelo | **E 80s**	25
☑ Tamarind | Avtar & Gary Walia | **Flatiron**	25
☑ Tocqueville | Jo-Ann Makovitzky | **Union Sq**	26
Tommaso | Thomas Verdillo | **Dyker Hts**	23
☑ Tratt. L'incontro | Rocco Sacramone | **Astoria**	27
Tratt. Romana | V. Asoli, A. Lobiano | **SI**	24
Turquoise | Sam Marelli | **E 80s**	21

GREEN/ORGANIC/ LOCAL

(Places specializing in organic, local ingredients)

NEW Aldea | Flatiron	26
Amy's Bread | multi.	24
Angelica Kit. | E Vill	21
Z applewood | Park Slope	26
Aroma | NoHo	24
NEW Aureole | W 40s	29
Aurora | multi.	25
Z Babbo | G Vill	27
Back Forty | E Vill	21
Barbetta | W 40s	21
Z Bar Boulud | W 60s	23
Barbuto | W Vill	22
NEW Bark Hot Dogs | Park Slope	–
Belcourt | E Vill	20
Blossom | Chelsea	23
BLT Market | W 50s	23
Z Blue Hill | G Vill	27
NEW Braeburn | W Vill	21
Broadway East | LES	22
Brown Café | LES	23
NEW Buttermilk | Carroll Gdns	23
Café Habana/Outpost | Ft Greene	23
Candle Cafe | E 70s	22
Candle 79 | E 70s	23
Caravan/Dreams | E Vill	20
Chennai Gdn. | Murray Hill	21
Chestnut | Carroll Gdns	24
City Bakery | Flatiron	22
Z Clinton St. Baking | LES	25
Community Food | W 100s	21
Cookshop | Chelsea	22
Counter | E Vill	20
Z Craft | Flatiron	25
Z Degustation | E Vill	26
Diner | W'burg	24
Dressler | W'burg	25
Egg | W'burg	23
eighty one | W 80s	25
Z Eleven Madison | Flatiron	27
Z Esca | W 40s	25
Falai | LES	23
Z Fette Sau | W'burg	25
Flatbush Farm | Park Slope	20
Fornino | W'burg	23
Frankies | multi.	24
Franny's | Prospect Hts	24
Gen. Greene | Ft Greene	20
NEW Get Fresh | Park Slope	–
Gobo | multi.	23
Good Enough/Eat | W 80s	21

Good Fork | Red Hook	24
Z Gramercy Tavern | Flatiron	28
Z Grocery | Carroll Gdns	27
Harrison | TriBeCa	24
Hearth | E Vill	25
Home | G Vill	21
Hundred Acres | SoHo	19
Ici | Ft Greene	21
Z Il Buco | NoHo	24
Irving Mill | Gramercy	20
Isabella's | W 70s	20
James | Prospect Hts	23
Z Jewel Bako | E Vill	25
Josephina | W 60s	18
Josie's | multi.	19
Le Pain Q. | Flatiron	19
Little Giant | LES	22
Locanda Verde | TriBeCa	22
Marc Forgione | TriBeCa	23
Market Table | G Vill	23
Z Marlow/Sons | W'burg	26
New Leaf | Wash. Hts	21
Palo Santo | Park Slope	23
Peaches | Bed-Stuy	–
Z Per Se | W 60s	28
PicNic Market | W 100s	20
Pure Food/Wine | Gramercy	21
Quartino | NoHo	20
NEW Recipe | W 80s	–
Rose Water | Park Slope	26
NEW Rouge Tomate | E 60s	22
Saul | Boerum Hill	26
Savoy | SoHo	24
Z Telepan | W 60s	26
Z Tocqueville | Union Sq	26
Z Union Sq. Cafe | Union Sq	27
NEW Vesta | Astoria	25
Zen Palate | W 40s	18

HISTORIC PLACES

(Year opened; * building)

1762 | Fraunces Tavern | Financial	16
1794 | Bridge Cafe* | Financial	21
1853 | Morgan* | Murray Hill	20
1864 | Pete's Tavern | Gramercy	16
1868 | Landmark Tavern | W 40s	17
1868 | Old Homestead | Meatpacking	24
1884 | P.J. Clarke's | E 50s	17
1885 | Keens | Garment	24
1887 | Peter Luger | W'burg	27
1888 | Katz's Deli | LES	23
1890 | Walker's* | TriBeCa	17
1896 | Rao's | Harlem	23

1900	Bamonte's	**W'burg**	_23_
1902	Algonquin	**W 40s**	_17_
1902	Angelo's/Mulberry | **L Italy**		_23_
1904	Lanza	**E Vill**	_18_
1904	Trinity Pl.*	**Financial**	_19_
1904	Vincent's	**L Italy**	_21_
1906	Barbetta	**W 40s**	_21_
1907	Gargiulo's	**Coney Is**	_22_
1907	Oak Room	**W 50s**	_18_
1908	Barney Greengrass | **W 80s**		_23_
1908	John's/12th St.	**E Vill**	_20_
1910	Wolfgang's* | **Murray Hill**		_25_
1913	Oyster Bar	**E 40s**	_22_
1919	Mario's	**Bronx**	_22_
1920	Leo's Latticini	**Corona**	_27_
1920	Waverly Inn	**W Vill**	_19_
1921	Sardi's	**W 40s**	_18_
1922	Tosca Café	**Bronx**	_21_
1924	Totonno Pizza	**Coney Is**	_22_
1925	El Charro	**G Vill**	_22_
1926	Frankie/Johnnie	**W 40s**	_22_
1926	Palm	**E 40s**	_24_
1927	Diner*	**W'burg**	_24_
1927	El Faro	**W Vill**	_22_
1927	Gallagher's	**W 50s**	_21_
1929	Eleven Madison* | **Flatiron**		_27_
1929	Empire Diner*	**Chelsea**	_15_
1929	John's Pizzeria	**G Vill**	_22_
1929	Russian Tea	**W 50s**	_19_
1929	21 Club	**W 50s**	_22_
1930	Carlyle	**E 70s**	_23_
1930	El Quijote	**Chelsea**	_20_
1933	Patsy's Pizzeria	**Harlem**	_20_
1934	Papaya King	**E 80s**	_20_
1936	Monkey Bar	**E 50s**	_18_
1936	Tom's	**Prospect Hts**	_20_
1937	Carnegie Deli	**W 50s**	_22_
1937	Denino	**SI**	_25_
1937	Minetta	**G Vill**	_20_
1937	Stage Deli	**W 50s**	_20_
1938	Brennan	**Sheepshead**	_21_
1938	Heidelberg	**E 80s**	_18_
1938	Wo Hop	**Chinatown**	_21_
1939	L & B Spumoni | **Bensonhurst**		_23_
1941	Commerce*	**W Vill**	_22_
1941	Sevilla	**W Vill**	_22_
1944	Patsy's	**W 50s**	_21_
1945	V&T	**W 100s**	_18_
1946	Lobster Box	**Bronx**	_19_
1950	Junior's	**Downtown Bklyn**	_17_

1953	Liebman's	**Bronx**	_21_
1954	Pink Tea Cup	**W Vill**	_22_
1954	Serendipity 3	**E 60s**	_18_
1954	Veselka	**E Vill**	_19_
1957	Arturo's	**G Vill**	_22_
1957	La Taza de Oro	**Chelsea**	_20_
1957	Moran's	**Chelsea**	_18_
1958	Queen	**Bklyn Hts**	_24_
1959	Brasserie	**E 50s**	_20_
1959	El Parador Cafe | **Murray Hill**		_21_
1959	Four Seasons	**E 50s**	_26_
1960	Bull & Bear	**E 40s**	_20_
1960	Chez Napoléon	**W 50s**	_20_
1960	Joe & Pat's	**SI**	_24_
1960	London Lennie	**Rego Pk**	_22_

HOTEL DINING

Affinia Dumont
  Barking Dog | **Murray Hill**   _15_
Alex Hotel
  Riingo | **E 40s**   _21_
Algonquin Hotel
  Algonquin | **W 40s**   _17_
Blakely Hotel
  Abboccato | **W 50s**   _21_
Bowery Hotel
  Gemma | **E Vill**   _19_
Bryant Park Hotel
  Koi | **W 40s**   _22_
Carlton Hotel
  Country | **Murray Hill**   _21_
Carlyle Hotel
  Z Carlyle | **E 70s**   _23_
City Club Hotel
  Z db Bistro Moderne | **W 40s**   _24_
Cooper Sq. Hotel
  NEW Table 8 | **E Vill**   _15_
Crowne Plaza Times Sq. Hotel
  NEW Brasserie 1605 | **W 40s**   _–_
Dream Hotel
  Serafina | **W 50s**   _18_
Dylan Hotel
  Benjamin Steak | **E 40s**   _24_
Edison Hotel
  Edison | **W 40s**   _16_
Elysée Hotel
  Z NEW Monkey Bar | **E 50s**   _18_
Excelsior Hotel
  eighty one | **W 80s**   _25_
Four Seasons Hotel
  Z L'Atelier/Robuchon | **E 50s**   _28_
Greenwich Hotel
  NEW Locanda Verde \| **TriBeCa**   _22_

Hilton Garden Inn			Royalton Hotel	
Lorenzo's | **SI**	19		Brasserie 44 | **W 40s**	20
Hilton Garden Inn Hotel			San Carlos Hotel	
Pigalle | **W 40s**	18		Mint | **E 50s**	21
Hotel on Rivington			Shelburne Murray Hill Hotel	
NEW Levant East | **LES**	–		Rare B&G | **Murray Hill**	21
Hudson Hotel			Sherry Netherland Hotel	
Hudson Cafeteria | **W 50s**	19		Harry Cipriani | **E 50s**	21
Inn at Irving Pl.			6 Columbus Hotel	
Z Lady Mendl's | **Gramercy**	22		Blue Ribbon Sushi B&G |	24
Iroquois Hotel			**W 50s**	
Triomphe | **W 40s**	24		60 Thompson	
Jumeirah Essex Hse.			Kittichai | **SoHo**	22
South Gate | **W 50s**	24		Standard Hotel	
Le Parker Meridien			**NEW** Standard Grill |	22
Z burger joint | **W 50s**	24		**Meatpacking**	
Le Parker Meridien Hotel			St. Regis Hotel	
Norma's | **W 50s**	25		**Z** Adour | **E 50s**	26
Loews Regency Hotel			Surrey Hotel	
Regency | **E 60s**	18		**Z** Café Boulud | **E 70s**	27
London NYC Hotel			Thompson LES Hotel	
Gordon Ramsay | **W 50s**	24		**NEW** Shang | **LES**	23
Maze | **W 50s**	25		Time Hotel	
Lowell Hotel			Serafina | **W 40s**	18
Post House | **E 60s**	24		Trump Int'l Hotel	
Mandarin Oriental Hotel			**Z** Jean Georges | **W 60s**	28
Z Asiate | **W 60s**	24		**Z** Jean Georges Noug. | **W 60s**	27
Maritime Hotel			Waldorf-Astoria	
Matsuri | **Chelsea**	22		Bull & Bear | **E 40s**	20
Marriott Marquis Hotel			Inagiku | **E 40s**	22
View | **W 40s**	16		Washington Square Hotel	
Mercer Hotel			North Sq. | **G Vill**	23
Mercer Kitchen | **SoHo**	21		Westin Times Sq. Hotel	
Michelangelo Hotel			Shula's | **W 40s**	21
Insieme | **W 50s**	23		Wingate Hotel	
Morgans Hotel			**NEW** Crudo | **Garment**	–
Z Asia de Cuba |	22		W Times Sq.	
Murray Hill			Blue Fin | **W 40s**	22
Muse Hotel			W Union Sq. Hotel	
NEW Nios | **W 40s**	–		Olives | **Union Sq**	22

NY Marriott Brooklyn			**JACKET REQUIRED**	
Morton's | **Downtown Bklyn**	24			
NY Palace Hotel			**Z** Carlyle | **E 70s**	23
Z Gilt | **E 50s**	25		**Z** Daniel | **E 60s**	28
Park South Hotel			**Z** Four Seasons | **E 50s**	26
Black Duck | **Murray Hill**	20		**Z** Jean Georges | **W 60s**	28
Plaza Hotel			**Z** La Grenouille | **E 50s**	27
NEW Oak Room | **W 50s**	18		**Z** Le Bernardin | **W 50s**	28
Renaissance Hotel 57			**Z** Le Cirque | **E 50s**	24
NEW André | **E 50s**	–		Le Perigord | **E 50s**	24
Ritz-Carlton			**Z** Modern | **W 50s**	26
BLT Market | **W 50s**	23		**Z** Per Se | **W 60s**	28
Ritz-Carlton Battery Park			**Z** River Café | **Dumbo**	26
2 West | **Financial**	22		**Z** 21 Club | **W 50s**	22

SPECIAL FEATURES

JURY DUTY

(Near Foley Sq.)

Acappella | **TriBeCa**	25
Arqua | **TriBeCa**	22
Big Wong | **Chinatown**	22
Blaue Gans | **TriBeCa**	21
☑ Bouley | **TriBeCa**	28
☑ Bouley Upstairs | **TriBeCa**	26
Bread | **TriBeCa**	19
Carl's Steaks | **TriBeCa**	21
Centrico | **TriBeCa**	20
City Hall | **TriBeCa**	21
Dim Sum Go Go | **Chinatown**	21
Ecco | **TriBeCa**	23
Excellent Dumpling | **Chinatown**	20
Fuleen | **Chinatown**	23
Golden Unicorn | **Chinatown**	20
Great NY Noodle | **Chinatown**	22
Jing Fong | **Chinatown**	20
Joe's | **Chinatown**	20
Mandarin Court | **Chinatown**	20
Nam | **TriBeCa**	21
New Bo-Ky | **Chinatown**	22
Nha Trang | **Chinatown**	22
Nice Green Bo | **Chinatown**	23
Odeon | **TriBeCa**	19
☑ Oriental Gdn. | **Chinatown**	23
Peking Duck | **Chinatown**	23
Petite Abeille | **TriBeCa**	17
Pho Pasteur | **Chinatown**	21
Pho Viet Huong | **Chinatown**	22
Ping's Sea. | **Chinatown**	21
Pongsri Thai | **Chinatown**	20
Red Egg | **L Italy**	20
Takahachi | **TriBeCa**	25
Wo Hop | **Chinatown**	21

LATE DINING

(Weekday closing hour)

NEW Agua Dulce | 3:30 AM | **W 50s**	–
Artichoke Basille | 3 AM | **E Vill**	23
Arturo's | 1 AM | **G Vill**	22
Baraonda | 1 AM | **E 70s**	18
NEW Bar Artisanal | 1 AM | **TriBeCa**	21
Bar Carrera | 2 AM | **multi.**	22
Bereket | 24 hrs. | **LES**	21
Big Nick's | varies | **W 70s**	17
Black Iron | varies | **E Vill**	21
Blue Ribbon | varies | **SoHo**	24
☑ Blue Ribbon Sushi | varies | **SoHo**	26
Blue Ribbon Sushi B&G | 2 AM | **W 50s**	24
Bocca di Bacco | 2 AM | **W 50s**	21
NEW Boka | 2 AM | **E Vill**	23
Brennan | 1 AM | **Sheepshead**	21
Cafe Mogador | 1 AM | **E Vill**	21
Cafeteria | 24 hrs. | **Chelsea**	18
☑ Carnegie Deli | 3:30 AM | **W 50s**	22
Casellula | 2 AM | **W 50s**	25
Cávo | 2 AM | **Astoria**	21
Chez Josephine | 1 AM | **W 40s**	20
Chickpea | varies | **Flatiron**	18
Coffee Shop | varies | **Union Sq**	15
NEW Cornelius | 2 AM | **Prospect Hts**	18
Corner Bistro | 3:30 AM | **W Vill**	22
Così | 1 AM | **G Vill**	16
Delicatessen | 1 AM | **NoLita**	18
dell'anima | 2 AM | **W Vill**	25
Ditch Plains | 2 AM | **G Vill**	18
DuMont | 2 AM | **W'burg**	22
Elaine's | 2 AM | **E 80s**	13
Elizabeth | 2 AM | **NoLita**	19
El Malecon | varies | **Wash. Hts**	21
El Paso Taqueria | 1 AM | **E 100s**	23
Empanada Mama | 1 AM | **W 50s**	22
Empire Diner | 24 hrs. | **Chelsea**	15
Empire Szechuan | varies | **multi.**	15
Employees Only | 3:30 AM | **W Vill**	18
NEW Emporio | 2 AM | **NoLita**	22
NEW Fat Hippo | 2 AM | **LES**	20
NEW Favela Cubana | varies | **G Vill**	–
Frank | 1 AM | **E Vill**	24
French Roast | 24 hrs. | **multi.**	17
Fuleen | 2:30 AM | **Chinatown**	23
Gahm Mi Oak | 24 hrs. | **Garment**	21
Gottino | 2 AM | **G Vill**	21
☑ Gray's Papaya | 24 hrs. | **multi.**	20
Great NY Noodle | 4 AM | **Chinatown**	22
NEW Harry's Italian | varies | **Financial**	–
HK | 1 AM | **Garment**	17
House | 3 AM | **Gramercy**	22
'ino | 2 AM | **G Vill**	24
'inoteca | 3 AM | **multi.**	23
Jackson Hole | varies | **multi.**	17
J.G. Melon | 2:30 AM | **E 70s**	21
Joe's Pizza | 5 AM | **G Vill**	22
NEW Joseph Leonard | 2 AM | **G Vill**	–
Kang Suh | 24 hrs. | **Garment**	21
Kati Roll | varies | **G Vill**	20
Knickerbocker | 1 AM | **G Vill**	20
Kum Gang San | 24 hrs. | **multi.**	21
La Esquina | 2 AM | **L Italy**	21
La Lanterna | 3 AM | **G Vill**	19
Landmarc | 2 AM | **multi.**	20

Menus, photos, voting and more – free at ZAGAT.com

L'Express | 24 hrs. | **Flatiron** 17
Lil' Frankie | 2 AM | **E Vill** 23
Lucky Strike | varies | **SoHo** 16
NEW Macao Trading | 4 AM | 18
   TriBeCa
Macelleria | 1 AM | **Meatpacking** 21
Maison | 24 hrs. | **W 50s** 19
NEW Mari Vanna | 1 AM | -
   Flatiron
Max SoHa/Caffe | varies | **W 100s** 21
Z NEW Minetta | varies | **G Vill** 20
Ollie's | varies | **W 100s** 15
Omonia | 4 AM | **multi.** 18
Pastis | varies | **Meatpacking** 21
P.J. Clarke's | varies | **multi.** 17
Pop Burger | varies | **multi.** 18
NEW Prime Meat | 2 AM | 19
   Carroll Gdns
Ramen Setagaya | varies | **E Vill** 19
Redhead | 1 AM | **E Vill** 21
Roll-n-Roaster | 1 AM | 20
   Sheepshead
Sahara | 2 AM | **Gravesend** 21
Sarge's Deli | 24 hrs. | **Murray Hill** 20
Schiller's | 1 AM | **LES** 18
Shorty's | varies | **W 40s** 22
NEW Sojourn | 1 AM | **E 70s** 24
NEW Sorella | 2 AM | **LES** -
Spitzer's | 4 AM | **LES** 20
Spotted Pig | 2 AM | **W Vill** 23
Stage Deli | 2 AM | **W 50s** 20
Stamatis | varies | **Astoria** 22
NEW Standard Grill | 4 AM | 22
   Meatpacking
Stanton Social | 3 AM | **LES** 23
SushiSamba | varies | **multi.** 21
Z Sushi Seki | 3 AM | **E 60s** 26
Tio Pepe | 1 AM | **G Vill** 20
Tosca Café | 1 AM | **Bronx** 21
Two Boots | varies | **multi.** 19
Umberto's | 4 AM | **L Italy** 18
Uva | 2 AM | **E 70s** 21
Veselka | varies | **E Vill** 19
Viand | varies | **multi.** 17
Vincent's | 1:30 AM | **L Italy** 21
Walker's | 1 AM | **TriBeCa** 17
NEW Walter Foods | varies | 23
   W'burg
Wollensky's | 2 AM | **E 40s** 23
Wombat | 2 AM | **W'burg** 23

MEET FOR A DRINK

(Most top hotels, bars and
the following standouts)
Ajna Bar | **Meatpacking** 19
Algonquin | **W 40s** 17
Amaranth | **E 60s** 18

Z Artisanal | **Murray Hill** 23
Z Atlantic Grill | **E 70s** 23
Aurora | **W'burg** 25
Z Balthazar | **SoHo** 23
NEW Bar Artisanal | **TriBeCa** 21
Z Bar Boulud | **W 60s** 23
Barbounia | **Flatiron** 21
Z Bar Masa | **W 60s** 26
Blue Fin | **W 40s** 22
Z Blue Water | **Union Sq** 23
Bond St. | **NoHo** 25
Boqueria | **Flatiron** 22
Brick Cafe | **Astoria** 21
Bryant Park | **W 40s** 17
Z Buddakan | **Chelsea** 23
Bull & Bear | **E 40s** 20
Cafe Luxembourg | **W 70s** 20
Cafe Steinhof | **Park Slope** 18
Centro Vinoteca | **W Vill** 20
City Hall | **TriBeCa** 21
NEW City Winery | **SoHo** 18
NEW Clerkenwell | **LES** -
Compass | **W 70s** 22
Z Daniel | **E 60s** 28
Z Del Frisco's | **W 40s** 25
Demarchelier | **E 80s** 16
Dos Caminos | **multi.** 20
NEW Double Crown | **NoHo** 20
Dressler | **W'burg** 25
8 Mile Creek | **NoLita** 20
El Rio Grande | **Murray Hill** 18
Employees Only | **W Vill** 18
NEW Five Leaves | **W'burg** 23
Flatbush Farm | **Park Slope** 20
Z Four Seasons | **E 50s** 26
Freemans | **LES** 21
Geisha | **E 60s** 22
Z Gotham B&G | **G Vill** 27
Z Gramercy Tavern | **Flatiron** 28
Harry's | **Financial** 24
HK | **Garment** 17
NEW Hotel Griffou | **G Vill** 20
House | **Gramercy** 22
Houston's | **multi.** 20
Hudson River | **Harlem** 19
'inoteca | **LES** 23
Z Jean Georges | **W 60s** 28
J.G. Melon | **E 70s** 21
Keens | **Garment** 24
Kellari Tav./Parea | **W 40s** 22
Koi | **W 40s** 22
NEW La Fonda/Sol | **E 40s** 22
Landmarc | **W 60s** 20
Z Le Cirque | **E 50s** 24
Le Colonial | **E 50s** 20

Lucky Strike | **SoHo**	16
NEW Macao Trading | **TriBeCa**	18
Maloney/Porcelli | **E 50s**	22
NEW Mari Vanna | **Flatiron**	-
Markt | **Flatiron**	20
Matsuri | **Chelsea**	22
Maze | **W 50s**	25
Michael Jordan | **E 40s**	20
Z Modern | **W 50s**	26
NEW Montenapo | **W 40s**	-
Z Morimoto | **Chelsea**	25
Z Nobu | **W 50s**	27
Odeon | **TriBeCa**	19
O'Neals' | **W 60s**	17
Orsay | **E 70s**	18
Z Ouest | **W 80s**	24
Park | **Chelsea**	16
Pastis | **Meatpacking**	21
Patroon | **E 40s**	21
Pera | **E 40s**	21
Piano Due | **W 50s**	24
Pop Burger | **E 50s**	18
PT | **W'burg**	-
Quaint | **Sunnyside**	23
Rayuela | **LES**	22
Sala | **NoHo**	22
South Gate | **W 50s**	24
Z Spice Market | **Meatpacking**	23
NEW Standard Grill | **Meatpacking**	22
Stanton Social | **LES**	23
STK | **Meatpacking**	21
Stone Park | **Park Slope**	25
NEW Table 8 | **E Vill**	15
Z Tao | **E 50s**	21
Tio Pepe | **G Vill**	20
212 | **E 60s**	18
NEW White Slab | **LES**	-
Wollensky's | **E 40s**	23

NOTEWORTHY NEWCOMERS (157)

Agua Dulce | **W 50s**	-
Aldea | **Flatiron**	26
Almond | **Flatiron**	20
An Choi | **LES**	21
André | **E 50s**	-
Anella | **Greenpt**	-
Anselmo's | **Red Hook**	16
Aperitivo | **E 40s**	20
AQ Kafé | **W 50s**	19
Arcane | **E Vill**	-
Armani Rist. | **E 50s**	23
At Vermilion | **E 40s**	18
Aureole | **W 40s**	29
Baoguette | **multi.**	22

Bar Artisanal | **TriBeCa**	21
BarBao | **W 80s**	21
Barberry | **W'burg**	-
Bar Breton | **Chelsea**	18
Bark Hot Dogs | **Park Slope**	-
Bati | **Ft Greene**	-
b-bap | **W 50s**	-
Bistrouge | **E Vill**	24
Bizaare Ave. | **Astoria**	-
Boka | **E Vill**	23
Bossa Nova | **W 50s**	21
Braeburn | **W Vill**	21
Brasserie 1605 | **W 40s**	-
Brooklyn Star | **W'burg**	-
Bussaco | **Park Slope**	22
Butcher Bay | **E Vill**	14
Buttermilk | **Carroll Gdns**	23
Café Select | **SoHo**	21
Calexico | **Carroll Gdns**	-
Caravaggio | **E 70s**	-
Casa La Femme | **W Vill**	20
Charles | **W Vill**	18
Char No. 4 | **Cobble Hill**	23
Chimney | **E 100s**	-
City Winery | **SoHo**	18
Civetta | **NoLita**	19
Clerkenwell | **LES**	-
Co. | **Chelsea**	22
Cornelius | **Prospect Hts**	18
Crudo | **Garment**	-
Dardanel | **E 50s**	18
Z DBGB | **E Vill**	23
de Santos | **G Vill**	21
Dhaba | **Murray Hill**	22
Dirt Candy | **E Vill**	23
Double Crown | **NoHo**	20
Ducale | **W 70s**	16
El Almacén | **W'burg**	-
Emporio | **NoLita**	22
Fat Hippo | **LES**	20
Favela Cubana | **G Vill**	-
Fishtail | **E 60s**	23
Five Leaves | **W'burg**	23
508 | **SoHo**	19
Flex Mussels | **E 80s**	22
Flying Cow | **W'burg**	-
Fonda | **Park Slope**	-
Fulton | **E 70s**	22
Get Fresh | **Park Slope**	-
Gus/Gabriel | **W 70s**	-
Haakon's Hall | **W 100s**	-
Hanci | **W 50s**	24
Harbour | **SoHo**	21
Harry's Italian | **Financial**	-
Hotel Griffou | **G Vill**	20

Restaurant	Location	Rating
Il Punto	**Garment**	20
Inakaya	**W 40s**	22
Inatteso	**Financial**	21
Inside Park	**E 50s**	17
Jo's	**NoLita**	-
Joseph Leonard	**G Vill**	-
Kajitsu	**E Vill**	-
Keste Pizza	**G Vill**	-
La Carbonara	**W Vill**	22
La Fonda/Sol	**E 40s**	22
L'Artusi	**W Vill**	21
Le Magnifique	**E 70s**	-
Le Relais/Venise	**E 50s**	-
Levant East	**LES**	-
Locanda Verde	**TriBeCa**	22
Lot 2	**Park Slope**	-
Lucas Steak	**Astoria**	-
Luce	**W 60s**	-
Lucy Browne	**W Vill**	-
Lugo Caffe	**Garment**	21
Lusso	**SoHo**	17
Macao Trading	**TriBeCa**	18
Mañana	**E 60s**	21
Marea	**W 50s**	26
Marfa	**E Vill**	-
Mari Vanna	**Flatiron**	-
Mesa Coyoacan	**W'burg**	-
☑ Minetta	**G Vill**	20
Momofuku Bakery	**E Vill**	21
☑ Monkey Bar	**E 50s**	18
Montenapo	**W 40s**	-
Mott	**L Italy**	-
Naya	**E 50s**	21
Nios	**W 40s**	-
No. 7	**Ft Greene**	23
Oak Room	**W 50s**	18
☑ Oceana	**W 40s**	-
Onda	**Seaport**	22
Opus	**E 80s**	23
Ortine	**Prospect Hts**	-
Perle	**Financial**	18
Permanent Brunch	**E Vill**	-
Porchetta	**E Vill**	24
Pranna	**Murray Hill**	20
Prime Meat	**Carroll Gdns**	19
Provini	**Park Slope**	-
Qoo Robata	**W'burg**	-
Quinto Quarto	**G Vill**	-
Recipe	**W 80s**	-
Ritz Asia	**G Vill**	-
Rouge Tomate	**E 60s**	22
Rye	**W'burg**	-
Salumeria Rosi	**W 70s**	23
San Marzano	**LES**	-
Saraghina	**Bed-Stuy**	-
Sazon	**TriBeCa**	-
Schnipper's	**W 40s**	17
Scuderia	**G Vill**	18
Seasonal	**W 50s**	25
Sel de Mer	**W'burg**	-
Shang	**LES**	23
SHO Shaun Hergatt	**Financial**	29
Sinigual	**E 40s**	22
Smile	**NoHo**	-
Sojourn	**E 70s**	24
Sonia Rose	**LES**	21
Sora Lella	**SoHo**	19
Sorella	**LES**	-
Spunto	**G Vill**	22
Standard Grill	**Meatpacking**	22
Sweet Emily's	**W 50s**	18
Sweetiepie	**G Vill**	14
Table 8	**E Vill**	15
10 Downing	**G Vill**	21
Terrazza Toscana	**W 50s**	-
Tonda	**E Vill**	-
Txikito	**Chelsea**	23
Umi Nom	**Clinton Hill**	-
Veloce Pizzeria	**E Vill**	-
Vesta	**Astoria**	25
Via dei Mille	**SoHo**	24
Vinegar Hill Hse.	**Vinegar Hill**	24
Vutera	**W'burg**	-
Walter Foods	**W'burg**	23
Watty/Meg	**Cobble Hill**	-
West Branch	**W 70s**	19
White Slab	**LES**	-
Ze Café	**E 50s**	21

NOTEWORTHY CLOSINGS (102)

Aesop's Tables
Ago
Alfama
Ama
Amalia
Avon Bistro
Baldoria
Bar Milano
Bar Q
Black Pearl
Bonita
Bull Run
Café des Artistes
Cafe Society
Caffe Bondi
Caffe on the Green
Cambodian Cuisine
Cendrillon
Centovini

Charles' Southern-Style Kitchen
Chino's
Chop Suey
Crave on 42nd
Deborah
Demaré
Dennis Foy
Devin Tavern
Diwan
Django
Elementi
Elettaria
E.U.
Evergreen Shanghai
Fiamma
57
Fleur de Sel
Frederick's
fresh
FROG
Garden Cafe
Giambelli
Grayz
Highline
Hispaniola
HSF
Il Nido
Jarnac
Kobe Club
Korhogo 126
La Belle Vie
La Cantina Toscana
La Goulue
La Grolla
Le Refuge Inn
Levana
Lever House
Little D Eatery
Lomito
Lookout Hill Smokehouse
Loulou
Lucy
Luxe
Madaleine Mae
Maroons
Merkato 55
Mi Cocina
Montparnasse
Neptune Room
Omido
Ono
Palm Court
Pampa Grill
Park Terrace Bistro
Payard

Persimmon
p*ong
Portofino Grille
Rainbow Room/Rainbow Grill
R & L Restaurant
Rio's Churrascaria
Roppongi
Roy's New York
Sheridan Square
Smith's
Solace
Spanky's
Stella del Mare
Suba
Sweet-n-Tart Cafe
Tempo
Tet
Thor
Tides
Todai
Tokyo Pop
Tomo Sushi & Sake Bar
Town
Una Pizza Napoletana
Via Oreto
Village
Wakiya
Zona Rosa

OUTDOOR DINING

(G=garden; P=patio; S=sidewalk; T=terrace)

Aleo | G | **Flatiron**	19
Alma | T | **Carroll Gdns**	20
NEW Anella | P | **Greenpt**	-
A.O.C. | G | **W Vill**	20
Z Aquagrill | T | **SoHo**	26
Aurora | G | **W'burg**	25
Avra | P | **E 40s**	25
Bacchus | G | **Boerum Hill**	23
Barbetta | G | **W 40s**	21
Barolo | G | **SoHo**	18
Bar Pitti | S | **G Vill**	23
Barrio | P | **Park Slope**	17
Battery Gdns. | G, P, T | **Financial**	18
Bistro 33 | S | **Astoria**	23
Z Blue Hill | G | **G Vill**	27
Z Blue Water | T | **Union Sq**	23
Boathouse | T | **E 70s**	17
Bobo | T | **W Vill**	22
Bogota | P | **Park Slope**	20
Bottino | G | **Chelsea**	18
Brass. Ruhlmann | P | **W 50s**	18
Bryant Park | G | **W 40s**	17
Cabana | T | **Seaport**	21
Cacio e Pepe | G, S | **E Vill**	20

Cafe Centro | S | **E 40s**	20
Cafe Fiorello | S | **W 60s**	20
Cávo | G, P | **Astoria**	21
Chimu | P | **W'burg**	22
Coffee Shop | S | **Union Sq**	15
☑ Convivio | P | **E 40s**	26
Conviv. Osteria | G | **Park Slope**	25
NEW Crudo | P | **Garment**	–
Da Nico | G, S | **L Italy**	21
Da Silvano | S | **G Vill**	20
Employees Only | G | **W Vill**	18
☑ Esca | P | **W 40s**	25
Farm/Adderley | G | **Ditmas Pk**	22
NEW Favela Cubana | P | **G Vill**	–
5 Front | G | **Dumbo**	19
5 9th | G | **Meatpacking**	19
Flatbush Farm | G | **Park Slope**	20
NEW Fonda | P | **Park Slope**	–
Gascogne | G | **Chelsea**	21
Gavroche | G | **W Vill**	18
Gemma | S | **E Vill**	19
NEW Get Fresh | P | **Park Slope**	–
Gigino | P, S | **multi.**	21
Gnocco Caffe | G | **E Vill**	23
Gottino | G | **G Vill**	21
☑ Grocery | G | **Carroll Gdns**	27
Home | G | **G Vill**	21
I Coppi | G | **E Vill**	23
Il Gattopardo | P | **W 50s**	24
Il Palazzo | S | **L Italy**	23
NEW Inside Park | T | **E 50s**	17
Isabella's | S | **W 70s**	20
I Trulli | G | **Murray Hill**	23
Jolie | G | **Boerum Hill**	21
Lake Club | G | **SI**	20
La Lanterna | G | **G Vill**	19
La Mangeoire | S | **E 50s**	21
L & B Spumoni | G | **Bensonhurst**	23
Lattanzi | G, T | **W 40s**	22
Le Jardin | G | **NoLita**	20
Le Refuge | G | **E 80s**	21
Marina Cafe | T | **SI**	19
Markt | S | **Flatiron**	20
My Moon | P | **W'burg**	19
New Leaf | P | **Wash. Hts**	21
Ocean Grill | S | **W 70s**	23
Pampano | T | **E 40s**	24
Paradou | G | **Meatpacking**	21
Park | G | **Chelsea**	16
Pastis | S | **Meatpacking**	21
Pete's Tavern | S | **Gramercy**	16
Portofino | T | **Bronx**	19
Primehouse | S | **Murray Hill**	24
Pure Food/Wine | G | **Gramercy**	21
Relish | G | **W'burg**	20
☑ River Café | G | **Dumbo**	26
Riverview | P | **LIC**	21
Sahara | G | **Gravesend**	21
Sea Grill | G | **W 40s**	24
☑ Shake Shack | G | **Flatiron**	23
☑ Sripraphai | G | **Woodside**	27
Surya | G | **W Vill**	21
Sweet Melissa | G | **Cobble Hill**	21
☑ Tabla | S | **Flatiron**	25
Tartine | S | **W Vill**	22
Tavern on Green | G | **W 60s**	15
Terrace in Sky | T | **W 100s**	22
Tree | G | **E Vill**	19
Trestle on 10th | G | **Chelsea**	19
Vento | S | **Meatpacking**	19
ViceVersa | G | **W 50s**	22
Water Club | P | **Murray Hill**	21
☑ Water's Edge | P | **LIC**	22
Wollensky's | S | **E 40s**	23
Zum Schneider | S | **E Vill**	19

POWER SCENES

☑ Adour | **E 50s**	26
☑ Bar Americain | **W 50s**	23
Ben Benson's | **W 50s**	23
BLT Prime | **Gramercy**	25
Bobby Van's | **E 40s**	22
Bull & Bear | **E 40s**	20
☑ Carlyle | **E 70s**	23
China Grill | **W 50s**	22
City Hall | **TriBeCa**	21
☑ Daniel | **E 60s**	28
☑ Del Frisco's | **W 40s**	25
Delmonico's | **Financial**	23
☑ Del Posto | **Chelsea**	26
☑ Elio's | **E 80s**	24
☑ Four Seasons | **E 50s**	26
Fresco | **E 50s**	23
Gallagher's | **W 50s**	21
☑ Gilt | **E 50s**	25
☑ Gotham B&G | **G Vill**	27
Harry's | **Financial**	24
☑ Jean Georges | **W 60s**	28
Keens | **Garment**	24
☑ La Grenouille | **E 50s**	27
☑ Le Bernardin | **W 50s**	28
☑ Le Cirque | **E 50s**	24
NEW Marea | **W 50s**	26
Michael's | **W 50s**	20
Morton's | **E 40s**	27
☑ Nobu | **multi.**	27
Norma's | **W 50s**	25
Patroon | **E 40s**	21
☑ Peter Luger | **W'burg**	27
Rao's | **Harlem**	23

Regency | **E 60s**	18
Russian Tea | **W 50s**	19
Sant Ambroeus | **multi.**	22
Smith/Wollensky | **E 40s**	23
Solo | **E 50s**	22
☑ Sparks | **E 40s**	25
☑ 21 Club | **W 50s**	22
Waverly Inn | **W Vill**	19

PRIVATE ROOMS/ PARTIES

(Capacity figures following name are approximate; call venue for details)

A Voce | 66 | **W 60s**	24
Barbetta | 100 | **W 40s**	21
Battery Gdns. | 300 | **Financial**	18
Beacon | 90 | **W 50s**	23
Ben & Jack's | 100 | **E 40s**	23
BLT Fish | 125 | **Flatiron**	23
BLT Prime | 100 | **Gramercy**	25
☑ BLT Steak | 32 | **E 50s**	25
☑ Blue Hill | 16 | **G Vill**	27
☑ Blue Smoke | 45 | **Murray Hill**	21
☑ Blue Water | 35 | **Union Sq**	23
☑ Buddakan | 60 | **Chelsea**	23
Capital Grille | 40 | **E 40s**	23
Cellini | 100 | **E 50s**	22
Centolire | 30 | **E 80s**	21
City Hall | 110 | **TriBeCa**	21
NEW City Winery | 18 | **SoHo**	18
Compass | 44 | **W 70s**	22
Country | 150 | **Murray Hill**	21
☑ Craft | 40 | **Flatiron**	25
☑ Daniel | 90 | **E 60s**	28
☑ Del Frisco's | 80 | **W 40s**	25
Delmonico's | 70 | **Financial**	23
☑ Del Posto | 200 | **Chelsea**	26
☑ Eleven Madison | 50 | **Flatiron**	27
EN Japanese | 25 | **W Vill**	23
☑ Felidia | 45 | **E 50s**	26
F.illi Ponte | 120 | **TriBeCa**	23
FireBird | 250 | **W 40s**	19
☑ Four Seasons | 300 | **E 50s**	26
Fresco | 45 | **E 50s**	23
Gabriel's | 36 | **W 60s**	22
Geisha | 25 | **E 60s**	22
☑ Gramercy Tavern | 22 | **Flatiron**	28
☑ Il Buco | 25 | **NoHo**	24
Il Cortile | 300 | **L Italy**	23
ilili | 42 | **Chelsea**	24
'inoteca | 30 | **LES**	23
☑ Jean Georges | 35 | **W 60s**	28
Keens | 85 | **Garment**	24
☑ La Grenouille | 70 | **E 50s**	27
Landmark Tavern | 50 | **W 40s**	17
☑ Le Bernardin | 80 | **W 50s**	28

☑ Le Cirque | 90 | **E 50s**	24
Le Perigord | 35 | **E 50s**	24
Le Zie 2000 | 22 | **Chelsea**	22
Maloney/Porcelli | 110 | **E 50s**	22
Matsuri | 56 | **Chelsea**	22
Megu | 50 | **TriBeCa**	23
Michael's | 75 | **W 50s**	20
☑ Milos | 24 | **W 50s**	27
☑ Modern | 64 | **W 50s**	26
Moran's | 170 | **Chelsea**	18
Mr. Chow | 35 | **E 50s**	21
Mr. K's | 50 | **E 50s**	22
☑ Nobu | 40 | **multi.**	27
☑ **NEW** Oceana | 80 | **W 40s**	-
Park | 170 | **Chelsea**	16
Parlor Steak | 40 | **E 90s**	21
Patroon | 60 | **E 40s**	21
Periyali | 45 | **Flatiron**	24
☑ Per Se | 65 | **W 60s**	28
☑ Picholine | 22 | **W 60s**	27
Primavera | 40 | **E 80s**	24
Raoul's | 23 | **SoHo**	24
Redeye Grill | 80 | **W 50s**	20
Remi | 80 | **W 50s**	22
Re Sette | 40 | **W 40s**	21
Riingo | 35 | **E 40s**	21
☑ River Café | 100 | **Dumbo**	26
Sambuca | 150 | **W 70s**	20
Shun Lee Palace | 30 | **E 50s**	23
Solo | 30 | **E 50s**	22
☑ Sparks | 130 | **E 40s**	25
☑ Spice Market | 30 | **Meatpacking**	23
☑ Tao | 26 | **E 50s**	21
Tavern on Green | 400 | **W 60s**	15
Terrace in Sky | 80 | **W 100s**	22
Thalassa | 150 | **TriBeCa**	24
☑ Tocqueville | 28 | **Union Sq**	26
Tribeca Grill | 120 | **TriBeCa**	22
☑ 21 Club | 500 | **W 50s**	22
212 | 80 | **E 60s**	18
Vento | 150 | **Meatpacking**	19
Water Club | 210 | **Murray Hill**	21

PUBS/ MICROBREWERIES

(See Zagat NYC Nightlife)

Alchemy | **Park Slope**	19
Black Duck | **Murray Hill**	20
Chadwick's | **Bay Ridge**	22
ChipShop | **Bklyn Hts**	19
NEW Clerkenwell | **LES**	-
NEW Cornelius | **Prospect Hts**	18
Corner Bistro | **W Vill**	22
8 Mile Creek | **NoLita**	20
Heartland | **multi.**	14

Jackson Hole | **multi.**	17
J.G. Melon | **E 70s**	21
Jimmy's | **E Vill**	20
Joe Allen | **W 40s**	17
Kingswood | **G Vill**	19
Landmark Tavern | **W 40s**	17
Neary's | **E 50s**	16
O'Neals' | **W 60s**	17
Pete's Tavern | **Gramercy**	16
P.J. Clarke's | **multi.**	17
Spotted Pig | **W Vill**	23
Walker's | **TriBeCa**	17
Wollensky's | **E 40s**	23

QUIET CONVERSATION

☑ Adour | **E 50s**	26
Allegretti | **Flatiron**	24
☑ Alto | **E 50s**	26
Aroma | **NoHo**	24
☑ Asiate | **W 60s**	24
NEW Aureole | **W 40s**	29
☑ Chanterelle | **TriBeCa**	28
Dieci | **E Vill**	22
Giovanni | **E 80s**	22
Il Gattopardo | **W 50s**	24
☑ Jean Georges | **W 60s**	28
Kai | **E 60s**	26
Kings' Carriage | **E 80s**	22
Knife + Fork | **E Vill**	21
Kyotofu | **W 40s**	21
☑ La Grenouille | **E 50s**	27
Le Barricou | **W'burg**	23
☑ Le Bernardin | **W 50s**	28
Lumi | **E 70s**	18
NEW Marea | **W 50s**	26
☑ Masa | **W 60s**	26
Mr. K's | **E 50s**	22
North Sq. | **G Vill**	23
NEW Oak Room | **W 50s**	18
☑ Per Se | **W 60s**	28
Petite Crev. | **Carroll Gdns**	25
Petrossian | **W 50s**	24
☑ Picholine | **W 60s**	27
Provence/Boite | **Carroll Gdns**	20
PT | **W'burg**	-
NEW Qoo Robata | **W'burg**	-
Rosanjin | **TriBeCa**	24
SavorNY | **LES**	20
Seo | **E 40s**	24
Sfoglia | **E 90s**	25
Square Meal | **E 90s**	23
NEW Sweet Emily's | **W 50s**	18
Terrace in Sky | **W 100s**	22
☑ Tocqueville | **Union Sq**	26

Tree | **E Vill**	19
Tsampa | **E Vill**	21
12 Chairs | **SoHo**	19
NEW Ze Café | **E 50s**	21
☑ Zenkichi | **W'burg**	25

RAW BARS

☑ Aquagrill | **SoHo**	26
Arté | **G Vill**	18
☑ Atlantic Grill | **E 70s**	23
☑ Balthazar | **SoHo**	23
☑ Bar Americain | **W 50s**	23
Ben & Jack's | **E 40s**	23
BLT Fish | **Flatiron**	23
Blue Fin | **W 40s**	22
Blue Ribbon | **multi.**	24
☑ Blue Water | **Union Sq**	23
Bondi Rd. | **LES**	18
Brasserie Cognac | **W 50s**	18
NEW Butcher Bay | **E Vill**	14
City Crab | **Flatiron**	18
City Hall | **TriBeCa**	21
City Lobster | **W 40s**	19
Craftsteak | **Chelsea**	24
Docks Oyster | **E 40s**	19
Ed's Lobster | **NoLita**	21
☑ Esca | **W 40s**	25
Fig & Olive | **multi.**	20
Fish | **G Vill**	22
NEW Fishtail | **E 60s**	23
NEW 508 | **SoHo**	19
NEW Flex Mussels | **E 80s**	22
Flor/Sol | **TriBeCa**	22
Giorgione | **SoHo**	21
Jack's Lux. | **E Vill**	26
London Lennie | **Rego Pk**	22
Lure Fishbar | **SoHo**	23
NEW Marea | **W 50s**	26
☑ Marlow/Sons | **W'burg**	26
Mercer Kitchen | **SoHo**	21
Mermaid Inn | **E Vill**	20
☑NEW Oceana | **W 40s**	-
Ocean Grill | **W 70s**	23
Olea | **Ft Greene**	23
NEW Opus | **E 80s**	23
☑ Oyster Bar | **E 40s**	22
Parlor Steak | **E 90s**	21
☑ Pearl Oyster | **G Vill**	26
Pearl Room | **Bay Ridge**	20
P.J. Clarke's | **multi.**	17
Primehouse | **Murray Hill**	24
Riverview | **LIC**	21
Shelly's NY | **W 50s**	19
South Fin | **SI**	19
Thalia | **W 50s**	19

Trata | **E 70s**	22
21 Club | **W 50s**	22
Umberto's | **multi.**	18
Uncle Jack's | **Garment**	23
NEW Walter Foods | **W'burg**	23

ROMANTIC PLACES

Aleo | **Flatiron**	19
Algonquin | **W 40s**	17
Allen/Delancey | **LES**	23
Alma | **Carroll Gdns**	20
Alta | **G Vill**	24
Asiate | **W 60s**	24
NEW Aureole | **W 40s**	29
Balthazar | **SoHo**	23
Barbetta | **W 40s**	21
Barolo | **SoHo**	18
Battery Gdns. | **Financial**	18
Blue Hill | **G Vill**	27
Blue Ribbon Bakery | **G Vill**	24
Boathouse | **E 70s**	17
Bottino | **Chelsea**	18
Bouley | **TriBeCa**	28
CamaJe | **G Vill**	20
Canaille | **Park Slope**	22
Capsouto Frères | **TriBeCa**	23
NEW Casa La Femme | **W Vill**	20
Caviar Russe | **E 50s**	25
Chanterelle | **TriBeCa**	28
Chez Josephine | **W 40s**	20
Conviv. Osteria | **Park Slope**	25
Daniel | **E 60s**	28
David Burke Townhse. | **E 60s**	25
Del Posto | **Chelsea**	26
Dressler | **W'burg**	25
Duane Park | **TriBeCa**	23
Eleven Madison | **Flatiron**	27
Erminia | **E 80s**	25
FireBird | **W 40s**	19
Firenze | **E 80s**	20
5 Front | **Dumbo**	19
Flor/Sol | **TriBeCa**	22
Four Seasons | **E 50s**	26
Frankies | **LES**	24
Gascogne | **Chelsea**	21
Gigino | **Financial**	21
House | **Gramercy**	22
I Coppi | **E Vill**	23
Il Buco | **NoHo**	24
I Trulli | **Murray Hill**	23
Jack's Lux. | **E Vill**	26
James | **Prospect Hts**	23
JoJo | **E 60s**	25
Jolie | **Boerum Hill**	21
Kings' Carriage | **E 80s**	22
Kitchen Club | **NoLita**	23

Kyotofu | **W 40s**	21
L'Absinthe | **E 60s**	22
Lady Mendl's | **Gramercy**	22
La Grenouille | **E 50s**	27
La Lanterna | **G Vill**	19
La Mangeoire | **E 50s**	21
Le Gigot | **G Vill**	23
Le Refuge | **E 80s**	21
Maria Pia | **W 50s**	19
NEW Mari Vanna | **Flatiron**	-
Mas | **G Vill**	27
Mr. K's | **E 50s**	22
My Moon | **W'burg**	19
Nino's | **E 70s**	21
Olea | **Ft Greene**	23
One if by Land | **G Vill**	24
Pam Real Thai | **W 40s**	22
Paola's | **E 80s**	23
Pasha | **W 70s**	20
Periyali | **Flatiron**	24
Petrossian | **W 50s**	24
Piano Due | **W 50s**	24
Piccola Venezia | **Astoria**	25
Pinocchio | **E 90s**	22
Place | **W Vill**	19
Primavera | **E 80s**	24
PT | **W'burg**	-
Quercy | **Cobble Hill**	22
Raoul's | **SoHo**	24
River Café | **Dumbo**	26
Riverview | **LIC**	21
Roc | **TriBeCa**	22
Sacred Chow | **G Vill**	20
Saul | **Boerum Hill**	26
Savoy | **SoHo**	24
Scalini Fedeli | **TriBeCa**	26
Sistina | **E 80s**	26
Spice Market | **Meatpacking**	23
Teodora | **E 50s**	20
Terrace in Sky | **W 100s**	22
Tocqueville | **Union Sq**	26
tre dici | **Chelsea**	21
Uva | **E 70s**	21
View | **W 40s**	16
Wallsé | **W Vill**	25
Water Club | **Murray Hill**	21
Water's Edge | **LIC**	22
Zenkichi | **W'burg**	25

SENIOR APPEAL

Allegretti | **Flatiron**	24
Arté | **G Vill**	18
Artie's Deli | **W 80s**	18
NEW Aureole | **W 40s**	29
Bamonte's | **W'burg**	23

Barbetta | **W 40s**	21
🚫 Barney Greengrass | **W 80s**	23
Borgo Antico | **G Vill**	18
Bravo Gianni | **E 60s**	22
Campagnola | **E 70s**	23
Capsouto Frères | **TriBeCa**	23
Chadwick's | **Bay Ridge**	22
Chez Napoléon | **W 50s**	20
Dawat | **E 50s**	23
DeGrezia | **E 50s**	23
🚫 Del Posto | **Chelsea**	26
Elaine's | **E 80s**	13
Embers | **Bay Ridge**	21
🚫 Felidia | **E 50s**	26
Fiorini | **E 50s**	20
Gallagher's | **W 50s**	21
Giovanni | **E 80s**	22
Grifone | **E 40s**	25
🚫 Il Tinello | **W 50s**	25
🚫 Jean Georges | **W 60s**	28
La Bonne Soupe | **W 50s**	18
La Mangeoire | **E 50s**	21
La Mirabelle | **W 80s**	23
Lanza | **E Vill**	18
La Petite Aub. | **Murray Hill**	20
Lattanzi | **W 40s**	22
Le Boeuf/Mode | **E 80s**	21
🚫 Le Cirque | **E 50s**	24
Le Marais | **W 40s**	22
Le Perigord | **E 50s**	24
Lusardi's | **E 70s**	23
MarkJoseph | **Financial**	24
Mr. K's | **E 50s**	22
Nicola's | **E 80s**	22
🆕 Oak Room | **W 50s**	18
Pastrami Queen | **E 70s**	20
Piccola Venezia | **Astoria**	25
Pietro's | **E 40s**	24
Ponticello | **Astoria**	24
Primola | **E 60s**	22
Quatorze Bis | **E 70s**	20
Quattro Gatti | **E 80s**	22
Rao's | **Harlem**	23
🚫 River Café | **Dumbo**	26
Rossini's | **Murray Hill**	23
Rughetta | **E 80s**	22
Russian Tea | **W 50s**	19
🚫 San Pietro | **E 50s**	26
Sardi's | **W 40s**	18
Saul | **Boerum Hill**	26
Scaletta | **W 70s**	22
Shun Lee West | **W 60s**	22
Tavern on Green | **W 60s**	15
Teresa's | **Bklyn Hts**	19
12 Chairs | **SoHo**	19

SINGLES SCENES

Ajna Bar | **Meatpacking**	19
Angelo/Maxie's | **Flatiron**	22
🚫 Asia de Cuba | **Murray Hill**	22
🚫 Atlantic Grill | **E 70s**	23
Bagatelle | **Meatpacking**	19
Baraonda | **E 70s**	18
🆕 Bar Artisanal | **TriBeCa**	21
Barrio | **Park Slope**	17
Blue Ribbon | **multi.**	24
🚫 Blue Water | **Union Sq**	23
Bobo | **W Vill**	22
Boca Chica | **E Vill**	19
Brother Jimmy | **multi.**	16
Bryant Park | **W 40s**	17
🚫 Buddakan | **Chelsea**	23
Butter | **E Vill**	20
Cabana | **multi.**	21
Canyon Road | **E 70s**	21
Chinatown Brass. | **NoHo**	21
Citrus B&G | **W 70s**	20
Coffee Shop | **Union Sq**	15
🚫🆕 DBGB | **E Vill**	23
🚫 Del Frisco's | **W 40s**	25
Delicatessen | **NoLita**	18
Dos Caminos | **multi.**	20
🆕 Double Crown | **NoHo**	20
Elephant | **E Vill**	20
elmo | **Chelsea**	16
Employees Only | **W Vill**	18
Félix | **SoHo**	16
Freemans | **LES**	21
Heartland | **multi.**	14
🆕 Hotel Griffou | **G Vill**	20
Houston's | **multi.**	20
Hudson Cafeteria | **W 50s**	19
Ideya | **SoHo**	21
'inoteca | **LES**	23
Joya | **Cobble Hill**	23
Kingswood | **G Vill**	19
Koi | **W 40s**	22
La Esquina | **L Italy**	21
Lure Fishbar | **SoHo**	23
🆕 Macao Trading | **TriBeCa**	18
🚫🆕 Monkey Bar | **E 50s**	18
Otto | **G Vill**	23
Pastis | **Meatpacking**	21
Peep | **SoHo**	18
Pete's Tavern | **Gramercy**	16
Schiller's | **LES**	18
🚫 Spice Market | **Meatpacking**	23
🆕 Standard Grill | **Meatpacking**	22
STK | **Meatpacking**	21
SushiSamba | **multi.**	21

SPECIAL FEATURES

NEW Table 8 | **E Vill**	15
Z Tao | **E 50s**	21
NEW 10 Downing | **G Vill**	21
Tribeca Grill | **TriBeCa**	22
NEW Walter Foods | **W'burg**	23
Xunta | **E Vill**	21
Zarela | **E 50s**	20

SLEEPERS

(Fine food, but little known)

abistro | **Ft Greene**	25
Aliseo Osteria | **Prospect Hts**	23
Amorina | **Prospect Hts**	25
Barbone | **E Vill**	24
Barosa | **multi.**	23
Brown Café | **LES**	23
Cafecito | **E Vill**	23
Café Katja | **LES**	23
Chiyono | **E Vill**	25
DeStefano | **W'burg**	23
Greenwich Grill/Sushi Azabu | **TriBeCa**	26
Gruppo | **E Vill**	25
Hibino | **Cobble Hill**	25
Il Palazzo | **L Italy**	23
Il Passatore | **W'burg**	24
Kai | **E 60s**	26
Ki Sushi | **Boerum Hill**	25
La Sirène | **SoHo**	23
Laut | **Union Sq**	24
Lazzara's | **multi.**	23
Le Barricou | **W'burg**	23
Luz | **Ft Greene**	24
Marc Forgione | **TriBeCa**	23
Matilda | **E Vill**	26
New Yeah | **Chinatown**	24
Niche | **E 80s**	24
Noche Mex. | **W 100s**	25
Omen | **SoHo**	25
Palma | **G Vill**	23
Petite Crev. | **Carroll Gdns**	25
Pukk | **E Vill**	23
Rock-n-Sake | **Chelsea**	23
Rosanjin | **TriBeCa**	24
Scalino | **Park Slope**	24
Seo | **E 40s**	24
Shanghai Café | **L Italy**	23
Soto | **G Vill**	28
Tevere | **E 80s**	24
Ushiwakamaru | **G Vill**	26

SUNDAY BEST BETS

(See also Hotel Dining)

Z Aquagrill | **SoHo**	26
Z Aquavit | **E 50s**	25
Z Artisanal | **Murray Hill**	23

Z Balthazar | **SoHo**	23
Z Bar Americain | **W 50s**	23
Z Blue Hill | **G Vill**	27
Blue Ribbon | **SoHo**	24
Z Blue Water | **Union Sq**	23
Z Bouley | **TriBeCa**	28
Café de Bruxelles | **W Vill**	21
Chez Oskar | **Ft Greene**	17
David Burke Townhse. | **E 60s**	25
Demarchelier | **E 80s**	16
5 Points | **NoHo**	22
Z Gotham B&G | **G Vill**	27
Z Gramercy Tavern | **Flatiron**	28
Lucky Strike | **SoHo**	16
Z Lupa | **G Vill**	25
Z Mesa Grill | **Flatiron**	23
Moran's | **Chelsea**	18
Odeon | **TriBeCa**	19
Z Ouest | **W 80s**	24
Our Place | **E 50s**	20
Z Peter Luger | **W'burg**	27
Piccolo Angolo | **W Vill**	25
Z Picholine | **W 60s**	27
Pomaire | **W 40s**	20
Prune | **E Vill**	24
Z River Café | **Dumbo**	26
Solo | **E 50s**	22
Tratt. Dell'Arte | **W 50s**	22
Tribeca Grill | **TriBeCa**	22
Z Union Sq. Cafe | **Union Sq**	27
Water Club | **Murray Hill**	21
Zoë | **SoHo**	20

TEA SERVICE

Abigael's | **Garment**	20
Z Asiate | **W 60s**	24
Danal | **G Vill**	20
NEW Double Crown | **NoHo**	20
Duane Park | **TriBeCa**	23
Kings' Carriage | **E 80s**	22
Z Lady Mendl's | **Gramercy**	22
Morgan | **Murray Hill**	20
North Sq. | **G Vill**	23
Russian Tea | **W 50s**	19
Sant Ambroeus | **multi.**	22
Sarabeth's | **multi.**	20
Sweet Melissa | **multi.**	21
Z Tamarind | **Flatiron**	25
Tavern on Green | **W 60s**	15
Tea & Sympathy | **W Vill**	21

THEME RESTAURANTS

Braai | **W 50s**	19
Bubba Gump | **W 40s**	14

Cowgirl | **W Vill**	16
Ninja | **TriBeCa**	16

TRANSPORTING EXPERIENCES

Ajna Bar | **Meatpacking**	19
☑ Asiate | **W 60s**	24
☑ Balthazar | **SoHo**	23
Boathouse | **E 70s**	17
☑ Buddakan | **Chelsea**	23
NEW Casa La Femme | **W Vill**	20
Chez Josephine | **W 40s**	20
FireBird | **W 40s**	19
Fraunces Tavern | **Financial**	16
☑ Il Buco | **NoHo**	24
ilili | **Chelsea**	24
Keens | **Garment**	24
☑ La Grenouille | **E 50s**	27
Le Colonial | **E 50s**	20
NEW Mari Vanna | **Flatiron**	-
☑ Masa | **W 60s**	26
Matsuri | **Chelsea**	22
Megu | **TriBeCa**	23
☑**NEW** Monkey Bar | **E 50s**	18
Ninja | **TriBeCa**	16
☑ One if by Land | **G Vill**	24
☑ Per Se | **W 60s**	28
Rao's | **Harlem**	23
☑ Tao | **E 50s**	21
Tavern on Green | **W 60s**	15
Vatan | **Murray Hill**	22
☑ Water's Edge | **LIC**	22

VIEWS

Alma | **Carroll Gdns**	20
Angelina's | **SI**	21
Antica Venezia | **W Vill**	23
☑ Asiate | **W 60s**	24
A Voce | **W 60s**	24
Battery Gdns. | **Financial**	18
Boathouse | **E 70s**	17
Bouchon Bakery | **W 60s**	23
NEW Brasserie 1605 | **W 40s**	-
Bryant Park | **W 40s**	17
Bubby's | **Dumbo**	18
Cabana | **Seaport**	21
Cipriani Dolci | **E 40s**	20
Fairway Cafe | **Red Hook**	18
F.illi Ponte | **TriBeCa**	23
Gigino | **Financial**	21
Heartland | **Seaport**	14
Hudson River | **Harlem**	19
Lake Club | **SI**	20
Landmarc | **W 60s**	20
Liberty View | **Financial**	19
Lobster Box | **Bronx**	19

Marina Cafe | **SI**	19
Metrazur | **E 40s**	21
Michael Jordan | **E 40s**	20
☑ Modern | **W 50s**	26
NEW Montenapo | **W 40s**	-
☑ Per Se | **W 60s**	28
Pete's D'town | **Dumbo**	19
P.J. Clarke's | **Financial**	17
Porter House | **W 60s**	24
Portofino | **Bronx**	19
Relish | **W'burg**	20
☑ River Café | **Dumbo**	26
River Room | **Harlem**	20
Riverview | **LIC**	21
Sea Grill | **W 40s**	24
South Fin | **SI**	19
Tavern on Green | **W 60s**	15
Terrace in Sky | **W 100s**	22
2 West | **Financial**	22
View | **W 40s**	16
Water Club | **Murray Hill**	21
☑ Water's Edge | **LIC**	22

VISITORS ON EXPENSE ACCOUNT

☑ Adour | **E 50s**	26
Anthos | **W 50s**	25
NEW Aureole | **W 40s**	29
☑ Babbo | **G Vill**	27
☑ Bouley | **TriBeCa**	28
☑ Café Boulud | **E 70s**	27
☑ Chanterelle | **TriBeCa**	28
☑ Craft | **Flatiron**	25
☑ Daniel | **E 60s**	28
☑ Del Frisco's | **W 40s**	25
☑ Del Posto | **Chelsea**	26
eighty one | **W 80s**	25
☑ Eleven Madison | **Flatiron**	27
☑ Four Seasons | **E 50s**	26
☑ Gari/Sushi | **W 40s**	27
Gordon Ramsay | **W 50s**	24
☑ Gramercy Tavern | **Flatiron**	28
☑ Il Mulino | **G Vill**	27
☑ Jean Georges | **W 60s**	28
Keens | **Garment**	24
☑ Kuruma Zushi | **E 40s**	27
☑ La Grenouille | **E 50s**	27
☑ Le Bernardin | **W 50s**	28
☑ Le Cirque | **E 50s**	24
NEW Marea | **W 50s**	26
☑ Masa | **W 60s**	26
☑ Milos | **W 50s**	27
☑ Modern | **W 50s**	26
☑ Nobu | **multi.**	27
☑ Palm | **multi.**	24

Milos | **W 50s** — 27
Modern | **W 50s** — 26
Morrell Wine | **W 40s** — 18
Motorino | **multi.** — 22
Nice Matin | **W 70s** — 20
NEW Oceana | **G Vill** — -
Otto | **G Vill** — 23
Ouest | **W 80s** — 24
Per Se | **W 60s** — 28
Picholine | **W 60s** — 27
Pomaire | **W 40s** — 20
Porter House | **W 60s** — 24
Post House | **E 60s** — 24
Raoul's | **SoHo** — 24
River Café | **Dumbo** — 26
Rothmann's | **E 50s** — 22
NEW Rouge Tomate | **E 60s** — 22
NEW Salumeria Rosi | **W 70s** — 23
San Pietro | **E 50s** — 26
Scarpetta | **Chelsea** — 26
Sharz Cafe | **E 80s** — 20

NEW SHO Shaun Hergatt | **Financial** — 29
Smith/Wollensky | **E 40s** — 23
Solera | **E 50s** — 20
Sparks | **E 40s** — 25
Tabla | **Flatiron** — 25
Telepan | **W 60s** — 26
Thalassa | **TriBeCa** — 24
Tía Pol | **Chelsea** — 25
Tommaso | **Dyker Hts** — 23
Tribeca Grill | **TriBeCa** — 22
Tse Yang | **E 50s** — 24
21 Club | **W 50s** — 22
NEW Txikito | **Chelsea** — 23
Union Sq. Cafe | **Union Sq** — 27
Uva | **E 70s** — 21
Valbella | **Meatpacking** — 25
Veritas | **Flatiron** — 26
Wallsé | **W Vill** — 25
Water's Edge | **LIC** — 22
Zoë | **SoHo** — 20

SPECIAL FEATURES

Wine Vintage Chart

This chart is based on our 0 to 30 scale. The ratings (by U. of South Carolina law professor **Howard Stravitz**) reflect vintage quality and the wine's readiness to drink. A dash means the wine is past its peak or too young to rate. Loire ratings are for dry whites.

Whites	95	96	97	98	99	00	01	02	03	04	05	06	07	08
France:														
Alsace	24	23	23	25	23	25	26	23	21	24	25	24	26	-
Burgundy	27	26	23	21	24	24	24	27	23	26	27	25	25	24
Loire Valley	-	-	-	-	-	23	24	26	22	24	27	23	23	24
Champagne	26	27	24	23	25	24	21	26	21	-	-	-	-	-
Sauternes	21	23	25	23	24	24	29	25	24	21	26	23	27	25
California:														
Chardonnay	-	-	-	-	23	22	25	26	22	26	29	24	27	-
Sauvignon Blanc	-	-	-	-	-	-	-	-	25	26	25	27	25	-
Austria:														
Grüner V./Riesl.	24	21	26	23	25	22	23	25	26	25	24	26	24	22
Germany:	21	26	21	22	24	20	29	25	26	27	28	25	27	25

Reds	95	96	97	98	99	00	01	02	03	04	05	06	07	08
France:														
Bordeaux	26	25	23	25	24	29	26	24	26	24	28	24	23	25
Burgundy	26	27	25	24	27	22	24	27	25	23	28	25	24	-
Rhône	26	22	24	27	26	27	26	-	26	24	27	25	26	-
Beaujolais	-	-	-	-	-	-	-	-	24	-	27	24	25	23
California:														
Cab./Merlot	27	25	28	23	25	-	27	26	25	24	26	23	26	24
Pinot Noir	-	-	-	-	24	23	25	26	25	26	24	23	27	25
Zinfandel	-	-	-	-	-	-	25	23	27	22	22	21	21	25
Oregon:														
Pinot Noir	-	-	-	-	-	-	-	26	24	25	26	26	25	27
Italy:														
Tuscany	24	-	29	24	27	24	27	-	25	27	26	25	24	-
Piedmont	21	27	26	25	26	28	27	-	25	27	26	25	26	-
Spain:														
Rioja	26	24	25	-	25	24	28	-	23	27	26	24	25	-
Ribera del Duero/Priorat	26	27	25	24	25	24	27	20	24	27	26	24	26	-
Australia:														
Shiraz/Cab.	24	26	25	28	24	24	27	27	25	26	26	24	22	-
Chile:	-	-	24	-	25	23	26	24	25	24	27	25	24	-
Argentina:														
Malbec	-	-	-	-	-	-	-	-	25	26	27	24	-